blue
rider
press

Substitute

Substitute

GOING TO SCHOOL

WITH A THOUSAND

KIDS

Nicholson Baker

BLUE RIDER PRESS

New York

blue
rider
press

An imprint of Penguin Random House LLC
375 Hudson Street
New York, New York 10014

ISBN 9780399160981

Printed in the United States of America
1   3   5   7   9   10   8   6   4   2

Book design by Michelle McMillian

To my wife Margaret, my daughter Alice, and my son Elias

CONTENTS

PREFACE

THIS BOOK IS a moment-by-moment account of the twenty-eight days I spent as the lowest-ranking participant in American education: a substitute teacher. I taught all ages, from kindergartners to twelfth-graders, and all required subjects—reading, writing, math, social studies, and science—plus a few electives here and there, like metal tech. I taught honors students and students in special ed classes—about a thousand children in all. I didn't have a teaching certificate, and I'd never taught in a primary or secondary school, but that didn't matter—all you need is a high school diploma, a clean criminal record, and a willingness to tolerate your own ineptitude.

I sought out the teaching job because I wanted to know what life in classrooms was really like. There are many books of educational advice, of theory, of hagiography, of gloomy prognosis—what's missing is a lived-through sense of how busy and complicated and weird and *long* every school day is; how many ups and downs there are, and how exhausting—and sometimes entertaining—school is, for students and teachers both. Forget curriculum, forget the parts of speech and the noble gases, the nature of prime numbers and the components of an argumentative essay: for many kids, going to school is simply about finding a way to get through six and a half hours of compulsory deskbound fluorescence without wigging out and incurring punishment. In these pages I've tried to convey, without exaggeration, the noisy, distracted, crazy-making reality of one fairly typical, not-terribly-poor-but-hardly-rich school district. I'm grateful to all the students who put up with my own fumbling attempts at doing my job, and to Sarah Hochman and David Rosenthal, of Blue Rider Press, who gave me the go-ahead to write this book. My wife Margaret, and my children Alice and Elias, to whom I lovingly dedicate this book, helped all the way through.

Before we get started, though, I should probably say something about my own schooling. I went to kindergarten at a private school in Rochester, New York—my mother paid for my tuition by painting circular murals of pelicans and polar bears that hung on the wall of the inner courtyard where we had lunch. For first, second, third, and fourth grade, I went to Martin B. Anderson School Number 1 in Rochester, where I had no homework, except once or twice a semester when we had to write a report. Once I saw a boy squash a praying mantis with his sneaker, a horrible sight, and once I saw another boy slammed into a wall by a teacher during a game of dodgeball. In third grade we learned cursive, and the teacher, Mrs. Newcomb, who disliked me because of my Beatles haircut, told me that I was going to injure my eyesight by reading an old edition of *Twenty Thousand Leagues Under the Sea*, set in tiny type.

In fifth grade, in 1967, I took part in one of the earliest experiments in voluntary integration: I got on a bus and rode, for an hour, from our middle-class neighborhood in Rochester to Clara Barton School Number 2, in what survived of the poor neighborhoods downtown after the bulldozing erasure of urban renewal. Number 2 was a brand-new school, and I was part of a small white minority. The work was not difficult—and there was an art class where I made a cast of my hand and threw clay pots—and I did practically no homework. I got beaten up once by some older kids, but not badly: that was my only adventure. For seventh grade I went to Number 23 School and was taught by a dashing man who loved basketball. I did nothing in seventh grade except eat Hostess Ho Hos and think about ten-speed bicycles and speed skates. No, not nothing: I completed one five-page report called "The Legs and Feet," with diagrams of bones and muscles, when we were assigned to write about transportation in New York State. Eighth grade happened in a special wing of Monroe High School, where the homework was minimal and bathrooms were scary and we had to swim naked in gym class, a hideous experience.

High school was, again, permissive and free of homework and other indications of "rigor": I went to a brand-new experimental public school called the School Without Walls, where I played music and took whatever classes I wanted and watched a lot of sitcoms on TV. While at School Without Walls I also audited courses at the University of Rochester—two literature classes, a history class, and a music theory class at the Eastman School of Music. I graduated a year early and typed my own transcript. And then I went to college—first at the Eastman School, and then at Haverford College, where I learned how to write and worked hard. That's the entirety of my formal education.

Now for my time as a teacher.

LEARNING TARGETS

In January of 2014, Regional School Unit 66—everyone just called it RSU66—offered an adult-education class at Lasswell High School in Lasswell, Maine, about fifty miles from where I live. It met one evening a week for four weeks. The class was called Substitute Teacher Training. I paid the thirty-four-dollar fee and signed up.

We met in a big white room on a frozen Tuesday night in February. There were eight students sitting at circular tables—a potter, a former seller of artists' supplies, a former nanny, an elementary school teacher recently moved from Boston, a student from the University of New Hampshire, the wife of a firefighter, a recent high school graduate who wore a brown knit cap, and me. Our teacher, Shelly, passed out a packet of information and said she was going to help us build tools and strategies for our substitute-teaching toolbox. (Her name wasn't actually Shelly—I've changed most names, places, and physical descriptions in this book so as not to cause embarrassment or grief.) Everyone who completed the class would receive a certificate and would get paid an extra five dollars per day of substituting, she said. So we would be making seventy dollars a day.

"I don't like to play sage on the stage," Shelly said, but she had a lot to talk about. She'd been an elementary school teacher before moving up to administration, and she spoke in a pleasant, cheerful, sixth-grade-teacher voice. She wore black flare pants and a gray knit sweater. The key to RSU66's approach was "voice and choice," she told us. Students should have a voice in the classroom, and they should and in fact did help to formulate each classroom's unique code of cooperation, using a technique called "power voting," which Shelly taught us. It involved brainstorming in groups of two and the use of many yellow stickers. For the power voting exercise I was paired with the former nanny. She'd recently had open heart surgery: when she sneezed, she winced.

Every classroom's code of cooperation was posted on the wall, Shelly said, and every class also had a series of "learning targets," which conformed to the Common Core standards recently adopted by many states around the country. For example, one ninth-grade learning target for social studies was: "Understands how the interaction of various religions has impacted history." But because students learn at different rates, and because RSU66's test scores, especially in reading, had been coming in too low, the district had adopted a performance-based approach, in which each child could theoretically master different targets at different times. The mission of RSU66, Shelly told us, was as follows: "To lead, to engage, and to inspire a community of respectful learners."

The district needed substitute teachers who genuinely liked kids, Shelly said. "I've had to dismiss a sub for throwing a box of tissues at a child. Not okay." She showed us some videos of the newly reformed elementary reading classes at RSU66, which used proven instructional techniques called the "daily five" and the CAFE method. CAFE stood for "Comprehension, Accuracy, Fluency, and Expanded vocabulary," but one of the district's teachers had rearranged it so that it spelled FACE, starting with Fluency. An appealing little girl in the video said the new approach was working for her: "I've never been much good of a reader or speller, and this kind of helps me. If I can understand reading, I can understand words and spelling more better."

Then Shelly taught us how to play a math game called What's My

Number? She'd used it on her sixth-graders with great success. Each of us got an index card. One of the would-be substitutes read her card: "I have twenty-four—who has two more?"

There was a silence. I stared down stupidly at my card, which said 26. Suddenly my heart thumped. "I do, I think," I said. "I have twenty-six. Who has ten less?"

Somebody said, "I do. I have sixteen—who has half of me?"

Another pause. An answer. A question. We went around the room doing mental computations, not always correctly. "Anyway, just something fun," said Shelly. She told us we might consider assembling a little canvas bag of puzzles, games, and "motor breaks," for those moments when a classroom was getting fidgety, especially toward the end of the day. "Any questions?"

The man who used to sell artists' supplies asked what time we might get a call from the sub caller.

"If it's middle school or high school, I think she starts calling as early as five or five-thirty in the morning," Shelly said. "Not only does she have to fill every spot, she has to give you time to travel." High school and middle school officially began at seven-thirty. "You don't want to arrive any later than seven o'clock." Elementary school began later, at nine a.m., so we'd need to be there at eight-thirty. There was a need for subs at all grade levels.

She also told us about the mandatory fingerprinting and criminal background check, which cost fifty dollars. We'd need to make an online appointment to be fingerprinted.

At nine o'clock, class was done. "I left for work at six-thirty this morning, so I'll be glad to get home," Shelly said. "Have a good night, everyone." We thanked her and walked out into the icy, gritty wasteland of the parking lot and drove home.

THE RECEPTIONIST at RSU66's fingerprinting office said, "The little boys' room is just down the hall on your left. I'd like you to get your hands nice and soapy and clean, and then take a chair, and Sharon will be with you shortly."

My fingerprinting session went poorly. Sharon, the fingerprint technician, held my hand and helped me roll my fingers over the little glass scanning window, but each time, after a moment of computation, an image of my fingertip would appear on her computer screen with little mauve areas superimposed on it that indicated biometric inadequacies, and then a rectangle would pop up saying REJECTED. After many tries and much sighing Sharon overrode the system and sent my flawed scans off to the identity service, IdentoGO, run by MorphoTrust USA, a subsidiary of Safran, which is a French manufacturer of aerospace components, bombs, and drones. "We'll see what they say," she said. Some people just didn't fingerprint well, apparently. "I had one woman in here, she was a pianist, and she'd worn her fingerprints away. Do you do a lot of typing?" I said I typed all the time. "That's probably it," she said.

ON THE SECOND TUESDAY NIGHT, I told Roy, the former seller of artists' supplies, that the idea of being in front of a class of kids frankly scared me.

"They say ex-military make good substitutes," Roy said. We laughed nervously.

"So, we can get started," said Shelly.

She introduced two women, Mrs. Norris, principal of Wallingford Elementary School—one of four elementary schools in the district—and Mrs. Ecklin, RSU66's director of special education. Mrs. Ecklin gave us an overview of some relevant vocabulary. Children who were diagnosed as having some sort of disability were given an IEP, or Individualized Education Plan; a list of IEP students in a class was usually to be found in the sub folder, along with any "accommodations" they were entitled to, such as extra help with taking a test. On the Individualized Education Plan were various codes: LD meant learning disability—for instance, dyslexia—ED meant emotional disability, S&L meant speech and language complications, and OHI stood for "Other Health Impairment," a catchall that included attention deficit disorder, depression, autism, deafness, blindness, and anxiety. "Anxiety is a huge one at the middle school and high school," Mrs. Ecklin said. "It's even trickling down to the elementary school." Kids who'd had cancer treatment were sometimes classed under OHI, because chemotherapy drugs can cause mental problems. "Unfortunately, the law is we have to label them to give them services," she said.

Mrs. Norris, the principal, said, "Never make the assumption—not that you would—that because a child has an identifying label that somehow is indicative of their intellectual capabilities. I'll never forget the child who was identified LD with an IQ of 142. When it came to phonemic awareness, he struggled, but when something was read to him, his capacity to understand it and give it back to you was off the charts. Every child should be treated as though he or she was your daughter, your son, your niece, your nephew, your grandchild—with dignity and respect and empathy. They did not leave their home that morning saying to themselves, 'I'm going to go to school and be as naughty as I can and make the teacher's life as miserable as I can.' I've been doing this for twenty-nine years. I've never met a child who's had that intent. Now, do things get in the way, and cause them to be quite challenging at times?" She laughed. "Yes! But you have to take a step back, and ask yourself what it is that they're lugging. Did they have breakfast that morning? Did someone yell at them? Did someone hit them? Did their brother lock them out? As a substitute, you don't know them and don't know their history, and you have to give them the benefit of the doubt. You have to assume, whatever it is that they're doing, whether it's yelling, screaming, throwing something, calling you a name, that there's a reason behind it that has very little to do with you. The more compassionate and empathetic you are, and the calmer you are, the more success you'll have."

Use humor, not the hammer, Mrs. Norris said. "Humor will defuse and be your friend. And if they say something funny—sometimes they'll say stuff and it's genuinely funny and it's not hurting anybody, it's just funny—it's okay to say, 'Hah, that was a good one.'" Then move on. But don't let chaos spread, she said. You can do a lot with a raised eyebrow, a warning look. "That's the biggest mistake subs make—they give kids too much rope."

Mrs. Ecklin said, "I've been in special ed for thirty years and it's the really naughty ones I really like."

Mrs. Norris said, "We both like quirky, naughty children. We love them. Kids know if you're pretending to like them or if you really like them. If you do really like kids and you show it, they'll eat out of your hand." Show that you're vulnerable, she advised. Apologize to a student for getting off on the wrong foot, even if the student was being a holy terror. "There will be days when you'll think, Okay, I wonder if Walmart needs a greeter. But you always come back. It's probably the most rewarding job you're ever going to do. Especially when kids get it and they tell you at the end of the day, 'I love you.' You might be the only person who says something nice to them—the only person who cares about them—all day long. Unfortunately that's the case for some of our kids. So do your best to make their day a really good day, no matter how they make your life miserable."

After some words of wisdom about fire drills and lockdown procedures and proper clothing, Shelly wrapped up the class and we went home.

ON THE THIRD TUESDAY, Shelly introduced three friendly, snappily dressed guidance counselors who were there to talk about Lasswell Middle School. The middle school had two floors, we learned, and it held sixth-, seventh-, and eighth-graders divided into nine teams, each with ninety students. The teams were named for great rivers of the world, Nile, Orinoco, Yangtze, Mississippi, Rhine, and so on.

The guidance counselors went into detail about emergency lockdown procedures and iPads—every student was issued an iPad—and class schedules. There was a certain block of time called STAR, which stood for "Students and Teachers Achieving Results," which seemed to involve silent reading. Substitute teachers deserved the same level of respect that everyone else at the school received, said the guidance counselors. Students must dress and act appropriately—no spaghetti straps, no short shorts, no T-shirts with references to tobacco or alcohol, no hugging, no kissing. No cellphones in class. We were to separate students who were being excessively chatty, they said. If a particular student was causing trouble, we should first try to "redirect" him or her, and if they continued to act up, then call the office. "When you call, you could say, 'I've tried to redirect so-and-so several times and they're not following directions and they're being disruptal.'" The guidance counselor paused, puzzled. "Disruptful?"

"Disruptive," Shelly suggested.

"Disruptive, thank you! I was an English major, which is scary."

We broke into groups and did some role-playing about how to deal with excessive chattiness and then I got very sleepy. I was on the verge of nodding off when I heard Shelly say, "Thank you again for coming," and the class was over.

I drove home thinking that as soon as you sit down in a class, even a class you're looking forward to, you begin to want it to be over. Even if you're really interested in what's going on—and I was interested in this substitute training class—there's an intense impatience to be done. I marveled that children were asked to sit in classes all day long. Such brightly lit classes, too.

A WOMAN FROM IDENTOGO called to set up a second fingerprinting appointment. I apologized to her for having hard-to-scan fingers. "It happens to a lot of people," she said. "Usually it's poor ridge quality, or oily fingertips." She said that if I failed three times, then they would just perform a "name check" on me—nothing to worry about.

I drove back to the fingerprinting office and washed my hands carefully twice. Again most of my fingerprints were rejected.

"See you again, maybe," I said.

"I hope not," said the fingerprint woman.

ON THE LAST DAY of substitute class, Shelly put out bowls of Reese's
Peanut Butter Cups at each table for us to eat. Mr. Clapper, a beefy man
with a coach's raspy, commanding voice, was there with two of his senior
staff—he called them "ladies"—to tell us how Lasswell High School
worked. Mr. Clapper had taught health and physical education for twenty
years, he said, and he'd coached the Lasswell football team, and then he
became assistant principal and still coached the football team, and now
he was Lasswell's principal. "We have a shortage of substitutes," he said,
"and a large part of that is because some of our subs are snowbirds. They
are someplace warm right now, as opposed to being available." He talked
about Lasswell's class schedule. "Our blocks are roughly fifty-seven
minutes long, and the students have six minutes to pass in between
classes. Lunch happens in three segments, so some of our blocks are
broken in two with lunch in between. And then we have one full block at
the end of the day."

One of Mr. Clapper's guidance counselors passed around a sample
folder of sub plans. "You'll get a roster that you mark off for attendance,"
she said. "You send one of those nice, trustworthy students right down to
the office to bring it down for you." She smiled. "They'll be back very
quickly, I'm sure."

The sub plans would include IEPs and health concerns, the guidance
counselor said. "If one of our students has seizures, that might be
something you would need to know." Substitute teachers really had to pay
attention to the bell schedule, she added. "Kids will work on you. They'll
say, 'We want to leave for lunch early, we're starving.' They'll badger you.
Don't let them do that. They're great kids and you'll enjoy them, but they
are teenagers, and they may try to pull one over on you." Every high
school student had an iPad, and iPads were for class work, not for games
or social networks. Cellphones should not be out in class—they could be
used between classes. "We want to keep hands off of kids," she added, "not

grabbing them, or putting a hand on their shoulder, or touching them in any way, shape, or form."

Mr. Clapper talked at length about lockdown procedures and fire drills. "We've been throwing curveballs," he said. For instance, they recently did a fire drill within a lockdown drill. Another time they sent a decoy class through the halls to lure students and teachers into thinking the lockdown was over, when it wasn't.

Shelley handed us evaluation forms to fill out, and signed certificates saying we had successfully completed the course. "So," she said, "you've gotten a picture of elementary school, a picture of middle school, and now you have a picture of high school. And you never really know how it's going to go until you set foot in each place." She gave each of us a last list of suggested educational games. "I've enjoyed doing this," she said. "Thank you for everything. Safe travels." We all said goodbye and thank you and waved at each other and crunched over broken bits of ice to our cars.

I SPENT A DAY FILLING OUT many pages of application forms for RSU66. There were actually two parallel sets of forms—one on SchoolSpring, a school employment website, and one on paper, with supplemental questions. I forwarded letters of recommendation and college transcripts, and I checked off that I'd be willing to substitute in all grades, at all schools. "Becoming a substitute teacher seems like the best, most direct way to learn how classrooms work," I wrote in the cover letter.

I dropped off the forms and waited. Soon I got a cardboard fingerprint card in the mail—IdentoGO had determined that I was not a criminal. I danced around the kitchen waving it in the air, and then I dropped by Shelly's office so that her assistant could make a copy. The next day I got an email: "Congratulations, Nick—you've been added to our Substitute Teacher List! You may begin getting calls as early as today."

I was a teacher.

SMALL BUT HOSTILE

The call came in at five-forty in the morning, plinking from under my pillow. Would I be interested in filling in for a day for a math teacher named Mrs. Prideaux, in a resource room at the high school? I said I'd give it a shot, and I kissed my sleepy wife and took a shower and put on my good shoes and a sport jacket and drove for a long time in the dark, over hilly rural roads, eating a toasted waffle. There had been a sudden thaw overnight, and the predawn traffic moved slowly through the side-sliding snowmist.

The buses, about twenty of them, were already queuing up as I reached the turn into the parking lot, where a sign announced that Lasswell High School was a tobacco-free area. I parked in the back, near the athletic field, a blank white plain with low shapes of cold fog slipping through the goalposts.

Hundreds of slow-moving, sleepy students were getting off buses and filing into a pair of side doors, supervised by several silent adults with clipboards. The idling engines of the buses made a heavy, steady noise; they exhaled plumes of exhaust, like cows waiting to be milked. There was a big stop sign on the door, ordering visitors to check in at the front office.

I told one of the grownups that I was a substitute and asked where the office was. He pointed down a hall. "Thank you for helping out," he said. I waved.

It was warm and brightly fluorescent inside—not loud. Students with expressionless early-morning faces were leaning against lockers or kneeling on the floor going through their backpacks or hugging in corners. One of the secretaries, a small, pleasant, quick-moving woman in a gray cocktail dress, gave me a folder full of papers and a lanyard with a tag on it that said SUBSTITUTE, and she took me to room 18 and unlocked the door. It was a small hot space, with about ten desks, some bookshelves, some cabinets, and a whiteboard. Taped to the wall was an information sheet on attention deficit disorder. The walls were cinderblock, painted a cream color.

"Here are your attendance sheets," the secretary said. "I've highlighted the different blocks that you have. All you need to do is mark them absent or tardy and then have a student bring them down to the office." There were two lunches, she explained, and I had Lunch B, which began in the middle of block 4, at 11:49 a.m.

I thanked her and she went away. I sat down at the desk. There was a SpongeBob jar on it filled with pencils and dry-erase markers, and piles of student papers and worksheets and abandoned notebooks. A teacher— plump and capable looking—stopped by to introduce herself.

"Anything I should know?" I said.

"There are some challenging kids, because this is all special ed," she said. "But Helen's had subs before and it goes pretty well. I'm close and happy to help if I can." She went away. I opened the folder and read Mrs. Prideaux's sub plans.

Six electric bongs came over the PA system, followed by a longer boop, and then a secretary's voice came on. "Good morning, please stand for the Pledge of Allegiance." I stood in the empty room, but I didn't speak, because there was nobody in the room with me yet. "I pledge allegiance to the flag of the United States of America," said the secretary over the loudspeaker, "and to the republic for which it stands, one nation, under God, indivisible, with liberty and justice for all. Please pause for a moment of silence." There was a moment of silence, another electric boop, and then she said, "Thank you, and have a great day." School was in session. It got very quiet. I had no students.

After a long time, the electric bongs bonged again, and it was the beginning of block 1. A girl walked in. "Hello," I said. "Hello," she said. She dropped her backpack by a desk. I asked her her name and checked it off on a list. She left. A boy came in and sat down and opened a container of diced fruit. I checked his name off on the attendance sheet. Another kid came in and began looking through the cupboards, opening them and closing them rapidly.

"How are you doing?" I said.

"Good," he said. In one of the cupboards he found a bag of cheese-flavored popcorn. He sat down.

"What's your name?"

"Jack."

"Hi, Jack, good to meet you. I'm Nick. Are you in this class?"

"No, but I usually come over here from across the hall and do work." He sat and ate popcorn, blinking sleepily.

I asked him what kind of math he was supposed to be working on.

"I'm doing something else, I'm working on history." He said he was researching the Vietnam War.

"Interesting," I said. "So who started it?"

He didn't answer.

"Hard to say, right?" I said. "Goes way back into the mists of time. People say Kennedy wanted to get us out of Vietnam. Do you think he did?"

"I think so," said Jack.

I read a supplemental part of the sub plans, which was in capitals. "ALGEBRA 2 STUDENTS WILL COME IN WITH BREAKFAST AND MAY BE A LITTLE LATE. I'VE BEEN SOMEWHAT EASY ON THEM BECAUSE THEY'RE GOOD WORKERS."

"People seem to wander in and out of this room," I said to Jack.

"Yeah, they do."

"So what do you like better, math or history?"

"Probably history."

More students stopped by the door, saw that I was a substitute, and left to prowl the halls in search of friends. A girl wrote something on a Post-it note and asked me to sign it. It was permission for her to go to the library.

"Should I have signed that?" I asked Jack.

"Probably not," he said.

I checked off some more names. They were juniors, it turned out. Some, who were taking Algebra II, were supposed to log on to a piece of software called MobyMax and take a test on their "core curriculum standards." Some took it, some didn't.

The bonger bonged again and some new students showed up. These were chattier. People were waking up now. I met a kid named Clyde who was interested in trucks and wore a plaid shirt and a baseball hat. He said he made good money by plowing people's driveways. His grandfather had gotten him a truck which was completely rusted out—you could see the road through the floor, he said, and it wouldn't pass inspection—so his father found him another truck on Craigslist for fifteen hundred dollars that he was happy with. Clyde told me that it was tricky to plow driveways right now, because the ground was starting to thaw. If it's a paved driveway, then you can just drop the plow down on the asphalt, but if it's a dirt driveway, you don't want to rip up the surface by plowing too deep. "You get a feel for it after a while," he said.

Another kid named Shamus came in, a quietly amused young man, also wearing a baseball hat, who turned out to have a girlfriend named Rianne. Rianne was round-faced and pale and wore very tight black pants and a black-and-pink-striped shirt and she worked at McDonald's. She'd worked until three in the morning the night before, closing the store. "I don't sleep," she said. That was how she got through high school, she said, by not sleeping. She leaned against Shamus with her eyes closed, while Shamus looked at videos on his iPad.

Shamus's friend Artie appeared—a loud, jokey storyteller, who liked to get as close as he could to dropping the f-bomb without actually dropping it: "I was like 'What the fffffff . . . udge?'" He was stocky and handsome, and he spent his time trying to find good-looking bathing beauties on his iPad from websites that weren't blocked. He was supposed to be doing a geometry worksheet.

Ms. Laronde, a young "ed tech"—a teaching assistant—came in to help Artie. She reminded him of the difference between complementary and supplementary angles. In a soft, faintly ironic voice, Ms. Laronde questioned and coaxed and prodded and finally got him to write his name at the top of the worksheet. That was all the geometry he did—he wrote his name. Besides that he told stories and said unexpected things. "My horrible fear is when you wake up and one of your eyes is swollen shut," he suddenly announced. "I'm probably going to die at the age of forty-five."

Ms. Laronde left to coach other students with Individualized Education Plans and Artie and Shamus began talking about milk. Artie said, "Boobies, cow boobies, that's where the milk comes from." He told a story about his little brother, who was seven. They were listening to Eminem and his little brother said, "Shut off those nigga beats." Artie said, "Those aren't nigga beats, those are cracker beats." Later Artie's father came home and asked what they'd been doing. His little brother said, "We were listening to cracker beats."

The sub plans said I was supposed to discourage a tall, wiry kid named Lucas from playing on his iPad. I tried. Lucas and his friend, who wasn't on the attendance sheet but who was allowed to visit, according to Mrs. Prideaux, were interested in watching YouTube videos of pickup trucks driving around in fields of mud—a sport called mudding. Some of the mudding trucks were "duallies"—trucks with two pairs of tires in the back. One truck was notable in that it had dually tires in the front and the back. "How can you even steer with duallies in the front?" Lucas's friend asked. They tipped their iPads in each other's direction: "Whoa, that's a nice truck!"

"That's badass, I have to say," said Artie, leaning over.

"Check this out," said Lucas.

A huge wave of mud spewed out from monster tires. "Oooh, nice," they said.

Adam, who had chewed-up fingernails, showed me a picture on his iPad of his four-wheeler. It had two speeds. You're supposed to drive up a hill in first, he said, but he'd had to shift to second to make progress. "It isn't dangerous unless you're stupid," he added.

The electric bongs happened again, and it was a new block. A sad girl showed up. She'd been crying because her boyfriend had broken up with her. Rianne hugged her and stroked her cheek. Shamus said, "I could put up my kickstand for you." Then, imitating a teacher, he said, in a low voice, "That is not acceptable!"

"I'll tell you what's not acceptable," said Artie. "What if I whipped down my pants and took a shit on your grave?"

Shamus and Rianne laughed. Later Rianne tried to take a nap lying on Shamus's lap.

Another teaching assistant showed up for a little while—very young, a recent graduate of the high school. He'd grown a goatee to look older than the students. He joshed with the young men about trucks, about jobs, about snowplowing, and about somebody's older brother. His name was Mr. C.

When the mudding videos got too loud, I told the trucker boys to turn them down—and they did. They were, in a way, polite. Every so often I would prod a student to work on math. "Math is like my worst subject," one of them said. "It's just stupid. I don't understand it. I hate it. It's a total waste."

But one kid, Colin, with a wavy shock of hair, sat silently the whole time, earbuds in, listening to music, crouched over, doing homework, erasing and rewriting answers.

When I stood up, several people said, "You're tall! How tall are you?"

The morning went by slowly. My head felt stuffed with cotton balls and I had trouble sitting up and looking authoritative. There was no coffee machine, so I sipped a Coke to stay alert. I sighed loudly at one point, and Clyde gave me a sympathetic look. "I hear you," he said. "I feel your pain."

The clock was an hour off because of daylight savings, which had just happened. "You're lucky you weren't here yesterday," said Clyde. "Everybody was grumpy. People were standing in the hallway yelling—it was bad."

Suddenly the bonger bonged for lunch. By the time I got out to the car I realized I didn't have time to drive somewhere and buy a sandwich, so I ate three Blue Diamond almonds I found in my car and drank the rest of my Coke.

Back at my desk, I studied the sub plans for what was supposed to happen after lunch. A girl, Charlee, had written a paper, and I was supposed to help her finish her bibliography, which needed to have at least three sources in it. She was sitting, staring into space, listening to music, looking goth but neat. And bored.

"So, you're working on a paper," I said.

Charlee nodded.

"What about the bibliography?"

She sighed.

"What are you writing about?"

"Oh, we had to write about an animal."

"An animal! That's pretty gripping, pretty interesting."

"Isn't it?" she said sarcastically.

"Of course, it depends on the animal," I said. "What did you choose?"

"The wolverine."

"I thought that was a shoe," I said.

"It could be a brand of shoe, but it's a damn wolverine," Charlee said. "I'll show you." She tipped her iPad toward me.

"Oh, it's a small, friendly, furry creature," I said.

"It's like me," said Charlee. "Small but hostile."

Artie called out, "Girl, get your ass to work!"

She began talking to her friend about what they were doing after school: they both had orientation and training at a Hannaford supermarket, where they'd just gotten jobs.

I was also supposed to encourage a certain boy, Logan, to finish a "health assessment" on suicide. "He only has one section left!" said the sub plans.

I went over to him. "So you're working on something about suicide?"

"Yeah." Logan was a serious kid, in a gray, zipped-up hoodie, with short hair and black eyebrows.

"And you've got one section left?"

"Yeah, I'm not going to do that, that's for extra credit." He showed me what he'd done. He'd been given a transcript of an actual call to a suicide prevention unit in which a despairing man talked ramblingly about how he had no reason to live, and about how much he wanted to die. Logan had, as asked, highlighted the "warning phrases" of suicidality with a yellow highlighter.

"That's quite an assignment," I said.

Logan said, "Yeah, I know."

"Well, you're almost there, you're on the home stretch, finish it up if you can."

He began playing a video game on the iPad, in which two hoppy animated creatures leapt up and down on a mountain range. Then his iPad froze. "My iPad froze!" he said indignantly.

And so the day ticked by. Nobody wreaked havoc or did anything too horrible. On the other hand, only a few students did anything that Lasswell High School would define as actual work. At a guess, I'd say that 1 percent of total class time—no, less than that—was taken up with algebra, geometry, health, history, language arts, or any other subject that the school was supposedly in the business of teaching. And yet, so what? I liked the kids and felt that given their forced idleness and the futility of their academic days, they were doing an impressive job of staying sane and keeping their senses of humor.

The means they had available to pass time productively had improved dramatically because of the iPad. In the old days, they would have made spitballs, or poked their neighbors—now they could watch mudding videos, which actually interested them, or take pictures of each other, or play chirpy video games. The iPad had improved their lives.

Nobody expected most of them to do academic work, it seemed, because long ago they'd been labeled as kids with "special needs"—even though in fact they were, judging by their vocabulary, their temperament, and their fluent way with irony, normal American high schoolers. They weren't masterminds, but that wasn't why they were in this room—they were here because they quietly refused to do work that they hated.

At the very end of the day, just before the bell rang, everybody gathered by the door. I began putting the computers away. (There were, in addition to the ubiquitous iPads, carts full of old Apple laptops.) Lydia, a girl with braces, in a pink sweatshirt, came in, very keyed-up and wild. She began throwing a pen around. I said, "Hey, hey, hey."

"Stop it, or the substitute won't come back," said her friend Shelby.

"I'll be back," I said. "I enjoyed it."

"See, he enjoyed it," said Lydia.

I felt like a figure of fun, but not so like a figure of fun that I didn't want to do it again. I hadn't helped anybody learn anything, I'd just allowed them to be themselves; I was there for a day to ensure that room 18 didn't descend into utter chaos. My role was to function as straight man, to give these kids the pleasure of avoiding meaningless schoolwork. And that was maybe a useful role.

The final six bells bonged and everybody surged out and the room was empty again. I wrote a note to Mrs. Prideaux saying that the kids had been good-natured and funny, and that I was grateful to have had a chance to fill in. As I was driving home, I remembered something Clyde, the snowplower, had said. "You've got your good kids and you've got your bad kids. And sometimes your bad kids can be your good kids."

And that was the end of Day One.

MYSTERY PICTURE

THE PHONE PLINKED AT 5:40 A.M. on Monday, St. Patrick's Day. Lasswell Elementary School needed someone to teach second grade, said Beth, the sub caller. "I'll do it, thanks," I said.

On the way there I bought two glazed donuts and two medium Turbo cups of coffee—one cup for later. The elementary school, a few miles away from Lasswell High School, was a low brick building in the middle of a wooded patch, with a playground out back: swingsets and a climbing structure sitting in a white field of ice. A jolly, pink-cheeked secretary signed me in and gave me a badge that said STAFF, which I clipped to my jacket pocket. The room was warm; I was already beginning to sweat.

In room 7, Mrs. Heber, the teacher who'd called in sick, was sitting at her desk, under garlands made of looped construction paper. She had a bad cold and looked as if she hadn't slept well; even so, she'd come in before school started to write up her sub plans and print out some worksheets. "You look like you have some experience under your belt," Mrs. Heber said. "Have you been a teacher?" I told her it was my first time teaching at the elementary level, but both my children had been through Maine schools.

"Well, there you go," she said. She stapled some pages together and handed them to me. I read a sentence: "Have the kids add 'I Found a Four Leaf Clover' to their fluency binder's table of contents." Mrs. Heber showed me the math activity worksheet, a grid of squares with an accompanying color key. "This is a little confusing," she said. "The kids won't have seen this before but it's really fun. As long as you get it, they'll get it."

"I hope you feel better," I said. "Thanks for preparing everything so well."

"Good group of kids," Mrs. Heber said. "I haven't told you about my little handfuls. My two handfuls are Parker and Benjamin. Keep an eye on those two—they'll try to get silly." She wished me good luck and left.

I drew up a seating chart to try to learn the children's names beforehand, gave up, and looked around, trying to get my bearings. The desks, made of wood-grain Formica, were tiny, arranged in a large square, with handwritten names taped to the tops—I'd forgotten how small second-graders were. The chairs were made of maroon plastic and they were stacked around the edges of the room, which had gray carpeting. The walls were crowded with a bewilderment of sights—calendars, headphones on hooks, yellow cardboard clocks with movable hands, a number strip that went around the ceiling, letter diagrams, a cartoon of parts of the body, a poster saying "How Do You Feel Today?" with pictures of children in various states of emotion, hand-crayoned figures of "ROOM HELPERS" mounted in plastic pouches against an electric-orange background. There was a bright yellow bookcase stuffed with a kaleidoscope of kids' books, and a green chalk blackboard superimposed with pastel Post-its and charts with primary-colored stickers going down the side. Behind Mrs. Heber's desk hung an intricate "Taxonomy of Educational Objectives," colored pink, aqua blue, pale green, and violet, with sub-objectives spelled out in rectangles. Under "ANALYZING KNOWLEDGE" was a box that said:

Analyzing Errors
in Reasoning
Identify logical
or factual errors
- Question the validity of
- Listen to insure
- Assess
- Expose fallacies in

Listen to insure? I started to get nervous—I couldn't take it all in, and I didn't know where anything was. Just then the teacher next door popped in to say good morning. "If you need anything let me know," she said. "They're a good group of kids, but they're very social. They love to talk."

"If you hear an uproar coming from this room," I said, "I'm sorry."

"Oh, you'll hear me, too," she said, which made me feel better.

A bell rang—an old-fashioned bell with a real clapper—and children began arriving in ones and twos. I said hi and they shyly said hi. Backpacks were hung on hooks, snowpants were removed, chairs were unstacked and distributed. "You guys really know what you're doing," I said.

"You're really tall," said one tiny girl, Anastasia—she was wearing several strings of green plastic beads in honor of St. Patrick's Day. Bryce, a tiny freckled boy, pulled out a chapter book from his backpack and told me he'd finished it last night—*The Lightning Thief.* I congratulated him. I'd forgotten that kids could have freckles. I found a stub of chalk and wrote "Mr. Baker" on the board.

I asked Anastasia if now was the time when I should pass out the four-leaf-clover poem for their fluency binders. "You have to ask the paper passer," she said. I asked who the paper passer was. "Tessa, but she isn't here yet."

Some children's voices came over the PA system, reading the date and the weather forecast in singsong unison. They told a knock-knock joke that I couldn't make out. The principal came on to announce several birthdays and to congratulate a team of Lasswell Elementary students who'd won an Odyssey of the Mind tournament over the weekend. Nobody in the class listened. Then, on cue, everyone grew quiet and serious and put their hands on their chests, and we said the Pledge of Allegiance together.

"Hi, everybody, I'm Mr. Baker, I'm the substitute," I said. "Is the paper passer here?" Tessa dashed over and began passing out the poem. A minor problem arose: normally poems destined for the fluency binder were copied onto three-hole paper, but this time, as several children told me, they lacked holes. "Oh, no," I said.

"I know where the hole puncher is!" said Anastasia. She rummaged on a side table covered with heaps of art supplies until she found it. The hole puncher began traveling around the room, punching holes in the four-leaf-clover poem, leaving a flutterment of paper dots on the carpet. A boy asked me for a Band-Aid—he had a red patch on his leg where he'd fallen on a snowdrift. "I'm so sorry," I said. "I think if you just let it air-dry and don't mess with it, probably that's the best thing you can do."

A plump girl with a kind face and pink shoes, Cerise, helped me take attendance—five students were sick that day, and two were there but were in a remedial math class. Another girl helped me take the lunch count— how many kids were getting a hot lunch, how many were getting SunButter and jelly, how many had brought their own lunch. When everyone had written the title of the poem in their table of contents and clicked their three-ring binders closed, it was time, according to the sub plans, to line up to go to Monday morning assembly.

Carter, who was smart and officious, told me the rule: silence in the hallways.

"The boys are always less good in the hall," said Ellie, who was also smart and officious. We processed, fairly silently, in a line to the cafeteria, where a murmuring crowd of children sat on the floor. The teachers stood against the wall; at a certain moment all of them raised their hands, holding up two fingers, and the assembly went quiet. In the front, a woman used a bucket and some milk cartons to show how many quarts were in a gallon and how many pints were in a quart. "Now, how many pints in a gallon?" she asked.

Two!

Eight!

Four!

A reading enrichment teacher read a poem by Natasha Wing, based on "'Twas the Night Before Christmas." It was about some children who catch a leprechaun in their house on the night before St. Patrick's Day: "They set all the traps round the room with great care / In hopes a wee Irishman soon would be theirs." The children stare at the captive leprechaun so that he won't disappear, and they demand that he tell them where he's hidden the gold. He tells them that it's buried under a rock in the back yard. But the leprechaun is a trickster: no gold for the children. End of poem.

"Now close your eyes and put your hands on your head," said the reading enrichment person. "Think of the characters. Think about the setting. Think about the beginning, the middle, the end. Think about the problem. Think about the solution." We thought about all these things. She asked who the characters were, what the setting was, what the problem was. Hands went up, the right answers came back. "You guys did it all," the reading enrichment teacher said. "You retold the whole story, problems, solutions—wow!"

We walked silently back to the room. "Can I have a drink, because my throat hurts?" asked a sniffly girl named Jessamyn. I said she could—there was a sink with a drinking fountain by the bookcases. According to the sub plans, I had to get through the four-leaf-clover poem quickly, because we had to have a spelling test and then snack time and then a reading of a Tacky the Penguin book before writing a story about a leprechaun. "Okay, guys, listen up," I said. "Everybody got three holes in their poem? Good. Everybody take a seat. Guys! So this poem is a— GUYS! Chip chip aroo! Hop! Hip! This poem is kind of weird and I need your help with it."

They quieted down and we read the poem together. It was supposed to

be funny—it's by a light-versist named Jack Prelutsky and it's about a
kid who finds a four-leaf clover that brings only bad luck—but the kids
didn't go for it. Perhaps it wasn't the right note to strike on St. Patrick's
Day, especially coming immediately after the poem about the trickster
leprechaun. I read:

> I barked my shin, I missed my train,
> I sat on my dessert.

"Ew," said Ellie. "That doesn't make any sense."

When we got to the end, Anastasia said, very simply, "I have a lot of
four-leaf clovers in my garden."

"I have grass in my yard," said Benjamin.

It was time for the unit 17 spelling test. Several kids suddenly
discovered that they needed to sharpen their pencils: there was a lot of
earnest grinding away at the fancy electric pencil sharpener hidden
behind the teacher's desk. They all knew where it was.

"All right, let's do this! Parker! Have a seat. Has everybody written
their name at the top of the page? GUYS!"

"Do you want me to clap them out?" said Tessa, with an eager
expression.

"Sure, clap them out," I said.

She frowned importantly and held her hands over her head and went
clap, clap, clap-clap-clap.

Immediately the whole class went *clap, clap, clap-clap-clap.*

About the spelling test, the sub plans said: "You read the words on the
pink sticky note, giving sample sentences for each word." I could do that.
"Were," I said. I made up a sentence: "We were going to Kohl's to buy a
pair of flip-flops. *Were."*

"Kohl's?" said several voices.

"Macy's?" I said. "Walmart? Somewhere."

"I've been to Macy's," said Jessamyn, who was wearing a yellow shirt
that matched her barrette.

I went on to the next word. "*Look*. Look before you leap, then leap like a madman and then look again. *Look*."

They wrote.

"Number three," I said. "*Down*. Down we go, deeper into the ocean than we've ever gone before. *Down*."

"Where there are some strange fishes," said Bryce, the boy who'd read *The Lightning Thief.*

"Leopard fishes," said Anastasia. "Glowing leopard fishes that have glowing eyes!"

There were twelve words altogether. The toughest one was *through*. I remembered learning how to spell it for the first time. After the test was over I wrote *through* on the board. "The beginning is pretty simple," I said. "T-H, *th*, and R, *thr*. But then you think, Hmm, there are all kinds of strange letters in there. It looks like it should be 'throg-hah.'"

"Throg-hah!" said Carter.

"But no, it's *through*. You have to journey all the way *through* those U-G-H letters to get to the end. Okay, and now it's snack time, folks."

Everyone pulled out their snacks. Some lined up at the sink to wash their hands. Cerise showed me where the Tacky the Penguin picture books were—propped on the ledge against the blackboard. People sucked on juice pouches and ate Goldfish crackers while I read the story of Tacky the Penguin's trip on an ice floe to a tropical island, where he meets a strange soft, hairy, gray rock that turns out to be an elephant. I secretly skipped some pages to get to the end. Must keep to the schedule.

Ms. Keeler, an amiable, gentle-voiced ed tech, came in to help while the kids wrote and illustrated a story about what they would do if they met a leprechaun. We spent almost an hour on this activity. I wrote *leprechaun* on the blackboard, and *surprise* and *favorite*. The class had, it seemed, developed a certain animus toward leprechauns. "I would hide in my room till it was morning time," said a girl named Evelyn. "I'd catch it in a jar and flush it down the toilet," said Ellie. "I'd dissect it," said Spencer, and he drew a black cage with a leprechaun trapped inside. "I would give it a piece of cake with poop inside," said Tessa—Ms. Keeler helped her spell *poop*. "I would steal his gold cake," wrote Dominic. "I would feed it cheese," said Marina. "I would feed it an elephant," said Jordan. Cerise was more affectionate; she said she'd keep her leprechaun with her forever. After the ed tech went to lunch, Tessa asked if they could use sparkly stickers to decorate their drawings, and I said sure—which was not the right answer. The sparkly stickers came from a sacred upper cupboard, and several indignant girls told me that the class was forbidden to use anything in the upper cupboard. "Yes we can, if the teacher says!" said Tessa. It took several minutes to sort that disagreement out—and then it was 11:10 and time for the forty-minute gym class.

I raised two fingers to signal for them all to be quiet. Again we traipsed wordlessly through the hallways. In gym they lined up along a line on the floor and the teacher put on Pharrell Williams's "Happy" at high volume. They started running around the gym in circles. "I'll see you at eleven-fifty," the gym teacher said.

Out in my car, I drank the second cup of coffee, staring at a dead oak leaf, resting. My knees hurt.

Back in gym, my class was finishing something called NASCAR, in teams of two. One child sat on a blue stool perched on a wooden square with rolling wheels, and the other pushed his teammate around the gym. Jayson and Parker won, they informed me, having pushed each other around the gym fifty-two times. Everyone was sweaty and completely wiped out. Tessa, whining, said she wanted to go to the nurse because her stomach hurt badly. I told her to try a drink of cold water. They all went into the bathrooms near the cafeteria and then they lined up in the cafeteria's lunch line. "This is your lunch break," said the sub plans.

I ate a sandwich at my desk and wondered if I'd taught anything at all that morning of use to anybody. It didn't seem as if I had. Did it matter? Yes, I think it did matter, more so in elementary school than in high school, because being able to read is a universally useful skill. The basic problem was that we live in a jokey, chatty world—which is a good thing—but a room full of eighteen jokey, chatty children is an inefficient place to learn.

I thought of my own second-grade teacher, Mrs. Richards—a dark-haired woman with a sly smile. She liked a report I did, "Workers Who Keep Us Well"—I drew a dentist's office, with a patch of cracked plaster on the wall, and a garbage truck with two men behind it holding garbage cans. The garbagemen kept us well, I wrote, because they took away all the garbage. Once I went up to Mrs. Richards's desk to ask her a question and unintentionally caught sight of her black, spiral-bound gradebook, where she'd written everyone's name in beautiful cursive. "Nosy!" she said, which hurt my feelings. She was a really good teacher. She taught us how to spell *elephant* and *umbrella*, and how to carry the one in addition. And she taught us the golden rule.

After lunch my class was hoarse and crazy tired. Three girls said their stomachs hurt. Parker, my "handful," was making roaring noises near the bookcase, and Jordan was singing "Who Let the Dogs Out." Cerise said, "Dominic said something not very nice to me."

"I'm sorry to hear that," I said. "Dominic, do not say not-very-nice things."

"If you don't have anything nice to say, don't say anything at all," said Anastasia.

Four children—including two of the roaring boys, as it happened—left to go to a Title I remedial program.

"It's time for silent reading," said Cerise.

"You are so right," I said, having studied Mrs. Heber's plans. "Silent reading, guys, it's time for SILENT READING."

And then a miracle happened. In a matter of minutes the whole class had pulled out little squarish picture books, or chapter books, or nature books. They all went quiet and they read or looked at pictures. Some sat on the floor. Some had their heads on their desks and their books balanced on their laps. It was so quiet I could hear pages turning. A whole half hour passed without any noise at all, except for once when my cellphone rang, embarrassingly. I was agog. What amazing children. What an amazing school.

Then it was one o'clock, and I peeked at the sub plans, which had grown as finely crumpled as old dollar bills from my having carried them around with me for hours. "Please read another Tacky book (or two)," they said. No! The Title I kids came back. The noise level rose four notches. Anastasia told me that Mrs. Heber had just finished reading the class *Charlotte's Web*. I couldn't bear to read another Tacky book, so we played a game. Someone read a sentence from *Charlotte's Web*, and left out a word. "Fern loved *blank* more than anything." Charlotte! No, Wilbur! "She loved to stroke him and put him to *blank*." Bed!

But soon I felt guilty that I wasn't following the plan, and I reluctantly embarked on the story of Tacky the Penguin going to a summer camp called Camp Whoopihaha, where they made s'mores. We talked about the way marshmallows burn at the end of a stick, and then a teacher dropped by to remind me that I had recess duty, and to say that I had to be absolutely sure that no kids strayed onto the large, hazardous ice pond that had formed a few days earlier around the swingsets. "Well," I said, slapping the big book closed. "I guess it all turns out okay for Tacky at camp. Tacky is DONE." There was a scramble of putting on snowpants and finding mittens, and the bell rang. Ellie and Cerise told me the rules of winter recess: If you had snowpants, you could climb on the snow piles; if you didn't, you had to stay on the pavement. If you were caught climbing on the snow three times without snowpants, you had to go stand by the wall. But fifth-graders could climb on the snow even without snowpants. I asked them what Mrs. Heber usually did at recess. "She'll walk around and make sure that kids aren't throwing snow or bullying," said Ellie.

Another substitute teacher, Ms. Healey—studious, quiet, in her forties—was on duty with me. She'd been substituting in the district for a year and a half, but she never took assignments at the high school. "High school is harder because they're full of themselves," she said. "I don't have the assertiveness that's necessary." Suddenly she called, "STAY OFF THE ICE! STAY OFF THE ICE!"

Two kids ran up to me and said, "Mr. Baker, there's a ball out on the ice."

"Yeah, the ball is going to stay there," said Ms. Healey. "Someday it will be retrieved."

A nurse came out to let us know that some kids were frolicking dangerously on a second smaller ice pond in the back; it was hidden behind a four-foot mound of gray snow.

"STAY OFF THE ICE!" called Ms. Healey.

"Mr. Baker, there's a ball on the ice," said Jordan.

"I know, that's just the way it is," I said.

After an interval of running and screaming and snowsuited misrule, all the classes lined up in five lines near the doors. There was some jockeying for position at the head of the lines.

"Mr. Baker, there's a ball on the ice," said Benjamin.

"I know."

"Another tip," said Anastasia quietly. "You can pick door holders."

"Thanks!" I said.

"Wait till everyone's quiet, then pick the quietest line," Anastasia said.

I let Ms. Healey pick the quietest line—I didn't want to hurt anyone's feelings—and I watched the faces fall of the quiet children in the lines who weren't picked. Anastasia was one of the door holders. We crowded back inside our classroom—snowpants were shucked off, more girls felt sick, Cerise had hurt her chin somehow, and Evelyn held an ice pack on her elbow after a fall from a snowbank.

Tessa, the paper passer, passed out the "Mystery Picture" math worksheets. One sheet was filled with a grid of squares, some cut in half by diagonal lines, with a row of numbers along the side, and a row of letters along the bottom. On a second sheet was a color key: D-8 = G, and G stood for green. I-11 = Y, and Y stood for yellow. The idea was to color in the squares according to the key, and if you did it right, you were rewarded with a blocky likeness of a green four-leaf clover against a yellow background. "Does everyone have a green crayon and a yellow crayon?" I asked. The roaring boys were roaring again by now; somebody was lustily working the crank on the paper towel machine; Tessa was singing

"Happy"; and my explanation, repeated four or five times, did not reach as many children as I would have liked.

Cerise, who was an artist, had, while I was across the room listening to a girl tell me about the time she broke her collarbone, embarked on her clover: it had wide, neatly crayoned green and yellow stripes against a white background. Two other girls quickly followed her example. Anastasia and Bryce did it exactly right. I walked around showing the confused kids how the numbers and letters corresponded to the squares. Anthony, who was smart but had some trouble talking, made a scribbly red and blue shamrock. "Did I mess up?" he said anxiously.

"Well, technically you were supposed to follow the numbers and letters, but it's a fine-looking clover," I said. "You just got a little carried away. I'll write a letter to Mrs. Heber saying I didn't do a good job of explaining the math activity."

"It's your fault!" said Anthony, laughing, relieved. "You'll get a bad note!"

After half an hour of effort on the mystery picture grid everything started to fall apart. The noise reached a sort of thick, chewy consistency, and then there was a string of tiny emergencies and entreaties. Somebody poured out a box full of plastic coins. Carter wanted me to ask him to add some numbers together in his head. Anthony, who was angry about something, found some fossil rocks, which made interesting noises when banged together. Twenty magnifying glasses rattled out onto a chair. Parker scrambled over a desk and had to be talked to. Tessa got hold of some glass marbles, which made a loud clacking sound on the table. Bryce wanted to list for me all the figures of Greek mythology he knew—I asked him who taught him to read; he said his parents had. Ellie showed me the bell the teacher dinged when it got too noisy, and she dinged it repeatedly—but by then Tessa had found a set of metal wind chimes, which also dinged and jingled. I waved my arms and clap-clap-clapped and ordered the class to start cleaning up.

"How's it going?" I said to Patrick, a quiet, pale boy whose shamrock sheet was untouched. He'd methodically torn the paper off most of his crayons.

"I don't know," he said. "I don't really pay attention that much."

I put him to work picking up crayon wrappers off the floor. Benjamin announced that he was one of two designated scrap-monsters, whose job was to pick up stray scraps of paper. Carter said his task was to check inside people's desks to be sure they were neat. Jordan was the supply shelf helper. "I tidy up there," he said. He began neatening the plundered box of sparkly stickers. "Great, excellent, I love it!" I said. I told Tessa to stow the marbles.

Dominic asked, "Have we been good today?"

"Well, yes," I said. "At the end it got kind of chaotic."

"Because if we've been good Mrs. Heber puts a marble in the jar."

I laughed. "You're kidding—the marble jar that Tessa poured out onto the table?"

"Yes."

More cleaning, some chair stacking, and then a voice came on the PA system—time for the first bus run. Half the class hustled off, backpacks bobbing. Some of them had a long bus ride to look forward to. "Bye!" I said. More chair stacking, and a second bell. More students left. A few last kids left for after-school class, which was held in the cafeteria. "Bye!"

And then the room was empty and still. I slumped in my chair. While I was writing a note for Mrs. Heber, the custodian came by and emptied the trash cans. I apologized for the disorder, especially for the blizzard of tiny paper circles from the three-hole puncher.

"Oh, don't worry about that," he said. "I have a backpack vacuum. This is not that bad. I've seen it worse than this. I've got eighteen classrooms, twenty bathrooms, two hundred and fifty desks, worktables, and so forth."

I whistled.

"Yep, I do that in under eight hours, five days a week. I've been doing it for eleven years. You have a good day."

Anastasia came by with her mother, who was, as it happened, a fourth-grade teacher at the school. "How did it go?" her mother asked.

"It went well," I said—half lie, half truth. "They're really nice kids." Which was truth.

To Anastasia I said, "Thanks for being in the class. You were great, very helpful."

"She said to me, 'I wish he could be a sub forever,'" said Anastasia's mother.

I thanked them and waved goodbye. I turned out the lights, washed my hands, and splashed water on my face. I felt like crying, from exhaustion or despair or joy, I'm not sure which.

At the office, as I handed in my STAFF badge, the jolly secretary said, "Are you ready for a nap?"

"Yep, it's nap time," I said.

She laughed. "So did you like the little people?"

"They're good people."

"Would you come back again?"

"Absolutely."

"Awesome."

Driving home, I again wondered if I'd managed to teach anything useful that day. Suddenly I remembered that I'd shown Anthony how to spell *found* when he was working on his leprechaun story. That was something. *Found* is a good word to know how to spell.

So ended Day Two.

DAY THREE. Tuesday, March 18, 2014
HACKETT ELEMENTARY SCHOOL, FIFTH GRADE

I SUCK AT EVERYTHING

"I DON'T KNOW if you're interested in subbing today," said Beth, at 5:35 the next morning. I wanted to sleep, but I said yes. "Great," she said, sounding relieved. I was to report to Hackett Elementary School, where I would be holding the fort for Mrs. Browning, who taught fifth grade. Fifth grade— that didn't sound too bad. I lay in bed staring at the ceiling, and then I made some coffee and brought a cup up for my wife, filled a thermos, fed the dog, fed the cat, made two sandwiches, and drove to Hackett, a small, unprosperous town some miles down the road from Lasswell. I passed a pizza shop and a for-sale convenience store, then a trailer park, and then some woods, and then a low sign in a snow pile that said Hackett Elementary School. I parked in a far corner of the lot and sat. It was a quarter to eight. A teacher got out of her car, hunched against the wind, carrying a full canvas bag, and made her way to the school entrance. Every morning a million elementary school teachers go to school to do their jobs. It was ferociously cold out, but clear—all the clouds had been blown out of the sky.

The school was almost identical to Lasswell Elementary, with a cozy, glassed-in office and a friendly secretary who showed me how to slide the magnetic strip on the door of my classroom in case of a lockdown drill. Mrs. Browning had left two pages of instructions and a stack of worksheets. "Students know that you will be keeping track of their dojo points," it began. "No peanuts allowed in my room ever. We have a student that is allergic to them."

Mrs. Browning's walls were crowded with signs and posters, including the same taxonomy-of-learning poster that Mrs. Heber had taped up. There was a good deal of advice about writing, carefully hand-printed in several colors of marker: "Reread all entries about seed idea, 'draft' in your mind." "Any sentences or words repeated? Can I think of different words or phrases to replace them?" "Is the first word of every sentence capitalized?" "Polish your work so it is ready for publication!" There was a lovely child's colored-pencil drawing of a desk that said "What Does a Clean Desk Look Like?" with pointers to important features: "Name tag left alone." "Only tissue box, water bottle and sanitizer on your desk." "Backpack hung up on rack, emptied and neatly put away." "All school supplies in box/bag in between books, or on top of them." There was a photograph of a penguin leaping up out of the ocean near a cliff. It said:

I MUST GO
MY PEOPLE NEED ME

Several lists of standard operating procedures were up on the whiteboard, including one SOP on tattling that said:

Being mean, trying to get someone in trouble
Making up things that are not a big deal

I heard a long, low buzzer that sounded like something from a prison movie. "What the hell was that?" I said aloud.

A reading specialist dropped by to warn me that the class could be rowdy. "They have a lot of energy," she said. "I'm sure you'll put your thumb right down on them." Then a hearty bald man appeared—Mr. Holland, the music teacher. "You're not Mrs. Browning," he said. I asked him if they did a lot of singing in music class.

"This time of year it's all singing, because they're preparing for a concert," he said. "We also do a lot of dancing and other types of movements."

"Sounds like fun," I said.

"Oh, we have fun in music," said Mr. Holland, "The only reason to do music is because it's fun. If it's not fun, don't waste everyone's time."

A few minutes later, the PE teacher showed up to ask me to tell the class to wear sneakers, because gym was inside today. "We did snowshoeing last week, but we're not doing snowshoeing this week," she explained.

Students began arriving and hanging up their backpacks. They were supposed to practice handwriting the letter *P* on a worksheet. I met Nash, Zeke, JoBeth, Rory, Danielle, Zoe, Carlton, Larissa, and two girls named Amber, and I made some headway with attendance. There were twenty-two kids in all; the noise level rose with each new arrival. "Put your hair up, Zoe," said Danielle. "I'm NOT PUTTING MY HAIR UP," said Zoe, in a remarkably loud, penetrating voice. An elegant, dark-eyebrowed girl wearing red lipstick, Nadia, sighed sadly. "It's usually crazy in the mornings," she said to me. "Especially after St. Patrick's Day. Top o' the morning to you! I just love saying that." I asked her how dojo points worked. "If they're being crazy, write their name down, and put a check next to it meaning they lost a point." Carlton was already being crazy, slamming his backpack around and making sudden screams and climbing on the chairs. He wore black pants with red stripes down the sides.

"Carlton, BE RESPECTFUL!" said Zoe.

"You're going to be totally good," I said to Carlton. "I can see it in your eyes. What are you interested in?"

"Football."

"What team do you like?"

"The Broncos. I'm going to try out for football next year."

"I'm NOT PUTTING MY HAIR UP!" said Zoe.

"Okay, hello, everybody," I said.

"GIRLS, GUYS, LISTEN!" Danielle shouted piercingly.

"Don't shout," I said to her. "As you can see, I'm not Mrs. Browning. I'm the sub, and I'm really hoping that you will use quiet, normal voices, and not shout, because it's a lot easier and saner if we do that. I'll write my name on the board, I'm Nick Baker. Mr. Baker."

"Mr. what?"

"Mr. Baker, like bake me a cake."

"Do you know Cassidy Baker?" asked Troy.

"No."

"Do you know Lance Baker?" asked Nicole.

"No." I wrote my name on the whiteboard.

"That's not a dry-erase marker!" said JoBeth.

"Oh, no," I said. I'd permanently defaced the whiteboard.

"It's okay," said JoBeth. "I know how to get rid of it!" She busily scrubbed my name off with a paper towel and some water until it disappeared. Carlton handed me a green dry-erase marker. "I KNOW WHERE EVERYTHING IS!" he said at the top of his lungs.

"Okay, but one thing you know is the less shouting you do the better," I said. "How's it going with the letter *P*? *P* is pretty important, *P* starts *peace and quiet. Peas.*" I couldn't think of any others.

Someone was slamming around binders; someone else was grinding loudly away on the mechanical pencil sharpener by the sink, sharpening his way through half the pencil.

"They're supposed to be working silently," said JoBeth.

"How often do you get a sub?" I asked Nash, who seemed rational and on-the-ball.

"Not that often, but when we do—" He shook his head. "Let me just say this before the day starts: Good luck."

"Oh," I said. "Maybe we'll learn a few things and, you know, have some fun. The only thing I don't like is shouting. How do you feel about shouting?"

"I'm not a big fan of it," said Nash, "but sometimes I will, when I get too angry. But that doesn't happen often."

Nash's friend Zeke pointed to an empty chair. "This kid here, Ian? He cannot control his anger. When it gets really loud, he gets mad and he loses control."

Nash said, "Yeah, when he's working and it's supposed to be dead silent in here, and it gets loud, he can't control himself."

The principal's voice came over the PA system. "Good morning, please stand for the pledge."

Everyone stood and turned, and then, instant uproar. The day before, it seemed, somebody had taken down the American flag and propped it in the corner, putting a small Irish flag in its place. I'd noticed the flag when I came in but hadn't paid attention to it—it was just one of innumerable colorful objects in the overstuffed, low-ceilinged room.

"Take it down!" said Zeke.

"No!" said several others—there was no time.

"WE NEED RESPECT FOR THE AMERICAN FLAG!" said Zoe.

But the pledge had already begun, and we took up the chanted words in progress: ". . . indivisible, with liberty and justice for all." When it was over, the class launched into a second singsongily chanted recitation, with words taken from a poster that hung on the wall. "TODAY IS A NEW DAY," the class said in unison. "I WILL ACT IN A SAFE AND HEALTHY WAY. I WILL DO WHAT I KNOW IS RIGHT. I WILL THINK BEFORE I ACT. I WILL TAKE CARE OF MYSELF, MY FRIENDS, AND MY SCHOOL. TODAY I WILL BE THE BEST THAT I CAN BE."

"That's inspiring," I said, when it was over.

"GUYS, BE QUIET!" screamed Zoe. How could so much voice come out of such a small person?

"So," I said, "we just said the Pledge of Allegiance to the Irish flag. We'll want to put the real one back up, won't we?"

"No," said Ross, "because the leprechauns did that."

I left the flag substitution for Mrs. Browning to correct. Several latecomers arrived and got settled. The principal said that the lunch choices were pigs in blankets, pizza, and SunButter and jelly. SunButter was fake peanut butter, somebody explained to me.

"I'M NOT PUTTING UP MY HAIR, DANIELLE!"

"Okay, guys," I said, "it's nine o'clock, quiet down, do work."

"No, it's nine oh three," said Ethan, and pointed at the clock.

"Nine oh three, thank you," I said.

"If someone is being wild, you can just send him to Mr. Pierce," said Larissa. "Yesterday was horrible." Mr. Pierce was the school principal.

"HAH HAH!" said Carlton, the loud boy she was referring to, hanging up his lunch box.

The class assignment, a carryover from the day before, was to write a few sentences about what happened over the weekend. Some kids had written more than a page and were done, others had written nothing. I paused in front of Toby, a boy with solemn eyes and round cheeks, who was running his hands through his hair. There was a blank piece of paper in front of him. "So what did you do this past weekend?" I asked him.

"Nothing," Toby said.

"Did you eat a cheese sandwich?"

"No, I had a ham sandwich."

"When you ate that first bite of ham sandwich, what did it taste like?"

"It tasted like ham."

"That's it! 'I ate a ham sandwich. It tasted like ham.' You are in good shape. Can you write that, please?"

Toby started to write, then stopped. Each letter he wrote seemed to be spun out of an odd backward circling motion.

We gathered for morning meeting near the whiteboard. All the students sat on the floor. Nadia explained that they were supposed to read what they'd written. Those who hadn't written could say "pass," or they could say aloud what they would have written if they'd written it.

Here's what was going on in their weekend lives. JoBeth was learning to balance a sword on her head like her mom: "It's fun but you have to be very careful, or you'll get stabbed badly." Danielle went to a monster truck rally and almost got a splatball egg at the mall. Sara made some origami figures. Nicole, Rory, and Troy played Minecraft; Nicole said there was a weird stalker guy following her around in the game. Carlton worked with his dad on his pinewood derby car. Nash raced in a pinewood derby and came in second twice but seventh overall. Zeke said he was going to go to monster trucks with his dad, but his dad said it was sixty dollars just to get in the front door, so his dad looked up the Harlem Globetrotters, and tickets for them cost three hundred dollars, so he took them to *The Lego Movie* instead, and then after the movie they were going to go to the gun show but they didn't. Zoe was going to get a new iPod but didn't. Toby ate a ham sandwich. Pauline, who was shy, went to the science museum to celebrate her brother's birthday, and a scientist rubbed a balloon on her head. Larissa was FaceTimed by two boys from class and then she whittled a stick with a knife for twenty minutes. Jess picked up her dog's ashes—she still missed him—and she slept over at her friend's and FaceTimed with two boys from class. Amber L. went to the doctor's to be tested for strep throat and then went to her aunt's house and then she rode her bike with her brother. Amber S. got a new bike and learned that the Girl Scouts have sold more than a million boxes of cookies in the state of Maine. Ian went swimming at the YMCA. Ethan started to write a book about a girl who uncovers secrets about her family and brings an evil creature to life, and then he decorated a cake with a whale for his mom's boyfriend, and afterward he learned that cake decorating was in his family on both sides: "I have cake decorating in my blood basically," he said. Amanda said the stove in her house caught fire and her brother helped her get out of the house. Nadia said she made a tunnel in a snowbank that was big enough that she could turn around inside it.

While they were telling their stories there were many interruptions: a secretary came by to ask how many people were having pigs in blankets, another secretary called on the intercom to ask if I could send the attendance to the office, and the three loudest girls repeatedly said QUIET! STOP TALKING! SHHH! GUYS, BE QUIET! SHHH! BE RESPECTFUL! GUYS, LET HER TALK! GUYS, STAY IN THE CIRCLE! GUYYYYYSSS!—unable to keep themselves from disrupting the proceedings with their scandalized scolding, even when I told them that their shouting "Stop talking!" didn't help at all and actually made things considerably worse. Also Carlton was doing chin-ups under his desk, and Nash was playing with his pinewood derby car.

"That was really great," I said at the end. "A little loud, but great."

We lined up for gym. As I was dropping them off to play kickball, Nadia, who had taken pity on me, said, "Mr. Baker, you look like somebody who would teach at the middle school, or high school."

I told her I wrote books for a living.

She said, "If you need help with anything, I'm always here."

I thanked her and went back to class to sit and drink coffee.

After gym came snack time. Everyone was irritable and full of resentments over the kickball game: the teacher had made several bad calls. Nash had gotten in trouble because Carlton lied, and the feud between the loud boys and the even louder tattletale girls was heating up. Somebody stole somebody's cookie. I lost my dog-eared sub plans and hunted for them among the polychrome clutter for several panicked minutes. The kids who had brought peanut-butter granola bars had to eat them at tables in the hall, outside the class, because of the no-peanut rule, but after they finished they got boisterous and a nearby teacher, Mrs. Clayton, came out and said, "You are disturbing a group that's in the back corner of my room!"

I herded them all back in. "That was a disaster," I said. I ordered everyone to sit down and be quiet, and I gave Amanda, the paper passer, a social studies quiz on the points of the compass to pass out. They were supposed to define the meaning of the following terms, using words and illustrations:

> compass rose
> north
> south
> east
> west
> northeast
> southeast
> northwest
> southwest

The sub plans said: "DO NOT HELP THEM! This is a test and I need to know if they know the answers." Well, a handful of kids knew the answers, but most were mystified. "I don't get what this means," they said. "I can't remember any of this." Many did not know what a compass rose was, and others had no idea how to define the word *north*. I didn't know how to define *north* myself—not that it mattered, since I was forbidden from offering hints. Sara remembered a directional mnemonic: Never Eat Soggy Waffles; Zeke changed it to Never Eat Soggy Whales. They all passed in their quizzes and I handed out a second social studies worksheet, in which they were supposed to draw the map of an imaginary city, with a key to symbols used, and a compass showing which way north was. Ethan began drawing a circus. Rory embarked on a map of the world he'd made in Minecraft. Troy worked on a map of a place called Skull Country. The noise level, post-quiz, swiftly rose to unimaginable heights, with shrill charges and countercharges flying around the room: WHAT THE HECK IS WRONG WITH YOU? GUYS, IT'S NOT RECESS! Ian—the one who got angry when it was supposed to be quiet and it wasn't—became enraged. He went over to the trash can, furiously tore up several pieces of crumpled paper that he found within it, and threw them on the floor. Then he picked up the torn pieces and put them back in the trash can.

The reading specialist appeared in the door with a quizzical expression. I apologized for the madhouse. I felt sick with shame. "I'm going to help you out here," she said. Suddenly her contralto voice boomed out. "I KNOW YOU CAN SHOW MR. BAKER WHAT YOU ARE NORMALLY LIKE," she said. The class got a little quieter—not much. "You guys need to do what is expected of you!"

Nash said, "Some people are doing it and some people are not doing it."

There was a scream of indignation from across the room.

"The people who are doing the right thing should continue to do the right thing, and other people will follow," said the reading specialist.

Sara said, "It's hard to do the right thing when everyone's distracting us!"

"You need to show Mr. Baker what you normally do," said the reading specialist, "because this will not make for a fun day for him."

She left.

I had them line up. Nicole and Carlton fought for position. "This is ridiculous!" I said. I told them they couldn't leave for recess until they got quiet, which of course worked—taking away recess time was one of the school's standard punishments. They began to file out, piloted by a teacher with recess duty. I stopped Nash and said, "Nash, if you only knew how loud your voice is."

Nash looked sheepish. "I know. I wished you luck! I did. I get angry."

Nadia stayed behind to offer counsel. "Usually if stuff gets this bad," she said, "you have to go to the guidance counselor and have her talk to us. A lot of kids have anger issues, and there's some not-nice kids in here." She led me to the guidance counselor's office, but the guidance counselor was busy talking to a parent. She then led me to the main office and pointed to a door. "Mr. Pierce is right through there," she said. "He knows the school very well."

I thanked her. "It must be hard for you," I said.

"Some people get so frustrated that they end up acting crazy," she said. "Like Ian. Sometimes he makes a sound like he's a gorilla. And then other people get mad at him, when really he's just frustrated."

"You've been very helpful," I said.

She went off to recess. I went to Mr. Pierce's office and introduced myself. "I'm not controlling the class well," I said. "They're very loud."

He nodded gravely. "They are very loud, yes," he said.

"I just wondered if you could come down and talk to them."

He said he would in a little while.

I sat at my desk, feeling guilty that the class had gotten so out of control that Ian had had to tear up the paper in the trash can. The sub plans said that after recess the class was supposed to work for half an hour on their mystery stories, critiquing each other's work using a checklist, but they hadn't finished their imaginary cities. Fortunately the imaginary-city task was supposed to be a two-day project. I was tired of the intense fluorescent light and I turned off the switch.

The class came bouncing and shouting back in from recess, blinded by the bright snow. "It's dark in here!" they said.

I had them take out their partly written mystery stories, which they were supposed to be recopying onto a half-folded piece of paper, thus leaving room for marginal comments. Amber S. was writing about a theft at a chocolate shop. She was supposed to think about whether it contained the required elements: feelings of excitement and anxiety, a plot twist, conflict, and a surprise ending. "What genre do you write?" she asked me, politely. Jess was busily writing down names of malefactors in the class and making dojo point checkmarks beside them. "I have a headache because it's so noisy," she said.

Just before lunch, the reading specialist came back. "Kids, show Mr. Baker a quiet line!" she said. "CARLTON! ZEKE! SHOW MR. BAKER A QUIET LINE!" She was having no luck. Fortunately at that moment Mr. Pierce arrived, portly and frowning. He stood by the whiteboard and waited. The class became still and downcast. He spoke in a quiet voice. "You need to do what you know is right," he said. "And if you don't, you'll spend the afternoon with me, so that others in your room can do what they know is right." He let that sink in. "I already have a letter written," he continued. "All that's missing is your parents' names and your name. Whoever comes down, I'll fill out a letter, with your name and your parents' names, and I'll send it home. And I'll give a copy to Mrs. Browning tomorrow. So I'm all ready. I'm willing to have company. But I'd rather not have it. All I ask is for you to do what's right. You're good people and I know you can do it."

Feeling duly chastised and contrite, we all walked to the cafeteria, where there was a massive molten fondue of noise. I went back and ate a second sandwich in my room, wondering whether this was in fact the worst day of my life. When I picked the class up half an hour later, Jess, a thin, sweet-faced girl with a pastel hairband, said, "At lunch some kids were saying you looked like Santa."

"Well, they have a point," I said. "I have a white beard."

"They say you're going to give us presents," said Jess. "I was trying to stop them because it's really rude. I could see them saying it in kindergarten, but not in fifth grade!"

"It's okay," I said. I held my arms out. "NOW, OKAY, GUYS—
TOTALLY QUIET! THIS IS SILENT READING."

There was a moment of relative silence, broken by Zoe. "Get your butt
out of my chair," she said to Carlton.

"READuh!" screamed Danielle.

"I'm serious," I said.

"Merry Christmas," said Carlton. Zeke snickered.

"THAT'S SO RUDE, CARLTON!" said Jess.

And then I lost it. I got genuinely angry. "Just sit in your chairs and
READ YOUR BOOKS. For god's sake! It's outrageous! I don't want to
hear ONE SOUND from any of you! NOT ONE PEEP!"

Perhaps because they could hear the true note of anger in my voice, or
perhaps only because Mr. Pierce had paid a visit, they all went silent. We
had half an hour of blissful, noiseless reading-to-self. Pages turned; the
heating system hummed. When it was over, I passed out a math worksheet.
The kids saw it and said, "Oh, no!" They clutched at their faces and
moaned.

It was a mystery picture grid, similar to the one I'd passed out the day
before in the second-grade class, except that this time the squares in the
grid were smaller—there were a hundred of them—and four colors of
crayon were involved. Each square held a single-digit multiplication
problem—"6 x 7" or "3 x 2"—and if you got the right answer and matched
it correctly with the color key and colored in the square, and if you
repeated that task a hundred times, you ended up with a crude likeness of
a train. Several obedient kids, mostly girls, set to work. Only a few students
knew their times tables; instead, they referred to preprinted times-table
matrices taped to the top of every desk. "They will try to be noisy," said
the sub plans. "Do not let them." Hah.

"This doesn't look like a train," said Danielle, disgustedly, when she'd
finished. I separated Nash and JoBeth, who were fencing with plastic
rulers, and I told Carlton to stand by the bathroom door because he was
talking incessantly about poop. The slower kids, sensibly, copied the train
shape from the faster kids' worksheets. Toby, the boy who said he'd eaten

a ham sandwich over the weekend, was in despair. Not one block on his page was colored in. He'd written his name at the top. "What's up?" I said.

"I suck at everything," he said sadly.

"No you don't," I said. "Just do what you can do. It's all right, it's really okay, don't worry about it, my man." I collected all the finished and partly finished and not-even-started mystery trains, and then, inwardly gnashing my teeth, I was compelled to hand out two more diabolical worksheets. One held a multiple-choice test of synonyms—the class did a good job of circling *difficult* as a replacement for *hard*, and *lengthy* as a replacement for *long*— and one sheet held a grim story about two boys taking a test, filled with twenty antonyms in bold. "They were calm because they were not really prepared but decided to give it their worst try." "Felix's pencil mended twice during the test because he was pressing too softly." "They were very anxious when they were finally able to finish and were able to turn their tests out." This sheet gave them a lot of trouble. "What's *mended*?" they said.

Toby asked me if he could sit at a table out in the hall, because he could concentrate better there. I said he could—he looked genuinely sad. A few minutes later, an enormous ed tech in a paisley dress ordered Toby back in the room. "They can't sit at the tables without supervision," she told me. "They know that." Toby obeyed, but instead of going to his desk, he climbed into a supply cupboard in the back of the room and tried to close the doors on himself. "YOU CAN'T BE IN THERE!" cried Nicole and Danielle, pulling hard at the doors as Toby's white fingertips held them firmly shut.

"Toby, come out of the cupboard!" said the ed tech. "COME OUT OF THE CUPBOARD OR YOU'LL OWE MRS. BROWNING A RECESS."

"He's really unhappy," I said to the ed tech, in an undertone. "He's been struggling. He told me he sucks at everything."

"Oh, he always says that," said the ed tech.

Toby emerged from the cupboard and put his head down on the desk, shielding himself with his arms.

Jess handed the ed tech the sheet that she'd kept of wrongdoers and, to my horror, the ed tech started to write all their names on the whiteboard.

I said, "Oh gosh, please don't write their names up there."

"Jess said you wanted me to write the names down," said the ed tech, annoyed. She erased the names and handed the paper back to Jess.

Jess, crushed, tore up her list and threw it away. The ed tech stumped off.

"Thanks for doing it," I said to Jess.

I collected the synonym-and-antonym worksheets. The last task of the day was for me to read to the class from *Danny, the Champion of the World*, by Roald Dahl, starting from where Mrs. Browning had left off, at the beginning of chapter two. I read to them about the BFG, the Big Friendly Giant, who catches children's dreams in glass bottles and makes magic powders out of them. *"A dream,"* I read, *"as it goes drifting through the night air, makes a tiny little buzzing humming sound, a sound so soft and low it is impossible for ordinary people to hear it. But the BFG can hear it easily."* I looked up. The whole class was motionless. Carlton's head was up; Ian's head was up; Nash's head was up; the tattletale girls were all intent on hearing every word I was saying. Everyone was listening. I kept going. I got to the part where the Big Friendly Giant uses a long blowpipe to blow his dream powders into children's rooms. The sleeping child breathes in the powder, and begins dreaming a marvelous dream. *"Then the magic powder really takes over—and suddenly the dream is not a dream any longer but a real happening—and the child is not asleep in bed—he is fully awake and is actually in the place of the dream and is taking part in the whole thing."* I reached the end of the chapter. "Wow," I said. "Should I read some more?"

"YES," said the class. It was the first time they'd spoken in unison since they'd said "I will be the best that I can be" at the beginning of the day. I read the next chapter, which was about kite flying. It was good, but not quite as good as the bit about blowpipes and dreams, and some kids got squirmy, but still, they all listened. Thank you, Roald Dahl—you difficult, arrogant, brilliant genius.

"You're an awesome storyteller," said Nadia.

The funny thing was, Dahl's story of the Big Friendly Giant had a residual effect. The class paid more attention to my voice afterward. When I asked them to pick up the paper on the floor and stack the chairs, they did it. I thanked each of them for spending the day with me, and some of them thanked me for being a sub. "Nash," I said, "you were going totally nuts in the middle of the day, and now you've pulled it together."

"I'm like that," Nash said. "I'm wild, and then I calm down."

"Well, thanks."

The buses were announced, and then the class was gone.

While I was writing a note to the teacher, on yellow lined paper, the night custodian came in to empty the trash. "How are you?" she asked. "You survived the day?"

I said I had. "They got a little wild."

"Oh, big-time," she said. Her husband was the day custodian, she explained, and he'd told her all about how wild the kids were. She had to do all the bathrooms by nine o'clock, she said. She used to have an assistant, but then the district had cuts and she lost her assistant. "But you know what? You do the best you can."

That's true. You do the best you can. End of Day Three.

YOUR BRAIN LOOKS INFECTED

I STARED AT THE RINGING PHONE uncomprehendingly, and then I remembered: I'm on call. Beth asked if I was interested in filling in for a seventh-grade math teacher, Ms. Nolton, at Lasswell Middle School. I was.

The middle school, hidden behind several fifteen-foot-high snowpiles in the parking lot, seemed new, with higher ceilings and a fancier entranceway than the high school—one of many schools built during Maine's era of relative prosperity, when Angus King was governor. My classroom, part of Team Orinoco, had cinderblock walls painted a gentle yellow, with a long row of Venetian-blinded windows down one wall. The chairs rested on the desks, which were arranged as a square within a larger square. There were two identical taxonomy-of-learning posters hanging in the room. One was in the back by a wall telephone, and another was affixed to a corkboard, just above an impressive chart of mathematical "benchmarks" for seventh- and eighth-graders, produced by the Northwest Evaluation Association. One benchmark read: "MA.03. AEE.03.02. Understands the solution to an inequality results in an infinite set of answers as plotted on a number line."

Inequalities, it turned out, was one of the topics Ms. Nolton wanted us to be thinking about on that day. But first there was homeroom. "Students are expected to be working, reading, or socializing quietly," said Ms. Nolton's sub plans. The students, who were giddy from reciprocal teasing, yanked the chairs off the desks and talked about music. The boys had faint mustaches, and their voices had just changed, or hadn't yet changed; some of the girls looked like they were about twenty-two.

"I'm allergic to Justin Bieber," said a flirty, sporty boy, Jason.

"Justin Bieber's amazing—no hate," said Sydney, a flirty, sporty girl with a wrist brace. "He makes elephants take dirt roads."

"Elephants love him," said Sunrise, who was thin and wispy-haired and secretive.

"My mom thinks he's weird," said Jason.

"I think he's a freak," said a loud boy, Evan.

"He's a weirdo with legs," said a super-confident girl, Cayden.

Georgia, broad-shouldered and theatrical, slammed her iPad pouch down on her backpack. "I don't like anything," she said. "Everything makes me mad. Even colors make me mad."

After the beep on the PA system we all stood and said the pledge, followed by a moment of silence. "Thank you, you may be seated," said the secretary on the PA system. "On the lunch menu today we have grilled chicken and broccoli on garlic butter noodles, with a garden strawberry and spinach salad, crisp celery sticks, and chilled grape juice, and milk choices." The students talked through the rest of the announcements, which were about intramural basketball, drama rehearsal, and a meeting of the yearbook committee. "Here's my pencil, I found it, yay!" said Sydney.

Next period was a STAR block. "What is STAR?" I asked William, who was staring at the floor. "Um, STAR is STAR," he said. A technology enrichment specialist named Mrs. Elton—an ample woman in a gray pantsuit with the voice of a caregiver in a nursing home for people with dementia—introduced herself. She taught STAR class on Wednesdays, she said, which was fine with me: these middle schoolers made me nervous. "Everyone should be reading for the first few minutes," she announced. The class went quiet; the boys sat on one side of the room and the girls sat on the other. Using purple marker, she wrote a list of science-related apps on the whiteboard: Little Alchemy, goREACT, Germ Blaster, NASA Viz, GeoMaster Plus, EarthViewer, Phases of the Moon, Black Hole, Powder Game Viewer. When she was done she explained that the students could download these on their iPads—except not right now. "We seem to be having Internet issues this morning," she said. "Has anyone had a chance to try Little Alchemy?" Nobody had. She went down the list, describing "fun apps" while the class stared at their hands or down at the blue-green industrial carpeting. When the Internet came back up, some kids downloaded Germ Blaster and GeoMaster Plus and Black Hole, and soon half the class was laughing and poking at their iPads. "Guys, little noisy," Ms. Elton warned. She looked at the clock. "Okay, guys, you can start packing up," she said, and the STAR block was over.

Next period I was on break, making some superstrong instant coffee for myself in the teachers' break room, and after that was an "advisory block"—a study hall. The students were supposed to take an online survey about technology, which they did, in extreme silence. Some of them listened to music on earbuds; two girls shared one set of earbuds. These advisory kids were easy—too easy, I thought. I missed the jokes, the bavardage. I got my computer out and read an article in *The Huffington Post*: "'Giraffe Woman' Has 11-Inch-Long Neck." The giraffe woman had begun her body modification program in middle school, by wrapping bent coat-hangers around her neck. Good lord. I could hear a science teacher next door explaining systems of classification—a restaurant menu, she said, was actually a way of classifying the food in a restaurant: appetizers, entrees, meat, fish, dessert. "I can't believe you're so focused," I said to the students. "Is this always the way it is?"

"No," said a boy.

At 9:55, the bell rang, and it was the beginning of my first actual math class. It was a high-level group, apparently, and they had lots to do: a half-page worksheet on number lines and coordinate planes, a "Scoot Sheet" of one-variable algebra questions, and several sets of problems on a website called IXL. They handled these fairly well. What broke the class's will, though, was a page downloaded from MathWorksheetsLand.com. At the top of the page was a cartoon of a hard-hatted man bearing down on a jackhammer. Below him were ten gnarly, closely spaced strings of variables that the students were supposed to "evaluate":

Evaluate $y^2+3/4x^3-3z^3$ when $x=4$, $y=2$ and $z=3$
Evaluate $(x + xy)-(-4y-3)x+6$ for $x=3$ and $y=2$

Several kids passed out small personal whiteboards, shaped like slates from one-room schoolhouses of yore, and everyone dutifully began crowding arithmetical calculations on them with dry-erase markers. They erased with their fingertips, or with neatly balled-up athletic socks, a bin of which were set aside for the purpose. The problem was that most of the students were shaky on the order of operations, and many had forgotten how to handle exponents. A few couldn't recall what seven times six was. They ended up with all kinds of strange answers on their whiteboards. Sage's fingers were blue from dry-erase ink. A plaid-shirted blond boy named Isaac called me over. "I'm having trouble with number four," he said:

Evaluate $6d+3d^2+3e-e/6d+d-e$ for $d=5$ and $e=2$

"That's a hairy bastard," I said, and we laughed helplessly at its absurdity for a while. Then together we jackhammered through it, variable by variable, making simple errors of arithmetic, correcting them, continuing. There was no answer sheet, so I wasn't altogether sure that our answers were correct. "Do the best you can," I said, and slumped in my chair. The bell rang; class over.

The next class, which was split in two, with lunch in the middle, had less work to do—just the Scoot Sheet, some simpler problems on IXL, and a test on graphing inequalities. I spent ten minutes pawing around in the sub folder and among the piles of papers on the desk, looking for the inequalities test. "There's something else she wants you to do," I said, "but I can't find it. So I think we should just talk. What should we talk about?"

"How awesome I am," said a small, plucky boy, Owen.

"How has seventh grade been going?" I asked.

"It has been the hardest year of my life," said Owen.

I asked them what the biggest adjustment was in going from elementary school to middle school.

"Waking up in the morning," said a smart kid, Thomas, with a voice like a patrician banker's.

"Ah, yes," I said. "Why does school start so early?"

Sunrise said, "It should be illegal for school to start before eleven. And illegal for it to end after eleven oh one."

"A sixty-second day," said Thomas.

"No, they'd just give you a ton of homework, think of it!" said Jason.

"If you were the superintendent of schools," I said, "how would you design the ideal school day?"

Mackenzie, one of the pretty, dominant girls, said, "I would say you didn't have to go."

"Then you'd miss out on the social aspect," I said.

"You wouldn't meet anyone in person unless you went to some sort of party," said Dylan.

"That's what they make the Internet for, and Facebook," said Mackenzie.

Her friend Darryl said, "I met my boyfriend online. He's thirty, and he's on Zoosk." The two of them laughed.

"That's kind of sketchy," I said.

"Joke," Darryl said. "I mean just like, we could go online and add random friends."

I said, "Let's say you absolutely had to require people to go to school Monday through Friday. When would you start the day?"

"Eight o'clock," Thomas said.

"Two a.m.," said Owen.

"I think twelve, for about an hour," said Laura. "We all could use forty minutes of schooling."

Thomas objected: "That would be twenty minutes of lunch and one class."

Darryl said, "I think we should all have recliners, that are really comfortable."

"Do you know how much recliners would cost for nine hundred students?" said Thomas.

Caleb, a realist, said, "I think it should be eight to twelve, four hours."

Sunrise spoke up again. "No!" she said. "The school day is not going to begin at eight. It's going to begin at twelve, and end at twelve oh one!"

I found a marker and, after inspecting it closely to be sure that it was a dry-erase, I wrote numbers on the board. "We've got one minute, one hour, four hours."

"I'd probably go with an eight-hour day every day," said a studious boy, Dana, who wore hearing aids.

"You're crazy," said Owen.

"The thing I've noticed," I said, "is that people mean well, but there's only so much you can do in a day. It seems like everybody shuts down after a time. You could compress what happens from, say, eight to two into half the time and still get learning done."

"You're right," said Thomas.

"So why do you think they leave the day this long?" I said. "There's something else to consider, isn't there?"

"Specials?" said Laura.

"Lunch?" said Caleb.

I said, "What about your parents?"

"They have to work," said Owen. "Daycare!"

"Exactly," I said. "All right, good. What else should we talk about?"

"Something fun," said Sunrise.

"Boys," said Darryl.

"I think we should talk about what our dream vacation would be," said Mackenzie. "My dream vacation would be going to Disneyland, meeting One Direction, going on rides with One Direction, and . . ." She trailed off.

Caitlin, another alpha girl, said, "My dream vacation would be getting dressed and then playing on my phone all day."

I asked them what One Direction was.

"It's a band," said Thomas, shaking his head.

"It's a big thing," said Caitlin.

"They're terrible," said Thomas.

"They're not terrible!" said Mackenzie.

"They are terrible," said Thomas. "Listen for yourself." He tapped play on a YouTube video. It didn't play, it was loading. Wi-Fi was slow again.

"They aren't even from America!" said Owen, who claimed to like thrash metal.

The music came on, One Direction playing "Story of My Life"; several girls sang along.

"Turn that off!" said Caleb.

The class began bad-mouthing Justin Bieber. A boy in the back named Regan was playing a video game.

"I was just looking to see if I was dead or not," he said when I asked him about it. "But I'm not."

"You are dead," said Max, the kid next to him.

Darryl said, "Did you know that if you get a blood transfusion from a twenty-five-year-old you can get his energy?"

"No," I said.

"My grandmother had a blood transfusion," she said. "She couldn't walk or anything, and then the next day after she got it she was painting walls and standing on ladders."

"I had no idea," I said. "Has anyone been to the hospital recently?"

"I was, last night," said Caitlin. "I choked on something and it got lodged in my throat."

"You were rushed to the hospital last night?" I said, startled.

"Not really rushed," said Caitlin. "My mom was driving really slow. I'm not eating chicken ever again."

Max said, "I almost died while eating ramen noodles."

The bell rang and everyone surged toward the door. "Are you guys coming back here afterward?" I said.

"Yes!"

"Good. Have fun at lunch," I said.

I ate a sandwich. Underneath my lunch bag I discovered the stack of twenty copies of the inequalities test, neatly paperclipped. Students were supposed to write a sentence describing the difference between an inequality and an equation—not an easy task—and they had to graph inequalities like $x > 49$. I watched a video from Khan Academy concerning the four quadrants of the coordinate plane. The bell rang again. My hardy band of educational reformers returned.

"Did you work at a college?" Mackenzie asked me.

"So what shall we talk about?" asked Thomas.

"I skinned my fingie," said Caitlin.

"I skinned my shoe," said Owen.

I flapped the batch of inequality tests in the air. "I found these things that she wanted you to do," I said.

"I'm sad," said Regan, as I passed the tests out.

"What are you sad about?" I asked.

"I don't know, things."

I said, "Life is weighing down on you? Remember this: Sing a happy song."

"Oh, can I sing?" said Sunrise. "Can I sing for you guys?"

"No," said Regan.

I waited for them to find their pencils. "This is actually a test situation," I said.

I walked around the room giving whispered hints, and then, when it seemed that a number of kids didn't remember how to graph an inequality, I asked Thomas to go to the board and give a demonstration. "Good job, Thomas," said Mackenzie. Memories refreshed, people labored away quietly. I took a bite of an apple. "Owen just blew on my face," Caitlin whispered. People began handing in their tests.

I looked at the clock. "Two minutes to go," I said. "And by the way, I really enjoyed having you in class. You guys are great. You're quiet and you're funny and you're charming—and you're delightful."

Owen laughed. "You're 'delightful,'" he said to Caitlin.

"Yes I am!" said Caitlin.

"Can you sub for us again?" said Thomas.

The bell triple-bonged.

"Bye, Mr. Baker!"

"Be our sub again soon, please!" said Laura.

"Have a good one."

"You, too!"

"Bye!"

The next class poured in and slumped down, waiting for something to happen. I took attendance. "I hope you're having a good day today," I said.

"I've been having an interesting day," said Georgia.

There was a loud bang from the far corner.

I spun around. "A sudden incredible sound just ripped the air wide open," I said. Somebody had dropped a textbook on the floor.

"It was Evan," said Brock, apple-cheeked and beaming.

"No it wasn't," said Evan, who wore a football jersey. "Brock does this all the time."

"Why does he do that?"

"Because he's Brock."

Lots of giggling.

I said, "What grade are you guys in?"

"Seventh!"

"Eighth!"

"Fourth!"

"Just ignore Brock," said Travis.

I passed out the half sheet on quadrants of the coordinate plane. "Do you know how to label the quadrants?"

"No."

"Kind of."

I went around to various desks, explaining number lines and Cartesian coordinates. It happens that each of the four quadrants on the Cartesian plane is designated by a Roman numeral—I, II, III, IV—and the Roman numerals go counterclockwise, for some reason. Valueless, instantly forgettable knowledge for most people, but these thirteen-year-olds had to know it.

"You have fifteen plump, beautiful minutes to do this lovely assignment," I said, and I bent with a flourish to pick up a sock eraser that somebody had thrown across the room. Instantly I knew I was in trouble: I had a bloody nose. Right when things were going well, too. I sat at my desk dabbing at myself with a napkin, hoping nobody had seen, hoping the bleeding would stop. How pathetic, I thought—I'd often gotten winter nosebleeds in school, because of the dry, overheated air, and now, back in school, I was getting winter nosebleeds all over again.

"Can we work in the hall?" asked Lily and Cheyenne.

"I think it's just as good to work in here," I said from behind my napkin. Somebody sharpened a pencil. I watched people explaining quadrants to each other. Alec walked up. "I don't know how to do any of these," he said.

"Just put your name at the top," I said. I took the napkin away from my nose and watched two fat, dark drops of blood fall. One landed on the top right corner of the sub plans, and one in the margin of a completed test from last period. Sniffing furtively, I quickly tore off the blood-dropletted bits of paper. I stuffed the scraps in my pocket. My nose seemed to have stopped bleeding.

"Quit it!" said Georgia.

Brock was causing a ruckus in the back.

"It was not me," said Evan, "it was Brock."

I walked over. Lily said, "If you have a problem with someone, write their name down or send them to the office."

"Why does everybody always blame me?" said Brock.

I stood in the middle of the room. "I WANT IT TO BE SILENT!" I said, in a ship captain's voice. "There are still a couple of kids working."

"I don't have any computational skills," said Cheyenne.

I looked at Brock's worksheet. "Are you done?"

I began collecting papers. The effort of shouting made another drop of blood fall somewhere on the blue-gray carpet.

"Oh!" said Trinity, who'd seen the drop fall.

"I'm sorry, I have a bloody nose," I said.

I covered my face again with the napkin. "I'm just going to talk to you like this."

"Just don't get it on any of the papers," said Trinity.

"You should go to the nurse," said Lily.

"I'm too old to go to the nurse."

"No you're not," said Lily. "I had a teacher that went to the nurse, and then she went home sick."

I handed the last stack of worksheets to her to pass out—the one with the jackhammer cartoon on it. I circulated, I explained the order of operations, I shushed, I joshed, I handed out compliments, but I was a wounded wildebeest of a teacher now. My inner sense of authority was compromised by the nosebleed, even though only a quarter of the class was aware of it. "Seriously, you're an atheist, you really are!" said Cheyenne to Luke, the boy next to her. I stopped by the chair of one string-bean of a student, Timothy, who hadn't made a noise. He was bent with his face inches from the desk, clutching his pencil with four fingers. "How are you making out?" I asked.

"I don't know," Timothy said, "is this right?" He'd filled a page of notebook paper with tiny numbers, some of them worked out to several decimals, some in the hundred thousands. It looked like something in *A Beautiful Mind*, and it was all wrong.

"I think you may have made a little technical mistake up here, maybe with the fraction," I said, pointing. "But you did some great calculations." Timothy began erasing.

"Aw, sugar!" said Georgia. She also began erasing.

"Sugar," said Brock.

Trinity, tall and full of casual sass, handed me her paper and turned to Devin and Mandy, who were sitting close together, sharing a pair of earbuds. "Are you guys like an old married couple?" she said.

"Shut UP!" said Mandy.

"Can I go get food from my locker?" Brock asked.

"Absolutely not," I said. But that gave me an idea. I told the class I'd be back in a second, and I hustled around the corner to the boys' bathroom to wash my face. I looked at the wild-eyed bleeder in the mirror. My shirttail was untucked and my substitute badge had flipped around on its lanyard so that it was blank. "You hopeless jackass," I said to my reflection, and laughed, tossing out the paper towels. I went back to class.

The noise level had not appreciably risen. I told Evan and Brock to go on IXL and finish up their word problems. Luke, who was caught up, had assembled a pretend gun out of three dry-erase markers, rubber bands, and a plastic ruler. "That's just wrong," I said. He took it apart.

Cheyenne got up on a chair. "There's a pencil in the light," she said.

I waved for her to get down. "That was meant to be there," I said. "When they designed this building they said there's going to be a pencil in the light."

"I put it there last trimester," Evan said.

"Are you lying?" said Trinity.

"No, I threw it, and it stuck into the tile," Evan said. "Then it fell. So I put it in the light."

"Why would you tell a sub that?"

I said, "You have made a difference in this school."

"Dude, your own mother hates you," said Travis to Brock.

Lily handed in her paper. "Mr. Baker," she said, "they're not allowed to have their hoods up in school." She gestured toward Brock, Evan, and Travis, all of whom had their iPads tilted against their backpacks so that I wouldn't see that they were playing video games. The three of them had their hoods up.

"Luke, honey, I need your help," said Trinity. Luke was quick with math. He went over to help her with fractions.

I walked Mia, who was bookish, through some minor algebra. "You want to get that x all by its lonesome self," I said, "so you first want to multiply by six."

It got quiet. I sat down and yawned. Some people sat by the heating register on the floor. "Five minus four is what?" Devin said to Mandy, prompting her. Cheyenne started brushing her hair. Eight minutes to go in the period.

Eventually I ambled over to the hooded boys. "I got work done!" said Brock.

"I'm so glad," I said. All three of them had quickly tapped their Minecraft games off their iPad screens.

"He's always like this, don't worry," said Evan.

I pulled up a chair and sat down. "What's your vision of the future?"

"Death," said Brock.

Travis and Evan laughed, and I did, too.

"Your life is huge," I said. I asked what Ms. Nolton was like.

"She's short," said Brock.

"She's nice," said Georgia, from several desks away. "She doesn't like Brock because he doesn't do his work. She yelled at us on Friday. She made Brock do pushups, and then she made Evan do squats."

"Georgia, that's my lotion!" said Cheyenne.

"She wants you to rub it on her back," said Brock.

"No!" said Cheyenne.

"Fifty pushups," I said sternly to Brock. "No, just do the opposite of whatever you want to do. Hoods are forbidden, as you know." I raised an eyebrow at the three of them.

"I look terrible with my hair," said Evan.

I said, "The thing that's interesting to me is that it's like you guys want there to be a rule so you can break it. If they had no rule about hoodies, nobody would care. It's not even that much fun to wear a hoodie."

"I know, but my hair's too long," said Evan. He pulled down his hood. A huge disorderly pompom of hair ploofed out.

"Oh," I said.

Brock said, "I'm like a ninja at night, when I play Manhunt."

I asked them whether manhunt was a video game or a physical game.

"It's a physical game," Lily explained.

"It's like hide-and-seek in the dark," said Brock.

"It's like hide-and-seek but with guns and clubs," added Evan.

Brock said, "Once I put on my hood, I'm like a ninja."

There was a commotion near my desk. Cheyenne, Georgia, Lily, and Mandy were arguing over the bottle of Aveeno hand lotion. "Mandy, I need that!" said Cheyenne.

"I see there are lotion problems," I said. "Unfortunately whatever lotion problems there are, they must be solved in the next two minutes." I pointed at the clock.

Backpacks were zipped up; iPads were put away in their cases and swung around like medieval maces. Lily and Mia began working together on their science homework. Travis went around the room gathering all the markers and the sock erasers.

Boop went the PA system. "Good afternoon," said the secretary. "Can I please have your attention for the end-of-day announcements." On Tuesday the swim team was victorious over Salter Creek Middle School, she said. She read off the first-place finishers. A pair of slacks were found on the stage in the cafeteria, and there were messages in the office for five students. "That will conclude afternoon announcements. Have a great afternoon."

Brock explained about chair-stacking. "The homeroom kids do the chairs once they come in," he said.

"There are kids coming into this class now?" I said.

"Yeah," said Brock.

"Oh my god." I'd assumed, because of the end-of-day announcements, that the day was actually over, but it wasn't. I studied the infernal sub plans one last time. "Students are expected to be working, reading, or socializing quietly," I read. "Absolutely no running around." There was a list of kids I should keep an eye on. They began arriving.

"I WILL ROCK YOU LIKE A HURRICANE!" sang a small, scrappy boy named Kyle, swinging his iPad case.

Luke stood in the middle of the room with his arms out. "We'll spin you around," said a girl. Luke turned slowly in place.

Chairs began going up on the desks.

Boop. More loud announcements, adding to the mayhem. "Dakota Cooper to the office for dismissal, please. Missy Tremain to the office for dismissal, please."

"Stop twirling," I said. "Stop twirling, stop twirling. STOP TWIRLING, otherwise you're going to fall down." Luke stood still. He looked woozy.

"Are you all right?" I asked.

"I'm fine. After a while I have to sit down."

He sat down.

"Is this normal?" I asked, meaning the level of end-of-day noise.

"Yes," he said.

"I broke my thumb," said Sydney, the girl with a wrist brace.

I asked her how.

"Reffing a wrestling match."

"BWAHAHAHA," said Kyle.

Boop. First-wave buses were announced. "Bye, first wavers," said Luke. The room suddenly became calmer.

"Why is it suddenly so quiet?" I asked.

"Because that fleabag of a kid is gone," said Luke, meaning Kyle.

"There are some people in here who are really annoying," said Sydney.

"I don't think boys get that their voices project everywhere," said Darryl, whose own voice was not soft. "Not you, Timothy, you're in every single one of my classes, and I never hear you."

"Ew, gross," said Georgia. She dropped something soft in the trash can. "It's a sandwich my dad made. He doesn't know how to make stuff."

Thomas said his favorite subject was social studies. He began drawing a tree holding the three branches of government; the elected officials and judges were twigs.

"That's a tree?" said Georgia.

I sent Max on a mission to collect fallen pencils.

Across the room, near a door, arose a minor unhappiness. Casey, one of the kids I was supposed to keep an eye on, had hit a girl named Brittany in the eye with the edge of his iPad case.

"Does my eye look infected?" said Brittany.

"Your brain looks infected," said Georgia.

I got Casey's attention. "Casey, what are you doing?"

"I don't know," said Casey, squirming against the doorjamb.

"Running around and hitting people," said Darryl.

"Will you stand still, so that I don't have to do something drastic with you?" I said.

Boop. "Melanie Delapointe to the office for dismissal!"

"Sorry," said Casey, to Brittany.

"It's cool," said Brittany.

Cayden, Georgia, and Darryl started singing "Wrecking Ball."

Boop. Second wavers left.

"Bye!"

I scrubbed at the two spots of my blood on the carpet until they were gone, and I wrote a short, fatuous note to Ms. Nolton: "The kids were excellent—friendly, funny, and quiet when asked." I turned out the lights. In the office I signed out and turned in my lanyard and apologized for not taking attendance during the first STAR period.

"That's okay," said the secretary.

"They were great kids," I said.

"So you'll come back?"

"Absolutely."

Later that afternoon I had a beer with Larry Reed, a retired social studies teacher from Marshwood High School, the school that my children had attended. Larry offered some helpful tips. When you introduce yourself, he said, write your name on the board, but don't say, "I'm Mr. Baker, I'm the sub." Avoid using the word *substitute* if you can, he said—because as soon as you say you're the substitute, you show the class that you have identified yourself with that role, and that undermines your authority. Also, get to know some students' names right away—kids like to be called by their names. "And let them know your expectations for the class," he said. "Not in a hardass way, but in a concise way, in a conversational way. Say, 'We have some work to do today, and here are my expectations. I expect you to be in your seats. I expect that when I'm talking, you're listening.' And tell them, again in a conversational voice, what the consequences will be of their not meeting your expectations. You can say, 'It may be that I will write you up for a detention. I may not be giving the detention, but I will be giving your name to the office.' Just leave it at that."

I nodded, taking notes. "The first test," Larry said, "is usually 'I need to go to the bathroom.' To which you can simply say, 'If you have to go, you have to go, but I expect you back within five minutes, and you are responsible for any work that you miss in that five minutes.' That tells them something, too."

Never make a threat that you can't follow through on, he said. "I've heard teachers say, 'If you don't be quiet, I'm going to throw you out the window.' You can't follow through on that. You can say, 'You're being disruptive, and next time you're disruptive I'm sending you out of here.' You want to be friendly, but you don't want them to be your friends."

Teach from your strengths, was Larry's last piece of advice. Tell them things you know. Have something up your sleeve that you can talk about, when the sub plans run dry. Never be in the position of having nothing to teach. "That's where the nightmares begin," he said.

Day Four, done.

TOAST

Beth called on Friday, sounding peeved, and said that a science teacher had suddenly gotten sick; they needed me again at the middle school. I said okay. I probably shouldn't have, because I'd hardly slept. My joints hurt, and I'd lain awake for hours writhing over a phone call I'd gotten on Thursday morning from Mrs. Fallon, Lasswell Middle School's assistant principal, about what she referred to as a "blood incident" from the day before. Several students in Ms. Nolton's class had mentioned that there had been an "issue with blood in the classroom," Mrs. Fallon said, and a custodian had noticed traces of blood in the sink of the boys' bathroom. And, she added, "Ms. Nolton said that there was a drop of blood on one of the whiteboards."

"Oh my god," I said. A whiteboard? I'd definitely been carrying around one of the personal whiteboards at one point. I must have bled onto it.

Mrs. Fallon had some advice. "I know it was your first day in the building, and by all accounts everything went really well," she said. "In an event like that, don't hesitate to go to the next-door teacher." It would be better, she said, not to use the boys' bathroom; I should use one of the teachers' bathrooms instead.

I apologized for bleeding all over the school.

"That's all right, it happens," she'd said. "We disinfected everything."

In any case, they wanted me back. I stumped downstairs to start up Mr. Coffee and frowned at the clock. It said twenty after the hour. Plenty of time to take a shower, I thought. But in my sleep-robbed brain fog, I misread the hour: it wasn't five-twenty, it was six-twenty. Still believing I was comfortably early, I made some sandwiches and drove north. Things weren't that bad, I reflected. I'd had a nosebleed. It happens. Get back on the horse.

The phone rang while I sat waiting for a stoplight. It was a secretary from the middle school. "Are you substituting for us today?" she asked. I said I was, I was on my way. "Because school starts at seven-thirty," she said, "and it's ten to eight now. We're just wondering where you are."

"Oh, no!" I said. "I misread the clock. I'm terribly sorry, I'll be there in a jiffy." I swore and gunned the engine up a long hill.

I'd screwed up again. Couldn't even read the clock. What was I thinking?

The parking lot was nearly full, but there was a slot near one of the far snowheaps. I was huffing and puffing by the time I reached the office. "It's unforgivable, really," I said to the secretary.

"Trust me," she said, "it's not the first time it's happened." She pointed me in the direction of Mr. Lyall's science class over in Team Ganges. It was a long yellow cinderblock room with lab tables that were filled with eighth-graders who had gotten to school on time, as I had not. However, as it happened, my presence was not yet needed: homeroom that day was devoted to something called "Advisor/Advisee," or AA, led by some sort of kindliness specialist, a Mrs. Dunne, who wanted everyone to study a handout from the Southern Poverty Law Center. "LADIES AND GENTLEMEN!" Mrs. Dunne said, over a steady hum of conversation. "LET'S TAKE A LOOK AND SEE WHERE WE'RE SIMILAR AND WHERE WE'RE DIFFERENT." The handout was meant to teach tolerance—it was about "friendship groups" versus cliques. Friendship groups were okay, but cliques were bad, because they often "exerted control over their members." Together she and the class went through a set of multiple-choice questions: *I _____ sit with the same people at lunch every day. (A) always, (B) sometimes, (C) never.* Most students answered "always." *When someone I've never talked to before speaks to me, I feel _____. (A) annoyed, (B) afraid, (C) excited.* Many said "annoyed." One said "afraid." *I _____ meeting new people! (A) hate, (B) don't care about, (C) love.* Some said "hate"; one girl said "sometimes." According to the answer key at the bottom of the page, if you answered mostly A's you should "ask yourself if you're in a clique." Everyone was talking at once. "SHHH," said Mrs. Dunne. "If I said hi, and I've never talked to you before, that's going to annoy you?"

"If I'm in a bad mood," said a girl, "yes."

"I'm fine about everyone," said a boy.

Further murmurs of dissent. Mrs. Dunne said, "I'm going to agree with you: the selections here kind of stumped me. I think we need a (D) answer—'I'm fine about meeting new people.'" After a while, she gave up on the tolerance lesson—the class just was not into it. She left.

It was my homeroom now. This was the moment to introduce myself and take command, but I had a strange attack of sleep-deprived shyness and didn't. I turned toward several kids sitting nearby. "So now normally what happens?"

"We have, like, free time," said Olivia, a short, bouncy girl.

A boy, Sean, asked me how long I'd been a teacher.

Not very long, I said—I'd taught some college writing here and there.

"Yeah, you look like a writer," said Sean.

"You kind of look like the guy on the back of *The Giving Tree*," said Prentice. He had small, puffy, amused, wicked eyes.

"Well, I've got a white beard."

"Can I call you Santa Claus?" said Olivia.

"Please don't," I said. "You can think of me that way."

"Do you give out presents?" Prentice said.

"No."

"You don't bring Jolly Ranchers in? You should, next time you sub at this school."

"That's a good idea," I said. I stood up and cleared my throat. "So—guys. I just want to say I'm sorry I'm late to your class. Mr. Baker is my name, and—um—I'm the sub." Bad, dumb, wrong. I flapped the tolerance handout. "I'm interested in this survey," I said, "because I have found, when I go into a Maine school, that the kids are nice. When somebody comes into your group, it's kind of a tricky thing. It's a delicate balance. You've got some friends and some people who are maybe a little bit new to the group, and they're not totally accepted but they're somewhat accepted. Everybody's trying to figure out their position. It doesn't seem to me that this is a terribly cliquish place. Do you think it is?"

"Yes," said Olivia.

"You can't say hi to everyone," said Sean. "Hi, Olivia!"

"Hi, Sean," said Olivia. "See, now we're in a clique!"

"Anyway," I said, "I don't know what they want you to do with these survey questions. I guess they want you to think about them and sort of become better people?" I stood for a moment. The class, having satisfied their curiosity about me, which was minimal, resumed their much more interesting conversations. They were a clique, and I was not a member. Why fight it? "And now you have a free moment to, ah, live your life," I said.

One of the secretaries came by to give me a batch of photocopied letters from the superintendent's office, urging parents to fill out a form that they'd recently received from the Military Interstate Children's Compact Commission. "The DOE"—Maine's Department of Education—"feels it would be helpful to know how many students we currently educate dealing with a parent/guardian serving overseas or based here in Maine and the unique difficulties these students face," said the letter. I handed out the letter; the kids stuffed it in the side pouches of their backpacks as the next-period bell bonged.

Mr. Lyall was in the middle of a unit on the periodic table and the chemistry of matter. The homework for the night before had been to choose one element from the periodic table—a poster of the table was on the wall—and build a small, three-dimensional construction-paper cube covered with fun facts about that element, held together with Scotch tape.

Some kids had thrown themselves into the project, making minutely detailed drawings on the facets of their cubes, using many colors of markers, and some had barely begun. Nobody was finished. I went around the room asking people about their elements, and making cries of wonder and admiration: "Wow, that's beautiful. That's amazing." One kid, Stephen, had made a yellow paper cube about neptunium. On one of its facets, he'd written, in tiny, careful letters, *Where you would "Bump Into" it: neptunium, because of its high radioactivity, is only used in laboratories. If you are not a scientist, you will probably never see it in your life.* A cheerful boy named Bruce, who had chosen selenium, was making some repairs to his cube. "It kind of got smushed cause my dog stepped on it," he explained. Melissa, a big girl dressed in purple, had made a cube about argon, with the chemical symbol in fat purple letters. *Even though it's not poisonous,* she wrote in yellow, *it can still cause suffocation.* Ryder, a boy in a blue button-down shirt, had chosen magnesium, which was used to make *JET ENGINES*—he'd surrounded the words with red flames. Over a drawing of a saucepan on a hot stove, he'd noted magnesium's boiling point: 1,994 degrees Fahrenheit, 1,090 degrees centigrade. *Plus it doesn't stink,* he wrote, in green letters outlined with black.

"My element was boron," said May, who was obviously organized and got all A's.

"Nice choice," I said. "Did you find anything interesting out about boron?"

"It's used in bleach, soap, and ceramics," she said promptly.

"Great work," I said. "What I like about this assignment is that for the rest of your life you'll feel a special affinity for boron, right?"

"Yes," she said, doubtfully.

After they'd deposited their element cubes in a plastic tray by the windows, they were supposed to read two chapters from a textbook called *The Nature of Matter* and answer some questions, but because of Mrs. Dunne's anti-clique survey, there wasn't time to do the reading. While they were putting final touches on their cubes, I skimmed the textbook to learn about the differences between physical and chemical changes.

Crumpling paper is a physical change, a burning match is a chemical change. Got it. A rotting apple is a chemical change, and rust is also a chemical change, because the iron reacts with oxygen in the air. I read one of the questions: *What kind of change occurs on the surface of bread when it is toasted—physical or chemical? Explain.* But . . . wasn't it both? The heat dries the bread, making it crunchy, which is a physical change, and the bread turns brown, which is a chemical reaction.

A peppy, bifocaled ed tech named Ms. Shrader appeared—actually she was a substitute, filling in for the regular ed tech, who worked one-on-one with Lisa, a quiet, affable girl who had a learning problem. Ms. Shrader helped Lisa with her element cube—she'd chosen copper—and then she came over to talk to me. She'd taught language arts, social studies, and gifted-and-talented at the middle school for twenty-five years; after that, she'd worked as an ed tech for high-functioning autistic students, which was a dream job. "That was the most fun I ever had," she said. Now she was a substitute. "This is what I did and who I was."

I asked her if getting her certificate had prepared her for being a teacher.

"Nope," she said. "My ed classes did not prepare me."

"Teaching is a whole new world," I said.

"It's so not what people think it is," Ms. Shrader said. She waved her arm at the students. "It's very easy to say you can do this, this, and this. But get in a classroom with twenty-five kids and find out how easy it is. It's not. Some things are possible, though. Kids want somebody to tell them what to do. You have to read the crowd. Some of these kids are on the bus at six-ten in the morning."

"It's a long day for them," I said.

"A very long day," she said. She checked the clock. "OKAY, GUYS, YOU CAN GO. SEE YOU LATER, HAVE A GREAT DAY!" Out in the cacophonous hallway, I heard her say, to another teacher, "Lord, have mercy."

I had a moment of stillness between classes, and a quick bathroom break, before twenty-two more fourteen-year-olds filed in, holding their fragile paper element cubes. Arsenic. Gold. Silver. Neon. "Why does neon glow?" I asked Tamara, whose cube was covered with bullet points and boiling points.

"Um, I can't remember," she said. I talked to Raymond, a smart kid, about depleted uranium weapons. Shelby told me about lithium. "It's found in the Earth's crust," he said. "When lithium touches water it lights it on fire. I'm not really sure how that works, since it's found in the Earth's crust." One of the tape dispensers ran out of tape and was refilled, but the new tape was not very good—it wasn't sticky enough. The students watched their newly taped cubes self-destruct several minutes afterward, seam by seam. We set that dispenser aside.

The students colored, they taped, they talked; I said, "Nice job, excellent, good going." The pile of finished cubes grew like a heap of alchemical treasure in the homework bin. This was a nifty assignment—there was something about having to turn a list of inert facts into a three-dimensional, decorative, faceted object that seemed to help kids think better.

I made a stab at teaching what was in the textbook, rather than merely ordering the class to read it, per the sub plans. If you make a smoothie, I said to them, is that a physical change, or a chemical change? Physical, they said. Good. If you take a bite of an apple and put it on the windowsill and wait for a while and it turns brown, is that a physical or a chemical change? Some said physical, some said chemical. I explained why it was chemical. "So—when you're done with your cube, just read the two chapters and answer the questions on page seventy-two and eighty-seven." I casually knuckle-tapped the numbers of the questions they had to answer on the whiteboard, as if I were a real teacher. Bethany was smiling to herself, working her thumbs on her cellphone. "Or just text your friend," I said. About two-thirds of the kids got to work on the assignment. Rodney and Bradley played catch with a uranium cube. I marched over, feigning sternness. "You want to come to the front and explain how depleted uranium works?"

"No," said Rodney.

"If it was a real cube of uranium, you wouldn't be able to bat it around like that, right?"

"Because it's one of the heaviest metals," said Bradley.

"Right." I opened Bradley's textbook and pointed out the questions they were supposed to answer. Nearby, Eileen, polite and deliberate, had carefully balanced her element cube on a marker set vertically on end inside an empty, dusty aquarium. "It's drying," she said. "It's inside the fish tank so no air will knock it over."

The tide of noise began to rise. Olivia, the bouncy, tiny girl in short shorts from homeroom, was flirting outrageously with the two uranium-cube tossers. "He's blushing," said Olivia. "Look at him, he's turning red!" I turned to talk to a kid named Winston in a Patriots T-shirt about nitrogen. "They used to have nitrogen tanks in paintball," he said. "It was so powerful they went to CO_2."

I asked him if he was a paintball man.

"I'm more of a snowboarder," Winston said. "My last run is tomorrow."

Next to him, Sam, a quiet kid, was using orange Sharpie to jazz up the *Kr* on his krypton cube.

"Does krypton make you weaken and fall to the ground?" I asked.

"No, it's a noble gas," he said. "It's highly unreactive." Math was probably his best subject, he told me.

Olivia came over. "I have a question," she said. "Can I get a Starburst?"

"No, but thanks for asking. What element are you working on?"

"Chlorine," she said.

"My best subject is tech," said Winston. "In tech, you can build stuff. I'm a hands-on person. We built a car out of wood, and we had to send it down a ramp a couple of times. And there was an egg in the car, a raw egg."

"First it was a hard-boiled egg," said Olivia. "They were trying to teach us you shouldn't text and drive."

"Then it was a raw egg," Winston continued, "and when the car hits sometimes the egg splatters. If you crash like that, it's going to be bam, you're gone. You have to protect the egg. I went down three times, and then I did the hill of death."

"The hill of death is where you have to stand on a stool," said Olivia. "I had to stand on my tippy-toes, that's honest."

"I had to stand on my tippy-toes," said Winston. "I lost my bumper, but the egg survived. I got a T-shirt for winning."

Class over. Twenty-two more students, twenty-two more backpacks, twenty-two more iPads in their black padded cases, sixteen more element cubes. "Top o' the morning!" I said, clapping my hands together.

"I'm walking on sunshine this morning," said a boy, Harley, with exaggerated zest.

"I'm Mr. Baker," I said. I successfully avoided saying I was the substitute—*they knew that*. While I was taking attendance, Renee stopped chewing gum, opened her large mouth, and yelled, "QUIET!"

"Don't say quiet, just be quiet," I said to her.

"Can I take the attendance down?" asked Harley, smirking.

"Don't trust him," said Renee, resuming gum-chewing.

They still had work left to do on their element cubes. Christopher, a gamer, wrote that chlorine was *a murderous gas*. The French had used it first, in World War I, he said: *The only problem was when the wind changed.* Joy had chosen tin. "It's very rare," she said. "Rarer than copper."

I asked her why it had that strange two-letter symbol, *Sn*. "Just to make life difficult?"

"It's because it's from the Greek," she said.

Courtney, the girl next to Joy, said, "My dad is a history teacher."

"Congratulations, Courtney," said Joy sarcastically.

Courtney had covered her gold cube with sumptuous stripes of golden crayon. "It's used in medications," she said, "and it's used in chips, in iPhones, that sort of thing."

"And you would never know," said Joy.

"This tape sucks," said Felicity, who was next to Courtney.

There was a scuffle across the room. "Ow, Lizzie, stop!" I felt like a waiter in a crowded Greek diner.

"What's happening?" I asked.

"We're massaging our necks," said Jessica, who had her hands around Lizzie's neck.

"These ladies are hurting each other," said Harley.

"IT'S A CHICK FIGHT! YEAH!" said Todd, who was shrimpy and high-voiced.

Nearby, Victor had drawn a large black spiral on one side of his cube. I asked him if it was a picture of the death spiral of the hafnium electron. "I don't know," he said.

Harley grabbed a textbook and slammed it on the table.

"Why would you slam the book?" I asked him.

"I don't know," said Harley.

"I don't know either," I said. "It makes a loud slamming noise if you slam it." I pointed out the question on page 87, the one about toast, and told him to answer it. "This question sums up the whole problem," I said.

Courtney, Felicity, and Joy came up. "Mr. Baker, can we work out in the hall?" said Courtney.

"People always ask me that," I said.

"We've got a bad class," Felicity said.

"You'll miss the social whirl," I said.

"I don't like the social whirl," Felicity said. "I like my friends."

"I did oxygen," said James, in a hockey shirt.

"What happens when oxygen comes into contact with the human brain?" I said. I laughed demonically, startling the boy. "Never mind." I took a huge breath. "WHEN YOU'VE FINISHED YOUR MAGIC CUBES—"

Harley was making a scene.

"Shut up, Harley," said Todd.

"No," said Harley.

"WHEN YOU'VE FINISHED YOUR MAGIC ELEMENT BOXES, THEY GO UP—"

"They're magical?" said Harley.

"Yes," I said, "because when they're done, you get a mark."

Todd had discovered the cube from an earlier class balanced inside the dry fish tank. "It's drying," I said. "It's got sparkles on it."

"I want to touch it," said Todd.

"No," I said.

"Stop it!" said Elizabeth.

More kids crowded around.

"Isn't it beautiful?" I said. "Perfectly balanced in its own little aquarium."

"That's Eileen for you," said Elizabeth.

"Did you see how he threw my pencil on the floor?" said Todd, pointing to Harley. "I should get him arrested."

Lyle, in baggy sweats, imitated a fussy teacher. "That is none of your concern, Harley. Turn around in your chair and return to your work."

Harley said, "I'm sharpening my pencil."

"He's sharpening his mechanical pencil," said Todd.

"So, what is a physical property?" I asked Lyle.

Lyle's eyes strayed to an open textbook. "*A physical change is one in which the form or appearance of matter changes, but not its composition,*" he read.

"You're artfully reading the textbook," I said.

"I have it memorized," he said.

"So if you have a rock," I said, "and you take a hammer to it—"

"That rock's going down," said Lyle.

We laughed and talked about blowtorches and states of matter.

"I'm so tired of winter," said Marielle, looking out the window. She had a long braid and a gentle, unformed face.

"I saw crocuses the other day," I said. "That means spring."

"It should be like ninety degrees outside by now," said Marielle. "We should be wearing shorts."

There was an odd momentary hush, one of those coincidental clearings in the verbal jungle that sometimes occur.

Todd promptly spoke up. "Get to work, children."

Harley said, "Todd's doing nothing but causing trouble."

"Is he disturbing the intellectual content of the class?" I said.

"I don't think there is any intellectual content," said Marielle. "You forgot, you're teaching eighth grade."

"Inner-lectual," said Harley.

"I like that," I said. "Innerlectual and outerlectual."

"Yummy," said Todd, rubbing his stomach.

"Inter-what? What's inter-lectual?" Jessica asked.

"Look it up," said Lizzie.

Todd was taking pictures of me with his iPad. I told him to stop.

Harley said, "iPads are stupid. I don't like them."

"Time to go," said Lyle. "I don't want to go. Can I just stay here?"

A general zippage of backpacks. The girls fixed their hair. I asked Todd what his next class was.

"Reading, with Mrs. Simmons."

"Whooo!" said a girl.

Class over; new class. Twenty-one children, each with a future life, each with a name to be called out. I signed and dated the attendance sheet.

Katylynn's hand shot up. She had a ring on her thumb. "Can we bring that down?"

"Yes, you can." Time to take control. "So I'm Mr. Baker, and WE ARE DOING SOME SCIENCE. And you've got some cubes, right? I have been really impressed by these cubes. Everybody picks an element and just goes wild with the art. And if you haven't gone wild with it, don't worry, you've just gone slightly wild." I turned to Katylynn and Roslyn, the two girls who were taking the attendance sheet to the office. "And gals? We need some Scotch tape that actually works. This Scotch tape is terrible. So if you could ask them if they could tell me where in the class the Scotch tape is, or if they maybe have some Scotch tape? Here we are talking about the scientific properties of matter. Scotch tape is actually supposed to be sticky. So we're going to get some better tape."

The noise was moving and growing.

"GUYS! If you've finished your cubes, that's tremendous, and if you haven't finished them, just pour your soul out into that cube. Everything about selenium or uranium or whatever it is you're doing. And then, when you're done, there are some pages to read in the textbook, and some questions, all about physical and chemical properties. Like when you take a bite of an apple is that a physical change or a chemical change?"

"Physical," said Anthony, a plaid-shirted polite kid.

"Right, and if you take a bite of the apple, put the apple on the counter, walk away, watch a TV show, and come back and the apple is brown, is that a physical or a chemical change?"

"Chemical," said Rita, with long straight hair.

"Okay! And let's say you're a miner and you carve out a bunch of stuff from a hillside and you melt it down and you end up with iron."

"Chemical?" said Anthony.

"Ah, but you're melting it," I said. "The difference between ice and water is physical, right? If you melt iron ore to make iron, that's sort of like melting ice to make water. Now, if you build a bridge with the iron and the rain comes and it reacts and turns to rust, what's rust?"

"Physical," said Anthony.

"Rust is a tricky one," I said. "You should know rust. Rust is a chemical change because the oxygen in the air is reacting with the metal. If you know rust, you've got the right answer to a question. Rust is a chemical change. So you're already there, practically. Just read that part of the textbook, firm up your knowledge, and answer the questions. Okay?"

Frederick, a charismatic boy in a baseball T-shirt, raised his hand. "Mr. Baker, I have a completely off-topic question. How tall are you?"

"I'm six four."

"Whoa, six four!" said Frederick.

"It was just the hormones in the meat," I said.

"Are you a basketball player?"

I said I'd played basketball, but not in school.

"Our team won the championships," Frederick said.

Frederick's friend Payson said, "Were you a science teacher at one point?"

"No, I never was a science teacher," I said, "and I never will be a science teacher."

"Except for right now," said Payson. "Right now you're a science teacher."

"You're right, my god, I'm a science teacher!"

Another hand went up, from a malicious cherub with spiky blond hair. "Misterbater?" he said. His name was Shane. His voice was just beginning to change.

"Mr. Baker," I said.

Immediate uproar. "That's Shane! Don't pay any attention to him!"

I didn't. I circulated, handing out compliments. "Iridium!" I said, admiring Aaron's cube. "What is iridium?"

"It's just a rock," said Natasha, willowy and impatient, sitting next to him.

"It's in meteors," said Aaron.

"It's in meat?" said Shane.

John was sniffing a quarter to figure out how silver smelled. He handed it to me. "Would you say that smell is 'musty'?"

I smelled the quarter. "It smells like old finger oil and dirt. I'm not sure if silver has much of a smell. But sure, why not? Musty." John wrote, *Smell: Musty*, on his cube.

"How do you like my *K*?" said Payson.

"Potassium! Beautiful *K*! Nice stripes!"

They went away for lunch and returned. Shane, having bellowed for half an hour in the cafeteria, had become a demon child. He drew on the floor with a Sharpie and then squirted a big plop of dish detergent on the black marks and began scrubbing the spot while trying to make an iPad movie of himself cleaning the floor, laughing.

"Whoa, stop, stop, stop," I said. "You're on the floor, Shane. That is a physical change in your altitude, and it will result in a chemical change to your grade. So please don't do that. Sit in your chair. Just do some work, okay? I have my eye on you."

As I walked away, I heard Shane say, "I hate that guy."

Class ended, and then, mercifully, it was STAR time. Some familiar faces were back, including Shane. They all, even Shane, "read" silently— meaning that they mostly poked at their iPads and listened to music—for twenty minutes. Then Shane raised his hand.

"Mr. Bakersfield," he said, innocently. "Can I call you Mr. Bakersfield? Like the Hell's Satans of Bakersfield?"

"No."

"Mr. Bakersfield," said Shane, "are you trying to grow your hair out on top?"

"My hair's pretty much gone on top," I said. "What about you? Are you trying to grow your hair out?" A girl laughed. That made Shane mad.

He began covertly jabbing a plastic ruler under his neighbor's backpack, trying to make it fall off the desk. "Stop with the ruler!" I said. Moments later he was silently pretending to whonk someone on the head with a textbook. I went over and pulled up a chair and lowered my voice. "What is the problem, Shane?"

"I'm ADHD," he said. "My pills begin to wear off around now."

"Oh, come on," I said.

"I swear to god!" said Shane. "Ask anybody."

I said, "Do you want not to be ADHD?"

"I don't want to be, but I am."

"Look, you're obviously smart," I said. "Just pull it together, okay? Just dial it back a notch. Can you do that? Thank you."

He calmed down a bit after that.

The secretary's voice came over the loudspeaker. "Please excuse the interruption for the afternoon announcements," she said. "There was a bracelet found today in the gym locker room area. Please come to the main office and claim it if it is yours. Students who are part of the cast of *Oklahoma!* will have a mandatory practice Monday through Thursday next week. Today's jazz rehearsal has been canceled." She read a long list of students who had messages in the office—parents were forbidden to text their children in middle school. I sat for ten minutes and watched the class chat and joke and raise minor hell. Let them. I wanted the day to be over.

But there was still forty minutes to go—end-of-day homeroom. "Hi, Santa Claus," said Olivia, the bouncy girl in short shorts. She began flirting with a serious, proto-gay boy named Michael. "You're so abusive, Michael!" she said.

"I am not," said Michael.

Olivia grabbed Michael's water bottle.

"Let my water go!" Michael said.

"Are you having a baby?" Olivia said. She turned to me. "There's ice cream in the freezer if you get hungry. I'm trying to lose weight."

"You can't lose weight," said Michael. "If you try to lose weight your body will compensate. Your body will just hold on to the fat."

"You're so abusive," she said to Michael. "Why did you tell Rodney to give James a lap dance?"

"I didn't tell him to do that!" said Michael. "He said he'd give me five bucks if I gave a lap dance to Melissa."

"How tall are you?" Bruce asked me.

"Six four."

"Wow, six four!"

"It means nothing to be tall," I said.

"WAVE ONE, YOU ARE DISMISSED," said the secretary. Six kids left the room. It was quieter now.

"You know how short I am?" Olivia said. "I'm just shy of five feet." She turned back to Michael. "Do you really want to be a teacher?" she asked.

"Yes," said Michael. "Like from kindergarten to fifth grade."

"I like kids a lot," Olivia said. "I like little kids, one-year-olds. One through like five."

They stacked some chairs on tables and picked up some stray pencils and I thanked them. "It's been a pleasure having you in class," I said.

"And people say I can't be nice!" said Michael.

"He can't," said Olivia. "He's abusive to me."

"I'm not abusive unless you're abusive to me," said Michael.

I asked what *abusive* meant.

"When you hit me, you're getting hit back, two times as bad!" said Michael.

I felt drained, numb, brain-dead. In the back of the room three of the remaining kids had begun playing hockey with a balled-up piece of paper, using their iPad cases as hockey sticks. "This is a long day," I said.

"A really long day," said Olivia. "I wish we'd start school at nine o'clock. They don't understand how crazy I am if I don't sleep. On Sundays I sleep till nine-thirty."

"You talk a lot when you don't sleep," said Michael.

"I talk a LOT," said Olivia. "Boys are always talking about . . . never mind." She looked at me. "Are you new here?"

"Yes, I'm very new here," I said.

"Do you like it?"

"Yes, I do. I like you guys. You seem like good people. Although sometimes things get a little out of control."

"I was listening to what you said this morning," said Michael. "You've got the wrong idea. Kids here are not what they seem. They spread rumors about me—bad stuff."

"So all that clique business they were talking about is true?"

"It's not cliques, it's more like gang warfare," said Michael.

"There are four girls in my class who are snobs," said Olivia.

"DUDE, DON'T OPEN YOUR LEGS, WHATEVER YOU DO!" said one of the hockey players.

"Hah-hah, please," said Courtney.

"Excuse me for a second," I said. I went to the back of the room. "What is this, air hockey, brain hockey? Just crank it back, okay? Keep the volume down."

I went back to Michael and Olivia. "So what are people snobby about?"

"Everything," said Olivia. "They think that they have everything, and they really don't. I'm kind of snobby myself." She asked Michael, "How do you think I am? I can be really nice, but I am very snobby sometimes."

I felt it was time for a platitude. "If everyone at school can find one or two people they get along with, that's enough, right?" I took a bite of an apple.

"I hate apples," said Olivia.

"There's one kid, you even say something disrespectful to him, he's going to punch you," said Michael.

"Do you know I got grounded for punching my mom?" said Olivia.

"Why did you do that?" I asked.

"She was being annoying. She was behind me and I was trying to go out the door, and she pushed me, so I turned around and smacked her, and when I got home she was like, 'You're grounded.' So I called the cops on her. I said, 'My mom's grounding me for punching her and I didn't punch her.' I lied about that."

I said, "You called the cops on your mom?"

"WAVE TWO, YOU ARE DISMISSED."

"Take it easy!" I said. They left.

I drove home. Day Five, check. At least I hadn't bled on a whiteboard.

OUT COMES THE EYEBALL

On Monday, Beth gave me a choice of several assignments—fourth grade, second grade, the middle school. She hesitated. "Or, there's an ed tech spot at the high school." I said I'd do it. I drove there slowly, stuck behind a heating-oil truck. Even so I got to the parking lot early. I parked next to a large gray snowpile and sat thinking about the strangeness of giving a kid like Shane, who seemed quite normal albeit sometimes irritating, a daily drug to control his behavior. The early sun cast interesting pink shadows on the rubble of frozen slush. I went inside.

"You are Lola St. Pierre today," said Paulette, the secretary, as I signed in. The ed tech room was just down the hall from the main office—a small chamber with a scatter of mismatched chairs and four desks and a file cabinet and not much on the walls. I shook hands with Mr. Bowles, the affable, black-shirted, striped-tied ed tech supervisor, and told him I was filling in for Mrs. St. Pierre.

A plumpish, friendly middle-aged woman, Mrs. Meese, looked up from her desk. "Mrs. St. Pierre is out, too?"

"Everybody's out," said Mr. Bowles.

"I'm shocked," said Mrs. Meese. They two of them began conferring. "Mr. Wakefield is in for Mrs. Batelle. So this gentleman here"—meaning me—"will be with Nina." Their eyes met—clearly it wasn't a good idea for me to spend the day with Nina. "Nina has boundary issues," Mr. Bowles explained. Better, he thought, if Mrs. Meese spent the day with Nina, and then I'd do ed tech duty in the classes that Mrs. Meese normally went to.

Mrs. Meese handwrote her Monday schedule, complete with room numbers and the names of the kids in each class I was supposed to keep an eye on—usually they were the ones with Individualized Education Plans—and gave it to me. "Our trimester has just begun," she said. "We're kind of just getting our feet wet here." The first class was English, with twenty-six students, one teacher, and two ed techs. "We both kind of police one side of the room each," Mrs. Meese said. "What we've begun in that room is we're reading a book. Mrs. Kennett has been reading and the kids have been following along." Next was a history class, then came Financial Algebra, then an elective called Community Safety, and then came a small literacy study group, where they were working on the difference between literal and figurative language. "The kids are going to need to highlight or underline things in the story," Mrs. Meese said. "So if you're familiar with all forms of language you'll be fine with that."

I thanked her for the helpful orientation.

"I'm glad you enjoyed it," said Mrs. Meese.

The English teacher, Mrs. Kennett, was about thirty, upbeat and appealing, wearing a red cardigan. Her room was painted a pale blue, and it had six six-sided, wood-grained-laminate tables in it; the chairs had tennis balls over their casters so that they wouldn't squeak. I took a chair near the windows and she walked to the front of the class and turned sweepingly to face them. "Goo-oood morning, folks!" Mrs. Kennett said, as if she were Robin Williams in *Good Morning, Vietnam.* "How are ya!"

Nobody answered. Five conversations continued.

"It's like ten degrees outside," said Mrs. Kennett loudly. "Who else is not okay with that?"

"I'm okay with it," said Jared, in a blue sweatshirt.

"Come on, it's the end of March!" Mrs. Kennett said.

"I actually lived in Alaska, so I'm okay with it," said Steve, who looked like a football player.

Anabelle, in a Hollister shirt, turned. "Steve, you were in Alaska? When was that?"

"I was like five."

"Five! You couldn't have been that acclimated to the Alaskan tundra yet," said Mrs. Kennett.

"He ran around naked," said Jared.

"Yeah, and I slept with the dogs outside," said Steve. "No, actually, we had a husky. Beautiful dog."

"I'm sure," said Mrs. Kennett. "I'm a big-dog fan. I like big dogs."

"I forgot my book," said Keith cheerfully.

"That's okay, we had somebody else forget their book. Who read the three pages you had to read?"

"I didn't!" called out a kid from the back.

"You should have!" Mrs. Kennett laughed. The book was a movie tie-in edition of Stephen King's *The Shawshank Redemption*.

"I read it," said Anabelle.

"I really think that the only way that you're going to get the most from this book is if I read it," said Mrs. Kennett. "And I'm willing to do that. It's okay with me."

"Woo-hoo!" said the kid in the back.

Mrs. Kennett said that over the weekend, she'd been to a place where they made maple sugar. "So, yeah, that was kind of cool. Anybody else do anything interesting over the weekend?"

"I worked at Market Basket," said Brandon.

"I took a shower," said Harmony.

"That's interesting," said Mrs. Kennett. "I have a feeling that's pretty normal, though."

"Nope," said Brad, a joker.

Noah, an upbeat kid with motor-control difficulties, said that he watched the Johnny Carson show all weekend.

The class was not under control. Everyone was talking.

"I found out," said Mrs. Kennett, "that I'm getting another niece or nephew this weekend!"

"We didn't even know you were pregnant," said Brad.

"No, so my sister-in-law is pregnant with her second. She's due in November. ALL RIGHTY! SO! SHHH. QUIET DOWN PLEASE! Before I read to you guys today, I'm going to hand out—please hold the moans and groans—I'm going to hand out—"

"UH!"

"AGH!"

"—your first assessment."

"MOAN!"

"GROAN!"

"This is an assessment that has to do with the narration standard that we talked about. The unreliable narrator. Knowing what it is, and using the book to talk about that." She moved around the class handing out the assignment.

Sebastian, one of the students I was responsible for, was drinking a bottle of mango juice. He was long-limbed, and made quick, decisive turns of his head, taking in what was happening and simultaneously ignoring it.

"I don't understand what the deal is with that," said Mrs. Kennett, pointing at Sebastian's mango juice. "It's a tiny bottle, and it's very expensive."

Sebastian shrugged, fished out a pair of earbuds from his backpack, and began untangling their cords.

Mrs. Kennett explained the project. It was going to be due in three weeks. "This is something that you're going to be doing as we read the book. This is a narration video journal. I was going to be really mean and have you guys actually present these things, but I know that there's a lot of anxiety around presenting in front of the class. So you can choose to present, which I'm pretty sure not many of you will do—otherwise you're going to be emailing them to me. It does kind of require you to use a little bit of technology as well. You're going to be videotaping yourselves. But I'll be the only one who has to see it."

"Steve, you have to wear a shirt," said Artie.

"Do the video in the shower," said Brad.

"OKAY! PLEASE LISTEN. Using your iPad, and iMovie, record four video journal entries, one for every twenty-five pages, that explains whether the narrator is reliable or unreliable, citing specific lines of text to support your argument. That's called evidence, and we're trying to create an argument that the narrator is either reliable or unreliable." Each video journal entry should be between one and two minutes, she said, and it should include a slide of each quote the student used.

Sebastian finished his mango juice, tipping his head way back and making a sucking sound to get the last of it into his mouth.

"I have a question," said Keith. "What if we don't have an iPad?"

"We're going to have to work around that," said Mrs. Kennett. "I realize that you're not the only one who's in that pickle. You might have to hand-write it, or type it if you have access to a computer." She went over the assignment again: analyze four quotations from four different parts of the book, preferably on video, in order to show whether the narrator is reliable or unreliable.

Sebastian began jamming the empty mango juice bottle against his tightly closed eye.

That was the plan, Mrs. Kennett said, and on Wednesday, they would start watching the movie version of *The Shawshank Redemption*, assuming it wasn't a snow day. There followed an interchange on extreme facial piercings, including one that exposed your lower teeth and made you look like a bulldog. "I have six tattoos," said Mrs. Kennett. "But some things I don't really get the point of, that's all. OKAY! Let's listen and follow along! Shhh."

Doing my job as an ed tech, I leaned forward and whispered to Sebastian to remove his earbuds from his ears so he could hear the story.

And then Mrs. Kennett began reading from *The Shawshank*

Redemption, taking up at the moment when the narrator and his convict friends are on the freshly tarred roof drinking Black Label beer. *"That beer was piss-warm,"* Mrs. Kennett read, *"but it was still the best I ever had in my life."* Instantly a concentrated, listening silence descended. The class, which had murmured and joked and made mildly rude comments without stop for ten minutes, was now still and perfectly attentive. Only two things, it seemed, really got the attention of students in RSU66: the Pledge of Allegiance, and fiction read aloud.

Mrs. Kennett was a good, uninhibited reader. Some words, like *coterie*, *Rotarians*, and *Nembutal*, stumped her, but she didn't hesitate over a sentence like: *If there were a few weevils in the bread, wasn't that just too fucking bad?* Using his teeth, Sebastian managed, after several tries, to pry off the red plastic ring from the mouth of the mango juice bottle. Mrs. Kennett came to a passage about Shawshank's prison leadership: *"The people who run this place are stupid brutal monsters, for the most part,"* she read. *"The people who run the straight world are brutal and monstrous but they happen to be not quite as stupid because the standard of competence out there is a little higher."* When she got to the part about Andy setting up the prison library, she stopped reading to say how important it was for the prisoners to get their high school diplomas. "He helped thirteen inmates get their high school equivalency," she said. "Think about that. You guys are in high school now. Can you imagine being in your thirties, or forties, and not even having a high school diploma? Or fifties or sixties?"

Brad said that his sister was twenty-six and didn't have her high school diploma.

"Not yet, but she's still pretty young," Mrs. Kennett said. "You always have time to go back. You just have to go to school, it's just part of life, you just have to do it. So let's move on."

There was a brief interchange about how Red was Irish in the book, whereas Morgan Freeman, who played Red in the movie, wasn't Irish, obviously.

"He could get a hair dye," said Dale.

"That would be a sight—a ginger," said Brad.

"He's got some freckles on him," said Kaylee.

"Obama's Irish," said Keith.

Later, when Mrs. Kennett read about a big draft in Andy's cell, somebody whispered, "Foreshadowing!"

Steve said, "It would be cool to have a scientific instrument that would go off whenever foreshadowing occurs."

"Or everybody in the room just coughs when we hear it," said Sebastian, who was making an origami crane out of green paper.

"Who wants to keep going?" said Mrs. Kennett. She read some more pages, but it was just about the end of the class now, and people were restless, getting ready to leave. "All right," she said. "So you guys have the rest of fifty-eight, fifty-nine, and half of page sixty to read tonight. That's like a page and a half. We can do this!"

The bell bonged. Sebastian was the first one out of the room. I thought, So this is the life of an ed tech in high school. I thanked Mrs. Kennett and went to history class.

The teacher, Ms. Hopkins, said she was just back from a conference on the teaching of history, and she was tired. She looked pale. "It takes a lot of energy to talk," she said. She asked me to make some two-sided copies of a worksheet, which I did, using the big copier in the teachers' break room. She passed out the sheets I'd copied, which had a list of words on them. Next to each word was a blank space to write its definition.

"I can't even handle the stickiness of this desk," said a disheveled boy, Marlon. "I spilled grape juice all over it. It's on my sleeve."

Cole, the kid behind him, whispered, "Shut your mouth, shut your mouth, shut your mouth, shut your mouth."

Ms. Hopkins closed the classroom door. "I don't want to see any technology out, put it away, we don't need it," she said. "We're going to go through these definitions. I'm going to give you pretty simplified definitions, so if yours are not simplified, or close to what I say, then I need you guys to write them down. These terms are like the basis of all this class. Starting with *foreign*. Can anyone give me a definition of *foreign*?"

Josh read from his iPad, hiding it behind his backpack: *"Characteristic of a country or language other than one's own."*

"That's pretty much right on," said Ms. Hopkins. "The simplified version that I have is just 'dealing with other countries.' When we say *foreign*, like *foreign affairs*, we're just talking about us dealing outside of our own country. Foreign affairs are not going to be unemployment— GUYS."

Two boys had been talking. "Sorry," said one of them.

"So if we're talking about Russia we're talking about foreign affairs." She asked for an example in US history where foreign affairs popped up. There was silence.

Finally Nicholas, wearing a red hoodie, raised his hand. "Different languages?" he said.

"Different languages, right," said Ms. Hopkins. "But tell me an example of the US dealing with another country."

Bethanne, a smart kid, spoke. "Trade, like when we get stuff from China?"

"Right. So these are examples, and if you don't have these you should be writing them down. Any trade outside of our country is foreign. The other issue you can put down here is war. World War I, World War II, the Cold War. Any wars that are outside of our country, that we're involved in, count as foreign." She paused. "A pet peeve of mine?" She wrote *WW1* and *WW2* on the whiteboard. "Don't ever write that, or that. That's not how you write *World War I* or *World War II*. You use the Roman numerals. I get some great essays in this class and they write *WW2*, and it just immediately makes your essay seem, like, not as good of an argument, because you don't know how to write the war. So, random side note, please make sure you don't do that."

She wrote *domestic* on the board and together she and the class defined it: it was the opposite of *foreign*. Then *isolationism*, then *diplomacy*.

"I can think of a case in our history when diplomacy failed," said Preston, a smart kid. "Nicaragua. That was when we started selling weapons to the Nicaraguans to fight their own battle."

Ms. Hopkins wrote *Nicarauga* on the whiteboard and paused. "I'm pretty sure that's spelled wrong," she said. She erased it and looked at the worksheet. *"Treaty."*

Bethanne read aloud from her iPad, not bothering to hide it. *"An official agreement that is made between two or more countries or groups?"*

"Yes," said Ms. Hopkins. "So it's a formal peace agreement between countries or groups. For this class we're really going to be talking about countries." She wrote *NATO* and *North Atlantic Treaty Organization* on the board. A student got it confused with NAFTA.

We moved on to *affect* versus *effect.* "These terms are confused a lot by students," Ms. Hopkins said. "This isn't necessarily like a US history thing, but it is two terms that you need to understand the differences of. Can anybody explain to me the differences between *effect* and *affect*?"

A boy raised his hand. "When you're saying *affect,* you're saying that you're going to change something. *Effect* is kind of used more as a noun. Like, 'The effect of being shot is death.'"

We turned to *conflict.* Bethanne said, "Even in our own country, we cannot agree on anything."

"Even in our school," said Marlon. "We can't agree on a grading system—we change it three times a trimester."

The Vietnam War was an example of a conflict, said Preston.

"The eternal conflict between the sexes," said Josh, with a flourish.

"Any war is going to go under conflict," said Ms. Hopkins, sipping from a cup decorated with a paisley pattern. They turned the worksheet over to see what the next word was. *"War,"* said Ms. Hopkins.

"War, a state of armed conflict," said Josh.

"I have kind of a long one," said Ms. Hopkins. "'Organized, and often prolonged, conflict. It usually includes'—you should be writing this if you don't have it—'usually includes extreme violence.' People dying and shooting each other and all that. Social disruption. Economic disruption."

Some of the students wrote *extreme violence* on their papers. More disembodied words floated through the still air of the classroom—*social, political, economic, isolationism*—each of them requiring a definition and an example. We got through these, one by one, but we still had *militarism, fascism, nationalism, communism, capitalism,* and *totalitarianism* to go. We were swimming in a warm, lifeless salt pond of geopolitical abstraction. Ms. Hopkins's throat was hurting more now. She told everyone to work on their own, and she sat down and put on some music: Journey singing "Love Will Find You." Then she played Joan Jett doing "I Love Rock 'n Roll." The students copied out the dictionary definitions of the disembodied words until the bongers bonged. I felt sorry for this class, and for Ms. Hopkins. I said goodbye and walked around the corner and down a hall to Financial Algebra, taught by Mrs. Erloffer, a short, tough veteran teacher.

She stood at the whiteboard going through the homework—the students were doing tax problems. For example, if somebody's taxes were $5,975, how much more tax would she have to pay if her income went from $42,755 to some higher amount? My head lolled and I read the inspirational posters on the wall. Below a photo of Einstein sticking out his tongue, a headline said, "As a Student, He Was No Einstein." Another poster: "The Best Way to Make Your Dreams Come True Is to Wake Up." And another: "You Get Out of Life What You Put Into It."

She dimmed the lights and showed a soporific PowerPoint. "So we're going to be constructing income tax graphs using compound equations," Mrs. Erloffer said. "We're going to use a flat tax, a proportional tax, and a progressive tax. Examples of flat tax. Is there anything we pay a flat tax on all the time?"

"Sales tax?" said a girl.

"Sales tax, that's right. *Proportional* is just another word for flat tax. And then we have the progressive tax system—that's when you pay different taxes based on the dollar amount that you earn. So—all these fancy words. I'm not going to make you know all these words, but if you hear them you'll remember that we talked about them in class."

The PowerPoint included tax problems with inequalities. "So let's check your understanding," said Mrs. Erloffer. "Can you write the tax schedule notation, interval notation, and compound inequality notation that would apply to a hundred and seventy-two thousand eight hundred and seventy-six dollars and ninety-nine cents? Let's write that amount down." She wrote the number down and showed how to notate it in several ways. "The tax schedule notation sort of wants it in words. Can you put it in words, now? You can do that. Here's the tax schedule. So, it's telling me that it has to be over what?"

A wispy girl raised her hand. "Over a hundred and thirty one thousand four hundred and fifty, but less than or equal to two hundred thousand three hundred."

Mrs. Erloffer nodded, writing the words on the board. "It's important to know where you fall in a tax bracket. I hope that you guys are all earning a hundred and seventy-two thousand dollars by the time I see you after you graduate. That would be awesome! Wish I earned a hundred and seventy-two thousand."

A boy muttered something.

"Huh?" said Mrs. Erloffer.

"I was just talking to Gabe," said the boy.

The soft rain of dollar figures continued, and I had to catch myself from dozing off at one point. "Simplify the equation and explain the numerical significance of the slope and the y intercept," said Mrs. Erloffer. Had she seen my sleepy head dip slowly down? I think she had, but she didn't say anything. As the clock made its final moves, everyone rubbed their eyes and started zipping up their backpacks. "We're not out of here yet," said Mrs. Erloffer. She finished graphing an equation, knowing, however, that everyone had zoned out. "So that's the significance of slope and y intercept, and we'll continue from here tomorrow." Six bongs and we rose to leave. I walked around the halls trying to find my way back to Mr. Bowles's room, getting lost twice. Finally I ran into Artie, from special ed math, and he told me where it was.

Mr. Bowles greeted me like an old friend. He said he'd just had an interesting talk with a student whose father was a bear-hunting guide. Several weeks before the beginning of bear-hunting season, the bear guides put out barrels filled with molasses, french-fry grease, stale pastries, and old donuts—black bears, it seems, are crazy for donuts. The bears become accustomed to feeding on the free junk food at the bait barrels, and then, on the day that hunting season opens, "hunters"—i.e., drunk, lazy barbarians—shoot at them from hiding places nearby. Each year, more than two thousand bears are killed in Maine at bait barrels. Mr. Bowles and I agreed that baiting bears with old donuts was unsportsmanlike and wrong. Then Mr. Bowles told a story about a time when he was surprised by a bear on a camping trip. "We sort of looked at each other, and then the bear turned around. The heart was really racing there for all twenty seconds of that encounter."

Drew, a rangy kid with a faint mustache, walked in and announced that he'd done a bad job of lacing up his boots. He joked with Mrs. Meese about how she was always late, while she ate something out of a plastic tub. "I don't like my last class," Drew said. "I don't like having my most hated class at the end."

"What's your most hated class?" asked Mr. Bowles politely.

"Bio."

"Oh, jeez," said Mr. Bowles. "You'd rather have that first?"

"Probably."

Mr. Bowles sniffed. "What's that smell, beef stew?"

"Barbecue chicken," said Mrs. Meese, chewing.

"I was way off," said Mr. Bowles.

"Yeah, I don't know how you got beef stew out of barbecue chicken," said Mrs. Meese.

"Smells kind of like orange chicken," Drew said.

"Nope," said Mrs. Meese, licking her fingers.

"That's my favorite Chinese food," said Drew. "I love it. When my dad was in the hospital, like he came out, we all went. Most of us had crabs' legs, orange chicken and stuff."

They talked about which restaurants were near the hospital—Five Guys, Denny's, Friendly's.

"You never know what to expect in a Chinese restaurant," said Drew. "We walk in the door, and there was a guy standing there who looked just like Elvis Presley."

"Was he singing?" asked Mr. Bowles.

"No."

"Wearing the white jumpsuit?" asked Mrs. Meese.

"Black suit," said Drew.

"Big fur coat?" said Mrs. Meese.

"No."

A few more kids came in. "Drew and I love to hate each other," Mrs. Meese explained to me. "He likes to pretend he doesn't like me. But I know deep down he really loves me."

"Deep, deep down," said Drew.

"So buried that no one will ever find it," Mrs. Meese said. "But it's there."

Drew ran his hands through his hair. "Last block," he said, "we talked about how we can afford to be a potato."

Mrs. Meese looked puzzled. "You can afford to be a potato? What was your vote on that?"

Drew said, "I had to vote whether I should stick my pencil in a socket and become a potato, or not stick my pencil in and stay a human non-potato. She's like, well, you've got to have the money to be a potato. And you're going to have to have someone to take care of you."

"What class was this in?" Mrs. Meese asked.

"Personal economics."

Mrs. Meese was still puzzled. "I'm thinking what does money and being a potato have to do with each other, buddy?"

"I don't know, she just brought it up. She was like, 'How are you going to pay for the medical bills and stuff?'" He walked over and sat by the window.

"Vegetable," said Mrs. Meese quietly. "Not potato."

I asked her how long she'd been an ed tech. "I started subbing in the fall of 2012, I think. And I was hired full time a year ago. When I subbed I was in every day. It got to the point where my phone never rang anymore, I was just pre-booked. They were just literally like, 'Okay, we just want you in.'"

I said that the school seemed to be full of good kids.

"What I found when I started subbing—the teachers are all very friendly, receptive to you being here, nobody has a problem with helping you with anything. And I've heard from other subs who have subbed in other places that their school isn't that way. The teachers in this school love having ed techs to help in the classroom, and I've heard in other schools it's not like that. The teachers actually don't want the help in the room. Maybe it's because it's another set of ears and eyes."

"And also," I said, "the ed techs can be the source of a little murmur of conversation."

"They can be," said Mrs. Meese. "That English class you were in this morning, that is a very big class. The math class, how'd that go?"

"Fine," I said. "I didn't do much."

"I've done that course seven times," said Mrs. Meese. "But this is the first time with that teacher, and she's doing it all different. So I'm walking in kind of knowing what's going on, but not knowing how she's going to be doing it."

I asked her about math requirements. Everyone had to take Algebra, Geometry, and Algebra II, she said. Financial Algebra was a half-credit course, and her kids didn't really understand it, but they tried. She packed up her lunch things and went over to talk to Drew. "I'm on this side of the room just so I can irritate you," she said to him. "I love it when I can irritate you, it just makes my day."

"I'll scare you," said Drew.

"You're not going to scare me."

"I scared you that one time, I can scare you again."

Mrs. Meese laughed.

"It'll happen again," said Drew.

"One day you're going to scare the living crap right out of me again," said Mrs. Meese. "I believe you."

Drew told us about an April Fool's trick one of his teachers did at his old school. "She took this teacher's keys to the lunchroom, and before they made the Jell-O, she told them, 'Put the keys in the Jell-O and serve that to her during lunch.' She got her Jell-O and saw her keys."

"I hope they cleaned her keys before they got put in that Jell-O!" said Mrs. Meese. "Yuck."

"One teacher was kind of short," Drew went on. "They put a pie over the door so that it fell right on him when he came in. It was the funniest thing I have ever seen."

The bell rang for block 4. I walked out to one of the modular classrooms in the back of the school, near the football field, where there was a community safety class taught by Ms. Accardo, a petite smiley woman with big hair and big moves. She looked like a dance instructor giving a TED talk. As soon as the bell rang, she said, "Well! Got some review stuff for you guys! After, of course, I do attendance!" While she called names, a kid named Ronald unwrapped a sandwich and began eating it. "Just so you know," she said, "the people listening to the iPads, if that's what you need to do in order to focus, I'm fine with that, BUT! If you spend time in class trying to find the right song, I do have a problem with that. So just a little FYI, wanted to get that out of the way."

She twirled on her feet and held out a finger. "Okay! What four things will clue you in about an emergency existing?"

"Behavior," said Ronald, chewing his sandwich.

"Unusual behaviors!"

"Smell," said Cayley.

"Unusual smells!"

"Sight," said Anabelle.

"Unusual sights!"

"Sounds," said Kiefer.

"Unusual sounds! Those are the four things. Very good. Okay. That will trigger, or should trigger, your rescue radar to go off. And why don't people get involved in rescue situations?"

"They don't know what to do?" said Kiefer.

"They don't know what to do!"

"They don't want to be responsible?" said Anabelle.

"They don't want the responsibility of helping! They don't want to get involved! And why don't they want to get involved?"

"Because they're afraid they might mess up?" said Andrew.

"They're afraid they might make a mistake! And what happens sometimes when people make a mistake and hurt somebody?"

"Get sued?" said Andrew.

"They're afraid they're going to get sued! What are some other reasons people don't help?"

Cayley said that you could be self-conscious.

Ms. Accardo made a slow, wide-eyed nod, turning to look at everyone in the class. "You're going to have a big old crowd of people, crowding around, staring at you rescuing somebody! Anything else? Sometimes people are scared of catching a disease. Or they're all grossed out, because sometimes rescuing people is nasty. It's gross."

Ronald raised his hand. "They think that people already have it under control."

"Yeah. 'Oh, there's people there! Somebody's taking care of that.' Big ole assumption! Okay, so what we're doing now is we're taking away a lot of those reasons for people not to get involved."

She told us how to obtain consent to help someone who is hurt. "What happens if someone is spewing blood all over the place, and they go, 'Get away!'?"

"Call 911?"

She pointed at the girl, Jennifer, who'd said this. "Call. You cannot tackle them! And put bandages all over them! Can't do it. Now, if they go, 'Go away'—and then pass out? A reasonable person would want assistance if they were unconscious and severely injured. You can help now—even though they said go away before they passed out."

But never try to do something that is outside your scope of training, Ms. Accardo warned. To illustrate this, she offered a vivid retelling of the tracheotomy scene in *The Heat*, which was, she said, "an R-rated flick with a lot of f-bombs." The guy's choking, and Sandra Bullock shouts, "I got this! Give me a knife!" She jams it into the guy's throat, and the blood starts spraying out, and she panics. The guy is practically dying, and she's horrified. The moral being that you don't know how to do something just because you saw somebody do it on TV. And always, always, Ms. Accardo said, before you help somebody, tell them what you're up to. "Your doctor tells you what he or she is doing. They just don't stick their hand up your shirt, right? With the stethoscope? They tell you what they're doing! You need to do the same, so you don't look like some creeper!" After giving us several more pieces of advice, she played a video about how to move a victim, using an *assist*, a *carry*, or a *drag*. We watched how to do a two-person seat carry. If the victim has a head or spinal injury, you must perform a *clothes drag*. "Support the victim by gathering the clothing behind the head and neck," said the male narrator, in a soothing voice. "Move the victim by holding on to her clothing, and dragging her."

"You don't HAVE to move the victim," said Ms. Accardo, after the movie was over—you only had to move the victim if the place where the victim lay prevented proper care. "Example! The person's on the bed, and you have to give CPR. You're just going to bounce them! You've got to get them on a firm surface to get compressions." The lunch bell rang and everybody left, leaving their backpacks behind.

"That was a pleasure," I said. "I didn't do anything, but I'm happy to be in your class."

"Well, thank you," said Ms. Accardo. "We're going to go to lunch, and then we're going to come back."

We went to the teachers' lunchroom, and Ms. Accardo introduced me to several teachers sitting at a round table. I started eating a chicken-salad sandwich. One of the teachers, Mrs. Plaistow, told a story of getting locked out of her lakeside camp cottage. She was out walking her dog, when her daughter went out to smoke a cigarette and forgot to bring her keys with her. Mrs. Plaistow went to a neighbor's house to ask for help. A fifteen-year-old kid came to the door in boxers. "That's all he's got on is boxers. Two black Labs barking their heads off. He says, 'I'll go over, we'll break into your camp.' His dad pulls on his pants, he says, 'I'll go over.'" The dad went to work on the door with a credit card. "Forty-five minutes, he struggled with that door," said Mrs. Plaistow. "I said, 'I feel so much better! You say you've never had a latch you couldn't get open, and you're struggling.' He goes, 'Don't remind me.' He goes off to get a sledgehammer to break the lock. Three hours, standing in the cold. The dog was happy, he was playing in the snow." She offered the son and the dad some deer-meat chili. "The dad says, 'You don't have to give us any chili. This is what neighbors do. Someday we might need something from you.' I said, 'That's probably doubtful.' He goes, 'Yeah, probably it is. But you never know.'" End of story.

Mrs. Rausch, a math teacher, talked about how, when she had to miss a day, she always left way more worksheets for the class than the substitute could ever get the class to do. Some subs just let the kids go wild and swing from the chandeliers, she said. Another teacher, Mrs. Thwaite, who sold Mary Kay cosmetics, invited Mrs. Plaistow and Mrs. Rausch to come over for facials on Thursday. Mrs. Plaistow accepted.

"Nothing's going to make my face look any better," said Mrs. Rausch.

Ms. Accardo and I walked back to the modular classroom. She resumed the lesson. "Two-person seat carry—anyone want to do that?"

Nobody volunteered.

"I had a kid break his foot out on the field," Ms. Accardo said. "Getting the wheelchair across an athletic field is not an easy feat. Way easier to get him into the building with a two-person seat carry."

She waited. Still nobody volunteered.

"So you're all good on how to carry people!" she said sarcastically. "No one wants to practice!"

"I want to drag someone," said Anabelle. "Can I drag you?"

Ms. Accardo got down on the floor. "Go ahead, drag me," she said. She pretended to be unconscious.

"Somebody videotape this!" said Ronald.

The girl struggled, but couldn't move Ms. Accardo. Kiefer stepped in to help, lifting Ms. Accardo's head.

Ms. Accardo opened her eyes for a moment. "I'll move my hair out of the way, sorry," she said. She resumed unconsciousness.

"I don't want to rip her shirt," said Anabelle. Eventually she successfully slid Ms. Accardo several feet over the floor.

We watched another educational video. "Most of us will experience some kind of severe injury at some time in our lives," said the narrator, while a loop of ambient new-age music played in the background. We watched actors moaning in pain from several gruesome soft-tissue injuries, and we learned how to apply pressure on a wound to stop the bleeding. When the movie was over, Ms. Accardo talked about how to deal with impaled objects. "You don't let the person take out the impaled object!" she said. "They have to resist the urge!" Her marker made squeaking sounds on the whiteboard as she drew a picture. "When there is an impaled object—let's say here's your arm, and here is the knife blade."

"Ew," said Cayley.

"God," said Ronald.

"Here's the knife blade, here is a blood vessel. Blood flow is stopped. Pressure, pressure." She erased the knife with her finger and, with a cry of agony, pulled an imaginary knife from her arm. "Now the knife is missing, and . . ." She drew jets of blood splashing out of the wound. "Squirt, squirt, squirt. Now it's open to bacteria, it's open to increased bleeding." She thought for a second. "You get something impaled in your eyeball?" She pretended to pull something out of her eye. "Aaaah, out comes the eyeball!" She told us where our various arterial pressure points were—"If you have a gusher, press on a pressure point"—and she warned us against using tourniquets. Finally, with a minute left, she asked the class to practice bandaging some wounds. I waved goodbye and hustled off across the parking lot to a ninth-grade remedial English class in the North Building, a separate one-story structure where all the freshmen were segregated.

The regular teacher was out. In her place was a fashionably dressed substitute of about sixty named Mrs. Carlisle, who wore artsy earrings and had a Florida tan. There were six kids in the class, crowded around two perpendicular tables in a room whose walls were covered with definitions and rules of grammar. The kids were slapping binders around and shouting. I introduced myself to Mrs. Carlisle as the substitute ed tech, shook hands with her, and sat down. "You need to calm down!" said a frowny smartass boy, Lance, loudly, to one of the binder slappers, Alan.

Mrs. Carlisle turned. "I have not had the pleasure of having you before," she said to Lance.

"You're in for a rude awakening," said Leanne, a girl with short black hair and goth makeup.

"There's something you need to know about me," said Mrs. Carlisle. "I'm not just some warm body off the street that's here to babysit you. I'm a school counselor, have been for twenty-five years, hope to be again. So with that said, I'm hoping that you're going to do the things you're supposed to do, so that I don't have to do what I'm supposed to do when you don't. Otherwise I'm very easy to get along with." Everyone was quieter after she said that she'd been a school counselor for twenty-five years. She handed out the first worksheet, which was about idioms. "You guys remember what an idiom is?" She read its definition: a saying that does not make literal, logical, or grammatical sense, but people within the culture understand its meaning. She said, "The example they give is, *Don't let the cat out of the bag.* Doesn't mean a cat's really going to pop out of the bag, okay?"

"Riaow!" said Leanne.

"So you need to use this idiom in your writing today: *a blessing in disguise.*"

"What does that mean?" asked Brianne, a big girl in a very small striped shirt.

"Think about it for a minute," said Mrs. Carlisle. "I heard one this morning. I was helping someone write, and their prompt was if anyone from the war had shared stories with them. One of the students was telling me that one of his stories was that his brother had to go to the bathroom. He was in Iraq, and then the bomb sirens went off, so he hit the dirt. The latrine that he would have gone to was blown up. It was a 'blessing in disguise' that the sirens went off, because he hit the dirt instead of being in the latrine. Okay?"

The class was silent, thinking this over.

"Or it might be," Mrs. Carlisle continued, "that when we had the snow the other day, I was going home, and a truck and a car had hit each other.

The side of the car was gone. Everyone was okay. They were all standing there talking. So everyone was safe, but it was one of those really slippery days. So it was a 'blessing in disguise' that I stayed late to talk to a teacher. Because otherwise I might have been that car. Do you get the idea?"

"Yep," said Leanne. "Kind of."

"So you can get started on that. I'm going to give you till ten after." She pointed to me. "And this is . . ."

"Nick," I said. "Mr. Baker."

Everyone laughed: there was another Baker in the class, Lance Baker.

"That's creepy," said Brianne.

"Smells like marshmallows in here," said Leanne.

"Do you girls need pencils?" asked Mrs. Carlisle. "Shh! Voices off!"

Alan cleared his throat phlegmily.

"Shh!"

The remedial grind of the pencil sharpener. Giggling. Muttering. Whispering. Tapping of pencils. Time passing.

"Ladies and gentlemen, you have four minutes left! I should not hear any voices!"

More muttering and giggling. Lance collected some of the papers.

"Take it away, squire!" said Leanne, holding out her sheet.

"What's a squire?" said Lance.

"It's like a butler," said Leanne.

"No way!"

Mrs. Carlisle asked Lance to describe what he'd written. "I wrote, like, two things," he said. "I'll do my second one, because it's funny. Most of you have already heard this. I saw a squirrel, and I went to go shoot at it. I missed, and it hit the tree, and it ricocheted and hit me where the sun don't shine."

Mrs. Carlisle cocked her head. "Okay, so how's that a blessing in disguise? I guess if you're the squirrel."

"It could have hit my face and put my eye out!" said Lance. "And then, my second one, I was sitting in my room, and I had my paintball gun in my hand."

"Oh, god," said Brianne, rolling her eyes.

"You're a dangerous child," said Mrs. Carlisle.

"And I had my hand over the barrel, and I didn't think it was loaded, and I accidentally pulled the trigger, and I had a huge bruise on the side of my hand."

"A bruise, not a burn?" said Mrs. Carlisle.

"It was a bruise," said Lance.

"Good thing it wasn't a flamethrower!" said a goofy kid named Samuel.

"I've seen kids get horrible burns on their faces from paintball guns," said Mrs. Carlisle.

"I got shot by one, it hurt," said Brianne.

"Are you sharing?" said Mrs. Carlisle, turning to her. "Go ahead, share."

"One day when my brother and I were home alone," the girl said, "he had a lighter, that he was playing with. I was in the other room, and I walked in, and he told me to see how hot it was, and I didn't believe him, so he threw it at me, and he burned me with it." She laughed. "If you have a lighter on too long, the metal will get hot. It left a mark on my shoulder."

"So how's that a blessing in disguise?" said Mrs. Carlisle.

Brianne pondered. "My dad came home?"

"She wasn't killed," said Leanne.

Mrs. Carlisle shook her head. "A blessing in disguise would have been if your dad came home *before* your brother had a chance to throw the lighter at you. You wrote a story, and that's great, but we still want you to know what the idiom means. And I'm thinking you're still a little confused."

Leanne said, "One time I was in a car with my mom. We were on the road going to my appointment, and I was listening to music, and next thing I knew, my mom's hand was on my chest. She hit the brakes really hard."

"The mom reaction!" said Mrs. Carlisle.

"And the car in front of us just, like, busted right into the other car in front of them," Leanne said. "So it was a blessing in disguise that my mom stopped before we actually hit."

"Remember when you popped a wheelie with the four-wheeler?" said Alan to Lance.

"I remember that!" said Lance. "I'll try anything once."

"I'm sure you will," said Mrs. Carlisle.

"He popped a wheelie on his four-wheeler and fell off the back of it," said Alan.

"Nice."

That was the end of assignment number one. Mrs. Carlisle gave instructions for the next worksheet, which had four pages. It was about figurative language. We had to underline and label each instance of figurative language in a story about an airport. Mrs. Carlisle said, "You should find one simile, one metaphor, two hyperboles, two examples of personification, one alliteration, three onomatopoeias, two idioms, and one allusion, okay?"

A shy girl named Misty raised her hand. "How do you find these if you don't even know what they are?"

"All you have to do is turn around," said Brianne. Everyone turned to read the definitions on the back wall.

Samuel began singing, "Oh no, moto peeya."

We did a little review. A simile compared two things using *like* or *as*, but a metaphor compared two things without using *like* or *as*. "So, the playground at Lasswell was an ice rink," said Mrs. Carlisle. "That's a metaphor." Evidently she'd been subbing recently at Lasswell Elementary School.

"An onomatopoeia is . . ." She trailed off, searching her notes. "I'm a little rusty, so I looked these up for you guys. It also, um, compares two things." She seemed doubtful and she looked at me. "Do you have anything to add?"

I said that an onomatopoeia was a word that sounded like what it meant. "So if the thunder goes 'rumble rumble rumble,' the word is trying to imitate what thunder actually sounds like. Or 'He squeaked loudly when he sat down on the tack.' The squeak—eek—is kind of a word that sounds like what it means." I felt myself blushing—it was the first teaching I'd done that day.

"Eek," said Leanne.

Mrs. Carlisle reviewed alliteration: "*Dunkin' Donuts* has the same sound where? At the beginning of the word. Does that help? Yes, no, maybe so? Get started and we'll see where it goes from there."

Leanne said, "Can I have my pencil?"

"Get out of your chair and reach for it," said Mrs. Carlisle.

The students hunched over the story and read it silently. Mrs. Carlisle and I compared notes, whispering. It was not a very good story, and there were some ambiguities.

After fifteen minutes, Brianne said, "I did not get any of this. We just started learning this."

"Don't get frustrated," said Mrs. Carlisle. "We can go through it together. These are tricky, guys."

We started with the first page, which said, *Jason could feel butterflies in his stomach as he entered the bustling airport. "This place is a zoo!" his mother exclaimed as she got in line at the ticket counter.*

Lance said, "I thought 'This place is a zoo' is a hyperbowl."

"Some of these could go either way," said Mrs. Carlisle. "I said it was a metaphor. But it could also be a hyperbole, because it's saying the place is a zoo. *Jason could feel butterflies in his stomach.* What do you think that is?"

"Nervous," said Brianne.

"Well, yeah, he's nervous, but what figure of speech are we using here?"

"A hyperbowl?" said Alan. He sniffed. "Somebody's using perfume."

"Personification?" said Misty.

"What is that smell?" said Alan.

"Can you really feel butterflies in your stomach?" said Mrs. Carlisle.

"No," said Leanne.

"So isn't it kind of like letting the cat out of the bag?"

"It's kind of a tickle in your stomach," said Lance.

"Unless you swallow a butterfly," said Samuel.

"Right," said Mrs. Carlisle, "but it doesn't say that Jason swallowed a butterfly."

Lance said, "Like when you go up the hill and the roller coaster drops down and it's like a tickle in your stomach. And then you look down and say, 'Waaaaaaaaah!'"

"An allusion?" said Brianne.

Mrs. Carlisle moved on. "How about *She got in line behind about a million other people.* Are there really a million people there?"

"Exaggeration," said Leanne.

"So if it's an exaggeration, what is it?"

"That would be an opanapo . . . ," said Alan.

"How about hyperbole? What's a hyperbole?"

Brianne turned and read the definition on the wall. *"An exaggeration that is so dramatic that no one would believe it to be true."*

"I know an allusion," said Misty. She found the place in the story that she'd underlined and read it. *"Jason noticed that the security guard looked more intimidating than Mr. T.* I found that!"

"Yep, allusion," said Mrs. Carlisle, checking her notes. "It's *making reference to something or someone.* Good job, Misty."

Farther down the page we came to another passage: *Jason placed his shoes, belt, and change onto the tired conveyor belt and walked through the metal detector.* Mrs. Carlisle said, "Tired purveyor belt! Can the purveyor belt really get tired?"

"It can break down," said Lance. "It can go, pkkkkk!"

"Is it really sleepy?" said Mrs. Carlisle. "No."

The PA system bonged. "Please excuse the interruption for a few announcements. Track practice will begin at two-fifteen in the gym, our first tangible sign that spring is indeed here. There will be a parent informational meeting for all boys' and girls' track athletes this Thursday at six p.m. in the auditorium. All parents are encouraged to attend."

"Make sure your names are on your papers!" said Mrs. Carlisle. "I should have six papers! I have five! I have Leanne's. I have Brianne's. I have Lance's, I have Misty's, I have—"

"This is not really a fanny pack," said Lance loudly. "This is a knapsack."

"Hobo sack!" said Alan.

"Ladies and gentlemen," said Mrs. Carlisle. "Push in your chairs."

"Lance is Hobo Joe," said Alan.

"Stack the chairs," said Mrs. Carlisle.

"We don't stack the chairs in this class," said Lance.

"If it's too hard for you," said Mrs. Carlisle, "I'll stack them after."

"We don't stack them," said Leanne.

"That's what I'm trying to say!" said Lance.

"Listen, why do you think we stack chairs?" said Mrs. Carlisle.

"So that people don't fall over them?" said Misty.

"How do you think the rug gets vacuumed at night, guys?"

"No idea," said Lance.

"The janitor!" said Brianne.

"Very good," said Mrs. Carlisle. "So we do it to be kind to the people who have to clean up your messes."

Samuel and Misty stacked the chairs. The bell for first wave bonged. "Bye!"

"Bye, guys, have a good day," said Mrs. Carlisle. "I'll make sure she knows that sheet was hard for you! I'm sure she already knows."

"Hope to see you again," I said to her. I walked to the office, saying hey to a few students I recognized. Paulette, the secretary, took my name tag. "Thank you very much," she said.

There was a crowd of students boarding their buses when I pushed out the side exit—fifteen idling yellow buses, packed with human flesh, ready to take people home. The windows were already getting fogged on the inside.

My car was very quiet when I got in. "All right, there we have it," I said aloud. "There we freaking have it."

That was Day Six.

WHAT THE HELL WAS THAT?

BETH HAD ANOTHER ED TECH ASSIGNMENT at the high school for me on Wednesday. My first class was US History, twenty-two tenth-graders under the practiced tutelage of Mr. Hawkes, who also coached hockey and had a powerful handshake. Mr. Hawkes knew how to take command of a class—he stood with his legs far apart as he took attendance, wearing a blue sports jacket and a black polka-dot tie, and he spoke with a remarkably loud voice. Half of the history students were missing, though—they were off interviewing for coveted spots at the regional technical school in Sanford, where those who got in could take half-day courses in the building trades, in landscaping and horticulture, in web design, videography, car repair, nursing, early-childhood education, and in other potentially remunerative fields. Mr. Hawkes referred the class to an online textbook; they could take a look at it if they wanted to. "Not that we use the book a lot," he said. "I'm not a big book guy." The assignment was to work on a chart about the antebellum era, but because so many kids were absent, he turned off one set of ceiling lights and put on a History Channel video called *America: The Story of Us*. Inspiring orchestral music came on. "*We are pioneers and trailblazers*," said the narrator. "*We fight for freedom. We transform our dreams into the truth.*

Our struggles will become a nation." The music surged. *"America—land of invention. Hot dogs, jazz, the elevator, skyscrapers. This is the story of the greatest innovation of all—the modern, vertical city."* I found a seat near the windows and relaxed; there was no one-on-one coaching I could do with a movie playing.

America: The Story of Us was heavy on the music and edited like a hard-hitting segment of *Dateline*, but it was good; most kids watched it, or at least half watched it. It began with the campaign to uncrate and assemble the Statue of Liberty, and went on to tell the story of the Bessemer process of steelmaking and Andrew Carnegie. Carnegie risks everything to build a huge plant in Pittsburgh, larger than eighty football fields. *"Inside: five tons of molten metal, three thousand degrees, hot enough to vaporize a man in seconds,"* said the narrator. Carnegie becomes fabulously wealthy. Cut to the Gilded Age. *"It's an era of obscene opulence. New York is a playground for super-rich industrialists and financiers. Wildly extravagant, they smoke cigars rolled in hundred-dollar bills, their wives' hats studded with diamonds."* Dramatic reenactments take us high up on a skyscraper during construction. *"They're up here eight hours a day. Meals when they can. No bathroom breaks."* Really? The roughnecks are Mohawk Indians and European immigrants. *"Two roughnecks out of five die or are disabled on the job."* We learn about Elisha Otis's elevator, and the density of new urban populations, and, in the shadows of the steel-frame buildings, slums and crime. *"Gangsters, murderers, thieves, and fear are on the streets."* Policeman Burns, the crime buster, gets tough, using the third degree. Jacob Riis takes photographs of poor families. Horse manure is a problem. *"Wagons are blocked by three-foot-high piles of human and animal waste."* George Waring builds sewers. Edison's bulb lights the cities, using power plants, conquering the night. *"As electricity comes to the city, more and more people come with it. By 1900—"*

Mr. Hawkes stopped the movie there, not wanting to get too far into the twentieth century yet, and he described what they'd be doing for the rest of the week. "Now you've got about ten minutes, so you can continue to pretend to find something to do," he said. Students sat quietly, staring at their iPads, listening to music. A teacher came by to borrow some Wite-Out. Six bongs.

Ms. Accardo's community health class, out back in the modulars, was next—but Ms. Accardo was absent. In her place was Mrs. Carlisle, the sub who had taught blessings in disguise on Monday. She was wearing jeans and leather boots with fur trim, and she had her bifocals on so that she could study the sub plans. "The first thing you are doing today," she said, "is you're going to need your iPads and you're going to go on Edmodo and find the stress management folder. You're going to read about the physical effects of stress on the body. You need to take notes on that. So get all your giggles out now." Several kids had forgotten the group code for Edmodo and asked Mrs. Carlisle for it. She didn't have it: subs weren't allowed to tap into the school's digital resources. "They trust me with you guys, but not with a piece of machinery—just lives."

Cayley, putting away her hairbrush, tried to remember the Edmodo group login code. "It's GLU3 something something something," she said.

"Can you two look on with people?" said Mrs. Carlisle. "Because we're going to be moving on."

"I don't understand what we're supposed to do," said Kim, in layers of pastel.

Reading over Kim's shoulder, Mrs. Carlisle said, "When you have a tension headache, what happens to your body due to stress?"

"You get a headache," said Kim.

"Yes . . . but." Mrs. Carlisle waited.

"You start crying?"

"How do you know you have a tension headache?" said Mrs. Carlisle.

"Your head hurts?" said Kim.

"But where does it usually hurt?"

"Your head?"

"The back of your head," said Mrs. Carlisle.

"Really?"

"Yep." Mrs. Carlisle rubbed her head. "It starts back here. It's good that you don't know this. Adults know this because they live it."

"Does that happen to Ms. Finn?" said Cayley. "Is that why she always walks like this?" She hunched her shoulders and held her head at a weird angle. Eric, in a gray T-shirt, laughed.

"I don't know, honey," said Mrs. Carlisle.

"Some days she has that buff walk," Cayley said.

"Like a man?" said Eric.

"Yeah."

Mrs. Carlisle handed out a packet on how to manage stress.

Jeremy tapped his feet several times and turned to the girl next him, Steph, one of the pretty girls. "You smell like mangoes," he said.

"Really?" said Steph.

"I like mangoes," Jeremy said.

The class began writing about tension headaches and migraines, and Mrs. Carlisle told Kim how tense she gets when she goes to the dentist. "I had a fourth-grader dislocate my jaw, and I had to have my jaw wired shut," she said. "It wasn't good. I've not seen any kids here like the kids I used to work with."

After she'd collected the papers, Mrs. Carlisle had everyone relax. "Stretch out your legs. If you fall asleep, I am not responsible for what happens to you while you're sleeping. Your eyes have to be closed. Listen— you have to listen!"

She turned on the stress-reduction tape—an actual cassette tape in a tape player. We heard some glissy new-age chords, over which hovered a woman's infinitely soothing voice. She told us to close our eyes, to breathe in through our noses and breathe out through our mouths, to clench and unclench our toes. "Your body is feeling heavy and warm and soothed," the angel-voiced woman said, "as if you just came . . . from a warm bath. There's a sensation that you're sinking . . . sinking . . . you're sinking into the chair or surface below . . . you're feeling relaxed and secure as you sink deeper into the warmth . . . so soothed . . . so comforted." Lambent swells of ambient deep-chill music filled the classroom. Some of the kids were slumped on their desks, some had their heads thrown back with eyes closed. Cayley was studying her fingers. "You feel good about yourself . . .

about your body . . . about the world around you. This feels so nice . . . there's nothing to be concerned about." The kind extraterrestrial angel goddess took us hypnotically back in time. "Remember the days . . . when you were a child in the back seat of a car . . . coming home from a long, active day of fun . . . you were satisfied . . . worn out . . . kind of tired . . . you're in the back seat . . . possibly leaned up against a sibling or a favorite blanket . . . you hear the cars going by and the quiet music of the radio . . . you hear Mom and Dad in the front seat talking softly . . . as you allow yourself to drift into a peaceful contented sleep." She took us to the seaside, where the warm waves teased the sand. We heard the gulls crying. "Your hair dances with the wind," she said. "Enjoy this moment . . . your body is feeling so soothed and so relaxed . . . let your thoughts drift." The music swelled again, metamorphosing into a sort of trancelike chorale prelude of compulsory relaxation, and then it died away. There was silence. Mrs. Carlisle turned off the tape machine with an old-school click.

Eric sucked some drool into his mouth with a slurping sound.

Cayley said, "Is it over? That was *not* twenty-five minutes long."

"Are we supposed to pass these papers in?" said Kim.

Jeremy took a peek at his phone.

"Let's take a minute to wake up," said Mrs. Carlisle. "To process the tape. What did you think?"

Silence.

"Did any of you feel any of what she was talking about? Yes, no, maybe so?"

Silence.

"I think everyone just took a nap," said Tasha, rubbing her eyes.

"No," Mrs. Carlisle said. "I was watching."

"I enjoyed it," said Jeremy, loudly, with a smirk.

Steph turned and said, disgustedly, "You didn't do it!"

Mrs. Carlisle said gently to the boy: "I want to know what kept you from doing this exercise."

"I was just too cool for it," Jeremy said.

"How about a serious answer?"

"Honestly, it just didn't grab my mind."

Mrs. Carlisle described the homework. "You guys have in front of you a stress-anger goal packet." Everyone was supposed to set a stress-reduction goal and itemize a series of steps that would be necessary to reach it. "You need to pick a date for when you're going to start your plan," she said. "And before you get all stressed out about your plan to be stress free, think about some of the things you're doing now. For some of you it might be sports or music or your best friend. So don't let making a plan to manage your stress stress you out."

Jeremy was drumming his feet on the floor. It was almost time to leave. The bell bonged. "Bye," said Mrs. Carlisle. "Have a good day!"

Students shuffled out, bumping backpacks. When they were gone I told Mrs. Carlisle that I admired how she was able to go with the flow and make things work. "Thank you, I appreciate that," she said. Feeling oddly peaceful and content with my lot, I went off to an eleventh-grade history class with Ms. Day, where I was supposed to shadow Sebastian.

Ms. Day was a cordial young woman with a wry smile and thick hair cut short. "Today we're going to touch on Germany," she said, "and then we're going to move in on the rise of Hitler, and how Germany was able to accomplish all the things that it did. And how that happened is really correlated to a lot of things going on in the world today. History repeats itself a lot." She shivered. "I'm going to put my jacket back on, because it's freezing."

Ms. Day played a YouTube video of a recent TV news story about Lasswell High School. An art class at the school was learning to draw faces by making portraits of destitute orphan children in Haiti. The idea was that the Haitian orphans would then draw portraits of the Maine kids. *"In the face of sorrow,"* said the newswoman, *"a small message of hope, and a sketch of a brighter future."*

Ms. Day said, "So that was a cool way to start class. Good things going on." She began showing slides. "Okay, *fascism*. What do you guys have about fascism? Ron, what have you got?"

"Led by a dictator having complete power," said Ron.

"Good, led by a dictator having complete power," said Ms. Day. "Anyone else have anything different? Here's something else. I'm going to show you a definition. Yours does not need to say the exact same thing— you don't need it to be word for word. It just needs to have the same message. So: *fascism*. This system is led by a dictator—good job, Ron— having complete power, suppressing all opposition, and controlling all industry and commerce. In our system today, who would be a group of people that oppose the president a lot?"

"Hippies!" said Sebastian.

"No. Well, not really."

"Middle Easterners," said Chad, eating a Jolly Rancher.

"In our own country," said Ms. Day. "Obama's a Democrat, so what party opposes him? Republicans, right?"

"Yes!" Side conversations were in progress around the class.

"We can get through this if you guys let me talk," said Ms. Day. "We have Democrats and Republicans who are known sometimes to have opposing ideas. That are keeping each other in check, so that one party doesn't grow too big and one doesn't grow too small. They can kind of battle it out and find some common ground, ideally. A Republican can stand up there and say, I disagree with what our president's doing, and here are my reasons." She turned to Scott, who had his iPhone out. "Put it away, or it's going in the trash. You can't do that in a fascist society. In a fascist society, there is no opposition. There is one party, there is one ruler, and you all love them, and you do not say anything bad about them, and if you do, you're going to some sort of camp, or you're being killed, or you're disappearing in the middle of the night. Siberia, right? The Russians did that a lot. Siberian exile."

"Serbia?" said Chad.

"Siberia. It's like a tundra. Okay? No opposition. There's no lively debate. It is this way and that is the way it is." She described the free-market system, and compared it to the economy under a dictatorship. "If I want to go start a business tomorrow, I can." In a dictatorship all business is government-run, she said. "Two countries that had this type of government were Italy, with Mussolini, and Germany, with Hitler."

"I didn't know Mussolini was from Italy," said Sebastian, who was paying attention. "I thought he was Russian."

"No, Mussolini is Italy," said Ms. Day. "You should look up Italy. The way Mussolini takes over Italy is pretty crazy. He took his men—he was a big war hero—walked up to the capital, and took it over. He said, I run this country now. We're not really going to have time to go into it, but if you want to do some independent research, how Mussolini took over is pretty impressive and cool."

"He just walked right up?" said Sebastian.

"Yes, literally walked right up."

Fascism was extreme nationalism, often racism, Ms. Day said. "So under nationalism you should also have Germany and Italy. Make sure those countries are under that category as well. How could nationalism lead to racism? Give me an example."

"Slavery?" said Sebastian.

"Slavery, right. The United States was pretty proud of itself, but we had slaves."

Maria, with waist-length black hair, raised her hand. "Hitler," she said.

"Hitler. Germans are superior, but only the Aryan German is superior. Just because all these Jews are part of Germany doesn't mean they're German. They don't have the mark of the blond-hair-blue-eye, and they are the cause of all evil. That's how it gets spun, or turns into racism. Yeah, they live here, but they don't look like us, they don't have the same ideals as us. The United States with African-Americans is also a good example of that, too."

"Two questions," said Sebastian.

"Two answers," said Ms. Day.

"Back when Adolf Hitler was running everything, who was the country that came and defeated him?"

"It was another world war, so it was us, Britain, and France, again."

"And Adolf Hitler didn't have blond hair or blue eyes," said Sebastian.

"True," said Ms. Day. "Also what really ends up to be the defeat of Hitler, and we'll talk about this later, is he tries to invade Russia. He attacked Russia in the middle of the winter. So that starts to deteriorate the army, and it starts to fall apart. But until then, they are a steamroller. Germans aren't used to the Russian winter. It's like you've got someone from Texas coming up to Maine for the winter. If it's a mild winter we're like, Oh, this is awesome. T-shirts at like what, forty? Summer's going to kill us this year. Can you imagine it being eighty degrees? It was forty degrees a few days ago, and we were like, Wow, we should open the window, and I'm like, That's sad, it is eight degrees above freezing and I find it warm. I remember we went down to Florida for softball when I was here— it was my sophomore year. It's April there, and we're playing softball, it was like seventy-five, seventy-eight degrees, and we were all like, It's wicked hot, we're going to go back to the hotel and swim in the pool! And somebody was like, You realize the pools aren't heated here, right?"

Maria said, "It's not really refreshing swimming in a warm pool."

"No, it's gross. So—fascism usually has a strong military, use of violence, and terror—"

"Yes!" said Sebastian enthusiastically.

"Use of censorship, and the government rules the media." She talked about the repression of dissent in Germany, about censorship and propaganda. If there had been an Internet in the Third Reich, she asked, could German citizens have done a Google search for, say, "Bad Things About Hitler"?

"Yes," said Sebastian.

"Nope, not in Germany," said Ms. Day. "It would be blocked. It would say, 'No results found, Hitler is wonderful, somebody will be at your house in a minute to get rid of you.'" China was like that now, she said, and so was North Korea. "You don't know anything about the rest of the world, because why would you, you live in North Korea, where everything's perfect."

"Gangnam style," said Scott.

"That's South Korea," said Ms. Day.

She showed us a clip from a cable history show. A British voice intoned, *"Hitler comes to power legally on January the thirtieth, 1933. Within a few months, his dictatorship is firmly in place."* Newsreel footage of mass rallies followed, and paraphrases from *Mein Kampf* against the Versailles Treaty and on the need for lebensraum, and frightening images of thousands of German soldiers marching in step.

"That is a lot of people," said Sebastian.

The British voice continued. *"A pathological anti-Semite, Hitler has also taken on the mission of asserting the superiority of the Germanic, 'Aryan' race, menaced by the Jews. For him, the Jews were the cause of the Great War, Germany's defeat, inflation, unemployment. The next war will be a war on the Jews."* Footage of Dachau. Then the annexation of Austria. *"The clouds of war gather."*

Ms. Day stopped the clip. "Do you think Germany is listening to the Treaty of Versailles anymore?"

"No."

"No, they've pretty much thrown them the double bird, saying, 'We're going to do what we want.'" She showed a photo of a crowd waving at Hitler's motorcade. "You've seen the Zapruder film, when Kennedy drove through Dallas on the day he was shot?" she said. "People loved Kennedy. He was a very well-respected president. Which is rare. A lot of the time, no matter what great things they've done, we don't always agree with the person in power. That's fine. Like Lincoln. Not many people liked Lincoln. And then later everybody's like, Oh my god, Lincoln's the best! Sometimes you've got to give yourself a few years, and then people are like, Okay, he really wasn't that bad, he did a pretty good job. Clinton is another really good example. But Kennedy was really well-liked during his presidency. People were pumped that he was coming to Texas. You didn't see nearly, not even a fraction of, the amount of people come out that day to watch him drive through as you did with Hitler. So extreme, extreme, extreme nationalism."

Fascism, she said, usually comes out in a time of need, or a time of crisis. "So, major depression, extreme inflation. People burning money to stay warm."

"Good idea," said Sebastian.

"You have to be able to at least start to recognize how bad things were in Germany to figure out how it got to where it was," Ms. Day said. "How do you follow somebody like Adolf Hitler? How do you do the things you do to people? There really are logical explanations for it. Not saying that there are logical explanations for exterminating millions of people—that's not what I'm saying. I'm saying that it's logical to see how the public mass could be behind Hitler, and how he could get as much power as he did. He promised jobs. Six million people to eleven million people were unemployed at that time. So he promises jobs. And he accomplishes that. He promises revenge for the Treaty of Versailles. In Germany people were like, Finally, god, I hate that thing! I used to have an awesome life and then this treaty comes along and ruins everything I've ever loved. And he blames the Jews for the hardships. The public already didn't like the Jewish people, and their leader is saying we're going to take care of this. They don't understand what that means at this point, and I don't even think the plans were in place at this point, either, but they're like, Phew, okay, good. I don't really care what happens, because I'm not the one disagreeing with him. I'm not the one disappearing in the night. Because I'm going to get a job and I'm going to be able to afford to feed myself and feed my family again. They don't get to flash forward fifty years and go, Ooh, maybe we shouldn't follow this path. I'm freezing in my house, I'm burning my money, my kids are crying themselves to sleep because their stomachs hurt because they're hungry—and this guy says I can have a job in a month? All right, we'll see where this goes. I can't afford to not follow it."

Ms. Day talked more about the worldwide depression, and about reparation payments, and about the rise of fascism in Italy. Mussolini also promised change, also promised the restoration of Italy's power. "Remember, Italy is the site of Rome," she said. "The Romans used to own everything."

"They owned the Colosseum," said Sebastian.

"Italy historically always was very strong. And then in modern day they're just kind of fading into being a normal country. So this is out of the norm for them, and they want to regain that empirelike system. And this is what Mussolini says he's going to do. How many of you had a class where you literally did nothing? And you were like, Oh my gosh, I would rather them give me work every day, and just give me something to do, because sitting here for an hour, it just makes me so bored, I feel like my brain is turning into goo. We've all been there. Or you get left home alone for the weekend, and at first you're like, Yeah, I can do whatever I want! And by day three you're like, I'm so bored, can somebody do something with me? Give me a chore to do? That point where you get so bored you clean your room?"

"Or you clean the house!" said Sebastian.

"You hate cleaning your room so bad, but you're like, You know what, I don't even care, I'm doing something, I'm fine with it. Okay. Jobs were scarce, and you sat at home thinking about how hungry you were, and then somebody comes and starts putting order into society. As long as you kept your mouth shut, you didn't have much to worry about, right?" She showed another slide about the rise of Mussolini. "He built *four hundred* new bridges."

"How did he build bridges if he didn't have money?" Sebastian asked.

"He told people to do it. Go do it. You're not going to tell him no. With rocks and stuff. Four thousand more miles of road! All these people are out there working and doing it. Now, you throw a toll on that road, you're going to start making money back on it." That led to a discussion of toll revenues in highways around the United States. And then: Mussolini attacks Ethiopia.

"Everybody feels good when you have a strong army," Ms. Day said. "What kind of things do you use the military for? Defense and—?"

"Offense," said Sebastian.

"What's an example of offense in a war?"

"Football!" said Scott.

Ms. Day ignored him. "Going overseas, invasions, mobilizing! What country do you guys have that practices militarism?"

"China!" said Sebastian.

"Japan," said Ms. Day. In the twenties and thirties, she explained, Japan had a policy of glorifying the military's power and of maintaining a standing army. This was known as *Japanese expansionism.* "Now, what type of landmass is Japan?"

"Um, marshy!" said Sebastian loudly, just for the sake of saying something.

Mark, a smart kid, said, "An island."

"An island, good. So do you think they have a ton of resources, a ton of farmland? No. And they've watched all these other big countries go through this phase of, Here's my empire, isn't it pretty? And Japan says, I want to do that, too. And you can't do that without an army." So Japan takes over a lot of China. She circled her arm over a map of the region. "Saigon, all over here."

Sebastian was jumpy, talking a lot. "Sebastian, do you want to leave and go work in Mrs. Prideaux's room?"

"Oh, no, sorry," said Sebastian.

"Didn't think so." Japan had a need for dominance in the Pacific theater, Ms. Day said. "They saw Great Britain's empire, they saw Germany have an empire—didn't work out so well for them—the Austro-Hungary Empire was around for a while, the Ottoman Empire was around for a little while—Japan wants a piece of that pie. We're tough, we're awesome, why don't we have an empire? So let's go make one." She played another historical clip about Japanese aggression in China. "By 1938, the Japanese controlled the wealthier portions of China, and nearly half its population."

And then she showed a slide about isolationism. "Who practices isolationism?"

"China!" said Sebastian.

"America?" said Mark.

"America, good. What's isolationism?"

Ron read a dictionary definition.

"Good," said Ms. Day. "We're not going to get involved in your stuff. We're going to let you guys fight. Please look at us as just a friend of both of you. It's like being friends with a couple when they break up. You're just like, Whoa, I don't want to have to not be friends with one of you. I'm neutral." She talked about the focus on building infrastructure. "What does *infrastructure* mean? It actually means inside structure. What are some good examples of that?"

"The White House?" said Sebastian.

"The White House, sure," said Ms. Day. "But they weren't like, Well, guys, we need to repaint the White House, so we're not going to World War II. A lot of it is roads, bridges, highways. A lot of things like that were done under FDR. National parks. So making things nicer at home." The US stays out of the League of Nations. "They said, Jeez, we've already been in one world war, we're all set! We don't need to be associated in a club with all these other countries, we need to focus on our own country and do our own thing. We literally can't afford to go to war right now, can't do it. Everyone thought World War I was the biggest mistake. We spent a lot of resources to go, and it ended a year later. We lost a lot of lives during that time we were in there, and it doesn't seem like we've accomplished much, other than destroying Germany. Didn't seem like it was our war. And this is a really awesome political cartoon—"

The bell bonged, and everyone got up to go.

"It says, *League of Nations Bridge, brought to you by President Wilson.* And there's Uncle Sam leaning on—" The woman on the PA system drowned her out. "Alexa Starling to the main office, please. Alexa Starling to the main office. To the guidance office, Wayne Donnelly, Donald Bogan, Jon Sharpe, Ellis Wharf, Dylan Cadman, and Shastayne Peabody, to the guidance office."

I said, "I enjoyed that, thank you."

"Oh, good," said Ms. Day.

"I didn't do anything," I said.

"There was nothing to do," she said, "you're good."

"So in your class," I said, "typically what would an ed tech do?"

"Like if they were doing work," Ms. Day said, "you would kind of just be there for questions. It's hard subbing for an ed tech. My husband does it, too."

THE NEXT CLASS was a small one in the remedial literacy room in the North Building. Here I was subbing for a Mr. T. "Mr. T.'s schedule is a bit turbulent on Wednesdays," explained a teacher named Mrs. Pellinger. "You can just sit and join us and we'll have a study hall." I sat down on a plastic chair.

The teacher stopped in front of a very young, short-haired boy with a dreamy expression. "What are you doing, David, listening to music? Do you have work you need to do? Like some science?"

David pulled out a wad of worksheets. "I've got to finish this last piece of paper," he said, smoothing it flat.

"All right," said Mrs. Pellinger. "Let's do it. You'll be all caught up." She read the worksheet. "So you have to explain *oceanic spreading ridge*, *subducting plate*, *stratovolcano*, and the *continental rift*. Pick one and start with that." She looked around. "Remy's working. Just getting everybody to do something positive here."

Another ed tech, Mrs. Lahey, said, "Jared, I know you have plenty of stuff to do, plenty. So you need to find it, and do it."

Jared asked to borrow Dustin's iPad. Dustin held it to his chest with long, thin arms. "Sharing is caring," Jared said mockingly.

Jon, a pale, doleful kid with glasses, had an assignment from English class. "I'm trying to make a comic about a writer in the seventeen hundreds," he said.

"Okay. Do you have the facts?" said Mrs. Lahey.

"I've got a couple of facts," said Jon, "but it's junk, there's barely any. I'm a terrible draw-er. I looked at how many books he made, I think he made a lot of books."

"What's his name?" asked Mrs. Lahey.

"Jean-Jacques Rousseau."

I sat up. I'd just been reading about Rousseau in Nel Noddings's book on the philosophy of education. Mrs. Lahey looked at me.

"You know who that is?" she said.

I said, "He was a guy who had a theory of education that everybody was born innocent, and you shouldn't interfere with a kid at all, but just let him grow naturally, and we're all noble savages. He decided that we shouldn't have to have teachers or force kids to do anything. Lived in France." My heart was pounding with the tiny scrap of knowledge I had to offer.

"What do you think of his philosophy?" Mrs. Lahey asked Jon. "You just grow up, and we don't force you to do anything?"

Jared, listening in, said, "That would be awesome."

"That's one way of looking at it," said Mrs. Lahey, with a gentle edge. Jon nodded.

"We would have no discipline," said Jared. "But it would be bad, though. Kids need discipline."

"You need discipline sometimes?" said Mrs. Lahey. "You more than others?"

Mrs. Pellinger laughed knowingly.

Jared hung his head. "Yeah."

Dustin, who had a speech problem, said, "Then the people who could read, could read, and the people who could read somewhat, could take longer to get something done."

I remembered something else about Rousseau. I said, "He believed that it would all work out. But there was one problem with his philosophy, even if you agree with it. It only applied to men. Women were supposed to serve and prepare and make everything, and then the men would be able to go wild and have a free existence. It was completely gender un-neutral."

"Did you understand what he just said?" said Mrs. Lahey to Jon. "It applied just to men. The women were supposed to serve the men, do whatever the men needed them to do. And then the men could just go wild and do whatever they wanted."

Mrs. Pellinger asked me, "So did that mean the women had to be educated?"

I said, "He didn't believe that women should be educated, or should aspire to the learning that men should aspire to. Men should come to it naturally, but women should be held back. It was incredibly sexist."

Jon started writing some dialogue in a speech bubble. Mrs. Lahey helped him spell *woman*.

"So this is a class in reading?" I asked Mrs. Pellinger.

"I'm usually in a room with five students," she said, "but that room is being used for something else today. There's usually four students in here working on fluency."

"And I'm one of them," said Jon, looking up from his comic. "How do you spell *could*?"

"C-O-U-L-D," said Mrs. Lahey. "That's one of your spelling words." She checked her phone. "Nineteen emails!" she said.

Mrs. Pellinger resumed explaining plate tectonics to David. "What he's looking for is the whole thing about sea-floor spreading. The idea that the ridges in the ocean are coming together."

"Like one goes up and one goes under?" said David.

"Yep," said Mrs. Pellinger, "and they create a ridge in the ocean floor."

I looked over at the Rousseau cartoon. "Does he wear a wig?"

"Yes," said Jon. "A powdered wig."

He didn't want any help from me, so I let him be.

Mrs. Lahey sat next to Dustin to give him some help. Dustin was supposed to be working on learning how to set SMART goals. *SMART* stood for "Specific, Measurable, Attainable, Relevant, and Timely." Mrs. Lahey said, in her soft coaching voice, "If you get stuck and need some help, who are you going to ask?"

"Ghostbusters!" said Jared.

I laughed. Mrs. Lahey ignored him. "Who would you ask?" she said to Dustin. "Would you ask your teacher?"

Silence.

"Who's your teacher?"

"Mr. Salton."

"So that's the person you would go to first if you need help. If he's not available, who else could you get help from?"

"I don't know," said Dustin.

"Could you ask me? Could you ask Mrs. Pellinger? Who do you have for a guided study teacher?"

"Mrs. Giroux."

"Could you ask her? Could you ask another student in class? So there are a lot of people you could ask."

David's science worksheet was progressing. "How does a volcano change gradually," said Mrs. Pellinger, "and how does it change abruptly?"

"What does *abruptly* mean?" said David.

"Very quickly and very fast. *Gradual* means slow. If it happens abruptly it's going to make what?"

The bell went bong, bong, bong, bong, bong, bong.

"If it made a volcano that would be an abrupt change," said Mrs. Pellinger. Jon put his colored pencils away, slid his half-finished Rousseau cartoon into a binder, and left.

I walked to another tenth-grade history class, this one taught by Mr. Domus, a youngish, congenially rumpled man with a knit tie and a green shirt. "Come on in," Mr. Domus said. On the back wall of his room were hung the front pages of many old newspapers. "Guys, I need just a couple of minutes and then you can work, okay? First off, everyone needs to take out the sheet I gave you yesterday that broke down the project." They were working in groups on the antebellum reform era. "I don't care what sort of a presentation it is, that's totally up to your group. Make sure you're including background information. Make sure you're including the actual reform itself—the actual efforts that will be made. Make sure you're including significant leaders. And make sure you're including results. Brian, you have that look like you have a question. Fire away."

"I don't have a question," said Brian.

"Then why are you staring at me?"

Students put their earbuds in and began poking at iPads.

Mr. Domus came over and asked me how substituting was going. I said it was going fine, but I hadn't been of much use to anyone that day.

"It's hard to be a sub when the ed tech is out," Mr. Domus said. "You have no clue who is who and what's what. I think it's really just law. Legally they have to have an ed tech in the class if it specifically says in the IEP that a student has to have support."

Half the kids were out, Mr. Domus said, interviewing for the vocational tech program. There were only a hundred spots available. If you got in, you could come out with, say, a nursing assistant certificate. "That's what my wife did," he said. Later she became an RN.

I watched him wander the class, encouraging, joshing. The kids liked him. Soon it was lunchtime.

In the teachers' break room I took out a sandwich at a circular table. Mrs. Rausch complimented me on my Scrabble mug, which had a big N on it. She said she'd taught Mr. Domus. "Jimmy was a good student," she said. "I've been doing this for twenty-seven years. Isn't that crazy?" She'd gone to U Maine Farmington to get her teaching degree, as had Mr. Domus. She had a gripe about having to teach kids how to use graphing calculators, because it took them a very long time to understand how to use them. "They've been given iPads," said Mrs. Barrons, "and they can just type in the graph and touch it and it'll do the calculations. But we can't let them use the iPads because they can get online and they check answers, and they can email back and forth. So they have to use the graphing calculators. You have one piece of technology that's so easy, and one that's so clumsy to work with, and they have to use the one that's clumsy."

The two younger teachers at the table, Ms. Thwaite and Mrs. Sever, began an involved discussion about Mary Kay cosmetics. Mrs. Thwaite had bought an expensive Mary Kay starter kit, but she was unhappy with the people who skimmed off her commissions. "I don't feel they deserve anything from me, because they've not supported me." She still had more than two hundred dollars' worth of stuff to sell, and she was thinking of moving to Florida. "I think it sucks," Ms. Thwaite said. "I could cut my losses altogether and burn a bridge. I need to call them and ask them is there a way I can be affiliated with another director and another recruiter. I need to find out how can I disconnect from these people."

"Meanwhile, she's going to nag you and nag you to start doing the crap that she wants you to do," said Mrs. Sever.

"Really?"

"Oh god, yes," said Mrs. Sever. "Why wouldn't she? She wants you to achieve at that level so that she can get more money."

"It's a pyramid," said Mrs. Rausch, eating a stick of celery.

While I was at the sink washing my Scrabble mug I ran into Ms. Hopkins, the history teacher, who looked even paler and sicker than she'd been on Monday. She was waiting for the microwave to beep. I made a feeble joke about the need to practice isolationism.

She smiled sadly. "It's not possible if you're a teacher. You get something at some point."

"I hope you feel better," I said.

Mr. Domus was already back in class, having eaten some leftover pasta. "It's my wife's grandmother's sauce," he said.

"I love leftovers," I said.

"Oh, there's nothing better," he said. "Casseroles, soups, sauces. Her grandmother is a very old-fashioned cook and the stuff is just—oh, it's rich. We reap the benefits. They're as tight as I've ever seen a grandmother and a granddaughter. Works out good for me." He looked around. "Austin, we're not texting, are we, bud?"

"No, man!"

"Okay, just want to make sure I wasn't seeing things."

Renata flung her hands up and said, "This is so stressful! We are not a good team."

"We need to practice team-building skills," said Liam, one of her team members.

Heather's iPad was playing music. "I'm just putting on this awesome playlist," she said. "Eric Clapton, hmm—never even heard of him."

Mr. Domus made an appalled sound. "Really?"

"I'm no good with names," said Heather.

"The first group he was in was . . ." Mr. Domus closed his eyes, trying to remember. "Later it was Derek and the Dominoes. Cream. First it was Cream."

Mr. Domus and I agreed that "Layla" was a great summer song. "He's one of those guys who's lasted the changing times," he said. "He's that talented. That raspy rock voice." He went up to the front of the room to look up something on his computer.

Near me, Monica, a girl with a gold scarf in her hair, said to her group, "Did you see that really bad Skittles commercial, the banned one? The one that goes 'Taste the rainbow'?" (It's a spoof commercial in which a newlywed groom splashes Skittles candies all over his bride.)

Her tablemate, Wesley, said, "He's like, 'I'm coming!' He sprinkles *everywhere.*"

Monica said, "They put it on full screen, and they didn't tell me. They're just like, Watch this. I'm like, Okay."

Meanwhile, Mr. Domus had found one of his favorite Cream songs on his laptop. He started playing it over a pair of small loudspeakers. I asked him if teachers had played music in class when he was in school. "Mm, a little," he said. "There was still quite a mix of the new, modern-age teacher and the old traditional teacher of the sixties and seventies. It was much more rigid. We had fun, but it was a lot more work than it is now." RSU66 was a very spread-out district, he said. "Transportation is a huge issue, because no one can walk. *No one* can walk."

I mentioned that I'd heard that some of the bus rides took an hour and a half.

"If a kid does band," said Mr. Domus, "or sports, or stays to do work and can't get a ride, we do late buses. They don't leave here till four-thirty. So it could be five-thirty before he's home, after leaving at six a.m."

Brian called out, "What's this?"

"Clapton," said Mr. Domus.

"Guns N' Dandelions!" said Austin, which got a laugh from Mr. Domus—it was a running joke, apparently.

He turned back to me. "It's funny because I've always been an upperclassmen teacher," he said to me. "For nine years I did juniors and seniors. I had to switch this year. For juniors, you had your lower groups, and they were what they were, but the honors were really good. They were pretty driven, they were decent writers. They were good to be around. But I find that the sophomores are even better. The sophomore honors kids, they're like the perfect mix." He went off to the bathroom and I sat and listened to the class talk and work while more Clapton played.

Two girls, Lissa and Mary, were talking about a girl they knew. "She dyed her hair," said Lissa. "Did she dye it, or did she let it go back to natural? Because I do remember it was blond."

"Well, it was blond," said Mary, "but then it was darker."

"I'm never going to dye my hair," said Lissa. "Somebody told me I should dye it. I'm way too dark for that."

Austin said, "I was born a straight-up redhead."

Lissa turned to look at him. "So your hair was red, and then it turned blond, and then brown?"

"Yep," said Austin.

"And your eyes are like blue and green," said Lissa.

One group in the back was talking quietly about literacy rates in the reform era. Nearby, Jordan, in a varsity jacket that was too big for him, was telling a story about a time someone threw a fish at his head.

"I decapitated a fish once," said Isaac.

"You know what's worse?" said another boy, Jamie, who sat on the edge of the bad-kid group. "Running over a squirrel on a bike."

"Done that," said Isaac.

"No," said Jamie. "The squirrel went into the spokes and part of it went this way and part of it went that way and some hit my shoulder." He was smiling, although the memory pained him. He wanted very much to be one of the interesting bad kids.

"My dad killed a squirrel with our garage door," said Lissa. "It slapped down right on top of it."

"That's awesome," said Jordan. "My mom was driving in Florida, and it was really hot and she had the windows open, and a bird flew into her window and bounced into her lap."

Mr. Domus returned and began whistling to the music. "Which class are you heading to next?" he asked me.

"Biology," I said.

"Oh, wonderful." He pointed out where the science rooms were.

Renata had colored the rim of a Sharpie cap and stuck it on Liam's face. He couldn't rub the mark off. It looked as if he had a cut.

"Guys, fix my desks as we start to wrap up!" said Mr. Domus. The kids began straightening up the room. "Austin, what do you want to hear, buddy? I'll play you one song before you leave."

"Uh, like, Def Leppard!"

"POUR—SOME—SUGAR ON ME," sang Isaac.

Mr. Domus didn't want to play that. "How about this one?" He put on Def Leppard's "Photograph" instead, and turned it up.

"I know this one," said Lissa.

"Perfect!" said Wesley.

"I'm out of luck, out of love!" sang Def Leppard.

"Be sure my desks are nice and tidy!" said Mr. Domus over the music.

Students clumped by the door. When the bells bonged, Mr. Domus turned the music up louder. "I see your face every time I dream!" went the song.

"Have a good day!" Mr. Domus said.

Biology was taught by Ms. Bell, a cheery, spherical woman in her twenties, who, although she was naturally soft-spoken, had trained herself to yell-talk to be heard. "Okay! My rule is you guys can pick your own assigned seats, as long as you're in the first two groups of four! There should be plenty of seats! As long as you're in the FIRST TWO GROUPS OF FOUR you guys can pick your own assigned seats for attendance purposes!" The classroom was large, with black laboratory tables. "Sit anywhere you want as long as it's in the FIRST FOUR TABLES! Anywhere you'd like!" She passed around some work packets. "'Kay, LISTEN UP," she said. A kid made a retching sound. "By a raise of hands, how many of you are feeling comfortable with the Punnett squares and how to do them?"

Many hands went up. One hand went halfway.

"I'm good," said a boy, Troy, with a baseball hat on.

"What I'd like you guys to do for the first ten minutes! While I'm taking attendance! Grab out the Punnett square activity, and try those last two problems, and then I will quickly show you the answers, okay? So! Quietly work on those last two questions!"

"What if you already did them?" said Dennis smugly. He was wearing a pair of new Adidas.

"If you've already done them, then you can work on your next worksheet! Or study for your test!"

She pointed to two names on my schedule that I should keep an eye on in this class—Drew and Jamie. "They might need your help in writing for them."

Jamie seemed to be working fine by himself, so I sat down with Drew—he was the kid I'd met in Mr. Bowles's class, who had been thinking about how much it would cost to be kept alive if he'd electrocuted himself and become a potato. Drew nodded at me and began cracking his knuckles one by one.

"That is some serious knuckle cracking," I said. Drew smiled. "So did you get this worksheet yesterday?"

"I wasn't in yesterday, I missed the bus by a minute."

I asked him if he had a long bus ride.

"From the school to my house it's two hours," said Drew. "From my house to here it's like an hour and a half. I'm one of the first pickups, the last dropped off."

We went on a walk to get Drew a computer, because his iPad was broken and Ms. Bell had sent out a PowerPoint presentation on genetics that everyone in the class was supposed to have looked at. When we got back, a boy was asking how a widow has anything at all to do with a hairline. They were working on the heritability of the widow's peak.

Two kids, Ryan and Norman, were playing an irritating game with pennies.

The first question Drew had to answer was *What is genetics?* Drew didn't know. He didn't want to know. I talked about what a trait was. A cat could be all brown, for instance, or it could be brown and white. Genetics was about how that trait gets passed on.

"Like a skill or something," said Drew.

"Yes, it could be a skill," I said. "A monkey could be an astonishingly clever climber of trees."

"I inherited my tallness from my father," said Drew.

"Okay, that's a trait that you inherited. The study of that is genetics." After some coaching from me he wrote, using phonetic spelling, *study of how traits get inherited*. The second set of questions had to do with Gregor Mendel—who was he and what did he do. Drew didn't know.

Ms. Bell was helping another group of kids. "Sexual reproduction," said Ryan suddenly, in a loud robot voice.

"Hello?" said Michelle, an alpha girl, from across the room.

"What are egg and sperm?" asked Ms. Bell.

"Cells?" said the boy.

"In order for the sperm from a guy to get transferred to a woman, you have to have what?"

The boy muttered something.

"Alex, I want you to say the word. Three-letter word."

"Sex?" said Alex softly.

Michelle made a long peal of laughter. "I'm sorry," she said.

"I know, it's hard for you guys to actually say that," said Ms. Bell. "But that's what it's called."

I clicked forward in Ms. Bell's PowerPoint presentation till I came to some slides about Gregor Mendel. "He was obsessed with peas," I said, skimming the bullet points. "He kept growing pea plants, and asking, Why is this pea wrinkly, and this one's smooth? He was completely fixated on pea plants. He was a monk. He'd take the seed from a smooth plant and a seed from a wrinkly plant and figure out which is going to win. Spent his life doing that. Generation after generation of pea plants."

"He's researching these pointless things," said Drew.

"And yet it turned out to be an incredible discovery. His big discovery was that some genes were dominant and some genes were recessive."

Drew wrote *monk* and *grew peas* and then tried to crack his wrist. "For some reason I can never crack my wrist forward," he said.

"That's probably just as well," I said.

"I used to crack it over and over. It made a sound every time."

Next Drew was supposed to define *F1 generation*, *F2 generation*, and *gene*. We talked about what genes were while I scanned a few Wikipedia articles.

Drew said, "It's like in *Spider-Man*, when he first gets bit. He goes asleep, and in the dream it shows the transformation."

Yes, the genes were getting intermingled, I said.

Drew wrote that a gene was *a chemical that determines traits*. "Is freckles a trait?" he asked. "I got my eyes from my dad. Brown. My mom's eyes are blue. Brown's dominant over blue. I learned that in middle school."

"Right, so there's a brown-eyed allele and a blue-eyed allele. An allele is a possibility." Was this true?

"Like a dice," Drew said. For his definition of *allele*, he wrote, *different options for a gene*. We'd finished page one of the six-page worksheet.

Ms. Bell called the office on the intercom. "Can you let the nurse know that I just sent Tabitha Furness down for an allergic reaction to butter?"

"I swear," said Drew, "I'll have moments where I just can't write. I'll start writing and I'll just jumble it up." From the distressed look of his handwriting, he had some powerful form of dyslexia.

We slowly finished a page on dominant and recessive notation, and we stumbled through the words *homozygous*, *heterozygous*, *genotype*, and *phenotype*.

"This pencil's dominant over the paper," said Drew.

"*Phenotype* and *genotype*," I said, scrolling through more paragraphs from Wikipedia, "is a meaningless bit of needlessly complicated vocabulary."

"I'll forget it by tonight," said Drew. "Slough it off. I'll have a dream about it. Wake up sweating. 'What the hell was that?'" We laughed.

I said, "The genotype is the code, and the phenotype is what it actually looks like. Like if the pea is wrinkly or not. I guess the way to remember it is 'phen,' with the P-H, is physical, and 'gen' is genetics."

We did a few Punnett squares—those four-piece squares that allow you to calculate how many blue-eyed wrinkled peas will result from the union of two alleles.

"I have my dad's eyes," said Drew. "My sisters take after my mom physically, but the way they are is a mixture of my mom and dad. My sister swears like my dad. Everyone makes fun of her for that."

I asked him if he took after his mother in swearing.

"No, my mom swears a lot, too. But my dad swears more. I don't do a lot of swearing around the house—yet."

It was almost time for the buses. "I enjoyed that," I told Drew.

"I became a scientist," he said.

"I became a science teacher," I said.

"I'm going to tell my mom I was so smart."

Ms. Bell came by and told people how to turn in their papers. "I want you to put them in the bin, but facedown, and like this, so they're facing in the opposite direction."

Tabitha, who'd returned from the nurse, was holding her hand up.

Norman said, "It looks like it's inflamed."

"It was the popcorn," said Tabitha. "I put my hand in the bag of popcorn. Troy said it's Newman's Own, so it shouldn't have sunflower. The only other things I'm allergic to are coconut and nickel. Like pants buttons."

"Wait a minute," said Troy, chagrined. "One was movie theater popcorn and the other was Newman's."

"So you don't even know what you're feeding me?" said Tabitha.

"No," said Troy.

Tabitha shook her head. "That's an hour of doing nothing."

"Troy almost killed Tabitha," said Norman.

"What if I, like, lost the use of my hand?" said Tabitha. "How bad would you feel?"

"I would feel terrible," said Troy.

"I'd be waving around a stump for the rest of my life."

"Come on back in, guys," Ms. Bell called. "All the way in, close the door! Back away!" She passed around some jellybeans.

"I don't know, am I going to die from this?" said Tabitha.

"There should be no coconut in them," said Ms. Bell.

"Green apple!" said Ryan.

Tabitha popped a jellybean in her mouth. "This is like piña colada," she said.

I asked Ms. Bell how long she'd been teaching at the high school.

"This is my first year," she said, chewing a bean. Before that she'd done Job Corps and alternative ed with Sylvan Learning. Teaching at Lasswell High School was much easier than Sylvan, she said. "With alternative ed, you'd be lucky if you can get two out of the ten to work. They don't care. They don't want to be there. Education's not their priority."

I gave Drew a wave and drove home. Day Seven, done.

HE'S JUST A HAIRY PERSON

FRIDAY WAS A DIM, RAINY, SLUSHY DAY, and Beth again had me working as an ed tech at the high school. US History was my first class, taught by a Mr. Boxer, a confident, goateed man of fifty with an iron throat—he had the loudest, carrying-est teaching voice of anyone I'd heard so far. Mr. Boxer's students were working in groups on the same project that Mr. Domus's students were working on: antebellum reform movements. They'd been given a choice of five topics to investigate—temperance, abolition, women's rights, education, or religious reform—and they had to use three primary-source documents in their presentation. "A question came up in the other class in terms of what do I mean by *documents*," Mr. Boxer said. "So I want to take a look real quick—I figured by this point in time you guys knew what primary-source documents were, because somewhere along the way somebody should have showed you those, like in third grade." He chuckled. "Apparently that hasn't happened yet."

He stopped to take attendance, and then continued. Wow, his voice was loud—maybe that was really the secret. "MKAY," he said, putting some text from the Yale library website up on the overhead projector. "Let's take a quick look at this, just to make sure that you can find three documents that pertain to what you're talking about. Things like books that somebody would have written at the time." He began reading from the screen. "*Determining what is a primary source can be tricky, and in no case is this more apparent than with books and pamphlets. From one vantage point, books are the quintessential secondary sources.* But sometimes, because they're written by people who lived at the time, they can be primary sources. NEWSPAPER ACCOUNTS—if you can find something from a newspaper at that time. Government documents would count as a primary source. Manuscripts. Diaries, those sorts of things."

Mr. Domus came in. He'd had a problem in his class with a movie: after six minutes, it just stopped playing. "Should I try *The Story of Us*— see if that plays? It's good."

"Yes," said Mr. Boxer. "They can still answer a few questions with it." He continued. "ARTIFACTS." The class had begun to chat. "GUYS, I'M TRYING TO HELP YOU HERE. Visual materials. Pictures, political cartoons, art—those are primary documents. Music from the time period. Somebody's recording. Oral history. Those sorts of things are primary sources. Does that help you, in terms of what you are looking for? Mkay? You have to get your presentations ready for MONDAY—whichever one of the five that you're working on. If you need help, let me know, I can come around. Your presentation can be a Keynote, it can be a poster, it can be an iMovie trailer, whatever you think it needs to be. It doesn't need to be long. You're just giving a little bit more information on one of those five reform movements. Are we all set? GO! You've got the block. You will not have time Monday to work on this. You had all block yesterday."

The class got down to work, talking in low voices.

I walked over to a cluster of three upscale slacker dudes in dark T-shirts, Louis, Dolan, and Seth, who'd been squirting each other from a tiny canister of something. Louis was wiping his eye and sniffing. "So, guys, good morning," I said in an almost-whisper.

"Hello," said Seth, with an ironic smile.

"I'm filling in for Mrs. Brunelle, the ed tech person," I said. "Tell me what she does."

"She just kind of sits there," said Dolan. "I don't see that there's a point to being an ed tech. The job must suck."

I said, "It's an interesting job because you get to see people squirt each other in the eye with—whatever that was. What was that?"

"Listerine!" said Louis, scrubbing at his face.

"That must have hurt," I said.

"Yeah," said Dolan. "He thought it was funny, so I sprayed him back."

"How's my eye?" said Louis, looking up at me.

"Looks okay, looks good. So what's the reform that you're doing?"

"We're doing education," said Seth.

"Education! That is crucial." I suggested that they check out some of the primary sources on the Library of Congress website.

Louis turned to Dolan. "Why are you mad at *me*? You sprayed me like ten times worse!"

I asked them what they thought were some good primary sources to find out about education.

"Newspapers?" said Seth.

"Yes," I said, "and diaries—teachers' diaries, saying this was my agonizing day, students' diaries. Students saying the conditions are appalling, there are no chairs, whatever. You could search for 'primary sources education reform.'"

They looked away; they wanted me gone, and I couldn't blame them. I got up and looked around. Somebody in the front of the room dropped the f-bomb.

"Hey, LANGUAGE," said Mr. Boxer. "I don't care about much, but I care about that one."

I went over to Vera and Denise, two tough-looking young women, and introduced myself. I asked them if the ed tech normally talked to people.

"Not really," said Vera.

"Why is she here, then?" I asked.

They shrugged. "It's a job," said Denise.

"What reform movement are you doing?"

"Women's rights," said Vera.

I tried to steer them to some primary-source documents about suffrage.

Louis and Dolan were still arguing about the spraying incident. "You're not supposed to spray it all over the place!" said Louis. "You're supposed to spray a little."

"That's exactly what I did," said Dolan.

"No fucking way!"

"I sprayed from here, dude. From here."

Mr. Boxer put his pen down. "Guys, language! Stop! Jeez! Little bit unnecessary." He went back to grading papers.

I overheard Michelle, the girl from biology, say, "Should we add that it took almost ninety years for them to get the rights that they wanted?"

Three-quarters of the class was discussing their chosen reform. They'd found some Internet sources and they were dutifully pasting political cartoons into Keynote slides. Mr. Boxer, doing the rounds, cautioned a student. "Be careful with education," he said. "Make sure you go antebellum. Don't do education reform today. We've seen what education reform looks like today—you're the living, breathing experience of that. It's gone well!" He laughed a fatalistic laugh. "Education didn't need reforming, at all. It was pretty good. It was okay!"

Vera suppressed three sneezes.

Mr. Boxer glanced at the clock. "You've got twenty minutes, basically, to make sure you've got a Keynote ready for Monday."

Louis was still sniffing and hawking from the retributive Listerine squirt. I sat and read the assignment sheet. The students needed to spell out *the breakdown/details of the particular reform. What initial steps were taken to implement this reform? What did the initial reform call for (nuts and bolts of this reform)? Why COULD this reform be effective?* In addition to finding three primary sources, they had to come up with a bibliography. *This presentation will be scored based on the Antebellum Reform Presentation and Project Rubric,* the sheet said. I tried to look up some primary sources myself and got an error message from the school's Wi-Fi network: "The website you have requested may contain content that is inappropriate and has been blocked by this system."

The noise level began to rise. "REMEMBER, Monday these need to be done," Mr. Boxer warned. "You'll present then."

He turned to me. "The next class would be more fun for you to sit in," he said, in a normal conversational voice. "My AP US History class. We get to watch a little Cold War stuff today—a little duck and cover. My favorite video ever, with Bert the Turtle. It's awesome. It's the most unintentionally funny thing ever, the way they talk about how you can survive an attack."

The class gathered at the door. "ENJOY YOUR WEEKEND, STAY OUT OF PRISON," boomed Mr. Boxer.

I smiled. "You've got it down," I said to him.

"Thanks. It's a pretty good gig. Or at least it used to be a pretty good gig. Beats a real job, I guess."

Bong, bong, bong, bong, bong, bong. Why six bongs? We got the message at two.

Ms. Accardo, the high-energy health teacher, was back teaching in her modular classroom after some training days. She passed out a packet on suicide prevention. I read a few of the warning signs on the first page. Hopelessness was a warning sign, the packet said, along with statements such as: *Things will never get any better. There's nothing anyone can do. I'll always feel this way. How long does it take to bleed to death?*

"All righty, then!" said Ms. Accardo. She took attendance. "You're Jacob. You're Wesley. And you're—Maria? I'm not doing too bad when it comes to names. Okay, then. In this accordion pocket folder, if you have not yet passed in your anger management assessment, please do so. It's going to come around the room. If you did, awesome! If you did it electronically and you want to submit it on Edmodo, do it! Via email, you may do that, too. Whichever one it is that you want to do, whether it's electronically, a piece of paper, I don't care. If you have a piece of paper, put it in the second slot. Cool beans? All right, then! Anyone have a pink highlighter?"

Maria handed Ms. Accardo a marker and she tried it out on the whiteboard.

"It looks more purple than pink," she said, "so it's not going to work for our purposes. And I'm UNPLUGGING the pencil sharpener. You'll have to plug it in elsewhere if you need to sharpen a pencil in the meantime. Does anyone else need a folder, because your backpack is eating your things? There you go. You, too? Okay, anyone else need a packet, because your backpack's hungry? You're all good. All righty, then."

She looked down at her notes and got very serious. "Everyone comes from different backgrounds, different experiences," she said. "So it's really important to be respectful to everyone that's in the room. I personally lost a friend to suicide two years ago now. She had a lot of life events that were going on. She was suffering from depression. You know those commercials for medications that say, 'If you experience suicidal thoughts, contact your doctor right away'? They'd JUST changed her meds! She had a migraine for three days. So: the migraine, the depression with the new meds, and she was a breast cancer survivor. She didn't say anything to anybody. Her posts on Facebook were, 'My head is killing me,' but she was pretty positive. So—people may have friends or family, or maybe some symptoms within themselves. It's important to be respectful of everyone. You especially are going to see it, and hear it, first, before us."

Ms. Accardo said she was a mandatory reporter, meaning that she was required by law to report suicidal speech or behaviors. "If I suspect or know that someone is harming themselves, being harmed by someone else, or is going to harm someone else, I have to report any of those situations. It's required. Have to. That said, if you find that someone is in need of assistance, you can still come to me and talk to me, if you're comfortable with me. If you're not comfortable with me, I would hope that you would find somebody who you are comfortable with." Sometimes a student from an earlier year talked to her, she said. "Maybe you're concerned 'My friend will be so mad if I talk to you.' In this case, it's better to have an angry friend than a dead friend."

She put on a movie, made with the help of student actors, meant to illustrate various warning signs of suicide, one of which was the giving away of prized possessions. To someone who is seriously depressed, you're not supposed to say, "Come on, it's really not that bad." Never say that everything will be all right. Don't lie to cheer a person up. Avoid saying, "You'll get through this, you always do." Don't try to guilt the suicidal person out of feeling suicidal by saying, "Just think how everyone would feel if you killed yourself." Sometimes there's nothing you can do or say that will help. "Remember, if somebody you know does take his own life, it was his choice, and his own responsibility. As much as you may have liked to help, as much as you may have tried to help, you're definitely not the one to blame." The movie ended.

"This is way bigger than yourself," Ms. Accardo said. "People who are trained to respond can maybe more efficiently help. Give the support that you can to your friend, but get people in who can really do as they've been professionally trained to do." Don't minimize somebody's feelings. Don't have a huge party and invite all the depressed person's friends. "'Keg on me! Whooo!' Yeah, how about we don't? Because what happens to the decision-making process when you add drugs and alcohol? Poom, right out the window!"

Suicidal people can be agitated, restless, or irritated, she said. Their behavior may go through changes. She asked Jacob to read from the warning-signs sheet. He gave it his best shot. *"Personality more withdrawn, tired, ape—"*

"Apathetic."

"Indecisive or boi—"

"Boisterous," said Mrs. Accardo.

"Yes, boisterous. *Talkative, outgoing. Behavior: can't concentrate on school, work, routine tasks. Sleep pattern: oversleeping or insum—"*

"Insomnia."

"Insomnia, sometimes with early walking."

"Waking," Ms. Accardo corrected.

"No, that's walking," said Jacob.

"That's waking," said Ms. Accardo.

"Oh, that's my bad!" Jacob continued to struggle through the long list, which even included *Sudden improvement after a period of being down or withdrawn.* Everything seemed to be a warning sign for suicide. The last one was *Getting into trouble with school, or with the law.*

Haley, who had green bangs, told the class about prison inmates who made weapons out of toothbrushes by sharpening the handles, and Ms. Accardo said some prisoners were given "little silicone doodahs" with bristles that fit over a fingertip to keep them from making shanks. "Now you can brush your teeth all you want—there's no stabbing with silicone!"

The class began chatting away about prison violence. Ms. Accardo cut it short. "Anyhoo," she said. "Where it says more boisterous, talkative, and outgoing. Someone who epitomizes boisterous is Mr. Poulin. Hello! He's right up there and cheery! You know Mr. Poulin. Now, if someone was suddenly boisterous! And talkative! And outgoing! And yay, I'm fine! Why would that be a bad thing? Why would this be a suicidal warning sign?"

"They're trying to make people think everything's okay," said Ryan.

"Yes, sort of. It's related. Sudden improvement after a period of being down and withdrawn. This is a HUGE DANGEROUS THING. They have made the decision that they are going to make a suicide attempt. Everything that has been weighing them down emotionally is now—ah! 'You know what, Monday afternoon. It's all over.' They have a plan. They have a time. They have a date. Yay! This is a very bad thing. Because they know exactly when all of this depression and everything? Is ending for them. And it's lifting. Do you see how really alarming this can be? So just being a boisterous yoo-hoo person is not a warning. But the flip of a switch is. Sometimes families go, Oh thank goodness, they're back to their normal self!"

"No," said the class.

"You really need to get on it, if that's the case." She told us about a Lifetime movie she'd seen about a suicidal person who had quit the soccer team. "Hindsight's twenty-twenty," she said. "Have you heard that?"

"No."

She explained what it meant.

Maria said, "It's a puzzle until someone does it, and then—oh."

Ms. Accardo said, "My friend never left a note. So we can only assume what her reasons are."

She talked about some other figures of speech: "I could kill myself!" and "My mom's going to kill me!" She asked, "Is your mother really going to kill you?"

"It depends on what you do," said Haley. "I mean, not all mothers are the same. I ruined my sister's new white jeans, and I said, 'My sister's going to kill me,' and she put a knife to me, literally. That was like seven years ago. Brand-new white jeans. She doesn't live at home anymore, so I'm good."

A sleepy boy, Wesley, lifted his head. "What just happened? I totally missed that."

Ms. Accardo summarized. "She ruined her sister's jeans, and said, Oh, no, my sister's going to kill me, and then her sister held a knife to her."

"Literally," said Haley.

"Man," said Wesley.

"I'm glad you are now safe," said Ms. Accardo. We moved on to what things you should and shouldn't do. Show you care. Do not argue. Do not offer simple solutions. Do not promise secrecy. Do not try to forcibly remove a gun from somebody. "There's a guy that doesn't have a jaw on this whole side of his face because of that particular situation," said Ms. Accardo. "He grabbed a shotgun."

"Ooh," said the class.

"He's alive—but."

"That's what happened to my next-door neighbor," said Jacob. "He tried flipping his truck. He drank constantly. He tried six or seven times. We could hear him every morning puking."

Maria asked Haley where she lived.

"Geary Hill," said Haley. "Middle of nowhere."

"Seems like all the towns here are in the middle of nowhere," said Maria.

"All right!" said Ms. Accardo. "Go to role-play three." Everyone looked through the suicide packet till they found role-play three. It was about Christopher and Alexa. Christopher is a straight-A student and a varsity athlete. His parents are strict and want him to be perfect. But he got an F on a research paper, bringing his grade down to a C. Alexa finds Christopher in the library staring at his homework. Alexa asks Christopher if he's been crying. He says he's fine. *"Are you sure you're okay?"* says Alexa. Christopher says, *"Actually I feel a lot better! Now that I've decided not to do this test, I feel great! In fact, I'm not going to do homework anymore. I'm tired of being perfect. Tired of doing what other people want me to do. And tired of my life."* Alexa says, But you'll go to a good school and get a good job and make a lot of money. Christopher says he doesn't care. Alexa says that she's here for him. *"I admire all the work and effort you've put into school and sports. You can always talk to me."* Christopher says that Alexa is just saying that because she feels bad for him. *"I'm done,"* he says. *"The only way I can make my life my own again, is to take it from my parents."*

Bong, bong, bong, bong, bong, bong.

"We'll do scene two, role-play three next class," said Ms. Accardo. "Remember you can always come talk to me if you need to or want to."

I walked slowly back to the main building. A girl was laughing. "There's a button on that guy's butt!" she said.

A boy said, "I don't flip out on people!"

"Do you know what passive-aggressive is?" asked a girl.

Ms. Day, the history teacher, was giving her class a multiple-choice quiz to do on their iPads. She got everyone logged in. "So at this point, nobody should be talking," she said. I was supposed to keep an eye on Sebastian. He quickly tapped the answers to a set of vocabulary questions about *isolationism*, *fascism*, and *militarism*. "Wow, you're good," I whispered. I sat back and let him work. The class was silent. Ten minutes went by. "So, everybody's done?" said Ms. Day. "Awesome. Today we're going to watch a movie. We've been talking a lot about how it's hard for us to imagine now how a group of people followed Hitler. This movie is a true story of a similar thing happening. Keep in mind it is a true story."

The movie was called *The Wave*. "*The people selected for extermination by the Nazis were herded into concentration camps all over Europe,*" says the history teacher in the movie. "*The life expectancy of prisoners in the camps was only two hundred seventy days. They were worked, starved, tortured, and when they couldn't work anymore they were exterminated in gas chambers, and their remains were disposed of in ovens. In all, the Nazis exterminated over ten million men, women, and children in these concentration camps.*"

A girl in the movie asks, "*How could the Germans sit back while the Nazis slaughtered people all around them, and say that they didn't know anything about it? How could they do that?*"

Good question, says the teacher. He begins, in succeeding classes, to act like an SS officer, barking orders at students and haranguing them. They chant the motto "*Strength through discipline, strength through community, strength through action.*" Louder and louder they chant it, as the ominous music swells. Gradually they're brainwashed and turned into modern-day Hitler Youths, members of a movement called "the Wave." The teacher starts to get caught up in his own experiment. "*You wouldn't believe the homework assignments,*" he says to his wife. "*They do what I give them, and then they do more.*"

His wife is unhappy. "*You're becoming a guinea pig in your own experiment,*" she says.

A female student resists the Wave; her boyfriend throws her down on the grass. The Wave members gather in the auditorium for a rally and chant their motto. "*In a moment, our national leader will address us,*" says the teacher.

Ms. Day stopped the movie. "All right, guys. We're going to call it quits there. There's like five minutes left, we'll finish it on Monday. What did you guys think, so far?"

"Are you going to become that guy?" asked Mark.

"No," said Ms. Day. "Last class I said, 'Please don't ever chant at me, that looks terrifying.'"

Bong, bong, bong, bong, bong, bong.

I walked back to the modulars, but one of the ed techs said I should be on break, so I went to the teachers' lunchroom to make some instant coffee. The PA system came on. "The annual Swanson Academy college fair will be held on Thursday, April seventeenth. The LHS guidance office will be providing a bus for any junior interested in going. The field trip runs from nine-thirty to eleven-thirty and is a great way to start your college search. Permission slips are in the guidance office. Permission slips are due back by April tenth." I ate a sandwich and sighed, then I splashed cold water on my face to wake up.

In the hall, a girl said that a boy had sent her a picture of him wearing a hippie shirt and a bandanna. "He was like, Should I wear this?"

Her friend said, "He asked me, too. He always sends me pictures of outfits and asks me if they're gay."

The first girl laughed. "Bye, Molly."

"Bye."

Mr. Domus appeared and unlocked his classroom. We trouped in. Gerald, who was a sharp-eyed kid with crazy red hair, said, "I'm tired. I went to a dubstep concert in Boston last night."

Lauren, a popular girl, said, "You just randomly went to Boston for a concert?"

"No, my mom—"

"Had you been planning on going? Why didn't you tell me? Wait, your mom went? She likes dubstep?"

"No," said Gerald.

"I was going to say that's pretty cool."

"My uncle works there, so we got free tickets," said Gerald. "They put Xs on our hands, if you're younger than eighteen, for drinking and stuff like that."

"How long was it?" asked Lauren.

"From eight till twelve o'clock."

"When did you get home?"

"Two."

"And you came to school?"

"I slept for two hours in the car driving back," said Gerald. "My ears were ringing."

"Dubstep messes with the head," said Lauren.

Gerald said there were over a hundred subwoofers on the stage.

"You must have been feeling it in your chest." She looked up—her flirty acquaintance Garth had arrived. "Hey, Garth!"

Mr. Domus said, "Guys, look at me. How many groups are not done?" Hands went up. "Monday's your presentation, so you have to be done. Don't leave it for the weekend, because we know that's not going to happen. Right, Gavin, old boy?"

"Last time I did it," said Gavin.

"I was just saying hi," said Mr. Domus.

"No you weren't," said Gavin.

"Yes I was!"

"No!"

"If you're a good boy, after lunch, I'll give you a mint," said Mr. Domus. "Spence, you can come get yours now." Spence had finished his presentation. "All right, make this happen. You guys don't want to have to do work over the weekend, I can guarantee that."

Kevin was clapping his hands near his friend Wyatt's ear. Mr. Domus pointed. "Hey, I'm going to slap both of you in a second."

"Do it!" said Artie, the kid from remedial math.

"And then I'm going to email Mom and Dad and let them know, because they'll be fine with it." He leaned toward me and whispered, "The kids over there are the low-performing kids. So it's not necessarily a bad thing to go over there every once in a while and see how they're doing." The antebellum reform project had changed slightly, he said. "We're not making them find the three primary documents. That really threw the kids. Last trimester they struggled with that, and it was to the point where they weren't getting the other things done. So we'll tackle that in later projects."

I went over to Gerald and asked him what he was up to. "I'm doing the temperance movement," he said. He pointed to a picture of Carrie Nation. "I'm just looking up who she is." Artie and George, both wearing baseball hats, were supposed to be working with Gerald on temperance, but George was deep into a video game and Artie was quietly surfing for bikini women.

"Let me know if you need help," I said.

I read up on the temperance movement so that I could help Gerald.

"Mr. Domus, I have a really stupid question," said Allison. "When does the Civil War start?"

"Sixty-one. Eighteen sixty-one. No, that's not a stupid question."

"There are never stupid questions," said Brody.

"Yeah, there are stupid questions," Mr. Domus said. "I disagree. There are. Garth asks them all the time."

Allison said, "You'll probably realize that I ask a lot of them."

"No, dates are hard to remember," said Mr. Domus. "I can't remember a lot of dates, believe me."

There was another computer problem: Chris had sent a bunch of pictures to himself for his project and now his email wasn't working.

I went back over to Gerald, Artie, and George, and told them about the American Temperance Union and Lyman Beecher. "The state of Maine was the first state to go dry."

"Yeah, I know," said Artie.

"Terrible mistake," I said. "They thought if they made it illegal, people would stop drinking."

Artie didn't agree that prohibition had been a mistake. "Why is there a seatbelt law?" he said. "Why did they think people were going to wear their seatbelts?"

"People will actually do something as simple as wearing a seatbelt," I said. "But stopping drinking? People have been drinking for ten thousand years. In fact, they used to feed kids beer, because the beer was more sterile than well water. Prohibiting alcohol is totally unnatural. But they thought that if they could eliminate drink, they'd have a beautiful society."

"It wasn't a success," said Gerald.

"Right," I said, feeling myself getting carried away. "If everyone is forbidden to have liquor, only criminals will have it to sell. So the Mafia comes to power. That's why we had the St. Valentine's Day Massacre—they were fighting over turf, over the right to sell liquor."

Gerald showed me his first Keynote slide. "Should I put 'American Temperance Movement' or just 'Temperance Movement'?" he asked.

"It's up to you," I said. "I don't think there's ever been any other country that's gone so whole hog into temperance, has there?"

"I don't know," said Gerald.

Garth was passing out Pringles. "I stole them from my stepsister this morning. She was like, I got Pringles. Nope, now you don't."

I got Gerald to look up "antebellum temperance facts" on Google and we found a good encyclopedia article with some primary sources. Together we read a quote about suppressing "the too free use of ardent spirits and its kindred vices." Gerald began cutting and pasting.

Allison said that she'd gotten a bunch of irrelevant Google results for Lady Antebellum, a country music group.

I went back to my chair. Mr. Domus circulated. "I'm so tired," Gerald said to him.

"You look tired," said Mr. Domus.

"I went to a concert last night," said Gerald.

"Oh, did you?" said Mr. Domus. "Who'd you go see?"

"Xcision, in Boston."

"It's dubstep," said Lauren.

Garth said, "All dubstep is is robots getting it on." He asked Lauren for her phone number.

"You've been asking for my number since Wednesday!" said Lauren.

"I don't feel good," said Piper.

"I have a little headache," said Gerald.

"I always have headaches," said Garth.

Bong, bong, bong, bong, bong, bong. Lunch break. After the kids were out, Mr. Domus told me that George was diagnosed as autistic. He played video games a lot, and sometimes he got so deep into them that he took on the behaviors of the characters in the game. "Just so you know," he said.

I raced to Dunkin' Donuts to buy a coffee and got back just in time for the resumption of history class. Mr. Domus said, "Okay, guys, you've got, oh, twenty-three minutes. You want to wrap this up before you go. You don't want this over the weekend, kind of dangling over your shoulders."

"This week went by slow," said Gavin.

"I think the week went by fast," said Mr. Domus. "Last week was dreadfully, dreadfully slow."

"The week went by slow but today went by well," said Gavin. "Today's been good."

Mr. Domus was pleased. "The pace has been good?"

"Yeah. That's how I feel," said Gavin.

When the bell bonged, Mr. Domus put on Bon Jovi's "Livin' on a Prayer" and blasted it. The whole class sang along. "We're halfway there! We're living on a prayer!"

BACK TO BIOLOGY. Ms. Bell was out that day, replaced by a slow-moving, slow-thinking sub named Mr. Nelson, whose red plaid shirt was neatly tucked into his pants under his pumpkin belly. "Oh my god," said Cayley when she saw him.

"See, I told you you'd say that," said Cole.

Drew showed up, carrying a plant that he'd grown in a little pot: a four-leafed clover.

Two kids, Ralph and Nicholas, had drumsticks out and were tapping out rhythms on the tables.

"All right, guys," said the sub. "LISTEN UP. I got like five different packets to hand out. Let me pass them back. Can I get somebody to help?" Nobody volunteered, so I substituted as the paper passer.

"Are you guys drummers?" I asked.

"I'm in band, he's in percussion," said Nicholas.

"Worksheets are flying everywhere," I said.

"We already did this," said Paige, who had big arms and big cheekbones.

"Screw that, we ain't doing that again," said Cameron, sliding one of the worksheets away from him on the lab table.

Riley began a thorough pencil-sharpening session; I gestured to the drummers to put away their sticks.

"Do we just work?" asked Brooke. She had a ponytail and a scarf with horses on it that went with her pale blue pants.

"Hang on!" said Mr. Nelson.

More aggressive pencil sharpening, more drumming.

Mr. Nelson was a very deliberate man, and it took him a long time to take attendance. He handed me a folder with IEP plans for Drew and the two other special ed students whom I was supposed to be helping. "I think that's your crew," he said.

Cameron balled up a piece of paper into the smallest ball he could make, squeezing it and squeezing it.

"OKAY, WE'RE GOING TO GET STARTED," said Mr. Nelson. "This first packet, 'Phenotypes and Genotypes.' What's an organism?"

"A living thing," said Paige.

"Right, okay. An organism is a large collection of phenotypes." He turned to the drummers. "Guys, stop. Who can tell me the difference between a genotype and a phenotype? Anybody."

A blond kid named Aiden answered, "Phenotype is characteristics, and genotype is the genes, pretty much."

"Yep. Did you all hear that? Do you all know what DNA is? It's up on the ceiling right there. DNA is made up of codes, or nucleotides, which code for proteins. We call those genes. When we talk about simple genes, we have a dominant and a recessive on each one. Two different genotypes can have the same phenotype. Phenotype is what you can see. Like big nose, blue eyes, big feet, whatever. It's what's expressed. So that's the difference. So we're going to take a poll, basically, of all these different traits, and see what's in this population here, which ones are dominant. Who wants to be my tally person?"

Brooke raised her hand and took a position at the chalkboard. She was a take-charge girl; she wanted to stand in front of the class.

"You'll be my scorekeeper," said Mr. Nelson.

Drew yawned hugely.

"All right, guys, listen up. Who can roll their tongue?"

"Caleb can roll his tongue," said Brooke. Others could, too. Brooke counted eleven tongue rollers. She wrote the number on the board.

"Widow's peak!" said Mr. Nelson. "Who knows what a widow's peak is? If you pull your hair back, if you have a point, that's a widow's peak." Slowly he verified three widow's peaks. Brooke wrote a three on the board.

"Long eyelashes!" said Mr. Nelson. He counted; Brooke recorded. Three.

"Dimples!" said Mr. Nelson.

Brooke said, "Everybody smile right now! One, two, three, you've got one. Dylan, smile at me! No dimples." Dylan was, of course, devastatingly handsome.

Ginny, in braids, appeared in the door, apologizing for being late.

"Can you roll your tongue?" asked Brooke. "Are your knuckles hairy?"

The girl looked at her knuckles. "A little hairy, yes," she said.

Did she have long eyelashes?

"Yes, I do!" said Ginny. "I think I do."

Mr. Nelson inhaled and, glancing at the worksheet, said, "CLEFT CHIN."

"What the heck is that?" said Cole.

"Some people call it 'butt chin,'" Mr. Nelson explained.

We counted earlobes, whether attached or pendulous, and lips, thick or thin. Brooke pointed toward Drew. "You've got thick lips." She pointed toward Mason, who was one of perhaps four black or mixed-race kids in the high school. "You have thick lips," she said. Then she looked at her friend Polly. "You've *definitely* got big lips—I think we know why."

"Who's got regular lips?" Mr. Nelson said. "I see one, maybe two thick lips."

"What are we doing?" asked Riley suddenly. He'd been doing sneaky things on his iPad.

"I see seven," said Brooke.

"I don't think it's as common as you think it is," said Mr. Nelson.

"Fine," said Brooke. "I'll put two."

How many people had hitchhiker's thumb? How many had color-blindness? How many could wiggle their ears?

Jasmine could wiggle her ears, said Brooke. Jasmine, who was shy, held up her palm: No, thank you.

"I've seen her do it," said Cayley.

"We can vouch," said Brooke.

"Okay, GEOGRAPHIC TONGUE," said Mr. Nelson. Here the class took a wrong turn. The worksheet defined *geographic tongue* as "the ability to flip over the end of your tongue." In fact, geographic tongue is a state of affairs in which one's tongue develops darker rounded patches on its surface; it has nothing to do with tongue movements. Mr. Nelson, having done some misguided Internet research, projected a screenload of Google images of severe and shocking cases of geographic tongue, intermingled with half a dozen other horrendous oral conditions. He tapped one of the images on the screen. "Kind of looks like thrush, almost," he said, as the class gagged and gasped.

"That's hot," said Paige.

Mr. Nelson asked the students to stick out their tongues to see if anyone had mottled red patches.

"This is gross," said Cole.

"It *is* gross," Mr. Nelson agreed. "Anybody that has that, or even thinks they have it?"

Cole stuck out his tongue.

"That's hotter," said Paige.

"So no one has one of those gross tongues?" Brooke asked.

"There was more than one like that in the last class," Mr. Nelson said.

"Ew," said Cayley. "There are people like that walking around?"

Brooke, who had teacherly instincts, wanted to move things along. She got us through "claw toe," which included a discussion of foot binding. "All righty, then!" she said, imitating Ms. Accardo. "We didn't do hairy elbows."

"Who's got hairy elbows?" said Mr. Nelson. "Anybody?"

"What the heck?" said Cole.

Ginny inspected her elbow. "I've got this one hair," she said. "Does that count?"

Mr. Nelson felt that one hair did count. "I don't think it has to be a lot," he said. "We probably don't have any bushy elbows." He giggled to himself.

"How about you, Dylan?" asked Brooke, with a playful smile.

Dylan shook his head.

"Are you sure?" said Brooke.

Paige leaned toward Dylan's elbow and studied it. "There's like three hairs."

"That counts," said Mr. Nelson.

"I knew it," said Brooke. "He's just a hairy person."

Mr. Nelson began laboriously finding percentages.

"WHO is making noises?" said Paige. She held her hands over her ears. "Fricking Riley, he does this thing on his iPad where it vibrates at a frequency that only certain people can hear, and it gives you like the worst headache EVER. He's been doing it for the past three blocks of class, because he thinks it's hilarious. Everybody's like, Ow."

Mr. Nelson was lost in his arithmetic at the chalkboard. I read Drew's IEP sheet, which claimed that he had "emotional disturbances." I hadn't noticed any. Drew was an easygoing, likeable kid with dyslexia, who sometimes got fed up with his schoolwork.

Finally Mr. Nelson stood back from the board. "All right, so there's your result. It goes on the back page, guys."

Riley played the high-pitched iPad sound again, using an app called Sound Grenade. "Ow, stop!" said Paige.

"I'm not doing it!" said Riley.

"Yes you are."

Cayley said, "So, Riley, I told everyone in this class that you are a transgender cross-dresser. You're welcome."

Mr. Nelson said, "It looks like tongue-rolling is the majority."

A louder, lower-frequency squeak came from Riley's iPad.

"I'm going to have to fight someone," said Paige, getting up.

Cayley, Cole, and Paige began wrestling with Riley over his iPad.

"Ow—bitch!" said Riley. Lots of laughter from the girls.

"GUYS," said Mr. Nelson. "Guys, can you listen up, please."

The scuffling subsided.

"Thank you," said Mr. Nelson.

"Go away!" said Riley to Cole. "Stop posting your problems on Facebook! He's posting his ex-girlfriends. He's got a lot of them."

That reminded Paige of something a boy named Zane had done. "He was like, I don't have any ex-girlfriends. I was like, How is that possible? He's like, I kill them off after I'm done. I was FREAKED OUT. I was like, Get away from me. I don't want you near me." She looked across the room. "Ralph, stop hitting yourself."

More laughter. "You're such a dick."

"Don't talk about yourself like that."

"Guys? ALL RIGHT, GUYS, LISTEN UP. The typical Mainer is going to be a tongue-rolling, short-eyebrowed, bald-elbowed, hairy-knuckled, straight-chinned, dimpled person. Lobe-eared, thin-lipped, non-hitchhiker's-thumb, right-handed, non-ear-wiggling, smooth-tongued, and—uh—normal-toed."

"So we just write all of that for number one?" asked Brooke.

"Look at your data," Mr. Nelson said. "If the whole population breeded, and if you did a sample of the children, most of the population would have or not have the traits on here, statistically. Does that make sense?"

I showed Drew where to copy Mr. Nelson's statistical chart on the worksheet, so he could get credit.

"Bald eyebrows," murmured Ginny.

"What?" said Dylan.

"BARE-HAIRED KNUCKLES," sang Ralph, in a Bon Jovi falsetto.

The drumsticks came out again and began tapping out triplets.

Mr. Nelson read the last question on the worksheet: *"Do you think that if you moved to, let's say Mongolia, the same percentage of people would be tongue rollers? Explain why/why not."*

"Yes—or—no," said Ginny.

"We don't know anything about Mongolia," said Mr. Nelson.

"I was going to say because they speak a different language," said Ginny.

"It's a different gene pool," said Brooke.

"I think this is somehow related to languages where people roll their *r*'s a lot," said Mr. Nelson. "Like the French, maybe. I think it's a French trait."

"I am French, hundred percent, both sides," said Cayley.

"We don't really know anything about Mongolians," said Mr. Nelson.

"Hairy-knuckle syndrome!" shouted Ginny, and laughed.

"That's hot," said Paige.

"The Eastern cultures, they tend to have hair in the ears," said Mr. Nelson.

Peals of melodious laughter from the girls. "Oh my goodness," said Cayley. "My whole day was like this. Riley, is it raining?"

"It's melting out," said Riley.

"It better be."

Aiden got up and walked toward the door. He'd had it.

"Aiden, you're not done!" said Brooke.

"I am, actually," said Aiden.

"Are you guys writing the numbers down?" said Mr. Nelson.

I went over to the two drummers. "That's driving me insane," I said. "Is it driving you insane?"

"Not at all," said Ralph.

"Guys, back to your seats!" said Mr. Nelson. "You're not done yet. Listen up! I'm trying to give you the information you need. BACK TO YOUR SEATS."

The PA system came on. "Excuse the interruption! Nina Deloitte to the main office, please. Nina Deloitte to the main office."

Paige started putting up the chairs. "I'm done," she said with finality.

Bong, bong, bong, bong, bong, bong. First wave.

"THIS IS YOUR DATA," called out Mr. Nelson.

Half the students trundled out. I said goodbye to Drew.

"You were talking mad shit and she just like punched me in the face!" said Riley, as he left.

Mr. Nelson erased the board. He sat at his desk with his hands folded, waiting for the second wave to leave.

"Do you only do science?" I asked him.

"No, I'm all over," said Mr. Nelson. "Yesterday I was doing testing. Tuesday and Wednesday was the middle school, in the resource room. And then Monday, Freshman English." At night he was on call as an ambulance driver.

The bell bonged and the second-wave students trouped out. Jasmine said, "Bye, thank you," to Mr. Nelson. He and I walked to the office together and turned in our badges and said good night.

I walked to the car and turned the key. Antebellum reform, suicide, Hitler Youth, more antebellum reform, and amateur genetics, all in six and a half hours. "What the *fuck*," I said.

Day Eight, finito.

I CAN WRITE, BUT I DON'T WRITE

It was April Fool's Day at Lasswell Middle School. "You're Mr. Monette today, all day," said the secretary, Elaine. Mr. Monette's room was in Team Ganges, and he taught eighth-graders language arts. At the lockers outside room 83, Wyatt, with an orange Superman logo on his shirt, saw me and froze. "Wait, are you subbing for Mr. Monette?"

I said I was.

"Yessss!" He pumped his fists and did a little dance with his friend, who was wearing a cape: No real work for them today.

I found the staff bathroom and blew my nose and tried to wake up.

"Students are working on a unit on Conflict in short stories," Mr. Monette's sub plans said. "Their rough drafts should be completed today and their final drafts are due tomorrow." I cleared some space on the desk and poured some coffee from a thermos. Prentice sat down near me and stared into space. "How are you doing?" I asked. "Did you get enough sleep?"

"No," he said.

"Me neither." It was homeroom, so I didn't have to teach anything.

"Hey, Mr. Whatsyourname!" said Bethany, dressed as Wonder Woman.

A teacher came by. "It's Superhero Day," she explained. "Some of them have chosen to dress up, so that will create a stir."

"Sean, that's quite the outfit!" said Bethany.

"My sister's annoying," said Felicity, who was also dressed as Wonder Woman. "She's like, 'I'm cute, I'm real cute!' I'm like, 'Shut up, you're retarded.'"

"Don't tell her those words," said Bethany.

Felicity said, "She's like, 'Well, you're retarded, too.'"

Marielle sat down. "What's your name, Mr.—?"

"Baker. So it's Superhero Day?"

"Yes, it's Spirit Week," said Marielle. "We raise money. Right now we're raising money for a school in Cameroon."

I asked how the superhero outfits related to that.

"We have to bring in a dollar if we want to wear an outfit." Marielle rubbed her finger. "I burned myself."

"Toaster accident?" I said.

"No, ironing," said Marielle.

The PA lady came on. "Good morning, if you could please rise and say with me the Pledge of Allegiance." We rose; we said it. The lunch menu was hot buffalo-wing wrap-it-ups with shredded cheese, brown rice pilaf, romaine and tomato mix, carrot coins, chilled apple juice, and milk choices. Milk choices, there were always milk choices. She read the names of the artists of the week. "And here's another list, of students who will receive a super student award, due to their considerate and kind behavior to others." There were three boys and four girls. "Congratulations to these students," she said. "Wouldn't it be excellent to hear your name read on this announcement, too?" Then the president of the student council made an announcement. "Good morning, LMS!" he said. "Today is Superhero Day. I'm excited to see all the costumes people brought in to wear." He described the private school in Cameroon that was the recipient of superhero money. "There are a hundred and forty students in the school," he said. "The students get two meals a day, plus their education." The money raised by middle schoolers would pay for a storage tank for clean water, he said. "There is no running water at the school. Students have to carry water down the street in buckets."

The first-block students filled the room, and there were a lot of them. "I remember you from science," said John. I wrote my name on the board and waved my arms and shouted and got the class to look up. "I guess you're thinking about conflict today? Conflict in short stories?"

A quiet girl nodded; her name was Bailey.

I said I didn't understand what conflict was, and why we needed to look for it.

"I don't understand it either," said Bailey. She had a photocopy of Poe's "The Tell-Tale Heart" on her desk.

I said, "SO BAILEY'S READING 'THE TELL-TALE HEART,' which is about the scary heart that's beating and all that. What's the conflict?"

Shelby raised his hand. "He chopped him up."

"That's something that happened," I said.

"It's person versus person," said Aaron.

"I see, it's a fight," I said.

Melissa raised her hand. "It was person versus self."

"That's what they say, right, it's person versus self," I said. "I guess you're right."

The class went back to talking. I looked down at the sub plans. I had nothing to offer them. Somebody started noisily sharpening a pencil.

I raised my voice to Mr. Boxer levels. "HOW MANY PEOPLE have actually read the story that you're supposed to read?"

Lots of hands went up.

"So you're supposed to write a rough draft of an essay about internal and external conflict. Why do you think they came up with this word that somehow sums up all short stories? Why wouldn't it be that a short story is about what is beautiful and interesting in life?"

The class went quiet. Payson said, "Because there'd be no fun in that?"

I said, "Something has to go wrong?"

Payson nodded. "Something always has to go wrong in order for something else to go right."

I asked people to say what other stories they'd read.

"'The Sniper,'" said Harley. "It's about a guy who's on a mission. He had to shoot this old lady, and afterwards there was another sniper on another roof that shot him in the arm. And then he went down and realized it was his brother."

"Do NOT give away the ending, Harley!" said Tamara.

The conflict was easy to spot in that one, I said, because the people in it actually have guns. "How often in real life do people actually shoot each other?"

"Every day," said Katylynn.

"Every day somewhere in the world," I said. "But in your own immediate experience, in Maine."

Victor, who was small and freckled, said, "People shoot theirselves every day in Maine."

"That's sad," said Shelby, making a fake crying face.

"Shut up," said Victor.

"It matters what you're talking about," said Christopher. "I could shoot Rodney right now, in the face, with a paintball gun. It can hurt him. And maybe I want him to be hurt."

"Do you play paintball together?"

"No, I'm just saying if I shot him in the face, which I really want to do right now—"

"Don't shoot me in the face!" said Rodney.

"Let me ask you this," I said. "Guys, when you woke up this morning, what was the conflict in your life?"

"Going to school?" said Melissa, who was wearing a pink headband that morning.

The wall phone rang. I answered. The secretary asked if I'd taken attendance in homeroom. I said I'd forgotten to take it. She said not to worry. I said goodbye and hung up.

"Shut up, Chris," said Rodney.

I said, "When you realized you had to get up and go to school, what was your feeling inside?"

"Tired," said Melissa. "And I was disappointed. Pretty much. I hate going to school."

"So if you were writing a story about your day, the main conflict would be that you did not want to get out of bed?"

"Yes," she said.

By then the class had dissolved into eight separate conversations. I couldn't blame them: I was doing a lousy job of teaching this English class. Raising my voice to a shout, I said, "SO WRITE A DRAFT OF THE ESSAY."

"Can I take attendance?" said Melissa.

"Yes."

Melissa began checking off the names of everyone who was there. I asked her to look over the previous sheet, for homeroom, and try to remember if anyone had been absent. Jessica helped her. "Can I bring a buddy when I go to the office?" Melissa asked.

"No," I said.

"What if I get lost?"

Kimberly, dressed as Wonder Woman, handed Aaron one of her earbuds. "Put this in your ear," she said.

Payson explained to me how they were supposed to write an essay. First they had to fill out several pages of something called an organizer, and in the organizer they were supposed to write their thesis statement, which had to appear in the essay's introduction.

I said, "That sounds really—"

"Hard?" said Payson.

"Theoretical. So did you get a first sentence?"

"I do not have a first sentence," said Payson.

He showed me his paper. At the top, he'd written "The Snipper."

Shelby read it aloud: "The Snipper."

"That's a very different story," I said. "About a madman with some scissors."

Payson handed me his copy of "The Sniper," by Liam O'Flaherty. I read the first sentence aloud. "*The long June twilight faded into night. Dublin lay enveloped in darkness but for the dim light of the moon that shone through fleecy clouds.* I'm in it already. So what do you think you'll have for sentence one?"

Payson said, "For sentence one I'd probably say, 'My story is about "The Sniper."' And then I'd do my introduction. That would be on the upper line. I'd put my name, and then I'd put my story below that."

"Boom, you're on it," I said. "The name, then the date."

"But we have to use the organizer," Payson said. "My organizer is in my locker." He went out to the hall to get his organizer.

I asked Shelby what his story was. "I'm doing 'Thank You, Ma'am,'" he said. "It's about this boy named Roger. He tries to steal this big woman's purse, but then he trips. She grabs him and brings him to her apartment and talks to him and makes him dinner. Makes him wash his face. Gives him money to buy shoes." It turned out to be a story by Langston Hughes.

Kimberly was reading through a piece of paper filled with her neat writing.

"You've already gotten it written?" I said.

"Yes," she said. She was working on an extra-credit question: predict how a character in her story would react to a different conflict, using evidence taken from the text. "This is to get you a score four," she explained. "The essay only gets you a score three." She was writing about "The Tell-Tale Heart." "I like Edgar Allan Poe."

"He was kind of messed up," I said. "But it worked out for him." I found an apple in my jacket pocket and took a bite of it. I kept circulating.

Payson came back with his organizer. On one sheet he was supposed to list examples from the story that demonstrated four different kinds of conflict: character vs. self, character vs. character, character vs. nature, and character vs. society.

"Are you ever conflicted with yourself?" I asked him.

"Um."

Behind him, Aaron was lobbing balls of paper at the trash basket.

"How many times are you going to miss?" I said.

"That was like my second time!"

Payson scoffed. "Second time! That was like your fifth time."

"Just put it away," I said.

"We used to get yelled at all the time last year for doing that," said Payson.

I looked away for a moment. Aaron took one last shot and made it.

I made my way to the back of the class and asked May, who was wearing a denim dress and a cable-knit sweater, what a good first sentence would be.

"You just write what you wrote on the graphic organizer," said May, showing it to me. "The graphic organizer sets up how your essay is supposed to flow. Introduction, and then your Claim One, your Claim Two." She'd filled the organizer's boxes with tiny, elegant writing.

"That's really good," I said. "Let me ask you this, because you seem to know what's going on. Say writers grew up in a world where there were no middle school classes that taught the idea of conflict. Could they still write short stories?"

"I think most fiction stories have conflicts anyway," said May. "The writer doesn't necessarily need to know what conflict he or she is going to put into it, but the story will have it."

I said I guessed it was sort of like people who grow up and learn to speak and read well, but they may not know grammar.

"Yes," May said. "I believe that many people, when they're writing short stories, don't exactly know that they're creating conflict, but it naturally occurs."

"That's really helpful, thanks," I said.

"You're welcome."

I walked over to Victor. "How's it going?"

"Good," said Victor. He'd chosen to write about "The Tell-Tale Heart." "I also saw the movie," he said.

"Which is scarier, the movie or the story?"

"It depends. There are two versions of the story."

I asked Victor if he had a first sentence; he didn't. He still had to fill out the graphic organizer, he said. All he had was a thesis statement.

Christopher interrupted, asking to go out in the hall because the people near him were stressing him out. I told him he could go if he came back with a finished draft.

I turned back to Victor. "What if you didn't fill out the organizer?" I said. "What if you just started, and said, 'In "The Tell-Tale Heart," Poe blasts wide open the knowledge of the inner demons we confront, blah blah blah.' Don't use the *blah blah blah*."

"I want to use the *blah blah blah*," said Harley.

I read John's thesis statement, which was, *The vulture eye is really a weird part of the story.* I didn't remember the vulture eye. "What is it?"

"A guy kept shining a light on a vulture eye," said John. "It was really weird, because he just kept mentioning it."

I said, "It's sort of a random terror element?"

"Is it sort of like a random tattoo that kills people?" said Aaron.

"The Killer Tattoo," I said. "That's a really good idea." I told Aaron about Ray Bradbury's *The Illustrated Man*. "He's tattooed all over his body, and when people look close, the tattoos start to move." I turned back to John. "So now that you've got the thesis that you want to prove, why don't you just go out on the surfboard and just write the damn thing. Just wing it!"

He couldn't, he said. He had to finish filling out the organizer first. Rodney appeared. "I'm coming to help," he said.

"We don't want you to help," said Aaron.

Payson called out, "I can't feel my legs!"

I went over to James. "How's it going?" He flipped his iPad over so I wouldn't see that he'd been playing a game.

"It's going *well*," he said. His voice was just changing, and he had braces and a twinkle in his eye.

"You've got the worksheet?"

"I do."

"And it's looking good?"

"It is looking good."

"Gold plated?"

His eyebrows went up. "Silver? Or maybe copper? Can I get a drink?"

"Yes."

"Thank you." He hurried off, the inquisition over.

Some crumpled paper flew past my head.

"Did something just fly by?" I asked.

"He threw it," Harley said, pointing to Payson.

"What!" said Payson. "Did not!"

"Okay, I did it," Harley said. "It just hit my foot and I got angry."

I asked Harley if he was having an insightful and productive day. He said he was. He was wearing a black Batman cape.

Rodney said something in a black-accented falsetto that turned out to be from *The Cleveland Show.*

"Do you get your homework done at school?" I said.

"Most of the time," Rodney said. "I went from fifty to twenty-five missing assignments. I did nineteen the other day."

"Nineteen assignments in one day?" I said. "You must have been smoking!"

"Smoking what?" said Aaron.

Rodney explained what was at stake. "If you're over five missing assignments you get your iPad locked up. You can't buy apps, you can't play games." YouTube wasn't blocked, though.

"And it's weird," Aaron added, "because sometimes I'll try to look up some information for a project, and half the sites come up restricted. It's a pain because even if you do finish up all your work, it's a long process to get it unlocked again. You have to have all your teachers sign a paper saying that you got caught up." Both kids were using blocked iPads.

I said, "Well, now you've got to write an essay. You've got to just motor through it."

"I'm tired," said Rodney. "I'm always tired, and I'm always hungry. I wake up at five in the morning, and I don't get on the bus till seven o'clock."

Why did he wake up at five?

"I have a bunch of crap to do every morning," Rodney said. "I put my stuff in this one place every day, and I wake up the next morning, and it's everywhere, scattered through the house. I have two little sisters."

Aaron and Rodney began rehearsing pickup lines they'd gotten from websites: "Girl, did you just sit in a pile of sugar, because you have a sweet ass." And: "'Did it hurt?' Girl: 'Did what hurt?' 'When you fell from heaven.'" "I've used that one so many times," said Rodney.

I told them to get writing. "How hard is it to write a sentence? I mean, seriously. Come out all guns blazing! 'In Edgar Allan Poe's mind-blowing festival of terror, comma, the conflict expresses itself as boom biddly boom bang boom.'"

"I typed a story," said Rodney. He began explaining it and Christopher, who'd returned, tried to interrupt.

"Shut up, Chris," Rodney said. "I have so many people in this story. Shut up!" He held many single-spaced typed pages, maybe ten pages.

"Wow, when did you write this?" I said.

"Last month," said Rodney.

Aaron said he'd written a story, too, seventeen pages about Somali pirates, on his iPad, but the iPad died when he was updating it, and the school's tech person fixed the problem by doing a clean install, so he lost the whole story. The teacher told him he had to write it all over again.

Meanwhile Rodney had been silently rereading his opus. "There's a lot of mistakes on this page," he said. He handed it to me. It was a story about the adventures of a kid named Fat Andrew, who was always hungry. *"It's a good thing I bought a Twinkie!" Fat Andrew said. He reached into his pocket and pulled out a half-eaten Twinkie with dirt and hair all over it. "You still Big Daddy's little angel, you creamy pumpkin!" he said.*

"I want you to read this one part," Rodney said. "Read from *A* to *mermaids.*"

I read: *A car approached Fat Andrew and stopped. The man in the car started to scream and shout. His whole car started to shake. He started to rip his hair out. He reached over the dashboard and punched through the windshield. "What's that guy doing?" said Fat Andrew. The man got out of the car and ripped the door off. He bit all the tires till they were completely flat. Ripped the engine right out of the car. Then he ran away into the ocean and swam away with the mermaids.*

I congratulated Rodney. "Lot of good writing in there," I said. "Damn! Darn, I mean."

"It's all right, we won't tattle," said Rodney.

Did everyone in the class have to write something like that? They nodded.

"Mine was really good till they had to reinstall the iOS," said Aaron.

The wall phone rang. The secretary was looking for a student who wasn't in the class. I hung up, discovered I was still holding my apple, and took another bite.

Katylynn and Tamara were quietly looking at pictures of animals on their iPads, trying to find out which one had the longest lifespan, as part of an assignment for science class. They'd found a kind of lizard that lives for a hundred and forty years. "I want to be a koala bear," said Katylynn. "I would be an urchin in the sea," said Tamara.

Katylynn reconsidered. "No, I would be a small dog. Like a Yorkie. One of the really cute small dogs, that would have a preppy dog life."

"I would be a golden retriever," said Tamara.

"Well, I would be a bigger dog," said Katylynn, "but they don't live as long. I'd be one of the smaller dogs that they'd carry in their purse."

I told them that I had a corgi at home.

"They're adorable," said Katylynn.

Tamara was Googling. "The oldest person in the world is a hundred and fifteen years old," she announced.

"I thought it was a hundred and twenty-eight," said Katylynn.

"No," said Tamara, "now the oldest living person is a hundred and twenty-three years old, Bolivian."

"They would just be a vegetable," said Harley. "They'd have to have people to do everything for them."

Tamara said, "In class, Prentice was like, 'I will die proudly at seventy.'"

"I want to live to ninety-five," said Katylynn.

Harley disagreed. "What if all your friends had died and you're just sitting there?"

Tamara said, "I wouldn't want to die alone for the simple fact that what if no one notices you're gone? You just stay there until someone finally notices. They open it up and there's a body there."

"I'm just going to live in an RV," said Katylynn, smiling sadly. "No one will notice me, and I will just—die."

They began talking about when the science project was due. I looked at the clock. Eight minutes to go. I went back to the cluster of jokers and sat down. They were listening to a metal band, Disturbed, and comparing more pickup lines. Aaron read one: "I think I'm a firefighter, because you'll find me where it's hot and wet."

Rodney said, "I don't know, I think the chicken tender one is better. I said it to one of my good friends yesterday, and she thought I was serious. 'Girl, you're like the dipping sauce for my chicken tender, but not in a rude way, in a honey mustard way.'"

I said, "So what would Mr. Monette be doing right now?"

"He'd probably be yelling at us," said Aaron.

"Does he yell a lot?"

"Only when people are loud like this," said Rodney.

Rodney said, "If I turn and look at Aaron like this, and say, 'How's your day going?' Mr. Monette will separate us." He waved at the girls who were laughing. "They can be as loud as they want and he doesn't do anything."

"He's got you targeted," I said. "Is that because you've got homework assignments due?"

"Yeah, those people do a lot of work," said Aaron, "so they can fool around."

I lowered my voice and asked them what the secret was to maintaining order in a classroom.

"It's fine like this right now," said Rodney, "but when everybody's talking, it's just bad."

"Be a friend," said Aaron.

"But see, that's what you're not supposed to do," I said. "If you become a friend, then supposedly you lose your authority."

"Allow people to have fun," said Rodney, "but don't let them carry it away."

Aaron said, "As long as they're doing their work, they can do whatever they want."

I said, "The problem is, I like talking to people. This is what I like doing. But getting you guys to actually finish an assignment is a whole different thing. Because you don't want to do it. And I don't—" I stopped. I didn't want to say that I really didn't care whether they wrote the conflict essay or not—that I didn't think doing it would improve their writing one bit—because that wouldn't make life any easier for them.

Rodney picked up my iPhone, which was on my desk. It was cracked and it had clear packaging tape on the back holding it together. He said, "I took one of the other substitutes' phones and I started taking random pictures of myself the other day. I spammed his phone. I used up all his memory. He laughed."

One table over, Christopher said, "Ow," and fended off a pencil attack from Harley.

"Guys!" I said. "How important is it to stab people in the head?"

I looked at the clock. It was 8:48 a.m., end of block 1. "It's been a pleasure," I said.

"You're here all day, right?" said Rodney. "I'll be back."

BLOCK 2 WAS IN MOTION. Frederick walked in and pointed at me. "I remember you!"

"I remember you," I said. "How's it been going?"

"Good. Baseball tryouts this week." He said he liked to play catcher and second base. "I can play anything. I can play the outfield, I can hit. But I'm best at catching."

I asked him how he learned to play.

"I played catch with my dad. He taught me how to throw. And then I started playing T-ball, and then it just came to me, and I learned to pitch."

"I can't pitch at all," said Raymond, wearing a polo shirt.

"It's hard," I said. "I'm not so good at it. It's a gift to get the ball going fast."

"You need to have a good mixture of accuracy and speed, and it's hard to get that mix," said Frederick.

I wished him well at tryouts, and admired Winston's superhero costume. "I like the boots, especially," I said. He was wearing tall hiking boots and his sister's tights. Lyle had on Incredible Hulk gloves

I said hello five times in different ways, at increasing volume, and said that I was Mr. Baker, filling in for Mr. Monette. The class went alarmingly quiet. "You guys have been reading these stories and thinking incredibly deeply about them. And analyzing them, and coming up with the conflict in your stories, supposedly."

A strange prerecorded crowd sound came from Lyle's Hulk gloves and everyone laughed.

"I didn't mean to do that!" said Lyle.

I asked how many had started their essays. Lots of hands went up, and I went around reading bits of what they'd written. "I have some grammar issues," said Anthony.

"Oh, let Mr. Monette worry about that," I said, skimming the first paragraph, which described a character who had "twisted the truth" to get what he wanted. The essay continued: *I will be explaining more in depth about how his internal and external conflicts that he experienced changed his personality. Without his external conflict, he would probably never have had to experience his internal conflict. After this introduction, I will start my next paragraph with his internal conflict.*

I suggested that he cut *that he experienced.* "Nice going," I said. "You wrote that whole thing in class yesterday?"

"Yes," said Anthony.

"Nobody writes anything in the classes I supervise," I said. "I don't know why that is."

The boy next to him, Sam, had read "To Build a Fire," by Jack London. "I thought it was depressing," he said. "Who wants to read about a guy who walks into the woods at seventy-five below zero and then dies? He wants to stab the dog but he can't because his hands are useless."

I told him I thought it was a memorable story, a killer story, especially the part where the snow fell on the fire.

"That must have stunk," said Sam.

I said, "I think you can start with what you just said: 'Who wants to read a short story about a guy who tries to build a fire and dies?' That's a very interesting question. You want to be true to what you actually felt. Because otherwise it's just a meaningless exercise."

Edith, in a facing desk, wearing slightly crooked glasses, was reading *The Hunger Games*. She asked, "Why do you have a rotten apple on your desk?"

I looked over at my half-eaten apple. "It's a scientific experiment," I said. "I'll put it away, it's disturbing you."

"No, it's fine, it's just weird," Edith said.

"You were the substitute when we were making the cubes," said Sam.

Edith said she was in the middle of the scene in *The Hunger Games* where the girl is up in the tree, planning to drop the killer beehive. "Is it okay for me to be reading this?" she asked.

"That's fine," I said. "You've already churned out the conflict-and-resolution essay, right?"

"No," said Edith. "I just don't want to do it." The graphic organizer bored her, she said. She'd read "The Monkey's Paw" and "The Cold Equations."

"The Monkey's Paw" was scary, wasn't it?

"No."

I asked her what "The Cold Equations" was about.

"This girl had to die because she was a stowaway," said Edith.

Sam, listening in, gave a long, detailed plot summary of "The Cold Equations."

"You know what I like doing?" I said. "You read the story, and then you close it and you say, 'What in this story was actually memorable?'"

Edith tapped on her copy of *The Hunger Games*. "There's a lot of memorable parts in this," she said, with a half smile.

"He picks boring things to read," Sam said, meaning Mr. Monette.

I read a paragraph or two of "The Cold Equations" and stopped. Sam was making no progress. "I have a hard time getting stuff on paper," he said. "I can explain something fluently, but if you ask me to put it on paper it's like I'm trying to write with a stick, basically."

"What if you told it to me and I typed it real fast, and we got it done in two seconds?"

Sam grimaced.

To Edith I suggested that she write about being conflicted about having to write the conflict essay when she really wanted to know what happened to the girl up in the tree.

"She's down from the tree now," Edith said.

Joy walked up with her completed essay about "The Tell-Tale Heart." Her thesis was that the main character was neurotic and experiencing several conflicts. *In this essay,* she wrote, *I will explain what these conflicts are, and what they caused the main character reveal.* I complimented her—nice paragraph, you're off and running! "To change this from a rough draft to a final draft," I said, "you just have to add a *to* before *reveal* and you're done."

Joy smiled and sat down. I sipped coffee. Derek, bunchy-muscled and curly-haired, made a pained expression and adjusted his chair.

"That chair is giving you problems," I said.

"No, wrestling is giving me problems," Derek said. "I got second seed in my tournament the other day. I lost to Blake Burnside." His essay began, *In this essay I will attempt to convince the audience that the main character in "The Sniper" has external and internal conflicts. The character traits and actions he performs give me reason to believe this statement. I also say that he is heartless, weather external or external. My first reason is that he feels no remorse for killing anyone except his brother. He congratulates himself on killing the man in the armoured car.* I nodded and asked, "What did you feel like when you finished this story?"

"I felt like this guy is a little bit heartless," said Derek.

"Did you feel that the story should exist?"

Derek frowned, thinking. "It should," he said.

"What if you were a person of criminal intent and the story pushed you over the edge and you started shooting people? Not you."

"There are a lot of stories like that," Derek said. "Sometimes you watch a movie about terrorism and you become a terrorist. But there are also movies like that that change people's lives in a good way."

Good point. I told Derek to take a look at the word *weather* in the third sentence. The boy next to him, Neil, had read Langston Hughes's "Thank You, Ma'am" and loved it. He'd already written his essay on it but he'd lost it, so he was starting from nothing again. I left him to it.

"I guess there's a lot of injuries in wrestling," I said to Derek.

Derek leaned toward me and said, in a whisper, "I injured my shoulder the other day. I'm whispering because I didn't report it as injured."

"Don't you want to save your body for high school sports?"

"Yeah, but the coach is intense."

"Too intense?"

"Not too intense," said Derek. "Just enough intense. We did well this season."

Sam came up and said that he'd found an external conflict in "To Build a Fire." The conflict was that a man warned the main character not to go out in the cold. "Good," I said. "Isn't that the story where he spits and the saliva freezes before it hits the ground? That's a beautiful image."

"Well, maybe not beautiful," said Sam. He went off to keep writing.

Many minutes went by. Nothing happened. The class was wondrously quiet. Everyone was working, or pretending to work, or reading. I had entered a teacherly zone. I was floating in a polar-fleece paradise of studious silence. I read some more of "The Cold Equations." I checked my iPhone. I unwrapped the end of a bar of coffee-laced chocolate made by Winnipesaukee Chocolates and gnawed off a piece.

After a while the silence became unbearable and I walked over to Bruce and said hello as softly as I could. His thesis sentence was, *My thesis is that the sniper, according to the external and internal traits, he is brave.* I suggested that he cut the *he*. Done. I didn't want to mess with the mystically whispery mood of the class any more than that. More minutes passed. Finally a loud zipper-pull of a backpack signaled for people to look up at the clock. The noise resumed. "Where am I going?" said Neil loudly. "Did you dye your hair?" Bethany asked Joy. Nobody said goodbye to me, which hurt my feelings slightly.

BLOCK 3 TRICKLED IN. A boy, Blake, was wearing red tights, a tight Lasswell wrestling singlet with a paper B taped to it, and a red bandanna on his head. Jessie, in a Catwoman outfit, offered to take attendance, but I couldn't find the class list. Courtney was writing on Rita's hand with a Sharpie.

"Hello! Hello! Hello! HELLO! I'm Mr. Baker and I'm filling in for Mr. Monette, and you guys are supposedly deep into and completely caught up in the idea of conflict. What is this nonsensical notion that every story has conflict? Is that true?"

"Yes."

"Yep."

"Maybe."

A group in the back was telling hall stories and laughing. Sean, dressed as Batman and wearing his father's Air National Guard boots, said, "Do you want me to get their attention?" He clapped five times loudly. Someone clapped back from the corner of the room.

I took a deep breath. "Do you think that—DO YOU THINK THAT when Poe sat down to write 'The Tell-Tale Heart,' he thought, All right, what conflict am I GOING TO HAVE IN THIS STORY?"

"No."

The noise was amazing, but I persisted in my little foolish, unenlightening speech. "WHAT HE PROBABLY THOUGHT is, I want to write the frighteningest, most disturbing thing—"

The noise was just too loud. I started to feel angry. "Hello! Guys! *JESUS CRAM.*"

All the kids in the back erupted in happy laughter. "Jesus cram," they said, "Jesus cram."

"I was trying to say *jeezum crow,*" I said. "So the question is!—" Nobody was listening. "Doesn't matter. I don't care. You've got work to do."

"Guys, you're rude," said Jessie.

Finally things settled down a bit. "So we're talking about Edgar Allan Poe," I said. "He's a small, very disturbed human being, who happens to be a genius, and he thinks to himself, I want to write the most terrifying, nerve-wracking story I can write. And then later on, generations of high school and junior high school students have to read through it and find the conflict in it. I've never understood that. I think you should just read the story and find out what happens. You're either entertained, and you like it, or you don't and you stop reading. Did anybody read the story and not like it?"

Nobody raised their hand.

"It's good, isn't it? Are you all pretty far along in writing about it?"

Nods.

"So all you have to do is put in a few touches, stuff in a few adjectives? Did anyone try to write a funny essay?"

"No."

"Why didn't you?"

"Mr. Monette would not allow it," said Sean.

"Yeah, he's not a very funny person," said Courtney.

"He doesn't do well with humor?" I said.

"No, and he doesn't say *Jesus cram,*" said Sean.

In the back of the room, the superheroes were gleefully imitating me.

"LET ME FINISH UP," I hollered. "I don't mind a general basic quiet murmur of talking, because I think you're all responsible almost-adults. But when the noise level gets to be a certain sort of cresting wave, then I'll make lots of gesticulations and angry sounds, and you'll quiet down, right?"

"You'll make angry sounds?" said Blake.

"Well, I'll say, 'Be quiet.' Is it possible to have fun writing this essay?"

"No!" said Roslyn, a big girl with a red streak in her black hair.

"Seriously?" I said.

"Yes, that is truly true," said Roslyn.

"Can I read your first sentence?"

"Yes, sir." She handed her paper to me. It was written in magenta marker. I read, *In "The Sniper," by Liam O'Flaherty, the sniper shows that he is strong and cares about his job. It also shows that he has to go through the many dangers.* Period. *The sniper was at war. All of a sudden* It stopped there.

"Mr. Monette helped me with it," the girl said.

"The many dangers what? That he confronts?"

"Yeah, I haven't finished it," said Roslyn.

What did she think of the story? I asked.

"I actually liked it because I like people getting shot and stuff," Roslyn said.

"You're very gruesome?" I said.

"Yep." Roslyn smiled. "I like war, and I just—I don't know—I like scary."

I said she was off and running. "And you've got a great color of pen, too."

The girl next to her, Natasha, said, "I'm doing 'The Sniper,' too, but I find it's very boring."

"That's because you love romance," said Roslyn.

Natasha said, "I think it's boring because he didn't even notice that he could have got shot—which he did!—when he lit the cigarette."

I said, "So it's not boring so much as it irritated you."

"Yeah, that's the word."

"Why don't you try to tell the truth about what you actually felt?"

"Okay, I will!" said Natasha.

"Oh, god," said Roslyn.

"You should not do that," said Prentice.

I read some more first sentences. Adam, in a Spider-Man shirt, had written: *In Edgar Allan Poe's story "The Telltale Heart" the main character reacted to the external and internal conflicts determined that he was mentally unstable because he killed the old man just because of the way his eyes looked, and then struggled with his own griefs.*

Suddenly, belatedly, I understood what was happening. Mr. Monette was forcing all his students to inject language about external and internal conflicts willy-nilly into their opening sentences. How touching, how desperate, how wrong. "Great, nice job," I said. "The only thing I didn't understand is, did Mr. Monette tell you to put that phrase in there, *reacted to the external and internal conflicts*?"

"Yes," said Adam.

"The rest of the sentence is great, but that phrase is sort of jammed in," I said. Could he perhaps put the phrase at the end of the paragraph somehow?

"He told us to put it in, and he insists," Adam said.

If he had to explain to an eight-year-old what the conflict was in the story, I said, what would he say?

"It's between the main character and the old man, and the main character and himself. He struggled with himself after he killed him."

"Right, because it's guilt," I said. "The guilt is coming back to get him. It's his own conscience. The only part that's hard to understand is your first sentence."

"Yeah, but he kind of wrote it," said Adam. "If it were up to me, I wouldn't put it in, but . . ."

"Okay, well, you've got a nice flow, good going."

I said hello to Trey, who was sitting expressionlessly, rubbing his crew cut. He couldn't write about "The Sniper," he said, because he didn't have his iPad. "It's in that closet right there."

"Are you in trouble?" I said.

"No, he just keeps it in there, and he gives it to me in class," said Trey.

"Are you having fun in this school?"

"No," said Trey.

"Why not? How can you design your day so you actually have fun here?"

"We can't have fun here till one-forty," Trey said, meaning at dismissal.

"Seriously, you don't enjoy any class?"

"Nope," said Trey. "I don't like any of it."

"Some of the classes, I have to admit, are kind of dry."

"Like this one," said Trey.

"Why don't you just tell the truth when you write? You seem to know how to talk, you're smart. Why not tell the truth?"

"Because I don't write," said Trey. "I can write, but I don't write."

"Are you in a superhero costume?"

"No."

"Well, I wish you all the best," I said. "Have fun, tell the truth, be kind, rewind."

"I'm going to go get my iPad," said Trey.

I turned to Blake. He, too, was writing about "The Sniper."

"Another sniper," I said. "You guys are sniping all over the place."

"I think Mr. Monette is trying to send us a message," said Blake.

I went to the next cluster, where Prentice was paying a visit to Courtney and Rita. "What's your kneecap called?" Courtney asked me.

"Patella," I said.

"See? I'm not going to remember that."

"Nutella," said Prentice.

I said, "So you read the story 'How I Ate My Donut Yesterday'?"

"I didn't read that one," said Prentice. "I read 'The No-Guitar Blues.'"

"You're the first person I've talked to that has read 'The No-Guitar Blues,' and that's very exciting to me," I said. "Did you physically move your eyes over the page?"

"Yes!"

"And so when you finished, what did you remember?"

"That he wanted to be a musician," said Prentice. "He wanted to get the money for this guitar he really wanted. He couldn't get the money, so he set out to do raking and mowing, but it was the wintertime, and nobody was hiring him. He found a dog on the side of the road, wandering around. He was going to bring it back to the owner so that the owner would give him money. He ended up finding an old guitar in the garage."

"So it had a happy ending," I said. "Do you have a guitar?"

"Yes, but I don't play it," Prentice said. "I look at it."

What did he have for a first sentence?

"Actually I've got nothing so far," said Prentice.

Leap into the unknown, I told him, like a parachutist from an airplane, and then I looked over at Courtney. She'd filled a page with writing about "To Build a Fire." I asked her what she thought was the most impressive moment in the story. "It's terribly tragic, isn't it?" I said.

"Mhm," said Courtney. "I felt bad because of the dog."

"Pretty sad," said Rita.

I said, "Why don't you tell the truth with your essay? You felt bad for the dog."

"You've got sparkle on your eyebrow," said Rita to Courtney.

"I know," said Courtney.

I read bits of her essay. *The environment was so cold, to the point where his body was numb. He tried to keep warm by making a fire, but the snow put it out.* I said, "Excellent."

Rita said, "I don't have my story yet because I was out for three days sick."

Blake jabbed at Adam with the corner of an iPad case. I leapt up. "Okay, that's the part I don't like. I don't like any poking at all. I hate poking! I literally hate it. And I will keep close tabs on that."

"You don't like it?" Prentice said, laughing.

"No, I hate it," I said.

"Why?"

"Because it's painful and disruptive!"

"Poking is painful?" said Blake.

"Yeah, don't even go there!" I said. "Here's a broken pencil for you. If you jab at somebody another time, I'm going to physically write you up. And make your life unhappy. I don't want to do that, because I actually like you. I actually think you're funny. I want you to do this."

"I don't want to have an unhappy life," said Blake.

"My life is great," said Prentice.

"I see so much conflict with iPad cases," I said. "It's like the case becomes a weapon."

"Mr. Monette's teaching us violence with these gruesome stories," said Blake.

Trey came back. "I can't do my thing because I looked in the cabinet and he must have moved my iPad or something."

"Here, dictate it to me," I said. "Tell me what you want to write. I'll type it out and email it to you."

"I don't have email," said Trey. "My iPad is all messed up. I don't even remember what the story is."

"Mr. Baker!" Natasha called. "Do you want to read my essay?"

"I do, very much," I said, "and I'll be right there."

"I took your advice and I wrote what I felt," she said.

I turned back to Trey. "What do you want to do right now? You're obviously bored and idle."

"I want my iPad but I can't find it," said Trey.

"Do you want to draw a picture?"

"I want to know where my iPad is."

"It's gone," I said.

"My ear's itchy," said Natasha, when I went over to read her beginning. The sniper, she said, wants to smoke a cigarette but he doesn't want to get shot. *Here is my evidence that supports my claim.* Then she quoted from the story: *"He paused for a moment considering whether to risk a smoke. It was dangerous. The flash might be seen in the darkness."*

"I have a couple more paragraphs," said Natasha.

"Excellent," I said. "Mr. Monette seems to like this phrase 'external and internal conflicts.' Is there a way to work that in?"

"I will."

I glanced around. Sean was rapidly typing his essay on his iPad, using only his thumbs. Prentice was unscrewing something underneath my desk chair, trying to set up an April Fool's prank. I shook my head at him. He stopped.

The class was on the move, and the noise was increasing logarithmically. "Ow, stop it!" said Courtney. I looked up and waved my hands above my head.

"All right, it's starting to get above the plateau!" I bawled. "The plateau of misery where the SOUND IS TOO LOUD!"

That settled them.

Michelle was quietly drawing a tousle-haired anime boy, with huge eyes. She'd written her conflict essay and put it away. "I get it, but I don't understand why we have to do it," she said. She fished it out of her notebook.

In the story "The Telltale Heart," Michelle had written, *the nameless main character shows that he is compulsive by his quick and determined decisions. He repeatedly asserts that he is in fact not a madman.*

The noise was bad. "How does Mr. Monette keep people quiet?" I asked her.

"I have no idea," said Michelle.

"Does he beat a gong?"

"No."

I read her description of the narrator's murder. *After he decapitated the body and cut the arms off, he shoved them under the floorboards, where later he dragged a chair onto that spot happily, talking freely with the officers.*

I said she'd given a very good précis of what happened. "Is the word *conflict* in your essay? Not that I personally care."

"No," she said.

"Well, if you're happy, I'm happy."

I sat next to Natasha and said, "So we've got one story about a character freezing to death in the snow, one story about a guy trying to mug an old woman, one story about a sniper, one story about a girl trapped in a spaceship and she's supposed to get killed."

Natasha nodded.

"Mr. Baker, I'm going to the bathroom!" said Blake.

"Okay," I said.

"Go to the bathroom!" said Courtney.

Prentice, who was sitting with his pals Sean and Trey in the middle of the room, wanted to talk about video games: Dead Space, Mass Effect, Grand Theft Auto V, FIFA, NFL.

"I played Call of Duty for like nine hours straight," said Prentice.

"How did that go for you?" I asked.

"My eyes hurt really bad," said Prentice.

"Your thumb was trembling?" I said.

"No, my thumb didn't bother me, my eyes hurt," said Prentice.

I asked them whether they liked having the iPads in middle school.

"I hate the iPads," said Trey.

"I'd rather have a laptop," said Adam.

"Me, too," said Rita, eavesdropping.

"You can tell if someone's playing a game on the iPads, whereas the laptops you can't tell," said Trey.

"Dude," said Sean, "Bruce has like thirteen missing assignments and he's not blocked!"

"Does it depend on the teacher?" I asked.

"Yeah," said Adam. "She checked it once and restricted some people and then she never checked it again."

I said, "So basically they get you hooked on the iPads and then they say if you don't deliver the goods we will take away the thing that makes you happy."

"Yeah," said Trey.

Prentice nodded. "They took my iPad. I don't really care."

I excused myself and walked over to Blake and Company. "Guys, I see frantic activity over here, and I don't know what it's all about."

Jessie the Catwoman said, "We're doing a communal thing."

They were folding cootie catchers using old drafts of essays. I told them that making cootie catchers showed spirit and leadership but to please do it more quietly. It was time for the class to go anyway. "Is this it for you?"

"Yeah, unless Mrs. Moorehouse lets us come in here for STAR," said Blake. "She won't let us. She is against fun."

"Blake, I know you have it!" said Roslyn.

"I don't have your iPad!" said Blake. "Why would I have your iPad? I don't have your iPad."

A teacher's loud voice came from the hall. "Go back into your class!" she said to Prentice and Sean. "Back into your class!"

Bong, bong, bong.

When everyone had left I sat in my room for a while without moving. Then I walked outside and around the far end of the building and got my lunch from the car. A woman was out for a stroll with her little dog. "Hello, little dog!" I said. I kept walking. "I give up with this shit," I muttered. I went back inside to the office and apologized for not taking attendance in homeroom.

Some teachers I didn't know were in the teachers' lounge, talking about which sub was going to cover a class in the afternoon. "There's a group of boys that can be trying," said one teacher.

Another teacher said that after there had been a substitute in his class he deleted all the iPad assignments that the students had done.

"You delete them without reading them?" said his colleague.

"Yes," he said. "They don't do anything anyway." The iPads had been a financial disaster, he felt. Any kid who messed up his iPad and had to have it restored should get a detention.

I took my leave. Shane, in a gray T-shirt with a flying baseball on it, was sitting at a table in the hallway serving some sort of detention. I asked if I could sit down with him.

"I don't care," said Shane.

"We had some good times in that class," I said. "But then you said your pills wear off in the afternoon and you get bad."

"It's not that I get bad," said Shane. "It's just that I start to lose focus."

"Well, it's a pleasure to see you again," I said.

"Yeah, nice seeing you," said Shane.

I WENT BACK INTO the room and sat down and squirted some sanitizer on my hands and clapped them together.

It was time for STAR class.

"Hello, Mr. Substitute!" said Olivia.

I gnawed more of my coffee-bean chocolate bar.

"What is that?" said Olivia.

I told her.

"Soylent!" said Aaron.

"Oh no, I got sparkles everywhere," said Felicity.

I said hi, hello.

"Mr. Baker, I need to go to my locker," said Harley.

"I understand your pain," I said, "and I want you to go to your locker."

"Hello, Mr. Baker, again!" said Bethany. "May I get a drink? It's really steaming in here."

"What happens in this class?" I asked May.

"We read until twelve-ten," said May.

"Twelve-ten or twelve-twelve," said Michelle.

"So it's supposed to be absolutely quiet?"

Michelle said, "We're supposed to silent-read. Plus a few whispers here and there."

I tried a stage whisper to get the class into the mood. "All right, so this is one of those beautiful moments of the day, I guess—it's actual silent reading."

"I don't like reading," said Victor.

"When does the actual silent time begin?" I said.

"Now," said May.

"Okay." I stage-whispered, "It's like we're floating in a cloud of cotton!"

The PA system came on. "Lacey Bissonette to the office to pick something up."

I closed the door. "Do you mind if I turn the lights off?" I whispered.

"Go for it," said Harley.

I typed some notes. Everyone's head was down. I could hear my stomach making digesting noises. How lovely to be able to hear one's own digestion.

Five minutes went by. The PA lady came on again. "Ashley Kimball to the office, please." I read the Thesis Statement Checklist from the Constructed Response Graphic Organizer, which the students were supposedly using to write about conflict in their short stories. A thesis statement had to: (a) be a complete sentence; (b) take a stand;

(c) have one main idea; (d) be specific; (e) generate discussion; and (f) not be a question.

At noon I announced that it was noon—no more silence. Bethany, Kimberly, and Felicity began planning a group Wonder Woman selfie.

Aaron and Harley and I discussed the selfie song and agreed it had a good beat.

Rodney, who was playing Flappy Bird, told me he'd tried out the pickup line about the pile of sugar with someone on the way to lunch.

"How did that work?"

"They gave me a dirty look," Rodney said. "They didn't know if I was talking to them or not, so I kind of faced the opposite direction and walked away."

I sat down near another cluster of talkers. "So what's happening? I feel I've lost touch with you guys."

"You want to get involved with our awkward conversations?" said Christopher.

"I do," I said.

"We're talking about cows," said Todd.

"Are there many kids who come from farms around here?"

"Almost everyone here," said Christopher.

A kid showed a picture of a cow.

"Oh, those udders!" said Todd.

Payson asked if he could go to the bathroom. I said he could. James asked if he could go to the bathroom. I said he could. Bethany asked if they could take the Wonder Woman selfie out in the hall. I said they could if they didn't make noise. I stood by the door.

May came up, wanting to go to the bathroom. I asked her to hold on for a second, so there wouldn't be too many people in the hall. "People are never like this when Mr. Monette's here," she said. "They're like actually reading." She told me I should tell them to get their work done and, if they didn't, fill out "instance sheets"—reports that they had to take home to their parents itemizing their misbehavior.

I said, "But don't you think it's kind of an unnatural situation to be cooped up in this classroom?"

"Yes," May said.

"I figure my job as a substitute is to give people a little more latitude, because on the days when Mr. Monette's here, they don't get any. Does that make sense?"

"Mhm," said May.

"Also, it's hard for me to keep order," I said. "I'm not very good at it, frankly. Thanks for the advice. I'll think about it. You didn't bring in your dollar today."

"I wasn't in yesterday and I forgot it was Superhero Day. I didn't realize it was today."

Payson, returning from the bathroom, mimicked May: "I didn't wealize it was today!"

I turned on him. "Hey hey, what was that? Please, say you're sorry, there's NO mimicry in this class."

"Sorry," said Payson.

"Good."

May said, "I wasn't feeling well yesterday." She left for the bathroom. I leaned out the classroom door and told the Wonder Women to wrap up their selfie. "I don't want to be on the hook for having created a ruckus."

"I'm just waiting for them to get ready," said Bethany.

They smiled, arm in arm, and Blake took the picture.

Back in the class Rodney called out, "Mr. Baker! Is this what you looked like in high school?" He flashed me a picture on his iPad of a proud, smiley middle school student at a science fair.

Christopher tried to grab the iPad. "Don't show him that! Don't!"

"What is it?" I said. "I saw a pickle there. Let me see."

I looked at the picture. Next to the smiley science fair boy, against a blue foam-core display board, was the headline "Things I've Shoved Up My Ass." Besides the pickle, there were cutout pictures of a hairbrush, a toilet plunger, and a baby's bottle.

I had to laugh. Aaron peered at it, shaking his head.

"Don't let anyone else see that!" said Christopher, with genuine alarm.

Felicity came up. "Mr. Baker, can we take the picture again, but with the whole group of friends? It'll be quick."

"Try to do it efficiently this time."

Blake, Bethany, James, Felicity, and their giggly friends posed for a popular-kid portrait.

"Don't let those morons get too loud," Aaron said, meaning the popular kids. "Just tell them to quiet down. That's what Mr. Monette does."

Rodney said, "Mr. Monette flips out."

Todd said, "He's like—" He waggled his cheeks rapidly and made a sound like Curly of the Three Stooges.

"He's got steam coming out of his ears," said Rodney. "His face is like on fire."

Michelle came up to show me another one of her drawings. "Isn't this creepy?" she said. The drawing was of an anime girl with strange striped ribbons around her neck. I said how much I liked the ribbons.

"Here's another one she drew," said Marielle, showing a picture of a girl with stitched-up Frankensteinian cuts on her face and arms, and a boy with a knife in his neck.

"Woo," I said. "Edgy."

"I need to go turn something in to the math room," said Blake.

"You just need to go see Miss Buckley," said Felicity.

"She's really hot," Blake said. He spun toward me. "You want to come?"

"No, I don't want to come," I said.

"Miss Buckley and the virgin little boy!" mocked Victor.

"Victor!" said Kimberly.

"What does Mr. Monette do at this point?" I asked again. I was running on fumes.

"He just sits there doing his work," said Felicity. "Yells at us, the whole class. He's like, 'You guys need to stop!'"

Bethany leapt and pushed herself lightly off the wall. A pen twirled through the air.

"Okay, the steam is going to come out of my ears," I said. "I like conversation, I like friendly things, I don't like plastic flying around, I don't like feet making contact with walls."

"Sorry about that," said Bethany.

"I like drawing flowers," said Olivia. "I'm really good at them."

In the back of the room Blake was shadowboxing with James. I told him to stop.

An ed tech wandered in looking for someone. "It's Superhero Day!" she said, and left.

Rodney made a disgusted expression. "She is so nosy. It can be dead silent in here, and she'll walk in here and be like bleh bleh bleh bleh bleh! I was suspended three times last year because of her."

"So there's bad blood between you?" I said. "Grudge match?"

"Basically," said Rodney, "because she's always looking over our shoulder and telling us what to do. And she's not even a real teacher."

"She's like a demon toad," said Todd. He pointed at Rodney. "He's a cactus, prickly on the outside. But full of water. And juices."

"You've got cactus milk," said Aaron. "Cactuses have milk."

I told them they needed to learn how to work under the radar. "You can have fun and do crazy stuff," I said, "but you have to not make noise that goes above a certain altitude."

"That's what I'm trying to say!" said Aaron.

"I was kicked out of two mental hospitals," said Rodney. "I had sharp objects on me. I hid them in my bathroom and they found out."

"You gotta have protection," said Todd. Aaron laughed.

"No, shut up—this is a true story!" said Rodney. "I was rooming with a twelve-year-old at the time. In the middle of the night, he stands up, halfway between our beds, and he just goes—" He made a long raspberry sound.

"Mr. Baker?" Payson asked me if he could go to his locker. I sat down next to Marielle and May. They had worksheets in front of them. "We're studying for art," one said. "We have a test tomorrow."

"Art history," I said, "or art?"

"Art, like clay."

"And you have a *test*?"

"We have to describe the process of making clay."

I said, "You'd think that one class, like art, you'd get a vacation from having to do worksheets."

"Nope," said Marielle.

Payson opened a YA baseball book called *Plunked*.

Felicity was imitating Mr. Monette's stare. "'What are you doing, Felicity! Get back to work!' He goes, 'Come here. What you said to me today in class really upset me!'"

I turned to Payson, who looked up from his book. "This is an amazing thing, this class," I said. "It's like watching fireflies at night. The little lights come on, go off, come on, go off."

Bethany was swiping through the superhero selfies. "Ew, look at how fat I look in that. I look like a fat blob!"

James twirled a calculator and Blake pounced on it. I said, "Sit down and don't make loud, sudden, crazy explosions."

"How long have you been a sub?" asked Bethany.

"Way too short a time to know what I'm doing," I said.

"But you've been our sub twice," said Felicity.

"Yeah, and I'm not getting any better at it."

Blake said, "Yes you are—you yelled at me today."

I picked up a sheet of paper on the floor, a worksheet filled with words, called "Find the Noun." I let the class be loud. They were keyed up because of the costumes and the photos and flirting and joking. I walked over to May, the girl who'd forgotten it was Superhero Day.

"I'm circulating," I said. "That's what teachers are supposed to do. I just wander all day."

"I'm just bored," said May. "I'm just sitting here being bored."

"You don't seem bored," I said. "You still seem attentive."

"I'm just so quiet all the time."

Todd said, "She's quiet because she was born from an egg. An egg that came from a bear. May of the Forest, kind of like George of the Jungle. The birds are her friends."

May smiled.

The three Wonder Women were really getting annoying—they were laughing loudly, talking baby talk, calling each other from across the room, full of the knowledge that they were favored by fate. Blake, meanwhile, was swinging around an iPad case and making chimp sounds. Soon he would be eating his own vomit. I thought of a white paperback that I'd read in college: *Asylums*, by Erving Goffman.

"Can I go get a pencil out of my locker?" asked May. I think she just wanted to be out of the class.

I hated how completely I'd given up. I didn't want to scream and yell to quiet them down, but I didn't want them to be loud, either. I wanted the day to be over so that everyone could go home and end this charade.

Rodney took Blake's calculator. "I don't care whose it is, it's mine now," he said.

"Did you do time in prison, seriously?" I said to him.

"Not prison," said Rodney. "Psycho ward."

"I've been to Parkeways once," said Todd.

"Clear Island Center for Youth," said Rodney. "I got in a fight in the cafeteria with a kid. I've been in a police program since I got out. I'm in a police program right now. Cadets."

"To learn how to be a policeman?"

Rodney nodded. Harley began pestering Todd. "Stop it," said Todd. "I will bring a piece of raw chicken into school and put it down your shirt."

"Do it!" said Rodney.

"I'll put lasagna in your pocket," said Harley.

"Okay, I'll eat it," said Todd. "I'll bring a gallon of milk to school and pour it all over you."

Bethany said, "I think it's time to go."

"Bye," called Rodney.

"Have fun, guys."

I had a free period and I sat and breathed and moaned and tried to get collected. The PA system came on. "Please excuse the interruption for the afternoon announcements. There will be no intramurals today. Student council has been canceled. Grade six, seven, and eight boys' lacrosse meeting tomorrow evening. There is no detention today. And now for a message from our student council."

"Hey, LMS, don't forget," said the student council member, "tomorrow is Sports Day. You'll be able to wear your favorite sports team's jerseys and gear." Again we heard about the school in Cameroon with no running water.

With twenty minutes to go before the end of the day, some students returned and there was big noise again. I asked Melissa what the worst moment of the day was.

"Mile run," she said. They'd run for a mile around the gym.

"I didn't run a mile," I said. "I walked around this room."

"That counts as your own little mile," said Melissa.

The PA lady said, "FIRST-WAVE STUDENTS, YOU ARE DISMISSED."

"Ow! Ow, my hair!" said Tamara.

Harley appeared in the room and walked quickly to my desk.

I said, "How's it going?"

"Good," said Harley. "Got a detention."

A grim-faced guidance counselor appeared in the door.

"What?" said Harley. "I was talking to him."

"And how would I know where you would be?" said the guidance counselor.

"I was talking to him," said Harley.

"You stopped in here when you saw me coming in the hallway." The guidance counselor led Harley away.

I was shell-shocked. I felt I'd missed several boats.

"Why is there glitter all over?" said Marielle.

I asked her, "What do you think I should write in the note to Mr. Monette?"

"We were really good," said Marielle. "We were a funny group."

"You were a funny group. How did the art thing go for you?"

"It was good. We had to pick an artist and we had to write about him."

Prentice put on some hip-hop and offered me a piece of gum. Everyone was mortally tired, counting down the minutes.

"Please excuse the interruption," said the PA woman. "Second-wave students, you are dismissed. You may walk to your buses."

"Take it easy, guys, bye," I said.

I turned in my ID at the office. Walked to my car. End of Day Nine.

DON'T KILL PENGUINS
CAUSE OTHER FRIENDS GET SAD

I WAS TRAPPED BEHIND a garbage truck on the way to the middle school, but I made it on time, almost. It was Pajama Day, and I was Mrs. Painter, a seventh-grade science teacher in Team Orinoco. In homeroom Brock, wearing baggy red pajama pants with hockey sticks on them, sang "Turn Down for What." I was determined not to screw up and forget to take attendance. I started shouting names and checking them off: CALEB. JASON. BRITTANY. REGAN. EVAN.

"Do you want me to bring that down for you?" said Brittany.

I nodded.

"Yesss!" said Brittany.

Outside a teacher said, "Guys, that was the seven-thirty bell. YOU NEED TO BE IN YOUR HOMEROOM."

"Can I go get a pencil?" Caleb asked.

"Why is everyone out in the hall?" I asked.

"Homeroom's boring," said Cayden.

"LUKE. TRINITY. GEORGIA. RUSSELL."

"He's not here," said Cayden.

"ARLENE."

"She's not here," said Cayden.

"As sickness ravages the school," I said. "BROCK. MANDY. ALEC."

"He's right there."

"Not even listening. Isn't that shocking? They just don't care."

A girl said, "GUYS, LISTEN!" There was no reaction. "Nah, they won't listen," she said.

"DANA. OWEN."

Owen said, "Oh, you're the awesome teacher!"

Ms. Nolton, the Team Orinoco math teacher—in whose room I had lately bled—opened the door that connected her classroom with ours. "Boys and girls, can I have your attention for just a moment? A reminder. Your field trip money and permission slips—many of you have not brought those in yet. Keep that in mind, for our field trip. Thank you." She disappeared.

I asked where they were going to go.

"Boston," said Georgia. "We're going to Quincy Market."

The PA lady told us to stand and say the pledge. Liberty and justice for all. The lunch menu was Mexican taco salad made with seasoned taco filling and corn tortilla chips, shredded cheese, shredded lettuce, chopped tomatoes, onions, salsa, and hot pinto beans. Plus a warm cinnamon puff, and pineapple, and milk choices. "The Lasswell boys' swim team ended their season with a stellar performance yesterday, beating Portland, Massabesic, and Saco at the Boys Swim Festival." She read off the first-place finishers. "If you see a swimmer today, give them a high five, because they swam swimmingly last night." There followed announcements about Spirit Week, drama rehearsal, band tryouts, chorus tryouts, and softball tryouts, all delivered in a cheerful singsong.

"This is the longest announcement I've ever heard," I said to Alec, who was staring into the middle distance.

The movie *Frozen* was going to be shown at two p.m. in the auditorium. "Students who are attending the movie, be sure you have all your stuff ready to go. And that will conclude our announcements for today. Thank you and have a wonderful day, everyone!"

I asked Alec if he was having fun.

"I'll have fun in seven hours," he said.

"There are cinnamon puffs for lunch," I said, trying to joke him out of his dejection.

"The food they have here isn't good food," Alec said. "They don't cook it good, so it doesn't taste good. It's all frozen stuff from Walmart."

Brock corrected him. "It's not from Walmart, dude, it's from the USDA."

I asked why some of the chairs had green tennis balls over their casters and some didn't.

"Cause kids are bad," Brock said. "Kids throw them."

Then it was STAR class and we talked about what people were supposed to be reading. "We have these huge packets every day to read," said Sage.

"I read what the teacher assigns me when I'm trying to fall asleep," said Darryl. "The other day I was reading for homework, and I fell asleep on the couch."

"I think you should expand the notion of reading," I said.

"You are awesome!" said Mackenzie.

"I'm not awesome," I said. "I just don't know what I'm doing."

"The last class with you all we talked about is One Direction, and we threw the socks," said Mackenzie.

"Oh, right, the socks," I said. "Good times."

Everyone went mum for silent reading. Mandy whisper-asked me if she could please just draw. I said she could draw a sentence and then read it—that amounted to silent reading. She seemed to like that idea and went off to get some markers.

I glanced at the sub plans, which were about some kind of math project, plus the five, no, six kingdoms of living things on planet Earth and something called a "dichotomous key." There was a picture of Linnaeus tacked to a corkboard on the wall, so I read up on him and on the history of classification, trying to dredge up what I remembered from junior high, which was outmoded anyway. The class's code of conduct was taped to the cinderblock near my desk, above the ever-present learning taxonomy poster, near a flowchart of learning targets. One target read: "Understands how changes in an organism's habitat and population size can influence the survival of a population." A big yellow arrow pointed to the target: "You are here!" The code of conduct was long and detailed, written in five colors of marker and decorated with tulips and smiley bears. It said: *I will not spread gossip. I will be honest and accountable for my own actions and behavior. I will pay attention to others when they talk and keep eye contact. I will look forward to learning.* And: *I will expect the unexpected.*

When silent reading was over, Ms. Nolton came in from the adjoining room to supervise the class. She made an announcement. "There are three or four surveys! You need to take the survey RIGHT NOW! The rest of you are working on your fraction flip books!"

"Sage, take my survey!" said Mackenzie, waving her iPad, where the survey software resided on a "learning management system" called Educate. "We created the surveys," she told me. "Once we get the results back, we're supposed to make graphs. My survey's about 'Would you rather.' Like, would your rather have to drink a stranger's saliva, chicken juice, hot sauce, or ocean water? I think a lot of them will say ocean water."

I asked her if by chicken juice she meant cooked or raw.

"Not cooked," said Mackenzie.

"Oh."

It was time to perambulate. Max was working on his fraction flip book, made of red construction paper. On each of the top flaps was a percentage, and when you flipped it up, it was supposed to show the equivalent fraction. "When you know how to do that, you are king of the world," I said. Max began spinning one of the lopsided, sliced-open tennis balls that had once covered the bottom of a chair leg. I told him to stop. Darryl wrote my name on the whiteboard, because I'd forgotten to. She underlined it with a curvy scroll, decorated with a flower. Dabney and Richard were talking about Power Rangers. Regan was playing hip-hop from his iPad speakers. Jade shouted, "Stop, you're going to rip it!" It was a relief to see that these seventh-graders were just as wiggy under Ms. Nolton's credentialed eye as they were with me.

"Are you taking a survey?" I asked Sunrise.

"I can't," she said. "I can't get on Educate."

"I'm sorry," I said. Educate. I wondered for a moment about how much money RSU66 had spent to lease and customize and troubleshoot this fancy, colorful software, plus Edmodo, Infinite Campus, IXL, and others. Probably a fair amount. Educate, a company founded in Alaska by a group of homeschooling data analysts from the oil industry, had sold its "mass personalized learning" system to low-test-score districts all over the country. "On the oil field everything had a meter. Lights, engines, pipes, even people, all had some sort of meter," said the company website. "The founders took a deep look at the needs and started to see that concepts behind finding and making optimizations with the oil industry were also applicable to education, with one major difference, the moral purpose behind enriching education versus enriching the wallets of the oil companies." Educate believed in the "personalized mastery paradigm." If you could log on to the website, great. If you couldn't, you couldn't.

Luke and Evan were reviewing the preliminary results of the poll they'd designed. "Six voted old age," said the boy, "and one voted being impaled by a narwhal horn." The other choices were drowning, having a heart attack, or getting shot.

"Why would I choose how I want to die?" asked Chase, who was still taking the survey.

I stopped near William. "I've taken all the surveys," he said.

"Was it fun?"

He shrugged.

I tried to get William going on the percentages flip book. "Let's say that it said I have twenty-five percent of all the stuff I need to graduate," I said. "How do you get from that to a fraction? What does twenty-five percent mean?" He'd cut out and glued the method he was supposed to follow from a worksheet. The wording wasn't terribly helpful: *The place value of the last digit becomes the denominator.* Then you were supposed to simplify the fraction.

William said, "It would be like twenty-five over a hundred?"

"Right! You just move the dot over two places and put it over a hundred."

Mackenzie interrupted with her interim results. "Five for chicken juice, ten for salt water, and one for a stranger's saliva," she said, reading off her iPad. More results were streaming in.

"I like saliva," said Chase.

Darryl said, "Oh? You would want to eat my saliva?" She was wearing a pair of huge Bigfoot slippers along with her pajamas.

Mackenzie said, "Now three for a stranger's saliva, eleven for salt water, and six for chicken juice."

Over the tumult, Ms. Nolton yelled from the doorway that one group from Team Orinoco still had not finished designing their survey.

"Jason, take Mackenzie's survey!"

Thomas was a movie buff, with a picture of Tim Burton on his notebook; his survey was long and complicated. He wanted people to choose their favorite movie from a list, including *The Little Mermaid*, *Wallace and Gromit*, and *Peterman*, which was autocorrect for *Peter Pan*. *If you could meet a movie director, who would you meet?* was another of his questions. And *Would you rather (a) go to a movie when you can meet the movie director, (b) go to a movie premiere, (c) have a private meeting with the movie director, (d) meet the director but never see his movies, (e) read his books rather than watch his movies, or (f) watch his movies and never meet the director.* Thomas had also asked, *What would you like to eat when you got to a movie?* and *How would you want to die inside a movie?* and *When would you like to die?* Most kids wanted to eat candy at the movies, followed by popcorn, but there were write-ins, too: Nutella, hot wings, "a burger," "everything," and soda.

Mackenzie took Thomas's survey. "*When would you like to die?*" she read. "*Morning, afternoon, evening, or midnight.* Hm. Midnight. I'd rather die at midnight."

The survey project was a great success—at least for many. I could hear an eager note in kids' voices as they compared results. Some were already graphing the incoming responses—circle graphs, bar graphs, line graphs—the software helped with that. "I've got to take my own survey!" said Thomas excitedly.

He asked me if I'd seen Blake on Superhero Day. "He was wearing his wrestling singlet, with tights."

"He was looking pretty cool," I said.

Thomas raised his eyebrows doubtfully.

Darryl looked up from doing something with a protractor. "I'd be like, Ah, put some clothes on."

"He was wearing a cape," said Thomas. "Well, towel."

Mackenzie said, "Everybody, announcement please. If you haven't taken our survey on Educate, we need you to take it now."

There was a group of slumpy loud girls in the back of the class who hadn't done anything. "They're probably discussing feminine things," said Thomas.

"They need to be separated," said Darryl.

"I hate separating people," I said.

"They're women, they can deal with it," said Thomas.

I went over. One of the girls, Marcy, was drawing a smoldering portrait of Ian Somerhalder, from *The Vampire Diaries*.

"Nice chin," I said.

"Ian Somerhalder is the hottest guy I've ever known. Me and him are"—she clasped her hands—"married. Married forever."

Nearby, Warren was swiping through pictures of pickup trucks, waiting for the results of his survey to come in. "My brother has a mudding truck," he said.

I asked him what his survey was about.

"Best basketball player of all time," Warren said. "Best NFL player of all time. Best soccer player. Best wide receiver. Favorite food."

"What if they don't know about sports?"

"They can just pick at random."

He'd also asked what everyone's favorite subject was. So far the results were: math, 22 percent; language arts, 0 percent; gym, 78 percent. Michael Jordan was winning the best-basketball-player question.

"We're going to get married," said Marcy to herself, as she sketched a lock of Ian Somerhalder's studiously disheveled hair.

I sat in a random chair and watched it all happen, singing Donovan's "Sunshine Superman" too softly for anyone to hear.

Ms. Nolton appeared in the doorway. "Off to your lockers!" she said.

Within thirty seconds everyone was gone.

Now it was time to pretend to be a science teacher. I found the chapter on biological classification in the Glencoe textbook, *Life's Structure and Function*, and read some of it.

"Can we take the attendance down?" asked Cheyenne and Caitlin. I gave them the signed sheet.

"OKAY, GUYS," I said. "HOOP! HIP! HOOP!" They went still. "So taxonomy. What's that about?"

"That would be a way to classify animals," said Jason. "Like if they had like the shape of a beak, we would be able to like choose different taxonomies."

I nodded. "There are certain people in this crazy world who really want to know where everything fits. And the main guy is this man"—I pointed to the picture of Linnaeus that was tacked to a bulletin board— "Linnaeus. Did you talk about him?"

"Not yet," said Lily.

"Linnaeus, about three hundred years ago, lived in Sweden—he was really smart, and he was interested in plants. He went around looking at plants. That's the first thing you have to do as a scientist, is actually look at things. And he would think, What's different about this plant? What's similar about that plant? He looked at all the living creatures and came up with a system, a way of dividing up, or classifying, all living things. What do you think he came up with? If you were a scientist, what would be the first category you'd come up with?"

"Living creatures?" said Sage.

I nodded. "You'd say everything living, and everything nonliving, that's good. And then you come down to the living things. Somebody says to you that it's terribly important, you're on a new planet, you have to classify all living things. What would you come up with?"

Long silence.

"Organisms?" said Jason.

"There are organisms. And you're looking at them. Some are big and green. Some of them are moving. They make grunting noises. Some of them fly. Some of them just sit there. How do you divide them up?"

"By the five or six kingdoms?" said Lily.

"Yes—but maybe the first thing you would do is say, 'These are plants, and these are animals.' That's the first thing that Linnaeus did, because he was a sensible guy. Very simple. And then microscopes came in. People started looking through microscopes and they realized that some things didn't look like a plant, and they didn't look like an animal. They were a blob of something that moved around under a microscope slide. So they thought for a long time. They thought, Hm, probably not a plant, probably not an animal. Probably something else. A *protist*." I wrote it on the board. "A protist just means a really little simple thing. There are all these fancy words, but basically they're just trying to figure out how life is organized." I looked down at my notes. "So then some years went by, more scientists looked at the stuff, and realized that there were many kinds of these things," I said, circling the word *protist*. "Some of them were really rare. They only found them because they went down to the bottom of the sea and found them living near the sulfur spouts at the bottom of the sea. So they came up with some rarer things." Darn, I'd forgotten their name. Don't panic. I held up the worksheet. "So you've got this worksheet, right? That says 'Classification Guide to the Kingdoms'? Do you have it?"

"No," said Jason.

"Yes, we have it," said Lily.

"Why are they called kingdoms? It's because it's like *Game of Thrones*, isn't it? Over here is the plant kingdom, and over here is the animal kingdom, and then there are these really bizarre kingdoms—there's the eubacteria kingdom. They make their own food, they're one of the oldest forms of life on Earth, they help you digest, they live in your intestine, they're small, they're disgusting. We move on. Another kingdom. The protists. The ones they saw when they looked down the tube of a microscope. And there was a controversy because of the kingdom fungi. What's a fungus? Is it among us?"

Sage raised her hand. "It's like something that feeds off dead or living plants and animals."

"Right! So if you had a mushroom here, and a weed over here, and they both pop out of the ground and they grow and they die, why would you not call both of those things plants? Or plantae, as they say? The scientists got really subtle, and they said, Well, plants use the sun to make their own food—they have chlorophyll—whereas funguses just live off of rotting stuff." I started writing on the board again, drawing lines. "They've got Animalia, just a Latin way of writing *animals*. Plants. Protists. And—what was it?"

"Eubacteria."

"Eubacteria! How do you remember that? It's hard to remember all these words."

"We have a silly sentence!" said Sage.

"No, we don't!" said Lily fiercely. "Not for those. That's how we remember the eight levels."

"Oh," said Sage.

I asked, "Did every group make a new silly sentence?"

"Yep."

"So what is the sentence that you use?"

"Donkey Kong Pays Charlie Only Five Giant Strawberries," said Sage.

"Great," I said. I looked down at my sheet. "Domain, kingdom, phylum, class, order, family, genus, species. Very useful to have that sentence. The *domain* is this giant umbrella term above everything. So that's Donkey.

And then Kong. Everything we've been talking about—plants, animals, fungi, eubacteria—all that is the kingdom level. That's the *Game of Thrones* level." I held up my finger. "There's one other kingdom, and it's kind of interesting."

Studying the packet, Lily called out, "Archaebacteria!"

I pointed at her. "Archaebacteria! When you say that something is archaic, what do you mean? Old."

"They're the oldest type," said Lily.

"Right. Archaeology is the study of old stuff—old rusting little bits of nothing that you dig up in the ground. Archaeology. So *archaebacteria* just means 'old bacteria.' In the earliest beginning of the world, when hot lava was spouting out everywhere, when the world's atmospheres were toxic and strange, there were these animals. One lives in hot springs—a bacteria that's able to live in really hot water, that's kind of amazing—and one in salty environments, like the Dead Sea. For three hundred years we've been talking about the difference between, you know, a corn plant and an oak tree. But here"—I tapped the words *archaebacteria* and *eubacteria*—"are the ones scientists are getting excited about now."

Then I decided to go AWOL from the worksheet. "Let me ask you one other really tough question. Could anyone go outside right now and know an oak tree when you saw it? Or a maple tree? Do you know the difference between them?"

"Nope," said Trinity.

"Yes, the leaves," said Luke.

"The leaves," I said. "So there's this huge scientific theory about all the living things on Earth. But usually what we need to know right here in Maine is the difference between a goldfinch, a robin, a hawk. You want to know what a moose looks like. That's the real world that we're living in. And this"—I waved the worksheet—"is the scientific world that involves all the species of the Earth. It's exhausting, actually. But once you realize that the first guy, Linnaeus, started in that simple way with just plants and animals, it makes sense. So fill out the packet and let me know if you have questions."

Trinity came up. "Can I go work in the hall?"

I told her to do the packet and then she could work in the hall.

Caitlin came up. "Can I work in the hall?"

"Buzz through this worksheet and then we'll see."

Lily came up. "Just letting you know. Mrs. Painter sent us a daily warmup that we're supposed to do. She wants it done and emailed back to her. So you may want to have everyone check their email."

"That's a very good point." I raised my voice. "Mrs. Painter has sent you an email with the daily warmup thing, and she wants it back."

I went up to Max. "Did you do the email thing?"

"I'm blocked," said Max. "I can't get email."

I told him what the email said. First list the six kingdoms. Then list the classification hierarchy. Then they had to say what a dichotomous key was, and why it was useful. "What does *dichotomous* mean?" I asked.

"I have no clue," said Max.

A wounded green tennis ball flew through the air. I ordered Devin, who'd thrown it, to put the ball back on the chair leg.

Caitlin was having trouble with Google Docs.

"Can I go get something out of my bag?" asked Devin.

I asked Lily what a dichotomous key was.

"A dichotomous key," she said, "is when you're trying to classify an animal, and it has certain features. It says, 'Pick A or B.' Say it was a cat and you picked B. Then it would say, 'Does this animal have a furry tail?'"

"Great, thanks," I said.

I walked over to Ashley, who was leaning her head on her hand doing nothing. "I can't concentrate." She was sniffly.

"Are you sick?"

"No, just a cold," she said.

I tried to get her going on the Google Doc quizlet, where she had to list the six kingdoms.

"I wasn't here for any of this," Ashley said.

I showed her where the kingdoms were listed in the packet, one at the top of each page. Caitlin came up holding a page of work. "Can I go out in the hall?" I said she could.

Everyone was having trouble defining *dichotomous key*. I couldn't blame them. "Why is it called a dichotomous key?" I said to the whole class.

"Because it is!" said Devin.

"Because scientists want to make a word no one knows?" said Ashley.

"Exactly," I said. "The scientists want to make a fancy word, because they want to sound smart."

"Yeah, and it's a pain!" said Ashley.

"Science is full of that," I said. "Doctors use fancy words like *febrile* for when you have a fever. But it's also because the words help them be more specific. So what is a dichotomous key?"

"A way to classify?" said Jason.

"It was just explained by that very smart person over there." I pointed to Lily. "All it is is a kind of flowchart. It says, Is it hairy, or is it smooth? Oh, it's hairy. Go down here."

A boy named Carl sneezed, rattling his chair.

I said, "Does it sneeze convulsively? Yes? Okay, it's Carl. That's a dichotomous key. All right? Thank you."

A neat, ponytailed girl sitting at one of the side tables, Jillian, seized her head in both hands and moaned in pain. "I'm in the middle of doing the dichotomous key, and I don't know what to do!" Part of the assignment was that they were supposed to create their own dichotomous key, in order to distinguish between an ostrich, a crab, an elephant, a fish, and a cat. She'd picked the elephant, and she'd written, "Does the organism have a long flimsy nose?"

Her friend Lindsey, in an Aéropostale shirt, who was making a dichotomous key for a cat, was farther along. Did the animal have ears or not have ears? If not, it was a fish. Was the tail long but skinny? Elephant. Was the tail long but furry? House cat.

"That's pretty good work," I said. "Seriously, that's pretty good work."

"See, that's what I'm having trouble with," said Jillian. Finally she came up with, "Does it have a long neck?"

"Ooh, yes!" I said. "You're flying now."

I went around the room lavishing praise on various half-completed dichotomous keys. "That's a seriously nice dichotomous key!" I said to Sage. "Do you know what *dichotomous* means? It just means cut in half. So you either go this way, or you go that way." I held up two fingers. "Di-chotomous. Cut in half."

Devin was poking fruitlessly at his iPad. "It's blocking my Google Doc," he said. His screen had a popup message on it: VIRUS SCAN WARNING. I told him to work on paper.

I asked Ashley how things were going. "Bad," she said. She'd gotten a D-plus on her BrainPOP quiz. On her iPad was a question about which kingdoms included eukaryotes. She had to look through the seven-page kingdom packet, I said. Each page held one kingdom.

"I have to look all through that?" she said.

"It's not that bad," I said.

"Yeah it is," said Ashley. "Look at all those words. Too many of them. I don't know where a eukaryote lives."

I started rattling around in the pages of the kingdom packet with her. "Okay, it says here that a eukaryote can be a unicellular organism. So then you go, Whoa, this is not a eukaryote, this is a prokaryote! So what's a prokaryote?" The packet defined a prokaryote as "a very simple cell." I felt a rush of exasperation. "You know what?" I said. "*Prokaryote* is one of those words you were talking about. It's a very complicated word that means 'simple.' Why do they do that to us?"

"Because they want to make money?" Ashley said.

"That's part of it," I said. I gave up. "So you've just got to poke around, look at the packet, and get familiar with it. That's how it works."

I went over to Evan, who again had a hoodie on to hide his hair. "Travis!" I said. "I know you from before. How's it going?"

"Lovely," said Evan. "He's Travis."

"I'm sorry," I said. "Every human being has a name. It's just too hard for me. Do you guys have the email from Mrs. Painter?"

"I might," said Evan. "She literally spams me with emails." He found it in his mail program.

I went back to Jillian, who'd been struggling with her dichotomous key. She recited the taxonomic ranking perfectly: "Domain, kingdom, phylum, class, order, family, genus, and species."

"Fantastic!" I said.

She'd finished her dichotomous key, too. "Now all I have to do is the packet."

Ashley had gotten a D-plus on her BrainPOP again. I'd carefully helped her find the wrong answer: it wasn't eubacteria, it was archaebacteria. "I'm sorry, that was my mistake," I said. This time she was stumped by *A vascular plant that seeds with fruits and flowers.* Together we flipped through the packet. Halfway down the Plantae page it said angiosperms *have tubes, flowers & fruits that produce seeds.* "Is it an angiosperm?" I said. She tried it on her iPad, which chirped: correct.

Jason was working on the definition of fungi. "They don't make their own food," he said. Devin and Carl were singing tunelessly.

Ashley's next iPad quiz question was: *Has cones, but no flowers or fruits.* More riffling through the packet. Was it a fern or a gymnosperm? I couldn't remember. "I'd say it's a gymnosperm," I said. "But I may be wrong." She tried it. A green checkmark appeared on the screen. Phew.

Travis and Evan were struggling with a stapler, slamming it around. "He jammed the stapler!" said Travis, whose packet had six staples in it.

"Oh, now you're blaming me!" said Evan. "I didn't even touch it!"

I asked who was good at unjamming staplers.

"I am," said Travis.

"You jammed it!" said Evan.

"That was the first time I touched it, Evan!"

"Don't throw it," I said. "It's an expensive piece of medical equipment."

Max looked up at me curiously. "It's medical equipment?"

"It is if you staple somebody with it. Like in *The Wrestler*. Did you see *The Wrestler*? He staples himself."

Lily came up. "I'm done," she said.

I said, "You are good. If you're done, what you have to do is recite a poem that you've memorized. No, do whatever you'd like to do, quietly. Congratulations on being done."

"Do you have a paperclip?" said Evan, still intent on fixing the stapler. I gave him a pair of scissors. He and Travis pried out the crumpled staple.

Luke and Carl were sharing earbuds, listening to "Truckin'" by the Grateful Dead.

Ashley finally got a passing grade on her BrainPOP. She was happy. And the stapler was working again. I got Evan and Travis to work on their Google Docs, and Travis to define *dichotomous key*. Evan successfully listed the six kingdoms. "You've done the warmup. My god, you're warmed up! Now what?"

"I get to relax for two minutes?" said Evan.

"Relax?" I said. "You just got warmed up. How many assignments are you behind?"

"Eleven," said Evan.

"I have twenty overdue things," said Travis.

"Holy crap," I said.

Caitlin came back from working in the hall. Class over.

A NEW GROUP CAME IN, leaping and screaming. "Can I take the attendance down?" said Laura.

Brittany said Alexandra would be late because she was getting an ice pack. I took attendance, shoutily.

"Can I take the sheet down?" said Brock.

"Yes."

"You said I could take it down," said Laura.

"I'm sorry," I said. "It's just too complicated." I gave the sheet to Laura. "ALL RIGHT. Mrs. Painter emailed you something terribly important.

It's a bunch of worksheets. You've got to answer some questions, and it's all about the subject of taxonomy. Do you know what taxonomy is?"

"Yep," said Georgia.

"What is it?"

"Stuffing animals."

Mandy sang, in a sweet voice, "Stuffing little dead animals."

"That's taxidermy," I said.

"Oh," said Georgia.

"So about three hundred years ago there was this guy named Carl. Carl Linnaeus. Did Mrs. Painter mention Carl Linnaeus?"

Dana, with hearing aids, pointed at his picture. "Right there."

"Right," I said. "He's one of those people who like everything to be in a certain slot. You know how some people are really organized? They can't just look at a parking lot full of cars, they have to figure out which cars have good mileage, which don't—they have to classify them. Some people have minds that work like that. Linnaeus did. He looked at the world—he lived in Sweden—"

This struck Mandy as very funny.

"He looked at the world, and he tried to figure out how living things were organized. Let's say you were Linnaeus, what would you do? What's the biggest distinction that you can find in living things? Some living things are stuck in one place, and they grow and turn green, and they have boughs. And some of them walk along, or hop, or fly. What would be the biggest distinction you could see?"

Silence.

Georgia said, "I don't know."

"Well, he took a stab at it, and he said, Okay, all living things are divided up into plants—and animals. Plantae and Animalia. Two chunks. Plants and animals. And then there were some microscopes floating around. People started looking down the tubes of the microscopes and they found that there were tiny little animals or plants—they didn't know what they were. They had one cell, and some of them moved around, and some of them had flagella that would help them move, and they thought, Gosh, is that a plant or an animal? We don't know. So they gave it a different name. *Protist.* So now you've got three." I talked about fungi—and that word, too, struck Mandy as funny. She was having a wonderful time.

When I had finished my spiel about the six kingdoms, Sunrise, who'd been standing near the desk, put her pencil in the noisy electric pencil sharpener.

"That was so considerate of you to wait," I said.

I told them what they had to do—watch a Keynote presentation on classification that Mrs. Painter had made.

An ed tech appeared, a Ms. Bishop, and began coaching a sprawly, wayward kid, Dylan. "What do you have to do?" she asked.

Dylan pointed to the whiteboard, which said, in red marker:

DUE FRIDAY
- Quizlet #4
- Brainpop—6 Kingdoms
- Kingdom Packet
- Mnemonic device
- Taxonomy key
- Darwin Finches (in class activity)

"All that stuff is due Friday!" Dylan said unhappily.

"You can only do one thing at a time," said Ms. Bishop sternly. "You can look at that list and go, 'Everything's due tomorrow!'—or you can say, 'What am I going to work on right now?' Do it, and you can cross it off the list."

Brittany said, "I'm going to do the kingdom packet, then BrainPOP, then quizlet."

"It's just relentless," I said. "The quizlets and the BrainPOPs keep popping."

Ms. Bishop made a mirthless laugh. She saw through me. She hated me.

Dana was trying to open Mrs. Painter's Keynote presentation. It wasn't working.

"I can't download it either," said Sunrise.

"A lot of kids are saying that they can't get it," said Ms. Bishop. She made an announcement. "If you can't see the Keynote, we'll make sure that Mrs. Painter knows. It's not an excuse to do nothing, though. Make sure to go on to something else."

"You have to download the Gmail app," said Mia.

"Some of the kids have restricted iPads, so they're not going to be able to download the Gmail app," said Ms. Bishop. Then she spotted something amiss. She made a beeline for Dylan, who had earbuds in.

"What are you working on?" she said.

Dylan looked up at her and plucked out an earbud. "I finished the thing," he said vaguely.

Ms. Bishop pointed accusingly at his iPad. "Busta Rhymes? You have so much work to do! You have everything done?"

"No," said Dylan.

"You're sitting here listening to music on YouTube?" She turned to me. "Mr. Baker? Dylan and I will be right back. We're going to go upstairs for a minute." She turned to the kid. "Come with me, please. Leave your iPad." They left.

"She's tough, isn't she?" I whispered.

"Yes," said Mia.

Brittany and Belle, who was growing out her bangs, came up and said they were wondering if they could go in the little room in the hall and work. "It's more quiet." I told them to blast through one of the assignments. If they did it well, they could go in the hall.

Georgia came up. "Can I work in the hall?"

"Get stuff done," I said. "If you have accomplishments, then you can work in the hall."

Alexandra was holding an ice pack on her swollen finger. "I really haven't gotten in trouble that bad this year," she said to Laura. Alec wasn't doing anything. I asked him if he'd watched the Keynote.

"My iPad is out of battery," he said.

"And you don't have a charger?"

"No."

"Is that a charger right there?"

"It's charging somebody else's."

Another kid at the table, Timothy, said, "I wasn't here for the mnemonic device."

I said, "Then don't worry about it. Just write you weren't here." I looked up. "THE NOISE LEVEL. THE NOISE LEVEL IS GETTING TOO HIGH."

Georgia came up saying she'd finished an assignment, so could she now go out in the hall? I said she could.

Belle said, "Where did my good pencil go! My mechanical pencil! Brittany! I actually wanted that pencil!"

I raised my voice again. "DID ANYONE GET THE KEYNOTE TO LOAD?"

"No."

Dana was helping Mandy do the challenge question, about the dichotomous key. "You can go, like, an animal without a backbone, and then you go off from that."

Mandy sang, "Twenty minutes to go till lunch."

I sat down on a spare chair near Brittany and Belle, who were collaborating, with mixed results, on their BrainPOP quizzes. I was losing steam. I said, "BrainPOP! BrainPOP! God."

Belle was drawing a picture of a fungus. "That's a hypha," she said.

"I want to see the Keynote real bad," I said.

"I doubt that," said Perry, who had on sunglasses.

Things were going fine with the iPads until two weeks ago, Thomas explained. "Then we got restrictions because some kids hadn't done their work. They ended up restricting half the team. Every student has complained about how the restrictions are so counterproductive. You can hardly go to half the websites."

"Exactly," said Mandy.

I was really hungry, and I began reciting the six kingdoms of crunchy snacks: the Dorito Kingdom, the Cheetos Kingdom, etc.

That reminded Thomas of something. "We did our mnemonic," he said. "Ours was 'Don't Kill Penguins Cause Other Friends Get Sad.'"

"That's brilliant," I said. "That's the best one I've seen. Do you think it's crucially important to know domain, kingdom, phylum?"

"It depends," said Thomas. "Some people want to be scientists."

Brittany said, "Some kids don't, they just don't care."

"I still think it's important, though," said Thomas. He tried to recite the list. "Domain, kingdom, phylum, class—uh." He fizzled out.

"Wait, I got this," said Belle. She closed her eyes and held her hands up. "Domain-kingdom-phylum-class-order-genus-species!" Thomas high-fived her.

Dana asked, "Can I go to the bathroom?"

"Yes."

Brittany said, "What's binomial nomenclature?"

Jeff, a low-profile kid, was tapping in answers to the BrainPOP. "How do you spell *vertebrate*?"

"You missed an *r*," I said. "V-E-R, vert. *Vert* means up and down. Vertical. Your spine is an up-and-down bone in your body." A green checkmark appeared on Jeff's screen. The next question was: *Father of taxonomy.*

Brock and Casey were deleting all their radio stations in iTunes. I asked them why.

"There's a song that's almost impossible to get," said Brock.

"But if you delete your station, then put it back on, you can get it," said Casey. The song was "Wild Boy" by Machine Gun Kelly.

A major slapdown of a notebook made me turn. A kid named Joseph was grinning crazily. "Do you know how loud that was?"

"No, I don't," said Joseph.

"It was loud," I said.

Georgia, who had returned from the hall, said, "They're boys, what are you talking about? They're all loud." She waved at Brock and Casey. "They scream at the top of their lungs."

"You don't look like screamers," I said, disingenuously.

"You don't know them very well, then," said Georgia.

"I'm a good boy," Brock said, smirking.

I asked them what they liked to eat for lunch.

"Pizza, if I can have it," said Casey. "I like cold pizza."

Sunrise finished her BrainPOP and said, "Mr. Baker, I got a D-plus."

Brock made an announcement: "Guys, it's almost lunchtime, praise the lord! Thank you, lord, for the food! Thank you, lord, for lunch!"

"You're a porta-potty," said Georgia.

"How do you spell *Jackson*?" Mandy asked.

"As in Jackson, Mississippi?" I asked.

"No."

"As in Michael Jackson?"

"Yeah."

I told her.

Time slid forward. The noise was like orange marmalade. Laura was helping Timothy spell *eubacteria* for the BrainPOP. Dana was fiddling with his dichotomous key. He was distinguishing between a penguin, a pigeon, an eagle, and a lion. If it was black and white, it was a penguin; if it wasn't, go to step two. Good. I looked at the clock. Lunch was at 11:55.

"We've got three minutes," said Laura.

"Were you tutoring Timothy?" I asked.

"Yes," said Laura.

"That was great. I really admire that, good work."

"I know, cause I'm awesome like that!" She flung her hair around.

"Well, you don't want to preen," I said.

"I'm awesome!"

I yawned. People started to ease halfway out the door. "Not quite yet," I called. "You've got two minutes."

Belle, Brittany, and Alexandra had turned the classification hierarchy into a clapping and chanting game. "We're studying," they said.

"LUNCH! LUNCH! LUNCH!" screamed Brock and Casey.

I ate an apple and sat sleepily and looked things up on the Internet. My mind and soul were dead meat. Mrs. Painter's sub plans said, "Any student who claims he/she is done can work on the remaining level 2 skills on the capacity matrix. There are plenty to choose from!" *Capacity matrix.* So much of what Mrs. Painter was required to teach was pseudo-knowledge — lists of tongue-embrambling Greek- and Latin-rooted words like *prokaryotic* and *heterotrophic* and *halophilic* that were perfect for tests because they were hard to remember. This was torture by word list. The uglier the word, the better, because it more efficiently showed who was willing to commit gobbledygook to memory and who wasn't. That was the true dichotomous key to Lasswell Middle School. (a) Is willing to master empty vocabulary week after week. (b) Is not willing. If (b), an ed tech will escort you away and fuss at you and restrict your iPad.

Pro means "before," and *karyon* is Greek for "nut." A prokaryote is a single-celled organism without a nut, or nucleus, so named by taxonomist Édouard Chatton in 1925. How helpful was that? *Many, many years ago I often went around with a sense of futility of all our efforts,* wrote a later taxonomist, in 1941. *During those periods I would go home after a day at the lab, and wish that I might be employed somewhere as a high-school teacher. Not primarily because I liked that better. But simply because it would give me some assurances that what I was doing was considered worthwhile.*

They came back. "Mr. Baker, how was your lunch?" said Brock cheerfully.

"Peachy good. How was yours?"

Casey picked a Cheeto off the floor and ate it.

"Germs!" said Georgia. "Ger-herms!"

A superball was bouncing around the classroom silently.

Ms. Bishop, the ed tech, returned. The room quieted down when she walked in the door. She leaned toward me. "The two guys that are sitting there near the back? They're looking at inappropriate stuff. So I need to have a little conversation with them."

"Okay," I said.

Brittany and Belle tried to recite the kingdoms. Brittany did it almost perfectly. "The kingdoms are: Eubacteria, Archaebacteria, prostates, Fungi, Animalia, and Plantae," she said.

"And Fungi!" said Belle.

"I pronounced one wrong," said Brittany.

"You are amazing," I said.

"I was voted by my seventh-grade class as valedictorian," Brittany said.

"I voted for her," said Belle.

"I need help," said Jeff.

The question was: *Two-word scientific name.* The answer was *binomial nomenclature.* Bingo. The next question was: *Plant that has tubes and cones.*

"That is called a *tube plant*," I said to William. "No, you need the sheet. The sheet is your friend." We found the answer. The next question was: *A kingdom of prokaryotes that live in extreme environments.*

Georgia was engaged in a hostile sort of middle school flirtation with Perry. "Perry punched me in the face," she said, laughing.

I walked over. "Is everybody happy over here? Happy stuff?"

"Yes," said Perry.

"I'm not happy!" said Georgia, hands on her hips.

I asked her to take a seat.

"What if I can't take a seat? What if this is not my chair?"

Ms. Bishop had left, so I went to the two boys in the back who'd been looking at inappropriate material. I asked what happened.

"I was being bad in the lunchroom," said Brock.

"How inappropriate is inappropriate?"

"I don't know," said Brock. "I was telling her I didn't want to do stuff and she got mad at me."

"Gymnosperm," said Sunrise. "Gym-no-sperm."

Georgia was dancing and poking at Perry.

"You've got a lot of energy today," I said.

"That's my anger," said Georgia.

"Where's your chair?"

"A ghost stole it."

I showed Perry the classification packet, page by page, and did a question with him so he knew how it worked. "Just fill this out and you'll have a world of knowledge at your fingertips," I said. "Do you want a cheese cracker?"

"No, thanks," said Perry.

I popped a cracker in my mouth. "Are you having fun?"

"No."

"Why not?"

"It's science!"

"Would you have more fun if it was math?"

"Yeah," said Perry. "Science has always been my weak subject."

"Do you like trucks? What do you like?"

"Fast cars."

He stuffed his earbuds in to get rid of me.

"Have fun with it," I said. "Fast cars and music, you can't go wrong with that."

I circulated three more times and poured myself some coffee. Suddenly, unexpectedly, the class began to leave. I must have been in a fugue state. "Bye, have a good one," I said.

"SO HELLO!" I SAID, to the next crew of twenty-two. "Hello, hello, hello. Taxonomy. Today it's all about taxonomy. If you were beamed down from a spaceship—first of all, you would NOT HAVE AN IPAD CASE to fling around and hit somebody with. If you were beamed down from a spaceship into a foreign planet—"

"I was!" said Owen.

"That's clear," I said. "And you landed, and you asked, 'How do I make sense of this planet?' what would you do? You'd have to look at all the growing things, all of the things that are alive, and you'd have to figure out how to classify them. If you came to this planet, what would be maybe the biggest distinction you could see?"

"Biggest distinction?" asked Caleb, with his chin on his hand. "That there's life."

"Right. Then basic things, like there's plants on the one hand, and animals on the other hand."

"And fungi!"

"So when Carl Linnaeus— GUYS! PLEASE! When Carl Linnaeus started to classify things, he did it just the way anybody in this room would do it. He looked around and said, Okay, the big distinction is between . . . ," etc. Then came the microscopes and etc. Kingdom packet etc. "So do the stuff that Mrs. Painter sent you, and you'll be very happy. And so will Mrs. Painter. And so will I."

"I forgot my charger in the last classroom," said Caleb. "Can I go get it?"

I heard more silly sentences. Dogs Kick Penguins Climbing Off From Giant Skyscapers. Dolphins Kill People Cause Of Fluffy Girl's Sweaters. Don't Kick Pink Cats Or Fun Guys Slaughter.

"Protista is my favorite of all the kingdoms," said Caleb, plugging his iPad into the wall. "It sounds Italian."

Sydney came up to describe her homework success. "I did mine on Notability, and I put it in Google Drive, and I put it on my iPad, and then I went onto my house computer, and took it out, and I did it, then I emailed it. My dad is a computer person."

Cayden said, "We can't get into the Keynote."

"Nobody's able to get into it," I said.

"Oh, okay."

"Wait, what are we supposed to do?" said Regan. Kingdom packet, kingdom packet, kingdom packet. I studied some plants growing in one of the aquariums.

"I'd be careful," said Cayden. "There might be a hornet in there. Last year I was in a science class with Miss Basset, and every day there would be two or three hornets in there. And it was my job to water them."

"Did you ever get stung?"

"No, I had one of them come this close to my face," said Cayden. "They kind of blend in with the plants. Owen! I need my pencil!"

"Are you making any progress?"

"I'm going to," said Cayden.

"I bet you are. Taxonomy. Not taxidermy."

"Taxidermy would be so fun!"

Owen sharpened a pencil for a full minute. "Can I go to my locker?" he asked. "My iPad's dead."

"That's because he doesn't charge it at home," said Jenn, who was smart and thin-boned and easily distracted. She was catching up, doing an old worksheet on binomial nomenclature. She had to use a key to figure out the scientific names for blue jay and Virginia waterleaf—*Cyanocitta cristata* and *Hydrophyllum virginianum*.

Chase and Caleb recited the taxonomic ranks. I nodded and gave them a thumbs-up. I said, "Think if you wanted to know about cars, and the first thing they did is say cars are all classified in this crazy way: *Hubcapia frontlightia*. What if you thought, I really love cars and I really love a certain kind of car?"

"The Ferrari Spider!" said Chase.

"You could become the world's expert in the Ferrari Spider without knowing the slightest bit about how cars are classified!" I said.

Chase was not interested in my disgruntled theorizing. "What's your favorite car?" he said.

"The one I'd buy right now is the Fiat," I said.

"I'd buy a DeLorean," said Chase. "And not just because of *Back to the Future*. Just because it's cool."

"It makes too much noise," said Mackenzie.

"And the engine stinks," said Caleb.

Chase showed me a picture of a Ferrari Spider. Then he said, "Jade! What are you doing?"

I went over to Jade and said, "I was sent over here to find out what you were doing, by certain of your colleagues."

"What's a colleague?" said Jade.

"A person you work with. Your schoolmates, your colleagues." I turned to Owen. "Are you a member of the Animalia kingdom?"

"No," said Owen. "I'm a eubacteria."

Mackenzie asked Chase how many questions he'd done for the archaebacteria page.

"Three," said Chase.

"There is no question three!" said Mackenzie. "It goes one, two, four, five." She laughed. "Three!"

Caleb said, "I found it. I found the Keynote."

"Seriously?" I said. "Damn. Nobody's gotten into it. Or at least they pretend they can't get into it."

Caleb began untangling his earbuds so he could hear the audio track that went along with the slides.

Marcy announced that she'd already listened to the Keynote. "I'm all caught up. Now I'm working on another level-two skill."

Chase showed me a 1929 Bugatti pedal-powered toy car, for sale for thirteen thousand dollars. "In Europe I saw a whole museum of stuff like that," he said.

Jade asked Chase how to answer a question about vascular plants.

"You're the smart one," Chase said. "You should know about that."

"About taxomony?" she said incredulously.

"Look at the Bugattis after you've finished your worksheet," I said to Chase. I watched him answer a question on the BrainPOP and then swipe back to the Bugatti page. "If you could do anything right now, what would you do?"

"Go to Burger King," said Chase.

"Do you have a long bus ride?"

"About forty-five minutes."

I asked him what the hardest part of the day was for him.

"Math," said Chase. "She handed us a test."

Darryl whooped; she'd gotten a right answer on her BrainPOP.

"The hardest part of my day," I said, "is when people start to get really noisy, and I can't get them to be quiet."

Chase said that Mr. Hansen had that same problem in English class.

Mackenzie and Jenn were taking selfies.

"My mom ran over my iPhone," said Jade, who was wearing Daffy

Duck pajama bottoms. "After she took my phone away, she ran it over. By 'accident.'"

I said that I'd dropped mine in the toilet.

"My mom did that," said Jade.

"Let me see," said Chase. He inspected the cracks on my phone, then handed it back to me. "Oh, wow, my Safari just logged out," he said. "Let's attempt to get it back."

"What did he call me?" said Jenn. "Sydney. SYDNEY! What did he call me?"

Sydney didn't want to say.

"She screams like a banshee," said Chase.

"Don't pull on people's clothes," I said to Jenn.

"Banshee," said Chase.

"I sense that things are falling apart," I said.

"Don't mind them," said Jade.

"Well, it's getting towards the end of the day," I said.

Jade said, "Everyone just wants to go, Whoop, out of here!" She started wrestling with her clothes and giggling. She held up a dry-erase marker.

"I threw it at her, and then it went down her shirt," said Owen.

"GUYS, THE NOISE LEVEL. BRING IT DOWN. BRING IT DOWN."

"Sorry, Mr. Baker," said Jade. She and Owen briefly struggled, trying to sit in the same seat.

"No, no," I said. "No."

"Sit next to Jenn," said Owen, "or in your own seat."

Jade wanted to sit next to Chase. She moved to an unoccupied seat.

"What scientific conclusions can you draw about this class right now?" I asked her.

"You can look at where they're grouped," said Jade. "Jenn would go with Chase, and those three would stay together. Mackenzie would go with them. Darryl would stay with them. Marcy would also go with them. And Sydney would go with them."

"What are you doing?" said Caleb.

"He asked me to classify the class," said Jade.

"Any unknown species?" said Caleb.

Chase asked me, "What's the function of a eubacteria?"

"It doesn't do a damn thing," I said. "No, it breaks stuff down, doesn't it?"

Chase began showing Sydney how to fold her lip down.

"I can't do it," said Sydney.

"Just fold your lip down! It's not hard, look!" He made a bizarre lip face and got a laugh.

Jade looked at the archaebacteria questions and sighed. "What's the answer to this one?" she asked Chase.

"You're the smart one," said Chase.

Jade turned to me. "Can you just like give me the answers and I'll write them down?" she said to me.

"I think you should do what you've got to do," I said.

I sat down in a different chair. "Are you here tomorrow?" asked Regan.

I said I was. "What that means, I don't know." I was making him nervous. "I won't sit next to you if you don't want me to. I'm just circulating. I'm like a little blood cell. Meanwhile you're busy." I looked at all the pencil writing on his kingdom packet. "I see massive progress."

Mackenzie said, "We're all really stressed out right now. We have so much homework. All these level-two things."

Kyle was passing the time by pretending to stab himself in the eye with his pencil. I looked at his packet. He'd answered question one on the protist page: *How are Protists, Archaebacteria, and Eubacteria the same? Different?* He'd written, *They have one cell.* He was stuck on the differences.

Owen's BrainPOP test crashed and he lost all his answers. He began it again.

"What are we doing tomorrow?" asked Caleb.

I looked at the whiteboard. "Tomorrow you're doing the finch exercise."

Jade said, "We could take a picture of all these people, and then write, *weird, awkward, short,* and *tall.*"

"You wouldn't want to make personal remarks, would you?" I said.

"That's why I didn't go with *sexy*, I went with *tall*, because he's tall."

Chase, who was pleased to be called tall, said, "I'm a socially awkward entrepreneur."

Jade started taking pictures with her iPad.

"No, no," I said. "Jade, hold it together. There's five more minutes."

Worse things were happening on the other side of the class: Darryl, Mackenzie, and Marcy had Sharpies out and they were marking each other with dots on the small of their backs. I got them to cut it out and took a bite from the unbitten side of my apple.

Owen sharpened his pencil aggressively. He checked the point. "There we go!" he said.

Music wafted from an iPad. Pictures were taken and discussed. Chase was a hub of activity. Darryl sang, "Eight six seven five three oh nigh-ee-ine." The whole class began singing it. I began singing it.

The PA lady came on. "Good afternoon, please excuse the interruption for the afternoon announcements." Intramurals. Drama rehearsal. The movie *Frozen*. Cameroon. Nobody listened.

"Thank you, Mr. Baker," said Chase. "You're going to be here tomorrow, right?"

"Yeah, I'll see you tomorrow."

Caleb said, "Thank you for your time."

"Thank you for your time!" I said back.

"I finished the test!" said Owen.

"He did not finish the test!" said Kyle.

"I did finish it! I finished it twice."

I suddenly thought, I love these kids. I really love these kids.

End-of-day homeroom. Brock came flying in with his arms out singing, "Humpty Dumpty sat on a wall!"

Jeff walked in looking worried. "Did you find a paper on the ground with my name on it? It said 'Jeff Lamarchais' on it and it said '*Frozen* movie' on it?" I hadn't. He hunted worriedly around the desks for the permission slip and then left.

Georgia walked in, saw the empty room, and said, "Everyone went away!" She left. A moment later the room was crowded again. Then it was empty.

"Brock, you're in trouble," called Marcy.

"What did I do now?" The room was full again and wild and loud. What the hell, it was Pajama Day.

I asked Luke what the highlight of his day had been, seriously.

Luke didn't want to say.

Evan said, "He sat with his girlfriend at lunch."

"'Girlfriend,'" said Luke bashfully. "Heh-heh."

Chair stacking. The first-wave kids left. Next to the door, where I stood, was posted the middle school dress code. Forbidden were short shorts, tank tops, belly shirts, basketball shirts without an undershirt, spaghetti straps, tube tops, spandex, spiked dog collars, spiked wristbands, bandannas, and pajamas.

Darryl, Mackenzie, Georgia, and Cheyenne, all dressed in pajamas, came in and put on One Direction. "This is the song we were telling you about!" said Mackenzie.

"Nice," I said.

Then they put on a beautiful John Legend song, "All of Me." They boosted the volume by putting the iPhone in a plastic cereal bowl and began singing along: "My head's underwater, but I'm breathing fine!" They moved their heads and held their arms out and swayed. "You're crazy, and I'm out of my mind!" They carried the bowl full of music away with them.

The PA lady came on. "Please excuse the interruption. For those of you who are staying for the student council's showing of the movie *Frozen*, to benefit the Tara School in Cameroon, we're going to begin calling down teams. But just a quick reminder that all school rules apply. There is no taking of any pictures. On your way down to the cafeteria to view the movie, please stop by the library and drop your bags and your iPads off, as you typically do for dances. With that said, could all student council members and Team Nile students who are staying for the movie please make your way to the cafeteria."

Cheyenne had done her hair in a new way, pulling it to the side. "Does this look totally unnatural?" she said. "Be honest with me."

"Yes," said Brock.

"It looks like you blow-dried your hair," said Georgia. "It looks really good."

The PA lady came back on. "Team Orinoco students attending the movie can make their way to the cafeteria."

"I want to get good seats," said Cheyenne. Everyone rushed off.

An excited roar came from the hallway. The full reality of what was about to happen was beginning to register. In the darkness of the cafeteria they were going to watch a beloved movie, and everyone would be wearing pajamas. It was a sort of sleepless best-friend sleepover involving hundreds of people.

When everyone was gone I went to the office. "You survived!" said the assistant principal.

"I'm in one piece," I said. I drove home.

Day Ten, over.

SHE STOLE MY GRAPE

On Friday, an early-release day, I drove to the middle school thinking about my eighth-grade science teacher, Mr. James, a kindly red-haired man with tinted aviator glasses and muttonchop sideburns and a handlebar mustache. Eighth grade in my section of the city was taught at Monroe High School, a brick monster of a place with guards in the hallways. Mr. James made us memorize the taxonomic rankings, and he taught us the classification kingdoms, but there weren't six of them back then, and they had different names, except for plants and animals. For reasons I couldn't fathom, Mr. James liked to hang out with the English teacher, Mr. Dean, who had slicked-back hair and a bunchy jaw muscle. Once I took a shortcut to my place in the cafeteria by walking over an empty lunch table. It took only a second. I sat down quickly, hoping that nobody had seen me, but knowing that I'd just done something very wrong and very stupid. A minute went by and I thought I was in the clear. Then I felt a hand take hold of my hair, which was long, and yank my head up hard. It was Mr. Dean, the English teacher, smiling a cruel smile. "You think that's funny?"

"No." My hair was held tight in his fist, pulling me up straight.

"I don't want to ever see you do that again."

"Okay."

He let go of my hair and walked away. I saw him across the room, talking to Mr. James and pointing to me.

Because Mr. Dean hated me, my mother talked to the principal and got me moved to a different section at Monroe, with four new eighth-grade teachers. My new science teacher wasn't nearly as good as Mr. James, but my new English teacher, Mr. Toole, was smart. He winked a lot, and he said I should buy a book of poems called *Reflections on a Gift of Watermelon Pickle*. I memorized a poem in it by William Jay Smith. Mr. Toole wore a three-piece gray suit every day, and he liked Shakespeare. He told me and my friend Nick, who was from Aberdeen, Scotland, to build a scale model of the Globe Theatre, instead of reading *To Kill a Mockingbird* for a month with the rest of the class. So we got to work. We found some Elizabethan plans and we used Popsicle sticks and toothpicks and pinkish plaster of Paris and made a horrible-looking likeness of the Globe Theatre that sat, quietly shedding bits of plaster, in the project room. We didn't read any Shakespeare. Later Mr. Toole told us to read Homer's *Iliad* and write an epic poem of our own. We did that, too. Mr. Toole was the best teacher I had, and he changed my life.

"HOW ARE YOU DOING, MR. BAKER?" said Brock in Mrs. Painter's homeroom. It was the last day, or half day, of Spirit Week: everyone was supposed to wear green and white, the school colors. Brock, Casey, and Joseph wore black hoodies and sat in a row—I told them they looked like the Supreme Court. The class was still hopped up from Pajama Day and singing snatches of songs. "Tomorrow, tomorrow, I love you, tomorrow!" sang Sunrise, who was dressed as somebody from *The Vampire Diaries*. She held out a handful of markers and asked me to choose my preferred color. I picked blue. On the whiteboard, she wrote "MR. BAKER IS HERE!" and decorated my name with blue flowers and stylized Smurfs.

"It smells like that weird hairspray," said Casey. He was looking at a Vine video.

The sub plans said, "Students are expected to be working, reading, or socializing quietly. They may use their iPads quietly." Brittany helped me take attendance.

"I have another song," said Sunrise, twirling. "Somewhere, over the rainbow!" Then she stopped. "Mr. Baker, Joseph has to leave, he's not in this homeroom."

"Joseph has to leave?"

Joseph slowly got up and slung on his backpack, shooting me a dirty look.

"Hey, I'm sorry, it's not my rule!" I said.

"I know," said Joseph.

Bong, bong, bong. The PA lady said, "Please excuse the interruption. Please stand and say with me." Pledge. We sat down. The lunch menu was "shaved turkey and cheese on a roll, wango mango juice or dragon punch, Goldfish crackers, fresh apple, mayo or mustard, and milk." No milk choices today, just milk. Drama rehearsals and girls' lacrosse tryouts were coming up. Numeracy students were to report to room 127. "Best of luck to Lee Baskin, who is representing LMS today at the state National Geographic GeoBee."

STAR time followed: delightful silence. One whispered question from Evan: "Can I use the restroom?"

"Of course."

The phone rang. Ashley was supposed to be in Mrs. Rivers's literacy class and she wasn't. She wasn't in my STAR class, either.

After half an hour, Mrs. Elton, the technology specialist, came by, per the sub plans, to do an "enrichment activity." She was wearing a red jacket with gold buttons over her giant bosom and had gold dangly earrings on her ears and she held a huge cup of Dunkin' Donuts coffee. She stood in the middle of the room. "Okay, guys, let's finish up with our reading," she said. "Today we're playing a group activity game called Spaceteam. Spaceteam is an app, which we turn our Bluetooth on to use. Who has seen *Star Trek*?"

Hands went up.

"You know when they're yelling out orders to each other—'Asteroid!'—and all that? This reminds me of *Star Trek*. You have to do different things on your iPad to adjust for, for example, an asteroid coming. They ask you to shake your iPad until it's safe. It's about taking orders, telling your team what the orders are, and they tell you what the orders are. So it's more or less about team-building, about direction-following, and a little bit about space." She divided the class into groups of four and explained the workings of the game. "You have to hold down on the green thing," she said. "You have to yell out orders to everyone."

The class stared at their iPads and began yelling orders to their teammates. *Ignite the grid saucer! Disengage the heliocutter! Activate rotogrid! Abort now! Asteroid, asteroid! Shake!*

"Are you guys getting the hang of it?" asked Mrs. Elton. I looked up Spaceteam, billed as a "cooperative shouting game." It looked like a clever, funny indie game, designed by a former team member at BioWare, but it was premised on rising tension and massive noise, and a class full of four groups of shouting Spaceteamers got unbearably loud fairly quickly. I sat watching the chaos grow, and I discovered that I disliked Mrs. Elton, this untalented gifted-and-talented specialist who had torn into the silence of my STAR class and made everyone play a game that forced them to yell nonsense instructions at each other under the aegis of "team-building." I wasn't the only one who was upset. Ms. Nolton from next door poked her head in and said, "Hey, guys—GUYS. Can I have your attention for a quick moment? I don't want to be mean or anything, but you guys are *really loud*. I've got a couple of people finishing up their testing in here. You guys are working really hard, and I hear good conversation, but since you're working in groups, can you keep the voices down?"

"They're playing an app like *Star Trek* where they have to yell out orders to teammates," Mrs. Elton explained. "It's a yelling game."

"Oh," said Ms. Nolton.

"We'll keep it quieter."

There was, of course, no way to keep it quieter. Even so Mrs. Elton began shushing everyone. "Girls, girls, quietly. Shh!"

"Activate saucer," said Chase.

"Who has green hair?" Jade said.

"SHH!" said Mrs. Elton. "What did we just say about yelling? Not appropriate."

Ms. Nolton opened her door again to say that her class was done testing.

"You heard it," said Mrs. Elton. "They're done testing!" A noise typhoon followed.

"Once you get to level six you get to shop and buy things," Mrs. Elton said, amid the yelling. "This is a good homeroom activity."

Class time was running out; iPads were zipped shut. Nobody had made out very well, and they'd had trouble sounding out the technobabble commands. "Okay, you guys pulled it together as a team, nice leadership here!" said Mrs. Elton. "GUYS, I want you to try this sometime, invite your friends to play with you. Some kids tell me they play on the bus. I don't know how they do that. A couple kids said they were going to play it in homeroom. Remember, if you get up to level six, you get to add more players, and you get to go shopping." Then she got severe. "I don't want you to be standing! It's not time to go yet! Did you have a good time?"

"Yeah," said Jason.

Thomas said, "One thing I noticed is that they sent different commands to both players."

"Yep, that is a challenge," said Mrs. Elton.

The PA lady came on. "Bridget Rice to the office, please."

"Goodbye, Mr. Baker," said Mrs. Elton.

"Take it easy, Mrs. Elton," I said.

"Engage the wormhole," said Dabney. "We were so close!"

Ms. Nolton appeared. "Sorry about that," I said. "They were all totally silent, and then she said, 'Okay, you're going to play a game that involves shouting.' I thought, Oh, okay."

"Wonderful," said Ms. Nolton. "The kid who had to make up his test still improved his score. It wasn't a huge deal."

I had a break from 8:26 to 9:13. I sat and breathed and thought of the way some people walk dogs. Some yank the leash to make the dog heel, and some let the dog smell the smells.

EVENTUALLY SOME STUDENTS gathered from the hall. I asked Perry what he was doing in Language Arts.

"We're making stories."

"Adventure narratives?"

"Um." He thought. "Fiction."

Alexandra and Brittany were discussing the merits of Vaseline as a lip gloss.

"Can I take the attendance down?" asked Brock. I said he could, but it was early yet. "Did you do the Brainplop, blah blah blah?"

"No," said Brock.

Georgia flumped in. "What are we doing today?"

"Brainplop, blah blah blah," said Brock.

Thomas told me that he'd watched the Keynote the night before.

A kid named Curtis said, "I'm not sure why I'm in here."

"I don't know why I'm in here either," I said. "What are you thinking about today?"

Georgia said, "I'm thinking about how I hate the tech teacher. We just hate each other. On his test today, I wrote *I don't know* for half the answers. And he hates me now, so I hate him."

I asked what kind of tech class it was—computers?

"Engines, cars, robotics, stuff like that," said Georgia.

"That could be interesting," I said.

"If the teacher was more interesting. Mr. Sterling hates me and my sister, and she's eighteen."

I signed the attendance sheet and sent it on its way. Then I threw my arms wide. "HAVE A SEAT, GUYS, IT'S CHAIR TIME."

"Share time?" said Casey.

"Chair time, green chair time," I said. "The classification of the entire universe is what we're looking at—again. And she's emailed you something exciting."

"Is it exciting exciting?" said Thomas. "Or are you just saying it's exciting so we do it?"

Joseph said, "It's boe-ring."

"It's about something interesting," I said. "It says, *List the six kingdoms.* You remember those archaebacteria that live in the saline solutions and they can withstand boiling water? That's pretty amazing. And then you have to do one more thing. You have to list one characteristic that each kingdom has. Like they might be unicellular, or they might be, whatever. That's for ten minutes. Ten happy minutes of doing the daily warmup from Mrs. Painter. So get the email, and warm it up! Then there's this thing called the Darwin's Finch Activity, that will just keep you laughing and happy."

William looked confused. I said, "Do you have that sheet that everyone's been flinging around for days?"

"This one?" said William, holding it up.

"Yes."

There was jabbering to my right. "She stole my grape," said Jeff.

Belle laughed.

I asked about their daily warmup.

"I already did that," said Belle.

"Did that," said Jeff.

"All I can say is, Gasp," I said. "Why don't you do six BrainPOPs and a squat thrust."

"*What* are we doing today?" asked Perry.

"Did you get the email from Mrs. Painter?"

"Yep."

"Did you answer the questions?"

"Yep."

"Then basically all you have to do is sit and zone out for the next five minutes till the other people are done."

He pulled out a muffin and began eating it.

"I broke my bagel chip," said Brock.

An iPad charging cord took flight. "Nothing needs to fly through the air," I said. "Just sit and do the warmup. It's a warmup! That's all it is!"

I went back to William. The question he had to answer was *Choose two traits that best describe the kingdom Protista.* I showed him the section of the packet that described the characteristics of Protista. "Can you graze your eyeballs over that paragraph?"

"They're gooey," said Dana, who'd been listening.

"What are?"

"Eyeballs."

"They're like saliva," said William.

"The Internet is very slow today," said Thomas. "I'm waiting for Portaportal to come up."

Georgia said, "Wait, *what* are we supposed to be doing?"

"The Internet is not working," said Brittany.

In a robot voice, Alexandra read: *"How—are—fungi—different—from—plants?"* Then she said, "Ugh!"

"Who knows about the Darwin finch activity?" I asked the class. "It's due *today.* Darwin owned a lot of finches, and he started measuring their beaks. He was trying to figure out how beaks would change shape based on what they ate. If they had to eat big, hard, hairy nuts—"

Brittany started laughing.

"—they had to crunch down on them hard, and they had to evolve a different shape of beak. So there's an activity where you measure the beak. Does that ring a bell?"

Timothy said, "I failed the quizlet because I had one spelling error."

"Don't step on my ring!" said Mandy.

I went over to a table where Jeff, Belle, and Dana were working. "This warms my heart," I said. "This guy's doing Darwin's finch! Measuring the beak!"

Belle was drawing some lifelike microorganisms, with spikes and squirmy mitochondria. "Whoa, those are some nasty cells," I said, approvingly.

Georgia said, "I have a question. Did you use to be a hippie when you were younger? You seem really like the hippie type."

In the seventies, I said, in high school, everybody was a hippie. "I had long hair. It's gone now, but that's what happens."

"Just the way you talk," Georgia said, "the way you choose to word things—you seem like a hippie. It's not a bad thing."

"Sometimes I get in a mood where I don't know why certain things are being studied," I said. "And yet they are being studied, and my job is to make them be studied. And then I get a conflicted feeling."

Jeff and Belle started tussling over a shared iPad.

"No physical struggling," I said.

"I wonder how many next assignments I have," said Belle.

"A lot," said Jeff.

"What happens to your iPad when you miss assignments? They confiscate it and blow it up, don't they?"

"They actually do something worse," said Jeff. "They make it so you can barely use it. This is all I have." He showed me his iPad, which had three lonely apps left on the screen. "I'm twenty-one assignments behind. It's because when I had my iPad wiped, I lost a bunch of them. It had a bug and it couldn't update, so they had to wipe it."

"So are you just going to burn through them and catch up, or you going to figure this year's blown, lost?"

"Blown," said Jeff.

I looked over Alexandra's shoulder. She'd answered a question correctly with the word *invertebrates*.

"Nice going," I said. I stood for a while, thinking. "It's amazing. I think that nobody's understanding, but gradually it sort of happens, like magic."

Across the room, somebody said, "Casey, I do *not* appreciate that kind of language coming out of your mouth."

Georgia said, "Thermophiles live in hot springs."

"You ate my grape," said Jeff to Belle.

"I'm sure you didn't need it," said Belle.

"I needed it for starvation and energy."

Thomas was stumped by a question: *Name three animals that are classified as platyhelminthes.*

"Flatworms," I said. "In high school they used to have to cut the platyhelminthes in half, and then they'd watch them grow the other half. That's the kind of sick stuff you do in high school."

"Like when you burn magnesium, to prove a metal can be burnable," said Thomas.

Georgia said, "Have you ever listened to the band Never Shout Never? They're indie. Listen to them. They're awesome."

"We've got to get ready to go to the next class," said Thomas.

I stood up. "That went by in a twinkling!" I said to the whole class. "Guys, you were so good, you actually got work done, thank you so much!"

BLOCK THREE ARRIVED. Jade and Caleb were already trading insults. "ALL RIGHT, TAKE IT DOWN, TAKE IT DOWN. Take it all the way down."

"Caleb," said Owen. "Take it ALL the way down."

I said, "Mrs. Painter has been kind enough to email every single one of you two emails. One of them says what you're supposed to do, which is a ten-minute warmup, and one of them IS the warmup. The Darwin finch activity is kind of neat. There's little green triangles and you get to resize them. Does anyone like resizing little green triangles?"

"Not really," said Owen.

"Well, you might find you do if you try it. Finish it, and you will be content, and we can talk."

"Cool," said Chase.

"Cool beans," said Darryl.

I walked around pointing at people. "Make sense? Everything's making sense?"

"I worked on the quizlet for like an hour, just trying to get everything correct," said Cayden. She opened the kingdom packet. "Oh my god, I'm never going to get this!" I got her going on archaebacteria.

"I finished the warmup," said Jade. "I'm a science nerd."

Kyle was trying to buy a pair of headphones from Luke with a five-dollar bill.

"I'm done with my level twos," Luke said.

"Are you some kind of a prodigy?" I handed him the book of science questions. "Do me a favor. Pick one question in this book that interests you, and show it to me."

"Fungi!" said Kyle.

"Do you like mushrooms on your pizza?" I asked him.

"Not really," said Kyle. "I like steak and cheese."

"Animalia is multicellular?" said Jenn, surprised.

I said, "You're an animal, right? And you've got a lot of cells. So you're multicellular, bingo."

"Oh, yeah," Jenn said. "A worm doesn't have a backbone?"

"Right. It's just pure muscular worminess."

Mackenzie couldn't get on the quizlet. "I got on it yesterday, and I tried again today and I couldn't."

"There's a lot of testing going on today, so the Internet is slow," I said.

BrainPOPs, Portaportal. Quizlet. Wi-Fi. BrainPOP. Packet. I told Darryl her voice was too loud.

"I know," said Darryl. "I'm just born to be loud. Kyle has a squeaky voice. I used to be like that."

"I want to see incredible progress," I said. "Just burn rubber."

"It's so hard on a half day," said Darryl. "Can I do cartwheels?"

"No."

Owen, sitting next to Regan, shouted, "Every one that he gets wrong, I get right!"

"Is everyone having fun, though?" I said.

"Yes," said Owen.

"You know what I'm doing tonight that's fun?" said Regan. "I'm going to a concert. And then on July eighth, I'm going to see Yes."

"I'm never going to get this done!" said Cayden, bouncing the palm of her hand on the top of her head.

Laughter from Owen about the BrainPOP: "He got the same ones wrong *again*!"

"I just spelled them wrong," said Regan, pacing around in circles. "I misspelled *vertebrate*. I used *chart* instead of *key*. So I got it right. I'm not doing it again. It's disgusting. I'm *not* doing it again!" He threw his iPad case in the trash.

"You know what," said Cayden. "I'm just going to do it in Connecticut. I have a long car ride, I'm just going to do it then."

"It is technically due today," I said.

"But we don't have class Monday."

"Oh, okay," I said. "What should we do right now?"

"Can we make one of those bombs out of baking soda?" said Jade.

"No, I don't think we should make bombs." Luke handed me back the question book, *How Come? Planet Earth*. "I'm going to ask some questions," I said. And if the question seems interesting to you, then say, 'I want to hear more about that question.' All right?"

"Sure!"

I read, *"How do cows digest their food?"*

"They gnaw it and they burn it in their stomachs," said Jade.

"Achaebacteria in their stomachs!" said Luke.

I said, "How do cats purr? There's another question. Why do they purr?"

"Sometimes they're stressed," said Darryl.

"Here's another good one," I said. *"How come so many animals have tails and we don't?"*

"To keep their balance," said Jade.

"That's good, like squirrels, when they're running up a tree. What are some other reasons?"

"When they're running fast, it helps them turn," said Dabney.

"Good. So here's what the super-scientific dude who wrote this, Kathy Wollard, says. *The fact is tails come from the sea. Scientists believe that life started in the ocean.* Don't talk. Be quiet. *Long before there were land animals, there were primitive fish. Fish evolved with tails because tails allowed them to move easily through the water.* Can everyone sit down? SIT DOWN."

"Kyle, sit," said Mackenzie.

I kept reading. "*Over time, tails specialized to do different things in different animals. Meanwhile, creatures like us that had no use for tails evolved tailless.* But you've got a tailbone, right? Once I had a sledding accident, I came off a hill and I came down, and my tailbone hurt so badly I don't even want to talk about it."

"I did that," said Jade.

"Oh my god!" said Darryl. "I hate it when the bone right there breaks in two. That happened to me."

"Ouch. *But before we're born, each human embryo—* Guys, dang. Dang."

"I like this, this is interesting, guys," said Chase.

"No it's not," said Sunrise.

I laughed. "Thank you. *Before we're born*—this is the crucial thing! *Before we're born, each human embryo repeats some of our evolutionary history. Tiny embryos start out with gill slits like fishes—*"

Owen was talking.

"We're LEARNING in here," said Darryl.

"Words are actually flying out of my mouth and going into people's ears," I said.

Caleb said, "If you guys be quiet, I'll give you a Jolly Rancher, okay?"

"Okay, I'll be quiet," said Owen.

"*And by their fourth week of development, human embryos have little tails.* So when you're a tiny infant in your mother's womb, you actually have a tail. Isn't that bizarre?"

"Not infant, fetus," said Luke.

"Jason had a tail," said Jade.

I said, "That's enough about tails, I think. Let's learn another fact, shall we?"

"No-ho-ho-ho!" said Sunrise, putting her head in her arms and pretending to weep.

"Maybe that's enough for now," I said. "Do you think that's enough? I could do *Why do animals become extinct?*" No interest. I flipped through the book some more. "*Why do fingers get wrinkled after soaking in water for a long time?*"

"It's like a prune!" said Owen.

"It's to increase their grip," said Jade.

"I don't believe that," I said.

"I read that somewhere," Jade said. "I don't remember where, but I read it."

A Jolly Rancher fell on the floor. Kyle made a lunge for it and put it in his mouth.

"That's messed up," said Caleb.

"I picked up a lollipop off the ground," Owen said.

"Ew!"

"You don't eat lollipops you find on the ground," Jade said.

"It was wrapped in plastic," said Owen.

"Okay, here's the answer to wrinkly fingers," I said. "*On hands and feet, skin is quite thick,*" I read. "*Submerge your hands, and the protein of the epidermis will slowly soak up six to ten times its own weight in water.* My gosh. *As the epidermis swells and swells, it pulls away from the dermis and folds into ridges and furrows.*"

"For gripping!" Jade insisted.

I said, "Not—well, okay, for gripping."

Meanwhile, rummaging in the bookcase, Darryl had discovered a different book of weird facts. "This is cool, can I read this?" she said. I told her to turn toward the class and circulate, and wave her arms around to get their attention.

"Circulate!" said Jade.

"I already read all those books," said Kyle.

Darryl read: "*Slugs have three thousand teeth and four noses.*"

"Huh!" Sunrise said, with faux amazement.

"*Writers once used bread crumbs instead of erasers to correct pencil mistakes,*" Darryl read.

"Wow!" said Sunrise.

"*A camel doesn't sweat until its body temperature reaches a hundred and six Fahrenheit.*"

"Wow!"

"That was awesome," said Chase. It wasn't clear if he was mocking or not.

Jade, tapping a page she'd found in another book, whispered to me: "Improved grip."

Darryl read, "*A baseball will travel farther in hot weather than in cold weather. Why is that?*"

"Because heat rises," said Owen. "And the bat's softer."

"Oh," said Darryl.

"Is it because the molecules are farther apart in the air?" I said.

"It doesn't have as much stuff to push against," said Luke.

"*The largest dinosaurs were vegetarian,*" Darryl read.

"See that," I said, "if you eat vegetables, you're going to become huge."

"*Panda droppings—or crap—can be made into paper,*" Darryl read.

"Crap, or scat," Owen said loudly.

"*It would take a jumbo jet about a hundred and twenty billion years to fly across the Milky Way Galaxy,*" Darryl read.

"I love Milky Ways," said the lollipop kid, Owen.

Jade stood and read from her book. "*Chewing gum burns about eleven calories an hour,*" she read.

Jade and Darryl started tag-teaming.

Darryl: "*Kids blink about five million times a year!* Do it, Jade, throw it back at me!"

Jade: "*Sea turtles weigh about as much as a water buffalo.*"

Darryl: "*If about thirty-three million people held hands, they could make a circle around the equator.*"

Jade: "*There are more plastic flamingoes than real ones in the US.*"

Darryl: "*Bakers in Turkey made an eight-thousand-eight-hundred-ninety-one-foot-long cake. That's the length of about one hundred fourteen tennis courts.*"

"Whoa!" said Kyle.

Jade: *"Spiders have clear blood."*

I said, "Spiders have clear blood, people. Know that!"

"Then how come when you smush them, it's like *ull*?" said Jade.

"They have clear blood, but their digestive system is a mess," I said.

"Ew."

Darryl: "Abracadabra *used to be written in a triangle shape to keep away evil spirits.*"

Jade: *"The average adult's skin weighs about eleven pounds."*

"So if you want to lose weight, take off all your skin," said Owen.

Dabney raised his hand. "It's a proven fact that when you wake up in the morning, you're three inches taller than you are at night," he said.

"Three inches?" I said. "No!" Suddenly the whole class began talking at once.

Jade said, "Did you know that *hippopotomonstrosesquippedaliophobia* is a fear of long words?"

The PA lady asked James Moran to please stop at the office before lunch.

"This was fun," said Luke.

Sunrise, who hadn't wanted to hear any facts, came up to me and said breathlessly, "Did you know that dolphins were evolved from wolves? I watched a documentary. If you look at a dolphin they have little like feet bones on both sides, but the feet have gone away."

"No kidding," I said. "That's a great fact! Nice going."

Jade and Chase were looking up a picture of a zedonk, a cross between a female donkey and a male zebra.

"Abracadabra," sang Owen. Several joined in with "I want to reach out and grab ya."

"What's that song?" said Mackenzie.

"Everybody knows that song," said Owen. "You have no sense of culture."

I looked at the clock. "It's time for lunch."

"Lunch!"

"LUNCH!"

"You don't have to scream *lunch*," I said. "Just go to lunch."

The early-release day should have ended right there. In fact, all school days should be early-release days, I thought, eating a peanut butter cracker. Nobody learns a thing after lunch—the cafeteria is an endurance roaring contest. Keep teachers' salaries the same—no, increase them— but cut their hours in half. That should bring in some new blood. And fire the worst of the ed techs and enrichment specialists—the ones who are paid bullies.

The kids came back, squealing and grunting. They were as sick of the Archaebacteria kingdom as I was. So what if the organisms could live in hot springs? About half the girls successfully measured the beaks of Darwin's finches, some of them working out in the hall; two of the boys did. Jade and Darryl became kooky and flirtatious, following several boys around, grabbing their shirts. There was a disagreement over a Jolly Rancher; Kyle lifted an unoccupied chair in the air and threatened someone with it. That was when I got genuinely angry. "PUT THE CHAIR DOWN AND SIT IN IT," I said.

"Can I go get my iPad?" Kyle asked.

"NO. Sit."

Later one of Kyle's friends brought him his iPad and he played some game on it defiantly. I ignored him. What did it matter? I left a fatuous note for Mrs. Painter and drove home.

Loud bad funny brilliant sullen blithe anxious children. If I were a real teacher, I would go completely nuts. I love them.

End of Day Eleven.

I DON'T JUDGE

Back in the office of Lasswell High School at seven-thirty in the morning, getting my day's schedule and ID badge. "There you go," said Paulette. "You're in room eighteen."

"Mr. Bowles?" I said.

"Yep, and your plans are on his desk in a three-ring binder."

Mrs. Meese, the genial ed tech, was already sitting at her desk. "Good morning," she said. "You are our illustrious leader today."

"That is a scary thought," I said.

"I'm sorry but that's how it goes around here," she said. She really was an incredibly nice person.

Ms. Gorton, another ed tech—with a kind-but-tough face and a yellow bandanna and a whiskey voice—showed me the schedule page in Mr. Bowles's binder, and I said hello to Drew, my dyslexic friend from genetics class, who was sitting in the corner with his feet up on the heating unit, listening to music and staring at nothing. He waved a hand in languid greeting, but he was not happy. Mrs. Batelle, a sharp-featured, bustling older gal, was responsible for him; she was riffling through his stack of overdue assignments. "There's one more short-answer part of the test," she said. "And then another part."

"Whatever," Drew said.

"We can work on that another time. You have your iPad?"

"Yep."

"Stupendous. Thank you, sir."

"You're welcome," said Drew.

"You're a good trooper. You want a Reese's?"

"No."

"All right. I'll owe you one, if you want."

She left, and then Drew shouldered his backpack and left.

Ms. Gorton shook her head. "Battle zones," she said. "The teacher and Drew. They don't see eye to eye."

I said how much I liked Drew.

"Yeah, me, too. It's a little like being in between divorced parents. It's hard."

She took off for her classes. Mrs. Meese and I were the only people left in the room. I read Mr. Bowles's binder and wrote out my schedule.

"Do you have any questions about what you're doing?" Mrs. Meese asked.

I asked where Mr. Masille's Intro to Tech class was.

"You've got to go to room forty-four, blocks one and five," she said.

The high school PA lady came on—noticeably less singsongy in her delivery than the middle school PA lady. She said, "To the guidance office! Sisely Giles, Becca Hamilton, Leslie Ingalls, Angelica O'Donnell, Linus Hopper, Susanne Lampe, Randy Holloway, Lexie Locke, Greta Altham, Francisca Archambault! To the guidance office!"

I walked to the tech room, passing a goth couple crammed into a kissing corner, staring into each other's eyes and squeezing each other's bottoms before their day of classes. The tech room had high ceilings and battered gray stools and several ancient-looking metalworking machines from which sprouted pipes and ducts and electrical conduits. There was a beautiful old Bridgeport drill press against a side wall. Mr. Macpherson, who was substituting for Mr. Masille, said hello. He was a handsome man in a blue button-down shirt and a black tie. He looked a little like James Caan in *Misery*. I sat on a stool near a large chipped C-clamp.

Bong, bong, bong, bong, bong, bong. The students said the pledge almost inaudibly, some not at all—maybe tech class was felt to be just outside of compulsory flag-pledge range. Mr. Macpherson barked out each student's first name—about fifteen of them—and said, "All right, I think you're all fully aware what you need to do today. Each one of you needs to draw two sketches of a possible maglev vehicle. The game plan is that once those are done, then we're going to group you. We'll have six groups of two and one group of three, where you can combine your ideas, and come up with one. Uno! *Ein!* One! Maglev truck, vehicle. Sound like a plan? All right, let's do it."

He brought out a box of model maglev vehicles from previous trimesters and set them on a table. There was a hum from the drop forge in back that covered up the murmur of students' voices. "Don't forget, whatever you design mathematically has to fit inside this track with minimal friction," he said.

I checked in on the two boys I was supposed to be keeping an eye on and went over to Mr. Macpherson's desk. "Let me know if I can make myself useful," I said.

"Here's what we're doing," he said. "We're going to give them four magnets, have them cut the cardboard, and as I said to them yesterday, they can go anywhere they want to with this." He showed me a maglev car with a toy locomotive glued on top that he'd built himself. "I have a model train collection," he said. He demonstrated how the car was supposed to slide down the incline, levitating on the magnets glued to its underside. The locomotive slid to a stop halfway down. "The tolerance, and the balance, has to be precise, and I'm thinking that there's a very slight drop in the ramp," he said—maybe a sixteenth of an inch. "This one clearly starts, and then it stops. The car has to be perfect." He placed a freight car at the top of the run. "This one goes good," he said. We watched it go down smoothly. I asked him why he thought maglev hadn't caught on more. "It's the expense factor," said Mr. Macpherson. "It's a matter of maybe forty, fifty years. They'll get it eventually. They'll have to get it, when petrol as we know it is gone."

Mr. Macpherson had been a sub at Lasswell for several years, he said. "I'm a retired college professor. So being involved in education is a piece of cake. A lot of people look at substitute teaching, they come in, they do it for two days, and they say nuh-uh."

He took one of the worksheets and held it up for the class. "Guys, now once you have your practice design, there's a sheet here, and I want you to put your first initial and last name. Print it, so it's legible. Let's get that done."

Everyone printed their name at the top of their worksheet.

Mr. Macpherson pointed at a slacker dude, Martin, wearing headphones. "Take that headpiece off," he said. "Once you've put your name on here, and you've got your designs, I want you to come to my 'office.'" He pointed down at his desk, which was in the middle of the room, covered with clutter. "I want to peruse them quickly before you move on. Come and see me right here. There's no fee to enter my office. But there is an exit fee." He smiled. "Is there anything in the world that you can think of, where you can get in free, but you have to pay to get out?"

"Jail."

"Jail, that's correct. Totally, totally correct."

Martin and his friend Dallas went up to Mr. Macpherson's desk with their maglev sketches. They planned to add a rectangular sail for added speed. Mr. Macpherson suggested they use a double thickness of cardboard. "And make sure you measure carefully. You may have to get it down to a thirty-second. You guys are good to go."

I asked Martin if they were allowed to blow on the sail.

"No," he said. "You're not allowed to add any force."

I wondered what a rectangular sail would accomplish, aside from adding instability to the car, but I didn't want to introduce doubt. Let them figure it out.

Another pair of students wanted to make a Spider-Man car.

"Where's the cardboard?" said Martin.

"I've got the cardboard," said Mr. Macpherson.

"Don, you want to make a hash spoon?" said another kid.

Mr. Macpherson continued to review designs at his desk

"He's hidden the cardboard," said Martin. "I'm really getting annoyed."

Finally Mr. Macpherson hoisted a box into view.

"All right, now," he said to the class. "In this box right here on the table there's cardboard, there's also a glue gun, there are some scales, scissors, and magnets."

He came over to me and spoke in a quiet voice. "I've got a little project for you," he said. "I'm going to turn you loose." He showed me a small piece of wood, about an eighth of an inch thick. He wanted me to find more wood of that thickness, which some students could use instead of the cardboard as a stable base for their models, since the cardboard was easily bent. He opened the door to Mr. Masille's dim, still, unbelievably messy office.

"You're going to have to be like a picker," said Mr. Macpherson. "Don't leave anything unturned. I'm subbing for Mr. Masille, and he's been here for like fifty years. He knows where everything is, but he couldn't tell you."

I told him I'd see what I could find. Mr. Macpherson had a shrewd face—what, I wondered, had he taught in college? Electrical engineering? Physics? I asked him. He said he'd taught physical education and coached hockey at Tufts for thirty-four years, and in the summers, he'd taught phys ed at Exeter. When he retired, he and his wife had wanted to buy a house in Exeter, but the prices were too high. So they ended up in Maine, where real estate was cheaper.

"I love Maine," I said. "Thanks for the mission."

"Good luck."

I spent a few minutes hunting around in Mr. Masille's lair, feeling like Peter Falk in *Columbo* except that there was no murder. The office was a wonderland of ancient shop books and binders and bolts and broken wrenches and dusty, left-behind student projects. There was no secret stash of wood that I could see. The place made me sad—I'm not sure why. I left and toured the busy wood shop in the adjoining room, where goggled students were using two-by-fours to build a wall with two windows and a door, while the teacher shouted advice at them over the scream of the table saw. I took a left and found I was in the welding area. Gloves and helmets hung on the wall. Nobody was welding, and there were no thin pieces of wood there, either.

I circled back to my gray stool. Some of the students were cutting their pieces of cardboard. A few of the magnets were very weak. "Be sure you test the magnets," said Mr. Macpherson to the class. A girl with a long blond braid, Laney, made her magnets jump and click together. She laughed delightedly.

"Not much luck?" said Mr. Macpherson to me.

"The scrap wood would have to be planed," I said.

He sent me back out to look for small pieces of sheet metal that we could cut to size using scissors. I pawed through a bucket near the drill press, but it held only heavy bars of steel with holes in them. Finally I found some smaller metal scraps in a different bucket and put them in the box with the glue and the maglev magnets.

"Guys, for weight on your maglevs you have the possibility of sheet metal," said Mr. Macpherson. "And you have nails, screws, washers, you name it. Use your imagination."

Laney and her friend had a glue gun but no place to plug it in. "Can you hook these ladies up?" Mr. Macpherson said to me. I found a spot for them at a table near an unused electrical outlet. They were discussing the possibility of a Christina Aguilera car.

"Dude, there's sheet metal," said Charles, one of my charges. I told him about the narrow spot in the middle of the track, where the cars tended to stall. He made some experiments with his cardboard chassis. "Yeah, it's totally crooked," he said. "Totally crooked."

Some maglev cars from earlier trimesters decorated a steel door. There was a furry mouse car made of cotton with paperclip ears, a car made of green triangles with yellow accents called "the Blurr," a mousetrap car, a car shaped like a house, a black bat car, and a car made from a real dollar bill, with a stabilizer fin in the back.

Mr. Macpherson seemed to want to keep me busy. He told me to repair one of the old prototypes with hot glue. It was made of a milk carton, but its magnet was dangling. There was only one glue gun.

I went over to the girls with the glue gun. Their car was going to be made of playing cards, but the glue wasn't flowing. "We tried it in that outlet, and it wasn't heating up, so we tried the other one," said Laney. I touched the business end of the glue stick; it was still cold. Using an old radio, I tested several outlets; all of them were dead. "Imagine a machine shop without a working outlet," I said.

"Yeah," Laney said.

Mr. Macpherson brought over two more broken cars from last year for me to repair. One looked like a bobsled. I told him the electricity was off, and he went off to find the other tech teacher, who knew how to turn it on. We sat on our stools and waited.

"We've got power!" said Mr. Macpherson, returning. Still the glue gun didn't work and the radio didn't play. I found a red reset button and clicked it. "Phasers on stun," I said.

The glue gun began dribbling and the girls began gluing. Charles came over and said he wanted to plug in the Shop-Vac and suck his face into it.

"Glue's working!" I said.

Martin and Dallas were tired of waiting for the glue gun. "Let's just call it quits, man," said Dallas.

"I want to bend some sheet metal," said Charles. He clamped a scrap of metal in a green Tennsmith manual brake bender and bent it. He'd taken tech before, apparently. He said, "Martin, come over and help me bend some sheet metal!"

Class was almost over. "GUYS, MAKE SURE YOUR STUFF IS SOMEPLACE SAFE," Mr. Macpherson said.

Charles called, "Guys, how come you're not helping me?" He bent another sheet metal scrap and held it up.

I tested the repaired cars and put the glue gun away in the box. Everyone gathered by the door, waiting for the bell. Heather was wearing a blue T-shirt with a tennis racket on it.

Mr. Macpherson asked, "What's the circumference of a tennis ball?"

"I don't know," Heather said.

"Eight inches," he said. "Anything else you want to know?" He began telling Heather the history of tennis, beginning with its royal origins in France. A member of the British army brought some rackets and balls to Bermuda in 1874, Mr. Macpherson said, and there a woman named Mary Outerbridge discovered the game and loved it. When she returned from Bermuda to Staten Island, she built the first tennis court in the United States.

Six bongs.

"Have a good day!" he said.

I shook hands with him. "Are you roving?" he said.

"I'm roving," I said. I thanked him and left.

NEXT PERIOD I WAS IN Mrs. Prideaux's remedial math class—the one with the cabinets full of snacks, where I'd spent the whole day the first time I'd subbed. My charges were Sebastian, who loved mango juice, and Jake and Pearl. Besides Mrs. Prideaux, who was standing on a chair finding some supplies in the cabinet, there was Mr. C., the young ed tech. "Eight kids," he said, "and they're all doing geometry. We're doing area today."

Mrs. Prideaux got down from the chair, and Pearl told her about a photograph that she'd seen in her grandmother's AARP magazine. "She looked like she was just in her fifties," said the girl. "She was ninety-one!"

"Wow," said Mrs. Prideaux, who looked about thirty. "We should be so lucky."

A boy named Taylor held up something made of pink and orange Popsicle sticks. "This is a gun," he said. "A loaded gun. I don't know where it came from, I just found it." He handed it to Mrs. Prideaux.

"That's so cute," she said, and handed it back to him.

"It's loaded and it's cute," said Pearl.

"Taylor, you know what you have to do," Mrs. Prideaux said. "You've got to finish that little assessment. And I think you have to finish your quiz, too."

Sebastian sharpened his pencil for a long time and sat down. From his backpack he withdrew three bottles of mango juice and set them in a row next to a suspension bridge that he'd made from yarn and Popsicle sticks.

"That's a lot of mango juice," I said. "Daily regularity. How's it going today?"

Sebastian shook his head. "I haven't slept in a long time," he said. "Too much stuff to do."

"Have you been making any of those origami cranes?" I asked him.

"Yeah."

"You can work on your core curriculum standards," said Mrs. Prideaux to Pearl.

Mr. C. began coaching Taylor. "She did the whole thing on the board yesterday," he said to her. "This whole thing adds up." He pointed to the sides of a triangle on the page of a workbook. "This, this, this."

"Sh! I want to get started!" said Mrs. Prideaux. "I have some people still finishing assessments in here. Taylor, hurry up!"

Taylor was indignant. Pete was slower than he was, he said. Pete, an elegant kid with a drawl and a fade haircut, said he'd already done the quiz.

"Guys, just finish!" Mrs. Prideaux said.

I whisper-asked Sebastian what he was supposed to be doing. "Do you have to take a test?"

"Mine's extra credit," he said. He got up suddenly to get something from the cabinet.

Mrs. Prideaux's finger went out. "Wait, no no no, Sebastian! Either you STAY IN YOUR SEAT over there, or—"

Sebastian said, "I have to get this! Or what? Or what?"

"You don't have to get anything!" said Mrs. Prideaux. She was mad, I think—understandably so—because both of us ed techs had been talking while she'd been trying to get the class started. But she couldn't get mad at us because we were on staff. There were too many adults in this tiny room.

Sebastian pulled out a workbook from the cabinet. It had his name on it.

"Can I get the work I have to do?"

"All right," said Mrs. Prideaux. "Just hurry up, sit down, GET STARTED!"

I looked at my sheet. Mr. C. whispered to me to stay with Sebastian. Sebastian, pissed off that Mrs. Prideaux had yelled at him, pulled a glue gun and a stick of pink glue from his backpack and plugged it in. "Nice glue gun," I whispered.

"I put passion in my pink," he said—an Aerosmith allusion, perhaps.

"I'm disappointed in you," Mr. C. whispered to Sebastian.

"I'm sorry?"

"You didn't tell me the cafeteria sells coffee."

"They don't," said Sebastian. "They sell coffee milk."

"I bought a coffee this morning," said Mr. C.

"Are you going to argue with me? You can argue with me all you want."

"Okay, fine," said Mr. C. "I'm not disappointed in you."

"I'm sorry, Mr. C.," Sebastian said. "I know about you and your coffee."

Taylor climbed on a chair and wrestled with something in the cupboard, looking for an eraser. A dead spider fell from a shelf onto Pete's head.

"Oh, that's dead," said Mrs. Prideaux.

Pete looked up from his test with a puzzled expression.

"He doesn't even notice that there's a spider on his head!" said Taylor, laughing.

Pete reached up, found the spider, and flipped it away, revolted. Somebody stomped on it. Hilarity.

I whisper-asked Sebastian if he'd finished reading *The Shawshank Redemption* in English class. "I buzzed through that in a couple of days," he said. He explained his Popsicle-stick bridge to me. "I'm trying to put more shapes on it. I have this triangle, I have the rhombus, I have the squares, but I don't have a parallelogram." He rubbed his face and rapidly shook his head, as if shaking off thoughts he didn't want to have.

"You all right?" I said.

"I haven't slept in a long time. I go to bed at eight and I stay up all night."

"Just lying there?"

"I take melatonin," he said. "I've had it for so long I guess my body's starting to get immune to it."

Mrs. Prideaux was explaining to someone how to find the area of a rectangle. "You're going to put the length and the width here," she said, tapping the paper.

"It's hard to get through the day when you haven't had any sleep," I said to Sebastian. "It's torture."

"Oh, yeah. I haven't slept in two weeks. I doze for an hour or so, and then I wake up."

"Area—whatever the length times the width is," said Mrs. Prideaux.

"Is that a side effect or something?" I asked Sebastian, figuring he was on some kind of hyperactivity drug.

"I have no idea."

I asked him what his parents said about the sleeplessness, still talking very softly, so nobody else could hear.

"I haven't told my parents, because I used to be able to sleep—once I went to my room, I was done. My parents will think I'm faking it or something. I'm not a fan of people not believing that something like that is a problem. I want it to be fixed. I'd probably get mad at them for unnecessary reasons."

"That's tough," I said.

"Oh, it is."

Pete was explaining to Mrs. Prideaux that he didn't understand one section of the test.

Sebastian looked down at the worksheet and crunched his eyes closed for a long time.

After a while, I said, "If you take some pills every day, they can cause sleeplessness."

"Yeah, I don't know what pills I take in the morning. My parents keep track of that. I'm supposed to keep track of the ones I take at night. I take an allergy pill, and I take melatonin."

"The pills you take in the morning may be making you lose sleep," I said.

"Yeah, and for the past couple of days I've been running outside for hours to lose my energy. I go to bed and I'm extremely tired, and I can't sleep."

"That's probably a side effect of the pills. If you were always a good sleeper before—"

"Yeah, I just haven't slept in weeks."

"Maybe you can talk to the doctor? Taper off? I don't want to presume."

"No, I get it. I just don't feel sane. I feel on edge all the time."

"That's not you, that's the medication."

"I'm so on edge," said Sebastian. "I can snap at any moment, and I don't want to do that. Sleep is a good thing."

"You're so right," I said.

"I'm afraid I'm either going to hurt somebody, or I'm going to hurt myself."

"And you don't want to talk to your parents about that?"

He shook his head. "I just want to figure it out."

"I think you've figured it out. It's probably your medication. If you're taking something powerful that brings you up, and they're giving you too high a dose, then that's why you're up."

Sebastian was silent. He was done talking about pills and not sleeping.

"That's one heck of a bridge," I said.

Mrs. Prideaux clarified a test question for Mr. C., who was helping Taylor with his quiz. The question was, "What are the properties of a rectangle?"

"He could put down that the opposite sides are congruent, or that the angles are ninety degrees—things like that," said Mrs. Prideaux.

Mr. C. sat back down near Sebastian and me. "What kind of coffee do they sell?" Sebastian asked him.

"I didn't check. I just knew that they'd just brewed it when I bought it, and it was pretty strong. Nobody else was getting it. They should charge for it."

"KOS is an isosceles triangle," said Mrs. Prideaux to Pete. "There are three other isosceles triangles here. Which are they?"

"See, I'm not the only one who didn't know they sold coffee," said Sebastian in an undertone.

"They'd probably make a lot of revenue if more people knew," Mr. C. said.

"People spend a lot of money on coffee," said Sebastian.

Mr. C. resumed coaching Taylor on the properties of a rectangle. "Two sets of parallel lines," he said softly.

Now that the glue was running, Sebastian affixed several more Popsicle sticks to the top of one of the towers.

"Last night we went and did backflips off the trunks of cars," said Taylor to Mr. C.

Mr. C. winced. "There's something about putting my feet in the air over my head that I just don't enjoy," he said.

Thin pink filaments of glue hung off Sebastian's bridge. "It's like a Spider-Man bridge," he said.

"Beautiful," I said.

He let the glue dry and looked at his worksheet. He wrote a few answers, scribbling them at high speed. "Mrs. Prideaux?" he said.

"Hang on," she said.

"I just have a question," said Sebastian.

"Done!" said Pete. He sighed with relief.

More pencil sharpening. This particular pencil sharpener was an expensive one, higher pitched than the middle-school pencil sharpener.

Taylor sketched a rectangle. Mr. C. measured the angles with a protractor. "Check this out," he said to me. "All ninety degrees."

"Nice," I said.

"I just drew it," said Taylor.

"Freehand," said Mr. C. "Now the area."

Taylor carefully added up the length of all four sides.

"Nope," said Mr. C. "That's perimeter."

"Oh, area."

"Okay, folks," said Mrs. Prideaux, "I'm going to give you a few more minutes, actually three minutes, and then we're moving right into the next section."

One of Sebastian's recently glued Popsicle sticks fell loose. He glued it back in place.

Mrs. Prideaux went over to Pete, who had his iPad out. "Put that away," she said. "This is your one warning. You're texting."

"It's not texting," said Pete.

"It looks like you're texting to me, or you're on Facebook. I don't care which it is."

"It was a blog."

"It doesn't matter."

"There's a difference, Mrs. Prideaux," muttered Sebastian.

"You don't do that in class!" said Mrs. Prideaux.

"I've done all the stuff you wanted me to do," said Pete.

"It doesn't matter! You could move right on to your core curriculum standards, or catch up on some of the old stuff that you haven't done."

"A blog!" said Sebastian, chuckling.

Taylor made an elephantine yawn.

"What the hell was that for?" said Sebastian. "The loudest yawn?" He stood up and stretched, quoting Eminem: "'Music is like magic, there's a certain feeling you get, when you're real and you spit and people are feeling your shit.'" Then he said, "Mrs. Prideaux, what's my grade in this class?"

"I'm not going to look that up right now," said Mrs. Prideaux.

"It's right here!" said Taylor, pointing to her computer screen. "Look it up for yourself."

Mrs. Prideaux and Sebastian went over to the computer. "Eighty-one," she said. "I hope you're not looking at the other grades. Taylor, you're missing a whole big grade in there. Sebastian, back in your seat."

Taylor raised a ruler and pretended to measure Sebastian's skull with it.

"Today is not the day you want to hit me with a ruler," said Sebastian. "Once I get more than three hours of sleep, I'll let you know."

Mrs. Prideaux stopped by Pearl's desk. She said, "When you measure the four angles of a quadrilateral together, they equal . . . ?"

I asked Sebastian how he passed the time at night.

"I listen to my music and read, basically. I don't play games. I have better things to do than assault my mind with that stuff." He leapt up and walked across the room again.

Mr. C. was showing Mrs. Prideaux a parallelogram that Taylor had just drawn. "He drew it freehand," he said. "It's right on the money all the way around."

"Sebastian! Back over, sit down," said Mrs. Prideaux. She grabbed a piece of chalk. "Now, I want everyone's attention up here. Taylor!"

"Wha?" said Taylor, pretending to be startled.

"I want your attention up here. We're going to do polygon areas today." She drew an octagon, with sides that were ten inches long. "To calculate the area of an octagon, we need to know what the perimeter is. So what is the perimeter of this octagon?"

"Eighty," said Dave.

"Nice job, Dave," said Sebastian.

"Yep, it's eighty," Mrs. Prideaux said. "Now the other thing that you will get is the apothem." She had an idiosyncratic way of pronouncing *apothem*: it sounded as if she was saying *opossum*, but with a lisp. "The opossum is a measurement from the side of the polygon to the center. So I'm going to say that this polygon has an opossum of thirteen." She wrote the formula on the board: "One-half times the opossum times the perimeter equals the area."

"So half the opossum?" said Sebastian.

"Yes, so I would put one-half times thirteen times eighty. And I will get—"

"Five twenty," said Dave, checking his calculator.

"Is it five twenty? Good."

"You're amazing, Dave," said Sebastian.

"So the area of this octagon is five hundred and twenty units. If I said it was inches it would be square inches." She drew a hexagon and asked Pete to figure out the perimeter. He was very nearsighted, so he went up to the board and peered at it.

"Have you gotten your eyes checked lately, Pete?" said Pearl.

"Yeah, I have. I'm getting contacts soon."

"Soon's not enough," said Sebastian.

"Why don't you wear glasses?" said Dave.

"Because with my luck, they would break in a week," said Pete.

"If you can't find your phone, how are you going to find a frigging contact that's about as big as your fingernail?" said Dave.

Mrs. Prideaux held up a handout. "I want everyone to find this page," she said. "We're almost done with this standard."

I made a pop-eyed face to entertain myself.

"Hiccups?" said Sebastian to me. "You've got hiccups?" He held out some Tic Tacs for me.

"I was just making a stupid face, sorry," I said.

"I don't judge."

Zeke snapped a pencil in two.

"Zeke!" said Mrs. Prideaux.

A teacher came to the door to talk to Mrs. Prideaux.

"Zeke's a troublemaker, don't make him mad," said Sebastian. "He will kill you. He's been to jail. Zeke! How many times have you been to jail? Don't lie!"

"Like, once," said Zeke slowly.

"That's one time too many, Zeke," said Sebastian. He began working on the handout.

"You're into this stuff," I said to Sebastian.

"I hate math," Sebastian said. "Hate math altogether. Hate geometry. I can do it but I hate it. Don't tell Mrs. Prideaux I said that."

Mrs. Prideaux was back, and circulating, helping people calculate the area of the first polygon on the handout.

"Can you do a polygon area on no sleep?" I asked Sebastian. "That's your challenge."

Sebastian looked at the problem, did some multiplying in his head, came up with the number eighty-four, then burped. "Excuse me," he said.

"Mighty mango," I said. I used my calculator and, with some prompting from Sebastian, came up with the same number, eighty-four.

Taylor left the room. "Taylor, come back!" said Sebastian. "He leaves for hours, then he comes back and doesn't know what we're doing."

"Next," I said, tapping the paper.

Sebastian counted the sides. "This one's a decahedron," he said. "Four point six two times thirty times one-half. Sixty-nine point three." Correct, check.

Sebastian and I began to race each other. I made a mistake and Sebastian pointed out where I'd gone wrong.

"What can I say, you're better than me," I said.

"Nah." In the middle of doing one problem, Sebastian heard someone across the room say the word *douche*. "Hey," he said. "No one says *douche* anymore."

Pete pointed at the figures on the chalkboard. "How am I supposed to remember that?"

"You are supposed to use the formula," said Mrs. Prideaux.

"Even with the formula I'm going to get confused," said Pete.

"But the formula is just one-half times the opossum times the perimeter."

My math sparkplugs were badly corroded, and I forgot to multiply by 0.5. Sebastian corrected my error. We got the same answer for the next one. "I was actually right," I said. "Praise the holy maker."

"The baby Jesus," said Sebastian.

We got to the bottom of the page. I sighed with relief.

Sebastian's hand shot up. "Mrs. Prideaux, I finished it."

"All right, good. On the back there's another whole page of fun and excitement."

Sebastian flipped over the paper to reveal several more complicated polygon problems involving square roots. The sample problem had an error on it. The area of an octagon that fit neatly within a square with four-inch sides could not be twenty-one square inches, because the area of the entire square would only be sixteen square inches. Sebastian went to Mrs. Prideaux and showed her the mistake. "You're right, it should be half," said Mrs. Prideaux. "Why did they do that? Why do they do these things?" She began telling the other students about the error in the example on the second page of the handout.

"Mrs. Prideaux, I finished it," said Sebastian.

"Very good," said Mrs. Prideaux.

I asked him what they were reading in Language Arts, now that they'd finished *Shawshank*. They were on to *The Things They Carried*, by Tim O'Brien.

"Potato salad," said Taylor. Zeke was abusing a yardstick. Mrs. Prideaux said, "When you get that yardstick in your hand, it gives you a feeling of power. It's not really a good thing to have."

"I'll take this to my next class," said Zeke. "I want to whack everybody. I just want to bash Tucker's face in."

"No, you don't," said Mrs. Prideaux.

"Yeah, I do."

"Zeke's a killer," said Sebastian. "Zeke has that face of killing. Mass murderer."

Bong, bong, bong, bong, bong, bong.

Mrs. Prideaux held the worksheets that she'd collected as the special ed students went off to their next class. "I don't know why they can't have nice simple little numbers," she said.

"All those radicals!" said Mr. C. "I won't be back till the end of the day. I'm teaching chemistry."

"That should be fun," said Mrs. Prideaux. She shook my hand. "Thank you, it was nice to meet you."

"A pleasure to be in your class," I said.

———————

"GOOD MORNING, AGAIN," said Ms. Gorton in Mr. Bowles's room. She was handing out candy from a plastic bag. "Can you have chocolate?" she asked Charles, one of the two kids I was in charge of for that block.

"I can have chocolate, but not peanut butter," he said. He had black hair sticking out from under a blue baseball hat.

"Can you have Skittles?" She handed him the bag.

"Oh, I like Kit Kats," he said.

I sat down next to Roland, my other responsibility, and introduced myself. Roland had a low voice and a baseball hat pulled low on his solid face. He looked about twenty-five.

Charles found some Zombie lip balm in his backpack and used it on his lips.

It was a sunny day, and I looked out the window at the brown, empty courtyard in the middle of the school. There was a robin on one of the benches. I turned to Roland. "Can anybody go out there? Or do we just look out sadly at the bird?"

"That's the honors courtyard," Roland said. "The next one is the teachers' courtyard. And the furthest one down is the senior courtyard. Technically. They're all shut down."

"Soon," said Ms. Gorton.

"Nobody knows," said Roland.

Charles said, "They told us this year that nobody was allowed in there. There was shenanigans. Littering."

I opened the window.

"We haven't had air in like three months," said Charles.

"These computers are up for grabs," said Ms. Gorton, piling up her binders in readiness for her next block. "Bye, guys, happy morning."

"Bye," said Charles. "Thanks for the candy."

He was working on a sculpture of a man kneeling, made of a soda bottle and coat hanger wire.

"Nice," I said. "Are those arms?"

"Yeah."

I pulled out an apple.

"You better bring food with you during school," said Charles, "because if you don't, you're going to be screwed."

"I just ran three miles," said Roland.

I asked him why.

"I have gym."

Charles said, "I couldn't run three miles if somebody bribed me."

"You'll probably have to at some point," I said.

"Nope," said Charles. "I've been postponing the inevitable for a very long time."

Roland said, "Waiting for the zombie apocalypse, when we're all going to die?"

"I'll be able to fast-walk," said Charles.

"The place that's safety will be exactly three miles away," said Roland, "and you'll have to run there."

"The place where it's safety is about seven miles away," said Charles. "My house."

I asked him if he had a zombie-proof air raid shelter.

"It's not really an air raid shelter," Charles said. "If we had a nuclear explosion, I wouldn't be fine."

"Your hamster?" said Roland.

"Actually, no one would be fine," said Charles.

I said, "I don't think we're going to get anything like that, do you?"

"No, no," Charles said. "A zombie apocalypse maybe. They have an animal-testing facility right in the middle of Kansas. That's where we get most of our food and it's Tornado Alley."

I said, "So the tornado releases the animals that are being inhumanely tested, they're pumped up on antibiotics, they're huge chickens, they leap out and they start terrorizing the countryside?"

"Yeah," said Charles, "and then we pretty much get the swine flu epidemic."

"I see," I said. "That's not good." I took a bite of my apple. "I know there's a lot of corn in the middle of the country."

"Pretty much you should grow your own food," Charles said.

Roland said, "I don't really care if there's a zombie apocalypse."

"Really?" I said. "I don't even like watching those damn shows. I can't stand these people staggering around half dead, I hate it."

"Walk normal!" said Roland.

Charles laughed. "I look at it like this. If you're prepared for the zombie apocalypse, you're prepared for almost anything."

"I hear you," I said. "But I don't even know how to shoot a gun. On those shows, they're always having to take them out somehow. I think I'd be the first casualty."

Charles asked me if I knew how to fire a cannon. I didn't.

Roland said, "You clean it, you pack it, stick the wick in. It's not that difficult."

A third kid walked in and sat down. He had long bangs and tired eyes and his name was Patrick. "Are you a new teacher here?"

"No, I'm filling in for Mr. Bowles. I'm Mr. Intestine. No, that's stupid, never mind, move on."

"You mind helping me with my test?" said Patrick.

"By all means. What's your test in?"

"History." His teacher was Ms. Hopkins.

He handed me the test packet. On page 1 it said, *Fill in the blank line with the correct ism.* The choices were fascism, militarism, isolationism, and totalitarianism:

Japan   _____

Always prepared for war   _____

Foreign policy of United States
after World War I   _____

System run by a dictator having
complete power, includes extreme
nationalism, and often racism   _____

Connected to the Soviets   _____

Focus of growth on industry and
military, low standard of living,
shortage of food and consumer goods   _____

"Death is the safest place," said Roland, still musing on the zombie apocalypse. "No, Canada is the safest place."

"Canada is not the safest place!" said Charles.

"They have no crime," said Roland. "The zombies would just look at the border and go, 'Nope,' turn around and walk away."

Patrick said, "My notes are on the computer. May I get a computer?"

"Let's just do it," I said. I pulled up a chair next to him. "So, Japan. They were very devoted to military life. The ism connected to Japan would be which one? Isolationism is what we were doing, saying we don't want to be bothered, right?"

"Yeah. So . . ."

"The Japanese were very militaristic," I said. "They were building submarines like crazy, they attacked us at Pearl Harbor. You gotta admit that."

"That's true," Patrick said.

I took another bite of my apple, waiting for him to figure it out.

He tapped his finger on the word *militarism.* "So that would be—Japan?"

"Bingo."

We looked at the next question, "Always prepared for war." The best match for that one also seemed to be *militarism.* "Hm," I said. "I guess you can reuse them?"

Patrick went off to ask the history teacher whether you could reuse the isms.

I went back over to Roland and Charles. "What's been happening over here?" I said.

"Basalt zombie stuff," said Charles. "My grandfather, up north, gets them all the time."

"Gets what?"

"Basalt zombies."

I didn't understand.

"People that are high on bath salts," Charles explained.

I said, "What do you do, make a smoothie of bath salts and become a zombie? What the hell?"

"Pretty much," Charles said. "It's to the point where you have to take off your clothes. You're pretty much burning yourself from the inside out."

"It's a form of, like, crack," said Roland.

"And it gives you a high?" I said.

"Well, more than a high," said Charles. "It gives you invincibility from gunshots."

"It's like PCP," said Roland. "They could get shot seven times and still be running at you."

"And it's bath salts?" I said. "I'm so out of it. You used to be able to buy boxes of the stuff."

"That's the street term for it," said Charles.

"It's not actual bath salts," said Roland.

"How do you spell *territory*?" said Patrick, who'd returned.

I told him. I turned back to Charles. "What do you mean they're zombies? Your grandfather takes care of them?"

"No," said Charles, eating his Kit Kat. "They just walk up to his house. They're screaming and yelling and having a spasm attack."

"Why are they there?"

"They're lonely up there. It's way way up Maine."

"Everybody seems to be reasonably under control around here," I said.

"Not necessarily," said Charles.

I asked what was supposed to be happening in the room right now.

"Nothing, really," said Charles.

Roland said, "It's a study hall, so we can work on things. And if we have nothing to do, then we just sit around and do nothing."

"You need a break in the day," I said. "Constant assaults of nonsense. I just learned about polygons. I never took geometry."

Roland said, "The hardest class I have is Algebra III."

"The hardest class I have is trash art," said Charles. "You take a bunch of random items, and you make something awesome out of it."

I went back to Patrick. "What did she say?"

"We can use the words over and over again."

"Beautiful."

He put *isolationism* next to the United States. Next to *System run by a dictator having complete power, includes extreme nationalism, and often racism*, he put *totalitarianism*. He had trouble reading the word *often*.

The phone rang and then stopped. Roland and Charles were talking about pandemics. "Most of us die," said Charles.

Patrick and I turned to the next page of the test. The first question was, *Italian leader during World War II.* I helped him spell *Mussolini.* The second question was *What did he want?*

"What does any dictator want?" I said.

"Control?"

"Sure, excellent."

Sebastian showed up. "I have a question," he said. "I was wondering if I could work in here."

I said he could if it was okay with his teacher. He left to ask.

Next question: *Pearl Harbor, who, when, where, why?*

I asked Patrick if he remembered anything about Pearl Harbor.

"No," said Patrick. "I wasn't here."

I told him about Pearl Harbor, and he began writing the date. "December seventh, nineteen forty—seven?"

I pointed down.

"Forty-six?" Down. "Forty-three?" Down. "Forty-one." Then he asked, "How do you spell *Hawaii*?"

He had to give three reasons why fighting in the Pacific was difficult for US troops. The islands were well fortified, I said, and the supply lines were long. "How do you spell *supplies*?" he said.

The test wanted him to define *two-front war.* I drew a picture. Patrick wrote, *War is happening in two diffrent places.*

He asked me how to spell *reparation*. He wrote about the attitude of the United States after World War I. He wrote about tanks versus horses in World War I. It wasn't an easy test. "Okay, I'm going to pass this in," he said. He left.

I went back to Charles and Roland, who were watching a trailer for a Japanese cartoon called *Attack on Titan*, in which the citizens of a walled city battle enormous homicidal naked people. "Is it lunch yet?"

"No."

I asked them what year they were in. Roland was a senior, and Charles was a senior, too, but he was going to be a super-senior next year. That got us on the topic of the movie *Super Size Me*. "I could have done without the scene of him puking," said Roland.

"And we didn't really need to know about his sex life," said Charles.

I said I'd once bought four fish sandwiches from McDonald's and set them up in a row in front of me and eaten them. "They were delicious," I said. "Now I don't do that anymore, because I think, The poor fish, there aren't that many fish left in the sea."

"I hate fish anyway," said Roland. "I like crab and lobster. I don't like shrimp."

Patrick returned holding his test, which the teacher had already gone over. I'd led him badly astray on one question—I'd prompted him to list the three Axis leaders, Hitler, Mussolini, and Hirohito, when he was supposed to list the "Big Three" Allied nations and their leaders. "Who were the three good guys?" I said. Patrick wrote down the USA and Russia, and then he was stumped. I did a Churchill impression: "We will fight on the beaches!"

"China?" he said.

"He was a British sort of man," I said.

"France?"

"British, English."

"Britain?"

"Boom."

After some more prompting, he ended up with Roosevelt, Stalin, and Churchill. He left. Then he came back smiling—he'd gotten an 80 on the test.

Roland, Charles, and Patrick packed up to go. Charles was off to work on his reading. "Before I got to this high school, I was an illiterate," he said. "I can read to a third-grade level right now. My comprehension is way up there, higher than the school average, but I've got dyslexia and stuff. When I was in kindergarten, they said, This kid will never learn how to read."

"Wow, that's kind of a triumph," I said.

Bong, bong, bong, bong, bong, bong.

Roland and Charles waved. "See you!"

The PA lady came on. "Mr. Nicholson Baker to the main office, please. Mr. Nicholson Baker to the main office."

My heart started thumping. What had I done?

In the office Paulette asked me if I was available Wednesday and Thursday. I told her I wasn't, unfortunately.

Walking back to Mr. Bowles's room, I heard snatches of conversation: "The dentist made my gums bleed." "You're wrong, very wrong." "It was like this weird fashion show thing." "Did we pass?"

Mrs. Meese was in Mr. Bowles's room talking to Lucas, one of the mud-truck aficionados from Day One—blinky, wiry, and slow moving. Drew was lounging out. I asked him how biology was going. He said they'd moved on from geographical tongues and hairy knuckles; now they were extracting DNA from wheat germ. "We're putting soap in it, like Dawn or something, and we're putting in rubbing alcohol. Next time we'll use a stirring stick to pull out the DNA, put some blue dye on it, and look at it."

"And then," I said, "you will witness the secret of life—a little blob of something on a slide."

"That's where babies come from," said Drew. "From test tubes." We were quiet for a bit, while Mrs. Meese helped Lucas with his history. "It's my least-favorite class, though," Drew said. "I didn't like it first trimester and I don't like it this trimester."

Drew liked English best, he said. "I'm learning how to make proper sentences. We watched a movie, too, *Boy in the Striped Pyjamas*, about the Holocaust. It was really interesting, I liked it. I mean I liked the movie, I didn't like what was happening."

Mrs. Meese was working with Lucas on his history—helping him spell *Roosevelt*.

Drew began eating an apple in a strange way. He ate one half completely, right down to the core, and left the other side untouched. That morning, he said, he woke up and didn't want to move, he just lay there. "People are always saying sleep is so important, and yet school starts so early."

"All right, Lucas, you did it!" said Mrs. Meese. She emailed his history assignment to his teacher.

Lucas came over to my side of the class and sat down. "What's going on?" I said.

"Nothing much," said Lucas.

"Drew's eating an apple," I said. "He eats one side at a time."

A girl came in looking for a paperclip to fix her shirt.

"I eat oranges like that all the time," said Drew. "It tastes really good to me. After I eat the orange peel, if I take a sip of water, I swear it's the best sip of water I've ever tasted."

"I'll have to try that sometime," I said.

Lucas looked up. "Peanut butter and mayonnaise," he said.

"Together," I said, "or apart?"

"Together," Lucas said. "I had to eat it when I went into solitary."

"Solitary what?"

"Juvenile hall," said Lucas. "That's what they give you, because they can't give you fluff, because it has sugar in it."

"No," I said.

"They make it look like it's fluff. They make it thick, but it's mayonnaise. If you go in the hole, that's what they give you."

"You were in the hole?"

"Yep. I punched a guard."

Mrs. Meese was explaining to a student how dot-dot-dots worked when you quoted a paragraph in an essay and wanted to leave something out. I leaned forward. Drew made a start on the second half of his apple.

"But you're a kid," I said. "How old are you?"

"Eighteen."

"You're a senior, right?" said Drew.

"Yeah."

I asked Lucas why he'd punched the guard.

"I went in there because I got charged with a Class A felony. I did like four months. I was in there, and the guard kept giving me crap, so I just punched him out. I did probably two weeks in the hole."

I said, "How much contact with the outside world did you have?"

"You go in the TV room. You only have two windows, and that's all you see. Woods."

"That's hard on your mind," I said.

"You'd think that people would see their mothers and stuff, but you don't want to do that. Somebody asks for an interview, you say no, or people will say you're a pussy."

I said I was glad it was over.

"I'm out now," Lucas said. "I done my time, and I'm doing good. I did anger management classes. Couple incidents here and there. But I'll say right now, any kid in this room wouldn't want to be in my shoes at that time. Any kid in this school wouldn't last three seconds there. When I was there, I was lifting weights, situps, pushups."

I asked him what constituted a Class A felony.

"Well, I quit school and took off. Walked down the street, and a kid owed me money, and he didn't pay me, and he punched me, so I punched him and knocked his head against a pole and slammed him with a shopping cart. I ran to Walgreens. I was sitting in the bathroom there for a while. Went home, went in my bedroom window, changed my clothes, acted like my bus came in. A cop comes to my house, he goes, 'Where were you around one o'clock today?' 'Home!' He goes, 'Nuh-uh.' I knew I was busted. I told my mom, I said, 'I'm done.' They took me to the station, read me my Miranda rights, said, 'You're under arrest.' I thought I was the toughest kid, but when I went in there, you ain't. I saw a kid ahead of me put his head right through a sheet of glass. The glass is this thick. He shoves his head, boom. He was bigger than that door. It took like four guards with shields to zap him down."

"Like riot shields?" said a girl, who was listening.

"Yeah, and he was in there. I'm like the shortest kid. D block is when kids are bodybuilders—you've got to get like fourteen cops to get at them. So I was in E block. I remember this kid would always scream at night. On and on. I finally said, 'If you don't shut up, in the morning, you make me lose my lunch this time, I'm going to go in there and beat the hell out of you.'"

The class had gone quiet. Everybody was listening to Lucas, while pretending not to.

"So he screamed that night," Lucas went on. "The guard goes, 'You lost lunch.' Because the kid wouldn't get up in the morning and they always took lunches from all of us every time. I didn't think they could do that. I told the kid, 'Come over here. We lost lunch?' So I peed all over his boots, the guy. I said, 'There's your lunch. You can eat that.' I went in the hole for that. Came back out, and the kid still screamed. His mind was messed up. When he first went in there, he was great, didn't scream or nothing. Three weeks in, his mind, it's like you're not there anymore. He was reading kids' books."

"He really lost it," I said.

"He really lost it. So at nighttime, the kids in the cells would crack their doors. The kids would fart into the door. One time I farted and a guard came by and he goes, 'Holy snap!' One time I broke a pen and put it on the shaving cream bottle. I put the shaving cream on the door handle so the guard couldn't open it. He tried to open it and all the shaving cream turned to, like, slime. So he goes, 'Yep, who did this this time!' Going into the shower he got me good. Pepper spray and oil and wax. That stings. He goes, 'How does it feel to be back?' So the kid was still screaming. Finally he followed me out for lunchtime. I went around and beat the crap right out of him. I said, 'You made me lose lunch for two weeks.' He stopped screaming after that. I'm sorry for that."

Mrs. Meese said, "Pearl?" She and Pearl began working on Pearl's English paper. Drew started talking to Mr. C.

Lucas didn't want to stop talking. "A new kid came in, trying to make a name for himself," he said. "He slit a kid's throat. So the kid came back and killed him."

"In juvie?"

"Oh, yeah, people don't know. They don't tell the outside world. Like if someone died, they won't tell. This one kid came in, new kid, they're beating him up every day. I went over to him. I said, 'What's your problem?' He goes, 'I'm not guilty.' I said, 'Everybody did something to come in here.' This girl got him in for drug running. She passed him the stuff and got him in there. He couldn't fight at all. He didn't know nothing about fighting. Kids would beat him up so bad that the kid wouldn't get up. I told him, 'Get up.' I went to Sergeant Stamm and I told him, 'He's going to die. The guys are going to get to him and he can't fight back.' In the shower I said, 'Watch your back.' They run up and stabbed him. I said to the guard, 'What did I tell you? He's going to die.' Sergeant Stamm goes, 'Yeah? So? This is your house, you're supposed to take care of it.' The kid made it out, and I go up to see him, and he says, 'I might take my life tomorrow.' I said, 'Don't do that.' That night he woke up, he made stuff out of sheets, a noose, jumped off the thing, killed himself."

Activity block was almost over and the class was noisy now. Lucas got up and I walked him to the door. "So I did my time, I came out, and I told my mom, my grandmom, my grandfather, I'm not going back in there for anything I do. I kept my promise ever since." Now he boxed, he said. "My dad coached me."

"That's quite a story," I said.

"I learned how to break someone's arm," said Drew, also standing by the door.

Bong, bong, bong, bong, bong, bong.

"Good talking to you," I said.

"Can you email that, Pearl?" said Mrs. Meese. "Lucas, thank you so much for all your hard work. Awesome job!" When the students were gone, she gathered some papers. I took a bite of a cheese sandwich. "This trimester just seems to fly for me," Mrs. Meese said. "I've got blocks one, two, and three, and I'm just busy, busy, busy, and then I have a little chill here, but yet, I'm busy. And then four and five I'm just busy, busy again." She bustled off.

Ms. Gorton came in to get a notebook. She asked how things were going. I said I'd just heard the whole grim story of juvie from Lucas. She shook her head. "If I listened to all the stories, my heart would be irrevocably broken," she said. "Bro-ken!" She left.

Mrs. Batelle and a third ed tech came in and began comparing notes on the isms history test, so that they could help Drew take it. I went out to make some instant tap-water coffee in the kitchen and said hello to Mrs. Carlisle, the sub who'd played the relaxation tape. Cutting through the library, I saw a poster on which was posted the SAT word of the day. The word of the day was *exodus*. Yesterday's word was *languish*, and before that it was *frank*, and before that *nullfy*, spelled without the *i*.

When I got back, the ed techs were shuffling fruitlessly through their history notes in order to find which of the isms was the correct answer to *What was the foreign policy of the United States after World War I?*

I put on my headphones and listened to some music. After a half hour Mrs. Batelle and Ms. Gorton went away and Mrs. Meese came back to have some yogurt. I told her that I was concerned about Sebastian. "I don't know how much to say," I said. "But I think he's taking some kind of med that is keying him up too much." I didn't say that whatever he was taking—Strattera or Concerta or some such—was on the verge of making him psychotic.

"Well, he's ADHD," said Mrs. Meese.

"Yes, but he said, 'I haven't been sleeping, and I haven't slept for days.' He's up, up, up."

"I had him first block, and he wasn't up, up, up, he was fine," Mrs. Meese said. "Some of that is to see how much sympathy he can get. But he is severe ADHD—I've never seen somebody as ADHD as he is. Right now he's on restricted pass, because he was signing out to go to the boys' room, but instead going to the cafeteria and hanging out with friends. He's not allowed to leave his classes at all."

We talked about Patrick, the mumbly kid who took the history test with me. Patrick would do anything to get out of a class, Mrs. Meese said. "He's a junior, and he's ricocheted in and out of this school five times, I think. His parents keep moving. First Kansas City, then Brunswick, then Greenfield, Mass. It was here, Kansas City, here, Brunswick, Greenfield, here, Portland, here."

"I think I saw him in the hall with a girlfriend, though," I said.

"Yeah, he's known her all these years. But he's not getting anywhere scholastically because they keep bouncing in and out of here."

"I feel sorry for some of these kids, seeing them struggle," I said. "They're barely able to spell, and I'm thinking, Is this the best use of their time?"

"No, it's not," Mrs. Meese said. "The issue that I see is kids that don't do book learning. They do hands-on learning. There's a ton of them in this school. Let them be a plumber or a carpenter or an electrician. But here's the problem. You can't be a plumber or an electrician or a carpenter now without going to college. There's no more coming out of high school and apprenticing under somebody."

I said, "They're being made unnecessarily miserable, and they think they're stupid, but actually they might well be a brilliant small-engine-repair guy, who just can sort of take things apart in his mind, who has that spatial sense. And yet here it's all about how many isms can you memorize."

"It's very frustrating," said Mrs. Meese. "My brother falls into this category. He's fifty-one, and he can do pretty much anything. But he's never had college. Right now he's working with a guy who is a furnace guy. He's learning under this guy, and he's doing fabulous. So my mother said to him, 'Why don't you apprentice under him, and get your license?' He said, 'Because there's no more of that, Mom.' He says, 'I've got to go to college. It's book learning.' He goes, 'I can't learn by reading an effing book.' When my brother was five, he was taking bicycles apart and remaking bicycles. And then he went to lawnmowers and minibikes. He took my mother's blender apart. You can blindfold him and tell him, 'There's a whatever motorcycle engine in front of you,' he'll put it back together. But he can't do it as a profession, because he has no college. He'd be a fabulous teacher. The f-bombs would be flying, I know that. He built a car from the ground up. He can weld like you've never seen anybody weld. He learned from my father. He learned all of it at my father's elbow. My father was the same way. He took my grandmother's washing machine apart—he wanted to know how it worked. Of course, she spanked him for that one—but it was the same idea."

Mrs. Batelle and Ms. Gorton came in with Drew and a new girl, Kendra, to do some more work on the history test. "Let's get this done, Kendra," said Ms. Gorton.

"It's nice and cool in here," said Drew.

Mr. Clapper, the school principal, came on the PA system. "Good afternoon, this is Mr. Clapper, can I have your attention for a moment? I would like to congratulate the class of 2014, and I'd like to announce the students in the top ten percent, in alphabetical order." He read off twenty-two names—eighteen girls and four boys. "Our honors essayist is Benjamin Young, our salutatorian is Tricia Hadden, and our valedictorian is Kelsie Mattingly. Congratulations to all of those students in the top ten percent of the class of 2014."

Kendra read a question on her test: "Give three reasons why fighting in the Pacific was difficult for US troops."

I sent some emails, after Drew showed me where to plug in the computer.

Drew opened a cupboard and found a can of antiperspirant. He gave himself a couple of quick squirts under his sweatshirt.

Mrs. Batelle looked up from her notes, hearing the hissing sound. "What are you doing?" she said.

"Deodorant," said Drew. "I'm sweating."

"That's okay, Drew," Mrs. Batelle said. "I thought you were having Jell-O pie or something."

Ms. Gorton said to Kendra, "We skipped this question yesterday. I want you to read the question."

"*What was the foreign policy of the United States after World War I?*" Kendra read softly.

Mrs. Batelle was reading an upcoming learning target assessment in Drew's binder. "Are you good at drawing?" she asked.

"I draw stick men," said Drew. "That's the best I can do." He yawned.

"Why don't you put away all your notes," said Mrs. Batelle. She handed him the learning target project packet. "And then, we can take a look at this. Okie dokie? *You are a reporter or a writer during World War II, and you have just witnessed or experienced one of the following events.* Fortunately, you were one American who was able to survive this horrific event. It's your job to explain this experience to the American people. So how would you explain it?"

"What experience?" said Drew.

"How, though," said Mrs. Batelle.

"You've got to pick an experience," said Drew.

"True. But how would you relate it to the American people. You're over there, you're not here. How would you get the news to the people, over the ocean to us? What's one way of doing it?"

"Boat," said Drew. "Boat? I don't know if they had planes."

"How else? 'Hello, hello?' What's this? A microphone!"

"Radio?"

"Radio. Or television? Did we have television in World War II?"

"Kind of, actually," said Drew. "I did a thing about TV last trimester, where I researched the history."

Mrs. Batelle said, "When did most households get a TV? I remember getting our first one, that's how old I am."

"Mostly it started getting popular around the 2000s," said Drew. "Close to there. Like around the 1990s, I think. Maybe a little later."

Mrs. Batelle pursed her lips. "I think earlier. Think about when I was born. We did this last year."

"Nineteen eighty-five?"

"I would love that. That was when my son was born. I was born in 1958, and I can remember a TV. Very vaguely. When I was about five years old, my dad had to go to the hospital and have his teeth out, to get ready for dentures. I was a little thing, and I remember going with my mom to the store to get a little tiny TV—"

Bong, bong, bong, bong, bong, bong.

"Is that our bell?" Mrs. Batelle asked.

Ms. Gorton nodded.

"Okay. Because in those days there were no TVs in the hospital."

Drew got up.

"This little tiny black-and-white TV," Mrs. Batelle went on. "And then we got the great big monster, and that big monster is still at my aunt's. It still works. So anyway, you'll be doing a project. You can do a cartoon strip, you can do a newspaper article, a radio show. Sounds like a blast! Now, Kendra, where do you go?"

"Metal tech."

"Mr. Partridge?"

"Yeah."

"He's a funny man. Bye."

Drew slumped off for biology. I packed up my briefcase and followed Kendra to metal tech.

"Sean, I like the new hat," said a kid out in the hall. "Nice and loose there."

"I like it, too," said Sean.

MR. PARTRIDGE HAD A BIKER'S PONYTAIL and a blacksmith's chest. I found the same gray stool I'd sat on in the morning and positioned myself behind Jamie, Lucas, and Ben—not too close, but not too far. A kid was using a mallet to hammer idly on a piece of metal, watching it bounce around. Two friends discussed a music festival they wanted to go to.

"Okay, a few moments of your TIME!" said Mr. Partridge. "There's two boxes. One that's graded, and one to be graded. If there's no paperwork, no name, well, who's this?" He held up a wrought-iron hook with a twisted handle.

"Ahem, Linus!" said a boy.

"No paperwork, goes back in the box. No job is done until the paperwork is done. Bear in mind, two pieces of paper for each activity project. Production guide, assessment sheet. On the sheet metal trades, the people that don't have it. Brian Kelso I don't have. Unless it's in the box with no paperwork. Rusty, no paperwork. Adam, paperwork. Roger!"

"I did it," said Roger.

"Well, it's not in the box. I'm not going to go looking for it! I'm looking for stuff all over the place here. Kendra and Rich, sheet metal! That's just the first activity. We're in the fifth week now!"

All this time Lucas and Ben had their heads crouched low over an iPad, conferring softly and smiling planfully.

Mr. Partridge said, "We got people working on the hook! We got foundry going on! The sugar scoop is that last sheet metal piece! You have to draw it out on paper." He held up a piece of paper with a shape drawn on it. "This is half scale. You do it full scale. Dimensions on here. You do your template with that. Bill is not here. I don't think we're ready to pour. Are we ready to pour?"

"Bill's is ready to be poured," said a boy.

"We'll wait for Bill. The foundry piece, everybody's doing okay. I got three or four sheets in yesterday for the foundry knowledge book work. It's an open book. Get the answers! Work together! I don't want to lecture all period and bore you to death."

Mr. Partridge walked around the class, checking on drawings. "You have an idea what I'm trying to do here?" he said to me.

"Yeah, I like the sugar scoop," I said.

"So basically, one, two, three," he said, pointing to Jamie, Ben, and Lucas. "Jamie does pretty good."

I paid a visit to Jamie. He was holding a small metal box that he'd made, using the brake bender. He showed me his paperwork. He'd gotten a 90. Now he was supposed to be working on plans for the wrought-iron hook with the twisted handle.

Another ed tech, Ms. Laronde, was talking to Ben and Lucas, who were still snickering over Ben's iPad. "Guys, I'm serious. Go ask Mr. Partridge for some work."

"I've done it," said Ben.

"When have you done the book work?" said Ms. Laronde.

"Last week."

"Did you do the drill press?"

"Yep," said Lucas. "First thing we did was that."

"Well, ask Mr. Partridge what to do, then."

Ms. Laronde went off to help someone else.

I went over. "Did you make that sugar scoop?" I said to Ben.

"Yes," said Ben.

Lucas thought this was very funny. Had Ben found somebody else's sugar scoop and appropriated it? Had he swapped his half-finished scoop for a fully completed one?

"How did you make it?" I asked.

More laughter from Lucas.

"Mr. Bowles showed me how to fold it," said Ben. "Do you have a Sharpie? I forgot to put my name on it. Mr. Partridge will get mad if it gets lost. I've just got to put my name on it, and I'll be done."

"You'll be done with work," said Lucas, laughing and thigh-slapping.

"So, Lucas," I said. "Thanks for telling me that unbelievable story. What are you up to now? Mr. Partridge said I was supposed to sit over here with you guys."

"You don't need to sit with us," Lucas said. "You don't need to watch us."

"That would cramp your style."

"Yeah, just do your own thing." Lucas pulled out the sheet of paper with a half-scale plan of an unfolded sugar scoop on it. "Ben, you remember how to do this?"

"Not really," said Ben. Snurfle snurfle. Either Mr. Bowles had done all the work for them, or they'd stolen or swapped a sugar scoop.

The blower in the forge came on. It sounded like the Bethlehem Steel factory back in its glory days.

Mr. Partridge checked on Lucas. "You need your paper template," he said. "Get the tape. WHO'S GOT THE TAPE? Mr. Bowles must have done the paper template for you."

"Give me some tape," said Lucas.

Mr. Partridge slapped down a roll of masking tape irritably. He turned to Jamie, who was talking to a girl.

The girl said, "Jamie, you know those silver things that hold things?"

"Vise grips?" said Jamie.

"You should know that by now," said Mr. Partridge. He showed Jamie how to measure the hook in order to estimate the length of quarter-inch iron he would need. "How many inches?"

"Sixteen," said Jamie.

"So you write that there. Mr. Baker, you can help him out. You got quarter-inch square solid, sixteen inches, and it weighs how much? How many inches in a foot? See where I'm going with this?"

Jamie and I began calculating how much material we'd need to make the hook. The noise of hammering and pounding was incredible. "How much is it per foot, twenty-five cents?" I said. We looked at a price table for quarter-inch iron.

"No, it's supposed to be forty-five," said Jamie.

"Okay, forty-five cents a foot," I said. "And you have sixteen inches."

Jamie thought. "Would that be forty-five times sixteen?"

I drew him a picture of a length of iron two feet high. "This thing is a foot plus another four inches. Twelve inches is a foot, right?"

"A foot," said Jamie, nodding.

"And then we're going to add one, two, three, four inches"—I made pencil marks—"and then we would have a total of sixteen inches."

"So would that be a dollar and thirty-six cents?"

"I think that's a bit much," I said, "because it's forty-five cents for this much, and then you've got to pay a little bit more money for the extra four inches. So if you've got four inches out of twelve inches, how many is that?" I wrote a four over a twelve. I was going too fast.

"Uh, eight?" Jamie was subtracting.

"You can turn it into two-sixths, or one-third," I said.

"Yeah, one-third, right."

"So now you've got forty-five cents, plus one-third of forty five." I drew three circles on the top of the piece of iron. "That second foot you've divided up into three pieces of four inches. What would be one-third of forty-five?"

Jamie groaned.

We divided forty-five by three on the paper. "Fifteen, boom," I said. "So forty-five cents for most of it, and then you're going to add fifteen cents for the rest of it. How much is forty-five and fifteen?" I wrote it as a sum, with a line under it.

"That would be a dollar and . . ."

"Let's do it," I said.

Jamie carefully added the numbers and looked at them. "Oh, sixty," he said.

"So it's going to cost sixty cents."

Jamie wrote down $.60 on the blank line. "Now I've got to sketch the hook," he said. "How do I sketch the hook?"

"Draw a hook," I said.

Jamie carefully drew a hook.

"Now you just have to make it," I said.

"No, I made it." He lifted a nearby hook from the table. It was perfect.

"Holy crap, you made that?" I said.

"Yeah, I put on the glasses," said Jamie. "I had to make this point first. And then, on the horn, you have to make the hook."

I read the directions. Twist with the vise grips. Reheat. Twist in the opposite direction. "Wow. Hacksaw, reheat, then punch. Did you do all this in one class?"

"No, a couple classes. And I made this, too." He handed me his tin box, which I showered with praise.

Jamie showed Mr. Partridge his math. Mr. Partridge told him to take the hook home and put the paperwork in the folder.

"Power!" called a kid near where the girls had been glue-gunning that morning. I showed him how to press the reset button to get current.

Mr. Partridge pointed to three boys in baseball hats sitting near Lucas and Ben. "They're the bonehead table," he said. "They're just gabbing. I won't give them much of a grade today, but at least I know where they are."

"This is a great class, though," I said. "You're really giving them a taste of a lot of stuff."

"Oh, I know," said Mr. Partridge. He shook his head grimly and pointed out that Ben had left the shop. Lucas was doing something conspiratorial with Ben's iPad. "If they're working, fine," he said. "If they're not, what are you going to do? They might get a three, which is a thirty, for the day. I look at it as time spent. I don't care if they do lousy work." He waved toward the kids who were hammering. "They're beating themselves up over there, but they're working. I get a few of them that show up once or twice a week. This is the fifth week. Fifteen absences, what do I do? I fail them. That's up to them. They know how I do things here." He pointed to Jamie. "This fellow, he works hard. He did the hook, he did the tray."

I sat down next to Lucas, while Mr. Partridge looked over my shoulder. "What happens now?" I said.

"What?" said Lucas.

"What do you have to do now?"

Lucas pointed at the template for the sugar scoop, and the sheet of tin from which it was to be made. "Something with that," he said. No eye contact. He had a pair of tin snips in front of him. Everything was ready to go.

"You've got to cut sixteen and a half," said Mr. Partridge. He marked the first place to snip with masking tape.

"Mr. Bowles messed this up for me," said Lucas.

"Who did the drawing?" asked Mr. Partridge.

"I'm going to say Mr. Bowles did," said Lucas.

"You're going to blame him?"

"He did, he really, really did," said Lucas.

"How come you didn't do it?" said Mr. Partridge.

"He told me, 'Do this, do that.' So I did, and he messed it all up."

Mr. Partridge said, "Well, maybe you ought to do your own, huh?"

"I was doing it," said Lucas, "but then he did it for me." He dropped a magnet on the piece of tin with a loud click and went back to Ben's iPad. Mr. Partridge tore off a small piece of masking tape and stuck it right in the middle of the iPad's screen. His thumb was enormous. Lucas squinted his eyes for an instant and decided not to fly into a rage.

"Those are the bane of education right now, Lucas," Mr. Partridge said, meaning iPads. "You're going to cut it, not all the way."

Lucas began halfheartedly cutting with the tin snips.

"You don't want to cut into the point, you want to stop before the point," said Mr. Partridge.

"Oh!" said Lucas sarcastically. He stopped cutting. Mr. Partridge demonstrated the right way to cut. Lucas snapped the magnet again.

"You watching?" said Mr. Partridge.

"Yeah."

Mr. Partridge put the snips down. "You do it, then." Lucas cut into the metal.

Mr. Partridge left. Ben returned. "I went down there, and she told me to walk out," Ben said to Lucas.

"You walked in, you walked out," Lucas said. They began talking softly together about iTunes passwords.

I took another shot at being a dutiful ed tech. "So, Ben, do you know how to do this, so you can show Lucas?"

"I don't remember how," said Ben.

"I know how to do it," said Lucas.

"If you know how to do it, you should just do it," I said.

They went back to the iPad.

Ms. Laronde came over. "Hey, Lucas."

"He's mad at you," said Kendra to Ms. Laronde.

"I know he's mad at me, but Lucas, you can't stay mad."

"I'm not mad!" said Lucas.

"You can't be on the iPad," Ms. Laronde said.

"Class is almost over," said Lucas.

"No, you have twenty minutes left."

Lucas feigned amazement. "No!"

"Yes."

"I don't want to do it," said Lucas.

"Can you work on it, please?"

Lucas said nothing. He looked down, waiting. Ms. Laronde stood there for a while and walked away.

Near me, behind Lucas and Ben, the three young men in baseball hats sat poking at their iPads. I watched them for a while, until I began to get mad. "Did you guys already do the stuff with the thing?" They looked up and focused on me. "You breezed through it and you're done?"

"We put our work somewhere and we can't find it," said one.

"So you spent the whole period doing nothing?"

"Yep."

I said, "All these machines around, Jesus!"

"We're not allowed to do anything else on them."

"Seems like a waste," I said.

"Yeah."

They returned to their screens.

Lucas asked Jamie if he knew somebody's password. Jamie, innocent, said, "I don't know her password."

Using common passwords, Lucas began trying to hack into an iTunes account. I watched them for a while, got up from the stool, and stood over them.

"So, guys," I said, "this whole time you've spent trying to scam the fricking iTunes, instead of learning something."

Lucas laughed, pleased that I sounded angry.

I pointed at the iPad. "This is a fucking screen," I said. "It's nothing. It's just nothing."

They were delighted with my swear. "It's fucking important!" said Ben.

I picked up the half-cut sugar scoop. "This is actually something real." I set it down.

"We do it because—ah—" said Ben.

"Tell him," said Lucas.

Ben didn't want to say. It had to do with a girl, I think.

I said, "Well, it's your choice."

Three people were hammering madly on their hooks.

I went back to my stool. Mr. Partridge dropped by. "How are they doing?"

"They just gave up."

He nodded. "They're done."

Mr. Partridge moved over to Jamie. "So how much did this cost?"

"I don't remember," said Jamie. Then he remembered. "Sixty cents!"

"Okay. You got money? I do have to charge something for the materials. We'll add it up at the end."

I slid my stool back to Lucas and Ben. "How well do you get along with Mr. Bowles?" I asked.

"Pretty good," said Ben.

I sat. Lucas said, "The first iPad I had got stolen. At the McDonald's parking lot. Then it got stolen again."

"Was it really stolen?" I said.

"Yeah, it was. I had food on top of my iPad. They didn't take the food, they took the iPad."

"My passionate door is open," said Ben.

I said, "Passionate door? What the hell? This is what I don't get. This room is actually real."

Lucas held up the iPad. "This is real. I'm holding it."

"I know it's real, but seriously. You can learn to make a freaking box."

"I don't want to make a freaking box," said Ben.

"But you did it. And Lucas didn't do it. And the guy came by and he saw you were looking at the screen and he thought, Screw it, I'll go and help somebody else. And then you lose your chance. I can't believe it."

"Two weeks ago, he did this," said Ben, nodding at Lucas. "And his got messed up, and when we came back, it was gone."

"It was stolen at McDonald's?"

"No, that was his iPad."

Lucas said, "Listen, he got his box done, and someone crushed it with a boot."

"But he did it again," I said. "He came back. I saw you did that template, I saw you did a good job with that. Now I'm supposed to help you, and I don't know what the next step is. But Mr. Partridge came by and was ready to show you, and you were blowing him off."

"I don't think we were blowing him off," said Ben.

"I don't mean blowing him off that way, I mean you just shrugged him off. It actually hurts his feelings if you do that."

"No it doesn't," said Lucas.

"Of course it does! Any teacher wants to teach. This guy wants to teach you stuff. He has skills, and he wants to teach you something. I watched the whole thing happen! I don't want to bore you, but it's like—" I shook my head. "So what do you guys want to do? In the end, do you want to do something with small engines?"

"I want to go in the military," said Lucas.

"Me, too," said Ben.

"All right," I said. "There you go."

Lucas said, "I'll paint my face black and put a towel over my head and go around with an AK-47 and go, Whoo-hoo!" He went into a Southern falsetto. "I'll shoot you, boy!"

Ben said, "My friend was in high school, he took a chair, he threw it out the window, and hit a car with the chair."

"You know what my dad did, dude, when he was here?" Lucas said. "You know those janitor hats? So he greased one of those and filled it up with water. Took a dookie in it and put it on the principal's truck."

"Wait," said Ben, "did he go here?"

"Yeah, here. The principal at the time says, 'That fucking kid!'"

"Last year my friends and I hated the principal so bad we put lobsters in his car," Ben said.

To Lucas I said, in a near whisper, "Your dad took a shit in a hat, and put it on the principal's car?"

Happy laughter. "Yeah!"

"ALL RIGHT, CHILDREN," said Mr. Partridge. "PACK UP. PAPERWORK UP FRONT."

Lucas and Ben bolted toward the door to wait for the bell. Jamie had been listening. "Those guys are toxic," I said to him. "You should stay away from them. You did really good work, by the way. This is a good class, it's real."

"My dad used to work at Bath, making ships," Jamie said.

"He made destroyers?"

"Yeah, and he used to shoot the guns," said Jamie. "He was in the army, too. He used to work for a company that makes jets."

I asked Jamie what he wanted to do.

"I like building stuff. I want to build machines. I love art, too."

Bong, bong, bong, bong, bong, bong.

Mr. Partridge sat down at his desk as his students trickled out of the room.

"I watched it happen," I said to him. "They're just transfixed by a stupid little rectangle."

"They're in another world," said Mr. Partridge. "They come in, they're late, they sit there, or they wander out. I grade every day. So far I got two, two, two, two, two. Five for the ones that worked. Jamie is about the best worker in here."

"He just told me his father worked at Bath Iron Works," I said.

"Good for him. I did five years there. It's a good experience. If you've got an in, that helps nowadays. I just happened to walk by in Portland at the unemployment office. Bath Iron Works was hiring. Nobody in there but the guy hiring. I got in. This was in 'seventy-three. When I started, there was three thousand people. When I left, there was five thousand people."

"It's great what you're doing here," I said. "And some of it will have an effect. A delayed effect."

"They'll never forget what they do here," Mr. Partridge said. "More so than the English or the math. I try to do shop math. I tell them to go on their iPad, look up metalworking. I ask them, What job would be your dream job in the metal area? I refuse to pass a kid who would mature better in a fifth year. I'm faced now with a couple kids. They want to graduate, but they're not passing. They want us to pass them to get the numbers up."

But sometimes, I said, a kid has to be tossed out into the world to realize what he really wants to do. "I wish I'd had a class like this," I said. Which was true.

"I started in high school," Mr. Partridge said. "I'm a welder by trade. I cut my first arc in high school, which I can get these kids to do. We're in a dilemma now in education. These are the programs that get cut."

We shook hands. Outside, as the buses idled, waiting to fan out over the countryside, it was beginning to rain. I drove home worrying about Sebastian's sleeplessness. And thinking what a hypocrite I was to make an angry speech to Lucas because he wasn't following the paper template and doing his sugar scoop. The only shop class I ever had to take was in eighth grade. It was taught by a trim, taciturn man, Mr. Harris, who told us to make keyhole chairs. No other kind of chair was acceptable; we had to follow his plans exactly. I used the jigsaw to cut the hole in the back of the chair—that was interesting—and I screwed in two of the legs, making pilot holes for the screws, and then I stopped. I looked around the room at eighteen children making the same thing. The chair, made of white pine, was one the cutesiest, ugliest things I'd ever seen—cutesy and so low to the ground that no grownup could sit on it comfortably. It was not a chair, it was an embarrassment, a pedagogical means to an end, and I despised it. I didn't tell Mr. Harris that I despised the assignment, I just didn't finish gluing it, or sanding it, and I didn't stain it with the dark oak stain that never looks good on pine, and I didn't polyurethane it. Mr. Harris gave me an F on my keyhole chair. Then, for the second half of the semester, he taught us drafting: how to write numbers and letters in blocky blueprint style, and how to use a T square and a triangle to make a three-quarter measured drawing of a rounded metal piece with two holes in it. That I liked doing—so I did it, and I got an A. One day a kid I was trying to befriend suddenly punched me in the chest, perhaps because I was good at drafting and he wasn't. The punch hurt a lot because that winter my nipples had oddly swollen adolescent nodules behind them. My eyes filled with tears but I didn't cry. Later Mr. Harris let each of us design our own piece of furniture. I made a Parsons table with a swiveling disk inset in the top, meant to hold our little black-and-white TV, but the TV couldn't swivel, because it was slightly too big for the disk. I passed the course.

To Lucas, the sugar scoop and the wrought-iron hook were like my keyhole chair—absurd make-work exercises with no value to him. Sugar came in a yellow cardboard box with a pour spout, after all. And what was he going to do with a wrought-iron hook except use it as a weapon? He clearly wasn't a pencil-on-paper kid, either—so he was probably going to fail the course, even with Mr. Bowles's daily help, and perhaps he would be forced to take a fifth year of high school. Was a fifth year going to help Lucas mature? He wanted to be a soldier and shoot people. He wanted never to go to juvie again. He didn't need more high school, he needed less high school. He certainly didn't need me fussing at him about how he was blowing off metal tech. On the other hand, maybe it did him some good to know that he was hurting Mr. Partridge's feelings.

Sebastian, though, Sebastian. Why was his doctor giving him those pills? Sleep is a beautiful thing.

And that was it for Day Twelve.

THERE'S NOTHING EXCITING
OR FUN HAPPENING TODAY

I TOOK SOME TIME OFF to write, and then I was back at it, driving to Lasswell Middle School on a Monday morning in May to take the place of Mrs. Lebartus, a sixth-grade social studies teacher on Team Rhine.

"Everything you need is right on the desk," said Mrs. Ricker, the language arts teacher next door. "They're a good group, but they do take advantage. The hairy eyeball is always good." She told me that I should be sure to eat in the teachers' break room and not in the classroom, because there were two kids with allergies. And she whispered a last bit of information: Rebecca, in a baseball hat and camo pants, looked like a boy but was in fact a girl.

A small boy, Jonas, sat down. I asked him what kind of things he liked to do.

"I just stay home a lot," he said, in a flat voice. "I like to play video games, because there's nothing to do. But normally up at camp I ride my bike."

I said hello to two more students.

"Did you like to ride?" Jonas asked.

I loved it, I said, I took my bike on trips through the mountains. "It's a feeling of freedom."

"Yeah," said Jonas.

I skimmed a chapter of the Prentice Hall *World Explorer* textbook while the children hauled chairs off the desks. "I need the broken chair," said Lexie. "My friend's going to sit here and she hates it when I give it to her."

Sunlight poured in on new-seeming tables. Maps and defined terms and learning targets were all over the walls. I said, "This is kind of a nice classroom. You've got carpet."

Lexie said, "We just had to have our carpet re-renovated, because we have peanut allergies, and right after we got the carpeting perfectly all done, like the next day, someone puked on it. It was awful."

Two girls came in, Ida and Amelia. Ida said she rode her horse over the weekend. "I fell off and almost broke my back," she said. "That's why I'm not sitting down."

"I almost broke my tailbone," said Amelia. "Somebody dared me to go on a swing and jump off the swing and over my bike. I did it, and I landed on the bike. And then yesterday I fell down the stairs."

"She's a disaster just waiting to happen," said Ida.

"I've broken like five bones," said Amelia. "I drink milk every single day."

Lexie said, "My dog got her tongue stuck on the doorstep. She had an operation when she was young, and now her tongue sticks out all the time, like this." She lolled her tongue out with a hangdoggy expression. "She was walking through the door and she got it stuck, frozen, and she couldn't rip it off. She's fine now."

"You're tall," said Ida.

There were three bongs. Everyone went quiet, thinking it was time for the pledge. "What happened?" I said.

Silas made a funnel with his hands. "Your attention, please," he said. "Please stand for the Pledge of Allegiance!"

Roxanne took it up. "Then he says, 'Please stand for a moment of silence. For lunch today, we have yadda yadda yadda.'"

"Could you put your name up on the board?" asked Carl.

"Good idea," I said.

"Why do they call it social studies if there's no social studying?" asked Ida.

The principal came on. "Please say with me." We pledged our allegiance and briefly momented our silence. Lunch was tomato soup with a grilled cheese sandwich.

"How tall are you?" asked Carl.

I sent off the attendance sheet.

Bong, bong, bong. Homeroom left, except the ones who stayed, and first block arrived. Rafe and Dennis were deep in a discussion about *The Hobbit.* "Okay, everybody, hello! Welcome to a class with a green carpet. How are you doing today? My name is Mr. Baker, I'm the substitute." I held up the textbook. "And we're going to be reading from this book, that matches the carpet. Who's good at passing out books?" Ten hands shot up. Books were distributed. When it got loud I said, "WOW!" And then I talked in a soft voice. "I like quiet. I love quiet. Everybody loves quiet, because you can think. We're going to have a guest attendance-taker who's going to be calling out names from the corner. Call them out!"

Lexie called out the names, nineteen of them.

When she came to Marisa, she said, "She's not from here, she's from Norway."

I flipped around in the textbook, looking for the right page. "Have you been reading from this book before?"

"Yes."

"What do you think of it?"

"Ugh!"

"What have you learned so far?"

"Landforms," said Jack. "Like mountains, rivers, like that. We've talked a little bit about culture, and we're on culture right now."

"You're on culture, my gosh, you're flying through life," I said. "Page sixty-four, guys. Page sixty-four!"

Dennis, in an orange T-shirt, was jumping around. "Gandalf, what are you doing?" I said. He sat down.

"We're going to be talking about migrating," I said. "Why do people migrate? What is migration?"

"You move from one place to another?" said Jack.

"Exactly, and why would you possibly do that?"

"Like if there was a war in your country?" said Ida.

"That's a good one," I said. "War is horrible and nobody wants to be around it because it causes mass confusion and insanity. So you want to get your kids away from it, your parents away from it, you want to escape it. What's another reason?"

"To start a new village or something?" said Amelia.

"Brilliant," I said. "Like the Puritans who came to this country. They were dissatisfied with conditions in their country, they were being persecuted, so they get on a boat. And then they're in a place that's unbelievably cold, has no food, has somewhat hostile natives, and they think, Why did we come here? Some of them went back."

Another hand, from Brady. "You can make a new home?"

"Maybe your earlier home was washed away in a flood," I said. "And you think, Well, it wasn't that good anyway, so why don't we just up and move?"

Marisa said, "I thought only birds migrate."

"Your parents were in Norway, right?"

Marisa nodded.

"So why did they decide to come to the United States?"

"My dad's job moved. He works for Ambra, which means 'ambergris.' Ambergris is whale vomit."

Missy said, "I want to work there."

"All right," I said, "so let's fly through the chapter and see what they actually say, because that would be nice, wouldn't it?" I read aloud from the textbook for a few sentences and came to a bit of history: *From 1881 to 1920 almost 23.5 million Europeans moved to the United States.* I said, "You can imagine: there were wars, there was hunger, there was a lot of desperation, and millions of people came here, and we said, like the Statue of Liberty, 'Give us your poor, give us your huddled masses, yearning to breathe free.'"

"Where are we?" asked Livia.

"We are on page sixty-four of 'Why People Migrate' in the green textbook," I said. I asked for a volunteer to read from a later paragraph, beginning with the word *demographers*, first explaining what a demographer was. Carl read: *"Demographers use the 'push-pull' theory to explain immigration. It says people migrate because certain things in their lives 'push' them to leave. Often, the reasons are economic. Perhaps people cannot buy land or find work. Or changes in a government may force people to leave."*

"Excellent," I said. "That was well read, and I didn't know about the push-pull theory. But it makes sense. Sometimes you're *pulled* to another place. It's like magnetic attraction. You think, I want to live in New York City! It's so much fun! And sometimes you're *pushed*, because things are bad and you want to leave."

Jack put up his hand. "Two things," he said. "Can I read? And can I go to the bathroom?"

"Yes," I said. "But you have to do both at the same time." Jack shook his head and left.

A boy named Edmond read a paragraph about the Cuban revolution and the Scandinavian exodus to Minnesota. Then another kid, Gus, volunteered, undeterred by the tumbleweed dryness of the prose. "Does she want us to read the whole chapter?" I asked. "Read until we drop?"

"No," said the class.

I skipped ahead, and asked Dawn, in the back, to take up with the Irish potato famine. She began reading almost inaudibly. "Really blast it out—sing out, Louise," I said.

"Hunger and starvation pushed people to migrate," she continued. *"Also England ruled Ireland very harshly. There were very few ways for the Irish people to improve their lives."*

I said, "Wow, little words on the page, little sentences. That was very well read, by the way. We're talking about unbelievable suffering and hunger and famine. And yet it's just little sentences on a page, and we can sit here happily in our class, and say, Yes, it was kind of sad, there was a big famine, the potatoes got sick, so nobody could eat them, and the Irish starved."

"What do you mean the potatoes got sick?" said Amelia.

"The potatoes had a disease," I said.

"The potatoes didn't have a doctor?" said Dennis.

"No. But the thing was that the British didn't help the Irish. That's the real scandal. England is an island. The Irish were starving and the British were right next door and they could have helped and they didn't—and it's shocking."

"Did the potatoes have the flu?" asked Dennis.

"Yes, they did. Flu is a form of virus, right? It makes you sick. Well, there are viruses that affect specific plants, and this was a virus, I think, that made the plants sort of turn black. They became inedible." (Wrong. I looked it up later. Potato blight isn't caused by a virus, it's caused by a fungus-like organism, an "oomycete.")

Lexie raised her hand. "Why don't they just chemicalize the potatoes to fix them?"

"They didn't have certain pesticides," I said. "But the basic problem is that when you plant a whole country with one kind of potato, then when the disease starts, it's going to spread and spread." I glanced down at the textbook. The next paragraph was about immigrants from Vietnam after the war in Southeast Asia. It was long and terribly written. "Let's not even read the next paragraph," I said. "In the case of the Vietnamese people who came to this country, is it push or pull? This is a tough one, because I don't know the answer."

"It's both," said Lexie.

"It's both!" I said. "Right? There was war. We had ravaged the country. Vietnam was not in good shape. On the other side, America is rich and there's lots to do here. Has anyone eaten at a Vietnamese restaurant?"

"No."

"I've eaten Chinese," Amelia.

"I've eaten in McDonald's," said Dennis.

I said, "That's close, but not that close. How about over in the corner, does someone want to read about other kinds of immigration?"

"I do," said Dayton.

"I wanted to read," said Missy.

"You guys like reading! Is this what happens in every class? People read and read?"

"No."

"I like talking, not reading," said Shawn.

Dayton began reading about the nineteenth-century deportation of convicts to Australia. From there the textbook jumped to ethnic groups in Yugoslavia in the mid-nineties. Then it hopped, without catching its breath, to Moroccan and Turkish laborers who leave their families behind and work in Europe. The prose was a time-tunneling parade of disembodied terms, countries without context, and statistics. "When does this class end?" I asked.

"Eight thirty-five," said Amelia.

"So we have to do a little more high-intensity learning and then you're going to rip through a worksheet."

Marisa pretended to tear the worksheet in half.

"Don't rip it up, just rip through it."

Lexie announced that somebody had written in her textbook. "It says, 'Go to page sixty.'"

I quieted the class down. "Lexie has come up with an observation about the textbook. Somebody has written, 'Go to page sixty.'"

"Then it says, 'Go to sixty-nine,'" Lexie said.

"Okay, so somebody has made one of those games where you jump around the pages—so what are you doing in that textbook? You are *migrating*. And that's what brings us back to 'Growing Cities, Growing Challenges.'"

"Oh, yeah!" said Dennis.

I read. "*One of the biggest challenges to today's nations is people migrating to cities from farms and small villages.* Does anyone play Call of Duty here?"

Practically every hand in the class went up. Rafe said, "Modern Warfare Three!"

"Okay, you remember when you're in the favela? GUYS! There's a big, prosperous South American city. And then there's this place with narrow streets. You're hiding, and shooting. That's the favela."

Lexie said, "What is Call of Duty?"

"Lexie doesn't play video games," said her friend.

"That's all right," I said.

"In this modern world," said Rafe, shocked.

"It's kind of a barbaric experience," I explained. "You spend your whole time looking through a scope and saying, 'I'm going to shoot that guy.' Anyway, the favela was a temporary city that grew up around the main city. So, one of the big migrations is when people think, I'm out here in the country, there's a jungle plant here, and I've got a hammock, that's about all I've got—maybe a few rocks—and instead I'll go into the city and make money, maybe I can drive a cab, whatever. But instead there's no place to live in the city, so they build this kind of shantytown, that's made of stuff they've found—sheets of tin, bricks. That's what they're talking about in this paragraph." I read some of it. "*In the past, most Indonesians were farmers, fishers, and hunters. They lived in rural areas.* They moved to urban areas—and then there's a bunch of numbers here. What do you guys think about numbers? Somebody says, 'Eleven million people did fourteen point five seven three!' How much does that help? Somebody says, 'It's a serious problem. Eighteen point seven three people are under the poverty line.' It doesn't help that much, does it? It's just a number. You know what it's doing? It's trying to impress you into thinking, Wow, it's big."

Amelia had her hand up. "I was going to say that," she said.

"We both agree. Good."

Livia said, "I don't know if this is true, but I heard that the smaller the place is, the more people live there."

"Maine's tiny," said Missy.

I said, "Well, Japan, for instance, is tiny. It's just an island, and it's jampacked with people. Hong Kong is—"

"What about Tokyo?" said Dennis.

"Tokyo! You've heard about those hotels."

Lexie said, "Yeah, they're just little chambers."

"They're like bee honeycombs," I said. "They say, 'Okay, sir, you'd like to go to your room?' They take you to your room, and instead of opening a door and walking in and looking out—there's your bed, there's the window, there's the bathroom—it's this little sideways telephone booth. You climb in. It's got a screen. It's got a bed, you can sort of sit up. You have to put on your pajamas outside, and you go in and sleep. So businessmen who work in Tokyo but live too far outside the city can spend the night for cheap in these strange hotels."

Dennis said, "I remember watching a Scooby-Doo movie where that happened."

"There's nothing in China like that," said Missy. "It's not packed at all."

"Well, it depends on where in China," I said.

We spent a moment talking about the men whose job was to pack people on the subways in Japan, and Rafe found a picture of the subway pusher-onners on page 55 of the very textbook we were using. I flipped forward and came to a bar graph. "They very badly want to teach us a graph," I said. I held open the book. "Bottom of page sixty-eight. We've got a pretty color, sort of a lavendery shade, and then we've got an orange color."

Dennis looked at the color key. "The orange is *ruban*," he said.

"Urban!" said several voices, correcting him.

I asked them what *urban* meant.

"Populated," said Lexie.

I nodded. "*Urban* is having to do with cities. Urb. You know, urb."

"Herb!" said Dennis.

"And rural has to do with—"

"Desert?" said Jack.

"Not enough people!" said Edmond.

I said, "Farming, outside of cities. Urban is hip-hop, funky—'urban music.' Urban is cities, rural is country. So when you look at this chart, what's going on? The light orange Creamsicle color, for urban, starts off small, and gets bigger. In 1800, which is two hundred years ago, very few people were in cities. Only three percent of the people were in cities. Then by 1960, it's a quarter, and now almost half the people are in cities. Yes, Dennis?"

"Why do people start living in the cities?" Dennis asked.

"Well, why would you want to live in a city?"

Gus's hand went up. He stood and said, "Can I say something to the class? Just because we have a substitute doesn't mean we can talk and be rude."

I said, "I appreciate your kindness in saying that, but let me tell you something, guys. I want to say something. You have not been rude. I've really enjoyed being with you, and I think it's been fun."

"Thank you," said Lexie.

"Can you touch the ceiling?" asked Amelia.

"I can jump and touch the ceiling," I said. "ALL RIGHT, GUYS! It's time now to do the review, really quickly." I went over migration, push-pull theory, and Cuba—they were supposed to know about Cuba on top of every other country that the textbook had fleetingly mentioned. I told them about the corruption of the Batista regime and mobsters with cigars and Castro's beard. And then we hauled out the double-sided worksheet, with twenty minutes left to go.

While everyone was looking for pencils, Gus came up and apologized to me for the class's rudeness.

"There's a certain amount of chaos that's just natural," I said. "Everyone who sees a substitute thinks, Oh ho! I expect that."

"There's a lot more talking than usual," said Gus. "It's starting to give me a headache."

"I'm sorry, man. I'm really sorry." I flapped the worksheet in the air. "THE WORKSHEET—the worksheet wants you to use your pen or pencil to explain in words why human beings migrate."

There was a moment of confusion about which side of the worksheet was page 1, until Jack explained that the holes for the binder should be on the left. "Lexie, hold it like this," he said.

I turned to Gus. "I'm sorry," I said again. "GUYS, now total and absolute concentration. Why do people migrate? The push-pull theory. Write something about the push-pull theory."

In the silence, Missy came up needing a pencil. I looked around the desk and couldn't find any. "Just use a pen," I whispered. "And if she gives you trouble, tell her that I couldn't find a pencil."

I went around the class helping people formulate half sentences about the push-pull theory. As I explained it over and over, it started to seem like a confusingly pseudoscientific term for something that was self-evident. "People are drawn to go to places that are richer or less dangerous," I explained. Was that push or pull? Obviously both.

"How do you spell *richer*?" said Lexie.

Marisa slowly spelled it for her.

"It doesn't look right," said Lexie.

Dennis and Rafe, in the back, were saying, "May the Force be with you!"

"No more *Star Wars*. We're talking the United States and the rest of this planet. Although you could talk about migration in outer space if there were space aliens."

"There *is!*" said Missy.

I said, "Okay, let's go to Main Idea B. *Why do people migrate within a country?*" I went around helping individual students with that one. "Why in one country would you go to another place? Looking for a job, maybe?" I checked the clock. "This class ends at—eight-thirty?"

"Eight thirty-five," said Amelia.

I needed to get them through this worksheet—that was my one goal— and I still had the whole verso page to do. "Guys, basically, lookit, Main Idea B. It's just a way of making you know this. It says, *Although many people leave their own country for others, migration can occur within a country, too.* All they want you to do is write down some supporting facts. Like, for instance, uhm—people might—"

Amelia, Lexie, and Marisa grabbed their pencils and sat expectantly, smiling, waiting to write down exactly what I said. I burst out laughing. "Look at you," I said.

"Why don't you give us two facts, very slowly," Lexie suggested.

"Why don't *you* give me two facts."

"Okay," said Lexie. "One is that McDonald's isn't healthy."

Amelia said loudly, "Did you know they feed chickens so much corn that they collapse on their feet?"

"Nice going, Amelia," said Dennis.

"That's from health class," said Amelia.

I said, "Let's say you wanted to be a chicken farmer."

"I would never," said Amelia.

"I would never, either," I said. "GUYS, LOOKIT. If you wanted to be a chicken farmer, and you desperately wanted to raise chickens in a nice way, so that they didn't collapse on their feet the way you learned in health class, but instead could walk around and peck and be happy chickens, maybe you would think, Well, I happen to know that in Maine, there are these nice people who raise chickens humanely, so I'm going to go to Maine and be a chicken farmer, and be near my friends, and we're all going to be organic together. Something like that. Main Idea B is just that you want to go places in your own country where you can make more money, or have more fun, where you can live your life the way you want to live it. Maybe there's just not enough food in your village, so you leave and go to another place. So now we've got to really *move*." I shook the worksheet. "The key terms!"

We worked on a sentence with a blank in place of *push-pull theory*. Amelia got the answer.

"Oh my gosh, yes!" I said. "Next sentence. *A person who* bleeps *from one place to another is called a* bloop." I wrote *migrant* and showed them how to tack on the prefix by doubling the *m*, for *immigrant*. "Okay, number seven! *A city or town is sometimes called a* blooping *area*."

"Rural area!"

"Urban area!"

"Urban area," I said. "*A less populated village is sometimes called a—?*"

"Rural?" said Jack.

"Rural area." I read the next question. "Uh-oh," I said, "here's one I don't know the answer to. I'm panicking, I'm panicking. *Many people move—"*

Two chair legs crashed together. I stopped.

"I didn't do that," said Dennis.

"You know, sudden loud noises are so unhappy-making, don't you think?"

Dennis made a fake sad face, and I had to laugh. Sixth-graders were great. Nobody was beating anybody up. Nobody was going to juvie. Male hormones were only just barely beginning to do their nefarious work. I went back to the question, misreading it. *"Many small people.* No, many big people. *Many people move from small towns to cities. This movement is called—"*

"My—gray—tion," said Missy in a bored singsong voice.

"Urbanization," said Amelia.

I pointed to her. "You got it. It's called urbanization!"

"No way!" said Dennis.

"Yep, urbanization," I said. "Have you discovered the secret about school?"

"You learn?" said Jack.

"They want you to learn big abstract words, like *urbanization.*"

"I don't want to learn big words," said Missy.

"What do we do when we're done?" said Lexie. "I wish we had a class where we learned everything about an animal."

"That's a nice idea," I said. "All right, in the last five minutes of intense and focused effort, you have to fill in words in column one and column two, one of these worksheety things that drive us all nuts. Column one. *A person who moves to a new country in order to settle there is—?* Is he an urban area? No. Is he an immigrant?" I made a bugle sound.

Pencils waggling, writing down *immigrant.*

I circulated, checking answers. "I see words forming on the page," I said.

Gus was having trouble with question 6. Stepping backward to get to the front of the room, I kicked Marisa in the ankle by mistake. "Oh, gosh darn it, what happened? Sudden catastrophe. I'm so sorry."

"It's okay," said Marisa.

"A question HAS BEEN RAISED," I said. "In the final seconds of our time together, a question has been raised about question six. *Which of the following is an economic reason why people migrate?* Tricky! *Economic* has to do with money. The answers are *They don't like the government, they can't find work, they're fleeing a war, they're persecuted for their religion.* Which one has to do with how much money they make?"

"B!"

"B. Does everyone agree? B?"

Question 9, about migration to Southern and Southwestern states, also confused people. I said, "Number nine, question about number nye-hyne!" Did they go to the South and Southwest to find better transportation, to find better schools, or was it C, to find better jobs and a warmer climate?

"I think it's C," said Dennis.

"I think you're right," I said. "The South is generally warmer. Of course, in Florida you have flying cockroaches, so that's not so good. Seriously. They're big."

Lexie raised her hand. "I went on a sleepover at my friend's, and it was her birthday, and we were outside—and there was this cockroach that was in their trunk, that they had transported from Florida? It jumped on me, and I screamed and I broke it in half, and the bottom half was walking this way, and the other half was walking this way. After that, a moose came over."

"And that is life in Maine," I said. Everyone launched at once into their own moose-encounter stories.

"OKAY, FRIENDLY PEOPLE. Pass in your textbooks, pass in your worksheets." It was time for them to go. Or no, it wasn't. Class ended at 8:35, said Amelia, not 8:30.

"Shhhhhhh!" said Gus.

"What should we do?" I asked.

"Maybe we can share something we did on the weekend," Lexie suggested.

"Ah!" I clapped once. "We're going to do an interesting unit right now on what I did over the weekend."

"I don't want to talk about food," said Amelia.

Rafe was up and thrashing. "GUYS! NO! SIT! SIT IN THE CHAIR! IN THE CHAIR. Physically in the chair. Physically in the chair. Physically *in the chair.* Very good. You are going to lead off with what you did this weekend. Listen."

"Uh," said Rafe. "I had my friends over."

"Wooo," said several girls.

"For a rave party," said Rafe.

"Okay, he had a rave party this weekend." I pointed to Shawn, in a blue polo shirt.

"I went fishing," said Shawn, "caught nothing, and lost my favorite lure."

Brady's hand. "I went to my little cousin's birthday, and they got him a dirt bike, and I was jealous, but I got to ride it."

Livia said, "Yesterday I went to the fairgrounds, and they were doing ATV racing. There were four-year-olds racing, and my grandfather raced."

Marisa said, "I had a dance competition and I won first prize."

"Congratulations!"

Missy said, "Okay! Outside I did twelve hours of softball. I did two games, three practices, and then I had a softball reunion. And my friend Sally slept over that day, too."

Lexie's hand went up, and she told the class the story of her dog's tongue freezing to the doorstep. "We had to kind of pull her off of it, and it was bleeding, and we got it wrapped up. That was like five in the morning. I went back to bed and I woke up at nine, and I worked at my riding place till twelve."

"Good. The tongue is okay, the dog is okay, guys, you've got to go, thank you all!"

Lexie continued her story as everyone left. "We call her Munch but her name is Tara. We call her Munch because she'll eat everything. She had a pyometra, an infection in the uterus, because she never had babies and we never got it removed, and even though she had an infection and couldn't eat, she still wanted everything. Everything, she'd eat." She walked to the door. "She even ate a stick!" She was gone.

WHEN I EMERGED FROM the teachers' bathroom, Mrs. Ricker stopped to say that there were some snack options in the teachers' lunchroom. "We have leftover chips and water bottles. Help yourself."

"Seriously?"

"Absolutely," said Mrs. Ricker. "We just ask that you eat it in the lunchroom because of the kids who have allergies."

Several cartons of snack-sized bags of potato chips sat on a side table in the lunchroom. There was nobody there. The copier was busily copying and stapling an assessment packet all by itself. The phone rang. I answered it. Nobody there. I hung up. Nothing like potato chips in the morning. I read an ad from Progressions Behavioral Health Services tacked to the corkboard: tutors were needed to help kids with developmental problems for twenty hours a week. The pay was ten to twelve dollars an hour. "We will train the right person," it said. A high school diploma or GED was required. I called my wife and told her about the push-pull theory of immigration, and then I went out to the drinking fountain and had a long drink of cold water. "Oh, yeah," I said. Back in class, I read more of the textbook. Many minutes passed. Eventually I heard lockers banging in the hall.

Roxanne came in with a boy. "That's Mr. Baker, our substitute teacher," she said.

"Hi," said the boy, whose name was Lester.

"We had a very lovely conversation with him this morning," said Roxanne.

I said to Lester, "Are you good at passing out textbooks?" Turned out he was. I took attendance. Hattie, here, Noelle, here, Jarrett, here, Cathleen, here, Foster, here, Jake, here, Sandy, here, Margo, here, Brett, here, Marylou. Marylou?

"I like to be called Lou."

"Lou. Are you here?"

"Yes."

"Good."

Roxanne, here. Kimbra, here. Jarrod, here. Haskel, here. Noah, here. Trent, here. Dean, here. Robert, here. Barbara, here. Andre, here. Lisa, here. Jerald. Jerald?

"He's absent."

"Oh, no, and I made a checkmark," I said. "What am I going to do?" I signed the form. "Anyone want to take this—"

Five hands up.

"I'm just going to go to the one closest."

"Aw, you walked past some people," said Sandy.

"Well, they weren't in front of me," I said, "but they were very well-intentioned people, and I really appreciate the enthusiasm. MIGRATION!"

"Vibration," said Noelle.

"That's what butterflies do," said Estelle.

I gave a little speech about how I liked talking and conversation, but not all at once, and loud sudden noises and explosions of merriment weren't allowed. "Everybody's got to get frowning and serious," I said. "Page sixty-four. Six four! Sixty-four. What is migration?"

Barbara, in a sweatshirt that said "Established 1987," said, "I don't know the exact definition, but when it's cold in one area, they move to a warm area."

"That's exactly right," I said. "Birds migrate. Butterflies migrate. Every year. When people migrate, it's a different thing. Say you were in a country that was ravaged by war. There's mud, broken vehicles everywhere, little fires. And you said, This is ridiculous. I don't want to have my family here anymore. You get on a boat, or you hike across a mountain, and you migrate somewhere. To escape something. And you might not do that every year, because you wouldn't want to go back. So let's read this chapter. Is that what you guys do sometimes? You sit and read it?"

"Yes."

"Do you sing it?"

"No."

"We do not sing it!" said Cathleen.

"Do you chant it?" I read the first line of the chapter in a hip-hop rhythm. Silence. "Okay, I'll start it off and then we can see how it goes," I said. "*Roberto Goizueta was the former head of Coca-Cola, one of the largest companies in the world. Yet when he came to the United States from Cuba, in 1960, he had nothing. This is how he described his escape from Cuba. 'When my family and I came to this country, we had to leave everything behind. Our photographs hung on the wall. Our wedding gifts sat on the shelves.'* Was anyone born in a different country?"

No hands.

"Was anyone born in Massachusetts?"

"I was born in Boston," said Jarrett.

Lester raised his hand.

"Where were you born?"

"Boston."

"Anybody else born in another state than Maine?"

Andre said, "Philadelphia."

"So why did your parents decide, 'We're done with Philadelphia, we want to migrate to Maine'?"

"They were sick of the crime," said Andre.

"They were sick of the crime! We're going to learn about something called 'push-pull migration.' Some people are pushed away from a place because they're sick to death of, say, the crime, or the hunger, whatever it is. Some people are pulled to a place. Okay, who wants to read? Who's got a large melodic speaking voice?"

Sandy read: "*From 1881 to 1920, almost twenty-three point five million Europeans moved to the United States. Since 1971, nearly seven thousand people migrated here from the country of—Vitnim.*"

"Vietnam."

"Vietnam," said Sandy. *"Over nine hundred ninety-five thousand came from Central America. And over four point two million came from Mexico. More than two point four million immigrants came from the Caribbean Islands."*

"Great," I said. "So we've got this globe, and it's sort of like waves are flowing over the planet. Why would *four point two* million people—that's a lot of people—leave Mexico and come to the United States?"

Sandy said, "I went to Mexico. It's because the water in Mexico is not very good. They don't filter their water. So you have to buy bottled water."

"Well, okay, when Americans go down to Mexico they get what's called Montezuma's Revenge. Serious digestive troubles. I mean *serious* troubles. So that's one thing. But what's happening in Mexico is it's poor, and people have no way to make money. So they sneak across the border, and they come to the United States and they work, say, at a hotel, cleaning hotel rooms. Or maybe they drive a cab. Gradually things go better for them, and they find a new life. There are huge forces that are pushing great masses of humanity all over the planet. Say in ancient Rome. Suddenly the barbarians come down from Northern Europe and take over Rome. That's a migration—and it's been happening for tens of thousands of years. Next paragraph, push-pull migration!"

Barbara read the first push-pull paragraph. Lisa, with long thin arms and a shy voice, read another paragraph. I told them about Fidel Castro, and the mobsters, and the wealthy Cubans who fled to the United States. "If you left a country because it was poor, and you went to another country, say Japan, or the United States, because it was rich, you're both being pulled and pushed. This is what they want you to learn. Push-pull migration. PUSH-PULL. If you know that, you're going to do swimmingly well on the worksheet. And that's the aim of life, isn't it? Anyone interested in the Irish Potato Famine?"

"I'm Irish," said Jarrod.

"Why don't you read that paragraph, then."

Jarrod read about the famine. I suddenly realized that the class had been quiet for a long time.

"So they came here and became Irish Americans," I said. "They enormously enriched our country. The great thing about America, for a while, was the Statue of Liberty. She said, Come on over! We'll take care of you. Doesn't matter where you came from. We had an open-door policy."

Next was more about Vietnam. I didn't want to read the paragraph, so I paraphrased it, and asked again if anybody had eaten at a Vietnamese restaurant. No. Chinese, yes. Thai, no. "Do people like sushi here?"

"Blech," said Robert.

"Caesar salad's my favorite," said Noelle.

Brett read from the number-filled paragraph about urbanization. *"In 1978, about four point five million people lived in the capital of Jakarta,"* he read. *"By 2000, its population was about eleven million. And demographers estimated that by 2015, the population will have risen to about twenty-one million."*

"So those are just big tiresome numbers that people are saying to you," I said, "but all of those numbers represent individual people who had to think about their tiny lives, and say, 'Where would my children be happier? Where would my aged father want to go? Let's figure out what we can do.' And sometimes the best thing for them to do is not to stay put, but to go somewhere. They do it by the millions, if things are really bad. So we go to this graph now."

"I'm not done reading," said Brett.

"Well, I think it was darn good. Darn good. And Jakarta is a beautiful name for a city. *Jakarta!*"

Lou said, "You should sing it."

Jarrett said, "Don't give him ideas."

We got to the orange and purple chart. The word for city in Latin was *urbs*, I said, which was pronounced "erps." We talked about people crowding toward the city of São Paulo. Worksheet time. Groans and chattering as the worksheet floated around the room.

"Can we work in groups of two?" asked Lou.

"Yes."

"Can we work in a groups of three?" asked Foster.

"Yes."

Trent, who was a tiny mischief-maker, started squirming.

"He's allergic to himself," said Foster.

"You guys are evil," said Trent.

"I'm a unicorn, but I lost my horn," said Roxanne.

Estelle shushed the class. Everyone went still. I sang the first few bars of the Pink Panther song. "Just try to keep the chat way down, or I'll have to say everybody work on their own, and that wouldn't be good."

"Rox, you're supposed to write down the meaning," said Noelle.

I went around nudging, prompting, giving examples, pointing to bolded words in the textbook. You might move to LA because you want to make video games. You might move out of New York because rents are too expensive. You might move to Nashville because you want to be a country singer. It has to be a powerful force, pulling or pushing, because it's a lot of work to migrate. Somebody who migrates is an immigrant, and you double the *m*.

Haskel told me about Skyrim, a video game. "Once you kill a dragon for the first time, you literally just *absorb its soul*."

I gave a three-minute warning for the first page. "Just scribble something down!" I said.

We slashed and hacked through the questions on the reverse side. Question 8 again gave problems. *"Many people move from small towns to cities,"* I read. *"This movement is called* FUNKADELIC. No, what is it called?"

"Migration!"

"Immigration!"

"Urbanization!"

"You're moving from small towns to cities," I said. "You're urbanizing."

I collected a few finished sheets. Jarrod found an inflatable world globe and threw it to Jarrett, over Robert's head.

"This is our planet," I said, catching it.

"Jarrod and Jarrett are torturing me," said Robert.

"Ask Robert where anything is, he knows it," said Roxanne. Where was Cuba? Robert knew. Where was Siberia? He pointed to Serbia, then found Siberia. Where were the Rocky Mountains? He found them. Where's the moon? Robert pointed to the air.

"This is Dubai," he said.

"Good. Okay. PUT YOUR NAME AT THE TOP. Grab your books. I want to see this room cleaned UP! Good work today! Lots of good concepts mastered!"

"I will be back for homeroom!" said Roxanne.

"Good, see you then."

"I might be back at the end of the day," said Kimbra.

"Hope to see you around."

"Are you going to be here tomorrow, too?" she asked.

"I don't think so."

"Noah, can I show you a handshake real quick?" said Jarrett. He shook Noah's hand and did a little shuffle and a double fist-tap.

NEXT BLOCK, a tall kid, Jerome, walked in. "Can I take the attendance down?"

"Yes, but we haven't taken it yet," I said.

"I'm just making sure ahead of time."

"That's so prepared of you," I said.

"I know, right?"

Another kid, Clint, came in, wearing an Apache helicopter T-shirt. "If you need help with the attendance, just ask me," he said.

"No, don't ask Clint," said Jerome, "he's the biggest troublemaker in this entire school."

Astrid said to Clint, "You got sent out of Ms. Plancon's room three times."

"Don't bring that up," said Clint.

"WELCOME," I said. I called out eighteen names, checked off seventeen, signed the sheet, and handed it to Jerome. "Okay, PAGE SIXTY-FOUR of this beautiful green textbook that actually matches the carpet. Page sixty-four. These pages are kind of shiny. They're covered with words. We're going to be talking about why people migrate. What do you do when you migrate?"

Brandon's hand shot up, and then he realized he didn't know the answer. He pulled his hand down.

Martha raised a hand. "You're sleepy and you don't wake up!"

I said, "That is an excellent try, but—sleep?"

"Hibernate," she said, her hand on her forehead.

Astrid, who had a loud singing voice, read the beginning of the chapter, and she read it well. We talked about Cuba, about persecution in Europe, about whether *Jamaica* was pronounced *Jamaica* or *Jameeka*, about how tall I was, and about the job description of a demographer. Amber found a definition of *demographer* in the back of the textbook. She read, "It's a *scientist who studies human populations, including their size, growth, density, distribution, and rates of births, marriages, and*"—she smacked her hand down on the page—"*deaths.*" There were two minutes left before lunch.

"Can you play basketball?" asked Kent. "Can you jump and turn and dunk the ball?" asked Kent.

"Oh, I did the flying double axel," I said. "They called me the Rocket. I was up there!"

"I'm going to call you Rocket!" said Kent.

"No, I wasn't very good at basketball," I said. "Besides height, you actually have to have skill. Can you palm the ball?"

"I can," said Kent.

I checked the big hand on the clock. "All right, guys, lunch."

"Bye, Rocket!" said Astrid.

"Bye, Rocket!" said Kent.

Ricky was hopping in place. "Can you let go of my foot?" he said to

Dougal. "I can't go downstairs like this!" He and Dougal hopped into the hall.

I went to the teachers' break room to get another snack pack of potato chips. Two teachers, Mrs. Yancey and Ms. Plancon, were eating leftover birthday cake and complaining about kids. Mrs. Yancey said, "I was like, 'In the future, if you're standing outside my door because you came to class, you need to not have a full conversation that I can hear from my desk.' They were like, 'Bleh bleh bleh,' while they were waiting at the door."

"They're wound today," said Ms. Plancon.

"Why? Why are they wound?" asked Mrs. Yancey. "There's nothing exciting or fun happening today."

I said, "I think they got wound up in my class, and I'm sorry."

"No, no, they were wound up from the start," said Ms. Plancon.

They resumed an earlier conversation about Jerome. Mrs. Yancey said, "I said to him, 'Aren't you a little bit embarrassed? We have a guest in our classroom today. This is the impression that she has of you—that you are that kid? Who makes that sort of comment?'"

"He doesn't care," said Ms. Plancon.

"We're starting our argumentative essays," Mrs. Yancey said.

"You'd think he'd be good at that!"

"I actually said that," said Mrs. Yancey. "I said, 'Spending all this time with you, I know that arguing is something you do really well.' So we're brainstorming all these topics. We had Haskel, who was saying stuff like, 'You know, I really think that the US military should be paid more, because look how much professional athletes make.' It was great. And then Ricky said, 'All hungry people should be fed.' Really just these neat, insightful social issues that they're coming up with. And Jerome says, 'Skechers are a ripoff.'"

Ms. Plancon laughed. "That's so . . . !"

"I'm like, 'Child, you have no soul!' They need to learn to think. Marty asked to go to the toilet. I'm like, 'Again?' And I'm like, 'What is taking you so long? What are you *doing*?'"

"He's done," said Ms. Plancon.

"Done for the year, or done with the activity?" Mrs. Yancey.

"I think he's done with the year," said Ms. Plancon.

I chewed a potato chip.

"I bought this thing called Stress Relief," said Ms. Plancon. "It's an aromatherapy thing."

"Did it work?" asked Mrs. Yancey.

"No," said Ms. Plancon. "But I'm going to pull it out. I am so wound right now."

Mrs. Yancey said, "They'd go, 'This stinks! What's that smell? Bleh bleh bleh!'"

"Take care," I said, softly closing the door.

My room was quiet. Textbooks and worksheets and backpacks lay on the desks, awaiting the return of seventeen children.

The school secretary arrived to tell me to call Beth, the sub caller.

I dialed 8 for an outside line. Beth said that a request had come into the central office for a tutor for a hearing-impaired middle school boy. It was a full-time tutoring job, all day, one on one, to help him catch up with his work, and it paid twenty-five dollars an hour. It went to the end of the school year.

"Wow, that's a lovely salary," I said. "The only thing is I kind of like being in class with these kids. Do you have any advice?" Beth said it was completely up to me. I said I'd call my wife and think it over and get back to her in five minutes.

I called my wife and told her the situation. She said I should do what I genuinely wanted to do. I heard noise from the hall. "Uh-oh, the students are coming back now," I said. "Love you. Bye-bye."

Clint was making crazy coughing sounds.

"Bye, Estelle," said Goldie.

"Hello! Hello!" I said. "Come on in!" As soon as I saw the kids take their seats and look up at me expectantly—this group of complete strangers that had become, for one day, my boon companions and fellow conspirators—I knew I couldn't possibly take the tutoring job. What, miss this madness?

Did I want to spend all day, every day, forcing a hearing-impaired boy to master a curriculum that I mostly didn't believe in? No. *I was a substitute.*

"I like piggies," said Goldie. "They go glump glump glump!"

"Where were we?" I said.

"How are you doing, Rocket?" said Kent.

"Do you have any candy?" said Rosabelle.

Out in the hall, a moving bolus of kids, thankfully not ones from my class, were making a racket. A little boy emerged from a nearby classroom and screamed, "LADIES AND GENTLEMEN! GO TO YOUR CLASSES!"

I closed the door, my eyes big. "Did you hear that? That was the loudest thing I've ever heard."

"Can I read?" asked Philip. Philip read, and then Jerome read. *"In the 1800s, many Scandinoo—"*

"Scandinavians," said Astrid.

"Oh, well, thank you," said Jerome good-naturedly. *"Many Scandinavians moved to Minnesota and Wisconsin. They wanted their own land, which was scarce in Scandinavia. Some also left to escape religious persecution."*

"So the Scandinavians were *pushed* out of their former lands," I said. "They said, We're tired of Sweden and we're tired of Norway, so we're going to roll up our sleeves nice and high, and we're going to—"

Jerome rolled up his sleeves and flexed his arms.

"Show off our guns," I said.

"Locked and loaded," said Jerome, quivering.

"And then we are going to move to the United States."

"What page?" said Clint. I told him. Clint read about Ireland, and he did it fluently. Then, as we talked about the potato famine, things went off the rails. Martha put her hand up. "Do you think there's going to be a World War III?"

The question irritated Jerome. "Why would you be thinking of that?" he said. While I tried to explain urbanization, he could not shut up. His mouth just kept going. Finally I said, "GOD. JEEPERS CRIMINY! BE QUIET. If I could teach you one thing in this class, what would the one thing be?"

"That I should have had a V8?" said Jerome.

"Be quiet," said Astrid.

I said, "If somebody is waving his arms like an idiot, trying to convey some idea, and you're sitting there going, 'I like my dirt bikes, I like my mudding trucks'—no, it's rude, right? And it causes people to give little speeches. Remember that."

"What's happening in Egypt?" said Dougal. "There's smoke coming from the cities."

"What page is that, sir?"

"Page sixty-nine," said Dougal.

"There's smoke coming from page sixty-nine, let's check it out." I found the picture. "All right, we've got a picture. Does anyone want to read the caption?"

Astrid spun around in her chair and said furiously, "SHHHHHHHH!"

"Oh my gosh," I said, impressed. "The spittle was spraying. Do you want to read it?" Astrid read the caption perfectly. It was unhelpful. *"Across the world, growing cities face special challenges,"* etc.

"So in Cairo, Egypt's capital," I said, "they're taking mud from the riverside, and what are they doing with the mud?"

"They're making homes," said Astrid.

"Right. And here's this modern city behind them. Great. We have blazed through the chapter. And now it's worksheet time. Who wants to pass out the worksheets?"

"I do, I want to be a suckup," said Jerome.

"I want to grow a beard just like him," said Kent.

"And while we're doing that, who wants to read another random word from the dictionary?"

Rosabelle flipped through the pages until she found the word *egg*. "There's two definitions," she said. *"Egg number one. Oval or round body laid by a female bird, fish, etc., containing the germ of a new individual."*

"The germ of a new individual," I said. "Isn't that beautiful? It's an egg. Next definition."

"To urge or incite," Rosabelle read, with help from me.

"This is kind of interesting," I said.

"Nuh-uh," said Clint.

"The germ of a new baby," said Jerome. "Looking good in the pan."

"Guys, EGG. Crack, birdie comes out. But there's also the second definition, which is 'urge.' I'm going to egg you on! Egg you on. That's a totally different word. I don't know why, but it's true. We just learned it. And now let's work on the worksheet. Ten minutes to do side one!"

A few minutes into the worksheet, Jerome stole Rosabelle's pencil and the class disintegrated. The girls screamed their outrage at the malicious boys.

Astrid said, "You want me to get them to be quiet? I'll sing."

Ruby said, "I can go get the teacher next door."

"I don't think that's necessary, do you?"

"Yes, because I can't concentrate," Ruby said.

Astrid began singing loudly.

"Don't sing," I said.

"I can't concentrate," said Ruby. She went next door.

A minute later, Mrs. Ricker stood in the doorway. "Okay, ladies and gentlemen, I understand you are to be doing a worksheet," she said. "You are to be seated and silent, doing that worksheet. This door is open. If I hear you I will come back, and it will not be fun for you."

"I'm sorry they made so much noise," I said to her.

"No, no, it's fine, sometimes they take advantage," Mrs. Ricker said. She went back to teaching her class. My class went funereally silent.

"See, that's what's embarrassing," I whispered. "That's embarrassing for me."

For the rest of the class, I made the rounds, helping kids with Main Idea B and questions 6 and 9. "I need some ideas," said Goldie. "Some people are too poor to pay their bills?"

"Put that down, good," I said.

They began handing in their worksheets.

"I've finished!" said Ricky.

"I've finished!" said Philip.

"Good, bring them up. Pristine. Good. Excellent. You are the man."

What a disaster. Once again I'd allowed the class to be hijacked by a feud between three of the loud-but-good girls and three of the loud-and-bad boys. I should have been able to shut it down with some kind of timely fierce threat display, but instead I'd tried to joke my way through, and it hadn't worked. I felt chastened and queasy and incompetent.

"Mr. Baker," said Astrid, "we're one minute late for locker break."

"LOCKER BREAK," I announced. What was locker break?

"What do you do if you're not done?" said Rosabelle. "I couldn't get much done, it was too noisy. Should I do it for homework?"

"Do you want to do it for homework? Or do you just want to hand it in?"

She handed it to me.

"I didn't finish," said Amber, who had left some lines blank.

"Don't worry about it, you did a good job with it," I said.

When they'd gone to their lockers and returned, when all the textbooks were piled and all the worksheets were handed in with names on the top, they made their daily forced migration to their next class. What a bust. I looked at the sub plans. "Now what are we doing, for flip's sake?" I whispered to myself.

NEXT. Theresa, a fleshy girl with cropped salmon-colored pants, held an ice pack to her face. "It's leaking already," she said.

"Wow, this is a huge class," I said.

"Twenty-two people," said Theresa.

"ALL RIGHT, SHHH," I said to everyone. "Mrs. Ricker's door is open, and she doesn't like loud noise, and I don't either, so be quiet, okay? I'm going to do something really unusual. I'm going to take attendance."

I called out seven names. "Are we having fun yet?"

"Yes," said Hugo.

I called eight more names. "You know," I said, "when they used to take attendance, and I was in class, I was always embarrassed when they would get to my name. My name is Nick. So I hate doing this, but I have to."

I called out the last seven names. Only Wesley was absent. "Who knows the way to the office?"

"Everyone does," said Avery, raising his hand.

"All right, you're the first person I saw to raise your hand."

Dede asked, "Why is there a dictionary on the desk?"

Because it was random dictionary word time, I said. "Just put your finger down anywhere on this page," I said.

"There," Dede said. Her finger was at *flexion*.

"*Flexion*, that's a good one."

"What's that?" said Dede.

"FLEXION," I said. I made two fists and flexed my arms. "Flexion. Flexion is *the bending of a joint or limb by means of the flexor muscles*. The FLEXOR MUSCLES." I snapped the dictionary closed. "All right, today there's going to be total silence, and total happiness. Total contentment. And total migration, because we are talking about, bada-bing, Why People Migrate. What is migration?"

Hands went up. "It's when people move," said Shannon.

"Right, butterflies migrate, but we're talking about people. There's incredible chatting to this side of the room, I don't like it. I will take names."

"Carson," said Shannon.

"I was in a car that got hit by a train and I got brain damage," said Carson rapidly.

"Yeah, sure," said Hugo. "He also said he played with gasoline."

"He said he was hit by a sniper," whispered Shannon.

I went over to Carson and looked at him. He shook his head rapidly and made a bubbling, laughing sound. "Hello," I said. He looked up at me with goggle eyes. I turned to a boy near him, Amos, who'd had his hand up. "What were you going to say?"

Amos said, "Migration is like when people move to different parts of the country, or the world, to get resources or stuff?"

"Excellent," I said. "This guy's good. Textbook, page sixty-four. Have you been reading this textbook, by the way?"

Yes!

"Have you been enjoying this textbook?"

No.

"Have you been loving this textbook?"

No!

"I have been *loving* this textbook," said Wendell, embracing it.

"What page?" said Brody.

"Six four," I said. "Was anybody here born not in the United States?"

"I was born in New Hampshire," said Shannon.

I whistled. "You're an immigrant!"

"I was born in York Hospital," said Amos.

Commotion.

"Carson, be quiet!" said Hugo.

I went back to stand in front of Carson and I gave him the hairiest eyeball I could manage. He shut his mouth.

"Where were you born, man?" I said.

"Colorado."

"So your parents decided to leave Colorado and come to Maine. Why did they want to come to Maine?"

"I don't know," said Carson. "They just did." He snarfled.

"So your parents *migrated*—oh, it doesn't matter. You don't care." I walked away from him.

"He does this all the time," said Dede. "My mother was an immigrant. She was born in Germany, and then she came to the US."

"Okay," I said, "and there's tons of people like that. This country is filled with immigrants."

Cole raised his hand. "My mom's grandfather came from Italy."

There was a roar from the hall.

I said, "And now there's a massive migration of kids down the hall. They're all from Scandinavia."

"Those are butterflies," said Everett.

"Those are some big butterflies," I said. I opened the textbook. "So they're going to start us off with a little bit of knowledge about the head of Coca-Cola."

"An intro," said Shannon.

I nodded. "An introduction. This man, Mr. Goizueta, was born in Cuba, he had nothing, he came to this country and became the head of Coca-Cola, and Coca-Cola is rich as anything because it's delicious, it's sweet, and it's nutritious, and if you drink a lot of it it will dissolve your teeth."

Brody said, "Did you know that Velveeta, before they put the color in it, is clear? My aunt's friend went to a Velveeta factory."

I read the quote from Mr. Goizueta. "Migration," I said. "The movement of people. Who wants to read a paragraph aloud? Do people do that in this class?"

Yes.

"Do they enjoy it?"

No.

"It depends," said Aurelia. "She picks people!"

"That are not raising their hands," said Theresa.

"You should call on Carson to read," said Wendell. "Because he can't."

Bad idea. I saw a hand, from Jonas. "Take it away!" I said.

"For centuries, people have moved from one place to another," read Jonas. *"This is called migration."* The parade of immigration statistics followed—*Groundhog Day* in social studies. A girl in the back, Lucy, read the push-pull passage fluently but inaudibly.

"Well done," I said. I gave them a capsule summary of the Cuban revolution, and then Aurelia read about the potato famine in a delightful, folksy-but-dramatic delivery. She was a natural. "Great reading," I said. "Think of how hard it is to make a decision to leave everything you know—all the streets, the countryside, your relatives—and go somewhere totally different. It's a huge, frightening decision. So something has to be really wrong in the place that you're at, or something has to be really right in the place you're going to." I was talking in a tired, serious voice. I wasn't trying to make jokes. The class was still and attentive. Even Carson was quiet, I'm not sure why. They seemed to want to hear about Ireland and Vietnam, and about migrations within a country, from country to city. "Does anyone here live on a farm?" I said.

Theresa raised her hand. I asked her what she had on her farm.

"Chickens, pigs, and calves."

"Great. Two hundred years ago, almost the entire population of the world lived in rural places—farms, tiny towns. Now it's very different. Now almost half the world lives crowded in cities. So this huge thing's happened, and it's called urbanization." I wrote the word on the board, and I told them about a time I went to Seoul, Korea. "It's one of the biggest cities in the world. You get on the subway, going quite fast—there are beautiful, clean, fast subways. An hour later you're still on the subway going through the town. It just goes on and on. It's gigantic." I described the capsule hotels in Tokyo, and I suggested that they have a look at the photo on page 69 of men building mud-brick shanties outside of Cairo. "Okay, now you know what you need to know to fill out the famous worksheet," I said. But watch out for the tricky questions, I warned— especially Main Idea B. "Think about your own experience. Why would you want to move to Boston? Or if you were in Boston, why would you want to move to Maine and start a chicken farm?"

"Chickens smell," said Theresa.

I told them if they did a good job on the first page, they could work with a partner. They went to work. An ed tech, Mrs. Morse, stole in as I was on my first tour of the class. She went straight over to Carson and stood behind him. His worksheet was blank. "You're not staying here unless you can get something done," she said.

"So?" said Carson.

"Come on, Carson," she said, in a flat, irritated voice.

"No," said Carson.

"We'll go down to the office and tell them no," she said. "Carson, get something done, or you'll be down in the office again."

"I am getting things done," said Carson.

"I don't need a wise comment," said the ed tech. "Come on." She led Carson away, nodding to me as she closed the door behind her.

"Who is she?" I asked.

"She's an ed helper," said Theresa. "She helps kids."

"And deals with them," said Everett.

"She just takes kids," said Hugo.

"She yells at kids," said Aurelia.

"She takes them away!" I said, in a mad-scientist's voice.

"She's a kidnapper," said Everett.

"She takes them out into space," Hugo said.

"She tickles them," said Wendell.

"She just takes them down to the principal's office to rot," said Aurelia, laughing. "I'm just kidding."

Theresa threw her melted ice pack away. I let Lucy and Rachel, who'd made progress, go out in the hall.

"I've finished," said Amos.

"How did you do that?" I said.

"I don't know."

I checked the worksheet. Everything was right. Rural, urban, push, pull. "Brilliant, nice job, Amos."

Brody said, "He's beating me up"—pointing to Wendell.

I grabbed a clipboard and held it up. "All right, I've got a clipboard. I'm going to put a blank piece of paper on top of it, and I'm going to write down anyone's name who is disturbing the peace and tranquility of this wonderful class. Okay? Thank you."

"What tranquility?" said Everett.

"What's tranquility?" asked Theresa.

Aurelia showed me her worksheet. "I don't understand this question," she said.

"Economic reasons push them to leave, don't they?" I said. "You can't find land, you can't find work. Sometimes a war pushes you. What are some reasons that would pull you?"

Amos interrupted to ask me what he was supposed to do.

"You are supposed to find a book from the magic book area."

Amos pulled out *The Big Book of China*.

"That's a good one," I said.

"Big books for small minds," muttered Everett.

"The only reason he has a big book is because he wants to read something else," Theresa explained. She was right. Amos slyly positioned a manga comic behind the propped-up China book.

Another ed tech appeared, Ms. Heath, and said hello. She went to work quietly helping people. No hectoring.

Everett handed me his paper filled with writing. "Whoa, you're using specific examples, man," I said. He'd quoted statistics from the textbook, and he'd filled the page with careful handwriting. "You are on top of it!"

"He's G/T," said Theresa.

"G/T, eh? Did you put your name at the top? That's all you're missing now. You'll fly through the back page."

"Can I work with a partner?" asked Everett.

"Yes."

Brody came up with a finished worksheet. "Excellent, very good," I said. "You are done."

Brody said, "What do you want me to do now?"

I looked at the sub plans. "Well, I think what she wants you to do is invent a cure for cancer. No, I think she just wants you to find a book, or talk to a friend, gently, quietly."

Shannon was done. I told her to read a book.

"Can I read one of my own books?"

"Of course."

Amos came back up to find something more to do. "You're reading that China book," I said. "Did you already read it?"

"Yes, I read it all," said Amos stoutly.

"Did you memorize it?"

"Yes, I did," Amos said. "I have a photographic memory. I'm learning all the symbols, fire, earth, water, wood, and metal." He gave me a wicked look.

One by one I checked the sheets. Mostly what kids wanted was for me to tap on the paragraph where a particular phrase that answered a question could be found. "How come you guys were much faster with this assignment than some of the earlier classes?" I asked.

"Because I'm smart," said Theresa. I admired the way she'd written her name with a flourish on the *T*.

"You're my favorite teacher," she said.

"I'm finished, what do I do?" said Chris.

"You can find a book, you can talk quietly to your friends. Something non-destructive."

Amos was standing, wanting another book. I said, "Do you want to read about Israel, or about the hungry planet?"

"I already read those," said Amos.

"I'll show you a good book." I pulled out *Charlotte's Web*, but he said he'd already read that. I flipped through some more.

"All of these have pictures," said Amos. "I don't like the pictures."

I pulled out a simplified version of *Frankenstein*. "This is a sort of dumbed-down retelling," I said.

"Dumbed down?" said Amos.

"If I'm done, can I draw instead of read?" asked Theresa.

"Of course."

Amos said, "I want to draw!"

"Yeah, draw, draw," I said.

Everett brought up his sheet again. On the reverse side, he'd written several small treatises on immigration, and his sentences were skillful. "Everett, you are good. That's all I can say. I can't say anything else."

"Thank you," he said.

"Just take another close look at the spelling of *immigrant*."

He looked at it.

"Spelling has no correlation with intelligence," I said. "But it is useful to spell things right."

"And then what do I do?" said Everett.

"You can read, draw, compose music, do whatever you want."

"I need help," said Wendell, pointing to a question.

I tapped the relevant paragraph. "It's usually hidden away in the text somewhere," I said.

Jonas came up with his sheet and I scanned it. "Oh, I like what you did here," I said. I pointed to *immagrant*. "Just check the spelling on that. I think you pulled it off of Everett's." I showed him the word on the whiteboard.

There was a whoop of laughter in the corner. I went over. "I'm your favorite student," said Aurelia.

I checked a few of their papers. "That's a work of art if I've ever seen one. Avery, congrats. Now you can read, you can create a new form of rocketry."

He held up his paper. "What am I going to do with this?"

"I don't know what you can do with it. It looks great. I'll take it and give it to the teacher." He'd also copied *immagrant* from Everett.

"He's going to sell it," said Wendell.

"Yes, I'm going to sell it on eBay," I said. "Rare, collectible worksheet, filled out by Avery. Well done. What happens now?"

"Now it's study hall," said Everett.

"With the same kids?"

"Yes."

Ms. Heath said, "Wendell, sit down at your desk." I was very glad she was there. With so many kids there were a million questions to answer. The speedier kids helped the slower ones, and in this way everyone's immigration worksheet got done, more or less.

Mrs. Ricker, the English teacher, came in through the adjoining door. "OKAY, LADIES AND GENTLEMEN. Remember last week, we instituted a study hall from twelve thirty-five to twelve fifty-five?"

Yes.

"Okay. That is twenty minutes for you to get some work done. It is not twenty minutes for you to socialize with your friends. It is twenty minutes for hundreds club, pronouns packet, whatever else it is that you have on our board that says 'Due whenever.' It is NOT social time. At twelve fifty-five you will go to your STAR class, and we are switching today. If you want to listen, I can go through the list."

YES.

"BUT I WILL NOT DO THAT IF YOU ARE TALKING. Because I will not talk over you. I will actually tell both rooms at the same time, just to save my voice. Give me a moment." She disappeared into her classroom and talked to them.

"Mr. Baker," said Brody, "can I go get my ruler from my locker?"

I held up a finger.

Mrs. Ricker returned and read off twenty-one names. "All of you go to Ms. Plancon's STAR. None of you should be asking me where you're going, because you're listening, right? This group is going to be with Mrs. Yancey." She read off more names. "If I just said your name, you're with Mrs. Yancey." She turned back to us. "Okay? Everyone knows where they're going? Give me a thumbs-up?"

Thumbs went up. She went back to her class.

I called Beth back. "I know it sounds silly because it's a lot of money," I said, "but I think I'd be happier filling in when you need me as a sub than committing to a Monday-through-Friday schedule till the end of the year." She said that was fine.

I helped Amos with a math exercise meant to teach order of operations. Aurelia's iPad wasn't working, so she rebooted it.

Theresa made a loud, revolted screech.

"All right, where's my clipboard?" I said.

"He just made me lick a pencil," said Theresa, pointing to Amos.

"Somebody's name is going to be on the board now," said Amos.

"Yeah, *Amos*," said Theresa.

"Do you feel a sudden wave of fear passing through you?" I said to Amos.

"Yes," said Amos. "But she did it to me, too. I have a red mark on my arm."

"It's all over now," I said.

"It's not all over, it never happened," said Amos. "So that means you'll never write my name on the clipboard."

"He looks constipated," said Aurelia, laughing, leafing through a book.

I said to Theresa, "Do you know *Lord of the Rings*?"

"Yes," said Theresa.

"I feel like Sauron. My eye looks over the classroom. *Wong, wong.* Nobody cares."

Aurelia, Theresa, and Amos began laughing themselves sick at a photograph in an art book. I glanced at it—it was a picture of a wizened, bare-breasted tribal woman making dinner in clay pots.

"I think it's a man," said Theresa.

"Does it make a difference?" said Amos. Wild giggling.

"That is totally out of control," I said.

"They keep on pointing this stuff out," said Theresa.

"SHH!" I said. "I'm on the hook. You've got to be quiet, you've got to be cooperative." I pointed to a hole in Amos's desk. "You've got a hole in your desk, man."

"It's been there for a while," Amos said.

Aurelia said, "He scrapes it."

"No I don't!"

"What do you know about the order of operations?" I asked. "What do you do first?"

"Parentheses," said Theresa. "Please Excuse My Dear Aunt Sally."

"Parentheses," said Amos. "Exponents. Multiply. Divide. Add. Subtract."

"You're my favorite teacher," said Aurelia.

"Thanks, it's very nice of you to say that," I said.

"You're the only one who can pronounce her name right," Theresa explained.

"That's why I like you," said Aurelia.

Study hall was over. Children shuffled in and shuffled out.

———————

STAR CLASS WAS IN SESSION.

"Hi, Hugo," said Marty.

"Hi, Marty," said Hugo.

"You're still my friend, right?"

Brandon came over. "I have to go to the library to take a test."

"Do you need a note from the librarian?"

"No, the health teacher is the librarian."

"Rocket! I'm here," said Kent.

"Okay, guys, listen," I stage-whispered. "The door to that room is *open*. It is silent reading, am I right? Because this is STAR. Every one of you will shine *silently*."

"Can we sit on the floor?" said Kent.

"You can sit on the floor if you're silent," I said. "I'm going to turn the lights down." The class began reading.

Mrs. Ricker appeared and saw kids on the carpet. "NO, NO, NO. You can't be seated on the floor."

I said, "I'm sorry, I said they could sit on the floor."

Mrs. Ricker explained to me that they'd decided to do a special activity during the first half of STAR, rather than during the second half. To the class, she said, "You're heading into my room. I will not talk over you, so settle down for directions. You must bring a pencil with you, and a positive attitude. Both of those things."

"What if we don't have a positive attitude?" asked Jarrod.

"Then shape up, buddy, shape up."

I asked Mrs. Ricker if there was some way I could help.

"Crowd control would be great," she said.

The doubled crowd assembled in Mrs. Ricker's room. "So who does not have a seat?" she said. "Grab a clipboard. Back up. Ross, grab a clipboard. Grab a clipboard. Ladies. Back up. Brett, you need a paper from the desk, you need to grab a clipboard. Okay, LADIES AND GENTLEMEN. We're going to be working on a learning target in this

STAR group. We're going to be rotating these STAR groups every five days. Clipboards are right here. As I was looking at the learning targets, I realized, Yikes, yikes, yikes, we don't have enough days to get through everything that we need to get through. So in this STAR group we're going to work on synonyms and antonyms. Most of you have probably done some synonyms and antonyms work in the past, and that's really okay, it just gives you a little background knowledge—right?—that helps you to be really successful when we do our synonyms and antonyms work. I know you're packed in here like sardines."

I saw that Rafe, from my class, didn't have a clipboard, so I handed him mine.

"All four legs of the chair need to be on the floor," Mrs. Ricker said to Carson. "OKAY, you are being extremely RUDE and I will not tolerate this behavior. If you are booted, it is a phone call home."

The PA lady came on. "Sydney Truslow to the office, please."

"And you will be having to explain to your parents why you were asked to leave. And that will not go over so well for you. You must be respectful. You're too large of a group for us to continue to have this go on. If you're booted, it's a phone call home, and that's not going to be pretty. I don't want to have to do it, but I will. We've got to get through this. Okay, synonyms and antonyms. Who has background knowledge? What's a synonym or an antonym? Which would you like to tell us all about?"

Dawn said, "I think they are opposite words to each other."

"Synonyms or antonyms?"

"I don't remember which one."

"Okay, I'm glad we're doing this. Dawn, choose someone in the room to help you out."

Amelia put her hand up. "Right here, Dawn, Dawn."

"Yes, Amelia, help us out."

"Synonym same, antonym opposite," said Amelia.

"Yes! Synonym same, antonym opposite. That is indeed true, and we've got this cool little presentation for you. Remember I said if you are talking THAT IS BEING RUDE. Okay? You think it's no big deal because you're talking, but if twenty of you are talking, it's a big deal. So ZERO. I think you can handle fifteen minutes of total attention here. Fifteen minutes."

She put up a slide. "Synonyms are words that mean the same thing. *Happy. Joyful.* Synonyms. And antonyms are words that mean the opposite. Let's use that *happy* example again. *Happy. Sad.* Antonyms. Opposite. Okay? So I gave you this handy-dandy chart. Nope, you shouldn't be writing on this yet, other than your name, because I'm going to give you some words, where you'll be looking at synonyms and antonyms. Synonyms for *happy*, right? You could say you're content, pleased."

Jarrod moved his chair, clicking its metal legs against the chair next to him.

"I am NOT happy right now, I am unhappy with your behavior. So *content, pleased, joyful, glad, cheerful.* All synonyms for *happy.* And on the flip side we have those antonyms. *Sad, miserable, gloomy, unhappy.* Those are our antonyms. So you have this chart thing, and this is how it's set up. You have the synonyms on this side, and the antonyms on the other side. So each slide that I show you is going to have the words. I'm going to go through them one by one, and you'll be tempted to rush through but I'm going to ask you not to, okay? Because there are a bunch of you, it's easier if we do it all together. You should have your pen or pencil ready. Find the side where it has Chart Number One, where it has the synonyms and antonyms for *beautiful.* Put your name on it, and the date. Name on it and the date. Are we all on the right page? Yes? We all have something to write with? Okay, so let's go through this. Word number one. They need to be spelled right, they're right in front of you, people. *Attractive.*" She put up a slide. "You can either write it in the synonym column or the antonym column. Is it a synonym or an antonym for *beautiful? Attractive.* When you are ready, tap your nose."

We tapped our noses.

"Don't poke your eyes out, just tap your nose. Okay. *Ugly.* Synonym or antonym? When you're done, tap your nose. You shouldn't be sitting so close to someone that you're seeing their answers. You're in your own space. Your own bubble. Next is *revolting*. Synonym or antonym."

"I don't know what that word is," said Shawn.

"If you don't know what it means, I want you to guess. We did *attractive, ugly, revolting*. Let's do *gorgeous*." She saw someone struggling. "Synonyms mean the same, and antonyms mean the opposite," she said. "Let's move on to *lovely*. Synonym or antonym? Okay, *stunning*."

Dede sneezed.

"Bless you. *Hideous*. Goldie, get out of her space. Thank you. *Hideous*. It's right here if you need to remember the spelling. If you can't see, come closer. And last but not least, *horrible*. Okay, put a hand on top of your head if you are all done. All right, so our next word, if you look at number two, is *dangerous*. So synonyms are the words that are similar to *dangerous*, and of course your antonyms are the words that are the opposite of *dangerous*. So let's have a look at these words. *Treacherous! Treacherous*. Is it a synonym or an antonym for *dangerous*? Next up is *harmless*."

Gus raised his hand. He had to leave for something.

"Okay, thank you. Ready? *Risky*. *Safe*. If you need me to slow down, just give me a wave."

Dennis waved.

"Are you being facetious? Do you know what that word means?"

"Um, not good?" said Dennis.

"When I say, If you need me to slow down give me a wave, you only give me the wave if you need me to slow down. Okay. *Protected*. Is that a synonym or an antonym for *dangerous*? *Protected*. Now, *secure*. Synonym or antonym? *Secure*. *Unsafe*."

Lester arrived late and sat near me. "You'll need a pencil or a pen," said Mrs. Ricker.

I handed him my pen.

"Okay, and we're at the last word, *hazardous*. *Hazardous*. So if you're done, hand on your head. If you're done, hand on your head. We've got a few people without hands on their heads, so they're still looking."

"Well, I can't see," said Dennis.

"Dennis, done? All right, next you'll see that the word that we're looking at is *smart*. If you're talking, that's rudeness, we will not tolerate rudeness. All right, so it's important that scuba divers are *smart*. Synonyms for *smart*, antonyms for *smart*. What means the same, what is something different. So, *sharp*. Synonym or antonym. *Sharp*. We're going to move on here to *intelligent*. Next up, *unwise*. Right smack in the middle here is *bright*. Three more. We've got *clever*. And next up is *foolish*. And last but not least, *brainless*."

PA lady piped up. "Flora Sayle and Rex Hoffman to the office, please."

Then the phone rang. Mrs. Ricker answered. "All right, all right, yes, okay." She hung up. "All right, so the students who—LISTEN CAREFULLY PLEASE. When you're talking, you miss directions. The students who are in Mrs. Lebartus's STAR, it is now silent reading time. It is silent reading time. If you took a chair from her room, you're going to bring the chair back. Also, the paper that you did—you need to return it to me. You will give it to me as you go in."

With hooting and the clashing of chair legs my students made their way back to our classroom.

"Hi, Mr. Baker," said Lexie.

"How are you doing? Day's almost over."

"Can we sit on the floor, Mr. Baker?" asked Marty.

"Please do."

I shut the door to Mrs. Ricker's classroom.

Rafe said, "I left my silent reading book in my locker, can I go get it?"

I nodded.

I went over to Theresa and Aurelia and asked them not to look at the book of international photography.

"I looked at it," said Theresa.

"She's never going to recover," I said. "Silent reading."

Theresa wandered off. I whispered, "Theresa! Theresa! Just sit."

Then we had seventeen minutes of soft, foam-core silence. Once in a while there was a sound of a turning page. The loudest noise I heard was when I squirted some hand sanitizer on my hands.

Suddenly, bong, the PA lady came on: "Please excuse the interruption for the afternoon announcements." She read off the names of twenty-five students who had to stop by the library, or report to the office for messages, or prepare for early dismissal. As soon as her voice came on the class began talking.

Then another PA announcement. "Natalie Whitman to the office for dismissal, please. Natalie Whitman to the office for dismissal."

Ear-blinding noise.

STAR CLASS BECAME HOMEROOM. More students arrived, and a few left.

"Elise Smiley to the office for a message," said a different PA lady.

Jerome, newly arrived, picked up an eraser to erase *immigration* and *push-pull theory* and *urbanization* from the blackboard.

"How did your day go?" I asked.

"Terrible," said Jerome. "Can I erase your name, or are you going to be here tomorrow?"

"You can erase it. I don't think I'll be here. I'm not sure, but I don't think so."

"No one knows," Jerome said. He wiped the board clean.

Lexie picked up the book of international photography, which was now sitting on Marty's desk. "Marty, can I throw away this book?" she said.

"No!" said Marty, from the back of the room.

"It's a perfectly good book," I said, "it just has some embarrassing pictures, that's all."

"*People,*" said Theresa.

"People," I said.

"Can I play the drums?" said Lexie.

"No, please, it's too loud," I said. "Does she play the drums in this class?"

"No," said Lexie. "They're right there." She pointed to an orange Frisbee-shaped gong thing on a high shelf.

"I don't see any drums," said Jerome.

Lexie reached up.

"She would not want you beating a drum right now," I said.

"She would not want us to smack one," said Lexie. She sat down.

"And—it's been a pleasure having you in class," I added.

Lexie brightened. "I know! We talked about McDonald's, and Cuba, and Scooby-Doo."

Jerome said, "And speaking of Cuban stuff, I would like to show you something, Mr. Baker, that I think you'll really really like."

"I am eager to hear it," I said.

"It's something from my favorite movie," said Jerome.

"What is your favorite movie?" asked Trent.

"You will soon know," said Jerome.

While Jerome tapped at YouTube, Lexie showed me a picture of her two dogs, Munch, the one whose tongue got stuck to the door, and Fleece, a tiny mutt wearing blue booties.

I said I liked the booties.

"She does not like them," said Lexie. "I also have a hamster. I also have a turtle. I don't have any pictures of him, though. He's so fat that his fat is sticking out of his shell."

"Here we go," said Jerome. He put his iPad down on my desk to show me his favorite clip from his favorite movie. A green-faced Jim Carrey began singing the Cuban Pete song-and-dance number from *The Mask*.

"Do you like Cuba?" Aurelia asked me.

"I've never been there, but I like it," I said.

"I like Cuba, and Cubans," said Aurelia.

"You like ze Cubanos," I said.

Jerome began doing the Jim Carrey dance.

"How tall are you?" said Aurelia.

I told her.

"I'm five nine," said Aurelia. "My mom's almost six feet."

Ida had brought out a tray of colored markers and began coloring her fingertips.

"Oh, don't do wacky things with markers right now, it's too late in the day," I said. I let out a huge sigh. "So that was Monday. That was Monday."

"We do fingerpainting," said Aurelia.

"In art class?"

"No, we've already been in art. I didn't like art."

Both Ida and Aurelia were coloring their fingertips. Eh, why not?

"How many times have you played GTA?" asked Trent.

"Not many," I said. "I wasn't very good at it, honestly."

"This is what we do, we make fingerprints," said Ida, holding up her marker-colored fingers.

"And then you go, boop," said Aurelia. She printed a blue fingerprint on the back of her hand.

I asked them how long a bus ride they had.

"I'm the first stop," said Theresa.

"I go home with my mom," said Aurelia. "She works in this school."

"That's convenient," I said.

"It's kind of embarrassing," said Aurelia.

"Embarrassing because she knows what you're up to?"

"She chaperoned my dance the other day!"

"My mom works with an old lady named Betty," said Lexie. "She's like ninety-seven years old."

"My great-grandmother was like ninety-nine," said Ida. "Then she got pneumonia."

Bong, first wave. Half the homeroom left.

"Bye," I said. "Have a good one!"

There was an uproar near the door, so I went over. "He tried to give me an Indian sunburn and I totally freaked!" said Trent.

"He did it to me," said Jerome "Look at that."

"That hurts," I said.

"It's friction!" said Trent. "Friction hurts!"

"Do you know what Lumosity is?" said Aurelia. "It's a game we play every day. It stretches your brain. It times how long and you get extra points."

"Sorry, just a sec," I said. "Do all the chairs have to be stacked up?" I remembered the sub plans, which said, "Please remind homeroom about putting chairs up."

"Now can we go to our lockers?" said Marty, after stacking two chairs.

"Are you trustworthy, and do you normally do it?"

"No," said Lexie.

"Yes," said Marty.

I let them go.

Aurelia demonstrated Lumosity. Ida and Marisa looked at horse pictures. A hallway commotion arose. "There's mayhem out here," I said. "Back inside." I got everyone in.

"Are you going to be here tomorrow?" asked Ida.

"Not sure," I said. "I'll see you if I am."

Marisa said, "I would like to show you the cutest video," she said. She showed me a funny cat video. I laughed at it. "And this one," she said. "Keep watching the dog, keep watching." The dog was sniffing and running madly in his sleep.

"Jeez, he's really going," I said. "I wonder if they have him on tranquilizers."

"This is even cuter," she said. She showed a video of a puppy that kept rolling back and forth on his back. "He can't get up! He can't get up!"

Near the windows, Theresa and Silas had started a game of inflatable-globe catch using two globes. "Theresa," I said. "Globes back in the globe area."

"Globes back in the globe area!" echoed Theresa.

Globes were stowed. "Thank you so much," I said. More turbulence by the doorway. "That guy Carson is out of control!" I went over. "Carson, how are you doing?"

"Good."

Mrs. Ricker had walked Carson over from her part of the hall. She smiled and said to me, "I just heard you're very cool because you played Black Ops and GTA Four."

"Well, I have a son who was into it," I said. "Now he doesn't play video games. I wanted to find out what that world was all about."

Theresa pointed at me. "He pronounced Aurelia's name right the first time!"

Mrs. Ricker's eye picked up evidence of disorder in my classroom. "They should stack the chairs and pick up things off the floor, and then they can just kind of sit tight."

I bustled back into my classroom to bark commands. "LET'S DO SOME SERIOUS STAIR CHACKING," I said. "Stair chacking?"

"Chair stacking," said Jerome.

"My mind reversed its polarity," I said. "Come on, guys, chair stacking."

Jerome went off to supervise a group. "Guys, he said stair chacking! Carson, stair chacking!"

"Stair chacking!" said Carson, grinning like a madman.

All chairs were stacked in under thirty seconds.

"Thank you, sir," I said to Carson.

Lexie, Ida, and Aurelia began comparing notes on a former teacher. Lexie said, "Mrs. Bentley screamed at my cousin and now she's so furious she's like, 'I will not go back to that school—'" She mouthed something more.

"Lexie, language!" said Theresa, who wanted to be in the group.

"No swearing," said Silas.

"You know you cannot say FUB in school," said a girl. "It's just not right." (FUB means "Fat Ugly Bitch.")

"WAVE TWO, YOU ARE DISMISSED, WAVE TWO, YOU MAY WALK TO YOUR BUS."

The boys heaved off, roaring and screeching; the girls said sweet goodbyes to each other. Bye, Lexie! Bye, Ida!

"Bye, have fun," I said. It was just a room of empty desks now.

Mrs. Ricker leaned in my door. "Thank you so much for coming in," she said.

"My pleasure, thank you for having me."

The stack of somewhat crumpled migration worksheets looked

impressively bulky, each class's work neatly arranged perpendicular to the next. I left a note for Mrs. Lebartus: her students were good-natured and friendly and funny, I said. I mentioned no names. The secretary waved goodbye when I dropped off my badge. My car was waiting, parked between two yellow lines. I sat in it for a while. Sixth grade. Treacherous, dangerous, harmless, risky, safe. I drove home.

End of Day Thirteen.

DAY FOURTEEN. Tuesday, May 6, 2014
LASSWELL ELEMENTARY SCHOOL, SECOND GRADE

WHEN YOU CLOSE YOUR EYES AND THINK OF PEACE, WHAT DO YOU SEE?

BETH CALLED AT FIVE FORTY-FIVE to ask if I'd like to be a substitute gym teacher at Lasswell Elementary. I'd been in a deep sleep, but the word *gym* made my eyes snap open: sweaty children screaming and running in circles for six solid hours. "I just don't think I'd be able to keep control of a gym class," I said. She gave me another choice: ed tech in a second-grade class at Lasswell. Sure. After she hung up, I lay in bed next to my sleeping wife, regretting having mentioned the favela scene in Call of Duty in connection with the problems of urbanization. Maybe the reason why the teachers in the break room had acted cool toward me was because I had undisapprovingly invoked hyperviolent video games, when they blamed those very games for the boys' inattention and wound-upedness and disrespectfulness. It was easy for me to be "cool" by making a few mildly subversive references, but they had to keep a lid on the lunacy day after day. On the other hand, what was wrong with Jerome writing an argumentative essay on why Skechers shoes were a ripoff? He was obviously smart. Why not let him run with it?

I bought a huge iced Turbo Dunkin' Donuts coffee and checked in at Lasswell, where it was Teacher Appreciation Day. I was substituting for an ed tech named Mrs. Spahn, in Mrs. Thurston's second-grade class. When

I got to room 5, Mrs. Thurston wasn't there. Two tiny human people were sitting at their desks. I found a chair and said hello and sat and sipped some iced coffee. One kid sneezed. "Bless you," said the other kid. The first kid sneezed again. "Bless you again," said the second kid. I read two posters taped to the wall. One said, "When you TEACH what you LOVE and SHARE what you KNOW you open EYES, MINDS, HEARTS and SOULS to UNEXPLORED WORLDS." The other held a quotation from somebody named Todd Whitaker: "The best thing about being a teacher is that it matters. The hardest thing about being a teacher is that it matters every day."

Mrs. Thurston arrived and said, "Are you Mrs. Spahn today?" She had on a high-waisted linen dress and her hair was pulled back into a black braid with a pencil poked into it. She went over the day's schedule with me and gave me Mrs. Spahn's folder. "She usually hangs out back here," she said. "Percy, Tyler, and Curtis are the three kids she works with in here."

"Thanks so much," I said. She wrote my name on the board. I read the sheet about Percy. It said, "At the main entrance, watch for a dark green van. This is Percy's transportation to and from school. You will need to go out and get him and walk him to Classroom No. 3, Mrs. Thurston."

A bell rang. I said, "I think I have to go out and meet him, right?"

"Yes," said Mrs. Thurston. Jeez, she could have told me. I hustled around the library toward the front entrance.

"Hi, Mr. Baker," said Cerise, the plump second-grader from Mrs. Heber's class.

"Hi, good to see you," I said.

Kids poured in through the front door.

"WALKING! WALKING! WALKING!" yelled a teacher.

At the end of the row of yellow buses, which were idling and puffing air from their air brakes, was a green van. The sliding door opened and a small boy got out. He was a good-looking, alert boy in a green shirt and black sneakers.

"Hey, Percy, how are you?" I said.

"Good."

"How long have you been coming to this school?" I asked.

"Since kindergarten," Percy said. We walked to class. He put away his backpack and sat down. "My mom hurt her arm on a pillow," he said.

"How'd that happen?"

"I have no idea. A pillow!"

I skimmed the sub sheet. "So you know how to do all this?" I said. "You need to get your sunglasses, headphones, snack bag, lunch bag."

"I have most things in my backpack," said Percy. He handed me a sheet of paper called a "Communication Log." I was supposed to note things down on it for Percy's parents.

"Are you Mr. Baker?" said Tyler. He was a little blond bony kid with a big smiley mouth.

I said I was.

"There's only one girl here, and the rest are boys," he said. "See, one, two, three, four boys, and you."

"I'm a boy," I said.

As more students arrived, he counted them.

Finally Mrs. Thurston looked up. "Okay, Tyler! You have morning work to do. Not wandering about. You all have morning work to do."

Tyler pulled out a spelling crossword puzzle. "Can you help me with this?" he asked me.

"Sure, let's take a look." I asked him whether he liked to go across or down.

"I'll go downwards," he said. He read the first word of the clue, which was *the*. "Three," he said, counting the number of letters in *the*.

I explained that you didn't have to count the number of letters in the words of the clue, you had to count the number of boxes for letters for that bit of the puzzle. There were six letters.

"Three," he said, counting the letters of *the* again. "One, two, three." I explained it again, and read the clue for him. "*The second day of the week.*" We both got confused about what the first day of the week was and tried *Tuesday*. But the sentence made it clear: *After a great weekend, it is hard to go back to school on* _____. Sunday was the first day of the whole week, and so they wanted *Monday.* Tyler wrote the word down in the square boxes, as I prompted him with letter sounds. When he was done, he laboriously wrote *Monday* again on the blank line, with light darting marks of his pencil. "We don't want to let anything be blank," he said.

I asked him if people called him Ty.

"Tyler," he said. "But I usually call me Ty."

We read the next clue. *Past tense of the verb "to find."* Zach _____ *James's glasses on the shelf.* Tyler was stumped. For *shelf* he read *shirt. Past tense* meant it happened a little while ago, I said. "You know the word *find*, like you find a candy on the floor?"

"Yeah."

"What if you *found* a candy on the floor yesterday? How would you say it?"

"I don't know."

"You'd say 'I found a candy on the floor,' wouldn't you?"

"Yeah!" He wrote the letters in the boxes, with help from me.

"Now I get it," Tyler said. He checked off clue number two, and tried to read four-down. *"What—"* he said. He coughed. He had a cold. *"What something is called,"* he read. *"What is your—?* Name!"

"You got it right off," I said. "First try."

"Now I need six."

"Right—six-across," I whispered.

"And it starts with an *E* and it ends with a *Y.*"

"Exactly, that's how it works."

Six-across was *Including all. The teacher gave a cupcake to* _____ *child.* Tyler coughed again and snuffled and wiped his nose with his sleeve. This was a tough one and he couldn't get it until I mimed *every* in the sentence. Then he forgot the *R* when he spelled it.

A three-note doorbell bong came on the PA system, and some children incomprehensibly chanted a greeting, a weather summary, and the lunch menu. They closed with a joke. "What did the egg say to the clown? You crack me up."

Tyler wrote *yellow* in the crossword puzzle.

Mrs. Thurston came by and pointed out to us that all the words in the puzzle were up on one of the whiteboards. "They're all right there," she said.

"We've been flying blind," I said. "That helps."

Mrs. Thurston put her hand on her heart. The class rose. We all pledged.

Percy came over, holding his worksheet. "Ta-daa!" he said. He was finished.

"Sir, nice job!" I said.

The students in the class next door sang "God Bless America."

Mrs. Thurston started collecting the crossword puzzles. Tyler and I were about halfway there.

A boy came up and said he was Curtis. My third kid. I asked him if he'd done the crossword puzzle.

"No. I didn't get time."

I asked Tyler what he was supposed to do now.

"I've got to get ready to go somewhere else," he said. He grabbed a binder and left.

I asked Curtis what he'd been up to.

"My dad's buying a new car," he said. "We're going to go camping and he got a car to sleep in. We're going to go gold-panning."

"You're going to search for gold?" I whispered. I didn't want to disturb the rest of the class.

"Yeah, the campsite we're going to has a place where you can go panning for gold."

"Amazing."

Mrs. Thurston was doing the rounds. "Andrew, you should be done by now. It's time to be done."

She gathered many of the students around her to talk to them about how to write a letter. *Dear* and *deer* were homophones, she told them. "There's a lot of chattering in the room," she warned. "What are you supposed to be doing when you're sitting on the floor?" She scolded a girl with a bad cough named Marnie. Then she said, "It's time to get ready for round one, please. Round one. BRITNEY!"

She gave me a stack of parent handouts to put into each student's cubby. "Marnie," she said. "I'm not sure why you're hanging out right there with that group. Please choose your spot and get started. Corey, you're not to be anywhere near Adrian all day." Ah, but Corey wanted to be near Adrian, who was wearing white corduroy pants and a red T-shirt. Mrs. Thurston raised her voice. "Corey, you now owe me a gem! You should be working right now, reading from your book bucket. If you are reading to self, you are not shopping for any more books, and I already gave you the directions for not being anywhere near Adrian. That's enough."

She began a grammar lesson in nouns and pronouns and verbs and adjectives, subjects and predicates. They had to underline parts of speech with different-colored pencils. Adrian, who wasn't on the floor with the more advanced students, asked if he could work out in the hall. I said I didn't know, it was up to Mrs. Thurston. "She says we can," said Adrian.

"Let me just check, because I'm a sub," I said. I whisper-asked Mrs. Thurston if Adrian could work in the hall. She said, "Adrian, you do not need to work out in the hall, we have plenty of space in here."

Percy said he needed to sharpen a pencil. I handed him a sharp pencil from a cup.

"I only use one kind," said Percy. "That's how I am." He sharpened his pencil, which had a special rubber grip on it.

"What about the rest of the stuff that you're supposed to take out of your backpack—the vest, the thermos, all that?"

"The vest should be in there," he said.

"Okay, if you know what's happening, that's good," I said. "So you finished that whole crossword puzzle?"

"Yeah."

"Find the noun," said Mrs. Thurston, across the room. "What is the noun?"

"*Spider?*"

"Why don't you underline the rest of the nouns. I want to see if you can do it on your own." Mrs. Thurston looked up. "Britney and Grace. You should be in your own space, please, and working quietly. Evan! I should not hear you talking."

"I wasn't talking, she was talking!"

"Coral, go find a different spot to work. Coral!" She explained to a smart girl, Ariel, that *these*, as in "these animals," was a pronoun used as an adjective. "It's showing you which kind of animals," she said. "So the adjectives are still part of the subject. If you said, 'The animal has five eyes,' the *five* would still be an adjective, because it's telling you how many eyes."

Ariel said, "If I said, 'A animal has five eyes—'"

"I'm hearing some chatting around the room!" Mrs. Thurston said in her admonitory voice.

"Are we ready for our quiz?" asked Ariel.

"I want you to read it through one quick time," Mrs. Thurston said, "and then I'm going to give you the quiz."

"YEE," said a smart boy, Stuart.

"Stuart loves quizzes," said Ariel. "Right, Stuart?"

"I love roller coasters."

"I've never, ever been on a roller coaster," said Ariel.

"You've never been on a roller coaster? I've been on an upside-down one," said Stuart.

"You're crazy. Hey, you want to know something? In a month and a half, I'm going to Disneyland. Well, Disney World."

Mrs. Thurston focused on Reed. "Have you finished reading the book?"

"No."

"You've got to read it through before you take the quiz. You're not following directions, there, Reed." Thirty seconds passed. "Reed! I'm watching your mouth move!"

Some of the kids could work just fine on their own, and some could not.

"Corey, if you're reading to self, I should see you with a book the whole time," Mrs. Thurston said. "Not looking around. Reading it."

Marnie's cough was bad. Mrs. Thurston gave some special help to some of the more with-it students. "Why do you think the author wrote this book?" she asked. "What was he trying to do?"

"He wrote it so people will learn about animals?" said Ariel.

"Most people don't know about the praying mantis," said Stuart.

"That's called inform. The author is trying to inform you about something. They're teaching you about it. The other thing that he could be doing is to entertain. So when you read a story like this one—" She pulled up *Buzz Said the Bee.* "Emmet, you should be looking at me and paying attention. I'm telling you something. This one's for entertaining."

"Can we read that one?"

"I've already read it," said Stuart.

"So with a book, it could be to *entertain*—you're just having fun. It could be to *inform* you, so that you learn about something. Or it could be to *persuade* you. The writing we had you do on Friday, telling me about what your favorite season was, was trying to convince me. Why is that season your favorite? You're trying to get me to change my mind." She handed out the quizzes and scanned the class. "I still hear some chatting in the corner over there," she said. Then, louder, "Marnie! You are not doing what you're supposed to be doing. You'll be spending some recess time reading, because you're not getting stuff done like you're supposed to be. You should have been reading this whole time. It was fine that you went and got a library book, but you're supposed to be reading it."

Curtis, who was very small and quiet, with rolled-up jeans on, came up and said, "Excuse me? Whenever I close my eyes, it hurts really bad. Whenever I close my eyes." He squinted his eyes shut for a while and then opened them.

I whispered, "Maybe you should just hold them open."

"I've just been trying to keep them closed." He sat down and resumed reading his book.

"Time to clean up soon," Mrs. Thurston said. "Marnie, what are you supposed to be doing? Get going right away. You're finishing up how you care for your dog."

Two girls gathered the colored pencils. "There's markers in here!" said one loudly.

"Girls!" said Mrs. Thurston.

"I know, but there's markers in here."

"Without talking," said Mrs. Thurston. "You're interrupting the entire rest of the class with it."

Percy was searching all over for a book. "I have to read it by tomorrow," he said. He found it in his desk: *A Book About Your Skeleton*, by Ruth Belov Gross. Now half the kids were reading softly aloud to a partner. Mrs. Thurston explained the two pronunciations of *bow*, as in "bow and arrow" and "take a bow." Adrian was playing with a set of cloth blocks on a tray. Each block had a letter on it. He'd spelled T I T A N I C. I gave him a thumbs-up.

Percy finished the skeleton book.

"You seem to be a fast reader," I said. "How did you learn?"

"Practice," he said. "I've just been reading a lot."

"Am I supposed to remind you to drink from your thermos?"

"Oh." He poured something into his thermos cup and drank it. Mrs. Spahn's sub plans said, "Prompt him to drink his water and tea. His thermos schedule is: First thermos finished by 11:00; second thermos finished by 1:00, and third thermos finished by 2:45."

Percy showed me a picture of a skeleton wearing a red baseball hat. It had red and yellow arm bones and green finger bones. We counted the number of bones that are in one hand. "How many bones are in your body?" I wondered. "A hundred?"

"Two hundred and six," Percy said. "It's in the back."

"Wow," I said.

"I think I'm going to read the book again, because we're going to do a quiz tomorrow. So I might want to read it again. I'm not that good at remembering the first time. I'm not a good rememberer."

"You seem pretty good," I said.

"I can remember things for, like, ten minutes. But after that I have a hard time remembering."

I asked him why that was.

"Maybe because I'm always thinking of a lot of other stuff? Like hundreds."

"What's in your thermos?"

"Water. That's my favorite drink. Tea's my second, and orange juice third. Soda I do not even like. Throw it away. Apparently I do not like weird food."

"So you like, say, a very simple cheese sandwich?"

He shook his head. "And I do not like cheeseburgers."

What did he like?

"Mm, chicken. Or pizza."

He read me a page of the skeleton book, which was nicely illustrated. *"Everyone has bones,"* he read. *"If you didn't have any bones, you would flop around like spaghetti."*

"Wow, you're quite a good reader," I said. "You don't mess around."

He kept reading. *"Every bone in your body is joined to at least one other bone. Put your thumb and first finger together. Can you see where your fingers touch?"*

Some animals couldn't do that, I said—for instance, a dog has to pick things up with its mouth. However, he can smell much better than we do.

"He can smell a lot better," said Percy.

I leaned over to the girl sitting near us. "Are we talking too loud for you?"

"Just a little bit," she said.

Percy kept reading, but now he whispered. He had trouble with the word *ligaments.*

"That's one of the longest words so far," I said. "Ligaments are like rubber bands."

"I think I actually know how to spell the word *through*," Percy said. "T-H-R-O-H."

I typed the word on my computer screen. "The way I think of it is, in order to get all the way through the word, you have to go through this O-U tunnel."

He nodded. "I'm a good speller. I actually know if there's a word that isn't spelled right."

He whisper-read another page. After so many halting readers I'd been helping recently in middle school, it was a joy to hear this gentle second-grader chug right along.

Mrs. Thurston was explaining compound words like *baseball* to her "normal" students. Percy told me how he jump-roped. *"You have two important joints in your skull,"* he read. "I like to swing a lot. Sometimes I actually swing for twenty-five whole minutes straight." He pulled out his vest.

"What's that for?"

"I wear it three times a day."

"For what?"

"I don't know. I wear it."

I pointed to a word. "Do you know this one? This is a tough one."

He looked at it. *"Cartilage,"* he read.

"Dang!"

"It is made of soft, rubbery cartilage," he read. "I'm a good reader!"

"All right, let me ask you a question. How many bones are in the body?"

"Two hundred six."

"Okay," I said. "I think you did a good job with this book."

He looked at the clock. "Wow, recess is in only seven minutes!"

"Do you like swinging in recess?"

"Yeah, but I also like playing with Tyler. Unless he owes his whole recess, like he usually does."

"Poor guy," I said. "Where's Tyler now?"

"He's in Mr. P.'s. He's the one who makes him owe so much recess. He isn't getting work done. I keep telling him to get his work done."

"Well, maybe he has a little trouble with reading."

"Yeah, he does. I try to help him out when he reads."

"That's good, because everybody learns at a different rate."

"First I sound it out for him, and then he usually knows the word. But he doesn't sound it out."

Mrs. Thurston said, "Eaman, I have a feeling that you should not be sitting anywhere near Jayson. You need to make better choices."

I sat back and yawned and whispered, "Holy shit," to myself.

I went over to Curtis. He'd learned how to spell *difficult*, which was one of the spelling words Mrs. Thurston had given them.

Mrs. Thurston was dealing out punishments to various children. "You already owe some recess time today," she said. "It's about the choices we make." The noise grew. "Uh, you know what? I'm having a really hard time hearing. And I shouldn't be. Coral, where is your attention focused? Britney, what are you supposed to be doing right now? I'm still hearing chatting from people sitting on the floor. What are you *supposed to be doing* when you're sitting on the floor?" Some of the kids had raised their hands, showing that they were ready to line up. She nodded to the hand-raisers to line up at the door. I stood up, figuring that I should.

Mrs. Thurston said, "Those of you who have more than five things in your folder? You are staying with me as part of your recess."

"I only have four things!"

"AND, if you have less than five things in your folder, you are quietly getting yourself ready." She pointed to a boy. "Wear your jacket, you can always take it off."

"I don't have my jacket."

"Whose job is that?" said Mrs. Thurston. "Whose job is it to get dressed in the morning?"

"Mine."

More hands signaled readiness. I asked Tyler what was up. He was trying to finish his crossword puzzle.

"I have things that aren't done," he said.

Mrs. Thurston counted the things in somebody's folder. "Four, five, SIX. Sit down!"

Tyler said something to me I couldn't hear, so I sat back down to be closer to him, accidentally sitting on my computer. "Whoa," I said.

"One time my dad almost sat on his tablet," Tyler said.

"Corey! Come get to work. You've lost some reading time. You're not reading out loud anymore, you're sitting here. I don't want you reading anymore to Alison. You've lost that privilege. Marnie! You've got tons to finish! Focus!"

Tyler and I murmured our way through another word in the crossword.

"Um, I'm not going to let the rest of the class go out, because I'm still hearing chatting in the line!" Mrs. Thurston said. "I'm still hearing chatting!"

Suddenly I realized that the chatting she was hearing was my murmured coaching of Tyler. I looked up.

"You go out for recess," Mrs. Thurston said to me.

"Oh, you're staying?" I said.

"I'm staying with them." She pointed to six sad laggards. She turned to Tyler. "You're focusing on what you need to do," she said.

I got in front of the line.

"Jayson, you're standing in the back for your ten minutes," Mrs. Thurston said. He had lost ten minutes of recess for an earlier infraction.

I asked her how long recess was.

"The bell rings," Mrs. Thurston said. "You'll know when to come back."

She stood beside the line of silent children, near Ethan, the line leader. They began chanting. "WHEN MY HANDS ARE AT MY SIDES, AND I'M LINED UP STRAIGHT AND TALL, MOUTH IS SHUT, EYES LOOK AHEAD, I'M READY FOR THE HALL." Mrs. Thurston gave a nod. "Ethan, you may go ahead."

"My gosh," I said. "That's excellent." I hurried along beside Jayson.

Jayson said, "We've been practicing that for SO LONG we know it."

The door leading to a cement sidewalk squeaked as it opened. "It's so sunny out!" said Jayson. "What are you doing?"

"I guess I'm on duty," I said. "Will you explain it to me?"

"I have to stand on the map." We walked around the side of the school and Jayson stopped on a ten-foot-wide map of the United States that was painted on the asphalt. Most of the kids sprinted off toward the playground. "Nice jacket," I said to Jayson, just to have something to say. The snow was gone, the frozen pond was gone; I could see revealed, along with the swingset and various climbing structures and a field of dandelioned grass, a large assemblage of bolted-together tractor tires, over which several kids were already screamingly scrambling.

"Look at all those tires!" I said. "This is where you have to stand?" Jayson nodded.

A girl ran up and said, "He has twenty minutes," and ran off.

"Ten!" called Jayson after her.

"Just ten," I said. I turned to him. "That's kind of a bummer."

"Mm."

I asked him what had happened, but he didn't want to get into it. He had a round serious face with straight black bangs and black sneakers and a jacket with white sleeves.

"Do you want me to go somewhere else?" I said.

"You have to go," said Jayson. "When my ten minutes are up, you have to come and get me."

"Okay, good luck!" I waved and walked toward the tractor tires, setting the stopwatch on my phone so that I'd know when to set Jayson free from his exile in the United States.

I made a slow wide circuit over the newly green grass, amazed by all the dandelions, and checked in with a young teacher, Ms. Fierro, who was standing in the shade near a picnic table with several discarded jackets on it. I asked if there was any place in particular I should be.

"You're supposed to stay with Percy," she said, when I told her who I was subbing for.

"Oh, okay," I said. "I'll hang tight with Percy."

"Not too tight, though," she said.

I said, "He seems perfectly—"

"I know!" said Ms. Fierro, shaking her head.

"He's got a weighted vest and all kinds of fancy stuff."

"And he's like one of the best students," she said.

"I don't get it," I said.

"Sometimes it's hard to get things," Ms. Fierro said. "I don't get everything, either." She laughed. I wandered off in search of Percy. A girl fell while she was running. "Are you okay, Sukey?" asked her friend, with two hands on her mouth. Sukey got up and kept running. Percy was standing near the swingsets waiting for his turn to swing. He wasn't with Tyler because Tyler was inside with Mrs. Thurston. I was hesitant to embarrass him, so I turned and went back to the asphalt United States—I felt sorry for Jayson, who looked abandoned and forlorn.

"How much time has it been?" he asked.

"It's been two minutes," I said. "I'll come get you, don't worry." I walked the grass some more. A little boy zoomed past me and turned, smiling, hoping I'd noticed. "Wow, that was fast," I said. A girl called, "Hi, Anna! Hi, Anna!" I loved these kids.

I walked over to the screamiest place, near the wide shiny slide. A cluster of boys were sliding down the sliding pole. A girl told her friend that her mom had decided to make gingerbread muffins, not gingerbread men. I looked over at Jayson, a tiny figure with white sleeves. I walked back to him and checked my phone. "Special time report," I said. "Six minutes, forty-five seconds." I looked down at the map. "You want to know where California is? You're standing on South Dakota. Over here is California. If you flew across the United States, and you landed right here, this is Maine. This is where we are. What state were you born in?"

"Maine," said Jayson.

A girl came up. "What are you doing on the map?"

"We're learning about the United States," I said.

The girl tapped her foot on Massachusetts. "That's Massachusetts," she said. She tapped on New Hampshire. "This is New York."

I showed her Long Island, and where New York State was.

"That's so big," she said. "You know what the biggest state is in the United States? Texas!"

"Can you find it?"

She tapped her toe on Texas. "I've got to go back," she said. She ran to rejoin her friends near the basketball hoop.

Jayson took a step over to Florida. "That's an interesting one, Florida," I said. "Florida is where they have hurricanes."

"Why is that one an island?" he asked, pointing.

"That's Alaska. That's near the north pole, and it doesn't fit on the map because it's not connected to these ones." I looked at my phone. It said nine minutes and something. Close enough. "And you, my friend, are free to go!"

Jayson walked off and found a friend.

I moseyed past two teachers. One was telling the other what to expect. "You're going to find parents who don't help their kids, and you're going to find teachers who are working so hard with those lower-echelon kids, whose situation could be prevented. And the kids in the middle get lost." Ms. Fierro, who'd told me to stay with Percy, was standing off to one side by herself.

"Sun, happy children, my gosh," I said to her.

"I miss the days when they had two recesses," she said. "I think they should have two recesses. For the second-graders, this is all they get for the day. It's over at ten thirty-five, and then it's all learning."

"They're burrowing away in there," I said, "doing the parts of speech, jeez."

"Yeah, I think next year they're not going to do this. This is an idea of the administration's. They thought they could use lunch for motor breaks, but lunch isn't like being a crazy wild child. You've got your head down, you're eating, it's very structured."

She made a no-no gesture at a boy. "They've started playing a game where a boy will hug a girl," she said.

I went over to Percy. "How's it going?" He was waiting for another turn at the swings.

Marnie walked up, coughing and limping. "I fell on the bench," she said.

"You hurt your leg."

"Uh-huh." She coughed and ran off. The sunlit wildness and screaming reached a crescendo and tapered off a bit. The bell rang. Everyone ran toward the asphalt map area to line up.

A boy held up a sweatshirt. "I found this on the ground," he said.

"Do you know what to do with it?"

"I have to bring it to lost-and-found with another thing I found."

"Can I take off my jacket?" asked a girl.

"Sure, just tie it around your waist," I said.

"Can I take off my jacket?"

The line leaders stood in front of their four lines.

"I'm a door helper," said a boy.

"So when do I tell people to go?"

"You pick which class to go first."

"Okay." I raised my arm. "Quiet. Hush it up!"

"QUIET," said a girl. "The teacher said."

I picked what seemed to be the quietest line, and they marched toward the door. The other lines followed. As we turned the corner I could hear Mrs. Thurston saying, "Voices off." Reed was in the middle of explaining to his friend why he was carrying his shoe. "Reed. Stop. Put your shoe on. Step out of line and put your shoe on. Voices are off in the hallway. Voices off in the hallway."

I held the door for a girl, who said, "Thank you."

"Oh my goodness, so much talking in the quiet zone," said Mrs. Thurston.

It was snack time. Curtis got out a juice pack and poked in a straw. "Do you like peanut butter and fluff?" he asked me.

"Oh, yeah," I said.

"It tastes good," he said.

Mrs. Thurston distributed Band-Aids and warned a boy not to put his milk on the corner of the desk. "You'll have spilled milk," she said. "Reed and Jayson, you should not be talking. You have work to do."

"Are you going to be at movie night?" Percy asked me.

"I'm not. What happens on movie night?"

Mrs. Thurston looked in our direction. "There's an awful lot of talking. The only voices I should really hear are Marc's, Dale's, and Tricia's. Everyone else should be quietly working."

In a whisper, Curtis asked me how old I was. I told him: fifty-seven.

"My great-uncle had a heart attack," he said.

Percy had a sheet of addition to do. He worked at it steadily. Curtis still hadn't done his crossword puzzle. Marnie coughed juicily on us.

"You should probably stay home tomorrow," I said.

"Adrian?" Mrs. Thurston said. "You're not interrupting anyone else's work, you're getting to work yourself."

Curtis and I whispered over his crossword.

"FOCUS," said Mrs. Thurston, to Reed. "Focus, focus, focus."

"Focus, hocus, pocus," said Lila.

"Focus, hocus, pocus," echoed Mrs. Thurston. She indulged the smart ones.

Curtis figured out the answer to one-down: *Monday*.

Mrs. Thurston had written a sentence with misspelled words in it on her easel. "Coral—go sit down and work," she said. "You have a desk all by yourself. You should be able to find more than one word spelled wrong."

Curtis and I sounded out the word *including*.

"Jayson, you should not be chatting. Reed, move over, you have more work to finish. Open your folder."

"I finished," said Reed.

"No, you did not finish. There are like three or four things in your folder. You don't just stick them somewhere else. You finish them. That's your goal, during snack time."

"I know," said Reed. He had several markers on his desk.

"Put those markers away. I took them out of your bucket yesterday. Go put them away where they belong. This is not what we do during snack time."

"I already cleaned out my bucket," said Reed.

"NO, I DID," said Mrs. Thurston angrily. "I went through all the buckets, and I sharpened a whole bunch of pencils, and I took all the extra erasers and pencil grips out that were sitting in there. They should not be in there. Markers and crayons should not be in those pencil buckets. Those are *for your pencils.* The art center buckets are over behind the art center table."

Curtis sounded out a clue: *Continuing to do something. We are _____ learning our spelling words.* We got the answer: *still.* I whisper-explained why a crossword puzzle was called a crossword: the words crossed.

Mrs. Thurston began a lesson on apostrophes. "Reed, who do I still hear talking? How many times have I said in the last ten minutes, 'Stop talking'? Tyler and Percy, that's not what I should see, that's why you're not seated together. Britney, when do I put an apostrophe in a word?"

"When it's someone's," said Britney.

"When it's someone's. You need an apostrophe-*s* if it belongs to somebody. So: *Mrs. Thurston's class* right now should be sitting quietly on the floor, listening." She told them about contractions. "You put two words together, and you pop out some letters. Where those letters pop out, you put an apostrophe. You have to find where those apostrophes go. I want you to write the sentences again correctly. There is an apostrophe in every one. I'm giving you a hint! There's only one in each sentence, not more than one."

"How about two?" said Taylor.

"Not two. And when you've finished those, please make sure you've written your letter about where you want to sit." She said the class had eleven minutes to finish the apostrophe sentences.

The sub plans said that Curtis, who had made no further progress on his crossword puzzle, had to go to the resource room at eleven-fifteen. "You've only got three left," I said. "You can finish it."

Mrs. Thurston turned in our direction. "Tyler and Curtis, did you write me a letter yet, about where you want to sit?"

They hadn't.

Tyler thought about what he wanted to say in his letter. "I have a lot of stuff coming out of my nose," he said. "Dear Mrs. Thurston, I want to sit at the blue table. From Tyler."

"Very good letter," I said. "Do you remember how to write *Dear*?"

"D-E-R? No!" Tyler had a revelation. "It's D apostrophe E!"

"You don't need an apostrophe," I said. "It's D-E-A-R."

"D-E?"

"A-R," I said.

Tyler was doubtful. "A-R?"

"A-R."

He took a shot at *Mrs.* by spelling it "misis." I showed him how to write *Mrs.*

"That's *merss*," he said. He had a point.

He pointed to a scab on my hand. "What's that?" I said it was psoriasis, a problem where your skin grows too fast. It wasn't a bad problem, I said, but it was itchy sometimes. "Does it gross you out?"

"No."

"Good." We began figuring out how to spell *Thurston*.

Mrs. Thurston came over and glanced down at our work. She said, "First thing on your paper is your—?"

"Name," sang Tyler, "and your number." The number was the number on his desk. Mrs. Thurston moved on. Tyler sang the name song over again happily: "First thing on your paper is your name, and your number," to the tune of "If You're Happy and You Know It."

"Good song," I said. "Okay, so you've got T-H-R. Add a U in the middle there, just for giggles." We had five minutes till Curtis had to take off for the resource room. "Thur-*ston*," I said. Curtis wrote STIN. "*Tawn*," I said. "Thurs-*tawn*."

"ThursTIN," Tyler corrected.

"I know it sounds like *tin*, but it's *on*. It's one of those weird words. Just stick an O in there."

"Mrs. ThursTIN is more better than TON," Tyler said. He refused to write the letter. He tapped his pencil on the desk and shook his head.

"What's going on, man?" I whispered. "Write that letter!"

"Mrs. ThursTAWN?"

"Yes, and put a comma after it, and go, pshoo."

"Okay, that is *crazy*. T-O-N?" He gave me a suspicious look, as if I was tricking him.

Marnie walked up and said she needed help with apostrophes. I got her started reading about the two kinds of apostrophes. Meanwhile Tyler had successfully finished writing *Thurston*.

"Then you write a comma," I said.

"What's a comma?"

I drew a comma for him. "It just looks like a little tadpole at the bottom of the line." I showed him where to put it. "It's kind of a neat thing, it just means a pause. All right, now, what do you want to say, real quick?"

"Dude, this is where I'm going to sit," said Adrian.

"I want to sit with Percy and Curtis," said Tyler.

"Good," I said.

He wrote *I want*. Then he said, "Which kind of 'to' is it?"

Marnie was prowling nearby us, bored, confused about apostrophes, and obviously ill. She held out her paper to me. "Marnie," said Mrs. Thurston, "that's not one of your choices right now. You're not to be interrupting anymore."

"Which is the simplest one?" I asked Tyler.

"T-O?"

"Right. So what do you want to do? Sit? Fly?"

"Sit. Sit next to Curtis and Percy."

"Tyler can't sit next to Percy," said Adrian.

"I'm sitting next to Adrian," said Percy.

"Adrian!" said Mrs. Thurston. "When I see your request, I'll see how many of those requests I can honor. Just let me know in writing what your request is—where you want to sit. Marnie, back to your work, hon."

Tyler and I sounded out *sit*.

Mrs. Thurston said, "Those of you who have finished our letters and our apostrophe pages, come on down."

Tyler and I successfully got the word *next* onto the page.

I raised a hand. "Is it time for them to go to the resource room?"

"Yes," said Mrs. Thurston. "Tyler and Andrew!"

"Okay, so you'll have to finish that later," I said. "You want to put that in your folder?" Tyler put the unfinished letter in his folder. It was a lost cause, anyway. He wasn't going to be allowed to sit next to Percy and Curtis.

When she'd gotten the class settled and in listening mode, Mrs. Thurston opened a book. "It's called *Dear Deer*," she said. "It's all about homophones."

Oh, great. I walked the resource room kids out to the hall. "Do I go with you guys, or stay?"

"You stay."

I went back to Mrs. Thurston's room and sat down to listen. A moose had just eaten eight bowls of mousse. "Oh my god!" said Grace, shocked.

"Have you seen the ewe?" read Mrs. Thurston. *"He's been in a daze for days.* A female sheep is called a ewe. When someone's been in a daze, they've kind of been staring off into space."

"Sometimes I do that," said Lila. "I look at something and I just start to stare."

"That's him," read Mrs. Thurston. *"The horse who is hoarse from humming a hymn.* When your voice doesn't work as well, when you've got a cold, you're hoarse. And when you're humming a hymn, like a song from church—"

Several girls started humming.

"Shhh! Corey, MOVE NOW. You are not to be near Adrian. Ever."

Mrs. Thurston kept reading. It was a pretty good book, if you were in the mood for homophones, or were perhaps stoned. The illustrations were cheerful, and the listeners laughed when the toad was towed to the top of the seesaw so that he could see the sea.

"One day," said Lila, "I was walking in my driveway, and I heard a rustle in the bushes. It was a female deer. I was scared and I ran inside."

"Usually they run away from you," Mrs. Thurston said.

Ten minutes and the book was done. "So, thinking about homophones," Mrs. Thurston said. "Some of them you might already know. Some of them now you know." She put the book down. "Moving on with math. Please stop talking. If you have a comment or question, you raise your hand. Everyone needs to get their journals, and a pencil, and come on back over here." A girl started singing her ABCs. "Uh, EXCUSE ME? You're grabbing your journals and coming to sit back down, not standing over there in the way. Someone else is still trying to get their journal." She got them all sitting down, with their journals open to page 180, in order to review yesterday's activity: they'd had to hold their arms open wide while a partner measured their arm spans with a tape measure. Arms measured, they'd tallied and graphed the results and made a block chart. All this had happened under the supervision of a substitute—Mrs. Thurston had been out all day—and she wanted to know how far they'd gotten. She used her iPad to project the worksheet on the whiteboard. "All right, so you should have had this part here filled in with tally marks, right?"

Yes, they said.

"Marnie, turn your paper, you need to be on page one eighty, not one eighty-one."

"I am on one eighty!"

"I'm still hearing talking. Ian, move. Move. Don't argue, just go. What was the first one that you listed for your arm span, in inches?"

"Forty-four," said the class, reading off of their worksheets.

"How many tally marks?"

One.

"Next number was what?"

Fifty-one.

"How many tally marks?"

Four.

She went through a long series of arm-span measurements and tally marks. "So which one had the most?"

Fifty-one, said the class.

They made a chart, going from lowest to highest. "Your papers should look like that," Mrs. Thurston said. "Yes? Hands up if you have that?"

Hands went up.

"Good."

They reviewed the bar graph. "Did you do the graph on your own?"

Yes. No. Yes.

"Good, that was what you were supposed to do. I have to check, because sometimes when we have subs, sometimes we don't know what's going to happen when we come back! Marnie, you'll need to fill in your graph."

As he listened, Percy sometimes made little stressed coughing sounds—he had a slight nervous tic. I ate a peanut butter cracker and watched Mrs. Thurston zoom through the rest of yesterday's math exercises. They'd had to draw five different ways to make forty-five cents, they'd had to make a ballpark estimate, and they'd had to read a thermometer. They'd had to find the "mode" in a group of numbers. "The most popular number is the *mode*," said Mrs. Thurston, in review. They'd had to do some things with simple fractions. "Reed, please stop doing that, that's not helpful. With the fractions, you're looking at what's colored in. One piece out of how many pieces? This is the what-do-you-know-about-fractions page. What's this shape?"

Triangle! Rhombus!

"There it is, rhombus—thank you, Tricia. If this rhombus is one, how many of those triangles would fit into that rhombus?"

Two, said a few.

"Two. If this is one, then one triangle would only be half of what was there."

Silence.

"We are going to do a whole lesson on that. Because on the next page starts unit eight. So it looks like, for most of you, we're ready to advance. We've been practicing our double-digit addition and subtraction. We've been practicing graphs. We've been practicing some of that beginning multiplication, in arrays. We've been practicing reading clocks. We've been practicing some measurement. Right? We've talked about our arm spans and our jumps. We've talked about the *median*." What was the median?

The middle, said Dale.

"The middle. The median is the middle. But you can't find the middle until you put them in order. That's super important. The *mode* is what, again? We just talked about it. The most what?"

"The most numbers in that thingamajig," said Grace, pointing to the projected chart.

"It's the most popular. Okay? You might think of it as the one that comes up the most. So when I look at those letters over there—that you wrote to me as to who to sit with—our *mode* right now for a person, as to who people want to sit with, is Dale."

"Oh," said Lila, smiling.

"Because right now there's three people who have requested to sit with Dale. He's the most popular person to sit with right now."

"I don't want to be popular," said Dale.

"Oh, popular can be good," said Mrs. Thurston.

She continued with her résumé of recent work in unit 7, paging quickly through the book. "We had some charts, we had some graphs that we read, we talked about doubles and halves, right?"

The class next door was having a motor break, loudly singing, "Wobble, wobble, wobble." Marnie and Coral joined in softly.

"We talked about those multiplication words—when I have lots of tricycles I can count how many wheels I might have. And fractions. Which tells me that we are ready for our"—she held up a stack of papers—"test."

No! Yay! Today?

The class got violently squirmy. Some of them were chanting along with the motor-breakers next door. Mrs. Thurston said, "Excuse me? What are you supposed to be doing? You shouldn't be banging pencils.

Still waiting for everyone to be listening. Coral. So, everyone who's ready for our math test, we will be putting our journals away, getting yourself set up with a privacy folder and a sharpened pencil and sitting quietly."

Pencils were vigorously sharpened. Privacy folders came out. These were tripartite, made of heavy cardboard, decorated with names and stickers, and they stood up on each desk, surrounding and fencing off every test paper, so that nobody would be distracted or tempted to copy an answer. Adrian made exploding sounds as he sharpened his pencil.

"Please stop, Adrian," said a smart girl.

"All right, looking around I see some of you ready," said Mrs. Thurston. "Marnie, you need to focus." Percy looked at me over his privacy folder. "Good luck," I said. Mrs. Thurston walked the class through the test to get them ready. "You have to read the questions," she said. "The first one says, *Three packages of paper towels, three rolls per package. How many rolls?* Don't just add them. I'm going to give you a hint. Draw a picture."

"Do we have to?" asked Stuart.

"If you know the answer already? No. But for most of you in here, you'll need to draw a picture in order to figure out what the answer is. The test has three of that kind of question. The ones at the bottom of the page are missing addends, just like your homework the other day."

"Homework?" said Jayson.

"There is a word problem. Marcus is the boy in it. There's a table to make a bar graph from, just like the table we worked on yesterday. Make the graph that comes from those numbers. Please stop making noise. There's a find-the-rule, there's an in-and-out, you find what the rule is. There are some three-D shapes. Do you remember what those are called?"

"Yes," said a few kids.

"There's another complete-the-table on the back. There's a find-the-median-of-two-sets-of-numbers. There's a find-the-median-and-the-*mode*. If you forget what those were, it tells you again: the middle number, and the most popular. Then missing numbers on the grid, using some bigger numbers than before. Last one on there is adding three numbers together."

Percy made one of his little nervous coughs.

"All right," said Mrs. Thurston. "Everyone's got pencils and papers, privacy folders are out. Voices off. We should not have noises. You're not looking around at anyone else's paper."

"I might look up at the ceiling once in a while," said Stuart.

"You might look over at the number grid, you might look up at the number line on the ceiling, you might go get cubes. Okay."

The class went to work. Mrs. Thurston came over and reminded Percy to put on his weighted vest. Silently he put it on and set a timer, which made loud beeps as he pushed the buttons. He didn't seem to mind. Coral sang softly to herself, her pencil moving, her head held to one side. Marnie coughed and went into the bathroom and locked the door.

"Drawing a picture often makes it much easier," Mrs. Thurston said softly, as she stepped slowly around the desks, her hands held behind her back. "I see a couple of you drawing pictures, and you're really understanding it. That's awesome. Reed, focus." Mrs. Thurston asked me if I'd written anything in Percy's communication log. I hadn't. The question was, *Did he need help at recess?* I put a 1, meaning no.

I whispered that I didn't understand why he needed all the monitoring. "He reads really well."

"He's done great," Mrs. Thurston whispered. He might not need an ed tech next year, she said, because he'd done so well this year.

The room became quiet, and we could hear the teacher next door doing a math word problem with her class: "Anthony, can you read number three for me, please?" she said.

Stuart finished his test.

"If you're finished, check to see if you have anything in your math journal."

"I have."

"How do you spell *trouble*?" asked a girl.

"Make your best guess," Mrs. Thurston said. "We're not counting for spelling. If we were testing spelling words, it would count. But we've not had that for a spelling word."

Mrs. Thurston paused at the bathroom door. "Finish up in the bathroom," she called to Marnie. "Come back and join us." To me, she whispered, "She's just kind of hanging out there, avoiding the work. It starts at this age and continues on."

Marnie emerged and sat down at her privacy folder and put her chin on her fists.

More people handed in the tests. Coral continued to sing happily. Percy's timer chirped in triplets, like a hotel alarm clock. He turned it off and put it away. He took off his vest.

Adrian read a question to himself, threw his head back, and said, "Ugh!"

"Can I go get some water?" Marnie asked.

"Go get some water, sweetie," Mrs. Thurston said.

Adrian read another question. He made a crazy throat sound. "ULHHH!"

"Adrian," Mrs. Thurston warned. "Shh."

Privacy folders were folded up. Percy handed his test in. Mrs. Thurston told him to go through his math workbook and finish the pages that he'd skipped over. "You still have tons of this to do. Big chunks." She turned more pages. "Little bits in different places. Okay?"

Percy turned the pages. "Can you please help me?" he said to me.

I pulled up my chair. He had pages and pages of half-finished math.

"Can you do that one?" I asked, pointing to a column of three two-digit numbers that were supposed to be added together. He did it. He moved on to some subtraction problems.

The spell of test-taking hadn't lifted yet. "Those of you who are working on unfinished work," Mrs. Thurston said. "If you've not finished your biography now would be a good time. If your biography's not done you have about ten minutes to work on it." They were supposed to be writing a biography of someone else in the class, including a colored-pencil portrait.

Tyler brought out his request letter. "*I want to sit next*," he read. He wrote *to*, and *Curtis*, and *and*. Then he said, "Perse's real name is Percy."

I told him how to spell *Percy* and we worked slowly through the spelling of *sincerely*. He didn't want to put his name after *sincerely*.

"How else will she know who wrote it?" I said.

He saw the point of that and wrote *Tyler.*

A line had formed of people waiting to hand in their tests. "Standing quietly in the line," said Mrs. Thurston. Tyler joined the line to hand in his letter. "Tyler, no! Go finish your biography, buddy." Tyler pulled out a piece of paper and began drawing a portrait of Percy, while Percy did more subtraction. Unfortunately, Tyler talked to Percy while he was drawing him. "Tyler, no talking to Percy!" Mrs. Thurston said. "You are not to be interrupting."

When he'd finished his Percy portrait, Tyler said, "I'm doing my word search." He pulled the unfinished crossword puzzle from his folder. "I want to do number seven," he said, which was *still. We are _____ learning our spelling words.*

"I want to do sixty-five!" said Adrian.

Tyler read, "*We are*—blank." He couldn't read *learning.* "Like," he guessed. "Love."

"Learning," I prompted.

"*Learning our sp*—"

"Sp, sp, *spelling words,*" I said.

He looked at the list of not-crossed-off words. "Still!" he said.

"Bingo," I said. "Good, so just copy out *still* into those boxes."

"Now I want to do number nine," he said. He couldn't read it. "Crazy," he said, shaking his head.

I started him off. "*A primary*—"

"*A primary color*—looks."

"*Like,*" I corrected. "*A primary color like*—"

"*A primary color like yellow and red,*" Tyler read. "Blue!" He began filling out the boxes.

Curtis's desk was clean and he was sitting quietly. "What's happening now?" I asked.

"Cleanup."

"Is it almost lunchtime?" I asked.

"It is lunchtime," he said.

I made a stifled sigh of deliverance and turned back to Tyler. He'd written *BULE* in the crossword squares. We got that straightened out.

"WHO WANTS THE WIGGLE SEAT?" somebody called out.

"Put that right in my writing folder," said Mrs. Thurston, "so it doesn't get lost in my pile, please."

"Can somebody give me a video game?" said Adrian. Percy laughed.

Tyler checked the remaining words. "I haven't did *pink*," he said. He copied it in the puzzle.

"I'M HEARING TALKING, BRITNEY AND GRACE! I should not be hearing any voices whatsoever."

"You are flying now, dude," I murmured to Tyler. He finished the *K*. "You're done," I said.

"The word search are easy easy peasy, easy peasy," he said happily. "I'm hot lunch." He went to wash his hands.

I went over the checklist with Percy. "You got everything?"

He nodded.

Mrs. Thurston took a position by the door. "I should have most everyone standing quietly in line. You should not be talking in the quiet zone unless you have something to ask me before we go to lunch!"

"Are you on duty today?" asked Dale.

"That's not something you need to ask me."

Mrs. Thurston stood straight and put her hands at her sides. The class began the hall chant. "WHEN MY HANDS ARE AT MY SIDES, AND I'M LINED UP STRAIGHT AND TALL, MOUTH IS SHUT, EYES LOOK AHEAD, I'M READY FOR THE HALL."

"Jayson, go ahead," she said. "Voices are off for the hallway."

We walked silently around the library, except for Tyler, who was quietly singing.

The cafeteria was a cavern of sound that got louder and louder as we got to the entrance.

"Marnie, walking please," said Mrs. Thurston. "Percy needs help opening his containers. He's raising his hand." She left.

I went over to Percy. "I got them open," he said. I took a position against the wall and watched two hundred children eat and shout.

Tyler came by with his food on a tray. I asked him where Mrs. Spahn usually stood.

"She just walks around and looks at people and sees if they're doing something wrong."

"Does she have a stern look?"

"She says, 'Don't do it again.' And if you do she takes away recess. Just walk around."

A teacher clapped the five-clap attention-getter and shouted something I couldn't make out about how it was already too loud.

Curtis came up to let me know that somebody had been bitten by a tick in recess.

"I love sausages," said Tyler, dipping his in a little container of syrup.

"I can't stand sausages," said another boy.

A four-foot-high yellow banner was taped to the back wall. The headline said, "When You Close Your Eyes and Think of Peace, What Do You See?" The rest of the banner was covered with hundreds of individual hand-printed messages, written by Lasswell Elementary students. *Unicorns. Florida and Disney. Buffalo. Nothing. I see people smile and laugh and play together. Freedom and candy. Lucky penny. The Nutcracker. Snow boding. Not fighting with sibs, no war, and to be nice to everyone. Video games. Darkness. Soccer.*

A teacher clapped her hands again. "HANDS UP. HANDS UP." Everyone put their hands up. "You have five minutes left—actually four minutes—to finish eating your lunch. Open up your milks! Open up your juices!"

The roar resumed. I walked around the tables saying, "Open up your milks, open up your juices!"

"Mr. Baker, Tyler thinks that there are no ticks in limes," said a troubled girl, Diana.

I shouted that the ticks came from Lyme, Connecticut, and carry a disease.

"It's a disease that makes your bones not work!" shouted Diana. "There are no such things as deer ticks!"

"There are deer ticks," I said. "They're very small."

"They're so small that you can't see them! I went to the zoo and I saw a python." She told me a long story I couldn't quite hear about a python eating a rat and about how her friend fell down in the bathroom.

"Wow," I said.

The sound of children rose to a full riot-gear fluffernutter death-metal maelstrom. How could human people endure this every weekday? I got a paper towel from a wall-mounted roll to clean up some milk that had spouted from someone's straw.

Another teacher came in to relieve me. "You're on break," she said. I had a half hour. I staggered to my car, famished. "I'm hurtin' real bad," I said aloud, slathering my hands with sanitizer in the hope that I could avoid Marnie's cold. There was just enough time to drive to the nearest restaurant, Dunkin' Donuts, to get another Turbo iced coffee for the afternoon. "What would be a good hot sandwich?" I asked the intercom.

"We have a new one. It's called Chicken Apple Sausage—it's really good."

"Okay, let's do that."

The sandwich, served by a small blond woman in a brown hat who'd probably gone to Lasswell High School, was very sweet and full of odd flavors, but I ate it anyway, and sucked down the coffee.

"What a nice day," said a teacher, back in the parking lot.

"I love it," I said.

"Me, too. I'll take all of this we can get."

The secretary buzzed me in and I went back to room 5. I was late. Mrs. Thurston's class was already on the floor, seated around Mrs. Kris, a learning enrichment social-workery woman who was dispensing advice on how to keep focused, listen, and not cause trouble for others. "Think about that this week, those skills, and work on that," she said. She was an extremely short older person, bejeweled, with a beehive hairdo and redrawn eyebrows. In a Mister Rogers voice, she read the kids a book called

When I Care About Others, by Cornelia Maude Spelman, which featured a cute bear and a cute cat. *"When someone is sad,"* Mrs. Kris read, *"I help him feel better." "I can imagine how others feel. And I treat others the way I want them to treat me."* I found myself wondering whether Mrs. Thurston would want to be treated the way she treated her students. "Do Unto Others" is a lovely maxim, but the golden rule doesn't operate fully in school: The children have no choice. They must go. Teachers are paid and choose to work there; children are unpaid and must endure rhombuses and homophones and tally marks and recess punishments whether they want to or not. Teachers have total power over their lives, and some of them are corrupted by it. Mrs. Kris read, *"I care about others. And others care about me."*

While Mrs. Kris read, Tyler got in trouble. He'd been fidgeting and pulling his arms into his shirt so that his sleeves dangled. Mrs. Thurston tapped him on the shoulder and they left the classroom together.

"So what I want you to do," said Mrs. Kris, "is I want everyone to think about something that you can do for someone to show that you care about them. Either here at school or at home. I want you to look down and think. Think of something that you will do for someone to show you care. When you have it, you can look up."

Marnie coughed.

"Cover your mouth," said Mrs. Kris.

The class on the other side of the divider was so loud that I could barely hear what most kids said they were going to do. Grace said she would help someone if they fell on the swingset. Marnie was going to help a friend who was being bullied, she said. Curtis said, "If it's a sunny day out, tell them, Isn't it a nice day out, and ask them if they want to come over to your house and play."

"Very nice, yes," said Mrs. Kris. "What about when you come in to school in the morning? Do you say hello to Mrs. Thurston with a big smile? That would show that you care."

Coral told a story about a time her little dog was bullied by a much bigger dog and she went to the big dog's owner to tell him. The owner put the big dog in the car and brought out a puppy from the car and got mad and said, "I have a little dog, too, I care about my dog!"

Stuart reminded Mrs. Kris that reading period was over.

"I know, I was waiting for Mrs. Thurston, who's out of the room. I don't want to leave until she comes back."

"I have something to share about my dog," Adrian said loudly. "I was at the ball game with my biological father. It was in the dog park—it was really funny—"

Mrs. Thurston arrived and whispered something to Mrs. Kris about Tyler's office detention. Adrian stopped telling his story.

"All right, I'll see you next week!" Mrs. Kris said to the class.

"That was so exciting," said Ariel.

Mrs. Kris put her finger on her nose and disappeared.

"REED, GO PUT THAT AWAY," said Mrs. Thurston. "This is why you're not finished with the things you're supposed to be finished with. In your desk or in your backpack. This is not playtime."

Percy came back to his desk. He was downcast. He took off his vest. Tyler was in hot water again. "He has to owe recess and go to Mr. Peterson's office," he whispered to me.

The class lined up. It was time for me to take them to gym class. "OH! I'm hearing voices!" Mrs. Thurston said. Then they chanted, "WHEN MY HANDS ARE AT MY SIDES, AND I'M LINED UP STRAIGHT AND TALL, MOUTH IS SHUT, EYES LOOK AHEAD, I'M READY FOR THE HALL."

I led them around the library to the gym, where they instantly began playing scream-and-chase, running themselves ragged. I said hello to the substitute gym teacher, Ms. Bithell, a tired, amused-looking woman in her thirties with a whistle and a clipboard. She was doing the job I'd refused. I asked her if I could help in any way.

"We're going to play dodgeball," she said. "So if you want to stay and get hit by the ball, you can."

At the far end of the gym, in the midst of the running and screaming,

Marnie had a coughing fit and bent over, her hands on her knees. She should definitely take a break, I thought, walking in her direction. Ariel sprinted over. "Marnie threw up," she said.

"Oh, god." I held my arms out near Marnie so that kids wouldn't track through the mess. "Don't worry, don't worry," I said to her. "Do you need to go to the nurse?"

Marnie wiped her mouth on some bunched-up fabric from her sleeve. "No," she said. "When I cough hard, I puke," she explained.

"Wow, okay." I told her to stay put while I got something to clean up with. Ms. Bithell came over. "I'll get some towels," I said. Jayson and Adrian charged toward us. "Watch out, watch out!" I said.

"Did you puke?" said Adrian. Two girls stood guard with Marnie near the wall, while Ms. Bithell went back to the middle of the gym. I asked Marnie if she was still okay. She nodded. Just next to the gym was the cafeteria, now empty and quiet. I saw the tail end of the roll of paper towels on the wooden dispenser on the wall, and I took it back to the gym and cleaned up the worst of the throwup.

Meanwhile, Ms. Bithell was trying to get the class to sit in a cross-legged crescent in the middle of the gym, so that she could teach them how to play dodgeball. "The longer it takes for you to learn to follow the rules, the longer we'll sit," she said. "It's difficult for me to be a substitute teacher if you don't listen."

I went back to the cafeteria and asked a woman in the kitchen if by chance there were more paper towels. She brought me a fresh roll. "Thanks a million," I said.

"Not a problem."

When I got back, Ms. Bithell was standing next to Marnie near the door.

"I'm going to take her to the office," she said.

"I'll do that," I said.

"Is it all cleaned up?" she said.

"It just needs another go-round."

Marnie and I went to the nurse's office.

"What's the matter, honey?" said the nurse.

"This happens a lot at home," said Marnie.

"What?" said the nurse.

"When I cough really, really hard—I start to feel bad," said Marnie.

The nurse looked at me.

"She's congested, so she kind of threw up," I said.

"Oh," said the nurse. "Where did you throw up?"

"I, um, my teacher wants me to take a break," said Marnie.

"In the gym," I said.

"Just have a seat and relax, honey," said the nurse. She told me the custodian would take care of cleanup.

"It's almost all done, I just didn't have any spritzy stuff," I said.

"I'll get that," said the nurse. She gave me a blue squirt bottle of disinfectant from under the sink. "You're too good. You're too nice."

Marnie asked if she could go to the bathroom.

"Yes, you can, honey," said the nurse.

In the gym, Ms. Bithell was beginning to take attendance. I spritzed and wiped until the floor was clean, happy to have something helpful to do. Far better to be cleaning up a puddle of child puke than teaching gym all day, I thought. I washed my hands in the bathroom and went back to observe the rest of gym class. "What does the word *dodge* mean?" Ms. Bithell said to the class.

"To throw the ball at someone?" said a girl.

"Throw the ball? No."

Another hand. "If someone throws the ball at you you move away?"

"Yes, moving away. So how would you dodge something? IF SHE'S DISTRACTING YOU, IGNORE HER AND MOVE RIGHT OVER THERE. YOU NEED TO GO RIGHT OVER THERE. And if I see you talking to someone, I want that person to say to you, Please stop. So. Why are you dodging? Why?"

"Because you don't know how to play the game?"

"Nope."

"To be safe?"

"To be safe, yes. Why else are you dodging? What are you dodging from?" The ball.

"All right, so the goal of the game is to throw the ball gently, from the waist down, and get as many people out as possible on the opposite team." She demonstrated the right way to throw, with the help of a kid from class. "I don't want anyone to get hit in the face. If I throw it toward you and you catch it, that means I am—?"

Out!

"I am out. So do I want throws like this?" She made an extremely gentle throw and her chosen helper caught it.

No!

"I know you're strong. But if I see anyone that's not safe, I will ask you to sit. If you get hit on the foot, are you out?"

Yes!

"If you get hit on the knee, are you out?"

Yes!

"If you get hit on the head, are you out?"

No!

"I don't want to hear people saying, 'He's out!' Just play the game. You need to be honest. If you hit someone, and they don't go out, just continue playing the game. Do you know what *honest* means?"

"Do not lie."

"Do not lie! If someone hits you and you don't go out, and you continue playing, is that being honest?"

No!

"No. I'm teaching you honesty, and fun, and good arm strength, and dodging."

She divided the class into two teams. Curtis ran up to where I was standing by the wall. "They called their team Thunderpussies," he said. He ran away.

"Go, go, go!" said Ms. Bithell.

A girl got hit right away and was hurt and affronted. "Are you all right?" Ms. Bithell said. She was. Another girl fell. "Do you want an ice pack? Do you want to go to the bathroom?"

Two of the boys began debating an out. "Don't argue!" said Ms. Bithell.

Marnie came back and began sprinting after the ball and flailing her arms and coughing. Finally I said to her, "Just sit it out, okay? Don't keep running around. You're sick." She rested for a while and then ran back in.

The class dodged and yelled for some minutes, and then Mrs. Thurston arrived. I told her that the sub had done a good job of cluing the class in about dodgeball—and that Marnie had thrown up. "She's not well."

"Most of it's the coughing," Mrs. Thurston said.

"ALL RIGHT, BOYS AND GIRLS," said Ms. Bithell. The class lined themselves up on the blue line as they'd been taught. "Raise your hand if you liked the game."

Most hands went up.

"Ah!" she said, relieved. "Tell me anything you didn't like about the game."

"Getting out," said a girl.

"OH, ON THAT BLUE LINE," said Mrs. Thurston. "We're getting ourselves ready." They chanted, "WHEN MY HANDS ARE AT MY SIDES, AND I'M LINED UP STRAIGHT AND TALL, MOUTH IS SHUT, EYES LOOK AHEAD, I'M READY FOR THE HALL."

We walked silently to room 5 and sat down. "We are reading to self, writing, or working with words," Mrs. Thurston reminded the class. "We're not making things. It's not craft time." Grace asked if she could go to the nurse. Mrs. Thurston said, "Are you bleeding or throwing up?"

"No."

Mrs. Thurston went around scolding, helping, threatening, and checking on progress. "COREY, what are you supposed to be doing right now? UNFINISHED WORK IN THAT FOLDER. Unfinished work in that folder. You're not just going to look at books, sweetie, if you're not done." She stopped by Tyler's desk. He was reading a picture book, not making a sound. "You're not supposed to be reading any words now, Tyler," Mrs. Thurston said, "you're supposed to be doing a 'picturewalk.' No stopping and looking at the words, you're looking at the pictures." She helped one kid finish a worksheet about the kinds of work dogs do. He was supposed to write down two main ideas. "Stop that," Mrs. Thurston said. "Hold the pencil correctly." Marnie was looking at the corner of an easel. "Marnie, that's not working," she said. "You can still work through a cold. If you have a cold, you need to focus and work. I've had colds so bad I couldn't even talk, and I was still here at work. You can do it."

"If you have a fever . . ." said Marnie.

"If you have a fever, and you're throwing up, then yes, you're not going to be at school, but if you have a cold, we need you here. You miss too much stuff if you miss school."

Marnie worked on a drawing for a while and showed it to me. She'd drawn spiders and zombie pigs. "They're like these big huge zombies with a half a pig," she said. "It's all about Minecraft. Me and Percy play it together. My mom has the movie *Slither*. It's a really horror movie. Ooh. I watched it." She coughed.

"I'm sorry you're so sick, kiddo."

"That's what my dad calls me—kiddo," she said. "Or goober."

"I think you should stay home tomorrow and rest."

"I don't know."

"Well, you should see what your parents say."

Mrs. Thurston announced that it was time for everyone to clean up.

"Time for me to put my cushion away," said Percy. He had a special textured cushion that he was supposed to sit on sometimes.

"Packing and stacking!" said Mrs. Thurston. She went through Percy's paperwork and told me to make a photocopy of today's log, on which I'd written what a wonderful kid he was. I made a copy in the break room and returned.

Mrs. Thurston was going over a subtraction problem, calculating the number of school days left in the year:

$$
\begin{array}{r}
176 \\
-144 \\
\hline
\end{array}
$$

She pointed to the ones column. "Is there more on the floor?" she said.

No!

"More on top?"

Yes.

"More on the top, you don't need to stop. Six minus four is—?"

Two!

Tens column. "More on the top, more on the floor?"

More on the top!

"More on the top, no need to stop. Seven minus four is—?"

Three!

"One take away one is—? Zero."

"Yay!" said a girl

"Thirty-two days left!" said a boy.

"We have to learn a *lot* in thirty-two days," said his friend.

"Adrian, your table's a mess. Marnie, you're supposed to be coming to sit down. Coral. You should sit down. Stop wandering and wasting time. Marnie, you're continuing to talk. If you're sitting on the floor, sit quietly please. Percy and Tyler, you're not talking right now. If you're talking right now you're not listening to directions. I still have folders here. Same people as usual, Britney and Coral. How are you going to have your homework at home, if you haven't even gone to go get it? If you continue to talk while I'm supposed to be reading, you will be sitting with your heads down. No! And Tyler, you're not supposed to be next to him anyway. Go sit behind Curtis, please."

When everyone was quiet, Mrs. Thurston opened a book and read from it. "'*Putrid cheese puffs!' It was nine o'clock, and I, Geronimo Stilton, was late for work—again! Pretty fast, considering I was not a morning mouse.*" She read rapidly, in little bursts, hurrying through the paragraphs. It was a story about a mouse. "*'Taxi!' I shouted, jumping into a cab. 'Seventeen Swiss Cheese Center.' Minutes later, we pulled up to my editorial office. Oh, yes, I forgot to tell you that I run a newspaper. It's called* The Rodent's Gazette. *I took the stairs two at a time.*" She heard a noise and looked up. "Coral, I'm TAKING A GEM. Right now you are not to be talking, you are supposed to be listening." She rushed on with the story. "*My head felt like it was about to explode. Even my whiskers hurt. I wouldn't wish this day on the meanest cat ever! I hate Mondays.*" She glanced up again. "Tyler, let go of the chair. You also left your snack on your table. If you're continuing to talk and make noises, there's no way for me to read."

The bell rang and reading was over. The class began to line up.

"Coral, right now you're supposed to be standing in line. Right now you're blocking the path. Come here. Take that, put it away. It does not belong on the floor."

"It's been nice spending the day with you," I said to Curtis.

"When would you come back?" he asked.

I said I'd be back if they asked me back. "I'm going to a different school tomorrow, Buckland," I said.

"Do you get assigned ones?"

I nodded. "Depending on who's sick, and that kind of thing." I asked him what his parents did.

Curtis said, "My mom takes care of a lady on Wednesdays and Fridays, and the day after Friday. And my dad checks out houses for banks. Sometimes he goes inside. He takes pictures of houses what don't pay for the bank. And there's some houses that are creepy. I've been to a creepy house."

"That's neat," I said.

"In one house there was a little door in the basement that was locked. My dad got in it, and there was a hook in it on the top. Creepy. I wasn't there. My dad said there was a house where the floors were really bad."

Mrs. Thurston made sure people had their eyeglasses put away in their glasses cases and their backpacks on, and she said goodbye to her favorite students. "Bye bye, butterfly," she said. "Give a hug, ladybug." Lila and Ariel hugged her. Tyler and Percy talked about a special substance in Minecraft called enchanted TNT. Because it was the end of the day, Mrs. Thurston didn't tell anybody to be quiet. When the three-note doorbell sound came on, meaning first wave was dismissed, she didn't make the class chant the hall chant.

"Out the door, dinosaurs!" she said.

I thanked her and walked Percy to the green van. The nurse greeted me in the office when I signed out. "This was our afternoon custodian," she said, meaning me.

I drove home thinking about the golden rule.

Day Fourteen was all done.

BUT WE DIDN'T DO ANYTHING

Buckland Elementary was another one-story eighties brick school in the middle of a nowhere of pine trees. Ms. Parsons, a secretary, gave me a sign-in clipboard and told me to put, under teacher, "Roving." "Do you have anything for the refrigerator?" she asked. I didn't. I clipped on my substitute badge.

She took me to the teachers' room. "We've had Teacher Appreciation Week this week," she said. "There's salads and brownies and fruit. Anything on the table, help yourself." She showed me around the cafeteria, the gym, the library, and the computer lab. There was only one other man on staff, so the small teachers' bathrooms were both unisex. "We're very small. We have eight classrooms. You can help out by opening the door when the kids come in."

The door was locked from the inside until the bell rang, so I held it ajar with my foot and pushed it open for each new arrival.

A brother and sister arrived carrying teacher-appreciation flowers. A girl with red fancy shoes and her mother came in, admiring the bed of tulips by the entrance. "Do you know what ants do to make flowers grow?" the girl asked.

"No, I don't, honey," said her mother.

"I do!"

They went inside. An early bus arrived. I said good morning a lot. "I love your beard," said a tiny blond person.

"Who are you?" asked a kindergartner.

"I'm a substitute here," I said.

"It looks like you're president," she said.

Good morning. Good morning. Good morning. Good morning, sir. Hiya doing? Good morning.

A slightly older girl was wiping away tears. I asked her if everything was all right.

"Yes," she said.

The early arrivals massed in the cafeteria. The principal, Mrs. Pilgrim, came by to say hello. "You're going to be the roving sub today," she said. "We're trying to do some assessments."

"Sure," I said.

Morning. Good morning. Hi, guys. Good morning.

A middle-aged teacher came up. "Can I help you with something?"

"I'm just helping people with the door. I'm a roving sub."

"Oh, okay," she said.

Another mother arrived with her daughter, who was wearing a flowery pink shirt and white, shiny shoes.

"Don't you look absolutely beautiful today!" said the teacher to the girl.

"I bought that shirt for three dollars at Marshall's," said the mother.

Ms. Parsons called out that she was still working on my schedule. "Five more minutes," she said. She went into the office. Through the glass walls I saw her put her hand on her heart. The school pledged allegiance.

Some latecomers arrived. Good morning.

Ms. Parsons walked me down to meet Ms. Collins, who taught fourth grade. "One of the teachers hurt her back, so she had to be out today. So it's just been one of those times when it's crazy."

Ms. Collins was a short-haired, self-assured woman with a naturally loud contralto voice. She told the class to do her a favor and close their computers. "I'm going to be pulling kids out one at a time to do assessments," she said to me. "I'll grab one, and then I'll send them back to get another student, and we'll do it like that."

She turned to the class. "So, boys and girls, what you are going to do with—" She turned and asked my name. "With Mr. Baker—that's easy!—to warm up, is you can play Around the World. You can go around two times." After that they were to work on their targets. "If you have papers that you're working on, you need to complete those before you start getting new ones. If you're all caught up, you can get another piece of evidence to work on, or you can go on IXL. We're not doing MobyMax today. Let's show Mr. Baker that we are good listeners. I will be back at ten-ten." A lot of kids went to mini-groups at 9:50, she told me. "I think a bell rings at nine-fifty. Kathleen, you need to finish your reading assessment, and Hannah, you need to finish your reading assessment. Marcus, I'm going to start with you." Marcus got up and went off to take his test with Ms. Collins.

I picked up a pack of Around the World math flashcards and the kids stood at their desks. "All right, guys, I'm Mr. Baker, and I think we need to do a little Around the World kind of thing." I held a card up.

"You have to flip it the other way," said Crystal, who had a side-scrunch of black hair.

"Tell me how to do it," I said.

"You turn the whole thing around, like this, so they can't see the answer," said Crystal. "You have to surprise us, too."

"And if you talk you get disqualified!" said Grant.

An ed tech—fifties, hoarse, toothy—came in and sat down. "You know what the trick is?" she said. "Keep it on the pile, because they can see through the cards." Her name was Mrs. Vaughn. She came over and picked up the pack.

"Why don't you do one," I said, "so I can see your technique."

Mrs. Vaughn began going through the pack. She took the game seriously. "Some of these cards are mixed up," she said. "Are you ready? Hope, you ready?"

"Are you all loose?" I said.

Mrs. Vaughn held up 8 x 3.

"Twenty-four!" said Hope.

Mrs. Vaughn held up an 8 x 7.

"Fifty-six!" said Joanna.

"Wow," I said. Mrs. Vaughn gave me the cards. "And—bidda boom!" I held up 7 x 9.

"Sixty-three!" said Elijah.

"Good," I said. "Cool as a cucumber. Who's next?" I held up 8 x 9.

"Seventy-two!" said Mitchell.

"Wow, you guys are fast," I said. I flashed an 8 x 5.

"Forty-five!" said Irene.

"Forty!" said Mitchell. Irene lost; Mitchell won. Public shaming. I dislike this game, I thought.

I flashed a 9 x 4.

"Twenty-four!" said Jasper.

"Eighteen!" said Lindsay.

"Twenty-eight!" said Connie.

"Thirty-six!" said Grant.

"You got it." How was this helping these kids learn their times tables? All it was doing was rewarding the smart kids who already knew them. For the minority who didn't it was just another brief storm of shame. "And—whonk!" I said, flashing a card. Eight times two.

Ada and Francie said, "Sixteen," at the same time. "Oh, a tie," said Mrs. Vaughn. "You know what, though?" She pointed to a skinny, squirmy kid, Felix, who was bouncing in his chair and tapping his feet. "You've got your last warning." He kept bouncing. "Five minutes," said Mrs. Vaughn. Felix slumped. "When I ask you to stop and you keep doing it, that costs you time. Hannah, we need you in your seat, please."

I did a few more. I sang a snatch of Daft Punk, "Around the World." I flashed 4 x 0.

"Zero!" said Tina.

"That zero is powerful," I said. "It takes over the whole situation." Finally I got to the end of the pack. Phew, we were done.

"Usually we do it twice," said Mrs. Vaughn.

Again? Shoot. I started at the top of the pack. Eight times ten.

"Eighty!" said Elijah.

Connie said, "Around the world in eighty days."

"Shhh," said Mrs. Vaughn.

"There's a book with that title," I said. I flashed a number upside down.

"They're mixed up in the pile," said Mrs. Vaughn. "Voices! Voices! Guys! You're fourth-graders! Shh!"

"All right," I said. "The magic—problem—is about to—arrive." I flashed 3 x 4.

"Twelve," said Hannah and Joanna, at the same time.

"Good," I said.

"That was Hannah," said a boy.

"I think it was a tie," Mrs. Vaughn said. "Voices! I'm going to go over to ask Ms. Collins if it counts doing the same answer. But that was still a tie, because she said it first. Yours was the second right answer. So, a tie."

"Good gosh," I said. Who the flip cared? I flashed a 3 x 9.

Jared was silent.

"Twenty-seven," said Hope.

"Jared!" said Mrs. Vaughn. "You should have trusted your gut on that one!"

Jared looked beaten down. I said, "Everybody has particular ones that are sort of their favorites. I know when I was in school I really liked eight times seven is fifty-six. I held on to that one. But everyone has ones that they use as islands in the midst of confusion. And here we go!" I flashed a 7 x 4.

"Twenty-eight!" said Dustin.

"Good," I said. I flashed a 6 x 9.

"Fifty-six!" said Mitchell. "No!"

"Fifty-four," said Ada. "That's my favorite."

"Nice," I said.

"My favorite's eleven times twelve," said Grant.

"What is it?" I asked.

"One thirty-two," said Grant.

"Wow, you're up in the stratosphere." I really wanted the game to stop now. I hated this game. "Where are we now, are we sort of in Japan? How far around the world are we?"

"I think we're in America," said Grant.

"We're getting back to America? You see the California coast? Here we go!" Nine times three.

"Twenty-seven," said Crystal.

The cards went on and on, with Mrs. Vaughn yelling and shushing. Finally it was over. I applauded the class. "Very impressive."

"BACK TO OUR SEATS!" said Mrs. Vaughn. "SEVEN! SIX! FIVE! FOUR! THREE! TWO! ONE! OKAY, GUYS, LET'S—SHHH!"

"How tall are you?" asked Joanna.

"Do you play basketball?" asked Elijah.

"CHECK IF YOUR NAME IS ON THE BOARD," said Mrs. Vaughn, "JASPER, I SEE YOUR NAME IN A COUPLE PLACES."

Shouting. Uproar. Jasper looked very unhappy.

I raised my hands. "Okay, guys, take it down. Way down. HEY! ALL the way down, please." They went quiet. "We're going to have an orderly transition here. Mrs. Vaughn is—"

"Gettin' sharp!" said Elijah, and laughed.

"—very authoritative," I muttered, out of earshot of her.

Mrs. Vaughn kept pacing around. "Mitchell, Lindsay, Jared, I want you to get started. Hope, I want you to sign on to IXL, on B-1! Hannah, at your seat! Fourth-graders! If I don't see everybody working within the next minute, you will be doing it at recess! Irene, I want papers. Work on your papers in your math folder. Tina, what are you working on? You have a division paper, don't you? You finished your division paper the other day—why don't you get another one for your target? Dustin and Mitchell, you've got FIVE SECONDS, and then you're on the recess list!"

Jasper was grimacing and crying because he'd already lost some recess.

"Jasper, I told you I'd take it back if you sat in your seat!"

"I *am* in my seat," Jasper said. "But you said I owed ten now!"

"No, you weren't listening," said Mrs. Vaughn. "I said, Go to your seat, and I will take the second five back. So you only owe me five, from earlier."

"What did I do earlier?"

"You were talking," said Mrs. Vaughn.

"I wasn't talking!" said Jasper.

"All right, stop, do your work."

I asked Mrs. Vaughn how long they were supposed to be doing work. "I'm happy to do something that's a little more fun for them," I whispered, "but I don't want to transgress."

Mrs. Vaughn said, "Why don't we give them a good ten minutes? I know when I used to sub I used to like to do different things." She resumed her high-volume policing. "Alex! What are you working on? You need a piece of evidence to pass in. I want you on IXL B-1."

"I have something else to do," said Alex.

"Then why don't you have a paper? Dustin, I want to see you working! Elijah, you've got your paper from the other day? I'm coming around, I want to see everybody working on something."

I whisper-worked with Lindsay on a division problem. Marcus returned from his reading test, and Kathleen left for hers.

"Trust your brain!" Mrs. Vaughn said at full volume. "Marcus, what's up! JASPER! You haven't done any work yet? Okay, girls!" She moved Tina and Connie away from each other.

A boy brought up a math paper to me. "That looks complicated," I whispered.

"OKAY, FOURTH-GRADERS!" Mrs. Vaughn said. "Before we go any further! Just because there is a sub in the room doesn't mean there are THREE BOYS in the bathroom at the same time. It doesn't mean there's more than one girl in the bathroom at the same time. You know you sign out, and if somebody's signed out, you stay here. Mitchell, did you sign out?"

"No."

"Then you owe me ten minutes. Alex, you owe me ten minutes. Dustin, did you sign out?"

Dustin nodded.

"Have a seat and get to work, then. And Alex, you will be doing work at recess if I don't see these problems done. What did I just say? Sit. Hey, smarty-pants, sit. Jasper! You're going to owe me more time!" Mrs. Vaughn was on a rampage, and the day had hardly begun.

I took a tiny chair next to Dustin, who was working on a page of geometry. He had to circle the shapes that were regular polygons, and then he had to write the definition of various words. "What's this one mean?" he asked.

"Dodecagon," I read. "It's a decagon plus two. What's a decagon, do you remember?"

"I remember," said Grant, next to him. "It's ten sides."

"Right," I said. "How many sides does a dodo have? I know, that's an impossible question. But anything that sounds like a dodo usually has twelve sides. I think. I may be wrong."

"No, you're right," said Dustin.

He went on to the next problem, a five-sided regular shape. I held up my hand, fingers splayed. *"Pent* is five. You know the Pentagon, in Washington, where all the generals plan wars? It's a building they deliberately built with five sides."

I went over to Irene, who was fuming at her computer. "I can't get onto my Educate, so I don't know what to work on." Her password was flower904 and it was being refused. I tried it for her, checking that caps lock wasn't on. Login failed.

"ALL RIGHT, GUYS," interrupted Mrs. Vaughn. "We have ten minutes before mini-groups. Mr. Baker would like to do something!"

I said, "I don't want to cramp your style . . ."

"No, that's fine," Mrs. Vaughn said. "Felix needs to still work. Ada can still work."

"Let's just keep going until everybody's happy," I said.

"WHY DOESN'T EVERYONE PUT THEIR MOUTH AWAY," said

Mrs. Vaughn. "Felix, you can finish yours at recess, because you owe me some time."

I asked Mrs. Vaughn if Ms. Collins ever read to the class. I'd found a world history factbook with a chapter in it about the industrial revolution. "During this time, no," she said. "But if it's interesting for them, that's fine. There's probably a lot of good things in there."

"I want to keep on doing math," said Grant.

"You can keep on doing math," I said. "I just thought I might read."

"You're very tall," said Elijah.

"So are you, my gosh," I said. "You've got nice sneakers, too."

Mrs. Vaughn pointed. "JARED, I NEED YOU AT YOUR SEAT. CRYSTAL, I NEED YOU AT YOUR SEAT. Mr. Baker is going to break things up a little bit."

I said, "Anyone who is still working on math, just keep going. Have you all read the Magic Tree House series?"

Yes!

"My gosh, you're way ahead of me. We could talk about something in world history."

"Yeah, yeah, yeah, world history," said Mitchell.

"VOICES!" shouted Mrs. Vaughn. "VOICES NEED TO BE OFF!"

"Can we take a vote?" said Lindsay.

"No," Mrs. Vaughn said.

"Well, a sort of informal vote," I said. "Do you guys know when women in this country got the vote? They weren't allowed to vote, right?"

Mrs. Vaughn pointed at a fidgeter. "NO, YOU'RE NOT DOING THAT. GUYS, YOU'RE NOT BEING VERY RESPECTFUL—"

Here I cut her off. "It's fine," I said. "Mrs. Vaughn, it's honestly just *fine*. It doesn't have to be pin-droppingly silent. It doesn't matter to me."

"Okay," she said.

"They're very nice kids," I said, "and I'm perfectly happy."

Mrs. Vaughn couldn't stop. "Jared, sit down right now!"

I told them about how an injection-molding machine worked, that it melted little plastic particles that came down in a tube and used a huge screw to squash the molten plastic into a mold. I told them about China, where they invented gunpowder. I showed them a picture of a steam engine and talked about pistons and expanding gases and paddlewheels. "Think of a world in which something doesn't exist," I said, "and one guy thinks, I want to build that. That's an amazing ability." Were there other inventions that they particularly admired? What did they use every day that they really liked?

"Basketball hoop," said Joanna. "We learned about it in my old school. The man didn't like that people were too pushy and stuff, so he made up a new game." We talked about basketball and volleyball for a while. The class was remarkably quiet. Mrs. Vaughn left to visit some other room. I asked the class for more inventions.

"Glasses?" said a girl, Francie, who wore glasses.

"Glasses! Now, that is an invention. How do you think they figured out that if you looked through glass, it would actually make you see better?"

"Telescopes, maybe, I don't know," Francie said. She began looking up the history of eyeglasses on her computer.

A specialist arrived to take Marcus and Felix to reading enrichment.

Jasper said, "Something else that was invented was the iPhone Five!" We talked about iPhones and Steve Jobs. I showed them the cracks in my iPhone 4s. "It still works perfectly," I said. "Now, that is a good machine."

"Steve Jobs had died by the time of the iPhone Five," said Grant.

"But he still lives on," said Jasper.

"Is this one invention?" I asked them, holding up my injured phone. No, said the class.

"There are dozens of inventions in here," I said. "There's a camera, there's a radio transmitter, there's a screen."

"I know who was the first person who wore spectacles," said Francie. "It was an ancient queen."

The watch was another great invention, said Dustin. Elijah raised his hand and described Foucault's pendulum. "It proves that the Earth does spin. Every hour it knocks a pin down."

Ada described a sundial. "They would have this round thing in the

SUBSTITUTE   [407]

garden. From the way the shadows would reflect on it they would tell the time."

We talked about hourglasses, measuring time by sifting sand. "Or they could burn a candle," I said. "And you can measure years of time if you just look at a tree grow."

Grant explained the counting of tree rings. "If you cut down the tree," he said, "and you count how many rings, that's how many years it has lived."

I said, "Why do you think there are rings in a tree? Anyone know?" I pointed at Irene. "Do you know?"

"No," said Irene.

"Because some parts of the year are cold," I said, "and the tree is hibernating, waiting for things to warm up, and some parts of the year are warm and it's growing like mad."

"Every year grows a new layer?" said Irene.

"It's growing a new layer," I said. "In the cold months the wood has a different kind of look than in the warm months." I told them what I knew about the dating of old wood using dendrochronology. "So that's another way to measure time. Okay. Are we done?" I was running out of steam. Ms. Collins still hadn't returned. "No."

Jared raised his hand. "One invention is the electric sharpener."

"Electric pencil sharpeners—yes!"

"We have one in class," said Francie.

"There's a little man inside of it with a chain saw," said Jasper.

"It wastes electricity," said Francie.

"Do you like the fact that electric pencil sharpeners make a lot of noise?" I asked.

"No."

"I think there's a little mouse in there, munching," said Tina.

We took the top off the mechanical sharpener and talked about the grinding gears inside. We talked about can openers. "What's another favorite invention?" I asked.

Connie said, "How about mirrors? When were mirrors invented?"

"Great invention!" I said.

"Charles Henry Gould invented the stapler," Elijah called out.

"Good research," I said. "Who invented the mirror?"

"I'll research that up!" said Grant.

"Me, too!" said Connie.

"Research it up," I said.

While they were doing that, I tried to write "Charles Henry Gould" on the whiteboard, but it was a fancy electronic whiteboard.

"You have to turn it on," said Tina. "Jasper! How do you turn it on?"

"I'm your technogeek," said Jasper, leaping up.

"I think I've figured it out," called Grant, one of the mirror researchers. "It's a person named Justus von Liebig. A German chemist. He created the modern mirror." Grant rapidly read a paragraph of an article from LiveScience: *"In the first century AD, the Roman author Pliny the Elder alludes to the first recorded use of glass mirrors in his encyclopedia* Natural History, *but the mirrors apparently never came into general use at the time."* Connie, who'd originally asked the mirror question, brought up her computer to show me the article.

"Good," I said.

"SmartBoards are a good invention," said Jared.

"These SmartBoards are awesome," said Jasper. "You plug it into your computer and into the projector, and when it comes on you just calibrate it with one of these markers, with your finger, and then whenever you press this down, you can draw green, and when you don't want it anymore, you use the eraser and wipe it off, because there's a sensor inside of it, and there's a sensor inside of the eraser." Jasper was clever—what was he doing getting yelled at by Mrs. Vaughn and sitting out recess?

"I know who invented the lock!" said Elijah. "The lock is James Sargent."

"Soccer was invented in China," said Grant.

"Someone invented school," said Jasper.

"Ah," I said. "Who invented school, and WHY?"

"I'm looking for who invented homework," said Jared. "I'm mad at him."

"Whoever did that is bad," said Tina.

Ms. Collins arrived with a handful of papers. "Sorry," she said. "I guess her clock was five minutes slow. Was it okay?"

"It was fine," I said, "we've just been talking about inventions."

"We were learning about world history," said Grant.

"Good," Ms. Collins said.

"They did some of their actual work," I said, "and then Mrs. Vaughn was getting mad at them for not being respectful, and I said, I'm just fine—and then, I don't know."

"Perfect," said Ms. Collins.

"They're very good with the math facts," I said.

"I drill them daily on math facts," Ms. Collins said. "I get you again in the afternoon." She turned to the class. "Have a seat, please! Let's log off the computers!"

I WALKED TO ROOM 2, Mrs. Wells's class of second-graders.

"Hi!" said the class.

"Class," said Mrs. Wells, "transition." She was in her fifties and expensively dressed. She intoned a two-note chant, "Class-class," and she touched a set of windchimes with her fingertips. "On three we should be looking at me. One, two, three. Thank you. All right, friends. Mr. Baker is a sub who's in our building today. I need to finish a little bit of testing, so he's here to help out for a little while. So here is what's going to happen. I said we would have a brain break, which we will. After the brain break, we'll get started with our reading today. And we'll go from there."

She had her computer hooked up to the projector, and she waited for the image to come on. "Thank you, Green Table, for waiting patiently and quietly," she said. "I am noticing that."

I said hello to Mrs. Colette, another ed tech. Mrs. Wells logged on to a brain break website called GoNoodle.

"Who's my helper today? Faith. You get to pick. Look up there." She pointed to some goggle-eyed cartoon figures. "Do you want Freckles

Sinclair? Do we want to go with Weevil LaBeevil again? Do we want to go to Zapp von Doubler? Oogles Fitzlemon or McPufferson? Tiny O'Flexem, Rad Chad, Flappy Tuckler, Tangy Bodangy, or Squatchy Berger?" Faith picked Squatchy Berger. A music video came on—an inspiring tearjerker of a song by Sara Bareilles called "Brave." One of the people in the video was an exuberant black kid who danced in a library with easy, beautiful moves—but because the kid was fat the class laughed uproariously every time he appeared. "I wanna see you be brave," sang Sara Bareilles, in the chorus. Over the song, Mrs. Wells told me what I should be helping the class with. "We've been working on biographies," she said. "So while I'm testing if you could just walk around and have them read a little bit of their biography to you. Maybe they can just talk to you about why their person became famous, or just anything they can tell you about their biography." More hysterical laughter at the fat black kid.

When the song was over, Mrs. Wells said, "Okay, friends, have a seat, please. I was just curious. I wasn't quite sure what was so funny about this video."

"The fat guy!" said Carla.

"That's not nice!" said Melody.

"That's rude!" said Terry.

"Eyes on me, please," Mrs. Wells said. "What I took away from the video was words about how to get your brave on. I like the fact that no matter what size or shape anyone was, they felt really confident to go out there and dance. And I know that if I were a person who was going out to dance, and I thought I was doing a good job, and people were laughing, that would probably make me sad. Next time we watch this video, I want you to look at it with new eyes, and the eyes I would like you to look at it with is, Wow, this is amazing that someone is out there and being confident about who they are. No matter what obstacles they might have. Maybe they aren't your typical-looking dancer that you would see on TV, but they're feeling good about who they are. Okay, friends, that's enough of a lecture."

I walked toward the front of the class and hit my head on the windchime. I muffled it with my hand.

"Now listen carefully to my words, please," Mrs. Wells continued. "On two. One, two. Blue Table. We are going to read for the first half hour. Just stop for now, Kevin, because listening doesn't mean moving a table. Thank you. Friends. I have asked Mr. Baker, when he comes around to read with any of you, he is going to talk to you about your biography. He is going to learn about your historical person. You're going to tell him about that person. Friends, I really notice that I have Melody's attention, because she's looking right at me. She's not coloring, she's not writing, and that to me shows me someone giving me level three with their bodies, which is cooperation. So, Green Table, go get your books and find your quiet spot. Jeremy, can you go get your book bin, I think I'm going to have Mr. Baker start with you. Red Table, go get your book bins."

"Why is your name Baker?" asked Carla.

"Because I bake enormous cakes," I said.

"Yellow Table, go get your book bin," said Mrs. Wells.

Jeremy and I found a side spot. He began searching through his book bin for his book, which was about Jackie Robinson. Jeremy had a snuffly cold but was friendly and cheerful.

"So what do you know about this guy, Jackie Robinson?" I said.

"Well, he was a great man and stuff," Jeremy said. "Because he was going to change the world. So like people could be black and play with like white teams and stuff?"

"Mm-hm," I said. "Excellent." He had a worksheet with four boxes to fill out. The first one was about Jackie Robinson's childhood. He'd written: *HEWSBRNINGORGA*. He was born in Georgia. I couldn't understand the rest, but Jeremy read that Robinson had moved to California. He started to write, *He wanted to change the world*. I said it would be great if he left a little space between words. "And just stick an *r* in *world*."

I could hear one of the better writers reading his long biography of Jackie Robinson aloud to Mrs. Wells.

"Are you going to be here for lunch?" Jeremy asked.

I said I was.

"My mom is coming for lunch," he said.

"Good. Just remember to leave some space between each word, so you can read it later."

Jeremy wrote about Jackie Robinson's mother as an influence: *SHEWSAGODMOM*. I got him to put another *o* in *god*, figuring that *good* was a useful word to know. Then he had to list two character traits "as evidence." He wrote, *HE HADTO RUNFAST*. Then he wrote, *YOU HAV TO FOCS ON THE BALL*. While he was working on *He was brave*, Mrs. Wells asked me to go over to a girl, Bonnie, sitting in an armchair. Soft study-time music played in the background. Bonnie was working on a biography of Betsy Ross. I asked her why Betsy Ross wanted to sew a flag. Bonnie said, "Because George Washington wanted a flag, because a war was going on. I think it was World War II, or World War I." She read me what she'd written. "*Betsy loved to sew and she had sixteen brothers and sisters.* That's a lot." She continued: "*Betsy went to work in an apostrophe shop.*"

I asked, "Do you know what an upholsterer's shop is?"

Bonnie said, "It's a place where they sew furniture and stuff."

"You are good. What else have you got?"

"George Washington wanted a flag," said Bonnie.

I asked her what she liked about the flag.

"I like the stars."

"I like the stars, too. Thank you so much, Bonnie."

Mrs. Wells sent me to visit Gerry, in a camo sweatshirt.

"Hey, Gerry, what's up, man?"

"Hm?"

"What's up?"

"Nothing," Gerry said. He'd been writing about Daniel Boone. "He used to not like raccoon caps, but he wears one."

"It's sort of a strange idea to wear a raccoon's skin on your head," I said.

"I wanted to buy one for five bucks at Cabela's," said Gerry. "But my mom wouldn't let me, because she didn't like raccoons." He read from his biography: "*Daniel loved the outdoors. He loved to trap and hunt.* He has a grenade. Right there!" He pointed at a pouch hanging from Boone's belt. I said I guessed that the pouch held gunpowder. (Actually it probably held shot.)

"Like black powder?" Gerry said. "My dad has a black-powder gun," he said. He read some more of his biography. "*Daniel built a road to Kentucky.*" Gerry said he'd driven up a mountain with a four-wheeler. "When we went, there was a lot of car pieces up there. Pieces of a broken car."

Gerry still lacked two "pieces of evidence" for his worksheet page on influences. Maybe Daniel's wife was an influence, I suggested. "Doesn't your dad help your mom and your mom help your dad?"

"A little bit," Gerry said. "My mom never helps cut wood. It's always me and my dad that cuts the wood."

"And what does she do that your dad doesn't do?"

"Cook."

Laundry?

"He don't do that," said Gerry. "He don't like being inside. He likes being outside." He put *hard working* for Daniel's character trait.

"Gerry, you're on it, man," I said. "Excellent."

"Thank you." He looked at my feet. "My dad has the same shoes, just lighter. My dad's boots he got at Cabela's."

"Does he have a coonskin hat?"

"No," Gerry said. "I have a rabbit hat. It's the two back legs. And it has the fur."

Mrs. Wells sent me over to Edgar, in a blue-striped shirt, who was writing about Abraham Lincoln, the sixteenth president. Lincoln liked the outdoors, Edgar said. Lincoln was honest and trustworthy. He'd taught himself how to read.

"Friends," said Mrs. Wells, "I have Tamara, Theo, Adam, and Ryan not in their seat. Will you please walk to your seats?"

I asked Edgar how he'd learned to read.

"My mom taught me," he said.

Mrs. Wells thanked me for helping, and I went to the tiny teachers' break room to have lunch, sitting next to a blue, bulbous Dasani vending machine that hummed and heated up the room. I wrote an email, and when some teachers assembled to have their appreciation party, I went off to the cafeteria to stand guard. The noise wasn't nearly as loud here as at Lasswell Elementary; there were maybe half as many children. Jeremy's mother was overseeing a section of tables. I shouted that I'd learned all about Jackie Robinson from Jeremy—that he was doing good work. She said she'd gone to Buckland herself.

"You're the president," said the kindergarten girl from before school.

"No, you're the president," I said.

Another girl showed me her container of kettle corn. I admired Jasper's sandwich. Mitchell flapped a piece of ham in the air and said his friend was a liar. Joanna needed a plastic knife and I got one for her. I made a peanut butter cracker disappear by palming it. "How did you do that?" said Jasper. I showed him how to hold up the cracker, following it with your eyes, and then when you pretended to pass it to your other hand, you secretly palmed it, while continuing to follow the now empty hand with your eyes. Three children began practicing with broken pieces of carrots and celery. Then it was time to be quiet.

"I SEE A LOT OF TALKING AND NOT A LOT OF EATING," said one of the parents who were volunteering for Teacher Appreciation Week. "You took a lot of food from the salad bar, especially the cantaloupe. Try and eat the cantaloupe, and some of your veggies, and then go to your main dish, okay? Thank you."

I taught several more kids how to do the magic trick, after making sure they'd eaten their cantaloupe. "It's called the Chinese egg drop," I said. Tina explained to me how to do a complicated card trick. A crowd of kids gathered around me, showing me their egg drop techniques. "Guys, you've got to sit down and finish eating," I said.

The bell rang. I clapped. "Time to get back to class! Pack it up! Pack it up and go!"

Mrs. Wells stood by the door with her hands up. Lining up began, table by table. Mrs. Vaughn, the ed tech, said, "Alex, go back and walk. Alex! Walk over and walk back. Shhh."

I led a line of students out the door to the playground for little-kids recess. A boy pushed a cart filled with balls along the sidewalk.

"Can I take off my coat?" asked a girl.

"Sure, take off your coat, by all means," I said.

There was a large wooden play structure with two upper rooms.

"Can I take this off?" said a boy, shucking off his sweatshirt.

"Can I take this off?" said another boy.

A kid named Wally was playing with a truck in the sand, right in the path of a girl who was swinging on a swing. I got him to move so he wouldn't be kicked.

"Mr. Baker," said Edgar. "I found a sticky note, and I don't know what it says. I just looked down, and I'm like, hm." He led me over to the Post-it note, lying in the grass. It said, *WECAN FRD 10 CRPS*. I couldn't make it out. I asked Edgar what he thought it said. "It says, *We can afford ten crops*," said Edgar. It was from a kindergarten project, he explained.

"You decoded it," I said. "You're a sleuth!"

A bright-eyed second-grader named Beth came up to tell me that she'd gotten her arm caught in the chain of the swings, and also she'd tried to kick the ball and she'd kicked the ground instead.

"Sounds like multiple injuries. Shall we bring in a helicopter and medevac you out?"

Beth shook her head.

Her friend said, "The chains really hurt on your arms when you get pulled back."

I said that they'd had a rough recess. "What are you going to do now?"

"Shake it off?" said Beth. "Do the hokey pokey?" The two of them danced around and ran off.

Harrison, a first-grader in a blue jacket, came up sniffing and frowning. "No one wants to play with me."

"I'm sorry," I said.

"I really need to play with someone," said Harrison.

A girl ran up and pointed at someone in the distance.

"He grabbed me by my shirt and ripped my skin," she said.

I said, "Is it bleeding?" She shook her head and ran away.

"Can you play with me, please?" said Harrison.

I told him I could watch him hang from the pole. Harrison hung from the pole for a moment and then dropped to the ground.

"They don't want to play with me," said Harrison. "Everybody don't wants to play with me. Everybody says, No, no, no."

"That's very frustrating," I said. I suggested he figure out something to do by himself, and then someone else would get interested in what he was doing and join in. I gestured at the trucks in the sand, but he shook his head.

"Nobody wants to play with me," he said. "That means nothing to do."

"You can count all the trees," I said. "You can count the blades of grass."

Harrison spotted someone he knew and walked away with small, stocky steps.

Three girls had arranged a collection of dandelions on a flat rock in the shade of a tree.

"Nice," I said.

"Gerry got hurt," said Tamara, running over. I walked toward Gerry. He was fine.

His friend Sammy asked me for the key to go inside. He needed to go to the bathroom. I told him I didn't have a key.

"I'll go in my pants," Sammy said.

"No, don't go in your pants," I said.

"Do it in my shirt," said Gerry. "It'll cool me off."

I told him to go to one of the other teachers who had a key.

"Just go pee in the woods," said Gerry, and laughed.

"That's how Daniel Boone would do it," I said.

"I know," said Gerry. "I did that at my house. Once I did it here when I was in kindergarten!"

"You just have to sneak behind a bush," I said. "Otherwise, maybe wait for a teacher."

Sammy started laughing. "We ain't supposed to do that out here."

"Okay, well, don't."

Adam said, "We saw somebody peeing in the woods. A little bit ago, we saw somebody doing that."

"I did that many a time," said a fourth boy, Neil.

Harrison returned. "No one wants to play with me!"

A parent volunteer came up, escorting a weeping boy named Dallas. "One of the kids jumped off onto his head."

"Oh, wow," I said.

"So I was going to go in and get an ice pack for him."

"That sounds like a great idea," I said. "And this kid needs to go to the bathroom."

"Come with me, buddy," said the parent, taking Sammy's hand. "We'll go in the front entrance."

Dallas said that his ear hurt where the other kid jumped on it. I looked at it. "It's a little bit red," I said. "You're being brave about it." He started to edge off toward the screamers at the play structure. "You think you can go back in?" I asked. Dallas nodded and ran off.

I retrieved a stray ball and watched a game of tag. A pretty, toothless girl came up holding a small yellow flower. "What kind of flower is this?" she asked me.

"I don't know," I said. "My wife would know. It's really pretty." She walked away, disappointed. Darn, I wished I'd known. If I'd known the name of that flower, I would have taught something important that day.

I was asked to adjudicate a complicated dispute involving a piece of orange plastic—not a Frisbee, a sort of light flying ring—that three boys wanted. The discussion went on for several minutes, and it hinged on whether one kid had abandoned it on the grass, or whether he was still playing with it.

In the middle of binding arbitration, a boy came up and said, "That kid over there, Mike, tried to stab me and my friends."

"Well, try not to be stabbed," I said, "and try to be safe."

A girl said, "A hornet's trying to land on her! A hornet's trying to catch her!"

The argument over the orange piece of plastic was settled and I walked to a different place in the grass. Theo ran over with two other kids and said, "Mr. Baker, Luke was grabbing me and pushing me around."

Another boy, Matt, said, "He almost chucked me down to the floor."

"And he's breaking the rules right now," said Mitchell. "No climbing up slides."

"That's a rule, is it?" I said. "Okay, let's do it. Posse time."

The four of us marched over to Luke. I said, "Are you Luke? How are you doing?" I read his T-shirt, which said KICK ME. "Listen, there's no grabbing and there's no climbing up the slide."

"It was by accident!" Luke said.

I said, "Were you climbing up the slide by accident? You just lost your way, and you said, I'll climb up the slide?"

"Yeah," said Luke.

"He forgot," said Faith.

"He thought it was something else," said Matt.

"Everybody forgets on occasion," I said. "But I just want you to know that's not so good."

A crowd from Mrs. Wells's class gathered. "He was trying to stab all of us!" said another kid, Roderick.

"He was trying to kick us!" said Terry.

"I wasn't going to," said Luke.

"Yes, you were," said Terry. "Show him!"

Roderick showed me his shoulder. Luke hotly denied being responsible for the red patch.

"Oh, for goodness' sake," I said. "Let's have a happy time. Let's do a little tap dance, come on!"

"I was on top of the monkey bars watching," said Melody, "and Luke was shoving and hitting."

The bell rang. All disputes ceased in a race for position in the line-up area. Balls went back into the four-wheeled ball basket.

"Can I hold the door?"

"Can I be a door holder?"

I chose some door holders.

Carla told me to count down from five to get kids to be quiet.

"I can't find my jacket."

A parent volunteer came up. "Come get your sweatshirts!"

I asked her if she had a key to get back in. She didn't. "We're stuck out here," she said, laughing.

I took a deep breath. "ALL RIGHT, FIVE! FOUR!" The kids joined in. "THREE! TWO! ONE!"

"Zero," said Carla.

"NOW WALK!"

We walked around the corner to the back entrance, hoping that a teacher would be there to meet us.

"Mr. Baker, are you going to be here tomorrow?" said Gerry.

"No."

"Aw."

The door, as it happened, was unlocked. The kids went in. I checked my schedule. I was on duty for second recess. I spun around and loped back outside, but nobody was on the playground. I heard the tweet of a bird. What the hell? I went back to the doors, which were now locked. I knocked on them but it was so loud inside that nobody heard. I knocked for a while longer and waved. A girl came and pushed open the door for me.

"I like your beard," she said.

"Thank you." I waited in the hallway for a while, and then it dawned on me that the second-recess children, the third- and fourth-graders, used a different exit. I went back outside. Innumerable people had already replenished the playground with confusion, screaming and swinging and being ignobly savage.

Two girls, both in white spring dresses, came skipping up and said their names were Valerie and Victoria. I said I was pleased to meet them.

"Hi, Mr. Baker!" said Tina.

"Hi, Mr. Baker!" said Jasper.

I sang some Daft Punk to myself. Then I saw a tough kid scrambling up the wide slide, crashing into people. I strode over and looked up at where he stood on the play structure, shielding my eyes from the sun. "All right, I saw it, you're busted!" I said. "You just went the wrong direction, man." He looked sheepish and slid down the slide. "Good, I don't want to see that going-up business. Follow gravity. Thanks."

A girl was panting. "Can you unfreeze me?" she asked.

"I don't think I can," I said.

She shouted, "Alex! Alex! Alex! No, Alex. Alex!"

A game of *Hunger Games* tag was in progress, which involved extreme screaming. The girls seemed to call out to the boys more than vice versa. The boys roared and windmilled their arms. At the swingset, a boy batted the girl swingers' feet as they came into range. "I make them scream and then I hit them in the leg," he said. I told him to stop.

Two ed techs were talking about buying a used car with eighty thousand miles on it. I kept walking, passing a second, smaller swingset, and there I saw something beautiful. Valerie and Victoria were swaying gently side to side, smiling with expressions of blissful contentment, each holding the chain of her partner's swing so that they would stay in sync.

"That's poetry in motion," I said. "Very graceful!"

"Thank you," they said.

As I walked away, one of the ed techs saw the girls and called a warning to them. They stopped swinging. When the ed tech went back to talking to her friend, Victoria and Valerie tentatively resumed their movement, making a small oval shape in the air. They were moving no more than an empty swing would move in a spring breeze. A boy who was playing tag said to the girls, "You're not supposed to be going sideways!" He ran over to the ed techs, who were looking in the other direction, and said, "They're going sideways."

The ed techs, Mrs. Malone and Mrs. Hayes, turned and lumbered over to the swingset. "I asked you to stop," Mrs. Malone said. "I'm going to put you on the wall if you don't." The girls stopped, but they continued to cross-hold each other's swing chains. "Now you can let go," said Mrs. Malone. They didn't want to let go of the chains, so they didn't. They loosened their grip but, for all of three seconds, they didn't quite let go. That ticked off Mrs. Malone. "Yeah, I think you should go on the wall," she said. "Five minutes. Five minutes!" Valerie got off the swings. Victoria, who was more stubborn, didn't. Mrs. Malone began counting. "One."

"But we didn't do anything," said Victoria.

"Go to the wall, five minutes," said Mrs. Malone.

Victoria said, "We weren't even going!"

"You were holding on again, that's why I asked you to stop."

"You said to stop going sideways, and we did!" Victoria began weeping.

"I said let go!" Mrs. Malone tried to pry Victoria's hand from the swing's chain.

"No you didn't!" said Victoria, holding on. "NO YOU DIDN'T. You said stop going sideways!"

"I'm giving you a choice," said Mrs. Malone. "Five minutes on the wall. Not a lot. But if you keep sitting here, then it's going to end up being a lot."

Mrs. Hayes said, "Just go to the wall instead of arguing."

"I don't want to go on the wall!" said Victoria, weeping bitterly, kneeling on the grass.

Why, amid the playground's screaming and shouting and roughhousing, were these ed techs punishing the two people who were calmly and happily and nonviolently making an oval shape in the air at an otherwise empty swingset?

I walked over to them. "I think I'm partly to blame for all this," I said—because I'd said that the girls' swinging was poetry in motion.

"They should still follow the rule," said Mrs. Malone.

"But then they got busted by you guys," I said. "I just wanted to add that to the mix."

"Thank you," said Mrs. Hayes. I watched them lead Valerie and Victoria toward the cinderblock wall of the back of the school—Valerie crestfallen and silent, Victoria still defiant. "I didn't do anything!" she kept saying, through her tears. "You said to stop swinging!" Mrs. Malone and Mrs. Hayes waited, arms crossed, while both girls sat down with their backs against the wall.

Mrs. Malone returned to where I was standing. "I just want to explain something," she said, "because it looks like we're being unfair and really mean. But sometimes the kids just keep back-talking and back-talking. That's what it's for, more than anything else. I've been told that they're not supposed to be swinging sideways. We had some kids get too rough. They fall off, and there are injuries and stuff."

"Really the riskiest thing is the play structure," I said. "I've been sort of hanging around there. So you're a teacher here?"

"I'm an ed tech, yes," said Mrs. Malone. "This is my second year here. I was a teacher for thirty-seven years, and I retired from that and came back as an ed tech."

"I see," I said. "That must be an interesting new experience."

"It is," she said. She strode off toward the play structure. I walked to the wall, where the two girls looked up at me with desolate faces. "I'm sorry all that happened," I said. Victoria wiped her cheeks. She was wearing a white barrette with a flower molded into it. "Thanks for being a good sport, I appreciate it," I said. I didn't want to make a speech criticizing the ed techs, so I just rolled my eyes and shook my head.

"Is five minutes over?" asked Valerie.

"Just about, but don't take my word for it," I said, "because she's the boss."

Back at the play structure, Mrs. Malone was helping another girl who was crying. "She said a bee went up her sleeve," Mrs. Malone said. "Do you have any good ideas about that?"

"Is it up there?" I asked.

The girl was sobbing and panic-stricken. "Yes," she said.

"You can feel it crawling?" said Mrs. Malone.

"No, but I know it's in there!"

"Let's just roll up your sleeve, okay?" I said. "You mind if I roll up your sleeve?"

I started to roll her sleeve up and the girl shuddered. "I think it stang me already," she said.

"You'd really know," I said. I asked her where she thought it had stung her. She pointed to her shoulder.

"I can't really roll your sleeve up much higher," I said, "so the best thing to do would be to go in the girls' room, take off your shirt, and make sure it didn't sting you. Shake out your shirt a little bit."

"I don't want to do that!" she said.

"I think probably it looked like it was going to go in there and then didn't," I said.

"Let's go check," said Mrs. Malone. As she walked the girl into the building, she remembered Valerie and Victoria sitting against the wall. "You can get off now," she called. They got up and straightened their dresses.

I went back to the wiggly bridge part of the play structure, where things were crazy. A boy chased a bee saying, "Bite me, too! Bite me!" Several girls were shrieking in full primal terror mode. However, nobody was injured, and nobody was trying to injure anyone, so I angled back around to the bigger swingset. Nearby, in the shade, three girls had set up a pretend tea table on a flat rock, with rock plates. It was almost time to get ready to line up.

Mrs. Malone reappeared. She said, "I don't think it's up there, either—the bee. I left her with the nurse, because the nurse had to take her shirt off. I think she's okay, but I didn't want to take the risk."

"Of course," I said.

While the lines were forming, I heard Mrs. Malone giving a full account of the side-to-side-swinging incident to Victoria's teacher. "I think she should lose fifteen minutes of recess," Mrs. Malone said.

"Absolutely," said the teacher.

I went back to Ms. Collins's class. "I don't think I have you till two-fifteen," she said.

"I'm sorry," I said. "Must be the noonday sun."

We looked at the schedule that the secretary had printed out.

"Oh, I thought that she had changed it," Ms. Collins said. "One-fifteen to two-fifteen. Okay, I'm wrong. You're right."

"Mr. Baker! Whoo-hooo!" said Jared.

I sat down. Ms. Collins said, "We have a lot of work to get done from one-fifteen until two-fifteen, until you go to computer lab. They're working on research projects. I keep extending the deadline. I'm not extending the deadline any further than this Friday. This is the last week we are spending on this, because I have a lot of other things I need to teach you in the next five weeks of school. This means every single one of you is going to be focused on your outlines, your rough drafts. Maybe you are revising. Some of the common mistakes—when I look at people's work—is people are forgetting to capitalize their states, or capitalize their capitals, and knowing that you need to put commas in between your city and your state when you're writing. Make sure you are revising for capitals at the beginning of your sentences, and punctuation marks. I'm not going to be in here, Mr. Baker's going to be in here with you."

"I'm happy to swap times, though," I said, "if you'd prefer."

"Nope, this is perfect," said Ms. Collins. "They should be able to work independently. Some of them are done with their final copy and they're working on taking that information and putting it into either an iMovie or a Keynote. But every single one of them should be working really hard during this time. I'm going to be pulling kids for some different reading assessments."

"So I should bop around and see how things are going?" I said.

"Yes, but just let me know anyone who's not using their time wisely. Thank you very much. BOYS AND GIRLS. Felix, I'm going to take you first for the assessment."

The class was more or less quiet, so I started doing the rounds. They were writing about their favorite regions of the United States. "Do you have to type that?" I whispered to Mitchell.

He nodded.

"Good luck, man."

I pulled a chair up next to Marcus, who had less than a line written and was not interested in doing anything. I asked him what region he'd picked to write about.

"Southwest," Marcus said.

"Southwest, that's fascinating! Do you like country music? No. What do you like? You don't like substitute teachers sitting down next to you asking you questions. What do you like about the Southwest?"

"Not really anything," said Marcus.

"It's just that it was your assignment?"

He nodded.

"Texas is down there, Florida's down there—no, Florida's not down there."

"Oklahoma," Marcus said.

"Oklahoma. There's a song about that."

Irene, nearby, sang a snatch of "Oklahoma."

I said to Marcus, "You've got to find something you like about the Southwest. Otherwise the world is just going to fall apart."

Elijah stood up. "Can we turn the lights off?"

Good idea. "You know what's in the Southwest?" I said. "The most amazing cactuses. They're fifteen, eighteen, twenty feet high, huge spines. Saguaro cactuses. Good luck."

I stood up and whispered, "It's so much calmer when it's dark, isn't it?" The class was almost as quiet as during silent reading.

Joanna said, "Do you think I should go to the nurse?" She showed me her arm.

"It's a bruise. It's probably not broken. So I would say wait. If it really hurts overnight, then worry about it. But not now. I think it's okay."

Hope was holding a towel over her eye. She'd gotten something in it during recess. "They used eight drops in my eye and they couldn't get it out, so they used a Q-tip."

"I'm sorry, that sounds like a nightmare," I whispered.

"Can I go someplace quiet?" Lindsay whispered.

I looked shocked. "You don't think this is quiet? Find a corner."

Back to Marcus's Southwest.

"What was the cactus?" he asked.

My computer wasn't logging into the network, so I drew him a saguaro cactus. Finally my Internet came on. "Check it out," I said, pointing to a page of Google images of saguaro cactuses. "They are enormous, they live for hundreds of years." I typed "southwest facts" into Google and got an *Encylopædia Britannica* article. "Do you like dry sand and lizards?" I asked.

"I like lizards," Marcus said.

"Well, there's definitely lizards down there," I said. "And spicy food, too."

I leaned toward Connie, who wasn't doing anything, and asked her how the typing was going.

"Good," she said.

A girl whispered, "Alex! Alex!"

Marcus handwrote, *I like how they have lizards.*

"Brilliant," I said. "You are in business."

He said, "What do you call those cactuses?"

I showed him how to spell *saguaro*.

He found a picture of a tiny bird that lived in the saguaro cactus. What kind was it? he asked.

"That is a funky bird," I said.

"Funky bird?" said Marcus.

"Don't write that down," I said. "It's a Gila woodpecker." I pointed to the name on the screen, in an article titled "The Saguaro Cactus and Its Greedy Guests," posted on Kuriositas, an educational blog. Marcus began writing *Gila woodpecker*, copying it letter by letter off my screen.

Jasper was doing something energetic and idle, making silence-shattering clicks of chair leg against neighboring chair leg. I pointed to his blank paper. "Let's see this thing take shape, man!" I whisper-shouted.

"I just started my outline," Jasper whispered back.

"Well, you've got to get flying," I said. "You've got to really kick it up a notch!"

Back to Marcus, who'd found a different bird—a hummingbird, dipping its beak into a saguaro bloom. He wrote *hummingbird*. Farther down there was a photograph of an owl, and one of bats pollinating a cactus by night.

"I like it," said Marcus.

"Kind of like a horror movie," I said. "They're long-nosed bats."

"Long-nosed what?"

"They're called long-nosed bats."

Marcus tried to write *nose*. "N-O-W? For *nose*?"

"Can I go to the bathroom?" asked Crystal. Of course.

I told Marcus how to spell *nose*. He studied a picture of a nest of paper wasps on the side of a saguaro.

"You think you've got enough?" I asked. "You almost do."

"Wait, what's that?" said Marcus, cursoring over to something on the screen.

"That's a red-tailed hawk," I whispered.

"Red-tailed hog?"

"Red-tailed hawk. It's a famous Southwestern bird. H-A-W-K."

Besides what he'd just written, he also had, *Oklahoma's capital is Oklahoma City*. And he had a title: "Saddle Up." Marcus's basic problem was that he couldn't read. What he was supposed to do was type what he'd handwritten into a Pages document.

"Good title," I said. "You made some good progress."

I sat down next to a Lindsay, who was almost finished. She was also working on the Southwest. I told her that Marcus and I had just found out about some birds that live in the saguaro cactus.

"And owls," Lindsay said. "Yeah, I know. I know almost everything about animals."

"Hey, she's not the only animal geek over here," said Grant.

"Can I go to the bathroom?" asked Elijah. I nodded. "Thank you," he said.

Another ed tech came into the room, Ms. Janecki. She seemed nice.

"Can I go get a drink?" said Mitchell.

Dustin showed me his Keynote. He had three pictures of the Northwest, with fancy spiraling transitions. "Oh my gawd," I whispered. "You're having fun with that. Now, where's your text?"

"I'm doing that right now," Dustin said.

"That's the most important part. The transitions are great, though."

Connie was working on the Midwest. She was at a loss for something more to say.

They make cheese in the Midwest, I suggested. "Tons of cheese. More cheese than we could ever eat."

"Ugh, I ate a lot of cheese yesterday and I felt so sick," said Connie. "I could hardly stand up in Miss Sandoval's class."

"Guys, too much talking over here," said Ms. Janecki.

The noise gradually rose as we approached the end of the hour. Grant and Elijah explained that I was supposed to pick two quiet kids to pack up the computers, but I could *not* pick anyone who'd asked to be picked. I picked Grant and Elijah because they'd done a good job of explaining, and hadn't asked. There were problems with saving typed documents to the server. "Can I share something before I go?" Ada asked me.

I said, "By 'share' you mean tell people about it? It's kind of chaotic right now. I don't think anybody's going to listen."

Ms. Janecki waved goodbye. "Have fun," she said.

Chairs were stacked. Random tuneless songs were sung. Connie used hand sanitizer. Alex punched somebody in the knuckle. Wrap it up, I said. Pack it up. Pack it all up. Everything packed up. Thank you so much.

You're packed up. Pack it up! You're packed up. You're packed up. Are you packed up? There you go! Everyone who's packed up go on this side of the room. Are you packed up? Pack your stuff up.

Then there was an uproar because Jasper and Jared discovered two bees in the window. Bees! Bees! Are you serious? Bees! The bees were on the outside of the window, but Jasper wickedly claimed that they were on the inside and screamed. Maybe kids were more frightened of bees now because of the killer wasp scene in *The Hunger Games*.

"Will you not go insane?" I said to Jasper and Irene. Sit down. Sit down right here. Sit down. Sit down, sit down, if you're all packed up, sit down.

"I need to do my job," said Irene. "I stack chairs."

"Go do it, then."

She sat on top of a stack of four chairs.

"Will you get down off the chairs, my dear?"

"I'm protecting them," said Irene.

I asked Grant what should happen now.

"We go in a circle and you can read to us from a book," Grant said. "But it's not usually this loud." I riffled through the bookcase and found a book called *Facing West*, about the Oregon Trail.

I said, "ALL RIGHT, ABSOLUTELY EVERYBODY, RIGHT NOW!"

Mitchell told me that everyone should line up to get ready for computer lab. I said, Okay, line up, line up.

Elijah said, "No, we don't line up yet. We still have ten more minutes."

We reached an apogee of noise and madness.

Grant said, "People think that because there's a sub, that they won't tell the teacher that people are yelling."

I got mad. "OKAY, SIT DOWN RIGHT NOW," I said. "Sit down. Right now. Sit. Everybody sit right down. Down. Down. Sit down. Sit down right now. Right here." I snapped my finger at Jasper and pointed at the floor. "Sit down there. Sit on the rug, right now."

Finally the din diminished. "I love this," I said. "This is so quiet. Is everybody happy?"

Yes.

No.

"Should I read something, or should I let you talk quietly?"

Read!

"LET'S TALK!" shouted Connie.

"Don't shout," I said. "Why would you shout?"

"I don't know," Connie said.

I sat and said nothing and waited for quiet. It came.

"All right," I said, "let's read a paragraph at random. So this is about a guy whose throat is very dry. That's a dramatic situation. Has anyone had a dry throat in your life?"

Me!

"Exciting stuff, eh? Had a cough? Okay, they're on the wagon train. They're trying to cross to Oregon in wagons, and it's hot and they're tired, and they're bored. Just as we are. Are we tired?"

Yeah.

No!

Let's have a party!

I read. "*'I'm tired,' Becky said as they started.* GUYS OVER THERE IN THE CORNER, WILL YOU SIT DOWN AND BE QUIET, PLEASE?" I waited again in my chair, looking sad. I felt sad, honestly.

"Guys, he's trying to read," said Hope.

"Really, just settle down, come on," I said. "*'I'm tired,' Becky said as they started. 'Come on now.' Ben took her hand. 'Today's walk will be easy.' But it wasn't. Before an hour had passed, the sun dried the soil to dust. The ironclad wheels of fifty-nine wagons crushed the dry grasses to a powder. Clouds of dust hung in the air by the time the Clarks' wagon finally passed. 'Carry me!' Becky begged. Ben didn't answer. The dust made his—* What is that sound coming from your throat?"

Jasper went still.

"Thank you. *The dust made his throat hurt. His chest felt tired and sore, and a tickle was teasing deep inside. 'Don't start coughing,' Ben told himself. 'Just don't start.'*"

Once again, I saw the power of fiction read aloud to bring a class of twenty Maine kids to a state of rapt, attentive silence. *"The harder he coughed, the less air he got, and the more scared he was. His face felt cold, and he was getting dizzy. Air! He needed air! 'Mama,' he heard Becky yell, 'Ben's face is all white.' Pa ran to help Ben up into the wagon."*

A hand. "Um, Ms. Collins is coming back," said Lindsay.

"It's two-fifteen," said Alex. "It's time to go."

"We should at least line up," said Lindsay.

I closed the book. "Okay, let's line up."

Everybody lined up, ready to go to computer lab.

Ms. Collins was out in the hall talking to a teacher. "I'm coming, sorry," she said. "Ooh, it's hot in here."

"Just like in that story," said Tina to me.

Ms. Collins took charge. "Guys, BEFORE WE GO, I want these chairs stacked, I want the floors cleaned up, so NOBODY should be in line. Let's all take ownership for this room, please. Clean up, clean up. I see papers on the floor." She dismissed me. "Thank you for your help, that's so nice."

"Bye, Mr. Baker," said Jasper.

I waved and, once out in the hall, studied my schedule. Room 7 was next. As I walked away I heard Ms. Collins's voice faintly through the door, saying, "Guys, nobody from group number one should be in line!"

How could they do it? How could these teachers spend all day saying "GUYS," month after month? How do they have the stamina?

ROOM 7 WAS FULL OF FIRST-GRADERS. When I told her my name, Mrs. Lurie, the teacher, said, "He must be good at baking cookies!" They were having quiet playtime, she said, until about a quarter of three, and then they could start to pick up. "My little guy," Mrs. Lurie said, pointing across the room. "The one with the football? Finn. Just make sure he stays focused." She left.

"Mr. Baker, can you do magic now?" said Danica. I recognized her from the cafeteria.

I said, "Can I see what you're doing? Are you building something with those blocks?"

"Yes," she said, "but can we see the magic thing with the crackers now?"

"I ate them all," I said.

"Disappear a marker," said Sawyer.

I held the cap of the marker up and explained how to follow it with your eyes. "Then you say, And now, I'm going to hand it to you. And you do *that*—and then you do *that*."

Whoa!

I did it for them very slowly, showing how the cap dropped in my left palm. Danica and Sawyer practiced. "How do magicians do it?" said Danica.

I said, "When magicians want to do a trick, they practice for days and days. They practice in front of a mirror until they know how to do it." I yawned.

"Keep on doing it," said Danica.

I said, "I don't know if I can do it, I'm tired. I'm exhausted!"

"Do it with the whole marker," said Danica.

That would be impossible, I said—it had to be something that the hand can cover.

"Mine can." Danica fumbled with the marker, throwing it behind her, and held out her tiny empty hand, smiling.

"Clever," I said. I asked Eliot how he was doing.

"Good," said Eliot.

"I'm glad to hear it," I said. "I'm tired."

"Pleased to meet you," he said.

"Good joke," I said.

Sawyer was going around the room demonstrating the Chinese egg drop.

I asked if Mrs. Lurie read a story sometimes.

"She already did," said Danica. She handed me an orange wooden block. "Do it with this block."

I made the block disappear.

"Do a magic trick with it!" she said.

"What do you mean? This is the only magic trick I know. My dad taught it to me a long time ago."

"Leo, go to the library!" reminded a boy.

"Leo, you've got to go to the library," said Danica.

I asked Leo why he had to go to the library.

"Mrs. Lurie's testing us."

"Have you been here all day?" Danica asked.

"Oh, man, have I been here all day," I said. "Have you been here all day?"

"Almost all day," said Danica.

"Everyone's been here all day, and it is getting *late*," I said. "It is time to get on the bus and go home."

"I hope so," said Noah.

I asked the kids who were listening what time of the day they liked best.

Noah said, "I like special."

Danica said, "I like computer lab and recess and lunch."

I went over to a quiet girl, Violet. "Hi! Are you doing anything fun? Can I give you this?" I made the orange block disappear.

Declan was leaning way back in his chair, almost falling but not quite. Adele, who had long black hair combed very straight, was drawing a computer on a folded sheet of paper, with the keyboard flat on the desk and hair fashions displayed on the computer screen. "That's my computer," she said. "I looked up hairstyles." She'd drawn the Apple symbol on the back.

Mike and Luke, the kid from the playground with KICK ME on his shirt, were spraying each other with bullets from pretend machine guns made of plastic blocks. I asked them to make a boat, a plane, or a fishing rod. "Don't make a gun. That just gets everybody in a tizzy."

"I want to make a Taser," said Luke.

I asked him not to make a Taser. "What if you made a . . ."

"Purple thing?" said Mike.

"What if you made a purple thing. And after you make a purple thing, make a yellow thing."

Danica said, "And after you make a yellow thing, make a everything thing!"

But Luke was hopping and bopping and shooting at shadows. "Dude, you are way, way too excited," I said. "Take it down, take it down. Why are you getting wild?"

"I don't know," Luke said. "I was outside."

"He just whacked me with that!" said Danica, pointing to Luke's half-assembled Taser.

Declan, reading Luke's T-shirt, said, "I put a sign on my shirt that said 'Pinch Me,' and people were starting pinching me all day."

Sophie and Madison pulled out a big box from under a shelf. In it were loops of colored plastic that opened and clicked shut. They began making a chain out of the loops.

"You have a beard!" said Danica.

"I sure do."

"Does it make your chin warm?"

Violet came up. "You know when you use the cube for magic? Where does the magic take the cube?"

I showed her the trick in slow motion.

"Oh." Violet went off to practice. This magic trick was the most successful piece of teaching I'd ever done. Thank you, Dad!

"We're making the world's longest chain," said Madison.

"I'm making the world's longest number," said Leo.

"What happened to your phone?" asked Danica.

I told her. Then I said, "Guys, in two minutes, we're going to have to stack the chairs and whatnot." I read aloud from a wall poster, in a rapper's voice: *The first thing I do is always the same. I pick up my pencil and I write my name.*

"Do you see how long this is?" said Madison, holding up the multicolored chains.

I said it was a very long chain.

"It's a necklace," said Madison.

I said, "It's a necklace for a very large person, with a very large neck."

"We're making it for our whole classroom," said Sophie.

It became even longer, and Sawyer began helping. "This is amazing," I said.

"Can you guys please not make it under my chair," said Noah, who was drawing.

A secretary came on the PA system: "At this time, please make sure all computers are returned to the computer labs. Thank you."

Time to clean up, I announced. The plastic chain was now fifteen feet long and out of control: wild laughter from Madison, because Sawyer had carried one end of it out in the hall. A scream.

"OKAY, KIDS, KIDS, RIGHT NOW," I said. "You don't have to take it apart. You can just carefully gather it up and put it in the box."

I went around repeating myself. Pack it up. Clean it up. Can you clean those pieces up? Just clean them up. Thank you. Good. Let's go, let's clean it up. Where's the box? Where's the box, my friends? There's the box! Beautiful. Sir, stray pieces. The blocks. Put that in the thing, please. Can you put that in there? Right in there. Sit down. Sit down right now. Sit down. Thank you. Will you pick that up? Thank you, sir.

I praised the sky in Noah's drawing. Then there was stair chacking, which went well, although I was semiconscious by this point. Finn was bonkers, so I had him take a seat in a different chair. I asked him what his plans were for the rest of the day.

"Um, play video games," said Finn.

I said, "You get a little wild sometimes, but I guess you can keep a lid on it, right? Do you know how to do that?"

He shook his head.

"Why not?"

"I don't know."

Sophie squirted some Germ-X sanitizer on her hands. I followed suit. So many kids had been coughing, I was sure I was going to get sick.

"Luke needs a motor break," said Eliot, pointing. "He's over there."

Mrs. Lurie came back. "How was it?" she asked.

"Fine," I said.

"Good!" She turned to the class and put her hands on her head. "OKAY, HANDS ON TOP?"

"NOW WE'LL STOP," chanted the class.

"HANDS ON TOP?"

"NOW WE'LL STOP."

"Let's get the rest of the chairs stacked," Mrs. Lurie said. "Declan, you have your glasses." She thanked me. "I'm all set now," she said.

"Thank you, guys," I said.

Adele ran up. "Do you like my computer?" She showed me her finished drawing of a Google Image search of hair fashions.

"I do," I said, "and it was nice to spend some of the day with you."

"Can you say thank you?" said Mrs. Lurie.

"THANK YOU," said the class.

As I closed the door I heard Mrs. Lurie say, "Finn, you're going to owe me a tack if you don't pick up."

In the very warm teachers' break room the teacher-appreciation food was still laid out. I asked if I could do anything to help clean up.

"No, but you can eat some of this food," said a teacher. I took a brownie.

Mrs. Parsons asked me to stand out by the door to make sure the kids didn't run when they met the buses.

The children flowed out into the sunshine.

Bye, Mr. Baker! Bye, Mr. Baker! Bye, Mr. Baker!

Mrs. Vaughn, the ed tech from the morning, was also standing outside watching for trouble. She noticed two boys who were hop-skipping toward their bus. "Michael! Felix!" she croaked. "Come on back. Felix, too. You were looking around, saying, Boy, am I going to get away with this?" Michael and Felix trudged back to the door, turned around, and again walked toward the buses. "Kathleen! Come back, and on the sidewalk!"

Bye, Mr. Baker.

Bye, have a good time! Bye! Bye!

Elijah said, "I'm going to throw up on the bus."

I said I hoped not.

Bye, Mr. Baker!

The buses started their engines, sudden snarls of torque, one after another.

"Is that it?" I asked Mrs. Vaughn.

"Yep, that's the end of the day," she said.

Day Fifteen, complete.

DAY SIXTEEN. Friday, May 9, 2014
WALLINGFORD ELEMENTARY SCHOOL, FIRST GRADE

SILENT BALL

BETH CALLED TO ASK if I wanted to teach first grade at Wallingford Elementary School, the school where Mrs. Norris—who'd given us those useful teaching tips in substitute training class—was principal. I said yes and ate a cheese-and-tomato sandwich as I drove, drinking coffee and hoping I wouldn't mess up in some basic way. Littler kids are more intimidating than bigger ones.

Wallingford Elementary School was made of brick and clapboard, built in the eighties, hidden behind trees half a mile from the village. A bell tower, which held a large, visible bell taken from the old, now demolished Wallingford School in the center of town, stood near the entranceway, with an American flag on a flagpole next to it. Mrs. Ferrato's class was in room 4—a small, neat, hypercolorful space with gray carpeting and miniature wood-grained desks and tiny blue plastic chairs and sunlight streaming in from two big windows. A large hemispherical desk was positioned in the middle of the room, near a set of plastic buckets with students' names on them, in colors of lime green, hot pink, and turquoise. On the wall was a chart in six colors that said, "Use Your Writing Voices." *VOICES* was an acronym: each letter stood for something to strive for in writing assignments. *V* was for "Voice": "I show my personality in my writing." *O* was "Organization": "I arrange my writing so readers can understand it." *I* was "Ideas": "My writing is clear, focused, and interesting." *C* was "Conventions": "I show pride in my writing by editing my work." *E* was "Excellent Word Choice": "I create images and evoke emotions with my word choices." And *S* was for "Sentence Fluency": "I vary sentence length, structure, and rhythm."

I thought of the kids I'd coached two days before at Buckland Elementary: many of them could barely form lowercase letters, or spell, or sound out a word—much less vary sentence length, structure, and rhythm. And I remembered my own first-grade class, taught by a sweet, plump, kind teacher who showed us how to spell *same* and *cake* and *run* and *sun* and *one* and *to* and *two* and made us read from the *Dick and Jane* textbook, in which nothing bad happened. I wasn't a precocious reader. A month before first grade began, with my mother's help, I'd struggled through *Green Eggs and Ham*, weeping over the unphonetic wrongness of the word *dark* (dah-erk?) but relieved and happy when at last I got to the last page and my mother as a reward made me pale green scrambled eggs and a small disk of greenish ham, which wasn't all that green because the ham was pink, and no amount of food coloring could change that. When I swallowed the celebratory eggs I could feel in my throat that I'd been crying. We did very little writing in my first grade—we certainly weren't able to "create images and evoke emotions" with our word choices—and although we learned how to write numbers, we did no math beyond addition and subtraction. The best thing that happened was when we were taken to a factory that made Millbrook bread, and I saw a piece of dough the size of a sofa tumbling around in a steel chamber while being poked at by kneading bars.

At Wallingford Elementary, in the hall outside room 4, were two other first-grade teachers. I apologized in advance for the waves of sound that would probably come from my room. They laughed. "There are always waves of sound," said one of them, Ms. Wisman, reassuringly. "They're a great bunch of kids, and you should have no problem. She leaves great notes."

Mrs. Ferrato's sub plans began with a description of something called the Clip-Up Chart, which was a row of laminated strips in seven different colors, one strip for each student. "If you spot a student going above and beyond during any part of the day, you can ask them to clip up to the next color," Mrs. Ferrato wrote. Whenever they "clipped up," by moving a plastic paperclip to a higher-value color, they earned a ticket toward a prize. "If there are students calling out or misbehaving, they will clip down. If they get to Orange, they owe recess." Well, no, I thought—not today. If Mrs. Ferrato wanted to set up a color-coded system of reward and punishment, she could certainly do that, but I wasn't going to be a part of it. I was weary of the practice of punishing kids for how they acted in the class by taking away their recess time.

At eight-thirty, the students would begin to arrive, said the sub plans. "They should hang up their coats and their backpacks, put their S.M.I.L.E. Notebook in the basket, check in for lunch and sit in their seat and work on morning work." SMILE was another acronym; it stood for "Students Managing Information and Learning Everyday."

I heard four mysterious beeps on the PA system and I found where the clock was on the wall. It's hard to explain why I was so nervous: it was partly that little children are mysterious beings, and partly because I genuinely believed in first grade. Everyone has to master the trick of decoding letters on a page—life is very hard in this country if you can't read—and I was the teacher, accountable for whatever they learned or didn't learn that day. I skimmed down Mrs. Ferrato's plans. There was something about the "Daily Five," and at ten o'clock I was supposed to "shake the purple egg." I wrote "Mr. Baker" on the board. Ready.

"Come on in, I'm the substitute," I said to the first arrivals, who stopped dead at the door.

"Uh-oh, it's a sub!" said a boy named Jake.

"How tall is he?" asked a girl in a blue ruffled blouse, hanging up her backpack. Her name was Emily.

"Can you touch the roof?" said Sarah.

Sarah tried to help Jake touch the ceiling by lifting him around the waist.

"Are you guys getting married?" asked a third girl, Leyla, slitting her eyes.

"No, of course not," said Jake. "I'm not going to get married."

"You said you would," said Leyla.

"I never, ever got married in my life," Jake said. "And I never will."

Several children handed in lunch money and checks for a field trip. I asked Emily what the Daily Five was.

"You do what you signed up to," Emily explained. "And when you shake the egg we come to the rug and we go to second round. We don't have to go to third round, but if you want you can."

Ah. I asked how many kids were in the class. Seventeen, said Jake. A young, pleasant-seeming ed tech named Ms. Boissiere came in to sit with Danny, a mildly disabled child who liked to throw his head back and smile.

The morning work was written in red marker on an easel. The first thing the kids had to do was to find the errors in

do you sea that butterfly

Then they were supposed to use *every* in a sentence, find the "base word" in *careful*, and do some subtraction: "Draw tally marks to show the number that is 20 less than 39." Emily brought up her paper and I checked it and put a star at the top, although I didn't fully understand what she'd done with tally marks. "Nice job, you're fast," I whispered. The sub plans said, "When you put a star on their paper they can sign up for Daily 5 and quietly read a book by themselves on the rug." Emily sat on the rug and opened her book, *Frozen*.

I helped Lee find the base word in *careful*. "When you take *care* of someone, you're careful, right?" I whispered. Another boy, Simon, had written an *every* sentence: *POTSAND BLSFLW EVERYWR*. He read, "Pots and bowls flew everywhere!" He had trouble with the butterfly sentence. I reminded him about capitals at the beginning of sentences, and question marks at the end of questions, and I asked him how many ways there were to spell *sea*. "There's S-E-E," said Lee, "and I don't know the other way," he said. I wrote more stars at the top of more pages. Suddenly I remembered learning how to make a five-pointed star in second grade.

Almost everyone had trouble with tally marks. Ms. Boissiere explained the tally technique to Destiny, referring to a number grid. She said, "You have thirty-nine, and with ten less, where would you go, Destiny? Up or down. Up, right. That would be ten less. So we'd go up one more time, to nineteen. So you now need to show tally marks for that number."

Joe also didn't understand how to find the base word in *careful*.

Beep. A PA lady said, "Please bring students to the gym for CARE time." *CARE* stood for "Creating A Respectful Environment."

We lined up.

"You're taller than our other teacher," said Simon.

"Hey, that's just the way it is," I said.

The whole school gathered in the gym—some students sitting on the floor, some standing. We teachers stood near our classes. The staff here was friendlier, less crabby, than at Buckland and Lasswell. One of the teachers was an alert-looking bearded man; all the rest were women. After a minute of mind-blowing noise, a teacher raised her hand and said, "Shhh," and the gym went still immediately. A second-grader in a light blue dress, with a bow in her hair, stood at the microphone and read: "Good morning, today is May 9, 2014. Please place your right hand over your heart for the pledge." The whole gym intoned the pledge in unison. "Please say the school rules," the little girl said. The gym chanted, "BE RESPECTFUL TO OTHERS, KEEP HANDS AND FEET TO YOURSELVES, LISTEN TO ALL DIRECTIONS, RESPECT ALL EQUIPMENT AND MATERIALS." There was one birthday that day, she said, Becca Hightower. Applause and cheering.

Becca took a bow and asked the CARE assembly to dance the turtle dance, so we moved our arms like flippers for fifteen seconds. Then the head of the parent-teacher committee, Mrs. Royer, came to the microphone, with applause. It was the last day of Teacher Appreciation Week, Mrs. Royer said. "Are we ready for the rest of the raffles?" Huge applause. She reached in a bucket and drew a name. A teacher won a twenty-five-dollar gift card from Applebee's. Gigantic applause. Another teacher won a ten-dollar Applebee's certificate. Yay! Another ten-dollar gift card. Woo! Two round-trip tickets on the Downeaster went to Ms. Carlough. Yee! Mrs. Newman won the beach basket, holding a striped towel, and sand shovel and pail, and sunglasses and sunscreen. Another teacher won another beach basket. Less clapping now for the winners. Mrs. Yates won a movie basket, with boxes and candy and bags of popcorn. Mr. Stowe, the sole male teacher, was going to win a spa basket, but that didn't seem quite right, so he won a movie basket instead. Woo-hoooo! Cheering. Mrs. Thornhill won the coffee basket. Mrs. Gaddis won the baking basket. There were a lot of prizes. What if Mrs. Ferrato won something? I wondered. I whisper-asked Emily to accept the prize for Mrs. Ferrato—just in time, too: Mrs. Ferrato won a garden basket. Then the parent-teacher raffle master said, "Thank you, and have a good day!"

The girl in the light blue dress said, "Have a fantastic Friday!"

We trouped back to our classroom, where there was time for ten more minutes of explaining tally marks and base words, over and over, and sounding out *every* and *butterfly*. "A lot of times, if you look at just the first three letters, you can get going and figure it out," I said. I asked Simon what thirty-nine minus twenty was. "Three?" he said. We looked at the number grid. Dwight had written *delicate* as the base word for *careful*. "You did something extra-special," I said. "But if you just put *care* I think you'll be in better shape."

"Darren got a paper cut," said Lee.

Darren held up his wounded finger. "That's a bad one," I said. I suggested that he hold his pencil in a different way so that the cut was out of the way.

All this was done in whispers. I looked up at the class and was flooded with gratefulness. "Guys, I really like how quiet you are," I said.

Anne-Marie came up to explain, shyly, that if people were doing good and sitting quietly they got to move up on the Clip-Up Chart. "If we do bad we move down," she said.

"I'll keep that in mind," I said. I took attendance, and then Emily reminded me that I had to make a lunch count. I read from the lunch menu on the calendar. "Lunch today is Monster University Mike's Popcorn Chicken, Sully's Savory Rice, Boo's Hot Broccoli and Squished—GUYS, HEY! IN THE CORNER? SERIOUSLY. Boo's Hot Broccoli and Squishy Steamed Corn, Mrs. Squibble's Oatmeal Roll and Chillin' Sliced Peaches, and of course, your favorite—milk."

Emily quietly but firmly told me the right way to do lunch count. "You stand up and you say, 'We're going to do lunch count,'" she said, "and then you say, 'Stand up if you're having . . .'"

I said, "Stand up if—MY DEAR FRIENDS. I really like it when there's no clash of voices. Thank you. Stand up if you are having popcorn chicken. Whoa, my gosh." Eleven popcorn chickens. One person wanted SunButter and jelly.

"Do you know about clipping up and down?" asked Sarah.

"I do, but I don't like to be mean right off the bat," I said.

Jake sat reading *Curious George.* I told him he was doing a great job.

"Mr. Baker? Jake can move up because you said he was doing a good job."

"On our clip chart," said Jake.

"When we get up to pink, we have a jewel," said Sarah.

"And three tickets," said Emily. "And if we get on purple we get two tickets."

"My mind is reeling," I said.

"Yellow is take away a ticket," said Jake.

"And orange is take away two tickets and recess."

"And red is when you call people."

"Not just people," said Jake. "Your parents."

"I see," I said. "That's helpful."

It was past time for morning meeting. Emily, who was a real stickler, told me that whoever didn't finish morning work had to do it at snack time.

"And if you don't finish it at snack time, you have to do it at recess," said Jake.

Simon took it upon himself to start ordering people to put books away.

I told him to sit down. "Then everyone will follow your lead."

"Have the students sit in a circle," said the plans. I was supposed to give one student a high five, and he or she was supposed to high-five the next student, and then the next, around the circle. This took a while. "Only one person talks at a time," said the plans. They were supposed to do something with the calendar, note the weather and the days left in school, and go over the day's schedule. I went off plan to ask the class if anybody had seen an interesting TV show or a beautiful flower, or had something else of note to report.

Emily raised her hand. "My brother's birthday was yesterday. He got a pogo stick, a basketball that glows in the dark, and *Willy Wonka*, the movie, and he got a video game. And his cake was this big."

Deena said, "My sister has a basketball that glows in the dark, too."

Simon and Randall were wilding out, so I separated them. To Randall, who seemed especially jumpy, I said, "I've got my eye on you, man."

Leyla said, "I watched *Chestnut*. It's about this dog that keeps growing. And there was two girls. One of them really wanted a puppy. There were two robbers from New York. They put the dog on the road. Then a truck was coming and the kid ran on the road, and then he grabbed the dog and went on the other side very quick, and then went back with the dog. And then Mother Agnes, she really doesn't like dogs, and they kept it a secret. And then one morning the two girls got adopted, and they—"

"That's good," I said, cutting her short as gently as I could. "I think what you want to do when you tell the highlight of a movie—that was a great summary—is you want to pick the most memorable moment, which was the moment when they save the dog."

A hand went up from Deena in the front. "Can me and Anne-Marie do the calendar?"

I said they could after one more kid said what happened last night.

"I watched *Beethoven*, which is about a dog," said Krista.

A secretary came on the intercom. "I need a lunch count." Eleven popcorn chicken, I yelled. Ms. Boissiere added that Danny was having chicken burger.

"Discuss the schedule," said the sub plans. Fine. "We're going to learn about nouns, verbs, and adjectives," I said. "We're going to shake the purple egg. We're going to have a snack. We're going to write, we're going to have lunch, we're going to go to the music classroom, we're going to read aloud, we're going to do some specials, then math, then pack and stack. There's so much to do today, it's almost overwhelming."

Randall was sniffing Simon's sweatshirt. It was time to dole out a worksheet called "Nouns, Verbs, Adjectives, Oh My!" But Randall couldn't get down to business. He rolled around, hummed, sprawled, blathered. I couldn't blame him. For all but one or two of these kids, it was too early to be studying the taxonomy of words, it seemed to me. They knew how to talk; they needed to know how to read and write. The parts of speech could come later. You can ride a bicycle without knowing what a sprocket or a brake clamp or a wing nut is. You can stand on tiptoe without knowing about the metatarsal arch. Pure brute decoding—reading and writing, memorizing all the unsoundoutable perversities of English spelling— that's what first- and second-graders needed, more than anything.

"I got a bug bite," said Anne-Marie, showing me her elbow.

I took a shot at putting grammar in context. I told the class, "Already, without anybody teaching you—even before you had a teacher—your brain soaked up literally thousands of words."

"Blee! Blop!" said Randall. Sit in the corner, I said.

I tried again. "In your mind are all these words, floating around. And what teachers are trying to do is say, Okay, let's take a look at this cloud of words and see what properties it has. What's the difference between this kind of word and that kind of word? And they came up with fancy terms, like *noun*, *verb*, and *adjective*." I handed out the worksheet, which said, *Write one noun, verb, or adjective, which can be associated with each place listed below. Example: the mall. People, shop, exciting.* The first place they had to think about was "your school."

"What's a noun that has to do with school?" I asked.

School?

Pencil?

"*Pencil* is perfect. Okay, a verb. Something you do at school."

Sarah's hand went up. *"Learn?"*

"Excellent. You guys really got the gist of it, good. And finally, this is the hardest one, what's an adjective?"

After some struggle, Leyla thought of *red*. Good—bricks are red.

The next place the worksheet wanted them to think about was the playground. They came up with *swing* for the noun, *play* for the verb, and then came the adjective. "Is the playground sleepy?" I asked. "Is the playground hot? Sometimes the playground is cold and icy. All winter long. Any suggestions?"

Fun?

"*Fun* is an adjective—or it can be an adjective."

While the class labored to print nouns, verbs, and adjectives, I got Randall to put his name at the top of the page. "Okay, beautiful," I said. I pointed to the instructions—find words that have to do with school. First, a noun. "A noun is some thing, like a desk, or a rug, or something that's in your school," I said to him. "That's called a noun. See that word right there? *Noun.* Tell me some thing in school."

Randall thought. "I do know something *around* school," he said. "Lots of caterpillars can be around school."

"Good, *caterpillars*, excellent." I wrote CATERPILLAR out so he could copy it.

"There's a book called *The Very Hungry Caterpillar*," he said.

As Randall wrote *caterpillar*, I helped Calvin think of a noun that went with *playground. Slide*, he said. Then I turned back to Randall. "Now something that happens at school," I said. "People talk, they run, they learn, they eat. Those are called *verbs*. Verbs are things that happen."

"Something I do at school is I think," said Randall.

"Yes, *think*! You got it. Randall, that was good." I explained what an adjective was. A color, or hot or cold, or bright or dark.

"Dark?"

"School can be dark," I said. "Especially when it's stormy out."

"One time I got so scared in a thunderstorm that I hid under one of these tables," Randall said. I showed him how to write *dark*, the very same word I'd had such a difficult time with about fifty years ago. Passing on the legacy.

Krista came up with her word list: *TV, look, awesome. Bat, hit, fun.*

Calvin said, "Joe is copying my paper."

"I'm not looking at his paper," said Joe. "I just have a noun and a verb, and now I need a adjective."

"Okay, keep your eyeballs on the page," I said. "What are some adjectives? A playground can be hot, it can be cold, it can be muddy, it can be crazy."

On and on we gamely grammared. Noun, verb, and adjective for the beach, for the doctor's office, for a baseball game. This was all lost time, it seemed to me, and for some kids it spread confusion and jitteriness, which on a normal day would then have led to their being "clipped down" and deprived of recess. *Adjective*—what an unlovely word for something juicy and squeezable and wild and elusive and fungible and adamantine and icy-blue. There were nouns and verbs and adjectives in play many thousands of years before anyone took the time to sort and name these abstractions. An eon of language precedes linguistics. You can write a three-decker novel or a whole history of Transylvania without knowing or caring in the least what the parts of speech are—and in first grade, unless you're an unusual little person who takes an Aristotelian pleasure in verbal classification, it's an unnecessary encumbrance and a distraction.

"So what happens at a baseball game?" I asked Randall. "Do they walk, do they run, do they sing?"

"Run!"

"And that's a *verb*." Randall wrote *run*.

Pencil, learn, red. Slide, play, fun. Bed, eat, fun. Water, play, fun. Sarah came up with *nervous* as a verb having to do with the doctor's office. I wished I didn't have to tell her that *nervous* was an adjective, and that she had to erase it and replace it with something like *worry*. Lee said that *game* was an adjective for the doctor's office. "Because when I go they give me a game," he said. Lee and Sarah were both making associative word herds, which was in fact a more interesting activity than this parsing exercise. I felt the minutes sifting by, wasted.

The finished worksheets went into the Done Box, and then I shook the purple egg, which lay on the whiteboard tray and made a sound like a maraca. Everyone began reading aloud to a partner. Joe got sad because he didn't have a reading buddy. I said I'd be his reading buddy. *"Up went the elephant,"* Joe read to me, guessing. I pointed to the picture of a giraffe in a tree and said, "It has a very long neck." I made the sound of the first letter: "Juh."

"Giraffe!" Joe said.

"Yes, good. Right. *Up went the giraffe.*"

"Up went the zebra," Joe read. *"Up went the elephant. Went up the—*I mean, *Up went the tiger. Went up—*I mean, *Up went the lion."* Then all the animals fell down from the tree house.

Joe read me another book, about dogs. *"Dogs do things that make me mad."* He had trouble sounding out *things* and *make.* On the other hand, he read *slobber* perfectly. What a great kid.

"Okay, brilliant," I said to the class. "And now I'm shaking the purple egg!" I shook it around my head. The class put away their read-aloud books and sat cross-legged on the carpet. Our next task involved a green plastic bucket filled with many bicolored plastic Easter eggs (slightly smaller than the purple noisemaking egg), each half of which had a word written on it with Sharpie. "Each student takes one half of the egg and must find their antonym partner," the plans directed. I asked someone to pull the eggs apart into halves. Sarah explained what an antonym was: an opposite.

"Oh my gosh, yes," I said. "Antonyms are opposite. You can remember it because you think of two ants walking towards each other, and they don't like each other."

"What if they're fire ants and normal ants?" said Emily.

I said, "A fire ant and a normal ant. Two ants, and they're antonyms. They want to go away from each other."

We talked about synonyms, and Emily said, "If it was *start* and *begin,* they would hop together, and that would be a synonym."

"Great!" I handed around the green plastic bucket, and each kid took out half an egg. "Now you want to find your antonym partner," I said. Immediately there was shouting and confusion. "Who has *hard*?" "Who has *down*?" Besides the noise, there was another problem: there were more antonyms than students, and many of the antonymic half eggs remained in the bucket. I decided to proceed one egg at a time. Deena's half egg said *start*.

I said, "We're going for antonyms. The opposite of *start* is . . ."

"Startle!" said Danny.

Nobody had *stop* or *finish*. What ridiculousness. Move on. Sarah's half egg said *begin*. Nobody had *end*, either, and a quick rummage through the bucket didn't turn it up. I found an egg that said *quiet*. What was the opposite of quiet?

Loud!

"I have *loud*," said Krista.

We got a few antonym eggs put together.

Anne-Marie raised her hand. "Mr. Baker, I can't hear you because everyone is talking."

I snapped my finger at Jake, who was hopping up and down. "SIT. I'm going to start taking names, and I mean it. I NEED ABSOLUTELY ONE VOICE AT A TIME. I want you to say what your egg says."

"*Easy*," said Jake. Nobody had half an egg that said *hard*, but I found it in the bucket. It seemed momentarily important to point out that there can be several different antonyms for a given word—for instance, the opposite of *quiet* might be *loud*, or *deafening*, or even, possibly, straying further afield, *rambunctious*. They all meant slightly different things. We got a few more eggs paired up, and then I pulled the plug.

"Okay, hand all the eggs in," I said. "That was loads of fun. Is it snack time yet?" I looked at the clock: 10:40. "Five minutes till snack time."

Calvin started shaking the purple egg. Don't play with the purple egg, I said.

"Mr. Baker, can we play Sparkle?" said Sarah.

I'd never heard of Sparkle.

"It's like if you get one of the letters wrong, you need to sit down," said Sarah. "If you get the word right, then you're still standing."

Emily said, "If someone says 'Sparkle' at the end of the word, the other person sits down."

It was another public humilation game, like Around the World. I said, "I'm very glad to know about Sparkle, but since it's already snack time we might have to do that a different day."

Joe said, "We have a snack bucket, can I go get it?"

"A snack bucket," I said. "Sounds exciting."

"It's not really exciting at all," said Joe.

Darren ate macaroni and cheese; Simon ate Ring Dings; Leyla ate Motts for Tots—little chunks of fruit. I ate a crunchy protein bar and listened to a girl named Tracy sing songs from *Frozen*. When they got too loud I told them to take it down a peg.

"We're not pegs," said Dwight.

"A notch, take it down a notch," I said.

"Why do you call us pegs?" asked Destiny.

"Can I read a book with you again?" asked Joe. He handed me the biggest book I'd ever seen. It was three feet wide and four feet high, some kind of crazily oversized picture book. We both laughed.

"We can't read those books anymore," said Emily. "Some kids make a mess of them and they rip them."

"Okay, wrap up your snackers!" I said.

I asked what time in the morning people woke up. Dwight said six. Calvin said five. Randall said, "I be awake all night." Finally snack was done and cleaned up, more or less.

To get their attention, I did the quintuple-clap thing. "Special flash report," I said. "What's happening next is finishing up the MOTHER'S DAY GIFTS AND CARDS. This is very important, because your mothers work hard, and they love you, and you've got to give them something. If you'd like to finish your card, you can. If you'd like to decorate the birdhouses, you can. And Ms. Wisman will be giving you a white bag to decorate, to hold the birdhouse." The birdhouses sat in a row on one of the art tables.

I sent Destiny next door to Ms. Wisman to find out when we were getting the white paper bags to decorate for Mother's Day. Destiny returned saying that Ms. Wisman had told her that we already had the white bags somewhere in the classroom. After some intensive searching we found the bags on a file cabinet behind Mrs. Ferrato's desk. I handed them around. "Decorate these bags for your ma. There's birdseed that's going in here, and the birdhouse, and the card. Decorate the front, make it beautiful, do something nice. It's your mom! You're taking them home today. That's very important. And then you save them up and you give them to your mom on Sunday."

What followed was the best forty-five minutes of the day. The kids colored the peaked roofs of the Popsicle-stick birdhouses with six different colors of colored pencil, and they thought about what kinds of birds might live inside them, and whether the birdhouses should have doorbells, and they put plastic baggies full of birdseed inside them (we found the bags near a window, behind some cups full of crayons), and they sang the melting song from *Frozen* and debated the dangers of hornets, and they decorated the white bags with stripes and circles and rainbows and *MOM*s, and they took care when putting the birdhouses into the white bags so that none of the Popsicle sticks were accidentally torn off—and then we arranged the big pink cards that they'd made earlier and the white birdhouse bags on the semicircular table, where they looked resplendent. Ms. Boissiere, the ed tech, went around giving praise. I read some of the letters glued inside the cards: "Dear Mom, I love you because you halp me win I fol daown. I like wan you gev me privig. I like going to Funtown Splahtan wsh with you. tHank you!" "Dear Mom, I love you mommy because. You care me like when I am sick or hurt. And like when it is bed time you read stories like the little mrmade." "Dear Mom, I love you MoM because you bring Me places. To the go kerts. You take cane of Me. You Feed Me. And Give Me love." My phone rang: it was my daughter planning a Mother's Day present. I went out to the hall to talk to her for a minute. When I came back in, Ms. Boissiere was saying: "Boys and girls, it needs to be a little bit quieter. If you guys can't handle it, we'll put it down, and you guys will be staying in for recess. Danny. You guys need to lower your voice a little bit. This is a fun activity, but you guys should not be hollering and shouting at people right in front of you, please. Thank you." Emily told Darren that he needed to color his whole bag. Darren came over to me. "Mr. Baker," he said, "do we need to color the sides of our bag?"

I told him he needed to follow his heart. "You don't have to do anything. What you're doing is making a beautiful bag that you think your ma would like."

The next fifteen minutes were supposed to be "Writing share/clean for lunch." There was serial bathroom-using and hand-washing. While several students played chirpy games on their iPads I made the mistake of trying to read some of the class a picture book I'd found on the shelf called *The Flying Dragon Room*, about a boy who leads his parents to a subterranean realm with a zig-zaggity ladder and an ubble bubble blower. I stopped after a few pages, because they were happier noodling with their iPads. "It doesn't matter," I said. "You're being very quiet, and I don't think I'll read any more." I sat and listened to the sounds of many tiny video games being played. Ms. Boissiere told me her story. She'd worked at the middle school for a while as an ed tech and then she moved to Wallingford Elementary. "I think I lucked out with my position here," she said. "Joan, who's in this room, is really good. I enjoy watching her with the kids. They're used to their routine. Joan was out on Monday, and the sub said, 'I try and follow the plans, but everybody does things differently.' It happens. But the structure and the consistency—it's big." She made an announcement to the class. "We're going to set the timer for two minutes, and then we're going to clean up and get ready for lunch, okay?" Randall hastily glued a crayon on his birdhouse to serve as a chimney.

The timer beeped. "Boys and girls, we're going to call the quietest table!" said Ms. Boissiere. The class went still. "Let's have Destiny's table." They lined up. "Tracy, Jake, you guys can line up. Sarah's table." When it got too noisy, she said, "Boys and girls, we can sit back down, and you'll be late for your lunch. Danny, go sit back down."

"I'm the line leader!" said Simon.

We walked to the cafeteria. Leyla took me aside and told me she'd gotten an eyelash in her eye. We got it out.

I walked back to the classroom. Mrs. Whitman was standing in the doorway, waiting for her class to line up. She asked me how it was going so far.

"They're really nice kids," I said, "but this is a hard job. You really have to admire teachers' ability to hang in there all day long, because it gets tiring."

"It does," said Mrs. Whitman. "It sure does." She turned to the line. "Okay, THREE, TWO, ONE, ZERO!"

I had twenty-five minutes for lunch. The sub plans said that after recess, which was between twelve-thirty and one, I was supposed to read aloud to the class: "Continue reading A-Z Mysteries. This book is on the easel." The book wasn't on the easel. I spent five minutes hunting around for any A to Z Mystery book with no luck, then hurried to the tumultuous cafeteria. Ms. Boissiere held her hand up and called for silence. "I AM HEARING LOTS OF SHOUTING," she said. "I am hearing people complaining about friends saying not-nice things to them! Let's all put our heads down and take a last minute at lunch to sit quietly, not talk to your neighbor, and think about what you're going to do this weekend! Think about how you can have a great Mother's Day on Sunday! Your voices are off, your heads are down!"

A minute passed, and another ed tech called, "MRS. CASTELLO'S CLASS."

When our class was called, we walked back to our room, readied ourselves for recess, and lined up again. As soon as the students were outside they fanned out and commenced screaming—all except for Randall and Simon, who fought over a pair of nesting orange traffic cones. Randall wanted to sit on one cone and hold the other cone to his chest, while Simon wanted to run around with his arm in a cone as if it was a lightsaber. While I chatted with a kindergarten teacher, an elegant girl in black pants and a black shirt with very short hair walked up and said furiously that the boys were not letting her play kickball. Her name was Renata. The kindergarten teacher, Ms. Carlough, took the boy kickballer aside. "We've been out here for two minutes and I've already had two problems with you. One more time and you're all done. Three strikes and you're . . . ? Out. What do you say to Renata?"

The boy said he was sorry, barely audibly.

"Good," said Ms. Carlough. "Anybody can play kickball."

I said to Renata, "I bet you're a heck of a kickball player. Are you good?"

"Pretty," said Renata.

"Good luck," I said.

"Thanks." She ran off to the kickball diamond, but meanwhile the game had dissolved. Renata stood on home plate, waiting, kicking the dirt. I chewed an apple. Simon and Randall ran back and forth over the field brandishing their traffic cones. Eventually a new kickball game started, and Renata walloped the ball toward second base and ran. One of the cone brothers, Simon, ran up to me and said, "Can you time me on your phone?"

I said I could, but first I needed to know what the A to Z Mystery was about.

"It's *The School Skeleton*," said Simon.

I started the timer and Simon dashed off, holding the traffic cone. He ran to the trees and back in forty seconds.

"Woo," I said. "You were a flash of lightning."

Using my phone, I bought an e-book version of *The School Skeleton* so that I'd be able to read it aloud even if I couldn't find the paperback in the classroom after recess.

A girl ran back with a huge bouquet of dandelions to show me. "I got them from all over," she said. "We're giving them to our teachers."

At one o'clock, the kindergarten teacher blew several blasts on a whistle. Renata, the kickballer, ran up. "I got no outs, one strike, and three home runs," she said. "Nice meeting you."

"Mr. Baker, someone called Darren a bad word," said Sarah.

"Oh, well, just let it go," I said.

Ms. Carlough said, "FIVE! FOUR! THREE! TWO! ONE! MADISON! GET IN LINE AND PUT A BUBBLE IN YOUR MOUTH!"

I walked my children in, with Simon at the head of the line. "Do you have anything I can put water in?" he asked. "I'm dying."

"Meow," said Tracy.

I found a cup for Simon. He drank greedily.

"Can we read the book now?" said Emily.

"Yes," I said. "Mrs. Ferrato said the book was on the easel, but the book isn't on the easel."

Emily found the book in somebody's book bucket. "We got to chapter three," she said.

"You are brilliant," I said.

The class was on the carpet and I was in my chair, with the book in hand. I said, "The last sentence she should have read you is, *Mrs. Eagle smiled slyly. 'About a vanishing school skeleton,' she said.* Does that ring a bell?"

Yes.

I read on. "*'What did you call your story?' Josh asked Dink at their lockers. It was three o'clock and everybody was going home. Dink grinned as he put on his jacket. 'It's called "Josh Stole the School Skeleton and Should Go to Jail Forever,"' Dink said. 'Hah hah,' Josh said.*" Near where Mr. Bones, the stolen skeleton, usually hangs, Ruth Rose discovers an adult-sized footprint in the dust. Mrs. Schottsky and Dink go over to inspect a footprint of a sneaker, with a zigzag tread. Dink wonders whether the thief made the footprint when he lifted Mr. Bones off the hook.

A girl raised her hand. "Can I go to the bathroom?" Of course. I read more pages. The principal, Mr. Dillon, isn't the skeleton thief, because he wears shiny tassel loafers with smooth soles. Mrs. Schottsky can't have stolen the skeleton, because she wears white nurse's shoes with special treads. We got to the end of the chapter.

"Can you keep reading?" said two kids in unison. I checked the clock.

Music was at 1:25. We had time to read chapter four, which had more talk about shoe sizes. They go back to Dink's house and eat some cookies. They measure a paternal sneaker, and Dink feeds his guinea pig with a chunk of cookie. I asked if anyone had guinea pigs.

"My cousin has two," Dwight said. "But his first guinea pig died."

More discussion in the book about the possibility of measuring teachers' sneakers. They redouble their resolve to find the skeleton. End of chapter four.

"Guys, I want to say that was excellent listening," I said. "I enjoyed that."

"Do you know where the skeleton is?" asked Darren.

"I do not know where the skeleton is." Dwight showed me how to mark where I'd stopped reading, using a paperclip. I asked what kinds of books they liked to read—scary stuff, or maybe nonfiction about volcanoes or insects?

"I don't like to read scary things, because it gives me nightmares," said Sarah.

"Anything but *Goosebumps*," said Dwight.

"What happens when you have goosebumps?" asked Deena.

If you go out on a cold day, I said, and the wind comes up, you get little things on your arm that are called goosebumps. "And when you're really frightened, also, you can get a clammy feeling, and you get goosebumps."

Lee stroked his arm. "You know how I know when I have goosebumps? Sometimes when I'm cold, my hair starts sticking up."

"I have a horrible dream, it's a nightmare about dying," said Leyla.

"It ain't going to happen," I said. "You're going to have a happy life."

Leyla wanted to tell me a long version of her dream but I said we had to go to specials, so I'd have to hear it later.

Joe asked me what a mosquito bite was, and I told him. We walked down the hall to music class. I had a half an hour to file papers. "Fill their SMILE Notebooks with homework in the Right Back To School side. Any reading logs that were turned in need to be put back into their homework folders for homework." So that was what the SMILE notebooks were all about:

homework and reading logs. What a mistake, I thought. Reading logs interfere with the seamless fickle joy of reading: they turn you into a page-by-page bean-counter of the waking dream. And homework, in first grade? Between first and seventh grade, I had a total of about ten pieces of homework. "Workers Who Keep Us Well" in second grade, plus a report on gorillas. A report on Rhode Island and a report on France in third grade. A report on Thomas Edison in fourth grade. Nothing in fifth grade. A study guide on *Lord of the Flies* in sixth grade. Practically nothing in seventh. My homework-free generation has done just fine. The first real homework I did was for Mr. Toole, in eighth grade, when he asked my friend Nick and me to write epic poems. There was, I thought, no need for homework, ever, in grade school or middle school. And there was way too much of it in high school.

But I was a sub, and my job was to enforce the status quo, so I spent ten minutes stuffing homework worksheets in the SMILE notebooks. I spent another five minutes reassembling the antonym Easter eggs in the green bucket. Then I called my wife and talked to her about the documentary movie she was editing. I told her about the Mother's Day bags and Popsicle-stick birdhouses. "Love you madly," I said. I stood outside the music classroom and peered into the window. The kids were dancing to a pop song. The PA lady came on, calling some kids to the office.

After music, my class was feral. I made an eraser disappear to get their attention. When they were quiet, I showed them the trick of how to do the egg drop. "You say some things that might not mean much, like 'Alaka zoomidoo, I'm going to make this eraser go to the zoo.' And then you go like this."

"I want to try!" said Tracy.

"I'll go get some more erasers!" said Jake.

"Can I tell you about the nightmare that I had?" said Leyla.

"Guys, please be quiet," I said. "We're hearing about a nightmare."

Leyla said, "I was watching this cursed mirrors thing, and then when I fell asleep I had a dream where it was the same kind of mirror as in the episode. There was one dark side, and I thought I saw this golden thing in the mirror. And then it hooked toward me, and I thought, I'm just going to get out. And then I dived toward it."

My sympathetic reaction was cut short, because Calvin was throwing crayons. "Kiddo? What the heck are you doing? Come over here and sit right there. Right there."

"Mr. Baker, your hair's falling out," said Deena.

"My hair's falling out?" I slapped my hands on my head. "Oh my god! It's seriously falling out."

The class's next task was one of those mystery picture grid things, where you color in the squares after doing something with rows of base-ten blocks.

"We know how to do it," said Simon.

"That's easy," said Calvin. "Easy, easy."

"Dude," I said fiercely, "if it's easy, let's see you do it."

While the kids were chattily coloring their mystery pictures, Ms. Boissiere told me that there was going to be a change to the schedule: she might be telling everyone to get their backpacks ready early. I went around helping the children who didn't understand the math mystery picture. The instructions said, *Use the base ten blocks to solve the problem. Write your answer on the line. Then color your answers with any color in your chart.*

"*Any* color?" said Krista. "You can choose whatever color you want?"

Well, no. You had to use the color that corresponded to that number in the number key, and the two possible colors were red or green.

Simon started to count loudly, "FIVE, TEN, FIFTEEN, TWENTY."

I made an announcement. "If you have to say numbers to yourself, say them in a whisper, so you don't distract the person next to you. All righty?"

The kids who finished quickly went back to making erasers disappear. "Does anyone want to know how to do the magic trick?" said Sarah. Ms. Boissiere began helping kids pack up their backpacks early.

Another ed tech arrived, and she and Ms. Boissiere conferred briefly. Then Ms. Boissiere took control of the class. "Boys and girls! Listen! I gave you guys a couple of directions. That was to grab your backpack and coat, and pack up your bag with your Mother's Day cards. I did not ask you to stack your chairs, Calvin, or sit on the tables. You guys are kind of not really listening, so it's making it very difficult for me to give directions. There should be nobody sitting on tables." Calvin climbed off the table. "We have a special treat this afternoon," Ms. Boissiere continued. "Mrs. Norris sent in cupcakes for us. So all the tables need to be cleared off. Put your names on your math packets and put them in the Not Done box." She handed out white cupcakes with white frosting and sparkles on top. "They're all vanilla," she said.

"Aw," said Calvin.

"These look awful scrumptious," I said, wolfing mine down. Something was afoot, though. Ms. Boissiere passed around some shark fruit snacks. I asked her what was going on.

She whispered, "It's Danny's last day."

While I washed the frosting off my hands, the other ed tech, Mrs. McChesney, said, "Should we say what this is about?"

Ms. Boissiere said yes.

"Boys and girls, I need you looking at me," said Mrs. McChesney. "Do you guys know why we're having this party?"

No.

Mother's Day!

"Nope, nope," said Mrs. McChesney. "I've got to wait till it's quiet and everybody's looking at me. I'll give you a few more guesses. What do you think?"

"Danny's birthday?"

"You are the closest one. Danny loves sharks, right? Danny is moving to go live with somebody else. He's going to be living pretty far away, so he's going to go to a different school. So we're all going to miss him very much. So we're having a goodbye party for him. So should we all say goodbye to him?"

Goodbye, Danny, said the class.

"We will miss you," said Mrs. McChesney. She gave Danny a shark book and a shark mug and a small rubber shark. Danny was happy and giggly. "Raise your hand if you want a second cupcake." Really?

I went over to Danny. "Glad I got a chance to get to know you," I said. "Hope things go well."

When the party was almost over, Ms. Boissiere thought of a number between one and ten. "Randall, you can go first."

"Nine?" guessed Randall.

"Five?" guessed Simon.

"It was three, so Simon is closer," said Ms. Boissiere. "So do you want some more shark gummies?"

Simon got the whole packet.

Ms. Boissiere said, "Everybody tell Danny how much you're going to miss him!"

WE'RE GOING TO MISS YOU, DANNY, said the class.

"I'm going to miss you one thousand times," said Simon.

"I'm going to owe you a million dollars," said Randall.

Anne-Marie went over and hugged Danny.

"Aw, are you guys getting married?" said Leyla. "Danny, are you moving to China?"

"No," said Danny, smiling.

Sarah turned to me. "I know how to remember north, south, east, west. Never Eat Soggy Waffles."

I started picking up the cupcake wrappers and the half-eaten second cupcakes. Ms. Boissiere clapped the class to order. "I think we have time for maybe one round of silent ball. But first you need to stack and pack." Mad chair stacking. "Wow, this table looks ready over here," said Ms. Boissiere. "Nice job, Destiny, Dwight, Calvin, Emily, looking good!" When everything was packed and stacked, Ms. Boissiere said, "You guys know the rules. You talk, you're out. You're over by the bags. If you talk when you're out, you're against the wall." Emily turned off the lights. "So starting now, no talking. You talk or make a noise, you're out. Danny, since it's your last day, you start. Go ahead." She gave the ball to Danny, who held on to it, laughing a snuffly laugh.

"Silent ball, remember," said Ms. Boissiere, warningly. Finally Danny threw it to Calvin. Then he cleared his throat noisily.

"Danny, you're out," said Ms. Boissiere. Danny went over by the backpacks and sat down. Calvin said, "No."

"Calvin, you're out," said Ms. Boissiere. "Nope, you're out. Calvin, you're out!" Calvin sat down on the rug.

Randall said something.

"Randall, you're out, sorry." Randall went sadly over to the backpacks and sat down. The ball hopped around the room. The girls were able to keep their mouths shut.

Calvin was fiddling with something. "Calvin, put that away," said Ms. Boissiere. Jake failed to catch the ball.

"Jake, you're out." Danny, Calvin, Randall, and Jake started snickering softly. "Shh! Boys on the rug!" Danny started laughing harder. "Shh," said Ms. Boissiere. "Jake, sit. Last warning."

Deena didn't catch the ball. "Deena, you're out." Tracy dropped the ball. "Sorry, Tracy," said Ms. Boissiere. "Jake, I said last warning, you go over to the wall."

Randall began clapping his hands softly and rolling his eyes. Calvin and Danny thought that was very funny. I didn't want them to get in more trouble, so I waved at them and whispered, "Totally silent."

"Go a little faster," said Ms. Boissiere to the remaining players. "All right, Simon, you're out." Huge snickering from the rug. Krista threw the ball wrong and said, "Oop."

"Sorry, Krista," Ms. Boissiere said. "Silent ball."

What a nightmare of a game—more public humiliation.

Ms. Boissiere checked the clock and abruptly took control of the ball. "I know we're playing a game, and it's Friday, but can I have you guys's attention one second?" she said. "Since Danny's leaving, I am actually leaving as well."

Aw, said the class.

"So today's my last day as well. But I just wanted to let you guys know that I enjoyed working with all of you, and I had a lot of fun."

"And I bet they had a lot of fun working with you," I said.

A bell bonged. "That was actually the bell," said Ms. Boissiere. "That was a great game of silent ball. Why don't you guys all go to the rug. If you're getting picked up or going to Y care, please grab all your stuff and line up. Grab your Mother's Day things, or else they're going in the trash."

I said goodbye to the kids who were lined up.

The PA lady came on and called about twenty names to the office. Simon was one of them.

Anne-Marie was sobbing. She hugged Danny again and tried to wipe her tears. Ms. Boissiere comforted her. "You know, he'll come back and visit," she said. "It's a good thing."

Randall pointed to my nametag, which said VISITOR. "Is that your name?"

"That's VISITOR," I said. "*V* for *visitor.*"

"What's that mean?"

"A person who is visiting the school."

The PA lady came on again to dimiss K through two.

Bye, bye-bye, I said. See you. Bye. Have fun.

I wrote a note to Mrs. Ferrato and neatened up her desk. The PA system came on. "Happy Mother's Day to everyone who is a mother," said Mrs. Norris, "and happy Teacher Appreciation Week. Thank you all." I found a last unmatched piece of an antonym egg, *good*, and matched it with its opposite, *bad*. I put the egg in the green bucket, turned in my badge, and drove home.

End of Day Sixteen.

NON-NEGOTIABLES

BETH CALLED AT FIVE FORTY-FIVE A.M. to say she had a job for me at the high school teaching Mrs. Kennett's tenth-grade English classes. I got there more or less on time, donned my substitute lanyard, greeted Paulette, and found room 15, Mrs. Kennett's classroom.

Above her desk Mrs. Kennett had taped pictures of her mom and dad wearing party hats, and her husband, who was a rock climber, and her daughter, in a princess dress, and her dog, with a Frisbee in his mouth. There was also a quote from *Through the Looking-Glass*: "Why, sometimes I've believed as many as six impossible things before breakfast." On the wall, in addition to the familiar taxonomy-of-learning poster, was a wall chart with advice on what to do before, during, and after reading:

BEFORE READING
- Activate Prior Knowledge
- Set a Purpose
- Identify Text Structure

DURING READING
- Visualize
- Take Notes
- Ask Questions
- Monitor Comprehension
- Reread

AFTER READING
- Summarize
- Connect
- Discuss

Activate Prior Knowledge! Identify Text Structure! Monitor Comprehension! It sounded like Spaceteam, the shouting-game app.

Steve, in a gray T-shirt, sat at one of the six-sided tables, his backpack in front of him, waiting for the day to begin. He looked about twenty and was built like a linebacker.

"What's been happening in here, anything?" I asked.

"Hm?" Steve said, politely plucking out an earbud.

"What's been happening in here?"

"We've been working on soundtracks," he said. "For our book that we just read."

Beep. The PA lady called Ron Bonacki to the main office, please. There were no sub plans on the desk, so I looked over a grading rubric for the soundtrack project. The assignment was to make a sort of playlist for Tim O'Brien's *The Things They Carried*, about the Vietnam War. "Choose 12 chapters to depict through song," said the rubric, downloaded from iRubric.com. "You will need to identify the mood and tone of each chapter and then find one song that best represents that. For each chapter, fill out an analysis form." The analysis forms were filled with blank lines, where students were supposed to write what they thought the mood of each chapter was, give quotations from the text that supported the assigned mood, give quotations from the lyrics of the songs, and offer an explanation of "how this song depicts the mood/tone of the chapter."

There was a full-page chart explaining what got you a good grade on the soundtrack project and what didn't. "Student is able to support all song choices with developed explanations, using lyrics and quotes that relate to the main idea of the scenes." That got you a 4. "Student does not have a grasp of the content. The explanations of the song choices do not show a relationship to the scenes chosen. Lyrics and quotes do not relate or were missing." That got you a 1. You also got a 1 if the analysis sheets had "four or more spelling, punctuation, and/or grammatical errors." Jeepers, I thought, how to lay waste to pop music and Tim O'Brien at the same time.

The head of the Language Arts Department, Mr. Markey, came by to give me a printed-out email of sub plans from Mrs. Kennett. Block 1 was the soundtrack project, he said. Blocks 2, 4, and 5 were all doing the same thing in my class and in his class—watching a YouTube video. He didn't say what the video was about.

The PA woman had announcements: "Drew Eschenbach to the main office. AP Bio students should be in the great room of the North Building to take your AP Bio test at this time. Nicholson Baker to the main office, please."

I hustled to the main office. Paulette had a change to the schedule. For block 3, I was covering for a chemistry teacher in room 22. The six beeps and the pledge happened while I was on my way back to class.

"So Mrs. Kennett is absent," I said to the class. "You've got an extra day to work on the soundtrack project."

"Awesome," said Kaylee.

Artie was in this class, and so was Sebastian, who seemed fine—jokey and cheerful and loud—getting more sleep these days, I guessed. He wasn't drinking mango juice this morning. Keith was eating a bagel with cream cheese. Mrs. Meese, the kindhearted ed tech from Mr. Bowles's room, walked around the class asking each kid if he or she had finished the project. "I think we should wait a little bit to take attendance," she said, "because I know some of them went to get breakfast."

Sebastian and Brad launched into a joshing argument. "You're such a jackass," said Sebastian.

I took attendance—it was a big class of twenty-six kids—while the students gossiped about iPad restrictions. Steve put his head down to take a nap.

I asked the class if they'd had any luck finding songs that went with the mood of the chapters.

"I've had no luck," said Steve, looking up. "I've been sleeping for the past week."

Mr. Clapper, the principal, stuck his head in the door. "You can disregard that third block," he said. "We're all set." No chemistry for me today.

Kaylee loaned me her copy of *The Things They Carried*. I read, *Henry Dobbins carried his girlfriend's pantyhose wrapped around his neck as a comforter.* I read, *You can tell a true war story by its absolute and uncompromising allegiance to obscenity and evil.* I said, "Theoretically everybody's read the whole book?"

"Theoretically," Pearl said.

"I don't want you guys talking at this table," said Mrs. Meese, to a crowd of big-voiced boys.

I let Mrs. Meese police the class. "What are you working on?" she asked, over and over. She had a nice, loose, jokey way of dealing with these "low-performing" students; she seemed resigned to the fact that none of them were going to do much in the way of actual work. I asked Steve if Mrs. Kennett had read any of O'Brien's book aloud.

"No," he said, "me and Keith read the last book out loud. We made a deal with her that if we read the book out loud to the class we didn't have to do the assignment."

I asked Brandon what chapter he was working on. He held up an analysis page for a chapter called "Enemies," half filled out. He said, "I've done like five of these. You're supposed to do eight. Or twelve, sorry."

I said, "For each chapter you have to fill out that same worksheet?" I hadn't quite taken that in. "My god."

"Imagine my enthusiasm," Brandon said.

"I can only dream," I said. "So how do you figure out the tone of something?"

"I don't know."

Mrs. Meese was full of enthusiasm and pep. "Three left to do?" she said to Harmony. "Good job!"

Keith said he had eleven analysis pages to go.

"It was due today," Mrs. Meese said. "You guys are lucky she's out sick."

"I have nine left," said Brad.

I asked Dale if any of the chapters had grabbed his mind.

He shook his head.

Jared slammed down his AriZona iced tea and burped.

"That was a bad one," said Anabelle.

Shamus told a story about his cousin being chased by a Scotty dog. He said to me, "I've written one word. *Love.*"

Pearl softly read aloud the first sentence of a chapter: *"But this too is true: stories can save us."*

"I like dancing to dubstep," said Dale, with his iPad blaring.

"DO IT," bellowed Jared.

"Guys, come on," I said. "Just do something. Do you have some headphones?"

"No."

"Why not?"

Pearl continued to read: *"But in a story, which is a kind of dreaming, the dead sometimes smile and sit up and return to the world."* She kept on going. The narrator, Tim O'Brien, walks into a village in Vietnam after an air strike. He sees an old man lying faceup, dead, with his arm gone, and flies feeding on his face. One of O'Brien's platoon-mates goes over and shakes the dead man's hand and says, "Howdee-doo." Later, his platoon-mate says, "Maybe it's too real for you." Pearl and a kid sitting next to her wrote that sentence down on their analysis sheets: *"Maybe it's too real for you."*

Bong. Mr. Clapper came on the PA system. "If I can have your attention just for a moment," he said. "Over the weekend, we had a technology glitch, where a thousand of our iPads, as several of you have found out, were accidentally put into lockdown mode. We're fixing the problem this morning. More information will be out shortly. So bear with us, and we hope to have this error corrected shortly. Thank you."

"A 'glitch,'" said Artie, with air quotes.

I loaned out my headphones.

"Fuckin' double-tap it!" said Jared. Jared and Artie watched a viral video in which a girl hits another girl in the head with a shovel.

Anabelle wrote about the chapter in *The Things They Carried* in which a nine-year-old girl gets a brain tumor.

Suddenly Jared blasted the first measures of "#Selfie." That got a laugh. Trevor shook his head and popped a Cheeto in his mouth. I went over to Jared. Had he gotten any of the worksheets done?

"No, not today," he said.

Shamus had written another mood word, after *love*: *caring*.

I looked at the clock. "So that's one word every twenty minutes."

"That's more than I usually do," Shamus said. He said he'd already chosen three songs and filled out three analysis sheets, and then he'd spent two days in ISS—i.e., in-school suspension—the week before, when the due date for the soundtrack project was changed. Mrs. Meese came over to say that if he didn't have the project done by tomorrow, when Mrs. Kennett was back, he'd get a zero. "You could have been working on it when you were in ISS," she said.

"But I never got the paper for it," said Shamus. "It's not my fault."

"It is your fault, because you got an ISS," Mrs. Meese said.

"Yes, but it's the teacher's responsibility to give me my work," Shamus said, reasonably.

"Then you talk to the teacher about it," Mrs. Meese said. "Check with her to see if she'll give you more time."

"I'm not trying to make a thing about it," Shamus said. "I was just asking a simple question."

"And I don't know the answer," said Mrs. Meese. "That's something that she has to answer."

"Okay." Shamus pulled the brim of his hat way down.

When Mrs. Meese had moved off to talk to somebody else, I tapped Shamus's copy of *The Things They Carried*. "I met the man who wrote this book," I said to him. "He put his heart and soul into it, and he wrote it as a work of fiction. He kept insisting that the stories are not true, but he's kind of presenting them as if they are true. What if you found out that, say, fifty percent of the stories were exaggerated, were not true, in this book? Would it matter?"

Shamus thought for a bit. "I would say that it wouldn't matter. I don't see how it would."

Dale handed me twelve pages, with some words and random song titles hastily scrawled on each one. "I'm done," he said, zipping up his backpack.

"You are finished, man," I said. "You are done."

"I'm DONE."

It was time to wrap things up. The kids who had taken out school laptops in place of locked iPads put them all away. Jared began telling the story of a movie called *The Maiden Heist*, with Morgan Freeman. "What the FUCK would be so important that you can't help your old friend Christopher Walken?" he said.

"Jared, you really need to watch the language," said Mrs. Meese, but since there were plenty of bad words in Tim O'Brien's book, which was assigned reading, she couldn't muster much outrage. What was interesting, though, was that Jared had a complete mastery of the Morgan Freeman movie. He could give a succinct off-the-cuff plot summary, and yet he'd done practically nothing on the analysis forms.

Mrs. Kennett wasn't to blame, though—she taught what the Language Arts Department at Lasswell High School told her to teach. And the Language Arts Department wasn't to blame either—filling out analysis sheets about *The Things They Carried* was standard operating procedure at American high schools. The people to blame were educational theorists who thought that it was necessary for all students to do literary criticism. If you want unskilled readers to read, I thought, make them copy out an interesting sentence every day, and make them read aloud an interesting paragraph a day. Twenty minutes, tops. If you want them to take pleasure in longer works, fiction or nonfiction, let them read along with an audiobook. Don't fiddle with deadly lit-crit words like *tone* and *mood*. And don't force them to read war books about shaking hands with corpses.

Bong, bong, bong, bong, bong, bong. The PA woman said: "All iPads should unlock themselves by the end of block two today. All iPads should unlock themselves by the end of block two today. Thank you." She read the names of about twenty-five students who had to report to the office.

Mr. Markey—curly hair, gruff voice, sleeves rolled up—came in with a projector to show the YouTube video, and we hooked it up to a school computer. "It's a video of Oprah interviewing Elie Wiesel," he said.

I said, "That's heavy-duty."

"Yeah—at Auschwitz," said Mr. Markey. "So they're walking around it and talking about it." I had a sinking feeling. The Holocaust, at Lasswell High School. Pictures of mass death in this pale blue cinderblock room.

As he left, Jared apologized to Mrs. Meese for his bad language.

"That's okay, Jared, don't be sorry," she said.

"They're going to write an essay comparing this video to whatever book they read," Mr. Markey said. "The idea is, what's the best form for teaching a particular audience about the Holocaust? The best thing for today is just to pay attention to the video."

I passed out the assignment sheet.

"Ooh, an assignment," said Chelsea.

She and her friend Madonna were debating whether they should get their hair cut at the hair salon at Walmart on Saturday: the Walmart salon was cheap and supposedly they did a really good job.

I skimmed the assignment sheet, which said, *In an essay decide which one of the mediums we have looked at is the best for telling a survivor's story. Defend your decision, but you must also acknowledge at least one counterclaim. In addition, be sure to use varied transitions to link your ideas and develop cohesion in your essay.* If you did that, you got a score 3. To get a score 4, you had to consider the problem of which medium is best *for a specific audience.* Every essay had to have a thesis statement, and the students were allowed one spelling mistake—these were "non-negotiables." "If I find a second mistake I will return it to you ungraded." On the back was a blank chart, to be filled out with the several qualities, or "criteria," that a Holocaust survivor's story must have, each of which was to be multiplied by a factor of importance, one through four, called the "multiplier." Students were asked to *assign values to each format and figure out its overall score.* The Holocaust assignment conformed to the following standards: Text Structures Level 6, Opinion/Argument Level 7, and Writing Process Level 5. It used the mass murder of Jews to evaluate the efficacy of various media.

"All right, my friends," I said. "Give me some examples of some books that you've been reading—because you're going to have to write an essay comparing the book that you've been working on with the video that you will watch." Gloria said she'd read *The Book Thief.* Madonna and Chelsea were surfing makeup options. "Dark mascara?" I said. "Would that be good? Good. So this video, called *Auschwitz: Death Camp*, is Oprah Winfrey talking to Elie Wiesel, who's a Holocaust survivor, in Auschwitz. The idea is to watch it and then compare it with one of the books that you've read." I held up the assignment sheet. "And you have to use these criteria. I wouldn't know how to do this, honestly, and I write for a living."

Having discovered that his projector had no sound, Mr. Markey brought all of his students into my classroom. Some of them sat on low cabinets or on the floor; the room was crowded and hot and dark.

We watched the video. It opens with Oprah standing on the railroad track leading into the front gates of Auschwitz, on a wintry day. We see a close-up of Hitler's eyes, and then, one minute into the movie, begins the parade of visual horror: pictures of piled, starved, naked Jewish bodies, bodies being bulldozed, bodies tossed into trenches full of more bodies. We were given a two-minute history of the war and the creation of concentration camps. Oprah said, *"When American and Russian troops finally liberated the remaining camps, all they found left behind were the dead, and the walking dead."* Elie Wiesel and Oprah talk, walking on the frozen pathways of Auschwitz, exclaiming at its vastness. *"This is the largest cemetery in recorded history,"* Wiesel says. *"I come here, and try to see the invisible, and try to hear the inaudible."* Oprah has her mittened hand in Elie Wiesel's arm, and Wiesel is cold—you can hear the shivering in his voice. *"I still don't grasp it,"* he says. *"It must have some meaning. What does it mean? That evil can triumph? We knew that. That humiliation exists? We knew that. But this, which was a scandal at the level of creation?"*

Wiesel is eloquent, and *Auschwitz: Death Camp* is a moving, freshly shocking, well-made video. But as I watched the kids sitting slack-faced, in plump-cheeked, polite silence, surreptitiously checking their text messages every so often, glancing up at the screen and away from it to think their own thoughts, adjusting their hair, while laughter and shouts floated in from the hall, I knew that this was the wrong documentary to be showing to a group of choiceless, voiceless high school kids at eight-thirty on a Monday morning, in connection with a compare-and-contrast media-studies essay assignment. The atrocity pictures kept coming, the staring corpses, the bodiless heads, while a violin played, and Wiesel read aloud from *Night*. And there was another problem: the particular copy of the video on YouTube that Mr. Markey had found repeated one section of the original program, so we were presented with some of the dreadful footage twice over. In the last fifteen minutes of the movie, we saw, displayed behind glass in the Auschwitz museum, a dark mound of empty cans of Zyklon B gas, and a low mountain of suitcases taken from Jewish families. We were shown a collection of confiscated baby clothes, more panned-across photos of bodies and charred faces—and then thousands of shoes, including children's shoes. *"Elegant shoes, poor shoes,"* says Wiesel. *"If these shoes could tell the stories of the lives of those who walked in them, imagine what they would say. Here it's like the camp itself: we were all together. A whole community of shoes."* And then, still in the same museum, Wiesel and Oprah walk along the gigantic glass-fronted display case of human hair, which looks to be more than twenty feet long and four or five feet deep. *"The first thing they did was to shave your head, from the corpses as well,"* says Wiesel. The hair was sold to factories, Oprah explains: *"At the time of the liberation, seven tons of hair was discovered at Auschwitz."* Wiesel almost can't look at the hair—it's too awful. *"More and more,"* he says. *"Oh my god,"* says Oprah. *"It's really unimaginable."* Wiesel says, *"They wanted to push their crimes to the outer limit, thus depriving us of the language to describe their crimes."* The movie ends with the two of them again out in the cold, shivering, standing near barbed wire. Oprah says she can't get her brain around the Holocaust, even now. *"Oprah, the death of one child makes no sense,"* Wiesel says. *"The death of millions—what sense could it make?"* Wiesel's last words are, *"Whenever people try to conduct such experiments against another people, we must be there to shout, and say, 'No. We remember.'"*

When the credits came on, Mr. Markey stopped the video. "Questions or comments right now?" he said. There were some small unhappy moans—no comments.

"Okay," Mr. Markey said. "Those who came from next door, let's go back next door. If you brought a chair, bring it back." Many clinks and shufflings of moving chairs.

I said nothing. I sat in my chair and felt dismal. A boy named Graham and his friend talked softly together about *Night*—how it compared to the video they'd just watched. They discussed the museum of hair.

Bong, bong, bong, bong, bong, bong.

Madonna and Chelsea were giddy after seeing so much death: as if they were cheerleaders, they chanted, "H! O! L! O! C-A-U-S-T, YEAH!" At least they could spell it.

I sat for an hour. I had lunch and listened to voices in the hall. The bell bonged again six times. "They asked to see your ID?" said a boy. A girl called out, "Garth! Garth Connolly!"

I continued to sit. A tall tousled kid appeared at the door. "Is Mrs. Kennett not here?" He said he usually sat in the room with her this block.

I said I thought her daughter had croup.

"Huh?"

"I think her daughter got sick."

"Oh, all right." He waved and left. I noted down the SAT word of the day: *prudent*.

In the hall, a girl said, "I'm not sick, I have allergies."

The PA lady said, "At this time, all chorus and chamber singers please go to the music room. All chorus and chamber singers to the music room." She read off fourteen names of people who had to report to the main office.

"Your butt's hanging," said a boy in the hall. A girl came in and stopped. "You're not Mrs. Kennett," she said. She left.

The PA system booped. "Happy Monday, Lobster Nation!" said a high schooler's male voice. "I'm Monk Bissette, and it's a beautiful day outside. I'm here with my best friend and cohost, the one, the only, Dr. Might B. Righty."

"Yo, wassup, Lobsters," said Dr. Might B. Righty. "Today the boys' and girls' tennis team has matches with Kennebunk. Matches begin at three-thirty p.m. Also the JV and varsity softball team travels to Bonny Eagle for a four-thirty game. The JV boys' lacrosse team hosts York at six p.m. Good luck to all Lobsters!"

Monk Bissette said, "Any student who has signed up for AP Government or AP History next year will need to attend a meeting on Tuesday, May thirteenth, during activity block in the auditorium. And our spring chorale concert will be held on Wednesday, May fourteenth, at seven p.m. in the auditorium. Mark your calendar today. See you there."

Dr. Might B. Righty said, "Also, reminder to all seniors again. Please, seniors, LISTEN UP. You must turn in your permission slips and ten dollars to hold your spot for our class trip. We're taking an awesome trip to Birch Point State Park, so PLEASE make sure you get that in by this Friday, all right—because we're going to have to start canceling buses or adding buses. So get that IN! And also get your dues in. We're graduating SOON, people. Get those dues IN!"

"That's all for now. I'm Monk Bissette."

"And I'm Dr. Might B. Righty. Stay classy, Lasswell."

More quiet. Mr. Markey came in to say he'd gotten his sound to work with the projector.

From the hall, two girls: "That's so cute."

"Oh my god, that's adorable."

I got the Elie Wiesel movie ready to play for the next class, which was split in two parts: twenty-five minutes of Holocaust, then twenty-five minutes of lunch, then twenty-five more minutes of Holocaust. I leafed through an anthology that sat on the desk until a boy named Thad arrived. "I'm guessing I'm supposed to be in here," he said. "I don't know."

I told him we were watching a video about the Holocaust. "It's seriously heavy."

Zach and Carter blew in. "Dude, she took my iPad with literally a minute left in class," said Zach. "Everyone was sitting and not doing anything. So I have to get it back next block."

"You got any food?" said Carter. Zach brought out a sandwich, which Carter rejected.

"Dude, you're making fun of my mom," said Zach. "You can't make fun of my mom."

Cece said, "Give me my headphones back."

"Are we watching a movie today?" asked Carter.

"It's not a cheerful movie," I said, passing out the Holocaust assignment sheets.

"What the?" said Paul, scrubbing his face.

Mathias and Pat were planning to go to the JV lacrosse game at six.

"I have a science Keynote to do," said Wynonna.

"Oh my god," said Phyllis. "I forgot about that."

"All right, hi, hello," I said. "HELLO."

Mathias and Pat just kept talking about lacrosse. I clapped my hands. "All right, so the deal is, I'm Mr. Baker, I'm the substitute, filling in. Hello, hi. Mrs. Kennett's child is sick, so she'll be back tomorrow. What you're going to do today is watch an incredibly depressing movie."

"Hah hah," said Cece.

"In which Oprah Winfrey takes a Holocaust survivor named Elie

Wiesel through Auschwitz. There are a lot of really tragic images. You're supposed to watch this movie, and while you're watching it, you will want to be thinking about whether it's a better way of conveying what is actually going on—"

Several conversations sprang up simultaneously. I stood watching their young, heedless mouths open and close. I waited for them to be quiet. Wynonna said, "Shh."

"The sound on the video is really soft," I said, "so if you want to hear it, you have to be quiet."

I started the video. "It's my girl, Oprah," said Remington.

"I can't hear," said Cece.

Oprah was saying, *". . . where it's estimated that one point five million Jews perished—here in the Holocaust, most of them Eastern European Jews."*

"Stop talking," said Phyllis. Laughter. Two softly muttered conversations in the back. Again, horrifying pictures of death on the screen.

I walked to the back. "Just be quiet," I whispered. "Just listen to the movie, okay?"

"Yeah, dudes," said Remington.

"Well, I can't hear it," said Cece.

"That's because you're talking," I said.

"When American and Russian troops finally liberated the remaining camps," said Oprah, *"all they found left behind were the dead, and the walking dead."*

"The *Walking Dead* TV show," said Remington, but nobody laughed. The class was listening now.

"Each time I come," Wiesel said, *"I try not to speak for a day or two or three, and just to go back and find the silence that was in me then. And I say to myself, How many of us did not live, and simply vanished?"*

They listened quietly for maybe three minutes, and then two boys started joking about the word "non-negotiable" on the assignment sheet. When Oprah said that Wiesel, on arriving at Auschwitz, smelled *"the stench of burning human flesh,"* they went quiet again. Phyllis and Wynonna began quietly discussing whether they should quote from this part of the interview, which led to more talk about whether one of them had handed an earlier assignment in or not. Somebody laughed.

"Guys," I said irritably, "watch the movie. Or don't watch the movie! It doesn't matter. Just don't make a lot of noise, okay?"

They were quiet for two minutes after that. Then more whispering arose like frail weed sprouts from the girls. Cece and her friend Christina simply could not shut up. What was I supposed to do? She was chatting rapidly about some grievance she had with a teacher while Oprah talked about the deportation of Hungarian Jews. I wanted to turn off the movie. *". . . were packed into the gas chambers by the thousands,"* Oprah said. *"As the toxic pellets mixed with air, cyanide gas was released, and felt like suffocation."* I waved at the loud table to be quiet. These high schoolers were being tortured to the point of numbness and indifference by gruesome imagery—those few who were paying attention—*and* the Holocaust was being trivialized through inattention, both at the same time. Why was this happening? Why was I a part of this? We came to the section that repeated. *"Once naked,"* said Oprah, *"mothers, their babies, children, the elderly, and anyone else deemed unfit to work were packed into the gas chambers by the thousands. As the tox—"* I skipped past the overlap. The conversations in the room continued. I went over to Remington and his knot of compulsive chatters and confiscated a disputed water bottle. "Just go to sleep," I whispered.

"How can we watch the movie if we go to sleep?" Cece asked. She was wearing a yellow shirt. She sounded just like the girl in the selfie song.

"Whatever," I said. "Just don't sit and talk."

But I had no authority. There were five separate conversations now. "I was like, Oh my god," said Cece. We came to the part where Wiesel is talking about the suitcases of the dead. Not a soul in the class was listening. It was almost time for lunch. I stopped the movie.

Bong, bong, bong, bong, bong, bong. The class left. "I have a boyfriend!" said Cece.

Mr. Markey came in to ask if the movie played all right. It had. I guess he thought it was a good assignment because mass murder is real. But it wasn't a good assignment. I don't want to be a substitute teacher who forces teenagers to shake hands with the dead. All they want to do is flirt and joke and get through the day.

Everyone came back from lunch, laughing and coughing. Christina pointed to the screen. "Are we watching this the entire time?"

"Yes," I said.

"Fabulous," she said.

I gave Remington his water bottle back. "If you're not interested in watching the movie, I understand," I said. "But just *don't* make a lot of noise."

"Yeah, girls," said Remington.

"Remington, shut up," said Cece.

I hit play. Wiesel and Oprah looked at the suitcases and the shoes, and the hair. The class talked quietly about their lives. I hissed, "Shh." I stood up. I wanted them to see the hair. We came to the end. I turned on the light.

"So how many here have read *Night*?" I asked.

"Never heard of it," said Cece, who was scrolling through things on her iPad. She read aloud a repost from a Tumblr blog: "*I was just about to fall asleep and then I sat up and almost screamed because I was struck with the realization and I discovered the ultimate truth of the universe: Teletubbies are called Teletubbies because they have televisions in their stomachs.*"

That pissed me off. I gave Cece a hate smile and I said to her, "Why don't you go up in the front and read that, to the class? Why don't you go ahead? I'd like to hear it. It's kind of a different approach."

"Do it!" said Remington.

"Go on!" I said.

"Do it, Cece, do it!" said Christina.

She couldn't have read it aloud, even if she'd wanted to, because the class was too noisy. Christina said, "I have four sisters, well, three sisters and it's four including me, and there's four Teletubbies, so we're each a Teletubby."

"I see," I said.

To anyone who was listening, I said, "Thanks for watching the movie. It's really too intense, I think, to show in a school. Too many dead bodies."

"Thad!" said Cece.

"You guys are so pathetic," I said aloud—and not in a whisper, either, although nobody heard me. I waited for a while—we still had ten minutes of class left. "Guys, can I ask you a question to think about? What's the difference between—" And then I stopped. Nobody had quieted down. I didn't exist. I tried again. "What's the difference between trying to tell—" I stopped again. I was going to ask them about the difference between watching a documentary and reading a book, but there was just no way, short of yelling like a maniac, to be heard over seven full-strength conversations. "It doesn't matter," I said.

"I want to hear the question," said Zach.

"It's not that interesting a question," I said. "It doesn't matter, because I don't care, and they don't care."

"Then don't bring it up," said Cece. "You make us curious."

"We were listening," said Zach, smiling.

I tried again. "When I watch a documentary like that, I—"

Cece made a disgusted laugh, and I asked her what she was laughing at.

"It's Cece, she always laughs," said Carter. "Just ignore her."

"The tallest sub in the world," said Cece, scornfully.

"I learned something from that movie," said a boy named Gibb. "They had to make handmade clothing, for children."

"In that movie, you learned that?" I said.

"That's what they said," Gibb said.

"What should happen now?" I shouted. "Independent reading?"

"I don't know how to read," Gibb said.

"But you know how to listen," said Zach.

"Come on, you know how to read," I said.

"I can read, but I can't read books," said Gibb.

I opened a window to let out some of the noise. Remington was recounting a dream he'd had: his brother was chasing him with a butter knife. Zach and Carter stood up. I asked them where they were off to. "We need to stand," one said. "We've been sitting down for too long."

I took a bite of an apple. Cece said she couldn't wait for summer. "You know how when you try to tie your hair in a knot," she said, "and it always comes out?"

"Yes, I always do that," said Christina.

"Because the more healthy your hair is, the loosener it gets," said Cece.

"Not really," said Christina, "but I hope so."

A large girl, Cloris, said, "Guys, I can't even tie my hair in a knot. I'm proud of my hair." She floofed it.

Kids in the back talked about basketball and video game upgrades.

Cece said, "I wanted to cry the other day because I found dark-chocolate-covered pomegranate, and all I wanted to get for my mom was dark-chocolate pomegranate and all the stores were out of it and I could not find it anywhere. And then I found it after at CVS."

I stood by the door, waiting for the bongers to bong. "What normally happens in this class?" I asked Remington.

"It's about like this," he said. "She'll yell at us when we get too loud, but she usually lets us do what we want."

Thad startled me by tearing up the Holocaust assignment sheet and throwing it in the trash can. "You just tore it up," I said.

I asked him what he'd like to do in the class.

"Play games."

"Dude, you've got a thirty-five in this class," said Zach.

"You don't need an education," Thad said.

"The rest of us have nineties," Zach said, joking.

"How's your mood?" I asked a silent girl, Betsy. "Stable?"

She made a seesawing gesture with her hand.

"I hate asking kids to do what they don't want to do," I said. "Nobody wants to sit through the movie."

Betsy gave me a pitying look. In the pecking order of the class, she was low, but I was lower.

"Twist the cap, Thad," said Cece.

Zach, Carter, and Remington were off to a math class. "Dude, you ready for the test?"

"No," said Remington.

"Everyone's failing that class," said Zach. "Culver's got like a thirty-eight."

Six bongs and they were all gone. I had a long stretch of quiet until the new class began to arrive. A girl named Amity sat down, checked her makeup, and asked me what the movie was about.

I said it was about the Holocaust. "And it is grim. It's seriously grim." I really didn't want to play the movie again.

"Hi, Amity, how are you today?" said Eugene.

Unenthusiastic response from Amity.

"How's your foot feeling?" said Eugene.

"Better," said Amity.

In the back, Wade did fist bumps with his friend Ross. "Yeah, break my knuckles. Come on, break them. Yeah!"

I passed out the Holocaust assignment sheets. "How's everybody doing? I'm Mr. Baker, I'm substituting for Mrs. Kennett. How does this class normally go? Do you talk about stuff, or do things, or have fun, or what?"

"Have fun," said Wade. "Strictly fun."

"Well, this will fit right in, then," I said sarcastically. "The Holocaust essay. May fifteenth it's due. You're supposed to watch this movie, which is Oprah Winfrey walking around with a Holocaust survivor talking about terrible things that happened. The point of this assignment is to look at the movie and think about the way you're learning about what happened, versus if you read, let's say, a book about the Holocaust, or if somebody writes a poem about it. You're trying to figure out which form will have the most immediate impact. Do you learn more watching a documentary? Do you learn more when you're in the immersive world of a book? I find I learn more sometimes watching a ninety-minute documentary than I learn reading a three-hundred-page book. I don't know about you. That's the question that this essay is all about. So watch the video and think about how much you're getting from it. It's got some appalling images. It's what you'd expect a movie about the Holocaust would look like."

"Shut up," whispered Rose, who was playing a number game on her iPad.

"What is your issue with him?" said Tom, who was also playing a video game. "Bear's done nothing to you."

"Is there tension?" I asked. "I feel tension right here."

"She has tension with me, I have none with her," said Bear.

"One more thing about the movie," I said. "These speakers are not very loud. So if you want to hear what somebody's saying, you have to be quiet and listen. Or else move sort of towards this side of the room. And even if you don't want to hear what they're saying, it would really be nice if you just were quiet."

Amity's hand went up. "Can I go down to the tech department to get my iPad looked at? It's still not fixed."

"How tall are you?" asked Wade.

"Six four and something. I never know. Let's watch the movie."

"You never know?" said Wade.

"Okay, the movie's going. Oprah Winfrey is talking!"

Oprah said, *"It is here, right here, on this railroad track, that a young teenage boy arrived in a cattle car, with his family, friends, and neighbors, in 1944."*

This class was quieter, it turned out. *"I thought, Maybe it's the end of history,"* Elie Wiesel said. *"Maybe it's the end of Jewish history."*

After a while, the little white laptop ran out of battery, and I had to plug in a power cord. "Hang on, guys, technical excitement here."

"Do you know Mr. C.?" asked Wade. "You and him should have a sub showdown."

I said, "Mud wrestling or something?"

"Pig wrestling," said Wade. "I'd put my money on you."

I positioned the laptop on a chair so that the power cord could reach it. We waited for it to reboot. Tom said he'd read *Night*. I asked him whether, so far, the book was more powerful, or the movie.

"The book, probably," Tom said. "He goes into details about what happened."

Rose helped me log back in to the school network. We messed with system preferences and display preferences. While I was fiddling, Tom threw out a pair of broken sunglasses. "Nothing gold can stay," he said, quoting Robert Frost.

"I say we just have a study hall," said Wade.

"It's the orange button," said Rose, pointing to the projector.

"I've been pressing it like mad!" I said.

Amity began braiding her friend Dolores's hair, saying that her father had texted her that he needed to borrow her hair straightener. Amity had texted him back, *"What do you need it for? Haha, don't want to sound disrespectful, I'm just curious."* She said, "What the heck does my father need my straightener for?"

"I told you," said Dolores, "he wants to straighten his hair." She swiped through her iPhone photos. "My brother's such a faggot."

"That's okay," said Amity, "because my brother's more of a faggot."

"Which one, Gregory?"

"No, Kenny."

"Oh," said Dolores. "I like Gregory."

No signal, still, coming from the projector. "This is really not happening," said a blue-bandannaed goth girl, Brandy.

"Does somebody have a beautiful piece of writing they want to read, while I fuss with this darn thing?" I said.

"Come on, Tom," said Amity.

Brandy said, "My poem consists of murder."

"Just murder?" I said. "Is there sometimes a happy moment?"

"No," said Brandy.

Amity got a text from her father about the hair straightener. "He says it's for 'uniform maintenance,'" she said. She sat for a while.

Dolores said, "I want to go home. I want to die."

All this time, I was trying to get the projector and the computer to handshake properly. "Maybe we could chat amongst ourselves," I said.

"Like a study hall?" said Rose.

"Very similar to a study hall," I said.

"I could read my murder poems," said Brandy. "Just kidding."

I said, "I think we should have an interesting chat about anything at all."

"How about the economy," said Brandy.

"The American economy," I said.

"No," said Amity. "Let's talk about the European economy."

Dolores suggested we play a game.

I said, "Like with winners and losers? I'm not sure about that." I gave up on the computer and stood up. "I just want three minutes of your time. Since I can't get this thing to play, I'm just going to tell you what happens. Elie Wiesel, the survivor, was there when he was fifteen, and he fortunately was one of the people rescued in 1945. So Oprah Winfrey takes him around, and they look at the big room where the Zyklon B gas came down from the ceiling. Zyklon B is a kind of crystal, and when it's exposed to air, it turns to cyanide, and it was used to kill people."

A girl in the back burst out laughing.

"It is hilarious," I said, giving her a sour look. "Then they go to this display that I had never seen before. It's human hair. It's a massive, twenty-foot-long display of human hair. And there are displays of the clothes that they confiscated from people. It's just a massively depressing immersion in one of the most horrible things that happened in human history."

Amity and Dolores started talking about their hair.

"What's up?" I said. "You're talking about *your* hair? What I want you to think about is, why would you want to subject people now to that tormented period? What is the point of seeing stuff that's that intense? It's about an hour of seeing dead bodies. Why would we want to do that? You're all eighteen, seventeen?"

"Sixteen, seventeen," said Tom.

"Is it a good thing for you to spend an hour looking at that much death and destruction? Is that good for your souls? Or what?"

Brandy said, "It's probably good for our ways of thinking. Not necessarily for our souls, but it could influence the way we think about things."

"We take things for granted," said Rose.

Brandy said, "If it speaks spiritually, it might actually benefit our souls, because we're wanting to connect directly with the event."

"Well, that's good," I said. "Because I was thinking that maybe you would watch something this bleak and you would think, What is life all about? If they're capable of doing something this horrible, why are we striving and struggling here?"

"It puts things into perspective," said Dolores.

"It puts things in perspective," I said. She was right. "So that's a recapitulation of what you would have seen if the technology had been working. Now, do you have lots of homework from other classes that you'd like to do? Would you like to sing 'Row, Row, Row Your Boat'?"

"I would like to read my murder poems," said Brandy.

"You would?"

"No, I'm not going to read them."

"You keep talking about it, as if you want to read them," I said. "You're desperate to read them. But you don't want to."

"She's afraid to share," said Tom.

"As are we all," I said. "All right, I'm going to be brave, and read a poem, gosh darn it. I'm seriously going to read a poem, if I can find it." I flipped around in the anthology looking for a Robert Frost poem I'd seen earlier.

"Is that documentary on YouTube?" said Eugene.

I looked up. "Yes. If you want, you can put in your earbuds and watch the documentary solo. 'Oprah Wiesel full documentary,' it's called."

Eugene got the movie going on his iPad, and then he connected the iPad via AirPlay to the projector by typing in a code. "There it is, I'm going in," he said. "I'm going in hard. We don't ask no questions."

The video came back on, and we turned up the volume. Oprah said, *"Bodies were burned in open pits. Holocaust survivor Elie Wiesel witnessed these atrocities as a boy, and gave the world his account."*

The class watched attentively, especially Brandy. When we got to the part that looped back and repeated, Eugene skipped ahead ten minutes. "I'm going to go hard with it," he said.

"You are really into that phrase," I said.

Oprah said, *"It was here in Auschwitz One that the notorious Dr. Josef Mengele, known as the angel of death, conducted sadistic medical experiments on prisoners, infecting them with diseases, rubbing chemicals into their skin, and performing crude sterilization experiments, in his quest to eliminate the Jewish race by any means possible."*

We watched in silence. When we got to the part about the display of suitcases, the video stopped again, buffering endlessly. Still nobody spoke. Nate tried to get it going again on his iPad, but the school's Wi-Fi was down.

"Well, thank you for watching what you could watch," I said. "It was a pleasure having you in this class." I listened as they talked quietly about random things—razor burn, water bottles, crutches, locked iPads—for several minutes.

Bong, bong, bong, bong, bong, bong. Mr. Markey came in to retrieve the computer and the tiny speakers.

In homeroom, while waiting for the buses, Madonna and Chelsea drew quite a beautiful magenta tree on the whiteboard. "You're such an A," said one girl.

"Language," said her friend.

Some boys stacked the chairs on the hexagonal tables.

An alert-looking kid named Braden was standing near me. "Are you energized?" I asked him. "Filled with knowledge and ready to confront the afternoon?"

"No," he said.

"Me neither," I said. "I'm exhausted. Is it an engine of oppression, school? Yes, no?"

"Nyeah," he said.

Six bongs. "Tootles," said Gloria.

I wrote a note for the teacher: "Dear Mrs. Kennett, All went well. Block 1 kids worked (with varying degrees of intensity) on the soundtrack project—and the rest of the day was spent watching Elie Wiesel. Mr. Markey was very helpful in setting up the A/V—and the kids were cheerful and good-natured. Thanks for letting me sub in your classes. Best regards, Nick Baker. P.S. I hope your daughter is feeling better!"

Outside, I saw Sebastian sitting by himself on the front lawn, plucking at a tuft of grass, waiting for his ride. I asked him how he was doing. "You sleeping better these days?"

"Eh," he said. "A little."

I walked out to the car and fished around for my key, which wasn't in my pocket. At the main office I told one of the secretaries that I stupidly might have left my car key in the classroom.

"Does it look like this?" She held up my key. "It's been on the counter all day."

Mr. Clapper, the principal, said, "Thank you for being here today."

"My pleasure, thank you."

Day Seventeen was over.

THE MAN WHO NEEDS IT
DOESN'T KNOW IT

Beth gave me a job as a ninth-grade science teacher. I got to Lasswell early and parked on a gravel path in a cemetery not far from the school. Among the gravestones were many little American flags poked into the ground, motionless, curled like upside-down sugar cones. I recognized some of the surnames from school—French names, from the Quebecois who came down to work as loggers and in the paper mills, and Scots names, descendants of the prisoners of war sent to Maine by Cromwell in 1650.

To work. At seven-fifteen I checked into the office and walked to the North Building, to Mrs. Moran's classroom, which was large and neatly arranged, with two pink file cabinets in front of the teacher's desk and inspirational quotes everywhere you looked. "Don't make lemonade, get mad, make life take back her lemons," said Cave Johnson. "Never, never, never give up," said Winston Churchill. "Don't fight a battle if you don't gain anything by winning," said Erwin Rommel. "Believe you can and you're halfway there," said Teddy Roosevelt. In the very middle of the whiteboard, in tiny red letters, someone had written

(Fuck
my
life)

The carpeting was black, with flecks of yellow and green and purple in a stain-hiding pattern, and pushpinned to a corkboard was a chart of LEARNING TARGETS MET! and seven festive diagrams of the layers of the Earth's atmosphere, all made by ninth-grade students. One was done in colored pencil, with a blue thermosphere and black stars. One was done in watercolor, with a yellow stratosphere. One was a circle cut out of mattress foam. And one was a yellow balloon with the layers drawn to scale in black marker: the troposphere, the ozone layer, the stratosphere, the mesosphere, and the thermosphere. I'd never heard of the thermosphere. All the chairs were stacked on the tables. Everything was waiting to happen.

Mrs. Moran's sub plans began with a capitalized command: "PLEASE LEAVE ME A NOTE TO LET ME KNOW HOW THE BEHAVIOR WAS FOR EACH CLASS." The class rules were: (1) listening to music was allowed in all classes during independent work; (2) students didn't have to ask to go to the bathroom, although they did have to sign out, and only one student was allowed to go to the bathroom at a time; and (3) "If iPads or phones become a problem you have the POWER to confiscate them." Block 1, from 7:30 to 8:28, was a "FREE BLOCK!" While I was reading the plans, a math teacher said hello. She looked done in. I asked her if there was anything I should know. She hesitated. "They can be challenging," she said.

Ten minutes into my free block, a guileless, big-boned girl, April, dressed in aqua knee pants and black sneakers, came in to work on her atmospheric model. She had painted a Frisbee blue and glued it to a piece of cardboard, surrounding it with white pipe-cleaner clouds. "Can you be honest with me for at least two minutes?" April said, bringing her project over to my desk. "I don't know if you're a mean person or not. How does that look?"

I told her I thought it looked very good. "You've conveyed what's going on," I said.

"That's the Earth," she said. "It was originally green, so I painted it blue, to look like the water." She'd made labels for the mesosphere and the thermosphere that she was going to glue onto the cardboard and she had some coloring left to do. "You see those ones?" She pointed to the "Student Exemplars" on the corkboard. "That's what I've got to get this to look like, but not exactly. In my own way."

She was 90 percent there, I said.

"Thank you," she said. She sat back down and began positioning the labels.

Long ago, I said, when I'd learned about the Earth's atmosphere, they hadn't mentioned the outer layers. "That's all new. I like your idea of using the Frisbee as the Earth."

"I have three Frisbees," April said. The one she was using for her project she'd found at the beach. "I looked down and I was like, Oh, interesting." One of her other Frisbees got broken. "And I got one for Christmas that was pink, and it glowed in the dark."

I said, "It's interesting to think of a Frisbee flying through space, in some giant game of ultimate Frisbee."

April began hunting around for something. I asked if she needed some colored markers.

"Nope, I've got about forty-five Sharpies. If you don't believe me . . ." From her backpack she pulled a large clear plastic envelope filled with every color of Sharpie you could think of. "Forty-five Sharpies," she said.

"You are set," I said. "That's more Sharpies than I've ever seen in one place."

"Sixteen bucks." She gave me a savvy nod, and went back to arranging the labels. "Tropo," she said softly. "Strato. Meso."

How easy and pleasant it was to be in a large classroom with one student, or two, or three—even four or five. Above five was when the noise problems began. One grownup can't teach twenty digital-era children without spending a third of the time, or more, scolding and enforcing obedience. What if we cut the defense budget in half, brought the school day down from six hours to two hours, hired a lot of new, well-paid teachers who would otherwise be making cappuccinos, and maxed out the class size at five students? What if the classes happened in parental living rooms, or even in retrofitted school buses that moved like ice cream trucks or bookmobiles from street to street, painted navy blue? Two hours a day for every kid, four or five kids in a class. Ah, but we couldn't do any of that, of course: school isn't actually about efficient teaching, it's about free all-day babysitting while parents work. It has to be inefficient in order to fill six and a half hours.

April was coloring in her troposphere. "You're in the home stretch," I said.

"What's the home stretch?" she asked.

"If you're in a horse race, the home stretch is the last bit of the race where all of the horses go full out—it's seconds away from the end."

I read aloud to April from the sub plans. Assignments were to be found, wrote Mrs. Moran, "in the lime green milk crate on my hot pink file cabinets."

"You can't miss it," April said. "She did that herself."

"She painted the file cabinets? That is dedication."

"She loves pink and she loves green."

I asked April which class she liked best.

"I loved Mrs. Tucker, the math teacher, and then she had to go out because of labor. She had a baby." She tipped her head in the direction of the math classroom and went down to a whisper. "Ms. Webb is a . . ." She shuddered. "She low-grades everyone. I shouldn't be saying this. Mostly everyone on this team had nineties. Now we're all down to fifties, forties. All she'll grade is our test scores. She'll grade our worksheets, that she gives us in class, but she'll put down a one, two, or three in responsibility. I don't like math at all. Most people on this team don't like her—just in general. Mrs. Moran I had last term. I fricking hated her. But now it's like, You're not bad. Mrs. Marsh is okay for English. She can be grouchy sometimes, and then other days she's perfectly fine with happiness."

I asked her what made for a good class—was it the kids, or was it the teacher?

"It depends on what kind of a day it is," April said. "It may be a gloomy day, but the teacher may be happy. I have a few classes with class clowns, which is hilarious. In this class, I cannot work at all. And we have you last."

"Everybody's tired," I said.

"But that's not really the reason I can't work. It's because of the loudness."

It's especially hard for a substitute to keep the noise level down, I said.

April said, "We have this sub, I don't know if you know him, he's Mr. C.? He'll just sit there and do nothing. Just like literally sit there."

"That's when you give up," I said. "I've done that."

"The kids try to overpower every single substitute on this team. The only one they don't overpower is Mrs. Carlisle. She likes it here. She's trying to get from being a sub to being a full-time teacher. Everyone loves Mrs. Carlisle." She stopped and held her hand to her mouth, thinking. "Technically, I should be working," she said. She took out a worksheet on which she was supposed to fill out the temperatures and kilometer thicknesses of the different atmospheric layers.

"Good luck," I said. "Don't let me bother you. I'm going to study up in case somebody has a question." I flipped through the geophysical sciences textbook.

Something else occurred to April. "It's nothing against you," she said. "It's just that we might not ask you for help."

"I know," I said. "It's sort of awkward to have a totally new person."

April said, "With a sub, pretty much the only class that gets their work done is honors. My class does no work. I will try to work, and the girl next to me, Marcia, she will try to work, too. And then there will be a girl named Daisy sitting there, where my purse is. At that table in the back. And there will be a girl named Jill. That one's blond. Daisy, Jill—all they do is goof around."

"I know what I'm in for," I said. "And I don't take it personally, because I think one of the things a sub can offer is a little break from the routine. But I feel sorry about people like you who are bothered by the noise."

April said, "I use my headphones, but then once I get sidetracked, it's like, Oh, I'm going to message my friends in class, and I'm not going to partake. I'll put my backpack in front of my iPad or use my best friend's phone. I use it for a certain messaging app. And then when I do try to work, it's like, Oh, there's not too much of class left."

I read the textbook and April worked on her work. Then I dashed out to my car to get a power cord. "Troposphere," I whispered to myself.

Two boys were laughing at the doorway to the North Building. "I've got gas, I'm telling you," one said.

Back in class, April was gone and a boy I didn't recognize pointed at me and said, "It's HIM." He was eating a bag of chips. He left. Others showed up.

"I'm going to go to the vending machines," said Penelope.

"That's a very important mission," I said. "And I'm going to write my name on the board."

I wrote "Mr. Baker" and sat down. My car key dropped out of my pocket.

"You dropped your key," said Rob. He picked it up and handed it to me.

Block 2 was called "Intervention," and there were only eight names on the roster. I asked Rob what the class was all about.

"Basically we make up work," Rob said.

"How's that going for you?"

Not well, Rob said—he was behind. "I got a concussion," he said. "I was out for a year and two months. I was hospitalized. And I got suspended recently." The concussion, his third, happened during a football game. "For two and a half months, it was constant headaches every day," he said.

I asked him if he'd stopped playing football.

"No, I'm playing next year."

"Dude, that's frightening," I said.

"My mom doesn't want me to play," Rob said. "My dad said I just have to be careful."

"How can you be careful? You're going to get creamed once in a while."

Six bongs. Class was in session.

"Especially if I play running back," Rob said.

Next to Rob was a kid called Bucky, who had a little mustache. "Do you play football as well?"

"I play basketball," said Bucky.

Rob said, "My sister's ex-boyfriend—we were playing basketball, and he was probably like fifty feet away from the hoop at one end of the driveway. The basket was behind his back and he just threw it up and got it in, from one end of the driveway to the other. I don't know how he did it. All luck, no skill."

Time to meet and greet other students. "Let me know if I can be of assistance in your endeavors," I said to Rob and Bucky.

Jill, the blond girl April told me about, brought in a five-color model of the atmospheric layers made of painted Styrofoam arranged like a wedding cake. She wasn't in the class this block, she said, but she didn't want to carry it around all day.

"Wow!" I said.

"It kind of broke on the bus," Jill said. She tried to find a place for it on Mrs. Moran's desk. "Just throw it on the ground—it's broken anyway."

"Don't reject it, it's beautiful," I said. "Believe in what you do!"

A stony-faced girl named Azure handed me a piece of paper. She wore a pumpkin-colored sweater whose sleeves went over her hands.

"Thank you," I said. "Do I deserve this yellow piece of paper?"

"Yes," she said. "Just keep it or throw it away." It was a tardy slip.

Bucky discovered that a Monster drink had spilled in his backpack. He pulled out his stick of deodorant and wiped it down with Kleenex.

Attendance. Robert, here. Dixon?

"He's not in this room right now."

Azure, here. William? William Boucher?

Azure pointed to Bucky. "He's right there in the hat," she said.

"And you're Bernard," I said to a kid in black. Bernard had an iPad mini. "You got one of them newfangled little iPads."

"My old one broke," Bernard said. "I got angry with it, and I smashed it against a pipe."

"He has a temper," said Bucky.

"You must have been pretty mad," I said. "Mad at your work?"

"At my mom," said Bernard.

Ah. Gerard?

"I think he has ISS," said Bucky.

"Yeah, he's in ISS for starting a fight this morning," Bernard said.

Rob said, "That's not what he's in there for. He was in a thing with Ms. Dahl, and he said some words."

"Bad words?" I said.

"Yeah," said Rob. "Words were said. He swore at her and called her a very inappropriate name."

Penelope, here. Noah, here. (So many Noahs!) Liam?

"Liam is in Mrs. Hoy's. You won't like her. Nobody does."

"It smells like paint," said Penelope, who had big retro glasses and wavy hair. She was making the exosphere by gluing down bunches of blue tissue paper.

Daisy Patten? Here. Marcus? Marcus Spinney? Here.

"Hi, Marcus Spinney," I said. "I'm checking you off. The thing is, taking attendance for this class doesn't mean a thing. It's only the first period that makes a difference. This is all just an exercise."

Dixon came back with a box of Kleenex. Noah tried to glue his finger to his nose. "I know that's one of the units that you're doing—nose gluing," I said.

Intervention, however, proved to be a small, calm class. "I love the way all this quiet working is happening," I whispered.

"The next class isn't going to be quiet," Penelope said.

I turned off a bank of lights to make the whisperiness last longer.

After five minutes Azure asked if she could wash her hands. Of course.

In the continuing bounty of quietude, Bucky and Bernard began stealthily playing Hungry Shark on their iPads. They whispered together about how deep the shark could swim. Later they moved closer to an electrical outlet so that they could plug in their tablets. Rob, the one who'd had three concussions, was at the same table as they were, writing something. Jill sat at a middle table with her boyfriend, Marcus, who had on a periwinkle-blue baseball hat. They were sharing earbuds. Marcus cracked his knuckles every so often. I read about the thermosphere, which is many miles above sea level and reaches bizarrely high temperatures during the day, hot enough to melt steel, but doesn't feel hot because the individual molecules up there are so sparsely distributed. Each hot molecule is like a burning spark in a walk-in freezer. In other words, the thermosphere is not hot, it's extremely cold. I read another inspirational quote on the whiteboard: "Fake it till ya make it!"

"I've got blue hands," Penelope said.

Five minutes before the end of the block, a guidance counselor came in to see how things were going. I didn't remember her at first—she was one of the women who'd explained lockdown procedures during substitute training. Mrs. Moran had left good plans, I said, and everything seemed to be going fine. As she left, she detoured past the table where Rob, Bucky, and Bernard were sitting. "What are you guys working on?" she said.

"Writing," said Rob.

Bucky and Bernard mumbled something about working on a Keynote and listening to music, having swiped Hungry Shark from their screens. "You should know what you're working on," said the guidance counselor. "Class is almost over, and I don't want to have to take away the music, or take away the iPad."

She left. "Was I supposed to be fussing at you for playing the shark game?" I asked Bucky and Bernard. "I figured that you would know what you need to do."

"I'm only missing one paper," said Bernard. "I usually do it in class." Bernard was probably lying—one of the main things that school taught, I realized, was how to lie to get by.

I turned to Rob, who had filled several pages with writing. "Whoa, words on a page!" I said.

"This is a book I've started writing," Rob said. "It's about this kid named Adam. He runs away from his house. He's running through the woods and he comes to a tree. He tries to catch his breath, and the tree grabs him and drags him into the ground. So he's drug underground, and then he has to try to find a way back up. There's a city under there that he sees, and this giant forest to the side. He's just getting to the gates, and goblins come up to him and confront him and say, 'State your business, or you die where you stand.' That's what I have so far."

"I like it," I said. "He's in jeopardy already. I love the idea of an underground world."

Rob pulled out a new, thick copy of *The Fellowship of the Ring* from his backpack. "I've read *The Hobbit* about ten times now," he said. "I just got this yesterday."

Penelope said, "I don't like reading a book after I've seen the movie."

Bong, bong, bong, bong, bong, bong. Gosh, that was an easy class.

"So this period coming up is pandemonium and craziness?" I said to Penelope.

"Pretty much," she said. "Just saying that now I'll be talking a lot."

"You have a complete character shift?"

"I have different friends in different classes," she said.

Before Rob left I asked him whether he was writing the book for himself or for a class.

"I'm writing it just because," he said.

A KID NAMED COLBY appeared and saw me. "She's out *again*?"

Another kid, Tucker, said, "Oh, hello. Your name is?"

"Mr. Substitute," I said. "Mr. Baker."

"Hello," said a third boy, Aiden.

"You having a good day?" I asked.

"Yes, I am," said Aiden. "You?"

"Yes, actually," I said. "The last class was great. Everybody was just sort of sitting, doing their thing."

Colby said, "This is probably the most active class you'll have today."

"What sort of activity will be happening? Give me the full rundown."

"We'll just be talking, not doing work," said Colby.

I said hello to a few more people.

"Can I take the attendance down?" asked Diana. Yes.

Four kids were clustered around one table at the far end of the room eating Doritos and talking about hashtags. "Is this the cool kids' corner?" I said.

"I'm the only cool person over here," said a long-haired goofball named Lionel. He was wearing a Kid Cudi T-shirt.

Students kept coming in. It seemed like a large crowd, but it was really only about fifteen. Plus an ed tech—"THE BEST Ed Tech EVER," according to the sub plans. Her name was Ms. Worrell.

"Aiden, that's not your seat, sit in your seat, please!" Ms. Worrell said.

"As soon as you walked in, everyone went tranquil," I said to her.

"They know that I'll be angry otherwise," Ms. Worrell said. "They're a little chatty sometimes."

I said I didn't mind. "But I'm a little bit looser than I should be. You should keep me in check, too."

Ms. Worrell laughed mirthlessly.

I gave a little spiel to the class. "So I'm Mr. Baker, the substitute, filling in. I'm very glad to have you in the class. And really today you're supposed to do what you need to do. Which is—" I looked at the plans. "The WebQuest Carbon Footprint. And then we have the project questions and the study guide. And we could maybe have a dramatic rendition of the troposphere? Have you done the layers? When I was in school there were none of these upper layers. The exosphere—amazing. Some people have used pipe cleaners, and some people have used little bunches of tissue, and it's all good." Colby poked Bucky. "And elbow management, it's called. That's when you keep them to yourself. I don't mind mild talking. What I don't like is the wave of sound that starts to build, and then it washes over you, and then one of us fusses, and it gets quiet, and then there's another wave of sound. Just talk *kind of like this*, and there won't be those crests. So, do it! Go to work! Let me know if I can help you in any way."

Ms. Worrell spoke. "Who still has yet to do the 3-D model? Let's see hands. Because it is due today."

"It's due Thursday," said Lionel.

"No, WebQuest is due Thursday," Beth said. "It says right there on the board, '3-D Model Project, 5/13.' Today's the thirteenth, Lionel."

Ms. Worrell turned to me. "I'm going to take my kids down the hall, someplace quiet, where I can crack the whip." She began herding some boys toward the door. "Down to the Dean's Den, please. Bucky, you're coming, too. Gather your belongings. I don't want you making eighty-five trips. Markers, paper."

I asked Lionel's table which iPad game was taking the world by storm right now.

"Piano Tiles," said Lionel.

"They got rid of Flappy Bird, that was a major major thing," said Hank.

"Some guy killed himself over it," said Tucker.

"No, those are all rumors," said Lionel. "He took it down because he didn't like the fame. The hate, and the fame."

"Couldn't handle the celebrity," said Hank.

"Just tear through the troposphere," I said. I pointed to the thermosphere layer. "This is where it gets nutty. It's hot, but it's far away? I don't like that."

"You don't believe in it?" said Lionel.

"No," I said. "I can't feel it, I can't taste it. It's a myth."

"Are bananas a myth?" said Hank.

"Bananas *are* a myth," said Lionel.

I laughed. "You insane person. I believe in bananas. Let's not question reality here." I liked Lionel. The three of them began using pipe cleaners and straws to build a planet Earth.

Bucky returned from the Dean's Den to get some pipe cleaners from the supply cabinet.

Aiden explained how the grading worked. If you did the worksheet about the layers, you automatically got a passing grade, even if you didn't do the 3-D model. So you could skip the 3-D model and still pass.

"Interesting strategy," I said.

Surprisingly, this class, too, was quiet. I watched some YouTube videos, and then I interrupted Tucker, who was now making a hat out of pipe cleaners, to show him and Lionel a video made by a GoPro camera hanging from a helium balloon that went nineteen miles into the air. "It hits these high winds," I said to him. "This is the only teaching I'm going to do today. We're almost done. The balloon is going to pop."

"They had an iPad attached to a balloon, and they flew the iPad up there," said Lionel. "The case that it was in kept it safe."

"I saw that," I said. "Bear with me now. It's going to pop. Nineteen miles high. That's a day's hike, but straight up in the air. That's more than a day's hike." We watched the camera fall to earth and land in a tree.

Hank brought out some Q-tips from the supply cabinet.

"Those are going to come in handy," I said.

"He has really dirty ears," said Lionel.

A man from the guidance department came in. "I want to borrow Aiden," he said. I went over to another jokey table and sat down. "It seems like there's a lot happening over here," I said. "I can't see why you couldn't use some of those pipe-cleaner shapes to, let's say, represent the troposphere as imagined by a certain N-dimensional alien who would think in alternative—"

"Did you just call me an alien?" said a sporty boy, Marco.

"Basically," said Diana. She pointed to Marco's pipe cleaner. "Is that a heart?"

Hank began looking in Mrs. Moran's desk for the glue gun.

"Do you have full permission to look in her desk?" I said.

"I do not even have half permission," he said.

The man from guidance returned. "Can I borrow Nora for a second?"

"What's happening?" I asked the class. "Everybody's being borrowed."

"They're looking for Nelson," said Hank. Nelson was a ninth-grader who'd gone missing the week before, after school. "He went out for a walk and then he disappeared."

Diana poked her finger in the glue gun. "Don't do that," I said. "That could hurt you."

Marco began crinkling up a water bottle.

"All right, guys, seriously," I said. "You've got fifteen minutes left. Apply yourself now—total atmospheric activity. Just layer it up, and do it, and you'll be done. And then you'll get, you know, an eighty-seven."

"Have you ever been poked with a soldering iron?" Lionel asked me.

"No. You've got it all arranged, so why waste all that good effort?"

Hank typed the wrong password too many times into Tucker's iPad and disabled it.

"Here's your hot-glue gun," said Diana to Marco. They began gluing down random pipe-cleaner shapes.

Penelope couldn't find any cotton balls, so she began pulling the cotton off the ends of the Q-tips.

"I got glue in my pants," said Diana.

Marco, showing off for Diana, tried to start a fire in a pool of molten glue. I dissuaded him.

Penelope was finished with her colored-tissue project. "It looks like a blob," she said.

"No, it looks like the planet Earth as interpreted by your tissuey sensibility," I said.

"Thank you," she said.

I checked the clock. "Eight minutes to go," I said.

"I'm here again next block, by the way," Penelope said.

"You're really spending the day in this classroom," I said.

"Oh, yes."

I stopped Marco from squirting hot glue on his teeth.

"That's a horrible idea," said Lionel.

"There are limits," I said.

"Tastes bad," said Marco.

"Why am I being responsible for you?" said Lionel.

I looked away for a moment, and when I looked back, Marco had commenced eating the glue stick as if it was string cheese.

I said, "NO, NO. I draw the line in the sand."

"It's a snack," Marco said.

"No, it's not a snack, it's a fricking glue stick," I said. "Don't eat that. Seriously. DON'T DO THAT."

"It's like gum," said Marco.

"It says nontoxic," said Diana.

"When they say 'nontoxic,'" I said, "they mean it's nontoxic if you're gluing stuff. If you eat sticks of it, it's probably going to be toxic."

"I just chew on it," Marco said. He spat out some pieces of glue stick into the trash can.

I asked Lionel what he was handing in.

"This finished piece of fine, fine work," he said. It was an eight-foot-long conceptual-art piece made of straws and pipe cleaners and yellow construction paper, the troposphere at one end and the thermosphere at the other. Very little was glued or taped down. He took a picture of it with his iPad. "Now I just have to put it up on eBackpack."

"Hey, guys, you know you didn't measure it out correctly, right?" said Diana to Lionel and company.

"Who measures?" said Lionel.

"You have to have it measured," Diana said.

"That's crazy," said Lionel. Actually he had done some rough measurements, jotting down kilometer distances.

"Dude, that's so off," said Marco.

"I hate you," said Lionel.

Bong, bong, bong, bong, bong, bong.

"Hear that?" I said. "Stack and pack."

ACTIVITY BLOCK WAS from 10:40 to 11:14. "It's the end of the trimester and they ALL have overdue work," said the sub plans. A big round boy in a maroon polo shirt introduced himself and shook my hand. His name was Stefan. He said, "Do you know a good riddle? I love riddles. They're the best."

I asked Stefan to tell me a riddle.

"What has four eyes, but cannot see?"

"A flounder," I said.

"Mississippi," Stefan said.

"Ah, nice," I said. He waited for me to tell him a riddle, but I couldn't think of one.

Stefan wasn't officially in this Activity Block, he was just visiting, he said. "I have you last today," he said. Ah, I thought, so he was one of the class clowns that April had told me about. "If you give me liquid, I will die," he said. "If you give me food, I will live. What am I?"

"A chocolate-covered cherry," I said.

Penelope said, "I would be like, Give me CPR!"

I looked at the attendance list. There were many more people in the room than were on the list. "Huge class, my gawd!" I said. I shushed the shouters.

"People come in from their other activity," Stefan explained. "They let their teachers know, and they come in here."

"They do their work and they're civilized and quiet?" I said.

"I'll let you determine that," Stefan said.

Melanie showed me her cotton ball project. "That's beautiful," I said. "Every ten miles is two centimeters. My god, it's to scale."

"A fire," said Stefan. That was the answer to his riddle. "What goes around the world, but stays in a corner?"

"An office chair," I said.

"No."

I guessed again. News? A satellite?

"A stamp," Stefan said. He pointed triumphantly at me. "Haaaaaah!"

Time to get started. "Okay, guys, hello. Hello, hello."

"Hi!" said Rhys, a girl with a hairband.

Ashton crumpled up an empty packet of peanuts.

"Shh, for a second," I said. "Quiet for a second with the peanuts. I just want to welcome you to this class. I like conversation, it's good, what I don't like is when the sounds kind of crest and get too loud. So just talk in a normal voice."

Stefan stood and boomed out another riddle, reading from his iPad:

"THE MAN WHO INVENTED IT DOESN'T WANT IT, THE MAN WHO BOUGHT IT DOESN'T NEED IT, THE MAN WHO NEEDS IT DOESN'T KNOW IT."

I said, "When you read that thing next time, just read it in a softer level."

"I will, I'm sorry."

Beep, the PA lady. "Please excuse the interruption for a few announcements. All students who've signed up for AP Government or AP History next year should report to the auditorium at this time. Congratulations to the girls' tennis team on their three-to-one defeat of Kennebunk yesterday." More announcements—about softball, baseball, yearbooks, and Project Aware, which was an antibullying initiative. Nobody listened.

I asked a catatonic but smart kid, Greyson, how he was doing on the Earth's atmosphere. He couldn't work on the project, he said, because he didn't have his iPad, and all his notes were on his iPad. I told him to make something with pipe cleaners.

"It's all got to be to scale," said Greyson.

"No, it doesn't have to be to scale," I said. I waved at the exemplars on the corkboard. "None of those are to scale."

"That's a different assignment," said Greyson. "It has to look like this." He showed me an exemplar lying on top of a bookcase.

"Well, then make it look roughly like that."

"Okay, I can handle that," said Greyson. "Uh, can I go to the nurse real quick?"

I nodded.

"Thank you," he said.

Lionel, Hank, and Tucker reappeared. "Come on in," I said.

Penelope called out, "Lionel, you're my favorite."

A sketchy-looking boy, Chris, dropped by. He stood, thumping his water bottle against a file cabinet, trying to decide if he wanted to stay in the class. I told him to take off his backpack and have a seat.

Chris said, "I don't trust some people around here, you know?"

"Just don't make loud noises with the water bottle."

The PA lady came on with an announcement about picking up cookie dough.

Chris stopped thumping the water bottle and instead twirled it in the middle of a table, saying, "Are you a man, or are you a woman?" Then he hopped up onto a low bookcase and sat. He began poking Ashton with a pen.

"God dang," I said. "What's up with you? Just get some homework out and pretend to do it. Put a piece of paper or a freaking iPad in front of you and do something with it. Don't poke. It's ridiculous!"

Chris finished drinking from his water bottle and commenced making crinkling, crackling sounds with it.

"Dude, this is pathetic," I said. "Take out some pieces of paper, put them in front of you, and make some marks on them."

"You heard the man," said Hank.

"Why are you telling me to get to work and not him?" said Chris.

"The reason is, he's sitting quietly and you're doing things with the water bottle. The water bottle is what's killing me."

"All right, I'm sorry," Chris said.

"It's that crackling sound. Doesn't it drive you insane? Obviously it has driven you insane."

"I like it," said Chris. "I play it on my phone, and that's how I go to sleep. You want to see a magic trick with gravity?" He took out a Verizon phone and put it on the table.

"I see what you did there, nice," I said. I did the Chinese egg drop with a thumb drive I had in my pocket.

"That was pretty good," said Chris. "It took me a second to realize it."

Ashton came up. "I have to go to the South Building and get that cookie dough."

"Go get that cookie dough," I said. "It's urgent."

Beep. The PA lady asked us to excuse her interruption. "Freshmen, if you sold cookie dough, please report to the New Caf at this time to pick up your order, thank you."

Stefan read me a riddle: "From the beginning of eternity, to the end of time and space, from the beginning of every end, to the end of every place. What am I?"

"A Milky Way bar," I said. "No."

"Read it again," said Tucker.

Stefan read it again.

"I got it right off," said Nora.

"It's going to be stupidly easy," said Penelope.

"What is it?" said Tucker.

"It's *E*," said Stefan.

"The letter *E*," Penelope clarified.

"Beautiful," I said.

"I get it now," said Tucker.

Melanie and Sisely came back staggering under a load of Otis Spunkmeyer cookie dough, in tubs.

"Mr. Baker!" Stefan said. "What's round on both sides and high in the middle? If you know it, don't answer."

"A cheeseburger," I said.

"I know this," said Penelope.

I said, "John Belushi? No. Sponge cake. I don't know. I'm bad at riddles. I can't do it. What's the answer?"

"Ohio," Stefan said.

"Ah. I'm going to find you a riddle," I said, wagging my finger. "I'm going to find you a mega-riddle."

Stefan said, "What can you catch, but cannot throw?"

"AIDS," said Chris.

Another kid found a riddle. "What gets wetter and wetter the more it dries?"

"I have the dirtiest mind ever," said Tucker. "Can I answer?"

"No," said Stefan. "A towel. It gets wetter and wetter the more it dries you."

"I get it," said Chris.

Sisely said that she'd ordered so much cookie dough that she'd had to make two trips to the cafeteria. "My mom's going to have to come in and get it."

"Mr. Baker, do you have a riddle for me?"

"I'm trying," I said. "I'm a little riddle challenged."

Beep, please excuse the announcement. "Anyone who hasn't picked up their cookie dough at this time, please go over to the caf, thank you."

"Any cookie dough left behind will be destroyed," I said. I browsed websites, trying to find a riddle for Stefan, but none of them seemed good enough.

Penelope read a riddle. "There is a boat with a lot of people, but at the same time there is not a single person on the boat. How is this possible?"

"There's more than one person on the boat!" said Stefan, wagging a finger. "You said there's not a single person, so there's more than one person. Is that the answer?"

Penelope shook her head. "They're all married."

"It's a couples cruise," said Lionel.

"What about the captain, and the crew?" asked Melanie.

"They're all married to each other. Marriage at sea," said Lionel.

"It's almost lunchtime, guys," said Chris, standing.

I read a joke from Garrison Keillor's joke book, which I happened to have on my phone. "How many surrealists does it take to change a lightbulb?"

Penelope had found another riddle. "What begins and ends with *e*, and has only one letter?" The answer was *envelope.*

"Do you have one for me, Mr. Baker?" said Stefan.

"I started to say it, but I was embarrassed and I moved on."

"No, say it!" said Stefan.

"How many communists does it take to screw in a lightbulb?"

"How many communists?" said Stefan. "That's just a messed-up joke." He had a riddle by heart. "So a man leaves his home in the morning, and kisses his wife goodbye. On his way home from work, he sees a man crashing through a power line. He immediately knows his wife is dead. How does he know this?"

Bong, bong, bong, bong, bong, bong.

"The answer is that THE WIFE WAS ON LIFE SUPPORT," Stefan said, over the din of departure. "That's such a messed-up riddle."

I said, "Have a good lunch, good lunch, good lunch, good lunch."

A HANDFUL OF KIDS ATE their lunch in the room. I took a long drink of water and washed my hands. One honors student, a hairy talker named Nolan, brought out a transparent spherical maze called a Perplexus Epic and gave it to his friend Ramsey to try out.

"Bollocks," said Ramsey. "It fell down."

"Roast beef and pepper jack today," Nolan said, chewing.

Haydon, who had droopy shorts and black sneakers, was looking at the stacked tubs of cookie dough. "Who bought cranberry oatmeal?"

"Ew," said Ivy.

"That is disgusting," said Ramsey.

Nolan had a lot to say, and he said it fast. He talked about red wine and chocolate, whether they were good for you or not, and he talked about whether or not North Korea was a threat to the United States. "North Korea is producing a licensed model of the 1946 GAZ M-20," he said. "That's what they're making. There's the GAZ 69, which is a jeep, and the GAZ M-20, which is a sedan car from the forties. Those are the two mass-produced vehicles in that country."

"You've got to ask why they are at that point," I said. "It's because the US bombed them till they were subsisting in caves. The country was devastated. The fact that they're now able to do anything is kind of a miracle."

"I think our being there in South Korea is intimidating North Korea," Nolan said. "Kind of like if you bother a porcupine."

I asked them why they ate in Mrs. Moran's room. Was the cafeteria really noisy?

"Yeah, it's not an enjoyable place," said Nolan. He was skimming local news stories at the same time he was talking and eating—stories about fires and cops and break-ins.

We sat silently for a while, and then Penelope said to Jill that one of the teachers on the team had been crying on Friday.

I said, "The thing that's hard—I'm sorry to interrupt you guys, but I'm lonely—the thing that's hard is that if you're a regular teacher, you actually have to get the kids to learn something. That's hard. A substitute can just enjoy it. People say funny things, do amazing projects, and I just take it in."

"It's a dream job," said Jill; Penelope laughed.

Six bongs.

HONORS GEOPHYSICAL SCIENCE was a huge class. I admired more models of the atmospheric layers. One used nesting rings, one used glass beads. I said, "Hello, hello, hello. I'm Mr. Baker, I'm filling in for Mrs. Moran, and she is OUT. How are you doing with the layers of the atmosphere, as they radiate upward? Some of them are hot and some of them are cold? You doing well with that? There are some incredible models. I have to say I'm really impressed by all the different ways that people have solved this problem of how to visualize layers of the atmosphere." A kid with a hot pepper on his shirt was talking. "So—Chili Pepper," I said.

"Did you just call me a chili pepper?"

"I'm just reading your shirt. All you need to do is focus down. Just give it everything you have. You're honors, right? Congratulations, let's have a moment of silence for that." I told them to work on their projects and to not be loud. "If I can be of assistance to anybody, let me know. That's it, enjoy. AND I MEAN IT ABOUT THE LOUDNESS!"

The Scotch tape ran out; I found some more in the cupboard. I met the kid, Joel, who did the yellow balloon and told him how much I liked its simplicity—just Magic Marker on a balloon. Grace took attendance for me while several girls made peals of laughter. Nolan said he'd made his atmospheric layers out of Jell-O, but the layers merged, so he now had four weeks' worth of Jell-O in his fridge. "I'm going to make it again out of cookie dough," he said. A girl named Mira had made her Earth using rainbow cake mix.

"That is way above and beyond," I said.

"Oh, why thank you," Mira said.

Linda, a tall young woman with blue-framed glasses, was tearing red M&M's and pale blue Necco wafers from the base of her gorgeous candy-themed project. Why the tearing?

"It had to be to scale," Linda said.

"Is anything to scale in this life?" I said. "No."

"I'm going to tell Mrs. Moran that," said Linda. "I'm going to say, Sorry, nothing's to scale in this life."

A bored kid, Wilson—the one wearing the hot-pepper T-shirt—was distractingly rolling a roll of masking tape on the desk. "I don't have my iPad," he said.

"Who cares about your iPad?" I said. "Do it in cardboard. Look at what people are doing. They're making works of art. There are pipe cleaners up there."

The honors students were not quiet and studious, they were flirty and jokey and loud, although they got work done, as April had said they would. There were many playful disputes over the glue gun, and I had to tell them several times to take it down a peg. Nolan talked knowledgeably about storage batteries and solar power and offshore oil drilling and a dozen other topics. A diminutive boy named Darcy said, "I mustache you a question, but I'll shave it for later."

"Ow, that hurt, you stabbed me!" said Linda, who was flirting with Joel—Joel was handsome.

Wilson bonked Case on the nose with a rolled-up piece of paper.

I asked Case his opinion of Mrs. Moran.

"She's really nice to everyone but me," he said. "She absolutely loves Nolan for no reason, and she absolutely hates me for no reason."

"You've got to win her over," I said.

"I almost got an ISS for messing with Wilson. Then he put shaving cream on my face twice. I told the teacher and she yelled at *me*."

Linda asked Joel, "What temperature did you put for the thermosphere?"

I urged them on, table by table. "All right, now label it! Let the art come bubbling out! All those pent-up feelings that are inside you, let them go."

"Is it hard being a writer?" asked Linda.

"Yes," I said. "It never gets any easier."

Wilson positioned a label on a cloud. "Feng shui," he said.

Five minutes before class ended a Hokusai wave of noise began. "SHHHHHHHHHHHHHHHHHH," I said. "Way down, way down, way down. Way down."

"Lay down?" said Wilson.

"Clean it up, right now," I said. "All the stuff that isn't yours. Go above and beyond. Right now. Wilson, I've got my eye on you, clean it up. Make me proud."

Bong, bong, bong, bong, bong, bong. Twelve forty-seven on a Tuesday.

"Have a nice day," said Linda.

"I broke my wrist the other day," said Wilson, on his way out. "A Salter-Harris fracture, on the growth plates."

"Wow, take it easy, man," I said. Bye. Thank you. Have fun. Good work today. See you.

ONE MORE BLOCK of Geophysical Science to go. The first person in the door was the riddler, Stefan. The class was in full-out bonkers mode, just as April had warned me. "Hold him down, punch him," yelled one of the class clowns. April said, "Can I go down to Ms. Miller at the end of the South Building for this block?"

"Because this class is too loud?"

"Yes!" she said.

I wrote her a permission slip.

A teacher appeared and began waving her arms. "Just go to class! Go to class! Go to class."

The PA lady: "Please excuse the interruption. All chamber singers and chorus members must be in the auditorium at this time. Thank you."

"That's you," I said, pointing at Vince, a shifty kid in a hunting hat.

Jill, Daisy, and Marcia were whooping and shouting at each other in Southern accents.

"They're having a girlie fight," said Stefan.

"Are you happy here?" I said to them, standing over their table. Then I gave my intro. "So you're DOING SOME WORK. That's what she wants you to do. Enjoy, have fun, and talk in really nice controlled voices, so we don't drive each other nuts. Catch up on what you need to do. Okay?"

Jill said, "You look nice and sharp today."

"Thank you so much, so do you," I said. I was wearing a linen blazer.

A ruler smacked down. "Line in the sand," I said. "Violence, things flying through the air, rulers smacking against the tabletop—all that is totally unacceptable. It will NOT be tolerated. I WILL drop the boom. It will NOT happen."

They all thought "drop the boom" was crazy funny and said it many times—drop the boom, drop the boom.

"Lower the boom," I said.

Bernard and Bucky were back. "How's your day been?" Bernard asked, conversationally.

"My day's been good," I said. "You've been a part of it. You were playing the shark game. Do the sharks eat people, or the people eat sharks?"

"Sharks eat people," said Bucky.

"So you're learning about nature," I said.

Vince offered to go make more copies of the project sheet.

"Vince is *on it*," I said. "He's off to make copies!" I looked around. "What the hay? People are under control here."

"That's because we're cool," said Jill.

"I know you're cool," I said.

"Too cool for you," said Jill.

"Too cool for school," said Marcia.

A quiet girl, Nancy, was stuffing a mound of dog-eared homework into her backpack. "That is way too much homework," I said. "What can you do about that?"

"I don't know," Nancy said, sighing. She zipped it away. With her permission, I lifted her backpack, which was ungodly heavy. "I have back problems now," she said.

The class continued quiet. How did that happen? "I just want to say, I love this level of work and inspired activity—thank you."

"Have you got a riddle for me?" said Stefan.

No, I didn't, I said, but I was working on it.

Vince came back with thirty copies of the 3-D model project worksheet. I turned off the lights. "Calmness," I whispered. Somebody's phone vibrated. Vince wanted to turn the lights back on so he could see his sheet better. "Let's try moving you by the window," I said.

"No, I'll just deal with the dark," Vince said.

It was so serenely calm in the room that eventually I got out my computer and typed for a while. After fifteen minutes, Jill suddenly looked up and broke the silence. She said, "Your lipstick's all over my rim!"

"Wow," said Daisy.

Jill described a commercial for Orbit gum—Sarah Silverman is pitching a TV show to some executives when her morning coffee cup comes in and calls her babe. She says, "We're not together." The coffee cup says, "I have your lipstick all over my rim." Jill said, "I just got that!"

"We're happy for you," said Bucky. Then more quiet working. I whisper-asked someone to open a window. After another ten minutes the talking began, first softly, then in normal voices. Bucky was snickering at a Mr. Bean GIF in an app called iFunny: Mr. Bean exuberantly crossing his legs next to a person in a body cast.

Marcia explained to Daisy how to make the atmospheric layers to scale. "For every ten miles, I did two centimeters," she said. "And then you put all the facts around it."

Somebody's phone made a crystalline ding. Daisy said, "I'm going to the office in ten minutes to do announcements. Wait, is that clock slow?"

"Yeah, she put it five minutes back," said Stefan.

"So we wouldn't start to pack up," said Jill.

"That's outrageous," I said. "Then you don't know what the actual time is." All day I'd been confused about when classes were beginning and ending: the bongers always seemed to be bonging early. The clock was deliberately set wrong—in science class!

I told Marcia that her project was a marvel. She'd produced little informational flags on toothpicks, mounted in bits of clay, bearing the height and temperature of each layer. Oh, Earth, you are a lucky planet.

"Tootle-ooh, guys," said Daisy.

Bong, bong, bong, bong, bong, bong. Stack and pack.

The chairs went up. A game of tabletop hockey began. "Another day of school," I said, "bites the dust."

Daisy came back, disappointed because there hadn't been any announcements for her to make. She cheered up quickly, however, shouting at Liam, who followed her around as she picked up trash from the floor. "You're making me uncomfortable before I punch you," she said. "I'll beat you up."

"I'll fuck you up," said Jill, in a growly black accent.

"Hey, hey," said Bernard.

"Fuck you," said Daisy.

I told Liam to stop following Daisy around and pick trash up in a different part of the room. Vince called Bucky a dickhead.

Bong, bong, bong, bong, bong, bong.

Bye, guys. Thank you. See you. Enjoy.

Bye, Mr. Baker!

I wrote a note for Mrs. Moran: "Thank you for letting me fill in in your classes—the kids were funny, alert, and (at times) focused—but always a pleasure to be around—best regards, Nick Baker."

I ran into Shelly, the teacher of the how-to-be-a-substitute class, in the parking lot. "How's it going?" she asked.

"Well, it was an interesting, stimulating day with the ninth-graders," I said.

"I heard that can be a challenging group," Shelly said.

"They're kind of hilarious, though," I said. "They know how to enjoy life. I'm not sure how interested they really are in the layers of the atmosphere above fifty kilometers."

"Only if it impacts them," she said.

"That's reality," I said. "But thanks a million, this has really been fun, and I've learned a whole lot."

"Will you stick with it next year?" Shelly asked.

"I may well."

End of Day Eighteen.

SIMPLE MACHINES

Beth called at 5:50 a.m. to send me to the middle school, where I spent the day urging Mr. Lyall's eighth-grade science students to fill out several worksheets on simple machines. I read to them from the textbook, and we talked about rakes and baseball bats as levers, and about the reduced friction on the puck in air hockey—all that went okay. But none of the students could do anything with the worksheet's main word problem: *A 600-N box is pushed up a ramp that is 2 m high and 5 m long. The box exerts a force of 300 N. What is the efficiency of the ramp?* Some kids plugged numbers into half-remembered formulas and got wrong answers—efficiencies of 200 percent. Many pencils were sharpened. Kimberly, Michelle, and Bethany talked about a vampire show. I was no help, because I'd never learned about newtons. By the third class, I gave up on trying to push the box up the ramp and, after a quick web search, wrote the name of a series of videos on the whiteboard: "10 Brilliant Rube Goldberg Machines." I tried to explain who Rube Goldberg was, but nobody cared. "GUYS! LOOK UP 'TEN BRILLIANT RUBE GOLDBERG MACHINES!' Watch those videos, and be enlightened."

"Do we have to?" said Katylynn.

"It's optional," I said.

Rita was drawing a tattoo on Roslyn's arm. "Do you want a tattoo?" she asked me.

"No, I want you to look up 'Ten Brilliant Rube Goldberg Machines.'"

"I hate machines! I'm a girl," said Rita.

I wrestled a ruler from Shane's hand. His pills were wearing off.

"What kind of music do you like?" asked Natasha.

About half the class watched the first Rube Goldberg video, in which many items burn and boil and fall and toil in order to turn the page of a newspaper. It reminded me of teaching.

"It makes no sense," said Aaron. "They broke a laptop just to turn a page of a newspaper."

I said, "So the question is, is that an efficient machine, or an inefficient machine? Bingo, you've learned the lesson."

More people watched the videos, one by one. They talked about them and laughed and were attentive. "Full screen!" said Roslyn. Even Shane watched them, looking over somebody's shoulder because his iPad was confiscated. I could hear the clicking sounds of the Rube Goldberg machines emanating from fifteen iPads.

Toward the end of the day, Todd showed me how to make a Chinese firecracker; Aaron told a story about his great-grandfather, who injured his nose while chopping wood; and Ryder said he wanted to be an air force pilot when he grew up. "My dad works at the air force base in Portsmouth. He used to repair the planes. Now he teaches classes."

What air force plane did he like best?

"F-18 Hornet," he said. "The Super Hornet. I like how it looks. It's my dad's favorite plane. I like the Strike Eagles, too." He brought out his iPad and scrolled through some beauty shots of Strike Eagle planes in various poses. Then he showed more pictures, scrolling slowly through a Keynote presentation he'd just made for health class. "That's my family," he said. "That's my mom, my dad, my sister, my mom again. These are my friends. That's my sister swimming. She's really good. She just needs to practice how her arms go into the water. I like fishing. There's me two days ago." He was holding a fishing rod in the picture. "And here's my quote." The quote was by Bernard Baruch: *Be Who You Are, Say What You Feel. Those Who Mind Don't Matter, and Those Who Matter Don't Mind.*

I wrote a note for Mr. Lyall. "Dear Mr. Lyall, Many thanks for letting me sub in your class. Classes on Work and Machines went well—some serious confusion over the reverse side of the Work and Power worksheet ("Using Machines"). Kids were good-natured, respectful, funny—Best regards, Nick Baker."

Day Nineteen was history.

STINK BLOB TO THE RESCUE

At 8:25 a.m. I was in the parking lot of Hackett Elementary School, putting on my linen jacket so I would look like a proper substitute teacher and jamming my giant squirt bottle of Purell into my briefcase. Hackett was the school where I'd spent that somewhat hellish day with fifth-graders two months earlier. But now I was seasoned, maybe.

Room 4, Mrs. Fellows's third-grade classroom, had three rows of wood-grain desks and red plastic chairs, some of which were already occupied. An ed tech, Mrs. Spaulding, a youngish high-octane gal in yellow denim pants who looked like a swimming coach, was in the room and the early-arrival children were doing arithmetic. "Everyone knows what to do," said Mrs. Spaulding. "Right, everyone?"

"Mhm!"

"Good morning," I said. A girl named Antoinette was wearing a tricolored floral hair ornament. "I like your sparkly bow," I said.

"There's a lot of bling in this room," Mrs. Spaulding said. "The girls love bling. Not the boys." She took me aside for a quick orientation session.

"They know exactly what to do," she said. "You've got a few young fellas who might give you a run for the money, but you'll see. All you've got to do is keep them busy and remind them to do quality work. They're good boys."

"Just to forewarn you," I said, "sometimes the noise gets a little loud in my classes."

"I can help you out with that," Mrs. Spaulding said.

I said, "I don't mind, actually. If it's bothering you, or if you think it's a bad thing, then yes. But I figure it's just part of what happens with a substitute."

Mrs. Spaulding showed me the sub plans, which were four pages long and said ☆ PIZZA PARTY TOMORROW!! in green marker at the top. "What we do in our morning meeting," she said, "after you introduce yourself, is tell them the expectations you have about quality work. They know what fun time is, which we don't mind—but we also know what transition time is. We also have kids that owe recess time today because of some behavior. They know, believe me. They're great students. But they're eight-year-olds, nine-year-olds. Read through the plans and if you have any questions let me know."

Mrs. Spaulding's one-on-one student, Nell, arrived. "We have a sub today," Mrs. Spaulding told her. "His name is Mr. Baker, and he's going to be a lot of fun!" She winked at me.

"Let's hope," I said.

The first half hour of the class was called WIN Time; WIN stood for "What I Need." They were doing adding and subtracting with regrouping. Regrouping involved drawing number blocks, turning a ten block into ten one blocks and ten one blocks into a ten block—Montessori with pencils. Not a bad thing.

Mrs. Spaulding was a talker. She chatted continuously through WIN Time—about the pizza party, about book buddies, about Mr. Baker, about regrouping, about the merits and demerits of the Kindle, about declarative and interrogative sentences. It was a wonder that any subtraction with regrouping got done, but it did. If she were a student, she'd definitely have lost recess. But she meant well. The room around us was arranged like an Istanbul bazaar, or a game of miniature golf, with little varicolored cubbies here and there for specific tasks, and its wall space and whiteboards were overlaid with posters and student art and flowery borders and learning targets and taxonomies of learning and codes of cooperation. A voice-level chart specified that *0* was silent, *1* was a whisper, *2* was regular inside, *3* was outside loud. A smiley cardboard pencil with a red tongue and goggle eyes held a scroll: "7 Good Writing Traits." The seven traits, each printed on a different bright color, were Ideas, Voice, Organization, Word Choice, Sentence Fluency, Conventions, and Presentation. "Voice is the soul of the piece," said white letters on a magenta background. "It's what notes the writer's personal style, as all his or her feelings and convictions come out through the words." Learning target ELA.01.WPL.01.03 was: "I understand that brainstorming ideas for a specific audience and purpose is a part of planning my writing." Under a big purple star hung an inspirational quotation: "Every time a bell rings an Angel gets their wings."

"Good morning, Patsy!" said Mrs. Spaulding. "You're the student of the day! Hi, Clark, how are you?"

"Good," said Clark.

"Good! You've got a new math sheet to do. Make sure you sign up for lunch! Hi, Dyann! Make sure you do your own work. These are four-digit numbers, kids, make sure you raise your hands if you have any questions."

She stopped talking for five minutes and let the third-graders do math. Then she started up again, in her number 3 "outside loud" voice. "This is Wilson Lemieux. We're going to send him to the nurse. He has the cheek disease. They call it the fifth disease. It looks like you have a slapped face. Morning, Cody. Morning, Donny. Morning, Emerson. Clark, sign up for lunch and get started."

The lunch chart was a red grid on the whiteboard. Each child put a magnetic-backed glass bead under chicken quesadilla, cheeseburger, SunButter and jelly, or "cold," meaning brought from home. Half the class was cold, and nobody was having SunButter.

Talia, a girl with a neat Louise Brooks haircut, showed me her drawing. It was of a girl with a large smiley head and Louise Brooks bangs, with tiny yellow hearts on a hair bow, and earrings with purple peace symbols on them, and green tights with hearts, and a skirt with a big peace symbol in the middle of it. Her shirt said, "Best Friends for Ever!" It was totally wonderful.

"Reese and Glenn, let's get started," said Mrs. Spaulding. "Have a seat. I want to see some effort on that math! If you're done you can practice your spelling words. If you have any unfinished work in your folder, do that."

The principal, Mr. Pierce, came on the PA system: "Good morning, please stand for the Pledge of Allegiance and school promise." After the pledge, the children and Mrs. Spaulding chanted the promise: "TODAY IS A NEW DAY. I WILL ACT IN A SAFE AND HEALTHY WAY. I WILL DO WHAT I KNOW IS RIGHT. I WILL THINK BEFORE I ACT. I WILL TAKE CARE OF MYSELF, MY FRIENDS, AND MY SCHOOL. TODAY I WILL BE THE BEST ME I CAN BE."

"Keep working, let's go!" said Mrs. Spaulding, when everyone had sat back down. "Cody!"

The principal told us the lunch choices, and then he said, "The winner of the pizza party from the food drive last month is—Mrs. Fellows's class."

That was us. The class leapt up and cheered.

"Nice going, guys," I said.

"Sit down and work," Mrs. Spaulding said. "Shh. Focus on your math. Study your spelling words. We've got five minutes before meeting."

A boy named Stanley came up wanting help with a word problem. Milkshakes cost $1.83 apiece, and somebody was buying a milkshake for himself and two of his friends. How much would the milkshakes cost in all? Stanley had drawn number bars and gotten the right answer. Micah, a shy boy, was having trouble with a question about a toy store. The storekeeper, Billy, had put 1,573 toys on the shelf. *At the end of the day, customers bought 862 of the toys. How many toys does Billy have left?*

Mrs. Spaulding raised her hand. "Eyes on Mr. Baker, please," she said.

"Good morning, everyone," I said. "I'm filling in for Mrs. Fellows today. I'm Mr. Baker. I'm going to try to do the things that you normally do in class, because this seems like a really good class. Some of it I might need your help with. And one of the things that's really helpful, when there's a substitute, is if one person talks at a time when you ask me questions, because the substitute is learning, too. I'm trying to figure out what works in this class, and you guys have it down to a science." I took attendance. Aubrey? Scarlett? Clark? Skylar? Patricia?

"Let him do the talking, please," said Mrs. Spaulding.

Reese? Wilson? Kennedy? Stanley? Donovan? Paisley? Emerson? Micah? Eric? Ruth? Nell? Glenn? Roberta? Dyann? Cody? Talia? Antoinette?

I said, "So, Patsy, can you do me the great favor of taking the attendance sheet and the lunch count to the office, please?" I called the class over to a gray area rug under the whiteboard for morning meeting.

Mrs. Spaulding continued with her two-note commands: "Pencils down! Chairs in! You kids know the ropes. GUYS. Stanley, give Mr. Baker some space! Everybody scoot up, let's make a nice circle! Who's got the list of who's sharing today? Can I have it, please?" She studied the list. "Okay, guys, LISTEN UP, PLEASE!"

"Did everybody get a lot of sleep last night?" I said.

"I got up at seven-thirty," said Dyann.

"I got up at like six," said Skylar.

"I think the flowers and plants do a lot of their growing in the middle of the night," I said. "They soak up all that water—"

"And the leaves on the trees!" said Mrs. Spaulding. "Who's sharing today?"

Aubrey, a wide-faced sleepy girl, said, "I get up at four, because I live at Russell Lake and I have to go to my grandparents', because my bus stop is at my grandparents'."

"Man, four a.m.," I said.

"Why, to feed the chickens or something?" Mrs. Spaulding said. She was irrepressible.

"No!" said Aubrey. "I have to get up because my mom has to get up early for work, and she has to drive me to my mimi's from Russell Lake."

"So, Patsy, what are you going to pass around for greeting?" said Mrs. Spaulding. "You want to get one of those stuffed animals?"

Patsy got a stuffed bear out of a blue bucket.

"Patsy, which way do you want to go, kiddo?" Mrs. Spaulding prompted, in her I'm-being-patient voice.

"Good morning, Ruth," Patsy said softly, and handed Ruth the bear. Ruth handed the bear to Emerson. "Good morning, Emerson," she said. Good morning, Clark. Good morning, Talia. Good morning, Cody.

"Paisley, squeeze in!" said Mrs. Spaulding.

"There's isn't room," said Emerson.

"Uh, there is room, Emerson, stop. Sh!"

When the bear had finished its trip around the share circle, I said, "Wow, you are a nice bunch of kids."

"THAT WAS VERY NICE, VERY QUIET," said Mrs. Spaulding.

I said, "And now what happens, Patsy?"

Patsy started to explain, softly, but Mrs. Spaulding cut her off. "We have a list of shares. Patsy, do you mind if Micah goes first? He has to leave."

Micah stood up. "This is my toy. It's a barracuda."

"Those are some serious teeth," I said.

Micah held up a piece of paper. "And this is a thing that tells you all about the barracuda. I just found it."

"Are there maybe two facts you want to share with us?" Mrs. Spaulding said. "Can you read two things for us?" Micah hesitated, and Mrs. Spaulding took his paper and pointed to the barracuda drawing posted on the whiteboard. "You can see up there who drew the barracuda, Mr. Baker."

I said it was a beautiful drawing.

"Micah's going to be a scientist or an archaeologist or something," she said. She read from Micah's barracuda fact sheet. "Let's see," she said. "It's a great swimmer. Likes to live near coral reefs. Do you know those big rocks that are under the ocean, that are very colorful? And he's sleek and flexible. So he swims like he's almost not swimming. Effortlessly."

Micah said, in his tiny voice, "My poppi was swimming under the water in Florida, I think, and he was scared because he saw a barracuda."

"Beautifully done, Micah, thank you," I said.

"Now sit down," said Mrs. Spaulding, "and you get three questions."

"How big do the barracudas get?" asked Eric.

"That's something we can research, guys," Mrs. Spaulding said.

I said to Micah, "You know what you can say when somebody asks how big they get to be? You can say, 'Well, they get to be extremely large.'"

"They get to be extremely large," echoed Mrs. Spaulding. "Second question!"

"Do they live in lakes and bogs?" asked Reese.

"They live in the open ocean," said Micah.

Dyann raised her hand. "I forgot my question," she said.

Glenn said, "What ocean they live?"

"Um," said Micah.

"Another good question," said Mrs. Spaulding. "There are a lot of different oceans. It would probably be, I would think, the Pacific."

I said, "Where did your poppi say he saw them?"

"That's right," said Mrs. Spaulding. "The Atlantic Ocean? Near Florida? Good questions, guys. Nice share. So, Micah, Stanley, and Cody, you kids need to go. Why don't you grab your math papers, if you're not done, if she doesn't have work for you."

When those three were bundled off, I asked Patsy to take it away.

"On Saturday I get to see my brother," she said. "Because it's going to rain on Saturday we were going to go to Funtown but now we're going to go bowling or to the movies."

I asked her if she used a big or a little bowling ball when she went bowling.

"Candlepin balls?" Mrs. Spaulding said. "The little balls? Where you don't have holes for your fingers."

"No, they have holes," said Patsy. "Or maybe not."

"I used to try to go bowling with those big bowling balls," I said. "I would fling the ball but my fingers were sort of stuck, and the ball and I would go flinging down the center lane."

"Micah just got a trophy for bowling," said Mrs. Spaulding.

Patsy told a long, inaudible story about losing at bowling.

"Three questions, guys," said Mrs. Spaulding.

Donny asked which bowling place she was going to go to, Ruth asked if she was going out to eat, and Clark asked how many balls you get.

"I think it's three, or six," Patsy answered.

"It's three for a frame," Mrs. Spaulding clarified. "Nice share, Patsy. Who's next?"

Eric had a magic trick to share.

"We have a lot of magicians in this class, Mr. Baker," Mrs. Spaulding said. "Sh!"

Eric pulled on a white glove and held up a Beyblade spinning toy. "I'm going to make this disappear," he said. The Beyblade disappeared, sort of. We applauded.

Question one was, had he learned the trick this morning, or had he been working on it for a while?

"I've been working on it on the bus," said Eric.

What did you use to make it disappear?

"Special magic power," said Eric.

What was it?

"A Beyblade," said Eric.

Paisley showed us her new thing of pink lipstick. "I'm collecting them. I got one orange, one red, and this one. And here's my book of jokes. What did the zombie like about school?"

Eric raised his hand. "That his brains fall out?"

"Nope," said Paisley. "Stiff competition. Why was the monster kicked out of class?"

Skylar said, "Because it kept on spying on people?"

"Nope, his eyes were on someone else's paper. And I might be going to Funtown over the weekend."

Mrs. Spaulding asked the first question of Paisley: Was the book a library book? Talia asked, "Do you enjoy reading?" Paisley said yes. Emerson asked, "What's your favorite joke?"

Reese was next. He said, "I'm not going to be here tomorrow, because my gram and gramp from Colorado are coming to visit. It's only for two days, which kind of stinks." Eric asked him if he was still going to play Pokémon. Mrs. Spaulding asked if Reese had been to Colorado. Jake asked what Nathan was going to do with his grandparents, anything fun? "I think we might go bowling," said Reese. "Tonight we're going to have clam chowder with them, with lobster in it."

"Will there be extra?" said Mrs. Spaulding, and winked at me. "Nice share."

For her share, Ruth showed a picture of her and her sister playing with a baby, and then she opened a large duffel bag and pulled out an ostrich Beanie Baby, one of a collection given to her by her mother. "I didn't bring all of them, because I have seventy-nine," she said. Her favorite was the ostrich; she stored most of her Beanies in a trash can in her room.

Talia said, "In five weeks I have to get braces." What colors? She didn't know, maybe gold. Gold and purple? She didn't know! Which teeth? "My four top teeth."

Sharing was done. I complimented the class on their ability to ask questions of one another. "Really good job," I said.

"So let's see how good we can transition back to our desks," said Mrs. Spaulding. "Put your shares in your backpacks, please! GUYS, QUIET TRANSITION! We're going into writing. Nathan, Spenser, have a seat, come on, guys. KEEP YOUR MATH HANDY FOR LATER. PUT IT IN YOUR MATH FOLDER, so you know where it is."

The sub plans said, "Pass out story about the stink bug. You can read as a group or have kids work in small groups." I passed out "Stink Blob to the Rescue," a one-page story with two pages of questions following it. Mrs. Spaulding said that three of the kids could not read the stink bug story because they had to finish a DRA, or Developmental Reading Assessment, beginning with Reese. "Put it away, Emerson, we're working on a writing workshop from Mr. Baker." She winked at me again.

"So this is a story called 'Stink Blob to the Rescue,'" I said. "You guys can help me read. What is a stink blob, anyway?"

Nobody knew.

"Let's see if we can figure it out from the first paragraph. *Mom senses danger. It's a villainous wasp—*"

I stopped, because Mrs. Spaulding was scolding Reese and I wasn't going to talk over her. She looked up and realized she was interrupting the class. "Reese, it's too noisy to do the DRA," she said. "I'm sorry, Mr. Baker," she said.

"There are a lot of tricky words in this, by the way," I said. "Words that are complicated for third grade. *Mom senses danger. It's a villainous—* What's *villainous?*"

"Bad," said Natalie.

"Bad! A villain is a bad person. Often in cartoons the music changes, and the villain has a cape. He's the bad guy. *It's a villainous wasp hovering just overhead. She quickly gathers her twenty-four nymphs under her triangular body.* And then take it away paragraph two, Emerson!"

Emerson read, "*The wasp ap—ap—apreech. Apreeches.*"

"*The wasp approaches,* good."

Emerson read on, haltingly, with help from me. "*Mom frantically waves her antennae. Not fazed, the wasp flies even closer. Mom turns her—*tongue?"

"Tough," I said.

"*. . . her tough, shield-like back and quickly buzzes her wings.*"

I reread the paragraph to suture it together, explaining what the word *fazed* meant. "Now what happens? Patsy."

Patsy read, "*The wasp ignores her threat and lands just out of reach. Mom kicks out her middle and back legs in another attempt to scare it off.*"

"Good job," said Mrs. Spaulding.

I said, "Whoever wrote this has really looked at wasps, probably through a magnifying glass. Her name is Sandie Lee. Good job." We kept going. The bad wasp loops in the air once and returns. A baby stink bug, called a nymph, creeps out from under her mom's body. The wasp darts toward it—but mama stink bug is ready. Reese read the next part. "*Mom's ready and silently drops her most powerful secret weapon . . . the stink blob. The wasp catches a whiff of this nox—* Nauseous?"

"That's a new word, gosh," interposed Mrs. Spaulding.

"Noxious," I said. "It means 'stinky.'"

Reese continued, *" . . . this noxious smell and zips away in the opposite direction. Lunch will have to wait."*

"Great reading," I said. "This is really putting a picture in your mind. We've got a battle between a wasp and a stink bug. And the stink bug has a secret weapon, which is what?"

"The stink blob," said several voices.

"The stink blob! It's a blob of horrible-smelling foul liquid that is going to protect her babies." What a fine story.

Scarlett read part of the next paragraph. To illustrate it, I drew a picture of the shield-backed stink bug and the wasp on the whiteboard, using green marker. "The wasp has a long droopy abdomen, and long waspy wings," I said. "These two creatures have a little tension today."

Eric struggled gamely through the succeeding few sentences. *"All stink bugs have a large triangular structure on their backs. This raised covering points towards their hind end and is called the* scutellum." Mrs. Spaulding talked quietly to her special student, Nell, throughout the reading, which just about drove me nuts, but I didn't say anything—it was her job, after all.

"So they gave you a crazy hard word," I said, printing *scutellum* on the whiteboard. "This is a word I don't know. It's a word most grownups do not know. And when it's a scientific word that most people don't know, and it never comes up in conversation, sometimes they put it in italics, leaning forward, to show you that we're being scientific. This whole thing is called the *scutellum*. And I think a *scuta*, in Latin, an old language, means 'shield.' It's the shield. It's the thing that protects that bug!" (Actually it's *scutum*.)

Dyann raised her hand, and read: *"However, the stench-gob is used only as a last resort since it saps the bug of most of its energy."*

Now that, I said, was a very interesting sentence. "This stink bug has to know that it is in serious trouble—so much trouble that it is going to use up all of its energy. It's like when you're playing one of those games, and your health is starting to go down. You're going to use up all your health to make this blob of stench."

Dyann read two more sentences and was stopped by the word *secrete*. "*When the young wander off they secret a scent trail.*"

"All right, here's a word that looks like *secret*," I said. "But there's a letter at the end. See that letter *E*? So when the young wander off, they *secrete* a scent trail. When you secrete something that means you leak it out of your body somehow."

Kennedy read last: "*If in trouble they send out a powerful alarm scent. It's Mom to the rescue as she follows this scent path right to her nymph.*"

I said, "The baby stink bugs are wandering around, and they're also secreting something. They're not secreting stink blobs, but they're secreting smell. That's how insects, ants, keep track of each other. Dogs do that, too, right?"

"Bloodhounds!" said Clark.

"They're insect bloodhounds. All right. That was fantastic reading, guys." I turned the page. "So there's a vocabulary activity, and I must say, these are some hard words." They needed some review, I thought, and I asked them what *villainous* meant.

"Listen up, guys!" said Mrs. Spaulding.

"Bad?"

"Bad, right. *Saps.* That's a tough one. If somebody saps your strength, it means they take your strength away. So *saps* means 'take away.' *Commotion.* If everybody in here were wild and crazy, what would that be?"

"A commotion."

"That would be a commotion. And you're not. *Noxious* is 'nasty,' right?"

Patsy raised her hand. "*Noxious* is like a really bad smell."

"A gross, nasty, noxious smell. *Secrete.* It doesn't mean 'secret.' When you secrete something, what are you doing with it?"

"You leak it out of your body," said Reese.

"Right," I said. "You might secrete blood. When you sweat, what are you doing? You're secreting sweat. We're just secreting people. So give it a shot, right now. Match each word with its definition. Don't forget to write your name at the top."

I went around giving hints where hints were needed.

"Do your own work," said Mrs. Spaulding. "Refer back to the text. It'll all be there."

One question stumped several kids. "I want to take a minute to talk about one really tricky question," I said. "It says, *Explain how the writer's style changes in the last two paragraphs.* Whoa. What's that all about? What is a writer's style? When a writer writes something, they can write it any number of different ways. You could write about this classroom like a scientist, and list everything and be very serious, or you could be funny, you could be kind of breezy and chatty. Or you could create a scary mood. That's the style that you use to write about something. So this question is why the style changed in the last two paragraphs. I frankly didn't notice that the style changed. Did you?"

They shook their heads.

I said, "But in the beginning, we were in a dramatic situation. Mom senses danger. The wasp approaches. Mom frantically waves her antennae. It's drama, it's excitement. It's a story. And then, in the last two paragraphs"—I switched to a BBC accent—"*Stink bugs range from six to twelve millimeters in size and come in various colors.* So it's much more scientific. That's what that question is about. Does that make sense?"

They labored at the pages of questions for a while. "Focus till snack, guys," said Mrs. Spaulding. She warned me that snack was in two minutes. "I'm just going to step out to the ladies' room, I'll be right back."

I tried to sum things up for the class. "So incredibly enough," I said, "you read through this story, which is filled with some seriously brand-new words—words that you never before saw, in some cases. What they used to do, when I was in school, is they would say, 'We've got to pick only words that kids would actually know at that very moment, or just a little bit harder.' This story is saying that a lot of times when you're reading, especially in scientific writing, there are going to be words that are a little bit confusing, but that's okay, because you can just charge on. That's what this thing is teaching you." I went over question 3, *Why are stink bugs called the "parent bug"?* While I was explaining how to skim back through the text to find the answer, Mrs. Spaulding came back and began shushing people loudly. "You have to be quiet while the teacher is talking," she said. I stopped to let her finish with her interruption. Then I said, "What do parents tend to do? They make sure their kids are safe. They're protective. The stink bug is unusual. Some insects just lay their eggs, wander off, and forget about it. They don't have any parental responsibility at all. But the stink bug actually takes care of its little ones, which is an unusual behavior in insects. That's why it's called the parent bug. But I must say, that phrase was snuck in there."

Ruth was puzzled by the very first question: *Why did the author write this article? (a) To explain how wasps hunt for prey; (b) to give information about stink blobs; (c) to tell you how nymphs protect themselves; (d) to give information about stink bugs.*

I said, "Why on earth did the writer write this article? Why did she write it? Well, probably because she's paid to write articles for schools. But it's also that feeling of pressure inside you. You want to say something. She'd learned about stink bugs and wasps, and she thought, Wow, I want the world to know this." I looked down the answers. "That is a toughie. All four of those are sort of true, but the question is what's the truest one. I would look at (b) and (d). One is to give information about stink blobs, and one is to give information about stink bugs. Now ask yourself, in this piece, we had all kinds of commotion. We had a stink blob, but we had lots of other stuff about—"

"Stink bugs," said Ruth.

"Stink bugs! So really the best answer is (d), to give information about stink bugs. One good clue you can use to find out is look towards the end of the piece. The end of the piece is usually going to talk about the main idea somehow."

"Shhh," said Mrs. Spaulding.

"Anyway, I think we're getting ready for snack," I said, "and thank you so much for your hard work."

"NO SNACKS UNTIL YOU CLEAR YOUR DESK," said Mrs. Spaulding. "Not stuffing your math paper in your desk, Stanley! You're going to go over that later. Mr. Baker can choose quiet kids that are ready to get snack."

"I know you're all going to be quiet," I said.

"FRONT ROW CAN GO," said Mrs. Spaulding. "Second row can go get their snack."

Reese brought up his portrait of his friend Eric. "He's half wolf," he said. "He's human in the morning, but he turns into a wolf. And he has ears, because he's also half anteater."

I took a bite of a sandwich. Spelling was coming up, and Mrs. Spaulding told me a class rule: "Try not to begin all your sentences with the letter *I*." She also said that the guidance lady, Mrs. Crane, was out today, and wouldn't be coming in after snack. Then she told Stanley to get a paper towel. "You're spilling." She said, "I'm like, is there a special password to get in that juice? OKAY, IN YOUR SEATS EATING, YOU KNOW THE RULES. Mr. Baker will let you know what's happening. We have to be flexible."

"What's happening is chewing, snacking, eating," I said. "Munching, cheesing."

"He's cheesing!" said Skylar.

"I'm banana-ing!" said Donny.

"Nice verb, I like that," I said.

Eric asked me how to draw a wolf. He wanted to keep up with Reese. I told him to use his memory. He drew a pair of scary eyes, and small ears. He made a soft howling sound as he drew.

"Stanley, in your seat," Mrs. Spaulding said. "We don't wander around at snack, sit down. SIT DOWN WITH THE BEVERAGE. Shhh!" She came around my desk looking for a packet of sticky notes, then went right back to being bad cop. "Reese! In your seat for snack, you know that."

I asked Reese how many cheese crackers he'd eaten.

"Three."

"Three down, three to go," I said.

"Well, three and a half," said Reese, holding up the one he was smilingly eating.

"Ooh, fractions," I said.

"Roo-ooh-ooh," said Eric.

I let a moment pass. "Okay, guys, finish up your snack," I said.

Immediately Mrs. Spaulding did the grade-school hexaclap. "I'M HEARING MR. BAKER SAY TO START TO CLEAN UP FROM SNACK. RIGHT NOW. MAKE SURE THE GARBAGE IS IN THE GARBAGE CONTAINER! DESKS NEED TO BE CLEANED OFF. Clean up from snack, Antoinette, let's go. Don't make me set a two-minute timer! Ten thirty-five, we transition! You need to finish those crackers, Emerson. I think during this next transition, Antoinette, Reese, and Dyann, and Patsy, you should be able to work on your DRAs, because this will be quiet learning. There shouldn't be any talking during this assignment, unless up goes the hand. We've done this many times."

Micah was drawing a fluorescent barracuda. "Hey, good coloring!" I said.

"GUYS, ALSO TAKE A LOOK AT WHO OWES RECESS TIME TODAY. We're getting a list from Mrs. Hearn, from yesterday."

Wilson, the kid with slapped-cheek syndrome, went off to see Nurse Chris.

"Amazingly efficient snack cleanup," I said, when the time seemed ripe. "I was looking out over a devastation of cheese crackers and juice, and now it's all gone. So, at ten thirty-five Mrs. Crane usually comes in and talks about feelings."

Mrs. Spaulding said, "He's telling you! Save yourself a question and sit down."

"Mrs.—"

"SITTING DOWN! EYES ON MR. BAKER."

I tried again. "Mrs. Crane talks about feelings and sometimes you role-play. Well, she has something else to do, and she can't be here. So Mrs. Spaulding—"

"SIT DOWN," said Mrs. Spaulding.

"Mrs. Spaulding and I have talked about it, and we've got a spelling worksheet. But since you'd normally be talking about feelings, when you look at these spelling words—*round, ball, blue, held, dark, girl, instead, past, rude, either*—when you write those words in a sentence, if you're stumped, and you want to write a new and interesting sentence with the word, let's say, *dark*, think about some kind of emotion. Think, I'll write an angry sentence with the word *dark*. Or, I'll write a funny sentence about the word *dark*. If you put some kind of feeling behind it, then you can write something interesting that sort of pops into your mind. If I said to you, Write a frightening sentence with the word *ball* in it, what would you come up with? *Ball?*"

"There is a live ball in a haunted house," said Scarlett.

"Okay, immediately—"

Mrs. Spaulding said, "I've got one!"

"—you're starting to think of this house," I said. "You're thinking of a strange, black, or maybe red, ball, hovering in the middle of a haunted house. All of a sudden, you're thinking, Wow, I've never imagined that before. So think if you can mix an emotion with a word." There was another hand up. "Mrs. Spaulding."

"I thought of like a ball of fire," Mrs. Spaulding said.

"A ball of fire," I said.

"Going across the prairie," she said. "A ball of rope! A ball of yarn!"

"And all they have to fight the ball of fire is one garden hose," I said. "So here are some spelling words to put in a sentence. Have fun with it. Remember, the sentences can go in any direction you want, and—"

"Mr. Baker," said Mrs. Spaulding, "these kids are amazing writers and readers. But they still have to do their work. On the back take the words, only the words, and alphabetize them."

"Oh, my gosh," I said.

Mrs. Spaulding said, "Who knows what *alphabetize* means? All together. ABC ORDER. And kids, remember capitalization and punctuation. Super-creative sentences, folks. I don't want all of them to start with *I*, either, please. And now we have to be super quiet, because we have three kids working on DRAs."

Emerson whisper-asked me how to spell *around*. I told him.

"Finger spaces," Mrs. Spaulding said.

I whispered to Talia, "Finger spaces, what's that? You put a finger between the words?"

Talia nodded.

"One or two of them can start with *I*," Mrs. Spaulding said.

Skylar said he wanted to use two spelling words in one sentence. I said to go for it. I told him how to spell *kick*.

Paisley read me two sentences: *The boy went into the haunted house, and it was too dark, so he left. I went outside and I saw a ball with flames from a lightning strike.*

"Very good," I whispered. "Good job."

She took a deep breath and went on to her third sentence.

Mrs. Spaulding came over. "I disappear in a little while to do lunch duty," she said.

"How sad," I said.

"I know," she said, laughing.

I went over to Cody, who had on a blue shirt. He wanted to write, "My shirt is blue," and he needed to know how to spell *shirt*.

Reese had used three spelling words in a single sentence: *There is a round blue ball going past.*

"You are good," I whispered.

Mrs. Spaulding seemed not to want to leave. "Focus, everybody," she said. "And underline your spelling words, too. Nice job, Nell."

I looked at the schedule. Mrs. Crane usually taught feelings from 10:35 to 11:15. It was only five of eleven. "Holy shit," I whispered to myself.

Donny raised his hand. "Does *dawn* mean 'night'?"

"Nice job, Stanley, I'm very impressed," Mrs. Spaulding said.

Glenn asked me, "Can I say 'I rode my test'? No. 'I rode my bike'?"

Dyann had written, *I held my sister's baby.* She whispered, "It's going to be true. She's having her baby soon, but I'm going to be holding him, so I just made up a sentence." She'd written, *Every body love's round things.* She said, "They're usually addictive."

"I like round things," I said. "I have one suggestion for you. Do you need that apostrophe? You might not need it. You might be home free without it."

Dyann had also written, *I'm a girl, I think.*

"I think so, too," I said.

For *past*, she'd written, *In the movie* Frozen *I like the part where she says the past is in the past.*

"Clark, turn around, that's five extra minutes," Mrs. Spaulding said.

Micah had finished his sentences: *The sky is blue. The sky is dark. I went around the ball. I held the car.* I asked him how he was with alphabetizing.

"I don't like to do that," he said.

When almost everyone was done, I wrote *past* and *passed* on the board. "This is a word that gives people trouble—even grownups have trouble with this one. *Past* versus *passed.* They sound exactly the same. But if you say, I ran *past* the car and waved, it's this one. If you say, I *passed* the car in the street, it's this one. And that is a diabolical and villainous plan that English came up with to confuse us. But that's the truth of it. If you said, 'I drove past a moose on the road,' which would it be?"

"P-A-S-T," said Talia.

"Right. Now, if you said, 'I passed a moose on the road,' it's going to be P-A-S-S-E-D, because the word is *pass.* I'm just throwing this out because it's something you're going to need to keep an eye on forever. I still make mistakes with it. Anyway, very good sentences, good alphabetizing."

"I have lunch duty now," said Mrs. Spaulding.

Kennedy started to talk.

"QUESTIONS, YOU RAISE YOUR HANDS," said Mrs. Spaulding. Then she left.

I announced silent reading, and turned off the lights. Patsy was still working on her DRA. She'd been assigned to read a book about Mae

Jemison, the first African-American woman in space. She was supposed to write down the most important thing she'd learned and she couldn't think of what to say, having already written that Mae Jemison was the first African-American in space. What more did they want? "You could say something about how it's important for all kinds of people to be able to succeed," I said.

After what seemed like an hour of throat-parching power-whispering, a buzzer buzzed ominously. "That means it's five minutes until lunch," said Antoinette. They had a half hour for lunch and then half an hour of recess, and I didn't have recess duty.

"Five minutes till lunch, everybody," I said. "Start thinking about thinking about thinking about getting ready." Shoes were changed, lunch boxes were distributed, and Paisley went off to get a light sweater. "Guys," I said to Jake and Stanley, "can one of you take responsibility for not bouncing off the other?"

Talia handed me a piece of paper that said QUIET. The class formed a line, I held up the QUIET paper, they obeyed, and we walked to the cafeteria.

"You're tall," said Dyann.

"Thank you, you're tall, too."

I ate a sandwich and crumpled up my paper bag and played some music and let the hour of not talking pass slowly by. At twelve forty-five, the crowd was back from lunch and recess, flushed, knackered, and happy. "Mr. Baker, can we open a window?" said Skylar.

"It was hot out there?"

"It was like a microwave," Skylar said.

"Mr. Baker!" said Paisley. "Why was six afraid of seven?"

"Because he might have gotten eight?"

"No, seven eight nine!"

Mrs. Spaulding had her eye on the clock and she began guiding us toward a state of preparedness. "Guess what, guys. Mrs. Hearn is on her way. You know what she wants. Clear desks. Time for literacy! Clean desks up! Desks clean!" She erased my stink bug and wasp drawings from the board.

Reese held up a bag with something in it. "This is my share. Can I squeeze it in? I forgot it this morning. My mom brought it in."

I checked with Mrs. Spaulding. "How about after math?" she said. "Mrs. Hearn's only here for twenty minutes. Don't let me forget. Stanley, is this your whiteboard? Pick it up, please. Come on."

Aubrey showed me her bug bite. "I've had it for like thirteen days now."

"You know, kids, you're doing a great job today," Mrs. Spaulding said, when everyone was seated and the desks were clean.

"That is true," I said. "It's been a pleasure to be in this class and to see what you're up to."

"Marker up off the floor, please," Mrs. Spaulding said. "Patsy, did you finish your DRA, kiddo? Good, good, good. We read this book, Mr. Baker, yesterday, called *Mr. Peabody's Apples*, written by Madonna. Did you kids like that book?"

Yes.

"Lot of messages in the book on using your words kindly towards people," Mrs. Spaulding said. "Kind of like what Madonna's been through, because she's so different, and vocal. It's nice to be different. Emerson, stick the ruler in your desk. It's a great book."

I said I'd always liked "Material Girl" and "Holiday."

"I love her music," Mrs. Spaulding said. "It's great workout music. It'll be my pleasure not to put any names up to owe recess, but you know, we have rules that we follow. Hi, Mrs. Hearn!"

Mrs. Hearn, the literacy specialist and guidance counselor, was a solid woman with turquoise beads and a reedy, carrying voice. "We're going to reread the story to refresh our memories," she said.

"Mrs. Hearn, this is Mr. Baker. Guys, nice transition. Go up so you can hear the story, let's go! Everybody, take a scoot forward! Everybody!"

"All right, *Mr. Peabody's Apples*, by Madonna," Mrs. Hearn said. "Artwork is by Loren Long."

"She's a great artist, Google her, ask your mom, she'll know," Mrs. Spaulding said.

"Look at this beautiful artwork," said Mrs. Hearn.

"Shhhhhhh," said Mrs. Spaulding. "Have you got a baseball game tonight?" she asked a boy.

"All right, you ready? Paisley, you ready? *In the town of Happyville, which wasn't a very big town, Mr. Peabody was congratulating his Little League team on a great game. They had not won, but no one really cared, because they had such a good time playing.* Isn't that how kickball is at recess? Who won doesn't matter, as long as you had fun."

After the game, on his way home, Mr. Peabody waves at everyone in town and they wave back at him because everybody's happy. Then, on the way past Mr. Funkadeli's fruit market, he takes a shiny apple without paying. A suspicious onlooker named Tommy Tiddlebottom thinks Mr. Peabody has stolen the apple and he skateboards off to tell his friends. The same thing happens again the next Saturday, and the rumor of Mr. Peabody's purported apple thievery spreads. Nobody but little Billy Little, Mr. Peabody's biggest fan, shows up at the next Saturday's Little League game. Billy Little tells Mr. Peabody that everyone thinks he's an apple thief. Together they have a chat with Mr. Funkadeli, the fruit seller, where Billy learns that Mr. Peabody always prepays for his apples. Tommy Tiddlebottom, the rumor-spreader, is confronted with the truth and apologizes for his malfeasance. Mr. Peabody orders him to go home and get a pillow stuffed with feathers.

"Now, yesterday," said Mrs. Hearn to me, over the heads of the listening children, "they had to try to figure out why Mr. Peabody would want Tommy to get a pillow with feathers. And some of them were pretty close. Don't raise your hand, Paisley! You already know!"

"It was a lesson on predictions," Mrs. Spaulding said. "They did a real good job."

"They had to predict why Mr. Peabody would want Tommy to bring his pillow to the baseball field," said Mrs. Hearn. Emerson was twitchy. "Emerson, we're going to be doing work on this. This is to help refresh your memory. *An hour later, Tommy met Mr. Peabody on the pitcher's mound.*"

Mr. Peabody marches Tommy up to the top of the bleachers and orders him to cut the pillow in half and let the feathers flutter out—thousands of feathers, all over the field. Then he tells Tommy to go pick up the feathers. Can't do it, says Tommy. Ah, well, says Mr. Peabody, it's just as hard to undo the damage you caused by spreading that rumor. Each feather is a person. Tommy reflects on the truth of this statement. *"I guess I have a lot of work ahead of me,"* he says.

Mrs. Hearn said, "Why did Tommy say that: 'I guess I have a lot of work ahead of me'? Why did he say that? Clark."

"Because he had a lot of things to do," said Clark.

Mrs. Hearn went on toward the end of the story. "'*Indeed you do,' said Mr. Peabody. 'Next time, don't be so quick to judge a person. And remember the power of your words.'* Remember when we did *Donovan's Word Jar*? One word made people feel happy or sad."

"Reese, pay attention, please, hon," Mrs. Spaulding said.

"*Then he handed Tommy the shiny red apple and made his way home.* He handed him the apple to show him what, Marc?"

"Um, forgivingness," said Marc.

"Forgiveness," said Mrs. Hearn. She pointed to the picture. "And there's the pillow sewn back together and feathers floating in the window."

"The pillow looks like a baseball mitt," said Eric.

"It does, the way they sewed it, it does kind of look like a baseball mitt. I want—*ope*, I'm waiting! We're going to look at this paper. I'm going to pass out this paper so we can look at the questions together. If you're paying attention this will be easy p—"

"EVERYBODY SIT UP STRAIGHT, EYES ON MRS. HEARN," said Mrs. Spaulding.

"—easy peasy. Right?"

"Reese, take one and pass it along," said Mrs. Spaulding. "Pass it along!"

"Come on, quick, quick, quick!" said Mrs. Hearn. "Let's go, let's go, let's go!" A worksheet rattled. "*Ope,* I don't want to hear the papers doing that."

"Pass it along," said Mrs. Spaulding. "Emerson. Who hasn't got one? WHO DOES NOT HAVE ONE? Anybody else? Anybody else? Cody, you've got an extra one. Give one to Mr. Baker."

"Thank you," I said to Cody.

Mrs. Hearn told the class to put their names on the worksheets, plus the date and the name of the book, and the author. "Who's the author?"

"Madonna," said the class in unison.

The first worksheet question they had to answer was *What connection can you make to this story?*

"This is part of the DRA—that's why we need to know this," said Mrs. Hearn. "What connection can you make to the story? Have you ever thought something that wasn't true? Did you see something and you didn't understand it? Or you thought you heard something, but it wasn't really what you heard?"

The class nodded.

"Yes. All of you have come to me complaining about something, or to Mrs. Spaulding, and we figured out that it wasn't quite what you thought it was."

To Cody, Mrs. Spaulding said, "Stop flipping that around."

The next question was, *What do you think the author is trying to tell us in this story?*

"Don't say it out loud," Mrs. Hearn said.

"Do we write it now?" asked Scarlett.

"NICE COMPLETE SENTENCES," said Mrs. Spaulding.

"No, when we finish this," Mrs. Hearn said. "Tell me one thing the author is trying to tell us, Patsy."

"Words are really strong?" said Patsy.

"Words are really strong," said Mrs. Hearn. "Rumors spread really fast?"

"Don't always believe what you hear," said Micah.

Then they were supposed to write what the most important thing was that happened in the story, and why.

Mrs. Hearn said, "Got it? Tell me why, and back it up. Give me some proof of why it's the important part of the story."

They also had to name the most important character—impossible question—and where the story took place.

"Then it says, *Do you like this story, yes or no?* And you're going to flip your lovely paper over, and you're going to tell me why you liked the story."

"Can we draw a picture?" asked Patsy.

"Did I say anything about drawing? Or did I only talk about writing?"

"WRITING," said Mrs. Spaulding.

"Writing," said Mrs. Hearn.

"Or why you didn't like the story," said Mrs. Spaulding. "Tell me if you would recommend this story to a friend."

"SO DOES EVERYBODY UNDERSTAND THOSE SENTENCES?" asked Mrs. Spaulding.

"Is everybody clear?" asked Mrs. Hearn. "Any—"

"Glenn, sit down, please," said Mrs. Spaulding.

"—questions? Eric, questions? Cody, questions? Antoinette, question?"

"Can we skip around?" Antoinette asked.

"You may answer in any order you want," said Mrs. Hearn, "as long as you answer every single question. Except for the last one, where it says, *Do you like this story, yes or no?* I want you to save that one for last. Okay? Sound like a deal?"

"BACK TO YOUR DESKS QUIETLY, GET YOUR PENCILS OUT," Mrs. Spaulding ordered. "Shhh. Donny, have a seat. Back at your desks, pencils out. Super-good handwriting. Come on, Donny, back to your desk. Guys, complete sentences. Name and date."

Mrs. Hearn said, "We'll put *Mr. Peabody's Apples* up on the board for you." She asked me to write the title and author on the board.

"Antoinette, get in your own space," said Mrs. Spaulding. "Get your legs in your space."

"What are you doing with that?" said Mrs. Hearn, to Eric, who was fiddling with his Beyblade. "Put it away!" She got irritable. "EVERYBODY

SHOULD AT LEAST HAVE THEIR NAME AND DATE ON THIS PAPER ALREADY! What are you doing?"

"LET'S GO, LET'S GO!" said Mrs. Spaulding.

"Let's go, let's go!" said Mrs. Hearn. "High-quality work!"

While the pencils moved in their little levered circles, Mrs. Spaulding and Mrs. Hearn conferred.

"Can you write *Happyville* on the board?" Paisley asked me. I wrote it.

Glenn asked Mrs. Hearn if he had to answer the first question.

Mrs. Hearn said, "Yes, everybody can make a connection to this story, in some way, shape, or form. You have teachers, people play sports, there are all kinds of connections you can make. If this was a DRA, you would have to make a connection to this story somehow. Have you forgiven someone for saying something to you? Stanley, get over in your space! Aubrey, get the name of the book and the author on there. Let's go!"

"What's your connection to the story?" prompted Mrs. Spaulding. "It could be something outside the school."

"Come on, Eric!" said Mrs. Hearn.

Skylar raised a hand. "Can I do a connection with baseball?"

"I just said that," said Mrs. Spaulding. "Make it a good connection, though. Make sure it makes sense with the story! Super-good handwriting. I have erasers if you need them."

"You've got to answer *this* in order to answer *this*," said Mrs. Hearn, tapping Reese's paper with her lacquered fingernail. "You've got to tell me what the most important thing is in the story, why was it important, and which character did it involve. I like how people are restating!" said Mrs. Hearn. "Make sure you're restating! 'The author is trying to tell us . . .'"

I cleared my throat in a low wolfish groan that only I could hear.

"Come on, restate the question!" said Mrs. Spaulding.

"Everybody should be different!" said Mrs. Hearn. "Everybody should have a different connection. Eric, pull your desk back so there's a space between you and Cody."

Cody asked how you spell *friend.*

"F-R-I . . . ?" said Mrs. Spaulding.

"E-N-D!" said the class in unison.

Mrs. Spaulding wanted to hear it again. "Come on, kids, HOW DO YOU SPELL *FRIEND*?"

"F-R-I—E-N-D!"

Mrs. Hearn wanted to hear it again. "How can you forget!" she said to Cody. "F-R-I—"

"E-N-D!" said the class.

"Put it to a Madonna tune, and rock it," said Mrs. Spaulding. "We've been spelling that since—"

"Let's see your best Madonna move, Mrs. Spaulding!" said Mrs. Hearn.

Antoinette, Paisley, and Talia began dancing and chanting, "F-R-I—E-N-D!"

Mrs. Hearn cut it short. "Okay, FIVE, FOUR, THREE."

Silence. "Nice," said Mrs. Spaulding. "Eyes on the page."

"Mrs. Spaulding," said Mrs. Hearn, "I'm going to take Cody for ten minutes so we can go over some things."

Cody made a throttled roaring sound.

Mrs. Hearn pointed at me. "*Judge.* Can you put the word *judge* on the board?" I wrote *judge* on the board. She and Cody disappeared.

I whisper-helped three kids spell *rumor*.

Mrs. Spaulding helped a kid spell *something*.

I helped Micah write *I feel bad for Mr. Peabody.* I helped Glenn spell *by*, as in "Don't judge people by," and *own*, as in "Mind your own."

"One time I stoled one of my brother's toys," Glenn confessed to me. "I shouldn't have do it, but I wanted it bad."

"I finished my paper," said Talia.

"You are a speed demon," I said.

"So what do I do?" she said.

"I guess you just have to twiddle your thumbs," I said. I showed her how to twiddle her thumbs. "You can pass about five minutes that way, but your thumbs will get tired. No, do anything you want. You're doing good."

"Can I draw?" she asked. Of course.

Mrs. Spaulding said, "I'll take your papers for Mrs. Hearn. If you're not done, you'll be getting them back. If not today, tomorrow, maybe at recess, or first thing in the morning. We're going to get ready for Book Buddies. You don't need to bring a book. I think she's got some kind of project she's going to have us do. So give me your papers, sit down, and Mr. Baker can start lining you up. SIT DOWN, STANLEY. Thirty seconds. Good job. Everybody better have something written down. Stanley, you're going to work on this tomorrow. Leave your scissors here. The first-graders will be doing the cutting. LEAVE YOUR SCISSORS HERE. I'm not going down the hall with a bunch of scissors."

"Do we bring a pencil?"

"Do we ever bring a pencil to Book Buddies? No. Voices off right now. Show me when you're ready! SHOW MR. BAKER WHEN YOU'RE READY. Books away. NO BOOKS. Glenn, are you ready? Emerson!"

Mrs. Spaulding picked the quietest line, and cued me to tell them to line up. "Okay, line up," I said. "Do you guys know the way to Mrs. Latimer's class?"

Yes.

"You know everything," I said.

Mrs. Spaulding said, "Super-quiet walking! I'm at the end. Nope, don't take anything. Shh! Voices off!"

In the hall, just outside the door to a classroom, I spotted Toby, the fifth-grader who told me he sucked at everything, sitting by himself at a gray table. "Hi, I know you," I said. "How's it been going?"

"Good," he said. He looked broken and hopeless—he had a worksheet in front of him that he couldn't do. I hurried to catch up with the class.

Cody joined the line, after his talking-to by Mrs. Hearn. "Cody, your shoe's untied," said Mrs. Spaulding. "When you get to class, please tie it. Let's catch up."

Mrs. Spaulding, twenty-two students, and I stuffed ourselves in Mrs. Latimer's crowded first-grade classroom. "THIRD-GRADERS, VOICES OFF," said Mrs. Spaulding.

"First-graders," said Mrs. Latimer, "if you can hear me, and see me, then I need you to turn your voices off. Third-graders need to know how they're going to help the first-graders. My first-graders are going to get a new math journal. The very first thing you need to do when you get your new math journal is third-graders are going to help the first-graders rip out activity sheet nine. FIRST-GRADERS! James!"

"Eyes on Mrs. Latimer," said Mrs. Spaulding.

"It has—"

"SHHHH!" said Mrs. Spaulding. "Scarlett!"

"—a little perforated line, where you have to gently rip it out. Make sure you're just getting activity sheet nine." She ripped out the sheet, making a farty sound. Loud laughter. "It makes a funny sound," she said. "And then with scissors, first-graders, with the help of the third-graders, need to cut on the dotted lines. Be very careful not to cut off the numbers, because those are important. You need to cut them all out. Then, on the back of the journals, my first-graders need to write their initials. Third-graders, you can help them."

"Kennedy!" said Mrs. Spaulding. "Chair down! Shh."

Mrs. Latimer said, "When they are all cut out—Katie, keep the table still, please—then you will end up with your fact triangles. And then you're going to help them with their math, if you wouldn't mind. The way you use fact triangles—"

"LISTEN!" said Mrs. Spaulding.

"—is you hold them in your hand, and you put your thumb over one of the numbers. So let's say you put your thumb over the top—the top is with the dot—so the answer is five. So you ask your first-grader, 'What is three plus two?' Without them seeing the answer, they figure out that it's five. Then you cover another corner. And then it will be five take away two, and they would need to give you the answer of three. Then you turn the triangle around and you cover another corner. So you're quizzing them on their facts. There's quite a few of them here. So cut out, first; initials on the back second; third thing you do is you start quizzing your first-grader on their facts. Okay? Make sense? Careful cutting on the edges, Kai!"

Mrs. Spaulding said, "Third-graders, you hear that? We've all done this, haven't we?"

Mrs. Latimer went over the fact triangles quiz a second time. Each number triangle was called a fact family.

"Don't let these first-graders fool you, they're pretty smart!" said Mrs. Latimer's ed tech, Mrs. Huntley, who had an even louder, lower voice than Mrs. Spaulding's.

"Listen up!" said Mrs. Spaulding. Mrs. Latimer read off the names of the paired children. I followed Cody and his first-grader, James, out into the hallway with several pairs of trianglers. James was wearing a snappy cowboy costume. "How much does it cost?" asked Cody.

"Thirty-five dollars," said James.

"So the trick with perforation—" I started to say.

Cody ripped out the activity page roughly, leaving some of it behind in the book.

James made a sad cry.

"You're fine," I said. "Cody avoided the triangles."

I showed another first-grader, Taylor, how to fold the page back and forth over the perforation so that it separated better. "Just get it started real easy," I said.

The kids were in a rush to finish cutting out all the triangles.

"How tall are you?" said Reese, from my class.

I told him.

"My brother's six foot one. He's seventeen."

Was he at Lasswell?

"He's homeschooled," said Reese. "He goes to something called Reveal. It's a Christian program. My uncle is like six foot eleven."

"Amazing," I said. James was scissoring like mad. "You cut a lot of triangles there, sir," I said. "Good cutting."

Paisley's first-grader, Rosa, said, "I'm already done."

Paisley quizzed her, holding her thumb over one number on a triangle: "What's six plus two?"

"Eight," said Rosa.

Paisley turned the triangle. "What's eight minus two?"

"Um—six."

Cody began to wander among the pairs of book buddies, saying, "What, what, what, what? What, what, what? What, what, what?"

Sitting on the floor was uncomfortable; I wanted to lie down and take a nap. I said, "Cody, you've got to hang with your book buddy. He needs your help. He's working. Look at him work—encourage him. You've got to actually sit down on the rug."

"I don't feel like sitting down," said Cody, "because my legs hurt."

While standing, Cody put his thumb over a number and quizzed James. "Three plus four," he said.

"Six," said James.

"Seven," said Cody.

I showed James what three plus four was on my fingers. He understood.

"Seven minus three," said Cody.

"Four," said James.

"Excellent, breakthrough," I said. "That's how it works." I made an enormous yawn. "Excuse me."

"I get sleepy almost every day," said James.

"It happens to me around this time in the afternoon," I said. "I get the woozies. What are you going to do when you get home?"

"I have something very difficult to do," said James. "I'm building something in Minecraft." His class had earned an extra recess by filling up their pom-pom jar, he said.

Paisley said, pointedly, "Yeah, and Cody, we haven't filled up our marble jar yet."

Mrs. Spaulding collected the scissors.

Cody said, "If we earn our jar bank, we're going to have thirty minutes of recess."

"That is almost unthinkable," I said. "How far are you? Halfway there? She'll start tossing marbles in toward the end."

It was time to grunt and get up slowly from the carpeting.

"FIRST-GRADERS, GET ALL YOUR TRIANGLES!" said Mrs. Latimer.

"THIRD-GRADERS, IN LINE," said Mrs. Spaulding. "Eric, five minutes if you don't get up!"

We processed back to room 4. Reese said, "Nine times nine is eighty-one."

"That's some serious math," I said. "I know kids in sixth grade who don't know that. Some people have a hard time with math."

"Some people never learn their times tables, literally," said Reese.

In the classroom, Mrs. Spaulding said, "Everybody in your seats. FIVE, FOUR, THREE, TWO." A few stragglers rushed to their chairs. "EVERYONE ON YOUR BOTTOMS. Listen to Mr. Baker."

I began handing out pizza party announcements for all to take home. The announcement said, "Dear Parents, We earned a PIZZA PARTY tomorrow, May 16th, for lunch!!!! Our class collected the most food for the food pantry!!!! Thank you so much! You will not need to send your child with a lunch tomorrow but definitely send in the normal snack. Sincerely, Mrs. Fellows." At the bottom of the page was a picture of a pizza with a smiley face on it made of discs of pepperoni.

"So, guys, how are you doing with multiplying by one digit?" I asked.

"Shhh!" Mrs. Spaulding said. "Voices."

Eric came up to the board to demonstrate how to multiply 56 x 4. "Well, six times four is twenty-four," he said, "so I do the four down there and carry the two up there."

I asked him to stand a little to the side so people could see.

"Skylar!" said Mrs. Spaulding in the back, scanning the class for daydreamers.

"And then four times five is twenty," said Eric. "Plus that two. So it's twenty-two, and there's your answer: two hundred twenty-four."

We applauded. He was a whiz.

Patsy came up and did 56 x 8. "First you multiply six times eight, which equals forty-eight," she said. "You put the eight down, and you put the four up. And then you do eight times five, which equals forty, plus four, so it would be forty-four. And that's your answer, four hundred forty-eight."

"Nice job," said Mrs. Spaulding, as we clapped for Patsy. We did a few more problems. Some kids counted expertly on their fingers; most knew how to get the answer.

Then Aubrey passed out blue correcting pens and we went over the morning subtraction problems, one by one, painfully slowly.

"Everybody, eyes on the board!" said Mrs. Spaulding. "Clark!"

The class was getting tired of arithmetic and so was I. "Wow, there are a lot of numbers in life," I said.

"Ugh!" said Wilson

"Wilson!" said Mrs. Spaulding.

Subtraction problem 4 was $8,261 - 4,950 = $ _____. Kennedy did it at the board. "One take away zero would be one," she said. "And then six take away five would be one. And then you can't take nine from two, so you have to cross the eight out and put a seven, and then twelve take away nine would be three. And then seven take away four would be three." Phew.

As number fatigue grew, the class began to confuse multiplication with subtraction: one minus one became one, not zero.

"I'm going to put some names on the board if the voices don't stop!" said Mrs. Spaulding.

After math, said the sub plans, we were supposed to play Bingo, but the Bingo boards were not in evidence, and Reese wanted to present his share, a bird's nest. He walked around the class letting people touch it. "I think it's from a blue jay," he said. "It was on the last step of my porch. I saw it and I got my mom. She said my brother had found it and he put it on the railing, but it must have blew off. I was like, 'Hey, maybe I could share it tomorrow!' So here I am, sharing it. We have another one on the window by our upstairs bathroom. It's huge."

"Shh, hey, guys, be respectful!" said Mrs. Spaulding.

Skylar asked why it had a leaf hanging from the bottom.

"Because the bird made it that way," he said. "I can't exactly answer that."

Paisley asked why there was a bit of ribbon inside the nest.

"Because the bird put it in there," Nathan said.

"It must have liked it," said Paisley.

Reese said, "I just noticed that there's some kind of yellow-white hair around the top."

"Maybe it's your mom's hair," said Roberta.

"Maybe it's yours," said Reese.

Clark asked how he knew it was a blue jay's nest.

"I'm guessing," said Reese, "because the other nest outside our bathroom is a blue jay's, and it has a piece of that ribbon, too."

"Well done, good sharing," I said. "You know what it makes me think about, guys? If you were a bird, and your job was to make a secure home for your eggs, how would you do it?"

Paisley said, "I would get some straw, I would get some wood, I would get some paper, I would get everything I could take."

Reese said, "Paisley, you'd be a *bird*."

I said, "So once you gathered—"

"LISTEN, PLEASE. MR. BAKER'S TALKING!" said Mrs. Spaulding. "SIT DOWN, STANLEY, OR IT'S A CHECK MARK."

I drew a branch. "So once you gathered that stuff, how would you build the nest? Remember, birds are miraculous. They can do things with their arms, but their arms are wings. So they can't hold on to anything with hands. They have to do everything with their beaks. What's up, Stanley? So here's the bough. First you've got to pick a good spot, that's up far enough out of the way of cats, and raccoons. Then, once you've picked the right spot, you have to be an architect."

"COULD YOU PLEASE BE RESPECTFUL TO MR. BAKER?" said Mrs. Spaulding. "He's done a wonderful job today. Turn around, watch him!"

"Some birds use mud as glue," I said. "But then they do the thing you can see in this nest, which knocks me out. They make it soft and round and perfectly safe for the eggs, so the eggs won't get hurt, and they won't fall out. Have you ever seen a bird trying to build a nest?"

"Shh!" said Mrs. Spaulding. "He's talking, Reese!"

I said, "Every single piece of that nest had to be flown one at a time in the bird's beak. It's like making cotton candy."

"It's really soft," said Reese, stroking the inside of the nest.

"The bird is making something really soft that's the shape of an egg, even before the eggs are born," I said. "How do they learn how to do that? It's instinct."

"Mother Nature," said Talia.

"Mother Nature!" I said.

Reese was still feeling the inside of the nest. "It might actually be dog hair," he said.

I nodded. "We have a corgi," I said. "He sheds all over the yard, and the birds make nests of his dog hair."

Scarlett said, "I have a bush right next to my window, and in the middle we have two robins nesting in it. And three eggs. We watched it, and it took them six weeks to get that nest done."

"Six weeks!" I said. "Think how hard that is."

"I know how they made it," said Scarlett. "Can I go out to the board?"

"Please," I said.

"We have about five minutes before we start packing up," Mrs. Spaulding warned.

Scarlett started drawing how the birds in her yard built their nest. "They put three or four sticks. And then—my dog sheds like crazy. It's a German shepherd. And then they take grass and slip it in through the trees. And they start curving it, and once they've done curving it, and making it like a bowl, they go out in my back yard and get the moss that's on the ground, and they lay it in here, for the babies, and they nest in there."

A hand from Paisley. "Next door at my house, I looked in a bush and I saw a bird's nest. I actually saw a bird in it but I didn't want to disturb it, so I just backed out."

"That's a really good thing to do," I said. "These birds are really struggling to make their home, and be in private, and sometimes you want to just leave them alone, right?"

"Can I show how they built it?" asked Paisley.

"If you can in about twelve seconds," I said, "because we're going to start packing, stacking, racking, and flacking."

"So this is the bush that the bird—" said Paisley.

"YOU'VE GOT ABOUT THIRTY SECONDS, PAISLEY," Mrs. Spaulding said. "*Ope*, Skylar, talking!"

"And I'm right here," said Paisley, drawing herself on the board, "and I backed up. And once an egg fell on the ground and it almost breaked, but I picked it back up, and brought it to the mom."

"The saver of birds," I said. "All right, guys, thank you for being a really fun class to be with. Now, pack and stack."

"DESKS CLEANED OFF," Mrs. Spaulding said. "WE'VE GOT SEVEN MINUTES."

"And if anybody has 'Stink Blob to the Rescue,' hand it in," I said.

"Shhh! Mr. Baker is speaking!"

"Thank you," I said. "I'm just gathering stray copies."

Mrs. Spaulding went to full volume. "QUIET, KIDS, GO GET YOUR BOOK BAGS, PLEASE. PACK AND STACK. GUYS! MAKES SURE YOU'VE GOT THOSE YELLOW PAPERS IN YOUR BAGS. SUPER IMPORTANT."

Reese erased the spelling words from the board.

"Oh, stop it, Stanley," said Mrs. Spaulding.

Stanley slumped angrily in his seat. Mrs. Spaulding had given him a check mark. "I hate this school," he said to me.

"I'm sorry," I said.

"I've been here for *four years*," he said bitterly.

Reese wrote, "Mr Baker is the best," on the board.

"Aw, thanks, man," I said. "It was fun being in your class."

"CLASS, WE HAVE A SPELLING TEST TOMORROW," said Mrs. Spaulding.

"Thank you for being our sub," said Talia and Paisley.

"Thank you for being good students!"

I wanted them not to get *rode* wrong on the spelling test, so I wrote, "I RODE my bike on the ROAD."

"You should probably write 'on the side of the road,'" said Talia, with a serious expression.

"You're right."

Talia used an orange marker to put a caret in the sentence where the words should go, and I wrote "the side of."

"BACK AT YOUR DESKS," said Mrs. Spaulding, holding up her hand. "FIVE, FOUR. THREE. AT YOUR DESKS, EVERYBODY."

"Do we have any homework?" Kennedy asked.

"Just look at the stars and sleep," I said. "I don't think with a sub you should have to do homework. Do you?"

"No," said Kennedy. "So should I say to my mom the sub said no homework?"

"Yes. Tell her the sub said you did such good work today you can take the night off."

"I DON'T WANT TO SEE ANY YELLOW PAPERS OUT," said Mrs. Spaulding.

Kennedy wrote out a note in her day planner for me to sign: "Sub said I did so good so I have no homework." I wrote "It's true," and signed it.

The buzzer buzzed.

"DON'T FORGET SPELLING WORDS, AND LET'S SAY THANK YOU TO MR. BAKER!"

"THANK YOU," the class said in unison.

"Thank you all, thank you very, very much!" I waved.

"Mr. Baker, I have bus duty," said Mrs. Spaulding.

"Can I sit in the hallway?" said Stanley.

"Just hang out in here and be happy," I said.

"I don't want to hang out in here," he said.

"I'VE GOT MY EYES ON YOU GUYS, I KNOW YOU CAN BE GOOD!" said Mrs. Spaulding, before she ducked out.

"Bye, Mrs. Spaulding!" said Antoinette.

The second buzzer buzzed, but it wasn't quite time to go: we had to wait for third-graders to be called on the PA system. A soccer ball came out from somewhere and scooted around under the desks.

"Mr. Baker," said Reese, "do you want to see something that I drew?" He showed me a picture of a monster.

"Nice shading," I said. "Fire-breathing!" Reese's mother came to the door to pick him up. Great kid, great bird's nest, I said to her. When it was time, I said, "LINE IT UP AND BE QUIET! Lead the way."

Backpacks bouncing, they threaded their way through the hallways and out the front door, and one by one they leapt onto the high first steps of their buses. While I was back in the classroom writing a note for Mrs. Fellows about what a privilege it was to be in her class, Mrs. Spaulding came by. "Everybody's cool?" she said.

"Everybody's cool," I said. "Thanks for your help."

"The kids really enjoyed your sharing," she said. "They work hard. They're good kids."

"They're good kids," I said. "Thanks, take care."

I picked some stray pencils up off the floor, and stacked up the stink blob worksheets and the math papers. Easy peasy. I heard the janitor emptying trash in the hallway.

Day Twenty, finished and done.

KEEP YOUR DEAR TEACHER HAPPY

On Friday, Beth asked me to teach kindergarten at Lasswell Elementary School. I didn't want to. I'd been substituting all week, and I was tired, and I thought that kindergarten would be even harder than gym. The only vivid memories I had of my own kindergarten experience were that we'd done fingerpainting, which was fun, and that I'd once gone number two hugely in my pants during nap time: the teacher had handed me extra toilet paper under the door of the stall. "I'm not at all sure I'd be good at it," I said, "but I'll do it if you really need me to."

"Frankly I'm running out of people to call," she said. "You'll like them, they're cute."

The air was soft and the ferns were visibly unfurling on the way to Lasswell. I found the little flat building pocketed among the pines. "Are you ready for this challenge?" said the school secretary, signing me in.

"Yes, I am," I said.

"Awesome!" She gave me the keys to the room and a badge. "It's Mrs. Price's room," she said. "Room twenty-seven."

Mrs. Price's room was stylish and relatively uncluttered: six primary-colored tabletops served as two-person desks, and a comfortable-looking gliding rocker sat in the corner. On the whiteboard was a five-tiered voice-level chart: *0* was no talking, *1* was a whisper, *2* was table talk, *3* was a strong speaker, and *4* was outside. The class rules were framed in a border of rainbows and smiling cartoon clouds:

> Rule #1—Follow directions quickly!
> Rule #2—Raise your hand for permission to speak!
> Rule #3—Be a bucket filler!
> Rule #4—Make smart choices!
> Rule #5—Keep your dear teacher happy!

A framed plaque on a shelf said, "It takes a big Heart to help shape LITTLE minds."

Westin, who had a big, wobbly, laughing head, was the first kindergartner I met. "My other friends are coming in," he said.

Ava, with short brown hair and a collared white shirt, said, "You want to know what I saw? I saw a white frog at the bus stop, and in the bus I saw two baby flies. My bus driver kissed them. Not kissed them, killed them. He put them in a paper towel and threw them away."

"I've got a Chihuahua named Boa," said Madeline.

I asked if they'd known that Mrs. Price wouldn't be in today.

"I saw Mrs. Price at my friend's bus stop, and she was sick," said Madeline. She had a stuffed bird named Princess. "She was being bad in daycare, so I put her in time-out."

Westin wanted me to know about the system of rewards and punishments, which involved Tallies and Mighty Oh Nos. If the class got seven Mighty Oh Nos, then the teacher erased the row of tallies. "Mighty Oh Nos are because we do a bad job," he said. I told him I probably wouldn't be keeping track of Oh Nos or Oh Yeses that day. Hazel was the class star of the day, Westin said.

Just then Hazel walked in crying. She was wearing a shirt with big blue flowers on it.

"She misses her mom," said Madeline.

"Have a seat right here and tell me about it," I said to Hazel. "What's your mom like?"

Through shuddering sobs, Hazel said that her mom was nice and that she missed her a lot.

I asked her if her mom went off to work.

"She works at home," Hazel said. "She makes blankets."

"Are they soft blankets?" I asked.

She nodded. "They're baby blankets," she said.

"It's a great thing that you love your mom and she loves you," I said. "It's about the most important thing in the world."

Hazel smeared her tears and sniffed.

I told a loud kid named Garrett, in a Myrtle Beach T-shirt, to get some work out and do his thing.

"Do these kids know the SOPs?" I asked Hazel.

She shook her head.

"Are they supposed to be working at their desks?" I asked.

Hazel nodded.

"Listen," I said to her. "You're very brave and you're doing really good, and I'm going to help you all I can, okay?" She nodded. I thought a change of subject might be a good idea, and I asked her if she had any pets.

"Three dogs and two fish," she said. She said she didn't have to walk the dogs. "We let them outside to go to the bathroom." I asked her who in the class was her friend.

"Everyone," she said.

"That's very generous," I said.

She got out her morning work, Word Rings. Word Rings were done in pairs. One person held the Word Ring and played the teacher, while the other person had to read the words, which were written in marker on laminated colored paper.

"You know what I like about this classroom?" I said. "Everything is neat and organized. Is Mrs. Price nice?"

"She's *really* nice," Hazel said.

"Whoa, you're really tall," said Garrett, who was writing on someone's whiteboard.

I asked him to figure out what he was going to do at his desk.

"We don't have desks, we have tables," Garrett said.

"Then will you figure out what you're going to do at your table and/or desk?"

"Garrett gets into lots of trouble," said January. "Also Westin. He's been hurting people."

Westin was flinging around a prism-shaped eraser.

"Hi, Westin," I said. "What are you up to?"

"Nothing."

"Good. Let me have the eraser." I told him to pick a morning work.

A loud long bell rang, and I wrote my name on the board.

"Mr. Black?" said Garrett. "Mr. Blacker?"

"Are you kind of a baker?" asked Abby.

I said that maybe a long time ago my grandfather's grandfather's grandfather baked bread, but that I didn't much. "My wife bakes bread," I said. There was a sudden coruscation of sonic energy centered on Garrett and Westin.

"SHHHHH! MY NAME IS MR. BAKER, and I can tell you're a really good bunch of kids, and you're going to be absolutely great in this class. And one thing—"

Garrett started talking.

"SHH! One thing you're going to do is help me know what the next step is all day long, because Mrs. Price has arranged this class so that everything works really well—right?"

"Yeah," said Noah.

"So in order for the class to work today, you're going to have to do a little teaching of me about what the next step is."

A four-note bell came on the PA system. We listened quietly to the faint announcements coming from two first-graders. "The weather today will be partly sunny, with highs around seventy," said a boy. Lunch was pizza bagels or cheeseburger, green beans, applesauce, and milk. A secretary announced two birthdays. And then we lustily pledged allegiance to the flag of the United States of America.

I said, "When there's a substitute, the temptation is for the noise to get too loud. Have you had substitutes before?"

Yes!

"What happens when a substitute comes?"

"We listen!" said Madeline.

"Nice! If we're having a discussion, it's better if one person talks at a time."

"There's another word for it," said Ava. *"Polite."*

"Polite is a good word. I've already met almost all of you, and you seem like really polite kids. That's a nice thing to see. Makes me proud to be a citizen of the State of Maine."

I pulled out the attendance sheet. Angel, uncertain and plump-fingered, found her name on it.

"Mr. Baker?" said Madeline. "My body is feeling out of shape."

I called out names and signed the sheet. "All right, guys, gather around," I said. "We're going to be going to an art exhibit. So what do we do when we go to an art exhibit?"

To my startlement, the class began reciting the class rules in unison. "FOLLOW DIRECTIONS QUICKLY, RAISE YOUR HAND FOR PERMISSION TO SPEAK, BE A BUCKET FILLER, MAKE SMART CHOICES, AND KEEP YOUR DEAR TEACHER HAPPY."

"And I am happy," I said.

"Whoo-hoo!" said Abby.

"My dad is bald," said Angel.

"It's what happens sometimes to men," I said. "The hair just comes off their head."

Noah wanted to know what a pizza bagel was. I said that it was a little round bagel, circular, with a hole in the middle, and it had pizza topping on it. "It's quite delicious," I said.

"Mm, I want to have it," said Noah.

January said, "Mr. Baker, smile! Click!"

"Okay, line up, line up, line up," I said.

"Westin was a superstar yesterday, so today he has to go in the back," said Abby.

I said, "Guys, dear children, in line please, and quiet. And remember, we're going to go and see art that's done by some of the older kids, so we're going to be very respectful, and ask them questions about how they did stuff. Right? It might be a little loud in the cafeteria, but the key is not to add to the noise."

We turned several corners and plunged through the wall of sound into the cafeteria, which was lined with large drawings, in front of which children stood. A second-grade teacher said, "It's kind of like a museum. They're just going to walk around and visit the animals, and the rangers will have information for them."

We made a tour of the walls and saw two red squirrels, a fisher cat, a mountain lion, a bobcat, another bobcat with crazy eyes, a gray fox, and a black bear. Each drawing was mounted on a large sheet of red or brown construction paper, with a page of facts next to it. We came to an opossum, and a three-foot-high exuberantly crayoned moose. We saw beavers, raccoons, and an ermine. "Owls and martens eat ermines," said the fact sheet. "They are ferocious hunters." There was a skunk, another red fox, two gray squirrels, a lynx with very good eyesight, a porcupine with thirty thousand quills, a white-tailed deer, and a woodchuck. "A woodchuck is also called a whistlepig," explained a second-grader. "They use a high-pitched whistle to warn members of their colony." I didn't know that. I loved these crazy animal-happy kids.

We paused to get our breath when we were out of the cafeteria. Ava said, "I can't believe I actually saw my sister!"

"I saw my sister, too!" said Madeline.

"I saw my daycare teacher!" said Jaydon.

"One voice at a time," I said. "I want to tell you that you were very good. We stopped at each person's art. We didn't hurt anybody's feelings, and we listened to what they had to say. They really worked hard. That huge white-tailed deer, that enormous moose! You did a great job of admiring the work that they did, so thank you."

Ava said, "My sister was the last one, and I hugged her, and she hugged me back and picked me up, and she was the white-tailed deer."

Madeline said, "I saw my sister, and she got tackled by a little midget. And the little midget was me. She's nine and I'm six."

Westin said, "I saw my friend Jason from my old school. He was gone and I never saw him again. And now I saw him."

During snack and book-reading time, Noah ate Yum Yums, January ate carrot sticks, and Garrett stood on one foot. A boy named Rick arrived late. I asked how many wanted pizza bagels. "I know what a bagel is, and I know what a pizza is, but I just don't know what they look like together," said Jaydon.

I said, "Imagine you had magical powers, and there was a pizza over here, and a little bagel over there, and you could go shwish, and put them together. You'd get a little round bite-sized bagel with pizza sauce and cheese deliciously sprinkled on top. It's hot. It's good."

"Oh!"

Four people wanted pizza bagels, two wanted cheeseburgers, and three wanted SunButter and jelly. The rest had home lunch.

"I have a whole lot of dandelions and we're planting a whole bunch of things in my garden," said January. "Orange and pink flowers. I got a pretty purple one, and it's really pretty. It's going to be a bush."

I opened a container of applesauce for Abby and said, "I talked to a guy last night who had planted one thousand five hundred strawberry plants."

"Whoo," said Abby.

"He's a strawberry farmer," I said. "He said they have a special machine to put the strawberry plants in the soil."

"I have a blueberry plant," said Hazel.

"I'm going to bring a robot to school," said Jaydon. "I'm going to ask it to make flowers and strawberries everywhere."

Angel showed me a book of minerals that she'd gotten at the book fair.

The book had plastic pouches inside that held several minerals, including a speckled wishing rock of Dalmatian jasper. Angel held it up for the class, but nobody was looking.

"Time out for a second," I said. "Angel's got an amazing book. Instead of being filled with pages, it's filled with . . ."

"Rocks," said Angel. She held out her book so that people could see.

"These rocks are from all parts of the world," I said. "These rocks, when you pull them out of the ground, they don't look good. They look kind of jagged. Then they put them in a special machine, which is called a tumbler. It's like a giant dryer, and it goes around and around, with all the other rocks, and all the rocks tumble and tumble, and they start to get smoother and smoother, and shinier and shinier, until finally they're smooth and shiny like this one here, the crystal quartz."

I asked the class if they knew where rocks came from. Many hands went up.

From the ground! From the dirt! From the mountain!

"How would they get down in the ground and in the dirt and in the mountain?" I asked.

Abby said, "There's little ant holes, and they put the rocks in the holes."

Angel said, "I'm hoping a moon rock can fall from the moon, or I can go up there, with my family one time, and try to get a moon rock."

Madeline raised her hand and said that rocks come from grass. She'd seem them in the grass at her daycare.

"That's true," I said. "You think, How could a rock come from grass? Millions of years ago, when dinosaurs walked the earth, and they had big tall fields of grass, and no people were around, well, the grass would die in a marsh, and maybe the water would come. The grass would start to rot and go bad, and squish down, and then more grass would grow on top of that, and that would squish down. After a while you've got maybe two hundred feet of old rotting roots and grass, and it's getting very dark and squishy and marshy. All the water goes out, and it gets harder and harder. More dirt on top of that, squishing down really hard, years and years go by. Finally you have something that's so hard that it's called rock. It's called sedimentary rock."

"Rocks are actually kind of like a toy," said Abby. "Because you can use them for stuff. Like hopscotch."

Hazel said, "There's rocks at the beach and there's lightning at the beach that will hit rocks and break them down into little pieces at the beach."

"Okay, Hazel had a good idea," I said. "Another way that rocks can form. Some rocks are formed because they're melted. They could be melted down by lightning, or they could be melted down when they get so deep in the earth that there's so much pressure that they form a volcano. A volcano is when the pressure of the earth presses so hard on the rock that it melts and turns red-hot, and it forces itself up the cracks of the earth, and then squirts out the top of a mountain. That's lava, right?"

"And lava is so hot you can't even touch it," said Hartley, who was wearing a red-striped polo shirt and had a smart-kid's lisp.

Angel wanted to show off her book some more. "Do you guys want to have a closer look down on the carpet?"

Hazel said, "Sometimes a volcano can stop erupting, and it never goes ever again. It gets yucky and old, and it breaks down and becomes rocks again."

"Did everyone get a chance to see my rocks?" Angel asked.

Hartley said, "Mr. Baker, before even it forms into a volcano, it leaves a bigger piece of a rock with all these crystal rocks on top. It's like a pie, kind of. There's little rocks left on top."

January said, "Mr. Baker, can I share my stuffed animals?" Maybe after recess, I said, because it was book time now.

Abby said, "Excuse me? I got an A in gymnastics."

Madeline said, "Mr. Baker, did you know I found a green crystal? A green one. It was all green. It was a square."

"That's beautiful," I said. "Did you look really close inside and see the secret world of the inside of the rock?"

"I saw a little bit of white," said Madeline. "And little moving stuff. I think I could find another crystal and maybe my mom could let me bring it in. And one of my cat teeth looks like a crystal." She pointed to her incisor, which had silver on it. "This one, that had the surgery in it. It's silver because I didn't brush my teeth good. They're going to pull it out. I'm sure the tooth fairy will give me extra money. Maybe a dollar."

I asked her what book she was going to look at for the next five minutes.

"I don't really know," said Madeline. "I'm going to look at my library."

"Did you guys want to go over there with my book?" said Angel. "I'm trusting you."

Westin was unhappy because Angel wasn't letting him touch the rocks. Look but don't touch, she'd said.

"If you see something shiny and it's yellow, that isn't gold, right?" said Hartley.

"Westin, why don't you find a book," I said. "Find a *Hop on Pop* or something."

Madeline put on her glasses, which had cranberry-red rims. "I only need them for reading, and we're reading right now. I can only see far words. I'm farsighted. My sister's nearsighted. She can't see anything that good."

I ate a chunk of coffee chocolate. "It helps me wake up, boyoing!"

"Are you sleepy?" asked Abby.

"I'm not yet sleepy, but I don't want to become sleepy."

"Does your wife kick snore?" asked Abby. "I heard a thing about kick snore."

"You have a lot of stuff we can know," said January. "Remember you said about the volcano and the rocks? You are amazing."

"You're amazing!" I said.

"I know how to make oak trees," January said. "You need a nut, which is a acorn. Then you plant it in the ground, then you water it, and then it turns into a beautiful tree."

Madeline brought a book over to me.

"Can you read this page?" she asked. The book was called *Zendaya*, and it was a biography of a teen singer, Zendaya Coleman, from a Disney TV show called *Shake It Up*. "*In addition to* Shake It Up, *Zendaya also got to work on other cool projects. She sang on the three* Shake It Up *albums, and shot videos for several of the songs.*"

"Wow, that's a lot," said Madeline. "I know how to shake it up. You like shake it and shake it and shake it. The song tells you what to do to shake it up. You have to shake it up over here, shake it up over there."

I got her to sound out *Shake It Up*. "See that? *Shake It Up*. You read it."

At 10:10 it was time to get ready for recess. "If you need to use the bathroom, now's your chance."

"Angel! Hazel! You don't need to use your jackets, because it's warm," said Abby.

They lined up.

"I'm on recess duty," I said. "GUYS, shh. I'm on recess duty. I want happy playing. I don't want any grabbing. I like happy people who do not bump into each other, but have a good time playing. Yes, there's a question."

"Hi!" said Madeline.

"Hello," I said. "So are we on our way?"

Yes.

Hazel led us out the big doors and everyone scattered. A minute later, Ava ran back. "Mr. Baker, I saw a white little baby butterfly!"

"I watch scary movies," said Abby. "Yesterday I found a baby inchworm."

"Hi, Mr. Baker," said Hartley, from the top of the slide.

Percy ran up, the boy who wore the special vest in Mrs. Thurston's second-grade class. "I know you," he said. "You were an aid when Mrs. Spahn was out."

A kid toppled off the tires and hit his head. "I was trying to walk across that thing and something banged," he said.

"Take a moment to sit and make sure it's okay," I said. I brushed off the sand from his eyebrow. "Sorry that happened."

I met two staffers, Ms. Solano and Mr. Frank, who gave me an emergency walkie-talkie. I gave it a puzzled look and spoke into it: "Roger."

"Just hold on to it," said Ms. Solano. "I don't know how to use it, either."

"You press the button?" I said.

"If you need to," Ms. Solano said, "but you never need to, so it's okay."

Abby and Madeline ran up. "Mr. Baker, they said they finished their ABCs and I just got on." The rule was, they explained, that when there was a line at the swing, the people who were waiting got a turn after they'd sung the whole ABC song. But people were rushing. I stood and listened to Abby sing, "Now I know my ABCs, next time won't you sing with me."

The boy politely got off the swing and let Abby get on.

Another kid ran up to say that Adam had gotten hit by a basketball in the middle of his face and the big kids didn't even care. Adam was lying on the dirt, uninjured but unhappy.

I went over to the older kids. "Dudes, time out for a sec. If a kid gets hit by a ball, and it hurts him or he's sad, you want to take a moment to say, Are you okay?, and make him feel a little better. Got that?"

"Yeah, sure," said the second-grader. "Over here!" The basketball game resumed.

Garrett asked me if he could take off his sweatshirt. "Yes, but don't forget where you put it," I said.

There was another boy down on the grass. "He's just playing dead," said his friend. "It's just like *Over the Hedge*. 'We die to live, we live to die!'"

Angel had found three new rocks to add to her collection. "We should call that the space rock," she said, showing me a gray, angular fragment.

The bell rang. "Back up, please," said an ed tech at the door. "QUIET, STRAIGHT LINES." My class lined up quietly, but the ed tech picked another line to go in first: "Mrs. Harmon's class, good job, you may go in," she said. We were next. "Face forward, please," said the ed tech. She spotted Angel studying her book of gems. "No reading while walking, not safe!" she said.

Angel was happy, though. Her gem book had been a hit in class and on the playground. "A lot of people really like this book," she said.

"Angel, can I see your rocks again?" asked Abby.

Hazel had a mosquito bite. Westin told me that he and Garrett had chased a girl. "She was in second grade!" he said.

"You never know what's going to happen on the playground," I said.

"A lot of people like my book," said Angel, dancing—but there was a price. Ava, whom Angel wanted to be friends with, was tired of hearing about Angel's gems, and she moved to a table across the room. "Ava, come back," called Angel.

"Have a discussion about the seasons and the senses," Mrs. Price wrote in her sub plans. So we did. Winter seemed to be mostly about sledding wipeouts and hot cocoa, spring was about rain and butterflies. I wrote "grow" on the board, and "spinach," and "leaf," and then I handed Hazel a stack of worksheet packets to pass out. Garrett handed out the pencils. A reading specialist named Mrs. Willett arrived to take three children off to a remedial something-or-other. Before she left, she said, in her prison-guard baby talk, "if you are ready to do your paperwork, I need your pencils down, and both hands over your head. Now, who is ready? Caleb's ready. Stretch your hands up high. I only see a couple people ready. I don't see Hannah. Thank you." She left with Garrett, Noah, and Hazel in tow.

"All right," I said. "Once you are lucky enough to get a pencil—and that is a lucky thing to have, believe me—you get to write your name on that first page." The worksheet was titled "In the Spring." Page 2 said, *I can see* _____. Page 3 said, *I can hear* _____. Page 4 said, *I can smell* _____. And page 5 said, *I can feel* _____. There were big blank boxes in which the kids were supposed to draw pictures of the words they'd filled in. "Can you smell stuff in spring?" I said. "Not if you have a clothespin on your nose."

"No!"

"No, but you can if you don't, and most of us don't have clothespins on our noses, so we can smell things. Some of it's good, some of it's not so good. Does anyone have a dog? I love the smell of dogs' paws."

"Me, too," said January.

"Ew," said Angel.

"What are the lines for?" asked Westin.

"That's where you can write something, like 'I can see little baby birds in the nest.' Or, 'I can see cheese melting on the hot stove.' Or whatever you can see in springtime."

"I'm going to draw a bumblebee," said Westin.

"What do we draw on the cover?" asked Angel.

"Close your eyes and think, what is a picture of spring in your mind? It could be a puddle. Or when the grass finally turns green, and you lie on your back looking up at the clouds."

Ten seconds later Westin said, "Yay, I'm done with my first page: bumblebee."

"Can you help me spell a bird?" said Madeline.

I wrote *bird* on the board.

"I don't know how to spell," said Westin.

"Well, spelling is something that you gradually learn over a long time," I said.

Abby drew several beautiful trees.

"How do you spell *bee*?" asked Westin.

"Guys, you don't ask how to spell," said Abby.

That surprised me. "You don't? Why not?"

"Because that's what Mrs. Price says," said Abby.

"Well, I don't think it's a bad thing to ask," I said.

"How do you spell *peep*?" asked Westin.

"*Peep* is a wonderful word," I said.

"P-E-E-P," said Ava.

"Ooh, you are good," I said. I wrote the word on the board.

Jaydon wrote that he could see *C ∩C* and hear *S C E R N S*. He'd drawn a brown circle in the middle of the paper. I asked him what the first word was.

"Well, if you're inside, and your mom baked cookies, you could see cookies."

"Okay, great. And I can hear . . . ?"

"Screams, sometimes?" Jaydon had drawn a scream cartoon coming out of a mouth.

"Ava just don't want to do anything," said Angel.

"Don't worry about Ava," I said. "You worry about yourself. Each of you is in a rocket ship going to the moon of spring."

After I'd written *bumblebee* on the board, I went over to Ava. Her "In the Spring" booklet was blank. "Did you not want to do it?" I said. "What's the deal? I don't get it. I'm puzzled."

"She never does her work," said Angel. "Ever."

Ava began shaking her head back and forth.

"You're smart," I said, "you could blaze through it."

More head shaking from Ava.

I asked her if she liked running fast.

Head shake.

Running slow?

Head shake.

Walking fast?

Head shake.

"Is this something that doesn't interest you?"

She nodded.

"She just doesn't want to do it," said Angel. "She's always like that."

"Well," I said. "I guess you'd just prefer not to." Ava nodded.

Ava was obviously observant, an enthusiast of spring: she'd seen the white frog and the two baby flies killed by the bus driver. And she was a better reader and speller than the others. I told her she could get a book to read, but she didn't want to do that, either. Instead, she got out her poetry notebook. Poor thing: she was already fed up with being asked to do inane worksheets and she was only in kindergarten. Twelve more years to go.

I can smell my dog, wrote Abby. *I can feel my mom.*

I can see the sun, wrote Angel. *I can hear birds. I can smell flowers. I can feel the table.*

I can hear wind, wrote Rick. *I can smell grass. I can feel air.*

"Beautiful," I said. "Because when you move your hand, you feel air."

Madeline had drawn a wild strawberry plant. *I can smell pizza,* she wrote. *I can feel sun.* She said, "Cause when I put my hand up, it gets really hot."

I wrote *pizza* on the chalkboard.

"Now what can I do?" said Madeline.

"You can look in your poetry book," I said.

"Poetry *journal,*" corrected Madeline.

I let everyone work for a while. "WE'RE GOING TO BE MAKING A LITTLE TRANSITION PRETTY SOON," I announced.

"What's a condition?" asked Madeline.

"A transition is when you move from one thing, and you make a transition to another thing. Mrs. Willett is going to come in here at eleven thirty-five, so in about one minute."

"Who's Miss Willett?" said Jaydon.

"She is a . . ." I honestly didn't know what she was, officially.

"Writing teacher!" said Abby.

"She's a writing teacher," I said. "So what Mrs. Price wants you to do is do a little stretch, use the bathroom, do whatever you need to do to get your ya-yas out before Mrs. Willett comes, so you can be attentive to her."

Hazel stood and tipped from side to side. Hartley hopped around. Westin went berserk.

"Westin, you're getting a little too wild there, man," I said.

Angel handed Ava the book of polished rocks to look at on her own. "I made Ava happy!" she said. "I made Ava happy!"

"I love to see you smile," I said to Ava.

Mrs. Willett blew in, book in hand, Garrett, Noah, and Hazel following behind. "We'll do a mini-lesson," she said, "and then I'll send them off to their seats for writer's workshop. We're working on how-to books."

"Can we still finish this?" Hartley asked me.

"Just leave it right there," I said, "freeze it in time, and gather around to listen to Mrs. Willett."

"OKAY!" contraltoed Mrs. Willett, to the assembled multitude. She was an extremely sure-of-herself woman with spike heels and a silk scarf. "January's ready. I know you're ready for writer's workshop when you're sitting, crisscross applesauce! Garrett's going to come up here, I need to see him for a second." She sat him down at her feet. "Westin, what are you waiting for? Just sit right down, because I want to get started with the mini-lesson! Westin!"

I told Westin to cool it and asked Mrs. Willett if she wanted me to go or stay.

"You can stay and kind of listen in," she said, "and the two of us, when they're writing, we go around if they need help stretching out their words." She pointed around the double semicircle. "I see Garrett's ready, and Rick, and Jaydon, and Madeline, and Angel. Hazel's ready. What's the problem over there? We don't need folders right now, I just need you to sit and look at me!"

January walked over to me. "I have black stuff behind this ear," she whispered. "Can you send me to the nurse?"

I whispered for her just to sit for now.

"Mrs. Price has been busy!" Mrs. Willett said loudly. "Can everybody see this chart that she made?"

Yes.

"Yesterday she wrote the ideas on the whiteboard. Remember, with the marker? And then it looks like she copied it over and made a chart for us. So this is a chart to help us when we are writing our how-to books." The chart said "Learning from a Mentor." "Remember we talked about a mentor is somebody that can help us? There are people who can help us, and then there are books that are called 'mentor texts.'" She held up a book. "This is one of our mentor texts. Number one, we can learn the *title* of a mentor text. The title tells what the book is about. Can everybody tell us? What's this book about? You can all say it."

"Soccer."

"We learned a lot about soccer yesterday, reading this book. Number two, the *pictures* can teach us in a book. Number three, a *list* of things that you might need. In a how-to book you might have to tell the reader what they might need. And number four—that's the new part today, that I'm going to show you! I'm going to go back into *My Very First Soccer Game*, by Alyssa Satin Capucilli."

"Capasilly!" said Noah.

"I'm going to skip some pages. Here's one I wanted to show you. *Game time. Together we run and dribble. And pass. Our feet start and stop the ball. Teamwork! Is what soccer's all about. Step one. Put the ball next to the inside of your foot.* There's the arrow. *Two. Move the ball forward, back, or even side to side. Tap and run, tap and run. That's called*—?"

"Dribbling!"

"Dribbling. The author, Alyssa, did something on this page to help us. Something that's new that we haven't really talked about much, this year. Something that authors will do to help us. I see a couple hands. Garrett, that's distracting me. Thank you. Look closely. I see a few more hands. Abby, what is something that you're noticing?"

"Um, the person is kicking the ball," said Madeline.

"Yes," said Mrs. Willett. "The pictures match the words, right, Abby? We have talked a lot about that this year—that pictures teach us, and we need our words to match our pictures. I'll give you a hint. This is something new that she did that's *in the words.* Abby."

"Teamwork!" said Abby.

"Yes! What did she do to the word *teamwork*?"

"Teamwork is to work together," said Abby.

"It means work together. And look at this. I'm going to read it. *Teamwork is what soccer's all about.* This word, *teamwork*, starts with what letter?"

"*T!*"

"Yes, a *T*! Look at how it's been printed in the book, compared to the other words in that sentence. January, what do you notice?"

"It's blue," said January, "and all the other letters are black."

"Noah? Wait, January. Noah? Why did you move? You couldn't see? Okay. So, January, say it again."

"Because it's blue," said January, "and all the other words are black."

"I can't see," said Jaydon.

"January, sit down," said Westin.

"She was showing us," said Mrs. Willett. "She can sit down after."

"See right there?" said January.

"Do you see the blue letters that January was talking about? Westin, why do you think Alyssa C., the author—why do you think she put *teamwork* in blue? In a different color?"

Westin said, "Because teamwork means you're like, um, cleaning up?"

"Yep, helping," said Mrs. Willett. "Working together as a team. But I'm wondering why is it in blue?"

"Uhhhh," said Westin.

"Why do authors do that? Rick?"

"They's on blue teams," said Rick.

"Could be that they're on the blue team," said Mrs. Willett. "Abby?"

"Because teamwork is a really special thing," said Abby. "You have to really do it."

"Right! It's a really special, important word, *teamwork*. And we call that 'bold.' Can everybody say 'bold'?"

"Bold!"

"Important parts in *bold*." She pointed to Mrs. Price's chart, where that statement was item number 4. "So sometimes, Hazel, authors will put those important words—guys? I'm going to wait. That's distracting, Westin. I saw that Mr. Baker already spoke to you about that once, right? So now this is the second time. When authors want us to really remember something, that's very important in a how-to book, sometimes they'll put the word in bold. Either in dark black or in another color." Mrs. Willett showed us several more bolded words in the book. "Is writing words in darker pencil, or even with a different-colored pencil, is that something that you might try, with some important words? In your how-to books?"

Silence.

"Give me a thumbs-up if you think that you might go through your how-to book today, and with some important words you might try to make them bold."

Thumbs went up.

"Excellent! Excellent. Now I'm going to say a word, and if you think it's a really important word for a how-to book, and should be in bold, give me a thumbs-up. Or thumbs-down if it shouldn't. The first word is *the*. Is that a really important word? We need the word *the*, but in a how-to book is that going to really tell us how to do something?"

No.

In a book about flying a kite, she said, was *string* an important word? Yes, maybe it was. Hazel's how-to book was about giving a party. Was *a* an important word in that book? No. How about *balloons*? Yes. "So you have to really think," Mrs. Willett said. "You don't want to put every word in bold, but it's just something you can think about. Hands down for a minute, January. Do you have to put words in bold in your how-to book?"

No.

"No, this is just another strategy that you might want to try as a writer today. Because, Mr. Baker, wait till you see their how-to books!" She asked everyone to look through their how-to books and see if they wanted to add anything more, or if maybe they wanted to put some words in bold. "Now Mr. Baker and I will come around, like Mrs. Price and I do, but let's tell him, what do you do if you need some help?"

"You raise your hand," said Hartley.

"Yes. Because if everybody comes up to us, we can't help everybody at once. Questions. Ava?"

"What if everyone raises their hand?"

"If everyone raises their hand, what I'll usually do is I'll say, 'I'm helping Ava, and then, Abby, you're next.' And then you have to be patient. Because there's a lot more of you, and there's only two teachers."

Angel had a question—did every important word have to be in bold?

"No," said Mrs. Willett. "It's up to you. You're the writer. You might just pick a couple. Hang on, Garrett, we have a couple more questions. Hands to yourself, Garrett."

Abby wanted to know what to do if a friend asks for help and you help them and they keep asking for help.

Mrs. Willett said, "I'd just use my words and say, 'I helped you, now you need to do some work, and if you need more help, raise your hand for the teacher.' Okay. Great. If you have your writing folder already at your table, you may go start writing. If you need to get your writing folder, you may make a line and get your writing folder."

How-to books were in progress concerning How to Fly a Kite, How to Give a Party, and How to Brush Your Teeth. Most of the topics came from a list of ideas in the worksheet packet.

"I don't brush my teeth," said Jaydon. "I do, but I don't have time every day."

Madeline was working on How to Go to the Beach. Westin was doing How to Make a Sandwich. Abby was working on How to Make Friends. Noah was working on How to Walk Your Puppy. The first thing to do, Noah said, when you're walking your puppy is "tell your parents." I showed him how to write *PARENTS*. Rick was explaining how to go on a ride at Funtown. I showed him that the *E* in *RIDE* makes the *I* long.

January raised her hand and I sat down next to her. She hadn't opened her writing folder. "My ear really hurts," she said. "In this spot right here." She pointed to her tiny ear, around which her thin blond hair flowed.

"Hm," I said. "It looks a little red."

"Can I go to the nurse? With my friend? It feels like it's bleeding."

"Is it a bug bite?" I asked.

"No," she said. "It didn't start hurting outside, it started hurting when we were reading. There are some black spots when I—when I—"

"I think you have some sand in your ear," I said, peering. "Is that it, maybe? You feel the grinding grainy parts? If you check with the nurse, she'll probably say it'll feel better a little later, and she'll send you back."

"Can I just go?" said January. "She might just give me something or she might just take a look."

That made sense. "Do you know the way?" I asked.

"Yes. Sometimes people bring us. They stay there, and then they bring me back."

"Can you go by yourself?" I asked. "Because there's a lot of work going on right now."

"I'm going to ask if somebody will take me," said January.

Mrs. Willett said that January needed a note for the nurse. I found the nurse forms and wrote a note: "January says her ear is hurting and hopes you can take a look. Thanks!—Nick Baker (sub)."

"My stomach hurts," said Angel.

"Well," I said, "keep an eye on it, if it's possible to keep an eye on your stomach, and if it starts to hurt—"

"It does."

"Hang in there. January has hung in there for a couple of hours. Try to drink some water. Usually if you drink some water it makes it feel better." Angel had a long drink at the drinking fountain by the bathroom door.

Hazel wanted Mrs. Willett to help her with the spelling of *teeth*, but Mrs. Willett was, like many reading teachers, a believer in the primal importance of do-it-yourself phonetics, which supposedly built self-esteem and independent thinking habits—even when a kid was obviously eager to know what the real spelling was. "Just write the letters for the sounds *you* hear," she said.

Dissatisfied, Hazel came over to me. "I have a question," she said. "I wish my mom was here, because she helps me do my work faster. I don't know what letter makes the sound 'th.'" She'd written HOW TO BRS YOUR TEE.

The end sound in *teeth* was spelled with a *TH*, I said. Why not tell her, if she was curious? It was a useful sound to know.

Garrett wanted to spell *help*. Mrs. Willett helped him figure out the *H*. "What vowel says 'eh'?" she said. "Eh, eh. It's either *A E I O* or *U*. Eh, eh." Garrett finally guessed *E*. Then *L*. Then *P*. "Great! Garrett is stretching out his words, and he's hearing the sounds and then writing the letters down! Nice, nice. Noah and Westin, I want you to focus on your own how-to books. I'm going to go help Madeline."

"I don't know how to write *animals*," said Garrett.

"Then just do your best," said Mrs. Willett. "Write the letters for the sounds that you hear."

I looked up at the blackboard and the whiteboard, where I'd written *pizza* and *bumblebee* and *butterfly* and *ground* and *peep*. I was violating pedagogical principles by telling the students how to spell those words— even though they'd asked me. Only a small group of short "sight words"— words like *and, out, in, eat, yes, cat, cake*, and *them*—were exempt from the make-your-best-guess requirement. Mrs. Willett was, it seemed to me, prematurely forcing kindergarten kids to write, and at the same time forcing them to write wrong. In practice the obligatory self-invented spelling made for sentences encoded in a weird phonetic Linear B that nobody, not even the struggling writer, could parse an hour later. It made for sadness, too. Some phrases were composed almost entirely of one-letter words.

I whisper-asked Jaydon how old the kids were in the class.

"Five," he whispered back.

"Did you get *animals* written, Garrett?" asked Mrs. Willett. "You know how to stretch it out. Write the letters you think of."

"I don't even hear any, really," said Garrett.

"You have to help yourself here, Garrett."

"How do I help myself?" said Garrett. "I don't even know what that means!"

"This is what it means," said Mrs. Willett. "Say 'ah nuh mulls.' What sound do you hear at the beginning of 'ah nuh mulls'?"

Angel said her stomach really hurt.

"Let's check back after lunch," I said. "If you're in agony, then you should go to the nurse."

"My back hurts," said Madeline.

"Oh my god," I said. "Everybody's suddenly gotten hurty."

Mrs. Willett's voice was so loud and distracting that Ava began shushing her. "Shh! Shh! Shh!" Mrs. Willett didn't notice, fortunately.

"Garrett," she said. "Ah nuh mulls!"

"*N* again?" said Garrett.

"If that's what you hear, write it down," said Mrs. Willett. "Helping yourself means for *you* to stretch out your words."

"*Z*?" said Garrett.

"No, it sounds like a *Z* but it's an *S*," coached Mrs. Willett. "Just one *S*."

Angel took a magnifying glass out and looked at the warped room with it. She was upset that Hazel hadn't returned from taking January to the nurse.

Time to wash up for lunch. "HOW MANY OF YOU WROTE ONE MORE PAGE TODAY?" asked Mrs. Willett.

Some hands went up.

"HOW MANY OF YOU WROTE TWO MORE PAGES TODAY?"

A few hands.

"I'm on my third one!" said Rick.

"Very nice," said Mrs. Willett. "You know we can't lose anything, so where does everything go? Noah, where does everything go?"

"In your folder."

"Yep, IN YOUR FOLDER. Jaydon, ho boy. I'm going to help you, because you've got a lot of stuff out of your folder."

January and Hazel returned from the nurse. "There was a tick in my ear!" January said, wide-eyed, to me. "It was this big!"

"Ew," said Mrs. Willett, overhearing.

"They had to bend my ear to get it out," said January.

"And it ate some blood of her skin," said Hazel.

"January, you are brave," I said.

"I was saying, 'Ow, ow, ow,' because it kind of hurted," said January. She showed me where the tick had been hiding out behind her ear, under her earlobe.

"OKAY, FRIENDS," said Mrs. Willett. She did the five-clap clap. "When your folder is put away, and your table is clean, you can wash your hands for lunch! Westin, that's a messy folder. Messy, messy, huh?" She looked at me. "Good thing you sent her to the nurse," she said, meaning January.

Angel was in the corner holding her stomach. "She can't breathe," said Abby.

"When I take a big breath, I still can't breathe," said Angel.

"I'm sorry, kiddo," I said. "We're going to keep an eye on it. After lunch, we're going to take a look.

"Did she use tweezers?" I asked January.

"No, she uses a little cup, and then she pinched it out. It looked just like a spider. It was a dog tick. It still stings right now."

She went off to tell Mrs. Willett about it in detail.

"You're cool," Noah said to me.

"You're cool," I said to Noah.

"Well, it's gone now, honey," Mrs. Willett said. "You were brave. Have you washed your hands? Noah, show Mr. Baker our quiet lunch line!"

"Mr. Baker, we have lunch in here because it's a half a day!" Noah shouted, beaming.

"Oh, honey, it's not a half a day," said Mrs. Willett. She chuckled.

"It's Friday!" said Noah, in a screech.

"Right, but we don't have half days every Friday. Just once in a while. Today you have a *whole day of school.*"

Squeals and moans and more screeches.

Westin had a loose tooth and was trying to pull it out and dance a jig at the same time. I told him to sit down for a second. When he'd gotten himself together, he took a place in line. It was 12:25 p.m. I raised my hand for silence.

"We have to wait until the line is ready!" said Mrs. Willett. She pointed at Hazel. "Oh, you look ready. Noah looks ready."

"I feel ready," I whispered. My stomach growled audibly and Abby suppressed a laugh. I told Angel that I hoped she felt better. "Thanks a lot," I said to Mrs. Willett.

"You're welcome," she said.

In the cafeteria, Ms. Carlough, the young kindergarten teacher I'd talked to at the playground on Day Sixteen, asked me how it was going. I said it was going pretty well.

"I had two absent today, so I only had fourteen kids," she said.

"It's kind of a miracle how they slowly learn to read," I said. "I can't imagine how it happens. But it happens with almost everybody."

"Especially around this time," she said, as we walked back to the kindergarten hallway. "They tend to bloom around April. In the fall, not as good, but by the end of the year, they seem to be doing a lot better."

I washed my hands and ate a cheese sandwich, and then I remembered that Garrett had left his sweatshirt on the playground. It was on the picnic table, just where he'd left it.

Mrs. Thurston, the second-grade teacher, had lunch duty that day, and she was in a bad mood. She had her hand in the air. "WHAT ARE YOU SUPPOSED TO DO WHEN I HAVE MY HAND UP?" she said. "I SHOULDN'T EVEN HAVE TO PUT MY HAND UP RIGHT NOW, BECAUSE *NONE OF YOU* SHOULD BE *SPEAKING*. WHEN YOU CLEAR YOUR TRAY, YOUR HEAD GOES DOWN. AND YOU DO NOT TALK FOR THE REST OF LUNCH. THIS IS A HABIT YOU NEED TO BE IN. Every grade you go to does this. IT'S AWFULLY NOISY FOR A ZERO NOISE LEVEL."

My class was sitting with their heads down, looking sufficiently cowed and compliant. "Shall we go?" I said, after a suitable interval. We marched roomward.

Angel said she still felt bad.

Garrett started crying. The dark blue sweatshirt I'd found wasn't his, and he'd also misplaced his lunch box. The sub plans said it was star share time: "The star shares something s/he brought in, then takes 5 questions, comments, or connections. The star picks out a graph from the easel bucket. You all conduct the graph."

Angel held her stomach, which was not small, and looked disconsolate, waiting for me to write a note for the nurse. She didn't remember how to spell her last name, which was Deschaine.

Garrett was having a meltdown, kicking backpacks, looking for his sweatshirt. He was sure somebody had stolen it.

I found the nurse's office notepad. "You have a stomachache, right?"

"No, I can't breathe," Angel said.

"My teddy's not feeling very good," said Madeline.

January took Angel off to the nurse. Hazel couldn't take her because she was the star, and we'd come to star share time.

Hazel took a seat in the thronelike gliding rocker, and I sat next to her. "OKAY, SHH. This is star share. How was everyone's lunch, good?"

Good.

"After lunch I felt like I was going to puke," said Abby.

"Well, that happens when you eat," I said. "Okay, Star Hazel, take it away. You can share a thought, an idea, something that you have."

Hazel held up her bracelet and her necklace, both of them plastic and sparkly.

"Three questions, comments, or connections," said Madeline.

"No, five!" said Abby.

Westin said, "I really like the gold ones. Not the blue ones, or the white ones, or the green. Only I like these ones." He touched the gold hearts on the bracelet. "And I hope you have a fun time with them."

"Well done," I said.

Madeline said, "I like your bracelet and your necklace because they're really pretty. And silver sparkly, and green, and blue, and white are my favorite colors."

Ava said, "I like it because it has everything's favorite color. I like it and I hope you have a fun time with the necklace."

Abby said, "I like the necklace because it has blue and green on it—"

"And white," Westin interjected.

"Shh," I said.

"And white," said Abby. "And I hope you have a fun time with the necklace."

I said, "When you're having a conversation with somebody— CAN YOU PUT THAT DOWN? And come over here?" Garrett was carrying around a cardboard tube.

"GARRETT, STOP," said Abby. Garrett put the tube down.

"Thanks, Garrett," I said. "When you're having a conversation with somebody, you want to bring them out. You want to ask them questions about what they're doing. Instead of telling something about your life, you ask them something about their life. So if she was talking about that bracelet, I would say, Oh, that's beautiful, where did you get it? Or, What made you choose that color? And then she has to say something else. So, where did you get the bracelet?"

Hazel suddenly got shy.

"Nowhere?" I said. "Just found it on the street?"

"You're funny just like Mrs. Price," said Madeline.

Garrett was in a tiny death spiral of disruption. "Garrett, will you sit right over there next to that green chair, please, RIGHT NOW."

"I don't want to," Garrett said.

"Well, then you're going to have a consequence," I said.

"You're supposed to put his name on a sticky if he's being naughty," said Hazel.

"Very naughty," said Rick.

"Wicked naughty," said Hartley.

"He's fine now," I said. "He did what I asked. Just relax, guys."

"I wish Mrs. Price was back here," said Hazel. "I miss her."

January and Angel returned from the nurse. Angel was okay. "I love you, Ava," she said.

I got out the graph, chosen by Hazel. "Have you ever given someone a flower?" asked the graph. Then it said, "Color in the box above your answer." On cue from Hazel, Westin put a tally mark saying he'd given someone a flower.

"Mr. Baker, Garrett's talking," said Angel.

"Will you not worry about that? Just have a seat." Angel was in a bad mood because the nurse had found nothing wrong with her.

One by one, very quietly, the children put check marks saying whether they had or hadn't given someone a flower.

"I like this quiet!" I whispered. "I can practically hear a cricket chirping."

"Can my bear do it, too?" said Madeline. "Please?"

I said she could give her own checkmark to her bear. Westin made a farting sound in his hand.

"Do not make rude noises with your hand, sir," I said.

"Okay," he said.

"One more," I said. "Garrett's got to make a check. Give us your honest response."

I added up the tally marks. "Okay, thirteen to nothing, people gave flowers!" I said. Next Hazel was supposed to pick out a book to read aloud. There was only a little time before gym, so I told her to pick a short book. We co-read some of *Hop on Pop.* *"We are all tall. We are all small."* Angel started screaming. There was a tiny bug in the class. "It's a sting bug!" said Madcline. I said, "It's a tiny little bug, just trying to find a way out. It's not going to sting anybody, believe me," I said. I skipped ahead in the book. *"He, me,"* I said.

"HE IS AFTER ME," recited the class. *"HIM, JIM. JIM IS AFTER HIM."*

"You guys are really starting to read! When you started this school year, could you read this book?"

"NO!"

"Your brains figured all this out. That's pretty incredible." I read on. *"Three, tree. Three fish in a tree."*

They roared it out: *"HOW CAN THAT BE?"*

An unhappiness arose because Angel said that Abby said that Noah was stupid. "She's telling me that I said stupid and I didn't," said Angel.

"Guys, I want to say something very important," I said. "Which is that I've watched all of you. I'm a hundred percent convinced that every one of you is an incredibly good kid. In general, you're good listeners, you're good workers, you're nice to each other. Every so often, there seems to be a tension. As far as I can tell, the things that you disagree about are very tiny. If you didn't let yourself be bothered by what somebody else did, it probably wouldn't be a bad thing. So my suggestion is to just sort of go with the flow." The class was listening, so I went on. "And here's the thing that I understand about this school, that I can see. People tell you what to do all the time. Isn't that true? All day long, you're being told what to do. It's exhausting. I would be exhausted. In lunch, they tell you what to do. In recess, they tell you what to do. Line up, and be quiet, do this and do that. And there's a lot of learning you have to do. It is hard, and I understand that. I want to say, I really admire you guys. I mean it. From my heart. I admire what you're doing." I didn't want them to see that I had tears in my eyes, so I looked at the clock. "And now it's time to go to gym, where they will also tell you what to do."

"You're funny," said Madeline.

"You're funny just like Mrs. Price," said Abby. She tried to hug me and made kissing noises.

"Okay, okay, thank you," I said, fending her off.

We pomp-and-circumstanced to the gym, and the doors opened. "Just a jog, not a run," said Mrs. Weld, the gym teacher. "Just a jog! Noah! Westin!" Pharrell Williams's "Happy" came on while they ran. I used the free half hour to squirt several more squirts of sanitizer on my hands and call my wife, who'd found a dead bat in the living room fireplace.

Half the kids were lined up along the side of the echoey gym. I said hello to Ava. "Jaydon, you may line up!" said Mrs. Gym Teacher. "Angel, you may line up. January. Westin. Garrett, you may line up. Nice job. You're sweaty because you worked hard today. That's very good!"

In the hall Madeline said, "Noah was following me, and he was swinging with me at recess, so I think he loves me."

"How exciting," I said.

"Does my hair still look good?" asked Angel.

"It's still got some tent in it," I said. "You look really nice."

"Thank you."

"You, too!" said Madeline politely.

Friday folders were handed out one by one, chairs leapt up clankingly on tables, a line formed at the door.

"Ava cut in line!" said Westin.

"She didn't cut, she was there already!" said Angel.

"But she got out of line!" said Westin.

I said to Westin, "Let me ask you, as an intelligent observer of life, how important is it to you to be number two or three or four in line? Does it matter? It doesn't matter to me. I'm going to be here in the back of the line. I don't care. Doesn't matter. I'm happy. You're supposed to walk the playground for fifteen minutes. Mrs. Harmon is on duty."

"Mrs. Arm?" said Rick.

"Mr. Baker?" said Hazel. "When you wrote your name on the board this morning, it won't come off."

Again I hadn't used a dry-erase marker. I scrubbed at my name furiously. Luckily it came off, all but a ghostly residue. "I thought maybe it was going to be there forever," I said. "Can you see it?"

"No," said Hazel.

"That's what I like to hear."

Ava had disappeared. I found her hiding behind some stacked chairs in the back of the room.

I opened the door to the little playground and watched them all take off. They weren't walking, they were running. Some were running backward. I said hello to Mrs. Harmon, who had a kind face.

"This is an arduous day for them," I said.

"Oh, we make them work," Mrs. Harmon said. "Most of our activities are morning-based, because by the afternoon, it's too much for them. So it's nice to have the afternoon for specials, and to kind of veg."

During my fifteen free minutes I went to the office to find out where the lost-and-found was, so I could take Garrett there—then I had recess duty. Without the first- and second-graders, recess was a lot easier to oversee.

January came up with a grievance. "Mr. Baker, I asked them to stop and they're still not stopping. They're following me, and I'm not liking it."

"Dang. Well, let's take a walk, and I'll keep them off you."

"I want to play by myself," January said, "but they want to play with me and I don't want to." She pointed out the two boys, who had retreated to the shadows of the play structure.

"Do you want me to talk to them, January, or just hang out here?"

"I want you to talk to them." She led me toward Enoch, in a white mesh shirt and camo pants. "He's hiding from you," she said.

To Enoch I said, "If somebody doesn't want to be followed, don't follow them. You know that. Makes sense, right?"

He nodded and scuttled off. Some girls found an anthill. A scrimmage of boys screamed.

"Mr. Baker, I'm a math genius," said a girl named Hadley. "I know ten times ten: a hundred. Two times two I think is twenty?"

"Do ticks like big grass?" said Noah.

"Yes, they like tall grass," I said. "But you won't necessarily get a tick just because you walked in tall grass."

"We sat in it, too," said Noah. "I got a tick once. It bited me. Is it time to line up, because I really want to line up!"

Westin opened his mouth and screamed, "LINE UUUUUUUUUUUUUP!"

January came over. "They're chasing me again." I told her I'd given Enoch a talking-to. She ran off.

The school secretary came up, saying that January's dad was there to pick her up for a doctor's appointment.

Westin called, "JAAAAAAAAAAAAAAAAAAAAANUARY!"

"Westin, that's not necessary," I said.

"You'll sleep good tonight," said the school secretary. We filed back inside; Garrett saw his sweatshirt and made a cry of joy.

Five minutes into the end-of-day chaos, Jaydon said, "I think I'm going to throw up a pizza bagel. It's coming back out."

"Don't let it," I said.

The bell rang. It was the principal, asking for our attention in order to name the Team Lasswell campers of the week, Marie Ballard and Lewis Hook. "Marie is a hardworking student who exemplifies what it takes to be a good friend. Lewis is a dedicated student in all areas of school, who is always in search of a way to make improvements and progress. Congratulations once again to Marie and Lewis for being named this week's Team Lasswell campers of the week."

Mr. Mullins, a bus conductor, began calling out the digits of bus numbers. "TEN SEVENTY-THREE!" he bellowed. "TEN SEVENTY-THREE."

"Mine is thirteen seventy-three," said Madeline.

"I'm zero five seven one," said Garrett.

Mr. Mullins bellowed, "ZERO FIVE SEVEN ONE! ZERO FIVE SEVEN ONE." Then he called, "TWO TWO FOUR! TWO TWO FOUR. THIRTEEN SEVENTY-ONE. THIRTEEN SEVENTY-ONE."

"GUYS, CAN I HAVE YOUR ATTENTION," shouted Hadley, the

math genius from the playground, in imitation of Mrs. Thurston. "TEN TIMES TEN IS ONE HUNDRED. REMEMBER THAT! OKAY? I DON'T HAVE TO YELL!"

A girl from the class next door said, "What's your name?"

"Mr. Baker."

"What color is the sky?"

"Blue."

"What's the opposite of down?"

"Up."

"Oh, no, Mr. Baker blew up!"

Ava said softly, "Mr. Baker, Westin lied."

He did?

She nodded.

"Let me tell you something," I said. "It's been great having you in class. I like the fact that you can read that *Hop on Pop* like nobody else. You're a very interesting person. Keep it up. Do you want me to say something to Westin?"

"He said I was cutting in the line," she murmured.

"THIRTEEN SEVENTY-THREE. THIRTEEN SEVENTY-THREE! TWELVE SEVENTY-ONE! TWELVE SEVENTY-ONE!"

To Westin I said, "Did you say something you shouldn't have said about Ava?"

"No," said Westin, "Garrett lied about—"

"THIRTEEN SEVENTY-TWO! THIRTEEN SEVENTY-TWO!"

That was Westin's bus. He bounced off.

"THIRTEEN SEVENTY-FOUR! THIRTEEN SEVENTY-FOUR!"

That was Ava's bus.

"How long did it take you to memorize all those numbers?" I asked Hadley.

"Five years," said Hadley.

"TWELVE SEVENTY-TWO! TWELVE SEVENTY-TWO!"

Bye! Bye! They were all gone, except Jaydon.

I walked Jaydon to Y care. He said his parents worked really late. He sat down at a cafeteria table with eight other Y care kids, whose assignment was to write about the best thing that had happened that day.

My note to Mrs. Price said, "What a pleasure it was to spend the day in your classroom—the kids were attentive, good-natured, and full of ideas! Thank you for letting me sub—Best regards, Nick Baker."

I locked the door and signed out.

"You ready for a nap?" said the secretary.

"A nap might come in handy, yes," I said. And that was it for Day Twenty-one.

HE PARTICULARLY DOESN'T LIKE THIS PARTICULAR SPOT

Monday morning's sky was an astonishing blue, and Beth had me going to the middle school to spend the day in the numeracy room, normally overseen by Mrs. Massey. The numeracy room was a quiet, gray-carpeted interior space with ten iMacs on tables, ten expensive-looking office chairs with fabric cushions and rolling wheels, and a bank of six smoked-glass windows that looked out on the second-floor hallway. If you did remedial time in numeracy, every kid on your team knew it. It was like being in an anthropological display in a museum.

The school district had learned some terrible news over the weekend. Nelson, the ninth-grade boy who'd gone for a walk and disappeared, was found dead, after a weeklong search. He'd fallen while climbing in an abandoned granite quarry.

Mrs. Yates, a math teacher, unlocked the numeracy room and showed me where the blue student folders were, in the top drawer of the hanging file cabinet. "They're going to ask you if we're doing Spelling City this week," Mrs. Yates said. "We are not doing Spelling City, which is math vocab. Mrs. Massey and I decided that we're going to stop doing that, because we're getting near the end of school and they have to concentrate on making benchmark. Even though we have sixth-, seventh-, and eighth-grade students, some of them are at fourth-grade level."

Nobody showed during homeroom. Lunch was a hotdog with crisp potato wedges. Information packets for summer girls' basketball were available at the office. Talent show practice would be held after school. I squirted sanitizer on my hands, ate some Winnipesaukee chocolate, and waited for someone to talk to. The problem of the day, written on the whiteboard, was 1,870 divided by 34.

Block 1 was Cher, Claire, Serena, Waylon, Hunter, and Roan. Serena's folder wasn't in the file drawer. "Waylon's probably not coming," said Roan. Serena, tall and black-leotarded, had made a hangman's noose out of red string that she had cinched around her finger. "I looked up cool knots on YouTube," she said.

"She's going to hang her finger," said Hunter. "It's kind of weird. My dad found a noose in our basement."

"Hunter's dad found a noose in his basement," I said to the class.

"Creepy," said Serena.

Waylon appeared, a droopingly cherubic kid with bags under his eyes. "I'm sorry I was late," he said. "I forgot about it."

"Can we take the day off pretty much?" asked Hunter.

"Nope, you know what a stickler for detail I am," I said.

"There's an Indian burial ground out there, I swear," said Cher, waving in the direction of the soccer field. She'd untied her noose and was trying to retie it. "I don't remember how to do this."

"There's a lot of mathematics to knots," I said. "I'm not a math person—"

"Nor am I," said Cher.

"—but there are whole departments of universities where they study the mathematics of knots. It's really interesting."

"I would hate that job," said Serena. She'd retied the noose bigger and made as if to put it over her head.

"No, no, no, no, please don't do that," I said. "That would not be good."

She put the noose around her wrist.

I asked if everybody had done the Problem of the Day.

"I can do it, I just don't really want to," said Hunter.

"Why don't you want to? It just doesn't call out to you? If it was divided by thirty-six and not thirty-four would you want to? No?"

"I don't like division," said Hunter.

Serena flipped her noose.

"You could hang a troll with that," Hunter said.

"All you do is ballpark it," I said, poking at the number 1,870 on the board with the tip of the marker. "Just look at that thing and say, Thirty-four, wow, that's about halfway between thirty and forty, hm, hm, and I know that five times thirty is one hundred fifty, maybe I could bump it up a notch, maybe not, let's try five, that kind of thing."

"Yuh! Spider-Man!" said Serena.

"Did you say 'Spider-Man'?" said Cher.

"Who's got a guess for this one?" I said.

"Two," said Serena

"Six," said Cher.

"Okay, so you say, I'm going to commit myself to six—temporarily. You try six. You go six times four is—"

Claire chanted, "Six times four is—"

"Twenty-four!" said Serena.

"Good, and then you go six times three is—"

"Eighteen."

"And then you add the two, and oh no! It's too high! So you know it's got to be one down from that. One down from six is—?"

"Five!"

"Now we're cooking with propane," I said.

"Burning, really burning," said Hunter.

We multiplied by five. "Then you draw the line, that beautiful line," I said. We subtracted. My marker cap fell off. "Then you drop the end of your pen."

"And then you do five again, so it's fifty-five," said Cher.

"Oh my gosh!" I said. "Subtract it out. Zero. Check! Do you feel all limbered up?" I looked over the sub plans. "Let's do some Fast Math!" FASTT Math, with a second T that people seemed to ignore—the acronym stood for "Fluency and Automaticity through Systematic Teaching with Technology"—was a bundle of remedial math games and exercises sold by Scholastic.

"I don't do Fast Math here, I don't think," said Cher.

"Cher has to finish her test first," said Serena. She'd put the noose around her tongue and was tightening it so that her tongue muscle formed a dollop of flesh.

"I just saw something I shouldn't have," I said. "God. Take that off right now."

"It's like a rat, hanging," said Hunter.

"That's mean," said Cher.

"Carry on, guys," I said. "I want to see real math happening."

"I feel laughy today," said Serena.

Waylon and Roan signed into Fast Math on their computers. "Would that be thirty-six?" asked Waylon slowly.

I said four times eight was not thirty-six. "It's close to thirty-six."

"Four times eight?" said Roan, listening in. "It's twenty-eight. No, six and six is twelve. Thirty-two."

I pointed at him. "Thirty-two!"

I went over to Cher and Serena to get them chuffing on Fast Math. "It looks not too bad," I said. "It's just little multiplication stuff."

Serena pretended to pull up on the tiny noose, flopping her head to the side as if hung. "No, I did not hurt myself," she said.

"I must report it," I said. "No."

"Mrs. Ritter, the nurse, already knows," Serena said.

"That you tried to hang your finger?" said Hunter.

"That I made this. I'm friends with her. I saw you walking in this morning when I was in her office."

They keyed in passwords and up came the Fast Math multiplication fact grid.

"Isn't that a thing of beauty?" I said. "It's got colors, it's got numbers." It did look pretty snazzy.

"That's going to take me a long time," said Cher, "because I'm not very good at these."

"I suck at threes," said Serena. "I don't know threes for the life of me. Threes and eights."

"I started with my zeros," said Cher.

"Anything times zero is zero," said Serena.

"I know," said Cher.

"Threes and eights are tough for you?" I said.

"And sevens," said Cher.

"Can you do three times seven?" I said.

"Twenty-one."

I said, "Okay, that's a good one. That's like an island. Think of yourself in a kayak, and you know that you can survive on that island. And then there are some other islands that you actually know."

"My cousin's a tutor here," said Serena. "I can't see how people can be smart in math."

"It's a part of your brain that some people have and some people don't," I said.

"You know you only use like ten percent of your brain?" said Serena.

"That's what they say," I said, "but I don't believe that. I think we've got this complicated brain, and we can't even comprehend how much it's doing, so we say we're only using ten percent."

"I bet we're only using ten percent to think, and learn," said Serena. "The rest of it is feelings and emotions."

"Your brain has to decide what to forget and what to remember all the time," I said. "You create little priorities, and you think, I want to blow this off because it's tiresome. However, I would like to learn how to make a noose."

"You want to?" said Serena, brightening. "It's real easy."

"No, no, I'm saying, as an example."

She demonstrated with her red cord. "You do this, and then you lay it down, and then this is up here, and then you do like that, and you fold it over, and you bring it under and you wrap it around to the top—"

Hunter looked over. "Why are you teaching the substitute how to make a noose?"

Serena laughed. "And then it just *slides*."

I said, "So you've got three times seven. That's your island. You're in the kayak—"

A jovial bald man, Mr. Fields, opened the door.

"Here's my noose," Serena said, holding it up.

"Do you have a moment?" Mr. Fields said to me.

"He was explaining an island concept," said Serena.

"Beautiful!" said Mr. Fields. "Hopefully you're listening!" He took me out to the hall, crushed my hand in a handshake, and spoke in hushed tones. "You've got a student over there in the orange shirt named Waylon Grant. He has some issues with emotional stability. If he tells you he needs to go to the nurse, you should let him go to the nurse. Because of the audio hallucinations he's hearing, and the threats that they're making to him and to others, we should discreetly follow him down to the bottom of the landing, to the bottom of the stairs as he walks his way down to the nurse's station."

"Is he under any medication?"

"Oh, YUH. He says right now he's okay. But the voices are talking to him. He's able to talk them away, but that doesn't always work. He has not presented a problem to anybody, other than he gets himself all super anxious. Just wanted to let you know that."

"Good to know," I said. "Thank you very much."

I went back inside. Cher said, "Why do I have to be in here if I only have two wrong on this whole test? Two hundred nineteen times seventy-two! I suck with word problems, and I didn't even do it."

"Well, let's work on some of that," I said. "But first of all, I'm just telling you that it would be good to know something like three times eight—right?"

"Twenty . . ." Cher rolled her eyes, puffed out one cheek, and pushed it with a finger. ". . . four."

"Yeah! Three times nine?"

"Are you going to be in here tomorrow?" asked Serena.

"I don't think so."

"Aw."

"Twenty-seven," said Cher. "I just did that one with my fingers."

"Right. So all this amounts to is making these happen a little more automatically. Right now, you're doing it, but it's as if you're wearing big boots, and the mud is sucking at your boots, and you're walking slowly up the path. You need to learn it so that it just comes like badoop badoop, and the only way to do that, really, is with flash cards."

"I have flash cards at home," said Serena. "They go all the way up to twelves."

"You should try it. I'm not an advocate of massive math education, necessarily—but the times tables are actually helpful."

"Lookit, I've got no circles on this page," said Cher, showing her placement test.

Waylon turned in his office chair. "Can you walk me down to the nurse's?"

"Yes, I certainly can," I said.

"Did Mr. Fields just tell you?" he said.

"He said that if you wanted to go to the nurse that yes, I would walk you down. Is it something you really want to do? I'd love to have you in the class."

"I don't know how long it'll be," said Waylon. "It might be really quick."

I turned to the class. "Guys, my dear friends. You are going to hold the fort totally calmly and responsibly—I'll be back in two seconds. I'm just walking down."

"I want to walk down!" said Serena. "Do you work at the high school?"

"I bounce around," I said. "Sometimes it's kindergarten, sometimes it's eleventh grade, you never know. But I'll be back."

Waylon and I made our way downstairs. I asked him how his day had been going.

"Good so far," said Waylon. "I just have to take a minute."

"How old are you?"

"Twelve."

"Twelve, good age! What floats your boat these days? What are you interested in?"

"Um, video games. I like Call of Duty and Minecraft."

The nurse wasn't in, but the assistant nurse was. "I'm fine now," said Waylon. His voice was light and soft. "I'll come back up if I have time."

"I hope you do. Good to get to know you."

"Thanks, you too."

Back in class I told the kids that I'd once had a terrible experience in grade school in a times-table spelling bee. "Total humiliation," I said. "I went home, and I realized that there were certain times-table moments that I knew, and others that I didn't. So are there ones that you really know, solidly?"

"Fives!"

"Zeros!"

"Tens!"

"Ones!"

I wrote on the whiteboard. "You know the zeros, the fives, the tens, and the ones. So: five times six?"

Pause. "Thirty."

"Okay, so thirty has a little hesitation, but zeroes you obviously know because everything always ends up zero, ten you always know, because you just add a zero, one because it's the same thing. So you can check these off."

"Oh, and elevens," said Hunter.

"Eleven times nine is—?"

"Ninety-nine."

"Okay. Let's move up in a level of difficulty. Let's try the fours. What's six times four?"

Serena started loudly counting by fours; meanwhile Cher said that it was twenty-four, because five times four was twenty.

"What you're doing is you're logicking out," I said. "You're outsmarting it. What you have to do is get it to be like pitching a ball, throwing a Frisbee, walking down stairs—something that your mind doesn't have to think about. So you just hear 'four times six' and blip, 'twenty-four.' If it's an automatic thing, then everything else is easier."

Hunter began scooting in his office chair. "He's gone to the time-out corner," said Roan.

"This is my diagnosis," I said. "This is the thing that you could do that would make high school just unbelievably much more easy for you. Get a bunch of flash cards from Hannaford's, and just do it."

"They sell them everywhere," said Roan.

"Mrs. Massey has thousands, but she made them herself," said Hunter.

Waylon came in. "Hey, good to see you back!" I said.

"I could make them in noose style," said Serena.

"We're going to really have a talk about this," I said. "It's serious. I mean it. I care about this, and I want you to, too. Actually memorize your times tables. They have to be like music in your mind. We could do it as a rap song. 'Eight times seven is fifty-six. Add another number and get your kicks. Nine times seven is sixty-three . . .'"

"How do you know these?" said Serena.

"I swear, all I did was go through the cards."

"Seven times seven is forty-nine," said Serena. "I remember because my fifth-grade teacher said, 'You are not leaving this room without knowing forty-nine!' The Forty-niners was her favorite team."

"That is your island," I said.

Serena and Hunter were doing more chair antics. Hunter said, "My fifth-grade teacher just told me—"

I said, "Can you not drag him around the room, because I would like to hear what you were saying. What were you saying?"

"We couldn't learn anything," said Hunter, "because the fifth-grade teacher just left me and Serena to sit. And she was annoying."

"Oh, yeah," said Serena, remembering. "She told me, Hunter, and Jocelyn to sit at the little table. We had to just sit there. And Issa. And then Issa went into the advanced!"

"I wasn't here in fifth grade," said Claire. "I was in Florida."

"I might be getting homeschooled next year," said Cher. "I've learned nothing here."

"You'd learn a lot being homeschooled," I said. "This school, because there are so many people, is sort of inefficient."

"I was homeschooled for a little bit," said Hunter, "I think it was in California, and I didn't do nothing. Why wouldn't I do nothing? It's warmer out there."

Serena was scooting in her chair now as well.

I said, "Guys, I like talking but what I do not like is bumper cars with the chairs."

"Californ-I-A!" said Serena, pumping her chair high with a lever. "Watch me shrink." She sank.

"Let's get something accomplished in this hour," I said.

"We can do a happy circle next," said Hunter.

"Duck duck goose?" said Serena.

"You can all sit around and we can share," I said. "We'll share math facts."

"No," said Cher. "You lost me at the math facts part."

"I am being paid," I said. "You're not being paid. I know that's bad. You should be paid to be in this school." Chair twirling. "Please don't twirl. We have to talk about math in some way."

"If you have us again on our team," said Hunter, "can we get all the teachers outside, and then can we do—what is it called?—wheelchair drag racing? I actually knew a guy who did that on the street, until he got hit by a UPS truck. I pushed him out in front of it."

"Is he all right?" I said.

"Somewhat," said Hunter. "It was a year ago."

"My dad broke three of his ribs in a motorcycle accident," said Claire.

"I broke both my legs in a motorcycle accident," said Hunter.

"I got pushed off a cement truck," said Cher.

Serena said, "My mommy broke her wrist while she was pregnant with me, falling off a hay   "

"Baler?" said Hunter.

"No, a trailer full of hay," Serena said. "My dad shattered his ankle in a car accident right before I was born."

"My mom fell off a porch and broke her face," said Cher, "and I just sat there and stared at her. And my dad was laughing. My dad laughs when bad stuff happens to people."

"That goes over real well," I said.

"I'm not joking," said Cher. "Every time I hurt myself, or one of us hurts ourselves, he just laughs. And then he'll get mad and bring us to the hospital."

"He's crying inside, right?" I said.

"I don't know. He starts crying when he laughs."

"My hair's annoying me," said Serena.

Cher suddenly remembered something. "Oh, my dad gave a baby a lemon," she said. "He laughed so hard, I thought he was going to pee his pants."

"So, guys, what am I going to tell Mrs. Massey?"

"That we worked very, very hard," said Serena.

"I want to see serious product," I said. "I want to see output. *Seven times seven is forty-nine.* All of them have to be like that. I'm giving you a piece of knowledge that will help you." In high school it would help them, that is. After high school, did it matter? Not so much.

"I finished my Fast Math," said Roan.

"So you've got to go to your folder, right?"

"I don't have a folder," said Roan.

Serena laughed.

I found Roan's folder in the stack. "Roan, Roan."

Roan laughed. "I didn't know I had a *folder.*"

I turned to Waylon. "You made it through Fast Math?" He nodded. We pulled out a worksheet he was supposed to have finished.

"It's really hard," he said.

"I WANT SILENCE," I said. "We're actually going to be working here." Waylon and I whisper-worked on a two-digit multiplication problem, while the others murmured. "You start on the far right, right?"

"Mhm," said Waylon. "Three times one is three. Five times three is fifteen. And then you put a zero. So it would be ten, eleven. One thousand one hundred seventy-three."

"Wow, your mind is chugging right along." Waylon and I worked on problems for a little longer, and then Waylon said, "I'm so tired. I woke up last night, really early. It was like one in the morning."

"What's interfering with your sleep, my man?" I said.

"I don't know. I should probably talk to my doctor about it."

"Do you have any medications that you take that would interfere with your sleep?"

"No," Waylon said. "Well, I take some medicine, but I've been taking it for a long time and my sleep has been good."

I asked if he'd adjusted the dose recently.

"When I was at the hospital, yes, but that was like two weeks ago, and my sleep has been good. But the last few nights it's been bad."

I said, "It's probably the meds, because it's been two weeks. It takes a little time. Is it a higher dose?"

"Yeah."

"So what's happening is your body has now been filled up to that new level, and that's why it's interfering with your sleep, probably. Don't you think? You're not getting enough sleep. That's horrible."

Waylon sat.

"I sleep so hard," whispered Serena to Cher, having overheard.

"I'm really tired," Waylon said.

"I'm sorry, man." I looked down at his worksheet. "Let's try this one, it's simple, and then we can have accomplished something. Five times seven."

"Five times seven." He counted on his fingers. "Five, ten, fifteen, twenty, twenty-five, thirty, thirty-five?"

"Good. So you write that down, and you put the little three up there."

He yawned. "Yep." He slowly wrote a little three.

"So you go five times two is ten. Would you add the three to it?"

"Yeah, you would."

I helped him along. "And then five times four is twenty . . ."

"Plus one would be twenty-one?"

"Bingo."

He yawned again. "Sorry, I'm just tired."

"I hear you. What if you slowly tapered off that stuff, whatever it is?"

"I can't," Waylon said. "That would be bad. I need it for my anxiety. Or else I'd be crying all the time."

"You think so?"

"It's what happened last year. The first day of school, when I moved back up here, I just was crying all day."

"It's partly that you missed your family, isn't it?"

"I don't know. But I was just crying all the time."

"So that's why the doc said take this stuff?"

"Yeah, Paxil," Waylon said. "Have you heard of that?"

I said I had. "It's pretty powerful stuff."

"I'm on thirty milligrams," he said. "It's kind of a high dose."

"Time to go," Hunter announced.

"We have to leave right now," said Waylon.

"Okay, hope to see you again," I said.

"We were supposed to leave like a minute ago!" said Serena.

"Take care, guys, see you around."

JUDE, LORRAINE, AND CRIMSON came in for block 2. I handed Lorraine and Crimson their math folders. "Jude, have you got one of these?"

"No."

"That's so sad," I said. The sub plans said that every student had at least one folder. I looked through the file cabinet. "Yes you do. You've got two of them. Extra bonus file."

"Not funny," said Jude.

"You never know what you're going to find in the file drawer," I said.

I refiled the folders from last block—distended, goiterous dugongs of arithmetical confusion—and squirted sanitizer on my hands, wiggling my fingers to feel the cool as the alcohol dried.

Jude asked for some scrap paper. There was none. "I think she actually ran out yesterday," Jude said.

"Do you know where the central scrap paper supply would be?"

"No."

Math class without scrap paper. I tore off a piece of paper from my Moleskine notebook and gave it to him. He was working a Fast Math problem: nine divided by one-third.

"Holy Toledo," I said. "Do you remember how to do that?"

"Yeah. Can I steal a pencil?"

"Pencil shortage," I said, and handed him a pencil.

While Crimson slapped away at her keyboard, playing a Fast Math game that involved ladybugs climbing on a vine, Lorraine worked on a math benchmark assessment something-or-other. I sat and stared through the smoked-glass windows at the occasional student in the hall. "Did you get it?" I asked Jude. "Did you bust through to the other side of that fraction thing?"

Jude said, "Yeah, and then I came up with this one that was like five times ten minus six squared plus five. I was like, What the heck? Simplify it. I tried to, but to do it, there has to be a thirty-one up there. So I just guessed on that one."

Just then a tall expressionless fellow named Phoenix slouched in. "I went down to literacy but they sent me up here," he said.

"What do you want to do?" I said.

"I don't know. They just sent me back up here."

Did he, I asked, prefer literacy or numeracy? He didn't care. I said,

"What people are doing in here is Fast Math, where they fling numbers at you. Does that sound like the right thing to do?"

"Yeah."

A man from guidance opened the door and stared irritably at Phoenix. Phoenix said, "I went down to them! They said come back up here."

"She just called me again, wondering where you were!" said the man from guidance.

The phone rang. It was the literacy teacher. "Is Phoenix Crowder in your room?"

"She's looking for him," said the guidance person, leading Phoenix away.

I told the literacy teacher that Phoenix was just leaving numeracy. My four students worked in silence. Blobs of empty time moved slowly through the morning's digestive tract. I felt my eyelids getting heavy, so I bit off some more of my Winnipesaukee bar. The crinkling of the foil made Lorraine look up. "Busted," I said, chewing. "It's coffee chocolate."

"What is it?" said Lorraine.

"It's just some coffee chocolate. I'm not just sitting here eating chocolate. That would be bad. It's coffee chocolate, so it's good."

"Must be a lot easier than having to drink coffee," said Jude.

"I hate having to go off and mix instant coffee and rush back," I said.

"I notice that any time a teacher leaves, it's just chaos," Jude said.

After twenty minutes, Jude left, smiling enigmatically to himself. I looked up the side effects for Paxil, which had a black-box warning about suicidality. It was not supposed to be given to children. Waylon was definitely a child, and he was so drugged that he could barely lift a pencil. Two of the listed side effects were sleeplessness and auditory hallucinations. If a Paxil patient heard voices he was supposed to call his doctor immediately.

Elaine, the secretary, dropped in to ask if I could substitute across the hall for a language arts teacher on Wednesday. Yes I could.

Lorraine and Crimson gathered their belongings and said goodbye. Anita, Susanna, and Sutton were block 3's fresh arrivals. They didn't speak to each other, and they looked sheepish as I handed them their folders. Their math worksheets had goofy names, like "Mad Minute" and "Five Minute Frenzy." I asked them, "Do you think it's helpful to have a special little room where people come to catch up in math?"

Anita, who was henna-haired and neatly dressed, thought it was. "But it's kind of weird to say, Oh, we have to leave for numeracy because we don't know how to do math."

I could see how that might be awkward, I said. "However, you probably have things that you can do better than other people can. I mean, seriously."

"I can ride horses better than they can," said Anita.

"Yeah, put them on a horse and see what happens," I said.

Anita said she owned a Haflinger, which was a strong horse. When she rode her Haflinger, she had to use a special bit. "My aunt has a shire-draft cross and also an Icelandic," she said.

The three of them did Fast Math and worksheets for the rest of the hour. Nobody talked. They were smart, undisruptive, compliant students who were no good with figures: having to serve time in a remedial room was a new and mildly mortifying experience for them. They thanked me when they left.

Block 4 was empty, and then I had a half-hour lunch break. I ate a sandwich slowly at my desk and drank a fizzy water, leafing through a history textbook called *The American Republic* that I'd found in a stack of discards in the teachers' break room. People glanced in at me through the windows. I felt as if I was myself serving an all-day in-school suspension. Occasionally there was a shout from the hall. The yellow walls of the numeracy room were bare, the corkboard was bare, and the whiteboard was bare except for the problem of the day—there wasn't even a taxonomy-of-learning poster to jazz up the place. The bald special ed teacher, Mr. Fields, came by to talk about Waylon.

He said, "The word on the grapevine was that shortly after we spoke, he had to leave, right?"

"He did," I said, "and thank you for alerting me. He talked to me a little bit. I don't know how much to get into it with you, but . . ."

"Nobody really knows the answers," Mr. Fields said.

"He's taking a lot of Paxil," I said. "He said, 'I can't sleep'—he just volunteered this—which is a side effect. And there's a side effect where you hear voices. I'm not a doctor, but it seemed to me like an awful lot of Paxil that he's taking."

"He particularly doesn't like this particular spot," said Mr. Fields, pointing at the floor. "He doesn't like math. So this happens regularly when he comes to school."

"He's a very nice kid," I said. "I'd be happy to spend time with him. We had a nice chat as we walked down."

"Oh yeah, he's always nice. For all these things that he's hearing, that are always telling him to do something terrible, he's never done any of that stuff. When you hear it, you go, Wow, that guy? He just doesn't come across that way."

"That's the thing," I said. "I think it's the side effect of the drug rather than the actual state of his own mind."

"Well," he said. He waved.

"Anyway, I appreciate the heads-up," I said.

Bong, bong, bong.

A thin, smiley eighth-grader, Birdie, came in and shut the door. "Yay, a substitute," she said. "I've been waiting for this."

Another girl, Corinne, entered and sat.

"There's a new kid coming, named Lorne," said Birdie. "This is his first day in this class. I don't know if he'll come, because I don't know if he'll remember."

I said, "So what she was thinking you guys should do is Fast Math, and your folders have some stuff in them. Let me know if I can help in any way."

"Do you want me to like work for five minutes, and then if Lorne hasn't come here I can go get him?" Birdie said.

Great idea, I said. I asked her if Fast Math helped.

"Yeah, it does," said Birdie.

"Can I go to the bathroom?" asked Corinne. She started to sign her name on the bathroom sign-out sheet.

"Oh, I don't think you need to sign that," I said.

A third girl, Zena, came in. "Sorry I'm late," she said.

Birdie and Zena started talking about Nelson, the boy who died. "Did you hear about that kid?" Birdie asked me. "They found him dead in the quarry."

"That's just horrible," I said.

"Yeah, he told his mom he was going for a walk," said Birdie.

"His mom said it was normal," said Zena. "He always goes on a walk. That one day he never came home."

"My sister knows him," said Birdie. "He was in my sister's grade."

The poor kid! The poor family! There was nothing more to say. The two girls swiveled in their chairs and did Fast Math for a few minutes. Lorne came in and allowed the door to shut with a click.

"Lorne, how are you?" I said.

"Good."

"So we've got Fast Math," I said, "and all kinds of happy things." I was starting to sound like Bill Alexander on *The Magic of Oil Painting*.

Birdie said, "He doesn't know how to get on Fast Math."

"I'll set him up!" said Zena.

"They're going to set you up," I said. Lorne gave me a half smile. He was curly-haired and slow-moving and handsome.

"This seems like a good school," I said to Birdie. "Good people, anyway."

Birdie made a skeptical sound.

"You think they're too strict, piling on the homework?"

"The teachers are horrible about homework," said Birdie. "They give us way too much. I wish we'd just have work at school, and family time at home."

"I totally agree," I said. "As a dad, I watched my kids go through Maine schools, and it was hours every night."

Birdie said, "My mom gets home at four, so when she comes home I'm still working on homework. The only time I see her is when I say good night."

"That's sad," I said.

"I know. Except for the weekend."

"This is the one childhood you've got," I said.

Zena said, "Mrs. Massey hasn't set Lorne up for Fast Math."

"Oh, no, what will we do?" I said. "Lorne, why don't you take a look at the riches of this folder."

"Oh ho," said Lorne. He opened the folder, which contained a placement test.

"Have fun," said Birdie to Lorne. "And Lorne, I'm telling you right now, whatever you get wrong, that's the worksheet you have to do."

"So do not get it wrong," I said.

"Do you want to see my folder?" said Birdie. She lifted it up. It weighed about a pound. "So do your test, just saying. I didn't even try when I took the test, so now I have all this."

"May I borrow a pen?" said Lorne.

"There's one right here," said Birdie.

Zena's keyboard began clicking as she played a bowling game in Fast Math. Corinne brought up a finished worksheet.

"You're all done?" I said. "Great. Do you have something you can read?"

"I have other worksheets to do," she said.

"Endless worksheets in life," I said.

Zena threw out some gum. "Mrs. McCardle said, 'Are you still chewing gum in school?' I go, 'It's really tasty, though.'"

"Really tasty," said Birdie. She noticed an appointment book in a corner that Susanna had left behind. "Her boyfriend is in the next class," she said.

Zena volunteered to take it to the office with Birdie.

"It sounds like a two-person job," I said.

"You can trust us," said Zena. They left.

"Can I go to the bathroom?" said Lorne. "Do I have to sign out?"

"Technically, yes," I said, "but I'm a substitute, so the normal rules don't apply."

Corinne worked quietly. The two girls returned. "We got it to the office, safe and sound," said Zena.

"Do you know how to do proportions?" Birdie asked me. Her problem concerned two rectangles, one eight feet wide and ten feet high, and the other sixty feet wide and forty-eight feet high—were they proportional? I drew the rectangles for her. I said, "The question is, is sixty over forty-eight the same as ten over eight? Proportional means if you shrunk this one down you could lay it right down on that one." We turned 60/48 into 15/12 and divided by three to get 5/4. "The point is you can simplify them to the point that you can say, Oh, they're the same proportions."

"Why don't they just say that, then?" said Birdie, going back to her chair.

A big girl named Janet swept in. She looked at the board and said, "What's going on, Mr. '*Baker*'?"

"Janet, I wrote you a letter," said Zena.

Janet looked at the letter. "That's bullshit," she said, and threw it out.

"Fuck you," said Zena.

Birdie laughed.

"Hah hah hah!" said Janet to Birdie. "You fucking . . . Mr. Baker, can we put on some music, as long as it's quiet, thanks!" said Janet.

"There's a ton of f-bombing," I said, "massive amounts of it."

"He's saying to watch your language," said Zena.

"Oh!" said Janet. She mock-tiptoed a few steps. "Okay," she whispered. "My bad, my bad." She turned on some hip-hop.

"Too loud," I said. "I'm sorry, that's painfully loud."

"Turn it down!" said Zena.

Janet looked in her folder. "What is this nonsense?" she said.

"Fast Math," I said.

"I'm doing it," said Janet. The girls all began whispering and f-bombing about someone named Anna.

"He just said not to swear," said Zena.

"I said, 'Freak you, Anna,'" said Janet.

"No, you didn't."

"Yeah, I did."

"Let's not be rude, guys," said Birdie.

"Are you in Ms. Scott's class?" Janet said to Lorne. Lorne said he was. "That teacher's hot," she said. "Those tight jeans? It's like she has no pants on."

Birdie went on with her grievances. "My math teacher, Mr. Lambert, he'll write something on the board and we copy it down, and when we need help he'll say, 'Look at your notes.' And then we'll say we don't understand, and he'll say, 'Look in the book.' And we'll say we don't understand the book, and he'll keep telling us to look at our notes."

"I got two days in ISS from him for asking for an eraser," said Lorne. "I was like, Hey, can I have an eraser? He was like, No, go to the office. I never got the eraser. That's what I'm bummed out about."

I asked if Mrs. Massey was into hip-hop.

Birdie said, "Mrs. Massey is like, 'I'm into jah-hazz, and classical blues.' I'm like, No."

Zena said, "Janet's watching dirty videos."

To Corinne, I said, "Thank you for actually doing lots of work."

Biggie Smalls came on Janet's iPad, doing "Big Poppa." When Biggie Smalls said, "Allow me to lace these lyrical douches in your bushes," Janet said, "Uh, I didn't—" and turned it down. She switched to Justin Bieber's "Stuck in the Moment" and the girls sang along tunefully, closing their eyes: "It's all fun and games till someone gets hurt."

"So cool," said Janet.

"Natasha is all about her tan," said Birdie.

"Natasha," said Janet with distaste. "Don't rub it in my face."

"It's not fair," said Birdie. "I'm pale."

"I have to go to spray tan," Janet said. "I don't tan. I just burn."

Zena looked up at the clock. "All right," she announced. "Class is over."

"Thank you for contributing," I said.

They were gone. I played "You Dropped a Bomb on Me," by the Gap Band at full volume. Nobody could hear me. When the door opened, I clicked it off.

BLOCK 5 WAS JUST A HANDFUL OF KIDS, three girls and two boys. "Are we doing Fast Math?" Erica asked.

"Is there a question of the day?" asked Jacqueline.

"There was a question of the day, but I mistakenly erased it," I said. "Should I put it up again?"

"No, it's fine," said Jacqueline.

"You shouldn't," said Sloan.

"We don't need it," said Jeannie.

I said, "I don't think you need it. You've got a lot of questions of the day. What is the meaning of life? All that kind of thing."

"What is the meaning of life?" said Erica. "Infinity pi!"

"It was a simple division question," I said. "And the answer was fifty-five. In Fast Math that bowling game looked pretty good."

"I like the ladybug one," said Deke. "I haven't done any other one this year. It's like a movie."

"Do we have to do Fast Math?" asked Erica.

"Absolutely must," I said. "There's no choice. You're in here. I'm in here. It's probably hypocritical for me to be saying you have to do Fast Math when I— GUYS, NO, NO, NO. No bumper cars, nothing like that."

"She lets us move around like this," said Jacqueline, scooting.

"If we need a pencil sharpened," said Deke, "we can just be like shooooo."

"It's funny," I said. "I think to myself, I don't care. And then I think, What would the teacher do? So then I drop the—lower the boom, and I fuss, and it's always about the wrong thing."

"BOOM, shaka laka laka BOOM," said Sloan.

"Do we still get our Jolly Ranchers?" asked Jacqueline.

"We need them right now," said Erica.

"I don't know where they are," I said.

"No, they're for Friday," said Jeannie.

"Ah, no, you see," I said. "They're for Friday."

"We almost got one," said Jacqueline.

Erica got an error message: "Unfortunately FASTT Math could not save your work. You will have to repeat today's lesson next time you log in."

I said, "You can just tell her that you did Fast Math today, but it didn't save your work. Try that. Saved by technology."

"Holy crap, I have a lot of work to do," said Jacqueline.

"I only have ten more assignments," said Deke.

"I might not be here tomorrow," said Erica.

I asked her why.

"ISS," said Erica. "I did something bad."

What was the ISS room like?

"I don't know, I've never been in there," said Erica.

"My brother's been in there twice," said Sloan.

"I got mad," said Erica, "and my friend was telling me to say it. I called a teacher the B-word."

"Bad friend," said Jeannie.

"She's not that bad a friend," said Erica. "I have no idea how to do this. Just look at all this I have to do." She made a whimper of despair.

We took a look. Her first problem had to do with the order of operations—i.e., Please Excuse My Dear Aunt Sally. "Can I write that on the board?" She wrote it on the board. "I don't remember what an exponent is."

"Like squared, cubed," I said. "One of those little numbers up on top." I wrote some exponents on the board.

"Can I go get a drink?" asked Jacqueline.

Sloan's paper had problems circled that he was supposed to do over. They involved something called the "least common multiple." Back in the day, it was called the "least common denominator," but times change.

Jacqueline sharpened a tiny stub of a pencil. "This is the funnest numeracy room ever," she said. "I think you should give us Jolly Ranchers."

"I do not," said Jeannie.

Erica was making another go at the first order-of-operations question.

"What's eight times seven?" I asked her.

"Thirty-seven!" said Erica. "What's eight times seven, people? Deke?"

"Forty-two," said Deke. "No, fifty-four!"

I made my little times-table speech again. "I just want to cut through all the underbrush, and give you a word of wisdom from a survivor. There are a lot of things that they're going to teach you in high school—"

"It's going to be junk," said Jeannie.

"A lot of it you're going to forget," I said. "One thing that will be useful to you your whole life is the basic times tables."

"You can always do a lattice," said Jacqueline.

"But you don't always want to draw a grid," I said. "All you have to do is go to Staples or Hannaford's—"

"Are you a survivor?" asked Erica.

"I am a survivor. I remember standing in front of a class in grade school, and they were doing one of those spelling bees except it was for multiplication, and I didn't know the answer, and I was humiliated. I got some flash cards, went through them, over and over again—and now, look at me. I'm a substitute teacher."

"Good story," said Jacqueline. "Makes me want to cry tears."

"So really, if you guys learn one thing today, learn eight times seven is fifty-six. I heard four different answers to eight times seven."

"It's fifty-six," said Jeannie.

"There you go."

"Seven times eight is fifty-six," said Jeannie.

I turned to Deke. "What is eight times seven?"

"Fifty-six," said Deke. "BOOM!"

"Did you *know* that eight times seven is fifty-six?" said Erica.

Deke began singing "Happy."

"What's two divided by four?" asked Erica. I did it on the board for her.

"Wait," Jeannie said, "if you do five take away ten you're going to get a negative, right?"

"Yes."

"Drop the pencil!" said Deke to Sloan. "Drop the pencil!"

"Guys, I want to see focused focus," I said. "Hyperfocus."

Erica said, "He has a pencil in his armpit."

Sloan dropped the pencil from his armpit.

"Deke, how's it going, man?" I asked.

"Delicious," he said.

"You've got your name down, good. This is the formula. Circumference equals two pi r. The radius is there."

"So you do two times three point one four times fourteen?"

"Exactly! So just do it. Have you got a calculator?"

"No." He went off in search of a calculator, and then he sneezed messily.

"That's nasty," said Jacqueline.

"I sneezed and it went out before I got my arm up," Deke said. "It was like, schwooo!"

"Disgusting," said Jacqueline.

"I didn't mean to," said Deke.

Jeannie shook her head. "This calculator is saying that two times seven is four."

"That's not right," I said.

"The one is faded," said Sloan.

"Then I need a new calculator," said Jeannie. "Deke!"

"What should I do?" Sloan asked, handing in his worksheet.

I said he should probably invent a new kind of internal combustion engine.

"Okay," he said.

"No," I said. "Learn the sevens times tables today. It only takes about twenty minutes. You know when a fly flies in front of a toad? The tongue shoots out and grabs the fly. The toad doesn't even have to think about it. What you have to be with that seven times eight is you have to be like the toad's tongue. It's got to be automatic."

"Say 'elephant juice,'" said Jacqueline to Deke.

"Elephant juice," said Deke.

"Say it to the person next to you."

Deke twirled in his chair to face Erica. "ELEPHANT JUICE," he said. Jacqueline laughed. Supposedly when you say "elephant juice" it looks like you're saying "I love you."

"I want to listen to music," said Jeannie. "But I can't."

I asked her what song she would choose to listen to.

"'You Only Live Once,' by Suicide Silence," Jeannie said. She said the first lines, leaving out the profanity. "'You only live once, so just go—nuts.'"

Meanwhile there was trouble at the whiteboard. "Stop," said Deke. "She's writing the F-word."

"No I'm not," said Jacqueline.

"Nine times seven is what?" I said.

"I don't know," said Jacqueline.

"Just learn that."

"Why?"

"Because if you learned one math fact a day, you would be in much better shape. Let me explain to you what's happening. They're loading wave after wave of stuff on top of this structure, and the structure that you've got is not helping you, because it doesn't exist. If you knew the nine-times-seven layer, it could hold the rest of it up."

"Sixty-three," said Jacqueline.

"That's right," I said.

"Can I clean the whiteboard, please?" said Erica. She erased the bad tiny words that Jacqueline had written.

Deke brought up his completed pi worksheet.

"Look at that!" I said. "Deke, nice job!"

"I know! Thank you."

"Can we play games?" said Sloan.

"Can we go for a walk in the hall?" asked Jacqueline.

"We've got four minutes left," said Deke. He lifted my green mug. "Hey, is this your cup? How did you do that?"

"It came in the store that way," I said. "It's called a crackle finish. At a certain moment, in the furnace, the glaze cracks and then changes color."

"It's cool," said Deke.

"Thanks," I said. I tried to make another speech but coughed instead. "I'm starting to really cough and hack, but I think you've done a wonderful job. I know I'm a bore, and I don't actually care about math personally, but I am the substitute math teacher, and I'm telling you, once you get those sevens down, the world is an easier place. Nine times seven."

"Thirty-six," said Jacqueline.

"Flip them around."

"It's time to go," said Deke.

I said, "You've got one and a half minutes to chat, share stories. How was your weekend?"

"I was sick all weekend," said Erica. "I had the flu."

"You seem healthy now."

"I saw her over the weekend," said Sloan, pointing to Jacqueline. "At Walmart. I almost bought candy, but I didn't."

They handed in their papers. "Well, that went just about as well as can be expected," I said.

"Yeah," said Jacqueline. "Have a wonderful day."

"You, too."

I tried to open the drawer to pull out the next set of folders, but it was locked.

I poked my head out in the hall. "Guys! Somebody locked the freaking drawer on me."

"Not me," said Jacqueline.

"Did Deke do it?" said Jacqueline. "He was over there."

"If you see Deke, will you send him to me?"

I struggled with the locked file drawer for a while. "Fucking torture chamber," I muttered. In the back of the top drawer I found a tiny key that fit the lock. Good. I got through ten seconds of "You Dropped a Bomb on Me" before the first of the last set of students slumped in. Block 6, block 6, block 6. The first girl was Livia. "I have a team meeting today, so I have to leave early," she said. "Can I have a cap eraser?" She found a stash of erasers in a lower drawer of Mrs. Massey's desk and took one.

Kent came in. "Remember, I called you Rocket?" he said.

I found Astrid's folder.

"Okay, I'm logged in," said Kent.

"Logged in to the matrix," I said. "What have you got? A fact grid. That's a joyous sight."

"Dude, I'm a master at this stuff," said Kent. "I'm so good, they call me the Monster. When they call you Rocket, they call me the Monster. I'm working on the twelve times table, and eight times four. Eight times four, thirty-two. Twelve times four, thirty-six. I'm a beast!"

"I'm almost done," said Jarrod. "I've just got a couple more papers."

"You're *not* almost out of here," said Rebecca. "Just kidding."

"I'm the closest," said Jarrod.

"Didn't you say you played Call of Duty?" said Kent.

"I don't want to talk about that now," I said.

They began slapping at their keyboards, doing their times tables. "You suck, Kent," said Jarrod.

More mad keyboarding. "Done!" said Kent. "First one done! One time, I was on fire. They had to call 911, I was so hot. I'm dead serious."

Jarrod began a geometry sheet. I read him the instructions in a Dr. Strangelove accent: *Describe each triangle below by both its sides and its angles.* Okay?"

"Okay," Jarrod said.

"Whose pencil is this?" Kent said. "It's my pencil now." He, too, embarked on a geometry sheet, which asked him to discriminate between equilateral, isosceles, and scalene triangles. I couldn't remember what a scalene triangle was, having never taken geometry in high school. "Scalene has no equal sides," Kent explained.

I pointed to a triangle. "That one has seriously equal sides," I said. "So I would hesitate before you write 'scalene.'" To give him a hint, I sang, "Isoscelee-hees, but I did not shoot the deputy."

"Can I go to the bathroom?" Astrid asked.

A kid named Bode brought up a placement test he'd taken. "What do I do now?" he said.

"I think you're done," I said. "You did Fast Math and you did this thing. I think you can read something, or check in with life, daydream. Is that permitted?"

"I guess so," Bode said.

"Can I check this?" said Kent. I showed him how to look up the answer key to sheet F-51 in the answer book. He wanted to know if I'd played Call of Duty on a PS3 or an Xbox. Livia needed help figuring out which were composite numbers in a long list. Seven was prime, but twenty-one and seventy-nine were composite.

Astrid returned from the bathroom and began talking quietly to Jarrod about whether a certain girl liked him. "She likes me as a friend," said Jarrod.

Kent said, "I play PlayStation Three, and I play Black Ops Two, or GTA Five, or I play Minecraft. And I have a YouTube channel. My name is hummertime. And I have a live stream, it's like an hour video I do of gameplays."

"Sounds like you take this very seriously," I said.

"This summer," said Kent, "I'm going to set up this thing where every view I get on my video I get a penny. If I get really popular and I get a million subscribers, that's kind of a little bit of money. Just from making videos."

"Pumping the traffic," I said.

"Do you know Adam Larousse, in eighth grade? I game with him and his brother. Me and him make Minecraft videos and crap."

"Minecrap?" I said.

"Never heard of that," Kent said. "Do you like my new kicks?" He showed me his Hyperdunk Nikes. "I got them customized, blue and black. Do you know the Dallas Mavs basketball team?"

"Can I have an eraser?" said Astrid.

I pulled out the bag of eraser caps from the drawer and made one disappear with the Chinese egg drop.

"I'm going to show *you* a magic trick," said Kent. "I'm going to make this eraser dissolve in my hand."

"With stomach acid?" I said.

"No, it's going to go through my skin, into my blood." He started rubbing the eraser cap vigorously against the palm of his hand.

"Don't hurt yourself," I said. "Looks like there's a little bit of a red mark."

"It happens." He rubbed and rubbed. "It's going to take a little while." He palmed the eraser and pretended to scrub it against his palm some more. Then he pulled the eraser out of his neck.

Bong, bong, bong.

When everyone was gone, and I'd written a note for Mrs. Massey, I went to the nurse's office, to tell someone in authority that I didn't think Waylon should be taking thirty milligrams of Paxil every day. Nurse Ritter was smiley and kind-faced, absorbed in braiding a girl's long beautiful red hair. "At some point I'd like to talk to you about Waylon," I said.

"Will you be in tomorrow?" she said.

I said I'd be in Wednesday.

"Let's talk then."

I drove home thinking about the dark circles under Waylon's eyes, and the soft, faintly despairing way he spoke. He'd seemed like a normal, articulate, polite kid going through his life in a Paxil trance, not sleeping and hearing voices. Why? Because he'd cried about having to go to school. Math made him anxious. Did Waylon need all this arithmetic in his life? Of course not.

Day Twenty-two was a wrap.

HOW DO YOU SPELL *JUICY*?

Mrs. Wallace's sixth-grade literacy intervention room was brightly lit, windowless, airless, and hot. I spent a long Wednesday there, goading "struggling readers" to work on a complicated assignment involving a book called *Esperanza Rising*, by Pam Muñoz Ryan, about a girl who leaves Mexico to make a new life in the United States. Each chapter of the book was named after the Spanish word for a fruit, a vegetable, or a nut, and the students' task that day was to pick one of these chapter titles and make a Keynote presentation about it on their iPads. They had to come up with at least five slides about, say, *las uvas* (grapes), and each slide had to contain at least three sentences. The first slide was to be an introduction, which described the qualities of the grape, employing words taken from a list of about a hundred and thirty food-related adjectives. The second slide was the "Why?" slide, about why people like grapes and what they make with grapes and what health benefits were derived from eating grapes. The third slide was the "Where?" slide, in which was revealed where grapes were grown and related information; the fourth slide was the "When?" slide, wherein you discussed the growing season of the grape and whether grapes were available year-round in Maine and how much they cost; and the fifth slide was the conclusion, which was supposed to be in two parts: *What did you learn that you hoped others learned about your fruit/vegetable/nut?* and *Do you think that you will try anything new that you learned about your topic?* In bold at the top of the sheet was a command, complete with typo: *MUST HAVE CORRECT SPELLING, PUNCTUATION, AND CAPTILIZATION.*

In the first block, a smart, funny struggling reader with braces named Kayley dozed off. "I'm so tired," she said. "And I'm hurt. I was on my bike. There was this girl and she was hogging the whole road. I went so fast down the road I had no control, trying to get a bug out of my ear. One hand on the bike, one hand trying to get the bug out of my ear, and then I fell. I slid." She showed the bandage on her hand. "And I slid on my hip, too."

Kayley eventually made an informational slide about papayas and gave me her student IEP log to sign. Had she been organized, focused, and respectful? I checked off the yes boxes and signed it.

When the next class came in, I asked them what happens to Esperanza in the book.

"She gets eaten by her undead father," said Aspen, another supposedly struggling reader. She managed, by the end of the hour, to create two slides about papayas.

Carson, who liked to make blubbling, blithering sounds, was in my third class of the day. "Puh-puh-puh-puh PAYA!" he said, in a goofy cartoon stutter.

"Let's pick one," I said, holding flat the list of chapter titles for Carson to look at. "Do you like nuts, berries, carrots? What do you like?"

"Carson, do you like *nuts*?" said Jeb.

Carson made a raspberry sound and giggled.

I pointed to *las papas*. "Do you like potatoes, Carson?" I asked. "Do you like french fries?"

"I love french fries," he said, in a normal voice. "I throw them out the window to give to the squirrels."

We broke for lunch; when Carson returned he began by making faux spastic noises. "GUHNEEP! MEEEEEP! MIGGA MIGGA NIGGA NIGGA!" He laughed explosively.

"You're having some trouble, man," I said. "Do you get sent down a lot?"

"No," he said, in his real voice. Then, giggling, he pulled out a handful of broken french fries from his pocket and stuffed them in his mouth.

"Ew, yucky, gross!" said Whit.

"I'm going to puke!" said Bronson.

"Sit yourself right down here," I said to Carson. "I want to hear how you read."

"I'm a potato," said Carson. "I don't read that book."

"Just start," I said. "Do what you can. The first word."

"Ethperantha!" he said, in what sounded like a saliva-rich Sylvester-the-cat accent.

"Okay, but do it in an American accent," I said. "Esperanza . . ."

He continued to read in his Sylvester accent: "*. . . almotht never left Mama's side. She thponged her . . .*"

"So you actually know how to read," I said.

"SpongeBob!" he said.

"*She sponged . . .*"

"*. . . her wiff cool watta.*" He read another line, and I realized he was imitating a disabled kid with a severe speech disorder.

"Peaches are awesome, yay," said Noelle, who was trying to concentrate.

Carson cleared his throat noisily, turned to Noelle, and then said, in a Southern accent, "Tryin' to read here, ma'am."

I asked Carson how old he was.

"Fifty-eight," said Carson.

I asked him again.

"Twelve," said Carson.

"Why are you so keyed-up?"

"BLIP!" He read a little more, using his disabled-kid accent. He was a good sight reader: he didn't hesitate when he came to the phrase *extra layers of newspaper*. I told him to read in an even, pleasant voice.

"Okay, then I'll talk in French," he said. "Jigga jugga bigga bugga. Vitta, vutta."

"Can we turn off the lights?" said Noelle.

I didn't answer; Carson had begun crawling under the desks. "UH UUUUUUUH!" he bellowed.

"Carson, do your work," said Jeb.

I told Noelle to have a look at her slides. "I've already done five slides," she said, which wasn't true.

"Then get your book out and read a page."

"I can't read that book," Noelle said. "All it is is gibberish! Half the words are gibberish."

I said, "If you know the word *gibberish* you can probably read the book no problem."

"It's Spanish," said Jeb.

Carson switched to making dog-panting noises and snorts. Finally I lowered the boom. "Take the book, find a page, read it, and don't make a sound," I said. "If you make another sound in the next five minutes, I'm going to send you directly downstairs. Just pull it together. You obviously can read. All of this is just an explosion of ridiculousness, right?"

"Yes," Carson said, nodding.

"Five minutes of silence," I said. "Otherwise you'll go downstairs, and that's no fun. People will fuss at you and you'll have notes written on your log, and everybody's unhappy."

"So, kind of like this?" said Carson. "YOU SUCK YOU SUCK YOU SUCK YOU SUCK YOU SUCK."

Enough. I stood. "All right, you're going down," I said.

"I'm going to read a book," said Carson, in his normal voice, picking up a random book.

"No, you're not," I said, "you're coming down with me. I said do it, and you didn't do it. Let's go."

"Whenever a substitute's here he's always like this," said Noelle.

Carson and I walked together down the long hall to the stairway. "Tell me everything," I said to him. "Are you messing up like this because you enjoy getting in trouble?"

"I have ADHD," Carson said, in his normal voice.

I said, "Whether or not you have ADHD, it's something you have to control."

Carson began walking downstairs backward, very slowly. "Bloomp, bloomp, bloomp, bloomp," he said with each step down.

"GET DOWN THE STAIRS," I said, pissed. "You're in some serious hot water." It made me nervous to have left the class unattended.

"Some serious what?"

"Hot water. Come on down."

He finally reached the first floor. "I'll just go back up in five minutes," he said calmly. His one goal seemed to be to make the substitute teacher mad. Well, he'd succeeded.

I walked down the hall. "Stay with me," I said.

"You're walking too fast for me," he said, dragging.

I swatted a copy of *Esperanza Rising* against my leg. "You STAY with me! You are sad, man. You are sad."

We arrived in the doorway of the guidance office, where two aides were talking and laughing. "You can leave Carson right here," one of them said. I loped back to my class. They'd all been sitting quietly.

"How do you spell *juicy*?" said Whit.

"You give it the *J*, give it the *U*—"

Noelle interrupted. "J-U-I-C-Y," she said loudly.

"Shhh, we're having calm," I whispered. "Peacefulness now." I wrote *juicy* on the board.

"Can we turn the lights off?" said Noelle.

"Yes," I whispered, "I love it when the lights are off."

The iPads glowed in the murk of the room, and there was silent Keynoting and reading for fifteen minutes. Because I'd walked Carson downstairs, my power over the class had increased. But I felt trembly and ashamed of myself for having lost my temper with him. If there was ever a person who needed a different setup, it was Carson. He needed a sympathetic tutor at home for an hour a day, paid for with public money if necessary. In a few years, his brain would calm down and he'd be fine. All middle school offered him was the giggly rapture of disruptiveness, the brief adrenaline surge of seeing which accents and forms of noise from his proven toolbox of chaos would drive a given teacher over the edge.

When Noelle and Whit began feuding, I had everyone in the class read aloud a few sentences each from *Esperanza Rising*. They all read surprisingly well—all except Margo, who refused to read anything because she was embarrassed. Sometimes they stumbled over a word like *clinging* or *temporary*. At the end of the hour, Carson returned to get his backpack. He held out his behavioral log sheets. "Sign these," he said, in his real voice.

I got a pencil. "*Respectful.* How respectful were you? A one?"

"Two," he said.

I checked two. "You had supplies, you had homework? You had a positive attitude? I think that's a two. You used appropriate language? Not so good, right?"

"I spoke French and English, yeah, that was fine," he said.

"No, I mean anytime people were trying to say anything, you were making all kinds of weird sounds, right?"

"No."

"Well, it's true, isn't it?"

"No."

I signed his sheets. "I'm sorry I had to send you down. I want to get to know you and I want things to go better."

"You know me," Carson said.

"I want to know the real you," I said.

"That was the real me!" he said, and left. He really just needed a tutor for an hour a day. Middle school was destroying him. I was part of the machine of his destruction.

Next class, Emily P. and Emily R. both chose to write about peaches, and Frankie chose the onion. It turned out that all but one of the kids in the class lived on Russell Lake.

"Russell Lake is trashy," said Frankie, looking up pictures of onions on Google.

"There's too many people, the houses are way too close," said Emily P.

"There's crazy people around Russell Lake," said Emily R.

"I'm the only person in here from Mossfield," said Rosabelle.

I asked her what Mossfield was like.

"Eh," said Rosabelle. "My neighborhood's trashy."

"How do you spell *tasty*?" asked Emily P. I wrote it on the board.

Peaches are so sweet and juicy, Emily P. wrote. *There yellow red and orange there round tasty and very soft the middle of the peach has a big pit.* Frankie lost his temper while trying to move a photograph of an onion into a Keynote slide. "I DON'T like doing this stuff!" he said. Over his laboriously pasted-in onion picture, he wrote: *Onions give you protein. They have amazing flavors.*

The Keynote app had just had an upgrade, and the resizing of text boxes worked slightly differently than it had, which made for some confusion. I thought of how many clouds of unknowing were enveloping these students during a single hour of a Wednesday afternoon at school: they didn't know how to spell, didn't know how to skim through search results in Google, didn't know how to pan for gold in a Wikipedia article, didn't know whether peaches had pits, didn't know what *varieties* meant in the context of fruits and vegetables, didn't know the difference between *they're* and *there*, didn't know how to use the updated version of the Keynote app, didn't know why Mrs. Wallace wanted them to make a Keynote presentation based on one of the foodstuffs mentioned in the chapter titles of *Esperanza Rising*, didn't know any of the Spanish words that were sprinkled throughout *Esperanza Rising*, didn't know what I as a substitute would or wouldn't allow them to do, and didn't know whether their being sent to a remedial literacy class meant that they were stupid. They had nothing but music to hold on to—music, and video games, and sports, and pictures of their dogs.

"I want to get a boxer," said Emily P. to Emily R.

"Can we have free time now?" asked Emily R.

I nodded.

"Thank you."

Rosabelle told me about a Wii activity she liked called Mii, where you make random people. "I've made myself," she said, "I've made Emily P., I've made my family." We talked about various iPhone disasters. "My brother had his iPhone, with all his pictures, in his pocket and he went into the lake," said Emily P. "He put it in rice but it still didn't work."

And then suddenly their iPads were zipped away and I watched my Russell Lake and Mossfield friends walk out the door. For the last block of the day I had only one student, Jacob. He was supposed to put on his headphones and use a piece of instructional software called System 44. "Please have him work quietly," said the sub plans. "He will try to chat." Jacob was a porcupine hunter, he told me, and a skeet shooter; he shot hundreds of clays every weekend, and he had to pay for his clays, which got expensive. "I'm on the Maine state team," he said. "Most of the time I get twenty-five out of twenty-five. My parents own a hundred and thirty acres in Wallingford, so I shoot a lot." He used a Beretta semiautomatic shotgun. "It's not like a normal shotgun—there's no kickback on it at all. It's my first year on the team."

"Impressive," I said. "Sounds like it makes you happy."

"Yep. Can I go to the bathroom?"

Two minutes later he was back. "Somebody in the bathroom wrote tons of swears on the door," he said. "Would you like me to go down to the office to tell the custodians?"

"You might want to wait till the end of the day," I said. "Nothing's going to happen now."

Jacob put on his headphones and let the jokey software man from System 44 teach him how to read better. After twenty minutes, he packed up to go. "Have you been living in Maine your whole life?" he said.

I said, "We moved to Maine about fifteen years ago—thank you for asking—when my kids were small. I was born in New York City and grew up in upstate New York."

"I don't know how you can live in New York City, with all the people," he said. "It feels so claustrophobic." Jacob was off to another literacy class, he said, where they read aloud to each other. "Have a good day. Are you going to be in here again?"

Maybe, I said. "I'll see you around."

"Bye," he said.

I sat for ten minutes, waiting for the day to end. When the dismissal bongers bonged and first wave was announced, I went to Nurse Ritter's office. She was out, but Waylon was there to drop off his chart. I asked him if he was feeling better.

"Yep," he said, with a cheerful note in his voice, but he looked sluggish and heavy-lidded. He walked slowly off down the hall. Nurse Ritter returned.

"I just wanted to briefly mention Waylon's situation," I said to her. "Waylon volunteered that he's taking thirty milligrams of Paxil. He seemed catatonic."

"Yes," said Nurse Ritter.

"Mr. Fields said take him down to the nurse when he's hearing voices. Well, that's one of the side effects of Paxil, as I'm sure you know. It seems like a hell of a lot of drug to be in his system."

"That's not all, either," said Nurse Ritter.

"He just seems like a guy who's seriously struggling with overmedication," I said.

"You and I do not disagree on that topic."

"I'm so glad to hear that," I said.

A girl with a knee injury came in to get her shoes. "I'm having a private conversation," said Nurse Ritter.

"My feet smell," said the girl. She left.

"I'm just thinking that there are long-term effects," I said. "And he seems like a wonderful kid, a really nice kid. He got sad when he started middle school, so he's been taking this monstrous thing ever since. I know you know this."

"I do," the nurse said. She spoke hesitantly, not wanting to say too much. "It's not like it's one provider. Unfortunately it's a societal and a cultural thing. We want that quick fix, and we think that it comes in a pill. And it's also very much about individual family culture. Sometimes this is a very strong current running through the family culture. As a school nurse, the best I can do is take every opportunity to offer suggestions to a family, and to try to educate a child. But ultimately I can only offer what I can offer. And I do offer!"

"I just thought, Wow, that's a lot of Paxil."

"Right, and if only that was all, but it's not. It's a sad story. The overmedication of children, and for that matter of adults, is problematic in our society. The prevalence is ever on the rise."

"Is it still on the rise?" I asked. "I thought maybe it had peaked out."

"No, it hasn't," Nurse Ritter said. She seemed as if she wanted to tell me more but thought better of it. "I appreciate your feedback. Just know that I'm very attentive to this issue. I'm working very closely with the providers to come to some terms. It's crazy. It's a lot, lot, lot of pills. We just don't know what to do with our feelings."

"Thanks so much," I said. "I'll see you again."

Part of the track team was out in the hall, shouting. I handed in my ID tag and waved goodbye to the secretaries.

Farewell, Day Twenty-three.

HAMBURGER WRITING

A WEEK WENT BY, and then I was back at Lasswell Elementary to relieve Mrs. White, a second-grade teacher who'd just had her knee replaced. "Good class, but a few strong personalities," said the sub plans. "Keep Blaze and Dorrie apart. Redirect Boyd and let him use the deadphones that are in his desk to block his ears so he can focus." Boyd was allowed to use something called the T stool, and so was Evan: "They can share it throughout the day." Both of them owed wall time at recess from the day before.

Blaze, a pretty, sprightly girl in a pink flowered dress, gave me her lunch money and showed me the T stool, which was shaped like a T and did not stand up by itself—the effort of staying balanced apparently helped "strong personalities" fidget less. The sub plans were four pages long and thorough. From 8:40 to 9:00, while Blaze passed out a worksheet on plural nouns, I drew smiley faces on turned-in homework. Then Tatiana led the class in the good-morning song, which went "Good morning, how are you? So glad to sing together, in any kind of weather. So glad to sing along, in song, together."

Tatiana went to the easel to read the morning message from Mrs. White, written in red marker. It was intentionally filled with mistakes:

"Good morning. it is a wonder ful wednesday please be a grate class for the sub and work hard Keep your morning werk paper at you're desk so you can correct it in an minute. Love, Mrs. White."

This class was full of good spellers and punctuators, and we corrected the mistakes without too much trouble, while Boyd and Evan roamed and chattered. The main problem wasn't Boyd, though—the main problem was the loud first-grade class on the other side of the room divider. Insulated floor-to-ceiling walls between classrooms are a good thing.

From 9:10 to 9:20 we turned singular nouns into plurals, and then I read the class some of chapter 11 of *Because of Winn-Dixie*, about a girl named Opal and a dog named Winn-Dixie. The kids loved this book. Opal, Opal's dad, and Winn-Dixie sit out a terrible thunderstorm on a couch, and Opal scratches Winn-Dixie behind the ears the way he likes. Suddenly Opal gets choked up because she realizes how much she loves her dad. *I loved him because he loved Winn-Dixie. I loved him because he was going to forgive Winn-Dixie for being afraid. But most of all, I loved him for putting his arm around Winn-Dixie like that, like he was already trying to keep him safe.* While I read it I almost got choked up.

"That was a good chapter," I said. "How many people here—quietly— have dogs?"

We went around the class hearing who had what kind of dog. Hunter had a black Lab. Blaze's dog's name was Hercules. Dorrie had a German shepherd named Cara who was three. Hugh had two dogs: "Stormy's brown and Cash is black," he said, "and they're both crazy. They run around drooling and they go to the bathroom in my room all the time when I accidentally forget, so it smells bad in there." Niall had a husky named Fang and a boxer named Jumper. Megan showed a picture of her dog on her phone. Denny had a German shepherd named Daisy. Rollo had ten dogs, one of which was a Chihuahua named Boss, and he had ten cats. "One of them is Cleo, and the rest I can't remember their names," he said. Braden had two dogs, one named Rita and one named Topper. Archer also had two dogs. "One is a golden retriever–Great Pyrenees mix. Her name's Tippy. And I have two cats that are sisters. One's name is Red, which is my cat, and my mom's cat's name is Pawsie." Agnes had a dog that was part a mix between a black Lab and an English springer spaniel. "She's really crazy and we have to train her. We can't have any cats because my dad's allergic." Boyd's dad had a pit bull named Wing.

Then Blaze handed out copies of *Scholastic News*, which carried an article about how to survive some common "summer bummers" like jellyfish stings, poison ivy rashes, tick bites, and sunburn. Boyd threw his copy of *Scholastic News* on the floor, and I banished him to a spot in some blue cushions off to one side of the group. Rollo read about the importance of tucking your pants in your socks. The shiny, flimsy pages of the newsletter rattled. We read about a chemical in broccoli that may work as a sunscreen.

"You know what's strange?" I said. "Everybody says, 'Oh god, I hate broccoli.' It's delicious."

"It's so good!" said Megan.

"Especially in mac and cheese," said Braden.

"I threwed it up," said Boyd.

"TMI," said Blaze.

It was windy and rainy out, so we had to have recess in the room. Blocks came out, and counting games, and checkerboards—all sorts of tabletop fun, most of which ended up on the floor. The room was destroyed. Hugh came up. "Me and Boyd owed five minutes on the wall from yesterday," he said. "I've already been there for two minutes, and he's been playing."

"I want to shake your hand, sir," I said. "Very responsible. Boyd, towards the end you owe me five, right?"

"Okay," said Boyd.

Denny said he had nobody to play with, so we looked at a book about wolves together.

When it was time for Boyd to serve his wall punishment, I sat next to him and asked him what he liked doing on the weekend.

"I go to my dad's," said Boyd, "and I like to go dirt biking. I used to have a miniature bike, but it's too big, so I have bikes about this tall now." He held his hand at his waist.

"It must be a bit frightening to get on a bike," I said.

"Yeah, it's real frightening," Boyd said. "Now I have a trail bike with a clutch and a shifter. I have a race bike, too. There's trails down at my grampy's shop. That's where I ride."

We talked about his little brother, about four-wheelers, and about how much he hated adjusting the loose seat on his pedal bike. Boyd, who had been a mad hatter up to that time, was perfectly able to have a calm conversation if he wanted to. He was not the problem—school was the problem.

"It's time to clean up," whispered Dorrie.

"TIME TO CLEAN UP!" I said.

"My waist hurts," said Agnes.

At eleven o'clock they had to take a unit 8 math test. Dorrie passed out privacy folders and everyone more or less settled down. But the test was too hard. Tatiana was stumped by this question: *There are three pennies in 1/5 of the pile. How many are there in the whole pile?* I drew her five rows of three pennies each. She sort of got it temporarily, but others didn't. Another baffler: *How much is ⅓ of twelve pennies?* I wanted to apologize to the class for these premature fraction problems. Three whiz kids could do them fine; for others it was just more fly-buzz of confusion in their heads. Second grade was too soon for this.

Agnes, who was done early, worked on an idiom assignment: draw a cartoon to illustrate "letting the cat out of the bag." Braden read. Dorrie and Blaze squabbled. Boyd and Hugh threw pencils. I collected the math tests and then drew Dorrie and Blaze aside. "I want you each to tell each other something nice right now. I need to see kindness."

"Dorrie, you're my best friend," said Blaze.

Dorrie said nothing and turned away. "Let's hear it," I said. "Something nice. Look at this beautiful dress Blaze is wearing. I'm going to count to three. One—"

"You look pretty today," said Dorrie.

While I was negotiating with the two of them, the rest of the class disintegrated into a state of lawless riot. "VOICES AT ZERO!" I said. It was time to do something called "Hamburger Writing." I waved one of the worksheets they'd filled out yesterday, taken from a website called SuperTeacherWorksheets.com. In the outlined top bun of a schematic drawing of a hamburger they were supposed to have recorded their title and main idea, which was "Memorial Day Fun," or some such. Then came three layers—the tomato layer, the cheese layer, and the hamburger layer—each of which was meant to hold a recorded detail of their Memorial Day experience. Underneath it all was the bottom bun, in which they were to write a closing thought. Niall's hamburger, for instance, had *going to Friendship park* on the tomato layer, *playing with my cousins for two hours* on the cheese layer, *playing video games* on the hamburger patty layer, and, on the bottom bun, *I liked Memorial Day.*

"So the top bun is going to be your main idea," I said.

"Ugh," said Hugh.

Now, while referring back to their "Hamburger Writing" worksheets, they had to write a rough draft of a paragraph about how much fun they'd had on Memorial Day, two days earlier. Pencils began twirling. Niall wrote, *On Momoriel day me, juliun, and Aunty sarah, Went to Freindship park for one hour than we went home.* Agnes wrote, *My great grandfather walked in a parade because he was in the army. Then later, me and my family had a BBQ with our firends Andrew and Lisa.* Rollo wrote that he'd found a baby bird in the garage. "It broked its wing," he told me, "so I saved it." Boyd, sitting under his desk, had figured out how to stick the cap of a pen to the tip of his tongue.

Next door, Mrs. Thurston's class began loudly chanting, "WHEN MY HANDS ARE AT MY SIDES, AND I'M LINED UP STRAIGHT AND TALL . . ." It gave me a shiver when I heard it.

"It's time for lunch," said Tatiana.

After lunch they went to music class, where they colored in likenesses of Beethoven, Bach, and Mozart. Evan's Beethoven had red wolf eyes. At 2:05 I took them back to our classroom to write several sentences about Tatiana, the Star of the Week, in the Friends Book. Tatiana liked a TV show called *Lub Ruts*, her favorite animal was a dog, and her favorite colors were blue and hot pink. Summer wanted to know how to spell *beautiful*, as in "Tatiana is beautiful." Dorrie became crazed with boredom and jealousy and walked around the room singing to herself and rummaging in boxes and washing her hands for minutes at a time.

The sub plans said that at 2:20 the whole class was supposed to build their read-to-self stamina during something called DEAR Time. DEAR stood for "Drop Everything And Read." I was required to time them with a stopwatch. According to a chart, the class had lasted for a full twelve DEAR minutes one day, three DEAR minutes the next day, and three DEAR minutes the day after that. I asked Solaris, who seemed smart, what I should do. "Do you think this class has got it in them to do DEAR Time?" The place looked like Grand Central Terminal.

"If you don't want to, we don't have to do DEAR Time," Solaris said helpfully.

Good, let's skip it and move on, I thought. I passed out a fresh worksheet called "The Beautiful Butterfly," which Mrs. White had printed out from HaveFunTeaching.com. Dorrie began a lengthy hand-washing session. I said, "Dorrie, come on, you're done, you're done, you're done! God dangit!"

Solaris read about butterflies, which have a thorax, an abdomen, and a nectar-sipping proboscis. *"The world's smallest butterfly,"* read Blaze, *"is* The Blue Pygmy. *It has a wingspan the size of a nickel."* Agnes read, *"The lifespan of most butterflies is only twenty to forty days. Some butterflies only live for three to four days."*

I had to banish Boyd to the pillows again, whereupon he was attentive. "Check that out," I said. "Our lives are almost a hundred years. Their lives are three days."

"That's so sad," said Blaze.

Braden said, "I knew a bug that only has a lifespan of one day. It's some kind of little yellow bug that lives in Oklahoma."

"Centipede?" asked Blaze.

"No," said Braden.

"How long do centipedes live?" asked Blaze.

"I actually once revived a cicada," said Braden. "I had this beer bottle cap, and I filled it with water, and then I put the cicada in there, and I circled it with rocks. I closed my eyes for a second, and when I opened my eyes, it started fluttering its wings."

Agnes said, "Male mosquitoes don't really harm you, they just make you itch. But female mosquitoes are even worse, because when they land on you, they do the same thing as male mosquitoes, except they spit something into your skin. And then you get sick, and you could die from it."

"Good thoughts," I said. There were five multiple-choice questions about butterflies they had to answer. The word *pygmy* caused some merriment. "Not pyg me, pyg you!" said Braden.

I found a chair next to Boyd. "I appreciate it," I said. "You sat quietly and you didn't go wild. Let me hear you read."

Boyd read me the first paragraph about the butterfly flawlessly, with almost no hesitation over *thorax* or *abdomen*. Together we went over his IEP log sheet. "Morning work I finished," Boyd said. "Math test I finished. I think today was great. So you put a little star."

"Mr. Baker, I have two pink monkeys," said Summer.

"I'm right in the middle of a conference," I said. "But wow."

Summer laughed.

"The only thing is sometimes you get a little wild," I said to Boyd. "You know that, right? Using your T stool as a weapon, that kind of thing?"

Boyd said, "It's just that for breakfast I have Crispix and then I have something that's loaded with a lot of sugar." I asked him if he took any medication. He didn't. "My brother does," he said.

Mrs. Thurston's head appeared at the door. She'd heard Hugh making noise in the hallway. "Next time he'll be spending some recesses with me if he makes that much noise," she said.

Hugh flumped in his chair.

"See, it reflects badly on me," I said. "You're bringing me down, you're bringing yourself down, and you're bringing human life down." We laughed at the ridiculousness of it all. "I know you're rational."

I signed Boyd's behavior log sheet. "And then I bring this home and I have my parents sign it and I bring it back," Boyd said.

Denny lay on the floor while Rollo poked at him. I called for chair stacking.

"Can we play Hangman?" asked Agnes.

"Well, the class is kind of out of control," I said. "As you can see."

She drew a scaffold on the board anyway.

A bell rang and they lined up. Tatiana walked up crying. "Mr. Baker, Hunter whacked me in the face with his backpack."

"I'm so sorry, kiddo," I said. "Right on your nose? I'm really sorry. Thanks for being a really nice kid in this class."

The first-wave buses were ready. "Bye, guys."

Megan was crying now, too. She said, "I said, 'Are you my friend?' and they said no."

"They get really hyper," said Agnes.

"Where's my skull?" said Boyd. He found a squishy foam skull in his backpack.

Second wave. "Bye, thank you!" I said. I listened to their voices die out as they jostled bus-ward. Next door, Mrs. Thurston began sharpening pencils for tomorrow.

Blaze left me a letter, written in six colors of marker: "TO Mr: Baker From Blaze I ♡ you Mrs. Baker your the best teacher in the world!" On the easel, Agnes had written, "Mr. Baker is the nicest ever." Below it Summer wrote, in small letters, "He sure is!"

I found a green Post-it and wrote a note for Mrs. White: "Students were great today—attentive, good-natured, and alert—aside from a few chaotic moments. Thanks for letting me fill in in your class."

I made sure the Memorial Day paragraphs were stapled to their respective "Hamburger Writing" worksheets and stacked them neatly on Mrs. White's desk, along with the butterfly papers, the math tests, the copies of *Scholastic News*, and the plural noun worksheets. I put *Because of Winn-Dixie* back where I'd found it, with the bookmark at the page where I'd stopped reading. My bottle of hand sanitizer was almost empty. I sat for a moment. Then I left for home.

Day Twenty-four, finito.

HIGH ON SUMMERTIME

The next morning I was in one of the modular classrooms at Lasswell Elementary in place of Mr. Seaborg, who was, judging by the newspaper headlines taped to his door, a huge Red Sox fan. His fourth-grade sub plans were handwritten on yellow legal paper. First there was music class, and then a math packet to do, then lots of other things. The last paragraph said: "If you have ANY issues with Micky, please send him to the office."

A girl named Stacy sipped iced tea and asked me if I'd substituted at Lasswell before. I said I had. "I've never done fourth grade, though. This is a whole new world for me."

Peter had a T-shirt on that said "Don't Fear My Awesomeness." A rowdy boy, Vance, came in with a fake mustache stuck to his upper lip.

"He has a whole package of them," said Colt.

After the pledge, they chanted a class chant: "WE THE STUDENTS IN MR. SEABORG'S AWESOME FOURTH-GRADE CLASS WILL LISTEN AND FOLLOW DIRECTIONS, BE SAFE, AND ACT RESPONSIBLY. WE WILL HAVE A SENSATIONAL FOURTH-GRADE YEAR. YEE HAW!"

While the class was off at music, I skimmed through *Hatchet*, the book Mr. Seaborg was reading to them. It was about a boy trying to survive in the wilderness after an airplane crash, and it looked good.

"Mr. Baker, look at my tattoo," said Juniper, a small bright girl with a ponytail. She had a flower on her arm.

"Classy," I said.

"I have to get another mustache," said Vance, retrieving a baggie from his desk.

For the rest of the morning, they did various math packets. There was a page of clock questions (*How much time has elapsed between 11:45 and 2:15?*) and a page of geometry questions (*Describe the difference between a rhombus and a parallelogram*), and they had to fill out a bar graph about Carla's international coin collection. Carla had thirteen coins from China, fifteen coins from Japan, four from Vietnam, and ten from India. *How many more coins does Carla have from China than Vietnam?* They also had calendar problems—Amanda was born two weeks after St. Patrick's Day, what date was she born on?

Mattie came up to have her packet corrected. "How's it going?" I asked her.

"Good," she said. "Actually, bad."

I looked at her paper, which had equations with small blank boxes in them representing variables. "What are you doing algebra for?"

"Because I'm smart," she said. But it was too hard for her. She couldn't get her mind around $\square - 10 = 5$ and $16 + \square = 74$.

I went over three elapsed-time clock problems with Micky, and he seemed to get it, finally. Using plastic coins, Vance and I practiced making change for a fifty-three-cent plate of buttermilk pancakes.

Everything they were learning so far was worth knowing, I thought: how to read a bar graph, how to make change, how to round up a number, how to go forward by weeks in a calendar and by hours in a clock. It wasn't easy for them, but it got them closer to somewhere they would eventually need to go.

The class started lining up. Micky and Juniper squabbled in line. "You look like one of those scientists in movies," said Vance.

Just as we left for the cafeteria, Micky doubled over, with something in his eye. "Don't scrub your eye," I said. "Grab your upper eyelash and pull it down over your lower eyelash. It'll make some more tears and it'll flush it out."

"It's gone," said Micky.

I had lunch duty, meaning that I walked around the tables saying hello and smiling at kids I recognized. Stacy showed me her plum and waved. After fifteen minutes, a teacher raised her hand. Everyone in the cafeteria raised hands and the teacher made a speech about how it was too loud. When she lowered her hand, the noise immediately resumed. Five minutes passed. "VOICES ARE *WAY* TOO LOUD," said the teacher. "AT THIS POINT YOUR HANDS SHOULD BE UP AND YOUR VOICES SHOULD BE OFF. IT IS MUCH TOO LOUD IN HERE TODAY, FOLKS. WE ARE BEGINNING TO EMPTY AND CLEAN TABLES. THAT DOES NOT REQUIRE TALKING."

Another two minutes passed, with noise again at full redline level. The teacher said, "OKAY, FROM THIS POINT ON THERE IS *NO* TALKING. IF I HEAR VOICES, YOU—OWE—RECESS!"

What a blessed deliverance to escape from the cafeteria—a giant sonic meatloaf. Twenty-five minutes a day of this torture would be enough to make any slightly jiggy person hyperactive. Yet most of them took it in stride.

Silent reading was up next. Carly opened her paperback of *A Wrinkle in Time*. I wrote a quotation from Samuel Johnson on the whiteboard. Nobody said anything for twenty-five minutes. The sound of pages turning was like distant cars passing on the road. I hated for it to end, but the sub plans said, "12:00 to 12:20—read aloud from *Hatchet*."

Emery told me where Mr. Seaborg usually sat when he read aloud— near the whiteboard. "Chapter sixteen of *Hatchet*," I said, "by Mr. Gary Paulsen. *And now he stood at the end of the long part of the lake, and was not the same—would not be the same again.*" I read for a page, and then, while our hero was hunting a bird, Micky hopped up to go to the bathroom. Vance and Isaiah got up to follow him. "We have to go with him," said Vance, "because he makes bad choices in there."

I followed Micky and his monitors to the bathroom and waited by the door. "You're not supposed to wait," Micky said,

"Just go to the bathroom!" I said.

The bathroom break completed, we got back in our places. I pointed to the Samuel Johnson quotation on the board. "Can anyone read this sentence to me?"

They read: *"The natural flights of the human mind are not from pleasure to pleasure, but from hope to hope."*

"You guys are good readers," I said. I told them a few things about Samuel Johnson—that he'd written the first really good dictionary of English, and that he was kind of twitchy.

"He had tics?" said Emery.

"Yes, he had all these tics. He was brilliant, but when he would walk down the street he would just be sort of—" I did an imitation of Samuel Johnson twitching and lurching. "He was a genius. And this is one of the sentences that he wrote that I really like. *The natural flights of the human mind are not from pleasure to pleasure, but from hope to hope.* Does anyone have an idea what that might mean?"

Juniper raised her hand. "Is it about people that are different and stuff?"

I said, "When you want something really badly, you hope to get something. You're desperate to see the TV show. You want to go to a movie. You want popcorn at the movie."

"We're not talking, everybody," said Peter to the class.

"Now, what happens when you get that thing?" I said.

"You get pleasure," said Emery.

"You get some pleasure—but how long does it last?"

"Not long," said Emery.

"And hope lasts a while," said Carly.

"That's it," I said. "You really, really want to be first in line. Or you really, really want to be done with school. Whatever it is. And when you get that thing, it's almost as if all of that wanting that you do just goes up in a puff of smoke. And you start wanting another thing. So what he's saying is that the most natural state of being is not a state of being where you're enjoying the thing you're doing, it's when you're hoping for the next thing. And that's kind of true, I think. Don't you?"

Yep!

Yes!

Isaiah raised his hand. "Kind of like if you want something, you hope for it, that hope always stays with you, but you might not get what you want."

I said, "So what he's trying to do is telling you something about human nature in one sentence, and I think he does it." Then I went back to reading to them from *Hatchet*. After Brian, the hero, kills the bird, a moose appears and starts bludgeoning him with her head. Brian crawls to the safety of a tree, ribs and shoulder aching. When the moose moves on, he retrieves the dead bird and hobbles to his hut, grateful to be alive. *"Such an insane attack, for no reason, and he fell asleep with his mind trying to make the moose have reason.* Space break!" I slapped the book closed. Now they were supposed to write something.

I read to the class from the sub plans. "Brian experienced many things for the first time during his experience in the woods. Describe one of these experiences with details from the story." A nice, simple assignment. Isaiah asked how many sentences long it had to be. There was no good answer to that, I said; they could write short sentences, middle-sized sentences, or even one long snakelike sentence that filled a page. "Just say to yourself, I'm going to write the best bunch of sentences I can, and I'm going to go pretty fast, because I have fifteen minutes to do it. Make them cry, make them laugh, make them weep."

"Just chunk it out, everyone!" said Isaiah, and he began writing.

Odette raised her hand. "I need to know how you spell *hatchet*."

I printed *hatchet* on the board.

They put their fourth-grade heads down and wrote and wrote. I read many paragraphs about Brian in the woods, Brian in the cockpit, Brian in the mud with the moose.

Odette wrote hers in neat cursive. Peter handed in his paper. "I didn't do too well," he said. "I did terrible."

I told him not to worry, and then I read aloud from the paragraph handed in by a quiet kid named Locke. *"I like the part when it was pitch-black out, and Brian was in the cave. Then a porcupine came in and Brian threw the hatchet, missed, and hit the rock on the face of the rock, and sparks exploded everywhere, and lit up the room, and so Brian saw the porcupine. He was spiked several times in the leg and had to pull out each one in agonizing pain."* I told them they'd all done good work, and they clomped out for recess while I ate a sandwich in class. Somebody else had recess duty.

Twenty-five minutes later, everyone was back. Juniper sat her tiny self down at her desk and began to cry. She and Micky had been fighting. "He was bullying me outside," she said.

"He *was* bullying her," said Emery.

"He was," said Carly.

"I was NOT," called Micky from the back of the classroom.

The class was quiet enough that I could hear Juniper sobbing into her fists. I crossed the room to loom over Micky.

"I wouldn't let her play a game with me," he said, "because she's been mean to me all day."

"Micky," I said.

"IT'S NOT BULLYING," he shouted. "JUST BECAUSE I DISINCLUDE HER FROM THE GAME!"

"Do not talk in a loud voice to me," I said. "Sit right here. We're going to talk quietly for a second. Do I need to send you to the office?"

"No," said Micky. "She's been mean to me all day."

"Kiddo," I said. "I've seen the two of you. I'll tell you something that you'll really profit from. A lot of the trouble you get into you're causing yourself, because you get wild."

"I just don't want Juniper playing with me," said Micky. "It's not a big deal."

"I won't send you to the office if you'll go over there right now and find one thing nice to tell her, and say you're sorry if she thought you were mean to her."

"I don't really know anything nice about her," Micky said.

"Are you kidding?" I said. "She's an incredibly nice kid. So are you." (Not strictly true.) "You just, for some reason, don't like each other."

"Since third grade, she's been mean to me. We were in the same class in third grade."

"Why can't you start fresh today?"

"She's never been this mean to me since third grade. It's usually when there's a substitute. And I'm tired of it. She distracts me from my work."

"You distract a lot of people," I said. "You've got a thing about getting a little wild. I want you to go over and say, 'I'm sorry you think I was bullying you.'"

"I have ADHD," he said.

"It doesn't matter whether you have ADHD," I said. "You can control it. I see you're smart. You can write. You can do stuff."

"Okay, I'll go say I'm sorry." He marched over and said, "Juniper, I'm sorry you thought that I was mean to you." He marched back and sat down.

"Thank you," I said.

To Juniper, I said, "I know that doesn't make it better, but at least it's a start. Okay?"

Juniper nodded.

"I'm hoping today could be the beginning of a beautiful friendship," I said, then chuckled at the remoteness of that possibility. Juniper laughed and wiped her face.

The sub plans said it was time for "Enrichment." An ed tech arrived with a cart full of laptops. She took Micky off to a Title I class. Juniper went to a reading class. Isaiah gave me a story of his to read. "It may be a little gross," he said. He'd read it aloud to the class a few weeks ago.

I read Isaiah's story aloud softly: *"I split my nose open one time when I was doing flipflops on my bed."* He hit the metal frame, he wrote, and blood came out like water from a squirt gun. This was when he was six. *"My brother ran around the room freaking out. It looked like a crime scene. Blood was on the floor, and my nose was hanging. My dad picked me up and scurried to the phone."* At the hospital they put three needles in Isaiah's face. *"They shot them in my nose to keep it from falling off."*

I moaned at the horror of it. "You're a survivor. Put it there, man." I shook hands with him.

"I still have a scar and it's kind of disformed a little bit," said Isaiah, holding his nose. I could see no sign of injury.

"It looks good," I said. "They did a good job—you're back together."

"Mr. Baker?" said Camille. "When I was five, a light fixture fell on my face, and I had a eighty stitches right here." She pointed to a scar at her hairline.

"No kidding, and you look perfect," I said. "You guys are amazing survivors."

Isaiah put his story away. Mattie gave Lewis an eraser cap.

"Whoa, this is a good class," I said. "Enrichment. Who's enriching their minds?"

"I don't know," said Stacy. "But I have to go to the bathroom."

With Micky out of the class, I didn't have to tell anyone to be quiet. Some added to their essays about Brian's adventures in *Hatchet*. Some pulled out their unfinished math packets. Odette showed me a division problem, 3,315 divided by 22, and we did it together. There was something soothing about doing one arithmetic problem slowly and carefully—just one. Emma and Hallie worked on their Wordly Wise notebooks. They quizzed each other, imitating the voice of the woman on the Wordly Wise website, on the meaning of *shun, furious, coax, clutch, caress,* and *prefer.* "You're building some serious vocabulary there," I said. Emma said that the reason Micky was in Mr. Seaborg's class was that Mr. Seaborg could control him, and they had a love of baseball in common. Mr. Seaborg was crazy about the Red Sox. "If you say Yankees in this class," said Hallie, "it's a swear."

Soon a troupe of fifth-graders arrived for a laptop software session, and many of my fourth-graders left—it felt like a whole new class. I rebooted an unresponsive laptop and handed a boy a box of tissues. Suddenly it was perfectly still.

"It's so quiet," I whispered. "It's wonderful."

"It's never like this," Stacy whispered back.

"Did you cast a spell over them?"

The fifth-graders were doing advanced math on IXL, and they were having trouble. Evan needed help finding the height of a cube whose volume was 729. We trial-and-errored it. Megan wasn't able to figure the height of a rectangular prism with a volume of 560 yards, a height of 8 yards, and a width of 10 yards. We got that one, too. Then Phil came up, wanting to know the length of a side-leaning shaded triangular area of 49 square inches and a height of 7 inches. I stared at the illustration for a long time. My mind ceased to function.

"She might know," Phil said, pointing to a small blond girl with a pointy mouth.

"Are you super good at triangles?" I said.

"I can try," she said.

"Mr. Baker, can I go get a damp paper towel?" asked Sierra. Yes.

I gave the blond girl, Tracy, the triangle worksheet. "Oh," she said promptly. "I would imagine that you would have to divide forty-nine by fourteen." I didn't believe her, but she was right: the answer was 3.5. A green checkmark appeared on Phil's laptop's IXL screen.

Phil put a fist in the air. "She's one of the smartest kids in our class."

"You're light-years ahead of me," I said.

The room's back forty became loud and jokey, so I went over there and asked them about their whispering skills.

"I don't have whispering skills," said a boy. "I have football skills."

"Can you play whisper football?" I said.

"Blue forty-two," he whispered, "hut, hut, hike."

"I got it right!" said Megan, across the room.

"Praise the lord," I said.

"I don't like math," she said.

The laptops went back in the cart, each with a dangling MagSafe charging cord, as a logjam of my fourth-graders returned. I asked Juniper what Micky had been doing during recess to bully her. "He wouldn't let me play the game that everyone else was," she said. "And he kept saying, 'Guys, everybody, Juniper doesn't know how to talk.' I don't really know how. I say *aminal* and *emeny*."

"That's so cruel, and so silly," I said.

"Mr. Seaborg says he's just trying to get a action out of me. A ride. I don't know how to say it. I don't know how to say a lot of words."

"You seem to be doing pretty well," I said. "I've noticed good words coming out."

The computer cart was closed and its padlock twirled. Vance's mustache bag reappeared. With five minutes to go, I put on "Imagine."

"Why are you playing music?" asked Juniper.

"Because it's been a long day," I said.

Isaiah said he liked country music—he liked Luke Bryan, doing "That's My Kind of Night." I'd never heard of Luke Bryan, but I found the song on YouTube and played it.

"This is my favorite song," said Isaiah.

"This is my mom's favorite song!" said Odette.

They sang along with Luke Bryan: "I got that real good feel good stuff, up under the seat of my big black jacked-up truck."

"This is my sister's favorite song!" said Mattie.

A bell rang and a grandmother in a flowered muumuu appeared at the door to pick up Aiden. We switched to Luke Bryan doing "Drunk on You." Four kids, crouching around my laptop and dipping their knees, knew the lyrics: "I'm a little drunk on you, and high on summertime."

The four-note gong sounded, calling kids for first-wave buses. Bye, I said. Lewis told me he liked a Christian song called "Do Something" by Matthew West. When I put it on, three kids knew it. "It's not enough to do nothing," they sang. "It's time for us to do something." Second wave was announced and in a fingersnap they all were gone.

"You survived another day with us!" said the secretary. "We're thankful."

Heck, I thought, I love this.

End of Day Twenty-five.

I KIND OF BREAK
MY OWN SPIRIT SOMETIMES

Beth said I had a choice: I could either teach first grade at Lasswell, or be a roving ed tech at the middle school. I slapped together some sandwiches and hissed northward through a rainy mist to the middle school—past a striped VW Beetle for sale, past a pile of stripped logs at a lumberyard, past a dead lump of a porcupine on the road.

"Everybody's out today," said Pam. I reported to room 232, special ed math, where a girl was eating a bagel. Mr. Fields, the bustling gent who had first told me about the voices in Waylon's head, was my dispatcher. I was going to do a tech block first, with Mr. Walsh, he said. "So, Nick, you're kind of tall. How tall are you?"

"Six four and change," I said.

"You were probably six five and change in your younger days," Mr. Fields said. "You haven't shrunk yet? You're over forty, aren't you? Heh heh."

"I'm fifty-seven," I said.

"Oh, you're a puppy!" Mr. Fields said. "Did you play basketball in high school?"

Actually, I said, there was no basketball team at my high school.

"Cut it out!" said Mr. Fields, amazed.

Cheryl, in the corner, asked for tissues, but the box was empty. Mr.

Fields said, "You can use a paper towel, Cheryl, and when you come back we'll have tissues, so you don't have to report us to the tissue police. See that look? Cheryl always gives you that look when she doesn't like what you said. Judy, beside her, is always a gentle soul. Beside her is Kelly, another gentle soul. Tyna, over there in the corner, is a very gentle soul, and Glenn, beside her, is something of a Mexican jumping bean. Over here we have the quiet duo of Billy and Gene, who are just enrapt in their video games. Hey, fellas, it's coming up on seven thirty-five, you know you should be off those contraptions. Thank you."

The principal came on the PA system. "Can I have your attention, please?"

"Yes you can, boss!" said Mr. Fields. "Hey, Gene, you should have that thing away. You can break the spell, do it!"

The class pledged its allegiance. Lunch was a hot meatball sub with shredded cheese. Band would meet from 9:55 to 10:40. A pair of glasses were found outside by the buses. The seventh-grade boys' lacrosse team had made a good effort as they faced the Falmouth Yachtsmen the night before. All library books were due back by June 10. "Please check your lockers, your closets at home, your bedroom, all other places where those library books may be hiding." Two students came on to announce a Team Orinoco dance, with special guest DJ Blake Burnside. "Enter to win an iTunes fifteen-dollar gift card and party like it's 1999 at our beach party, with drinks, food, and a lot of fun tattoos and leis." That concluded the announcements.

Bong, bong, bong. I followed Judy down to tech class. "WALK ON THAT STAIRWAY, BOYS," said an ed tech. "THAT'S VERY DANGEROUS."

Mr. Walsh, a compact baldie with a mustache, shook my hand and said I was supposed to work with Dana, who wore hearing aids. "He pretends he doesn't hear a lot."

Mr. Walsh called out names for attendance and I sat on a stool in the hot, bright room. There were a dozen educational robots arranged on a table. "Dana's not here," said Mr. Walsh to me. I said I'd just float around.

Mr. Walsh addressed the class. "OKAY! What we did yesterday was we did the Yucca Mountain sheet, explained the controls, gave you an opportunity to work a robotic arm." He had the loudest voice I'd heard yet in school. "We'll have a little competition today, to see who does it the quickest. We'll do that first, and after that we'll do the Fryeburg Fair."

"Caca or Yucca?" asked Jackie.

"Yucca," said Mr. Walsh. He turned to the whiteboard, which said CACA MOUNTAIN ACTIVITY. "Somebody changed that on me."

The class paired up, and each team of two picked out a robot arm and two "casks"—cylindrical wooden blocks meant to represent sealed containers of nuclear waste. The robot arms were black and yellow, and they made a high, revving, whining sound when they moved, like tiny chain saws. "I'll give you two minutes to practice," said Mr. Walsh, "and then we'll start the competition."

I read the Yucca Mountain activity sheet, which was professionally laid out, with copy furnished, so it seemed, by some sort of a pro-nuclear lobbying group. Maine's nuclear power plant, Maine Yankee, was closed in 1996, said the sheet, *after 26 successful years of electrical generation—* not mentioning that the plant was shut down by the Nuclear Regulatory Commission because it had falsified safety records. Nuclear waste was held in crash-resistant casks, the sheet explained, *specially designed to hold radioactive materials safely.* It briefly told the story of Yucca Mountain, the underground site in Nevada where American nuclear waste was supposed to go. *As of 2008, construction was stalled and at this time, it appears as though the depository under Yucca Mountain will never be built and millions of dollars will be wasted.* A callout offered reassurance: *You would have to live near a nuclear power plant for over 2,000 years to get the same amount of radiation exposure that you get from a single diagnostic medical x-ray.* I wondered what the residents of Fukushima would say about this activity sheet.

"I'd like to have everybody put their shoulder up to start with," Mr. Walsh said—meaning the robot's shoulder. "SHOULDER UP, ELBOW

OUT." The students worked their controllers with their thumbs. "If you should drop a cask, you need to put it back on the circle." He checked his stopwatch. "READY. SET. GO."

The clumsy machines swiveled and joggled and eventually took hold of their dangerous spent-fission cargoes, while their operators cursed and laughed. The object was for each team to lift two casks and place them into a plastic box and close the lid. Several casks fell on their sides.

"Be nice to James, he's special," said Forrest.

"You do it, I can't!" said Anna.

One cask rolled off the table onto the floor. "You just exploded the Earth," said Tucker.

The winning time was one minute, fifty-one seconds. "ALL RIGHT, WE ARE GOING TO MOVE ON TO THE NEXT ACTIVITY," said Mr. Walsh. I liked Mr. Walsh, who had discovered that the only way he could survive as a middle school tech teacher was to develop a voice like a union activist's and shout all talkers down.

"How many people have been to the Fryeburg Fair?" he asked, handing out an activity sheet. Many hands went up. He read to us from the sheet: the fair was the largest in Maine, with oxen pulls and wood-chopping contests and pigs and chickens and rows of porta-potties. "ALL RIGHT," said Mr. Walsh. "YOUR TASK. In this activity, you are an employee at Blow Brothers and your boss has told you to load four porta-potties into the back of the truck body. These are going to be your porta-potties, right here." He held up a handful of gray plastic cylinders, narrower than the wooden nuclear waste cylinders.

"Those are really skinny porta-potties," said Vicky.

"WHAT YOU'RE GOING TO HAVE TO DO—is you're going to have to put them in one of the five holes," Mr. Walsh said. The holes were drilled in wooden blocks, representing the porta-potty trucks. "You need to be careful. They're kind of difficult to stand up. And if I see anybody tipping the table, or shaking it, you'll be going somewhere. So don't be shaking the table. ALL RIGHT?"

He gave the class a few minutes to practice, and then the race began.

Robots clenched and whined and dropped porta-potties here and there. "I just spilled my bucket of pee all over you guys," said Tucker. "She's covered with it."

"I'm done, because I don't want to do any more," said Anna.

"Gavin cheated," said Jackie. The winning time, by a two-girl team, was two minutes, thirty-five seconds.

"LISTEN UP, WE'RE GOING TO STOP," Mr. Walsh said. "Bring the porta-potties up to me, put the robots in the middle of the table, and take your sheets with you." Tomorrow, he said, they would be doing robotic heart transplants, pretending to be cardiac surgeons at Maine Medical Center. When everything was put away, ready for Mr. Walsh's next group of roboticists, he said, "ALL RIGHT! I guess you guys can go. HAVE A GOOD DAY."

Back at math special ed headquarters, Mr. Fields described some of the students I might be asked to help that day. "Diane wears kind of like a red fleece and pulls her hair back, very plain girl—nice kid, works hard. Bobby Bowman is this big solid kid—"

"Kind of crew-cutty," said Ms. Quinn, one of the other ed techs.

"Crew cut, dark-rimmed glasses," said Mr. Fields. "He's a nice kid. He can do everything fine—he just kind of like daydreams a lot. He needs a little bit of 'Hey, hey!'" He banged a file cabinet with his fist. "'Are you in there? Anybody home?'"

"Don't hit him, though," said Ms. Quinn.

"No, he's very gentle, he doesn't take much of a prod. Another guy, Frank Wood. He's a shorter guy, about yea big and about twelve pounds. Tends to wear T-shirts, short brown hair, kind of goes in every direction."

"I thought it was reddish," said Ms. Quinn.

"Brownish blond, strawberry blond, something like that. Nice kid, very quiet, but he's not a real good reader, or a good writer, so he might need some help."

I had a free block, and I went out to the car and ate a sandwich until it was time to check in with Mr. Fields. He told me about more special ed students I might encounter. "There's one girl named Katy, or it could be her friend Lynda," he said. "We call the two of them the Katy-Lynda, because they're basically alike. Little kiddy girls. There might be a guy named Adam, and there's a guy named Shawn—he's a blond-headed kid. They might need help with the writing. Adam can do pretty much everything, he's just got to have a nudge. The girls are kind of helpless. But they can do more than they predict."

Health class was my next destination, taught by a long-fingered, tough-but-kind woman named Mrs. Fitzgerald. "Just hang out," Mrs. Fitzgerald said to me. I sat down at a table on the side of the room, near Katy and Lynda and the pencil sharpener.

"Today is your day to talk to me about big things that you read in your alcohol article," Mrs. Fitzgerald said to the class. "Your job is to teach the class, so I can just sit back and fall asleep."

"Sounds like a good idea," said Renee.

"Doesn't it?" said Mrs. Fitzgerald. "So say Marjorie starts first. She's going to talk about something that's a big thing to her that she learned about alcohol. And if I call on Ray next, Ray has two choices. He can make a connection to what Marjorie said, or he can come up with a whole new alcohol fact. Got it? This is what they do in college."

"Lots of fun," said Ray quietly.

"In some colleges, anyway," said Mrs. Fitzgerald. "Sometimes you're in a class of a hundred and fifty and they just lecture to you for eighty minutes. But sometimes there are discussion classes. You're expected to come prepared for class and you're expected to discuss. It's a big responsibility. So who would like to go first?"

Randy, in Top-Siders, raised his hand. He said, "I picked out from the article that you're actually more likely to hurt yourself and others and commit more crimes, and go to jail."

"Can anyone make a connection to that and explain why?"

Toby said, "It messes with your nervous system and your brain. You could think that something is completely normal and fine, when your real conscience knows it's wrong."

"So it affects thinking skills," said Mrs. Fitzgerald. "It's really hard to stop and think when you're under the influence of alcohol. How many of you have seen someone who has had too much alcohol, but they think they're just fine?"

Hands went up.

"Look around the room, that's your evidence," said Mrs. Fitzgerald. "When people drink alcohol, they think they're fine, because their brain is under the influence of what?"

Alcohol.

"Of what?"

Alcohol.

"And alcohol is a what?"

A depressant.

"A depressant, nice job. So I'm under the influence of a depressant, and I think I'm doing just fine. There's absolutely no reason I can't teach, there's absolutely no reason I can't drive. If your brain is not under the influence of a depressant, then you would look at me and say, I don't know what's wrong with her, but there's something way different about her. She can't even walk straight. She's mumbling and she's not making any sense. But my brain is telling me I'm just fine, because I'm under the influence of a depressant. Is it okay that people either love the Yankees or they love the Red Sox?"

Yes.

"Is it okay if you're friends with somebody who likes the opposite team? Can you tolerate that normally? Do you like it? Not particularly. I don't particularly like it when someone's a real Yankees fan, but I can still be friends with them, and I don't have to fight them. I don't have to argue with them, and I don't have to beat them up, and I don't have to kill them over it. But that's what people do when they've been drinking. There have been people at Fenway Park and at Yankee Stadium that have died because they have worn the opposite team's jersey. Emotions escalate, and people end up being shot or killed or seriously injured—over what? When we boil it all down, it was over what?"

A team.

"They liked a team that I don't like. Deal with it! Deal with it. But it's not easy to deal with it when you're putting a chemical in your body that changes the way you perceive things."

A tall floor-mounted fan sent a breeze of coolness over the drowsy class as we learned more about the horrors of alcohol. Melanie raised her hand to say that what she'd learned from the article was that alcohol is made by fermenting certain fruits. Mrs. Fitzgerald dismissed that fact as irrelevant. Alcohol was a poison, she said. Our liver filters out poisons, and alcohol is filtered out by your liver, therefore we know that alcohol is a poison. It couldn't help you get better grades, and it couldn't help you decrease the stress you feel from school. "We don't want to be drinking to decrease stress. Are you serious? You want to put a poison in your body to decrease stress? It's not a strategy to help you with stress. When you look at the reasons why teenagers use, I just want to tell you, they look like a bunch of excuses to me. You guys are too smart to use those as excuses. You guys are too smart to think that alcohol's going to relax you. You know better than that." What we needed were healthy relaxation techniques, she said. "Think of something that you personally do that decreases your stress, that makes you relaxed, that would be considered healthy."

"Play sports," said Randy.

Mrs. Fitzgerald nodded. "That's a healthy redirecting activity."

"Sit on my horse?" said Anita, who kept eyeing Randy.

"I draw," said Marjorie.

Mrs. Fitzgerald said, "What's the end result if I draw, or I walk my dog, or I lay across on my bed for a little while and just relax? Or I do yoga, or slow breathing, or I doodle, or I read or write?"

"It decreases stress?" said Marjorie.

"When I read, how does it decrease stress?" said Mrs. Fitzgerald. "For those of you that love to read, when you get yourself into a good book, how does that decrease stress?"

"You get distracted by it," Cary said.

"You get distracted by it," said Mrs. Fitzgerald. "If it's a good character, or a good plot, it kind of takes you away. When I get done reading, I don't feel sick, I don't have a really bad headache, I'm not vomiting in the toilet, I haven't said something or done something to somebody that I didn't mean to do. How about when you draw? What do you notice? You get better at it. When you drink, you get better at drinking, because your body gets more dependent on it, and it needs more to get the same feeling. People that practice drinking get very good at it. People that practice their drawing get very good at it. Which very-good-at-it would you like to do? You guys don't need alcohol. Am I going to feel better about myself if I feel sick? Am I going to feel better about myself if somebody shows me on their phone that they took a video of me doing really stupid things, and now it's viral?" Alcohol, she said, will not help you fit in at school. "Who are you going to fit in with when you're acting like an idiot? Other idiots. Is that who you want to fit in with?"

Mrs. Fitzgerald moved on to the dangers of driving while under the influence. "Think about your brain as like an iPad that has too many apps open on it. What happens to your iPad?"

It goes slow.

"It goes real slow. So under the influence of a depressant, my brain goes really slowly, and I have a hard time multitasking." That's what led to car accidents, and snowmobile accidents. She wrote "FETAL ALCOHOL SYNDROME" on the whiteboard and told us about it. "The baby's born addicted to alcohol," she said. "It has physical deformities, and/or emotional and mental disabilities." A boy raised his hand to ask how to spell *deformities*. "Women aren't using to hurt their babies, they're using because they're addicted to alcohol. They made a personal choice to go down the road of addiction. The alcohol is making the decisions for them."

It sounded like Mrs. Fitzgerald was a total prohibitionist, but in fact she wasn't. After about age twenty-four, you could drink. "If we could keep alcohol out of your hands, and out of your bodies, until your prefrontal cortex is fully developed, there wouldn't be as big an issue with alcohol in our country."

I walked—faintly querulous, wanting a cold beer—to the next class, which was taught by Mr. Fields. He handed a bag filled with empty candy wrappers to a girl named Paloma, who wore a blue plaid bucket hat. "Would it wake you up if you were to go up to the board and count out how many of M&M wrappers are in here?"

"Probably not," said Paloma. "The entire class is math."

He handed the bag to Bobby instead. "There's no food in there," Mr. Fields said. "We took the food out and fed it to other people."

"There's just two," said Bobby. He wrote a two next to "M&M" on the board.

He gave the bag to Paloma.

"Is it the hat that makes you so sleepy, or is it something else?" said Mr. Fields.

"I'm stuffy," said the girl. "Can't . . . breathe . . . through . . . nose." She counted out two Fruit Roll-Up wrappers and wrote a two on the board.

Roxanne counted one Three Musketeers wrapper. Whitney counted four Snickers wrappers. Bobby, up again, counted two Milky Way wrappers.

"Mr. Baker, can I leave you in charge of the bag of candy wrappers, so that Paloma doesn't wake up and start to go through it to see if there's a piece of candy left in there?"

Then Mr. Fields handed around another plastic bag, this one filled with arithmetic problems on slips of paper. Each student fished out four problems.

"Do you want to pick four as well, Mr. Baker?"

I said that I'd be honored.

"This is all about going over division by five and six," Mr. Fields said.

Bobby did his problems aloud: ten divided by five is two, thirty-five divided by five is seven, twenty divided by five is four, and eighteen divided by six is three.

Paloma was next. She spread out her four division problems. "I would really love to breathe," she said. Thirty divided by five is six. Thirty-five divided by five is seven. Forty divided by five is eight. Twenty-four divided by six is four.

"Do you notice anything about these?" Mr. Fields asked.

"Five and six seem to reoccur," said Paloma.

"Okay, anything else that you notice? Do you have any prime numbers as an answer?"

"I don't know," said Paloma.

"She has eight, four, seven, and six, are any of those prime numbers?"

"No," said Bobby.

"Seven is," said Mr. Fields.

They went around the class doing simple division.

"And Mr. Baker, what did you get?"

"I got fifteen divided by five equals three," I said. "Twenty divided by five is four, twelve divided by six is two, and ten divided by five is two."

"And what do you notice about your answers, if anything?" Mr. Fields said.

"I've got a prime number in there, three."

Mr. Fields tooted a large old-fashioned automobile horn and handed it to me. "Whenever you feel the urge, do that, and that means we have to go around and get another pick-four from people, and see what they remember. Any time you want."

"Okay," I said.

"Do a practice one."

I honked the horn.

"Do it a little louder so that it wakes up Whitney."

Honk!

Whitney screeched.

"That is loud," I said.

"Do it often," said Mr. Fields.

"Don't do it, it irritates me," said Whitney.

Mr. Fields shook the bag of candy wrappers. "Probability is the topic here," he said. "What does probability mean, Jaden, in your own words?"

"The possibility of it getting done?"

"The possibility of getting something done," said Mr. Fields. He wrote a capital P on the board. "That P just stands for 'probability.' Last week the big capital P on the board stood for what measurement, Paloma?"

"That if you put some more letters in there it would be my name," said Paloma.

"Thank you."

I honked the horn.

"Hey, okay!" said Mr. Fields. "There we go. Paloma, quickly. Eighteen divided by six?"

"Three."

"Thirty divided by six?"

"Not five," said Paloma.

"It is a five!" said Mr. Fields. "Twenty-four divided by six?"

"Gahhh!" said Paloma. "Four."

"Nice guess," said Mr. Fields, turning. "Bobby, ten divided by five. Don't be insulted. You've just got to know these things."

"Five! No. Two."

"Of course it is," said Mr. Fields. "You're just messing with us. All right, Mr. Baker. You should probably go and visit Mrs. Christian."

"Can I do it?" said Whitney, meaning toot the horn.

"I don't like giving the students control of this," said Mr. Fields, hugging the horn. "Chaos is sometimes good, but not today."

I went downstairs to Team Nile, where Mrs. Christian's seventh-grade science class was in the midst of a cell biology project. She briefed me on it. "They've all picked a system, whether it's a school, or a factory, or a sports team, and they're trying to figure out, like, what the nucleus would be in the school, or what the nucleus would be on a sports team." She pointed out several kids who might need help, warning me that some might not want help. I went over to Gabrielle, who was sitting and thinking her thoughts. She had a packet in front of her about parts of the cell. I didn't want to interrupt her, but I did anyway. "Can I check in?" I said. "What's your analogy?"

"What?" she said. She had a kind, despondent face.

"What's your comparison?"

"A farm."

"Great idea! So the nucleus is the place that everything is directed from? That's a tough one. What did you come up with?"

She paged through the cell packet. "I couldn't find anything."

I pulled up a chair. "What place on the farm is where everything gets made, and is sort of the center of the farm?"

"The barn."

"The barn, interesting," I said. "Not the farmhouse, the barn, I see that."

Gabrielle said nothing. Her packet was filled with words like *mitochondria*, *cytoplasm*, *ribosomes*, and *vacuole*, and she didn't know how to pronounce them, or what any of them meant.

"*Mitochondria,*" I said. "What are those? Those are the squiggly things, right?"

She was silent.

"I don't know what that would be on a farm. Do you have any rivers, or creeks, or irrigation ditches?"

She looked up at me and smiled slowly, waiting for me to go on to someone else, which I did.

Matthew had chosen a movie theater as his analogy. He'd drawn the plan of a movie theater on a blank piece of paper.

"Great idea!" I said. "Did you come up with that?"

"No," he said.

"So what would the projection booth be? Hm, interesting."

He stared at the page, waiting for me to move on. I swiveled and talked to a kid behind me, Cooper. "What's happening, man? Good stuff?"

He shrugged. "Yeah." He'd just written a definition for *endoplasmic reticulum*.

"That's a word, eh?" I said. "Good god, you sometimes wonder why scientists don't come up with simpler words. So what are you comparing yours to?"

Cooper looked up at me. "Jail," he said.

"Nice. So what equals a nucleus in a jail?"

"The warden?" Cooper said.

"Ah," I said. "Good one. And the endoplasmic reticulum? What does that do? I don't remember."

He'd written, *Moves stuff around. Made up of complex membranes.* "The guards?" he said.

"The guards, yeah," I said. "They push around those carts. Good choice. This is a pretty interesting assignment." I waited. Cooper didn't want me there. I was pretty much poison in this class. "Good luck," I said, and greeted Dawson.

"I'm doing the Boston Red Sox," Dawson said.

"I'm doing a grocery store," said Egan, the boy next to him. "It took me ten minutes to write all this stuff down."

I asked Egan what the nucleus was in a grocery store.

"The manager, because in a grocery store the manager is in charge."

"Good point," I said. "Do the bathrooms at a grocery store count? What would they be equivalent to? Or the cash registers? That's hard. This is a hard assignment. I kind of like it, though."

"Yeah, I can't remember what those things are called that get rid of waste," Egan said.

"Is it the mitochondria?" I said. "Or is it the endoplasmic reticulum?"

"The endoplasmic reticulum stores proteins," said Egan. "Maybe it's the mitochondria. The mitochondria gives energy."

"I've got a question for you," I said. "What would money be?"

"Money would be the protein," Egan said. "Because money goes into the store, and the endoplasmic reticulum stores it."

I said, "Then maybe the endoplasmic reticulum would be the cash register? Or the safe?"

"Yeah," Egan said, not entirely convinced.

I turned back to Dawson. "So the Red Sox," I said. "What would be the batting cage?"

"I don't know," said Dawson.

"I don't know either," I said.

"I think the proteins would be the food stands," said Dawson.

"I think the ribosomes would be the food stands," said Booker, who sat next to Egan. "Because ribosomes make protein, and food is protein. Depending on what you have in the food."

I read Dawson's definition of the nucleus: *holds the genetic information of the cell.*

"That's the coach," said Dawson. "John Farrell."

"The man," I said. "Good luck, dudes."

I crossed the class to a couple sitting together. "What's happening here?" I said to Fletcher, who swiped something away on his iPad.

"I'm trying to be stupid is all," Fletcher said.

"That's top priority," I said. "Are you doing one of these comparisons?"

"Huh?" said the girl, Vanessa.

"Are you doing one of these comparisons with the cell?"

"I already did that," said Fletcher.

"We already finished that," said Vanessa.

"I compared mine to a school," said Fletcher.

"Mine was the mall," said Vanessa.

"I like that," I said. "So what's the nucleus of a mall?"

"I don't remember," said Vanessa.

"I said mine was the principal," said Fletcher.

"Because the principal's office holds the genetic information?" I said.

"He controls the building," said Vanessa.

"And then what are the bathrooms?"

"Nothing," said Fletcher.

I sat in a chair on the side of the room for a while, waiting to find out how I could be useful. The class, I was happy to notice, was loud and shouty.

"Getting a little noisy in here," said Mrs. Christian.

I asked Matthew what he generally bought to eat when he went to the movies.

"I usually get candy and soda," he said.

"So at a movie theater, what is the ribosome?"

He pointed to the projector in his drawing. "That," he said. He'd written, *In a movie, you press play. A ribosome acts just like a projector.*

"Fascinating," I said. "How did you figure that out?"

"Mrs. Craig helped me." Mrs. Craig was the ed tech for whom I was substituting.

"Did you do any Golgi bodies?"

Matthew pointed to the ticket counter, which in his drawing corresponded to the Golgi apparatus.

"Holy crap," I said.

"I like my arrow," Matthew said. He'd drawn a fancy green arrow.

I was boggled by too many partial analogies. "It kind of scrambles your brain a little bit," I said.

"Sexual reproduction!" said Zoe loudly.

Back to Gabrielle. She had drawn a barn and some farmers. The farmers were the Golgi bodies in her comparison.

She pointed to *vacuole*. "I can't find that one," she said.

I flipped around in a textbook. "I think the vacuoles are more important in plant cells," I said. "You've got an animal cell. Maybe you can move on."

She needed to know what corresponded with *mitochondria*. I showed her a page of the textbook, which said that the mitochondria acted like a digestive system, breaking down nutrients. "So on the farm, what breaks things down? The soil, the insects in the soil? No, let's see. The tractor?"

"Animals?" said Gabrielle.

"The animals chew the grass and digest it," I said. "That's a good one. No comparison is exact."

"What is that one?" she asked, pointing to the words *endoplasmic reticulum*.

"I thought you'd never ask," I said, flipping around in the textbook. "It's a series of folding membranes in which materials can be processed and moved around inside the cell. What moves things around in a barn? A wheelbarrow?"

"A grain tub?" said Gabrielle.

"A grain tub. Do you know about farms?"

She nodded. She lived on a farm. We kept going. Ribosomes make stuff, I said.

"The cows?" she said.

"Cows make milk," I said, nodding. *Cytoplasm* was the next term she needed to analogize. I said, "It's a gloopy substance that's all around the cell. What's all around you on the farm? People breathe it, and animals breathe it, and plants breathe it."

"Oxygen?"

"Yes, air. Air's like cytoplasm, isn't it? What do you have to do now?"

"I have to put it into a Keynote," Gabrielle said.

"Oh, wow." I felt despair. The kids were supposed to half learn the definitions of the microscopic components of a cell, then half compare these definitions inexactly to another complex system that existed on a human scale, and then put their garbled comparisons into Keynote slides. And yet some of them were having fun with it. Some actual learning was happening.

"GUYS, START CLEANING UP, PLEASE," said Mrs. Christian.

As the classes changed over, Waylon, my overmedicated friend, showed up. "Hey, how are you?" I said.

"Not so good," said Waylon. "I'm having the same problems I had last time."

I asked him if he was still not sleeping.

"Last night I had a Benadryl," he said, "so I had a pretty good night's sleep."

Had he talked to his parents about cutting back on the Paxil?

"Yeah," he said. "They put me on Benadryl."

"They don't want to cut back on the dose?"

"We did."

"Oh, good," I said. "Is it easier to concentrate?"

He nodded.

"It's great to see you," I said. "I'm sorry it's still a problem, but I hope it goes better. Catch you on the flipflop."

"All right, bye."

I hotfooted it out to the car to get my day's schedule, which I'd left there by mistake when I ate a sandwich, and on my way back I saw Shane, my old nemesis from science class, on his knees on the grass, planting some flowers near the school entrance while a teacher looked on, her arms folded.

"We're putting in a memorial garden for Nelson," said the teacher. "Nelson was one of my students last year."

"That was really a sad thing," I said.

IN MR. FIELDS'S MATH CLASS, a new set of students were doing division problems taken from the arithmetic bag, and now there was another ed tech in the room as well, a young man named Mr. J. The kids had more energy than the last group, and Lynda, Katy, and Adam were interrupting each other.

"If you want to go to lunch on time," Mr. Fields said, "I suggest you be quiet now. If you want to be talking now, they'll go to lunch, you'll still be sitting here. Who's screwing who? Come on, get real, will you?"

After another round of division Mr. Fields brought the horn out and gave it to me. "When Mr. Baker blows the horn, we'll have to stop what we're doing and go around again."

He pulled out his bag of candy wrappers. "The candies have been removed to protect the innocent from the effects of calories." Again the students counted how many Twix wrappers, how many Snickers wrappers, how many etc. There were thirteen wrappers in all. "What we're talking about now is a thing called probability. What do you remember about probability?"

"It's everything added up," said Adam.

Mr. Fields asked Katy what she remembered about probability.

"It sounds like *probably*."

"And what does *probably* mean, in your world?" asked Mr. Fields.

"Yes, no, maybe," said Katy.

Adam said that probability was that maybe a car was going to break down.

"It's the chance that something's going to happen," Mr. Fields said. He wrote a capital P on the board, followed by a blank set of parentheses. "Last week, Adam, when we were doing area and perimeter, what did the capital P mean at that time?"

"Perimeter," said Adam.

"Thank you very much."

"Mr. Fields?" said Lynda. "You should write 'Pb.'"

"I'm not going to write 'Pb,'" Mr. Fields said, "because it's always written P parentheses, and that would confuse you." He pointed at me. "What do you say there, Mr. Baker?"

I booped the horn once and the ed tech, Mr. J., called out division problems. Thirty divided by five. Ten divided by five. Twenty-five divided by five. Three divided by six. The class got most of them right.

Then Lynda was asked to close her eyes and decide which candy wrapper she wanted to pull from the bag. "Twix," she said.

"So you've got two chances out of thirteen," said Mr. Fields. "The probability, out of that thirteen, in one pick, is two out of the thirteen. Mr. Baker, can I ask you to come over here and be the official eye-watcher on Lynda, and make sure she is not peeking?"

"I trust her," I said.

Lynda reached in, eyes closed, and pulled out a Twix wrapper.

"Dang it!" said Mr. Fields.

"You must know the feel of a Twix wrapper, texturally," said Mr. J.

"I hate it when I have to pay off a debt," said Mr. Fields. He arranged a display of mints for her to pick from. "Just so you know, I haven't washed my hands in a week or two." Lynda took a mint. "Give the winner a hand."

"Boo," said Adam.

Adam reached in, hoping for an M&M wrapper, of which there were two. "Mr. Baker's got his eyes on your eyes," said Mr. Fields. "Adam knows he's a cheat."

Adam tried to sneak a peek

"No, no, no, no," said Mr. Fields.

"Just look toward me," I said.

Adam pulled out an M&M wrapper. "I got it!" he said.

"He also only had two chances out of thirteen," said Mr. Fields.

After several more reachings in, it was time for lunch, and he passed out more mints. "When you come back, we're going to play a little game that has to do with flipping dimes."

The class was filled with the sound of chewing. "What you guys don't need is sugar," said Mr. J.

"I NEED SUGAR," said Adam.

To get out the door, each student had to do more division. "You have to get at least two of these right," said Mr. Fields. "Ten divided by five!"

"Ten divided by five is . . . five," said Adam.

Mr. Fields shook his head. "Twenty-five divided by five?"

"Five!"

"That's rolling!"

"I don't understand why they didn't teach them the times tables," said Mr. J. to me, in an undertone, while the class called out wrong answers at the door. "They completely took the rigorous memorization out of it. They do this lattice stuff, have you seen that? It's insane. It's the most classic case of if it ain't broke, don't fix it." He left.

"Forty divided by five is?" said Mr. Fields to Lynda.

"Nine."

"Try that again."

"Eight."

"Thank you very much. Thirty divided by six?"

"Two."

"Try this one. You've got to get it right to get out of the door. Twelve divided by six."

She didn't know.

"How about this one? Forty-five divided by five?"

"Nine!"

"There you go," said Mr. Fields. "You're out the door, bye-bye."

When everyone was gone, I said, "You really make it fun."

"Next class I won't be that good," Mr. Fields said. "I'll be tired."

I told him I'd just been talking to Mr. J. about the times tables. "He was saying that kids didn't learn their times tables in elementary school. Which does seem to be true. But I've been substituting in the elementary schools, and they're much better at it now. They can really spit it out."

"Good," Mr. Fields said. "Otherwise they get up here and, come on, it takes them five seconds to maybe pull it out?" He gathered up his candy wrappers. "And my next class will be even slower." He seemed wiped out.

In the teachers' lounge, two teachers were comparing notes. "So he gets up and throws his essay in the trash," said one of them. I ate an apple and, when it was time, went to the cafeteria to do lunch duty. Another substitute, an old-timer, had a pocket full of lemon drops. That was his secret to getting kids to volunteer as table-washers, he said: "I bribe them with candy."

One more class to go: seventh-grade biology with Mrs. Painter in Team Orinoco. "Yesterday you finished diagramming mitosis and meiosis, and comparing and contrasting the two," Mrs. Painter said to the class. She sounded flat-voiced and tired. "That should be done by now. If it's not done, you need to do it at home, or before you start your capacity matrix. Today, as a whole class, we're going to watch a video on how plants reproduce. We're going to talk about the video. Afterward, I'm going to give you your last capacity matrix. It has every assignment on it that you'll have to do from now until the last week of school."

Howard, a little jumpy kid, raised his hand. "Do we work through the last week of school?"

"If we're not done," said Mrs. Painter.

"What if everything's done, then what?" asked Whitney.

"We'll deal with that when we get there—if we get there," said Mrs. Painter. She reviewed asexual and sexual reproduction. "How many parent cells are in mitosis?"

One!

"How many parent cells are in meiosis?"

Two!

She called us to the front of the room and turned on the YouTube movie. *"Today's topic is the exciting process of plant reproduction in angiosperms,"* said an animated amoeboid female-voiced blob named Pinky. *"A fruit develops from the ovary of a plant, which doesn't exactly sound appetizing. Pumpkins, green beans, tomatoes, squash—these all developed from the ovary of a flowering plant."*

Mrs. Painter stopped the video. "Who knew plants had ovaries? Raise your hand."

"What are ovaries?" said Whitney.

"Female baby-making parts," said Maureen.

"Oh, I know all about that," said Whitney.

The video resumed—and Pinky began bombing us with vocabulary. We heard about *stamens, filaments, anthers,* and *pollen,* which was the sperm of the plant. Then the female parts: the *pistil,* the *stigma,* the *style,* and the *ovary.* Next came the *sepals* and physical pollination, effected by a bee. More words from Pinky followed at a brisk trot: Pollen grains held two kinds of cells, a *tube cell* and a *generative cell.* The tube cell grew down into the *tube nucleus,* and the generative cell traveled down the tube cell into the ovary, where it divided into two sperm cells, both of which sought out a component of the ovary called an *ovule.* Each ovule had an *egg cell* and two *polar nuclei.* One sperm cell fertilized the egg cell, while the other sperm cell joined up with the two polar nuclei to form a *triploid cell* that would develop into the *endosperm,* in a process called *double fertilization.* Pinky's cheery voice made me sleepy, and by the time we got to the two polar nuclei my head started to droop. I think Mrs. Painter saw me dozing off, and I felt bad about that.

"Okay, this is what we're going to do," said Mrs. Painter. I straightened up in my chair. "Before you work on your Keynote, I'm going to give you a sticky note and have you write one thing you learned about plant reproduction, and one question that you have. Based on what you guys put down, I'm going to make a mini-lesson for tomorrow, so we can get the missing parts. Back to your seats."

Paloma and Bobby, from Mr. Fields's class, sat at a table near me by the windows. I waved at them. "What's up back here?" I said.

"NOW YOU ARE TRANSITIONING BACK TO YOUR TABLES," said Mrs. Painter. "THIS IS A REDIRECT I SHOULDN'T HAVE TO BE MAKING."

She passed out sticky notes. Paloma said something softly to me I didn't hear.

"I'm what?"

"You're the quietest teacher I've ever known," Paloma said.

"Oh, no, I'm very talkative," I whispered, "it's just that when I'm an ed tech I don't like to disrupt the class. When I'm actually a teacher up there I flail around and talk loudly."

"What do you teach?" asked Bobby.

"Anything they want me to," I said.

"You're like a go-to?" Bobby said.

"I'm a sub, so science, English, whatever."

"That's what my mom was," Paloma said. "Now she's studying to be a nurse."

"How's it going for her?" I asked.

"Pretty good. She's in the middle of classes."

Bobby said, "My mom was thinking of going back to college. Then she found out that the people in the program who'd graduated couldn't get a job anywhere. So she's not."

I said, "A lot of people are starting to think that it costs too much to go to college. There's a lot you can do without it."

"I wanted to go to college to be a psychologist," said Bobby. "Then I thought about that, and now I want to be a firefighter. I'm fourteen, and I can start now."

"At fourteen you can be a firefighter?" I said.

"Well, you can be a junior firefighter. Not a Grade A real firefighter, but they train you to be a firefighter."

"I'M READY WHEN YOU ARE," said Mrs. Painter. "HOLD ON TO YOUR STICKY NOTES. I'm going to collect them after we go over our matrix. On your capacity matrix, you need to put your name on it, and date started, which would be today. So six four twenty-fourteen. This is what you're going to be working on from now to the last day of school. All of the assignments that you have for the rest of the year are right on this paper, front side, back side."

I studied the capacity matrix, which was a sideways chart filled with boxes. Down the left side were learning targets and "Baby Steps," and a box that said *Knows key terms*. To the right were levels of achievement— Emerging, Partially Proficient, Proficient, and Advanced—and lists of activities: BrainPOPs, quizzes, and projects, including an interesting-sounding "Build a Beast Project." On the far right were boxes where Mrs. Painter could sign to show that each learning target and Baby Step had been successfully completed. To score a 4, the highest possible score, a student had to demonstrate *a higher order of thinking from Marzano's Taxonomy*—Robert Marzano being the Colorado-based educational consultant who was the source of the neo-Aristotelian learning poster that was up in almost every classroom.

"Since you guys are losing your iPads next week," Mrs. Painter went on, "I am going to give you the time today to finish your BrainPOPs and the vocab. I'm going to save the mini-lesson that we were going to do today until Monday. WHAT ARE OUR LAST TWO LEARNING TARGETS? Someone raise your hand and read one of them. Maddy. Whitney, find your paper and point to them. Learning target one and learning target two. *Understands how variations in the behavior and traits of an offspring may permit some of them to survive a changing environment*."

"Wha?" said a voice.

"What does that mean?" said Mrs. Painter. "What are we asking, what do we need to know? Alton?"

"Like possible adaptions, physically and mentally, adaptions to get along with their surroundings and circumstances."

"Exactly. Did you hear that, Whitney?"

"Yes," said Whitney.

"What did he say?"

Whitney said nothing.

Mrs. Painter turned to Alton. "Repeat it, because you said it very well."

"Like mental and physical adaptions to be able to cope with surroundings and circumstances."

"Exactly. So we're looking at how animals or plants have adapted to allow them to be able to survive in a changing environment. The next learning target is *Understands the physical and behavioral features of plants and animals that help them live in different environments.* So what do you think we're going to look at there? What do you know about biomes, different biomes? What were you going to say, Anne?"

"I was going to say it's about what an invasive species needs to invade a new space."

"Yes, you can talk about what an invasive species needs in order to be invasive. Or what else, Roy?"

"It's how the animal or plant adapts to the environment, such as a woolly mammoth had a fur coat to survive in the Arctic."

"Right, we talked about a polar bear versus a black bear. We talked about why you might not find a black bear in a polar region, and then we talked about the characteristics of a polar bear and of a black bear, and why they have those physical traits for their environment. For the 'I Will Survive' activity, we're going to talk a lot more about that sort of thing. So basically we're going to be talking about adap—adaption, and physical and behavioral features that allow plants and animals to survive in a particular environment. This will be your last set of key terms for the whole year. Are you excited?"

"Woo-hoo," said a boy.

"IF YOU HAVE NOT FINISHED YOUR CELL KEY TERMS, you need to make sure you do that. IF YOU HAVE NOT FINISHED YOUR MITOSIS/MEIOSIS DIAGRAM, you need to do that. IF YOU HAVE NOT FINISHED YOUR COMPARE AND CONTRAST, you need to do that. Don't worry about plant reproduction, because we're covering that as a mini-lesson. Today you should be at your new key terms, starting them or finishing them, and then moving on to your BrainPOPs. Remember, you're not going to be having your iPads after next Tuesday, so you need to be working hard so you can get those BrainPOPs done. Otherwise you're going to have hard copies of those quizzes."

"Uh-oh," said Howard.

"Yeah, not fun," said Mrs. Painter. She pointed to the whiteboard. "Your BrainPOP list is right here. It tells you exactly what to do. We'll go over the matrix further tomorrow. When you're done with them—"

The class began to talk and boisterize.

"ALL EYES ON ME FOR ONE SECOND. If you finish a task on your matrix, I will need the evidence of it and your matrix. So if you finish your key terms, bring me your key terms and evidence, so I can sign off. If I sign off on it, that means you got maximum points. I'm not going to write the grade on your actual assignment. I'm going to collect these at the end of the class and then put it on Educate, so it will be right there."

I watched the class resignedly dig through backpacks and pull out iPads and find pencils and get to work. Key terms: *prophase, metaphase, anaphase, telophase, identical daughter cells, heterozygous,* and *homozygous.*

"It just goes on, doesn't it?" I said. "It just keeps going on."

"Long, long, long, long, *long* day," said Paloma.

Bobby showed me a drawing he'd made of a man in a camouflage outfit, with a gas mask.

"Are you going to be here tomorrow?" said Paloma.

"No, I'm sorry to say, because I like this school," I said.

"You don't seem like someone who'd teach at Lasswell High School," she said.

"How do you know that?" I said.

"I don't," she said.

I said, "Have you heard bad things about Lasswell? I've taught there. It's not that bad. It's not that great, but it's not that bad."

"One of my brothers goes there," Paloma said. "All the teachers there, except for two teachers, all of them hate him. He got suspended for four days because he broke two rulers."

I misheard. "What rules did he break?"

"They were metal, and he broke them and bent them into a duck. They thought he was making a gun, so they sent him to the office."

"Oh, come on," I said.

"I know, right? It was this round-bellied thing, and the other ruler went up like wings. He was *making a duck*."

Bobby paged through his notebook of drawings for me to see. "Beautiful," I said. "So you've got this all done, the meiosis and mitosis aspect of life?"

"Uh," said Bobby.

I leaned toward a third kid, Cedric, who was absorbed in fitting a metal spring to the top of his pencil. "How's it going?" I said.

"Terribly good," he said.

I looked at his mitosis and meiosis sheet, which was half done. "You're on it," I said. "All these vocab words."

Mrs. Painter caught my eye and pointed toward a quiet kid with a peach-fuzz mustache named Melvyn, who needed help. Melvyn was comparing and contrasting mitosis and meiosis. He had written *sexual* and *asexual* in the correct boxes.

Suddenly there was a tiny incident. "I'm going to walk out of this classroom," said Howard. "Can Asa help me?"

"Howard, you don't need help," said Asa.

"I'm stupid," said Howard.

"Howard, last call," said Mrs. Painter.

"I need help, because I'm stupid," said Howard.

"Lazy?" said Mrs. Painter.

"No, I'm stupid. I *am* stupid."

"Well, I'll help you," said Mrs. Painter, "but you do not need help."

Meanwhile I found a page in a textbook that gave the steps of mitosis. "It's kind of a dance," I said. "Have you ever seen a movie of it?"

Melvyn shook his head.

"You see the chromosomes waggling around, like square dancers, and they go off on two sides of the cell. And then the cell pinches off, and boom. Here's how they explain it. They use fancy vocabulary, but basically, the chromatids move to opposite ends of the cell, and then they form a whole new nucleus, and then it starts to pinch, *like a balloon with a string tightened around it*, and then they're divided, by gumbo. And off they go."

Melvyn needed to write down one more fact about mitosis. I read some more of the textbook. "Mitosis is happening all the time in your body, right?" I said.

"Mhm," said Melvyn.

"Your cells get old and they die and you've got to get more cells." I read from the textbook: *"Cell division allows growth and replaces worn out or damaged cells.* It's the basic way you keep fresh. It's different than meiosis. With meiosis, you get an egg and a sperm and you end up with a whole new baby. You're not replacing anything, you're starting from scratch." Oh, these words! Who were the cruel authors of incertitude who came up with such similar-sounding, hard-to-remember, Greek-rooted terms for processes that, in humans at least, had such different aims and frequencies of occurrence? Mitosis happens hundreds of billions of times a day, throughout our bodies; meiosis happens only in ovaries and testicles. Melvyn wrote *Replaces dead cells.*

Once Melvyn had written the ways in which mitosis and meiosis were different from each other, he then was supposed to list the ways they were similar. Finally he had to make a Venn diagram, referring to both lists. He had trouble keeping the two words distinct in his mind, and my increasingly clumsy attempts to explain just confused him. Finally he went off to get help from Mrs. Painter.

"Crap, I better do the BrainPOP," said Paloma.

I said, "You better do that BrainPOP, because if you don't do that BrainPOP—"

"There won't be any BrainPOP left," she said.

"Paloma, are you done?" called Mrs. Painter from across the room.

"Yep!" said Paloma. Then, in an undertone, "Nope."

"Are you on the first one or the second one?" asked Bobby, who was drawing the hand of his cartoon soldier.

"The second one." Paloma began playing part of a BrainPOP on the life cycle of the cell, but she forgot to plug in her earbuds. The BrainPOP narrator's voice filled the room: *"Prior to mitosis or meiosis—"* She turned the volume down.

"Whee!" said a girl.

Bobby asked Paloma the answer to a question about the life cycle of the cell.

"They live, and die," said Paloma.

"There's a funny song by the Cruisers, I think," Bobby whispered. He whisper-sang, "'Life sucks, and then you die.'"

"That's the worst song ever," said Paloma.

"It's kind of depressing," I said.

"It's not a dark song, it's a funny song!" said Bobby. (It's by the Fools.)

"Mrs. Painter," said a smart kid. "On the BrainPOP, I just finished doing natural selection and evolution, but whenever I hit save it always—"

"I know," said Mrs. Painter. "That happened to Eva, too. Just screenshot it. Not a big deal. You don't have to redo it, I trust you." She checked the clock. "THREE MINUTES, so if you're working on BrainPOP, make sure you either pause where you are, or don't start a new quiz if you haven't."

I watched the class begin its end-of-class routine. This is what they did five or so times a day: snatches of work saved on BrainPOP or IXL or somewhere on the network, papers handed in for grades or signatures or stuffed away, pencils stowed or abandoned, iPads zipped, backpacks shouldered, hair floofed, shirts pulled down in back where they'd ridden up. And at the same time, small heaps of key terms began to smolder and self-immolate in their minds.

"ALL RIGHT, THIS IS WHAT I NEED FROM YOU," said Mrs. Painter. "I need you to close your iPad. Leave on your desk your evidence, if you have any, and your capacity matrix. I'm coming around. If I need to sign off on an area, you need to let me know. HOLD ON TO YOUR

STICKY NOTES, AND WRITE YOUR INDIVIDUAL SOP ON THE BOTTOM."

"Obviously, we're all stupid," said Paloma.

"We're not stupid," said Bobby. "Just under-intelligent."

"It ain't over till it's over," I said. "Seems like you've got a lot on the ball to me."

Mrs. Painter collected Paloma's capacity matrix. When she was gone, Paloma showed me two anime drawings she'd made in colored pencil—both of short-haired youths in jumpsuits with multicolored hair. "This one is a boy, but he totally looks like a girl," she said.

"Wow," I said, "these are nice. When did you do these?"

"This one I did last night, and this one I did two nights ago."

I said how good they were—they were good. "I love the hair."

The principal's voice came over the PA system. "Your attention, please, for the end-of-day announcements." He began talking about the girls' soccer team.

"VOICES OFF," said Mrs. Painter, but everyone kept talking.

"Don't let them break your spirit," I said to Paloma, quietly.

"No," said Paloma. "I kind of break my own spirit sometimes. I stopped drawing once my dad died. That was a year ago."

"I'm so sorry," I said.

"I just got back into it," she said.

"Attention, girls' lacrosse players," said the principal, "practice has been canceled today. Attention, students, we will be collecting iPads next Monday and Tuesday. Please bring in all the equipment that was issued to you at the beginning of the school year." Sports physicals for next year were available for free on June 17 with the school nurse, he said. "And that's going to conclude the announcements for this afternoon. Have a great evening, everybody."

"Thanks for your help," said Mrs. Painter, holding a handful of sticky notes.

"It's a pleasure," I said. To Paloma I said, "Good luck with your art."

"Bye," she said.

On the way out I ran into the potter from February's substitute training class. She'd done some time at Hackett Elementary and at the high school; now she was a long-term sub at the middle school, teaching math.

"Lordy," I said.

"It's easy," she said.

"Oh, it's a piece of cake," I said. "I'm glad you're on the job."

"You, too."

I sighed and unlocked my car—all set with Day Twenty-six.

THAT'S JUST THE WAY SCHOOL IS

I WAS SITTING in Mrs. Compton's third-grade class at Wallingford Elementary at eight-thirty in the morning when Mrs. Hulbert, the teacher next door, came by to let me know that the school was going to be having a lockdown drill that morning in the cafeteria, just after snack time.

I had a substitute ed tech in the class, Ms. Lamarche. "This class can be pretty chatty," she warned me.

"I don't mind," I said.

"My hair used to be long," said a boy named Andrew, rubbing his head. "Yesterday I got a haircut."

"It looks good," I said. "Summer's here."

"I've been in this room quite a bit," Ms. Lamarche said, "so if you have any questions, feel free to ask." When more kids began arriving, she took charge of the lunch count. "MAKE SURE YOU GUYS MAKE YOUR LUNCH COUNT ON THE BOARD, NOT ON THE IPADS, OKAY? And Marshall, we'll be watching you today."

Mrs. Compton's sub plans said that a student, Colleen, had selective mutism and spoke to nobody. "If it is necessary for her to respond to you, have her use a whiteboard." I was supposed to write, and I did write, the following things on the board:

—Make your lunch choice
—Hand in library books
—Finish Lulu packet
—Check Showbie Morning Business for 5 worksheets!
—Read on your Kindle if finished

Most kids chose "brunch for lunch"—French toast sticks with syrup, a sausage patty, a hash brown patty, and oven-baked beans. Andrew went around letting his classmates feel his shorn head. "Everyone on the bus made fun of me," he said.

Mrs. Compton was a great believer in the digital future—so much so that she had the children learning penmanship not with pencils or pens in hand, but with iPads flat on desks: the kids had to trace, with unsteady fingertips, over the dotted image of cursive letters on their screens. That morning they were learning to handwrite the letters *p* and *g* on their iPads. Book reading happened on Kindles, and Mrs. Compton was a follower of the CAFE method of reading—Comprehension, Accuracy, Fluency, and Expanded vocabulary—which she itemized in a wall chart with a green polka-dot background. *Comprehension* was especially taxing and meta-cognitive: "I make and confirm my predictions. I check for understanding. I determine the author's purpose. I retell the story. I find cause-and-effect relationships. I distinguish between fact, opinion, and propaganda. I make connections text-to-text and text-to-self." Below the green polka dots was a display of reading comprehension strategies that Mrs. Compton had found somewhere online, each personified by a cartoon animal. Digger the Dog determined important ideas. Kit-Kat Connector activated background knowledge. Jabber the Reteller, a toucan, synthesized and retold. Questioning Owl asked questions before, during, and after reading. Iggy the Inferring Iguana made inferences and predictions. Another wall poster offered writing advice: "Choose a *strong* idea. A strong idea is clear and exact. Narrow down general topics. Each paragraph should have a *topic sentence*. It will tell the reader what the paragraph is mainly about." There was a tip sheet on how to stretch a sentence:

Who? My cute puppy.
What? My cute puppy curls up.
Where? My cute puppy curls up on the rug.
When? My cute puppy curls up on the rug each night.
Why? My cute puppy curls up on the rug each night to
    chew his bone.

Math required a math vocabulary wall chart, which included *factor*, *product*, *median*, *mean*, *mode*, and *range*—the last four defined with the help of a poem:

> Hey diddle, diddle,
> The median's the middle;
> You add and divide for the mean.
> The mode is the one that appears the most,
> And the range is the difference between.

The word *average*, one of the few math words employed in everyday speech, had apparently been scrubbed from the arithmetical lexicon.

Near the windows and the large, loud turbo-fan—which I kept turning off, because it was loud, and Ms. Lamarche kept turning back on, because the room was hot—there was another wall chart for common problems. "I have to go to the bathroom." "I have to go to the bathroom, but somebody is already out and it's an emergency." "I don't know what I'm supposed to be doing." "I don't know what this word is." "I don't know what the directions are or mean." "I finished my Math Menu and already signed up to take the assessment, now what?" "I finished my Literacy Menu and already signed up to take the assessment—now what?" No answers or solutions were given: instead, there were square barcodes that children could scan with their iPads using a scanner app in order to summon an official, digitally delivered response.

Marshall, in a red T-shirt and black basketball shorts, was the difficult kid, and Ms. Lamarche bossed him around and shouted at the class to focus; I tried to be Zen-like about her fussing because she knew the class well and wanted to be in charge. After fifteen minutes of cursive iPad practice and arithmetic and miscellaneous Showbie Morning Business—Showbie is a "paperless classroom" iPad app—we went to Care Time in the cafeteria to recite the school rules and pledge the pledge. When we had all reassembled in class, I talked about why cursive had been invented, and then I timed them, to see if they wrote five letter *P*s in a row faster when they printed or when they wrote in script. I told them to have a close look at the beautiful cursive General Mills *G* on the Cheerios box.

We lined up to go to the library to hear the librarian, a gravel-voiced gent named Mr. Merlier, read from *Whistle in the Graveyard*, a book of ghost stories. "This is a free time for you," said the sub plans. I spent it buying an ebook of *Lulu and the Brontosaurus*—the class was in the middle of reading it on their Kindles—and chanting, "'Out of the night that covers me, / Black as the pit from pole to pole.'"

In the library at 10:20 a.m., Mr. Merlier was finishing a story about a pirate who swore an oath to guard some buried treasure in Bonavista Bay, on the coast of Newfoundland. "You know pirates," Mr. Merlier said. "An oath like that is a blood oath."

"Can you show us the picture?" said Philip.

"You're looking at the only picture there is," he said.

"There is another picture!" said Philip.

"Where are you talking about?"

Philip paged through and found a picture of a pirate's head.

"Please have a seat," said Mr. Merlier. "You watch too much television and too much video, obviously. You need a picture for everything. Try your imaginations. Had you been born in the time when there was just radio, maybe your imaginations would be stronger. You need to work on that. Be quiet." He read, *"THEY LEFT ONE MAN—they left one man on the beach who had taken a solemn oath never to leave the treasure unguarded."*

The pirate band never returned, Mr. Merlier continued. Years went by, and the treasure-guarding pirate grew old and died and became a ghost, who still haunts Bonavista Bay. Once some men tried to dig for the treasure, but they were so terrified they went mad. Nowadays, though,

Mr. Merlier said, the ghost is tired of his guard duty. One night, not so long ago, the ghost stopped a fisherman and told him to return alone at midnight and drip some blood on the ground; if he did, he would possess the treasure. The blood could be from a chicken, the ghost said, or perhaps from a cut in the fisherman's wrist. The fisherman was terrified and ran away. *"Everybody knows that the ghost is honor-bound,"* Mr. Merlier read. *"He took an oath to scare off people, even though he really wants somebody brave enough to come along and dig up the treasure.* OKAY, GUYS, I want to wish you a good summer."

"That book is awesome," said Rianna.

Cormac wanted to know where, exactly, the treasure was.

"We don't know the specifics," said Mr. Merlier, "but it's on Bonavista Bay. You need to find out where Newfoundland is first. And then you'll need to find the bay. And then you'll need to do a little digging, to find out where from the locals, maybe send a letter or two, or an email."

We chuffed back to class. Because of the lockdown drill, snack had to happen quickly.

"SHHHHH!" said Demi.

"Whoa, that was a power shush," I said.

Ms. Lamarche said, "All right, everyone, listen! WE HAVE A FIVE-MINUTE SNACK. SO EAT UP QUICKLY, PLEASE."

"Why do we only have five minutes?" asked Sabrina. She'd brought out a bag of Keebler Bug Bites—graham cracker cookies in the shape of dragonflies, caterpillars, and ladybugs.

I told them we had to practice a lockdown soon. "CHOW DOWN," I said. "Snack it up."

In a back corner of the room, Marshall, Devin, and Jonas were crouched over their juice boxes.

"This is the man cave," said Jonas. Colleen walked over.

"Get out of the man cave," said Marshall to Colleen.

"No, I didn't hear that," I said. "You say, Welcome to the man cave. Come on in."

"Hah hah hah, you can't come in," said Marshall.

"That's ridiculous," I said.

"It's called a man cave," said Devin.

"It can be a man cave that has guests," I said.

"We are the guests," said Jonas.

I asked if there was a woman cave. Evidently there was. I took a bite of a sandwich.

"LET'S FINISH UP OUR SNACKS!" called Ms. Lamarche.

"Stop chewing," I said. "Just keep it in your mouth. No, finish chewing. We're going to get ready for the lockdown procedure."

"What lockdown procedure?" said Imogen, eating a Fruit Roll-Up.

Mrs. Hulbert came to the door. "MRS. COMPTON'S CLASS. We should be lining up, putting our snacks away. We're going to be practicing in the cafeteria, and then outside at recess."

I said, "You've got to be focused, thoughtful—"

Ms. Lamarche blasted over me: "YOU GUYS, I WANT TO SEE A LINE, PLEASE."

"Mr. Baker," said Porter. "Devin and Marshall are sharing their food."

"I think your name is funny," said Jonas.

"I'M GOING TO START MY TIMER," said Ms. Lamarche. "WHATEVER IT TAKES YOU GUYS TO LINE UP AND BE QUIET IS WHAT WE'RE GOING TO DO DURING RECESS. Caroline! I WANT A STRAIGHT, QUIET LINE, PLEASE. YOU GUYS KNOW THE RULES." She roared so loudly this time she made herself cough.

The cafeteria was three-quarters full and even louder than during lunch. Mrs. Shorter, one of the teachers, shouted the crowd down. "BOYS AND GIRLS. IF WE HAVE A LOCKDOWN IN THE CAFETERIA, WE ALL NEED TO GO INTO THE KITCHEN. In the kitchen there are places that we go. We have the office, which is the first room. We have the storage closet, which has food in it, the second room. We have the back room. And we have the chemical room. Also, we have the refrigerator, the walk-in cooler. Your hands cannot touch anything in any of those rooms!" The day before, Mrs. Shorter said, when they'd done a similar drill, there were a couple of issues. It got crowded in some of the rooms, especially in the chemical room, and it was impossible to close the door. Also, there might not be an adult in the room with you. "You need to be responsible for NO TALKING in that room. YOU ARE NOT LOOKING FOR YOUR FRIENDS. YOU ARE NOT CHOOSING THE ROOM YOU GO INTO. You're going to a space as a space! IF YOU WALK INTO THE REFRIGERATOR, yes, it's going to be cold, but you will not freeze. In the refrigerator, there's a second door. That's the freezer. We're not going into the freezer."

"We will freeze!" said a boy.

"No, we will not," said Mrs. Shorter. "Yesterday, our best time was a minute and ten seconds. Our goal is to somehow get it under a minute. Remember, your first job is to get yourself to a safe place. Okay! PLEASE SECURE THE BUILDING!"

A hundred children pushed and shuffled as quickly as they could into the kitchen and found a space to stand in the cooler, the chemical room, the storage room, the back room, or the office. All five doors were shut.

"We're still not getting through this doorway fast enough," said Mrs. Shorter.

Everyone flushed back out to the cafeteria. "I smell hotdogs," said Devin.

Mrs. Shorter gave some pointers about moving deeper into the kitchen faster, being silent, and not holding hands. "We also noticed room hopping," she said. "If you're in a room, it's not who you're with, it's the fact that you've gotten yourself to a safe place. Remember, this is for your safety! Okay, PLEASE SECURE THE BUILDING!"

The second trial did not begin well and Mrs. Shorter stopped it partway through. "That was horrendous," she said. She started them again. I timed them on my phone. One minute, thirteen seconds.

"Nice job, guys," I said.

"You're tall," said a boy.

We went outside to practice another lockdown on the playground. Wayne brought along the red emergency bag, which held a key and a whistle and a walkie-talkie.

Mr. Stowe, the teacher who'd won a spa ticket, was master of ceremonies for this drill. He wasn't a shouter; I liked him right away. "Three loud whistle-blows tells you secure the building," he said to the group. "When you hear the three whistles, it is your job, as quickly as you can, to rush behind the basketball hoop and down to the trail. It's kind of muddy, so our feet might get a little dirty, but that's okay. We are going to walk down the trail. If it were a real emergency—"

"You would run," said Rianna.

"You would be going as quickly as you can, and you would continue on that trail, all the way to the center of Wallingford to make sure that help was on the way. Today, we are just going to walk probably fifty yards or so down the trail. It needs to be silent. Right now you're just going to be playing."

The kids sprinted off to play.

"Do you want to be in charge of the whistle?" Mr. Stowe asked me.

"No, I don't want to be in charge of the whistle!" I said.

Mr. Stowe inspected the whistle dubiously. "Lisa was the one who used it yesterday, and now she's out today. Hm." He wiped the whistle off thoroughly with a shirttail and blew it three times.

The children racewalked down a narrow trail through woods. Marshall and his confederates shot off at top speed. Mr. Stowe yelled and I tongue-whistled to call them back.

"Oh my gosh, look how far they ran," said Myra.

We walked back to the building and lined up.

"I was running like never before," said Clayton, who was winded and hot.

When my class had lined up, I said, "Excellent emergency management training activities. Nice going."

"I ran all the way down the trail," said Marshall.

Mr. Stowe reviewed the drill—what went well, what didn't go well. Everyone had moved quickly, and hadn't tried to stick with their friends. "In a real emergency, continuing to run like that is the best thing you can do. For today, I would say that some of you went a bit farther than fifty yards. And we could have been a little bit more quiet. I know it's exciting, we're running off into the woods, but we need to be as quiet as we can."

"We went like seventy yards," said Cecil, back in class.

"We went like seventy thousand yards," said Marshall.

"We went like ninety yards," said Cormac.

"EVERYBODY SIT IN THEIR SEATS, PLEASE," said Ms. Lamarche.

Each kid had a Math Menu on his or her iPad and was supposed to do what it said for forty minutes. Every time a student tapped in the correct answer, the iPad chirped like a smoke detector with a low battery. I went around asking what nine times seven was. Half knew, half guessed or looked it up on the matrix taped to their desks. The sub plans said they were supposed to be working quietly, so I bellowed, "EVERYBODY BE QUIET, RIGHT NOW. You simply cannot concentrate if everybody's talking this loudly."

The intercom came on. "Is Imogen Reynolds there today?"

Yes! said the class.

"Okay, thank you."

Imogen had a bad cough and went to the nurse. Ms. Lamarche turned the fan on—gosh, it was loud. Wayne wanted help with a word problem: *The amazing upside-down carnival is coming to town, and they need help filling out their brochure. Can you fill in the missing information?* He had to find the perimeter of the roller coaster and several other rides in a chart, but he'd forgotten what perimeter was. We worked out the answer, which was eighteen feet. Why was the roller coaster so small? Why was a third-grader doing perimeter problems on his iPad when he still hadn't mastered addition or subtraction, or his times tables?

"What's nine times seven?" I asked Cecil.

"I'm past my nines, I don't remember them that good."

"For today, just remember that one. What's nine times seven?"

"Sixty-three," he said.

Every time I helped somebody with some higher-level problem, I asked him or her what nine times seven was. Some couldn't learn it, some could. "Burn it into your brain," I said. It didn't matter, except in school.

"Burn it, burn it, burn it," said Jonas.

"My brain's going to be illegal!" said Clayton.

A few kids were doing clock problems, but most were struggling with perimeter measurement. Demi showed me her screen: *The perimeter of a square family room is 36. How long is each side?* After five minutes of coaching and drawing pictures and counting out wooden blocks, she got the answer. It was obviously too hard for her. Because so much happened on iPad screens, the class was out of the habit of using scrap paper to draw shapes and lengths.

"Mr. Baker, I don't get it," said Elijah. *"The perimeter of a square piece of tissue paper is one hundred twenty centimeters. How long is each side?"* In order to answer the question, Elijah had to remember that a square was made up of four equal sides, and then, after sketching the square, he had to construct a proto-algebraic equation in his head:

$$\square + \square + \square + \square \text{ equals 120 centimeters}$$

This expression, he had then to understand, was the same as

$$\square \text{ times 4 equals 120 centimeters}$$

Then he had to remember how to divide 120 by 4, which relied on his knowing that 12 divided by 4 is 3. His iPad finally chirped with the right answer, but Elijah, I'm sorry to say, was lost.

I swerved back to tutor Wayne, who'd been hit with an even harder problem: *The perimeter of an air hockey table is 26 feet. It's four feet wide. How long is it?* After five minutes of drawing pictures and thinking about the nature of rectangles, Wayne got the answer, and his iPad chirped. He sat back, smiling and relieved. Along the way he'd tried to multiply 26 by 4, and he'd insisted that half of 18 was 8. Perimeter problems could wait. The quick, cute iPad lessons were luring these third-graders out to sea in little rowboats and leaving them there to sink.

Many intelligent, successful grownups, I happen to know, never memorized their times tables. Life doesn't need you to know them—but middle school does, and high school does. Otherwise you end up in special ed classes playing Fast Math bowling games or in Mr. Fields's room, guessing quotients whenever a substitute teacher honks a horn. I looked up at the class. "ALL RIGHT, IT'S GETTING A LITTLE NOISY, MY FRIENDS," I said. "WHAT IS NINE TIMES SEVEN?"

SIXTY-THREE.

"Good."

Imogen came back from the nurse with a note. "Imogen has wheezing in lungs. Called home and left message. She states she feels better—please send her back with any difficulty breathing. Marianne (nurse)."

"I have allergies and it's making my lungs hurt when I breathe," said Imogen.

"I'm sorry, that's a bad feeling," I said.

Kirstin, one of the smart girls, came up. "Mr. Baker, I forgot what it's called when you're doing multiplication and you're adding it."

"Repeated addition!" said Wayne and Porter simultaneously. "JINX."

"Double jinx," said Porter.

"Triple jinx," said Wayne.

"Okay, okay," I said.

"You can't do that," said Caroline to Jonas. Jonas was taking pictures with his iPad.

"You called me a toilet," said Jonas.

"What's nine times seven?" I asked Caroline.

"Sixty-three," said Caroline.

"You are good," I said. I turned to Jonas. "What's nine times seven?"

"Eighteen?"

"Mrs. Compton says we're not allowed to take pictures," said Caroline.

"Don't take pictures, for gosh sakes! And don't worry about it!"

"Mr. Baker, how do you spell *repeated*?" said Kirstin.

I spelled it for her. Marshall, tipping, fell off his chair.

"You all right?" I said to him.

He nodded.

"Mr. Baker, look," Porter said. His iPad said that he'd mastered three skills.

"You mastered three schools, good. Skulls? Skills. What's nine times seven?"

"Um—sixty-three?"

"I love the sound of that." The clock said noon. I did a Frank Sinatra imitation, "It's time—to go to recess!"

Rianna sang, "Get rid—of all the kids."

"I don't want you to go," I said. "I miss you guys."

"I wouldn't miss Marshall, if I were you," Rianna said.

"He's all right," I said. "I can handle him."

"I can't," said Rianna. "He's annoying."

"He always fools us and makes us mad," said Sabrina.

"CLEAN UP," said Demi.

"CLEAN IT UP," I said. "WHAT'S NINE TIMES SEVEN?"

"SIXTY-THREE!"

"Oh, yes! I want that achievement in your heads today."

"Mr. Baker, can I use the bathroom?" said Cormac.

"Use it or lose it," I said. "ALL RIGHT, SHH! I HEARD A SUDDEN CLASHING OF LOUD VOICES. It's like swords clashing together, and it hurts everybody's ears. The exciting news is that recess is on. I'm going to be out there, watching you like a hawk, hoping you have fun. Let's line up."

We went outside. Imogen had a clipboard and a pencil with her to work on math, because she'd been in the nurse's office. "You're not watching me like a hawk," said Porter.

Mrs. Hulbert announced that there was no kickball for the rest of the week. I asked her what happened.

"We've had fights."

"Nobody can agree on the rules," said Mr. Stowe. "I've been recommending all year just a list of rules that are laminated and posted, so we all can agree."

"Certainly makes sense to me," I said.

This was Mr. Stowe's first year at the school. "First year anywhere, I guess," he said. He'd gotten a philosophy degree at U. Maine Orono, and then he'd worked as a substitute for a while, and then as an ed tech, and then he got his teaching certificate.

"They're lucky to have you," I said. "You have a good way with the kids."

"I'm trying," he said. "It doesn't always work."

I watched some basketball happening for a while. Imogen came up to ask what we were doing in the afternoon. I looked at the plans. Lunch, silent reading, and literacy worksheets, I said.

"Oh, no," said Imogen. "I don't like worksheets."

"I don't either," I said. "I just like talking to people."

She pointed at the ground. "That's a bunch of ants," she said.

"They work all the time," I said. "After a rain they have to dig."

"Dig the little hole that they fall through," said Imogen.

"They have to take out the little grains of sand," I said. "It's a lot of work to be an ant."

"Especially when you're so small," said Imogen. "When I was living where my dad is living now, we used to have carpenter ants chewing our wall. All the time."

"We have them, too," I said. "After a while the wood turns to powder."

"Especially when you have a little brother that likes poking holes in the wall."

Imogen sat under a tree and worked on her clipboard for a while. Then she coughed and said, "Ow."

"Ouch," I said. "That's deep in there."

She showed me what she'd written on her clipboard: "Dear, Mr. B, Today the class was grate!! Love Imogen."

"I'm glad," I said. "Let me ask you this, and answer me honestly. Does it drive you crazy that the teachers are always telling people to be silent, to be quiet? They're always saying, 'I hear people talking!' Does that drive you nuts, or is that just the way school is?"

"That's just the way school is," Imogen said, smiling.

"It sometimes hurts me when a teacher suddenly says, 'You will give me five minutes of recess!'"

Imogen said, "Yeah, I saw you like blinking a couple times."

"Did you catch that? I didn't know anyone caught that. Anyway, it's all good, right?"

"Mm," she said.

We looked out at the playground for a while. "Will you be happy when it's summertime?"

"Yes!"

"LINE UUUUUUUP!" called Devin, Sabrina, and Demi.

Balls went into wire baskets. Lines formed and went quiet. At Mr. Stowe's signal, we snaked inside, with chosen door-holders holding the doors. It was time for lunch. "QUIET IN THE LINE," I said. My class walked off to the cafeteria.

Ten minutes later, three girls, Myra, Rianna, and Sabrina, returned carrying their brunch-for-lunch lunches and their lunches from home. "Can we sit in here?" said Rianna.

"Everybody keeps barging into all of our fights," said Myra.

"We need to talk," said Sabrina.

"Yeah, we need to talk and work things out," said Rianna.

They pulled up chairs around a table near me and, using several colors of Sharpie, began making behavioral charts for each other, and for several other students who weren't there, with boxes to check yes or no.

"Do you need to talk in private?" I said, eating a sandwich at Mrs. Compton's desk, under the American flag. "I can move."

"No, it's okay," said Sabrina.

"We have to work this out ASAP," said Rianna.

"If we keep yelling at each other, Mrs. Compton will have to move us."

They talked seriously, at times formally, coloring in their charts, drawing lines with rulers—almost as if they were playing house or having a tea party. They were playing guidance counselor. Myra wrote, "No fighting, no bullying," at the top of her paper. "That's just a reminder," she said. The problem, I gathered, had to do with secrets told to two of the boys and withheld from some of the girls. There was a fair amount of giggling.

"Sabrina, eat over your tray," said Myra.

"Whenever we get in a fight, we write yes, and each box is for each day," said Sabrina.

"How about we have a *Y* for yes, and an *N* for no, since we have such tiny boxes?" said Rianna. She wrote an abbreviation key. "Y equals Y-E-S. N equals N-O."

They ate for a while.

"I'd say we worked everything out pretty good," said Rianna.

"For today, should we put yes or no?" asked Myra.

"It should be no, because we're working it out."

They wrote "N" in the today boxes, and "talk" in the boxes for how they'd resolved their disagreement.

Cecil came in. "What are you guys doing?"

"We're talking about our privates," said Myra.

Wild laughter. "Ew!"

I stood. "It's after one o'clock. It is SILENT READING. SHHHH." I turned the lights off.

"Can we keep going?" said Myra.

I whispered, "No, it's absolutely silent reading. You're going to have to continue this meeting tomorrow. I like what you're doing, but you've got to table it now."

A specials teacher came to take away several students.

I turned off the fan. Merciful joy of no fan. "Marshall, sit down!" I hiss-whispered.

"WHOO-HOO, WELCOME BACK!" said someone's iPad reading app.

"Turn all the sounds off, and just use your eyeballs to read the words," I said. "Eyes, words—no sounds."

"Use your eyeballs," said Demi.

The room became hot. I inspected the fan, which turned out to have a low setting. It had been on high the whole time. I moved it closer to the window and turned it on low. Marshall said that Mrs. Compton allowed some kids to listen to books with headphones. Fine.

"Oh, thank you, Your Majesty!" said an iPad.

Finally the parachute of silence spread over the class. All we could hear was the now tolerable fan and Mrs. Hulbert in the next room yelling to her class to line up.

Marshall continued to fidget. "Marshall!" said Ms. Lamarche. She coughed loudly and talked nonstop to the kids in the back of the class. She seemed to be physically incapable of whispering.

When the half hour was over, I said, "Okay, it's Showbie time. Get your iPads out, get them warmed up, get them revved up. There should be worksheets for you to do."

"God, there are three of them in there!" said Jonas.

"Ugh," said Devin.

Marshall, meanwhile, had left for an alternate space-time continuum. "Flip around in your chair, Mr. Sir," I said. "With your feet on the floor."

"Yeah, yeah," said Marshall.

"And your mind in your head."

I glanced at an iPad to see what the first worksheet was. It was about idioms. "Does anybody know what an idiom is?" They didn't seem to know. "It's a way of saying something without actually saying it. Be quiet, please. So if you say, 'It is hot as a bee's bananas outside,' which I don't think means all that much—"

"It just means that it's really hot," said Elijah.

"Right. So here it says, *Casey is always on time. She is always . . .*" Jonas was talking to Marshall. "Dudes? What is happening? Why don't you stand up and read this one for us, please. Right now."

"Okay," said Jonas. *"Casey is always on time. She is always on the dot."*

"What does 'on the dot' mean?" I said.

"Um, they're early?"

"Right on time. It's an example of something called an idiom. I liked the way you read it in a loud voice. Why don't you try another? Jonas's going to read this one in an even louder, ringinger voice."

"The pizza was selling like hotcakes!"

Another ed tech arrived. She began having a chat with Ms. Lamarche, while I tried to explain the meaning of "chip on your shoulder." I asked whether "Who let the dogs out?" was an idiom, not knowing the answer myself. The class ignored me.

"Can I tell you a joke?" said Clayton. "What do bananas always say when they're having fun?"

"What?"

"Go bananas!"

"Good one," I said. "What about 'shake a leg'?"

"What about 'break a leg'?" asked Myra.

"'Break a leg' means do really well, 'shake a leg' means get going."

The second Showbie worksheet was about a dentist. I turned off the fan and read it to them, with the two ed techs chatting in the back. The heck with them, I thought, I'll just be like the robotics teacher and roar over them. *"DAVE WAS A DENTIST,"* I read. *"However, he was a very special dentist. He was very, very tiny. In fact, he was smaller than a toothbrush."* Dave has a new patient, a lion, who is in terrible pain and can't eat. Dave goes into the lion's mouth, which smells very bad, and, taking stock of the situation while standing on the lion's tongue, he spots a bad cavity in one of the lion's back teeth. He fixes the cavity and the lion is happy. *"However, the next time Dave saw the zookeeper coming, he hid in his closet.* The end." They had to answer detailed reading comprehension questions about the story: *What was so special about Dave? What was the first thing he noticed when he stepped into the lion's mouth?* Etc. The worksheet seemed to be loosely based on William Steig's *Doctor De Soto,* but without charm.

"What was the smell like?" I said.

"Smelled like raw poop," said Cecil.

"Lions eat a lot of meat, so it probably smelled like bad meat," I said.

Imogen coughed horribly. Elijah sneezed. "Bless you," I said.

Ms. Lamarche turned the fan on high.

"How do you spell *roar*?" said Devin.

Their last Showbie assignment was to write an alternative ending to Judith Viorst's *Lulu and the Brontosaurus*, about a spoiled girl who wants a pet brontosaurus. It was an unusual book because it already had three endings, one sad, one happy, one mixed. "Write your own ending, and make it good," I said. "Make the sentences rich. Lots of description. MY FRIENDS, IT'S TOO LOUD. Marshall, sit down. SIT DOWN. When you've written your end, bring it up to me, I'll look it over, and then you can type it."

Kirsten brought her alternative ending up: every week, Lulu and the brontosaurus went ice-skating together. Good. I pointed to where she needed to capitalize and punctuate and she was off to type it on her iPad. In Caroline's ending Lulu tricked the brontosaurus by inviting him over for cake and asking him to close his eyes; while the dinosaur's eyes were trustingly closed, Lulu quickly built a wall around her house so he could never escape. Jonas's ending was not a happy one: Lulu called the brontosaurus a hag and the brontosaurus farted in Lulu's face and said he hated her. Cormac had Lulu inviting the brontosaurus to Thanksgiving dinner, whereupon she dressed him as a clown and played football with him—and the brontosaurus dropped all the passes. In Wayne's wrap-up, Lulu invited the brontosaurus over to play on a pogo stick; while bouncing on the pogo, the brontosaurus went to the bathroom and fell into his own poop.

"Right," I said. "I want to hear more about how a brontosaurus can go on a pogo stick."

"He has really tiny feet?" said Wayne.

"That's quite an achievement. If you want to write about poop, that's up to you, man. I think it would be better if you wrote about not-poop, but who am I to say?"

"Sorry," he said, chortling. "I already typed mine in. What do I do now?"

I referred to the sub plans, and made an announcement. "IF YOU'VE FINISHED YOUR LULU ENDING, YOU CAN DO PICTURE OF THE DAY, FLUENCY CENTER, OR SHUFFLE CENTER, whatever that is."

"I'll do Picture of the Day," said Wayne.

Sabrina said that Lulu and the brontosaurus didn't end up living together, but they did schedule a playdate. Colleen, the selectively mute girl, wrote: *Lulu asked the brontosaurus to be her pet, and she would give him leaves all the time, and would let him stay in the back yard. The end.*

"Nice going, Colleen," I said.

Rianna had filled a page with red printing. Lulu, she said, packed a pickle sandwich in her backpack and went for a walk in the woods, where she encountered a huge spider, who told her to give him something. Lulu took out her sandwich and gave the spider her backpack, and she kept walking till she got to the brontosaurus's house. He gave her a snack and a new backpack; she hugged him and returned home.

"Wow," I said. "I like the pickle sandwich and the backpack. Only thing is *huged*—just add a *g* there. Excellent. How old are you?"

"Eight."

Elijah had a happy ending: Lulu wished the brontosaurus a great brontosaurusy life and carried him home on her back. "At least, that's the most I know of his life," he said.

"Excellent job, man," I said.

I went over to Jonas and Marshall. "Dudes, you're pushing your hips together in the same chair. That's bizarre and ridiculous. Marshall, sit over here."

Porter's ending was that Lulu invited the brontosaurus over for Christmas. The brontosaurus got a Great Dane as a present, and Lulu got a stuffed animal.

Porter said, "Mrs. Baker—I mean Mr. Baker—what do I do now?"

"Now just give it up," I said. "You're done. You're so far done that you're done beyond done."

"What do I do?"

"Well, you've got Picture of the Day, Fluency Center, or Shuffle Center. What is Shuffle Center anyway?"

"It's what Colleen's doing, see her?" said Porter, pointing across the room. "So I do one of those three? What happens if I do all three?"

"Then you'll just be in the stratosphere," I said. "Get a whole book and read it and memorize it and say it to me backwards."

Clayton said that when the brontosaurus came to eat strawberry three-layer cake he experienced a sugar rush and cracked his head open. Lulu brought him to the doctor and he was so happy that he tossed Lulu up in the air and she hit Jupiter. She came down stupider.

"Mr. Baker," he said, "Devin is on the app store and he's not supposed to be on the app store."

"Should we bring in the app police?" I said.

Clayton made a siren sound and we strolled toward Devin, who got out of the app store at high speed.

"Quickly changed it, did you?" I said to Devin. "Do you remember the story about Lulu and the brontosaurus?"

"No."

"You do not? Where the heck have you been all my life? They've been reading it aloud in this class."

"I forget," said Devin.

Imogen, whose desk was near Devin, had put her head down, feeling terrible. She sat up, coughed, turned on her Kindle, and summarized one of the endings of *Lulu*, in which the brontosaurus had cake and went home.

"I don't like that story," said Devin. "The girl has a big fat head." It was true, in the illustrations she had a very large head. I told him to read some of the book.

Marshall had written about the dinosaur smashing his head on a lot of trees until Lulu smacked him in the face.

"Looks like you are done," I said. "You can do Shuffleboard, Fluency Center, this and that."

Colleen silently brought up the work she'd done in the Shuffle Center. *an octopus is a boneless creature,* she'd written. *octopuses can grow at night. they can live for six months to a couple of years.*

"Excellent," I said. "I know you know this, but I'm just calling it to your attention. When you start a sentence, you want to start it with a capital, right?"

She nodded.

"You are in business," I said. "Thank you very much for doing it, You are hot stuff."

"Colleen's hot stuff," said Cecil. He'd written that the brontosaurus ate ten thousand cookies at Lulu's party, then excused himself to go to the bathroom: when he came out he felt much better. Cecil's deskmate Elijah was beside himself with hysterics over Cecil's story.

"I'M LIKING THESE ENDINGS, FOLKS!" I said. "A LOT OF GOOD WORK HAPPENED TODAY."

"Who did the longest one?" asked Myra.

"The longest one was by Rianna," I said. "Very long and very detailed, and it involved a pickle sandwich. I saw ones that involved ten thousand cookies, ones that involved bathrooms, I saw ones that involved cake, celebrations, Christmases."

Rianna, Myra, and Sabrina asked to go to the library.

I said, "You are very quiet workers, so I think you can go to the library, yes." I gestured toward the back of the class, where Marshall was raising hell. "Look at this pandemonium. *Pandemonium* means 'wild chaos.' You are calm. Thank you."

The intercom came on. "Mr. Baker? Can you please dismiss Jonas?"

Everyone said goodbye. Bye, Jonas, bye, Jonas, bye, Jonas!

"Good work today, Jonas," I said.

Devin was whispering into the fan. Had he read any of the book? He had. "How did it seem?" I said.

"I can't remember it. I don't have a good memory."

"Oh, okay," I said. "That's cool."

We were entering the horrific end-of-day limbo time. I thought maybe it would be a good idea to have some music, but while I was talking to Kirstin about what to play, things went wrong in the back. Wayne and Devin were making an iPad action movie in which Devin pretended to stab Wayne with a pair of children's scissors. Ms. Lamarche saw it happen and pushed herself up out of her chair. "ALL BOYS BACK THERE, I WANT YOU IN YOUR SEAT," she said.

"Absolutely right," I said.

"THAT WAS NOT SAFE," said Ms. Lamarche.

"What did I do?" said Devin.

"What did you do?" said Ms. Lamarche. "You stood over him with a pair of scissors, doing like this to his head. THAT IS NOT OKAY."

"It seems like toward the end of the day," I said, "people begin to fall apart."

"Oh, we do," said Cecil.

"Especially him and him and him," said Elijah, pointing to Marshall, Devin, and Wayne.

"I can fall apart," said Marshall. He pretended to lose an arm.

I said, "So what can you do to keep it together?"

"We can eat golden apples," said Wayne. (Golden apples are restorative in Minecraft.)

"Elastic bands!" said Marshall. "Glue? Staples?"

"Staple yourself together," said Wayne. "Make all kinds of butts on you. Butt, butt, butt, butt, butt, butt."

I said, "Your mission, and you don't have a choice about whether or not to accept it, is to stand up, go over there, get a book, and read three pages in it, right this second."

Colleen brought another piece of work up. She'd read a story about the *Mayflower* and drawn a picture of two of the people who died on the ship.

"Excellent. You've really been working hard this afternoon. Do you work this hard every day at school?"

Colleen nodded.

"Good."

I looked at a book with Marshall and we found a picture of a large land animal. "So what is this thing?" I said.

"A bison?" said Marshall.

"A musk ox, for god's sake. Can you believe it?"

"Have you ever seen a shaved yak?" asked Wayne. "I want to see a shaved yak. Shaved yak, shaved yak, shaved yak, shaved yak."

I shushed him. "I haven't seen you read a single page," I said.

"Shaved yak, shaved yak," echoed Marshall, more slowly.

"What are we supposed to be doing?" asked Porter.

"We're supposed to be enriching our minds with education," I said.

"I read three pages," said Wayne.

I looked at him dubiously.

"What?" said Wayne. "I read fast." He danced around, talking baby talk.

"Wayne, you're off the chain," I said.

Ms. Lamarche stood up. "OKAY, LET'S START PUTTING IPADS AWAY, PLEASE, AND START PICKING UP. FLOOR PEOPLE, PLEASE START PICKING UP. TECHNOLOGY PEOPLE, PLEASE MAKE SURE IPADS ARE PLUGGED IN."

I put on Lennon's "Imagine."

"That's so beautiful," said Rianna.

"MAKE SURE YOUR ROW IS STRAIGHT," said Ms. Lamarche. "CHARLIE! STUFF OFF THE FLOOR, PLEASE."

I stopped the song.

"The day's almost over," I said to Imogen, who was looking sicker than ever.

"Good," said Imogen.

"You'll feel better tomorrow," I said.

Ms. Lamarche was in motion. "HOW'S THE LIBRARY LOOK OVER THERE? CLAYTON!"

I went around with Clayton picking things up off the floor. "Who straightens up the rows, guys, let's straighten up the rows," I said.

Ms. Lamarche said, "IMOGEN, YOUR SEAT IS OVER THERE. WHY ARE YOU BACK HERE?"

Colleen brought up her Picture of the Day, a drawing of a happy swimmer. Her description said, *She's swimming. The girl is wet. There's waves. There's splashes. Brown hair. Mouth open. Blue bathing suit. Red cheeks. Blue water. Daytime.*

"That's a really beautiful thing," I said.

"Can I use the bathroom?" said Colleen. She could speak!

"Of course you can use the bathroom," I said.

Clayton showed me the ideal way to straighten a desk. "Keep them a little separate, but not too separate," he said.

"You've done good work today," I said.

"Thanks," he said. "I want to tell you a fantasy joke. What does the iPad say to the other iPad?"

"What?"

"Go to the app store and you'll get some more iPads!"

I laughed. "Do you make these up?"

Clayton nodded.

"What kind of music do you like?" I asked him.

"WHO IS IPAD FOUR?" said Ms. Lamarche. "ALL RIGHT, EVERYBODY, VOICES ARE OFF, PLEASE. IF I SEE YOU TALKING, YOUR NAME GOES ON THE BOARD, AND WE'LL START WITH RECESS TOMORROW. Marshall, you want to be the first one?"

"No."

"THEN GO SIT DOWN. Whose iPad is number four?"

"Myra," said the class.

"And she's not here, right?"

I put on Lennon again and sang along.

"LET'S PACK AND STACK, PLEASE!" said Ms. Lamarche. "Elijah, can you stack Colleen's chair, please. Philip, can you stack your chair, please? Devin, come clean off your desk! Devin! VOICES ARE OFF AND LISTENING, PLEASE. WHO'S TALKING?"

The secretary came on the PA system to read off an endless list of dismissals.

"All right, guys," I said. "WHAT'S NINE TIMES SEVEN?"

"SIXTY-THREE?"

"I love it," I said. They lined up. "Thank you very much for being in this class."

"Are you going to be here tomorrow?" Porter asked.

"I don't think so," I said. "Take it easy, guys."

"You have to go with them to the bus," said Ms. Lamarche.

"No, he doesn't," said Cecil.

"Yeah, he does," said Ms. Lamarche.

I walked down the hallways, humming "God Bless America" for some reason, and I watched the children leap onto the buses like reverse paratroopers. I waved at the faces in the bus windows and went inside, drank greedily at the water fountain, and said, to the empty classroom, "That just about does it." I put on "Imagine" and picked up stray scraps from the floor.

Day Twenty-seven was a wrap.

PLUTONIC LOVE

On Wednesday, Beth said she needed a ninth-grade English teacher at Lasswell High. At seven-fifteen a.m. I parked at the far end of the cemetery, where there were no headstones yet, and no flags, and plenty of room for new graves, and waited for it to be time to go to school. It was a perfect, windless, cloudless morning. I thought about life and death. The day before, in Oregon, about the time my third-graders were writing their madcap endings to *Lulu and the Brontosaurus*, an angry ninth-grade student had brought two of his father's guns to school. He shot one boy in a locker room, wounded a coach, and then killed himself in the bathroom. Pills? Rage? Why?

In the office, while I waited for Paulette to make copies of my schedule, one of the other secretaries told me what was happening at the high school. "We're about to have graduation," she said. "Getting those seniors through. Marching practice yesterday. Then, tomorrow night, graduation."

I set off for the North Building. In the hall, a male teacher looked suspiciously at me. "Can I just ask who you are? Are you a sub? It's just that you're not wearing a tag."

I told him I was supposed to get my tag in the North Building.

"All right, cool," he said. Everyone was watchful the day after a school shooting.

Mrs. Marsh's room was pale blue and still and the walls held many words and their definitions, some from the dark science of rhetorical analysis: *ethos*, *logos*, and *pathos*. A poster offered a quote from C. S. Lewis: "WE READ TO KNOW THAT WE ARE NOT ALONE."

A kid named Cobie came in with a dead iPhone and a cord. He'd forgotten his wall charger. "Just put it in my computer," I said. He hooked his phone up to my computer and left. I read more vocabulary words posted by Mrs. Marsh's desk: *placid*, *nuance*, *noxious*, *covert*, *abhor*, *allege*, and *appalled*. Minutes passed.

Six bongs. Nobody was in the room with me for block one. The secretary came on the PA system. "Please stand for the Pledge of Allegiance," she said. "I pledge allegiance to the flag of the United States of America. And to the republic for which it stands, one nation, under God, indivisible, with liberty and justice for all. Please pause for a moment of silence. Thank you, and have a great day." Since I had no students, I sat at Mrs. Marsh's desk and read some of the papers she'd been grading. They had errors of tense and number, but they were honest and thoughtful, and they were not about dinosaur poop. One was a study of Pentatonix, *a formidable music group that makes interesting arrangements*. One was about the history of hairstyles. *Once originality runs out, what do you have left? Old ideas. Stylists are usually just bringing back old trends. For example, the 1950s simple curled ponytail is coming back, but people are adding color and accessories to it*. Rockabilly bangs had recently come back, too—*not a very appealing design*. One essay dealt with the effect of music on the brain. *Music benefits the brain in mental, physical, and emotional ways*, the writer said. $x + y = 154 - 89x + 9x = ?$ *Do you know what it is? Are you doing this math problem with your headphones in? If you do, you're more concentrated than you would be even if the room was silent.* One was about video games: *Grand Theft Auto is a series of games where you are a character that fights for what you want. For example if you wanted to be Vice City's biggest criminal, you would be. You have to do different missions so you can get to be the biggest criminal, by violence, blood, sexual content, nudity, and never any good things.* In an essay about social media, a boy had written, *Young people's social time is mostly shrinking.* In the margin, Mrs. Marsh had corrected *shrinking* to *dimishing*—not much of an improvement, even if you added in the missing syllable. Cobie returned to get his phone.

The sub plans were brief. Block 2: "Take attendance. All students must work silently." Block 3: "All students must work silently and independently on final project for *Romeo and Juliet.* Please check off that they have accomplished at least one page of work." Activity block: "Take attendance. All students must work silently." Block 4: "Take attendance. Same as Block 3." Block 5: "Same as Block 3." The instruction packet for the *Romeo and Juliet* project said that the students were supposed to determine the theme of the play, and then (a) come up with a music playlist that was redolent of the theme they'd identified, accompanied by 1,000 words of annotation, or (b) retell in 1,000 words the story of the play in a fresh setting while evoking their chosen theme, or (c) write a 750-word critical essay analyzing their chosen theme. To get students going in the right direction, there was a worksheet offering some possible themes they could pick from. These were Youth, Avoiding Fate/Destiny, and The Power of Love. The theme of love in *Romeo and Juliet* supposedly had five subtypes, listed on a separate worksheet page: Divine Love, Romantic Love, Familial Love, Superficial Love, and Plutonic Love. Mrs. Marsh, unsure of the difference between the god of the underworld and the Greek philosopher, had invented a new and wonderful form of love.

The students in blocks 2, 3, 4, and 5 did not work silently or independently, needless to say. Most were fractious and snarky and full of an extreme end-of-the-year impatience to be done with school. Very few produced anything close to a page of writing. Shakespeare was not a hit; they all disliked *Romeo and Juliet* to varying degrees. Jill said she absolutely hated it. Brendan said, "I thought that it was the stupidest play I've ever read. You're fighting for no reason. You're falling in love with a thirteen-year-old. You're gay." He flat-out refused to work on the project.

Marcia, although she hadn't liked the play, had finished the assignment. She'd chosen love and violence as her themes. "Basically I said that Verona's in Italy, and Italy is known for romance," she said. "But Italians are also stereotypically known as being hotheaded. That explains why the Capulets and the Montagues have the rivalry." A kid named Myles wrote a good first sentence: *Shakespeare wrote a suspenseful tragedy about a forbidden love.* Another student, Malcolm, wrote two sentences: *Italy, the country of love and violence. Verona is full of hot-headed people with funky outfits.* Joel's dramatic retelling began: *This baffling story of a cannibal and a sadistic, crazed butt-stabber starts in a German slave dungeon on a cold, stormy, normal German day.* Lionel's version replaced the people with animals, and it began: *"You slimy muck, you. You filthy scumbucket," yelled Tibalt. "Be parted, tools," commanded Denvolio. As the fray continued, the many animals involved were scratching, clawing, and biting each other, until through the streets gallops a donkey, and on its back lies a wee man, with a regal oversized hat in uniform.* Stefan had come up with an excellent title and nothing more: "A Heartwarming Cold Steel Love."

But the big and little things that happened that day had nothing to do with Shakespeare. Myles was yelled at for dumping a water bottle onto the pavement outside. Vince got suspended for harassing somebody. A kid named Titus Brown, in a Harley-Davidson sweatshirt and a Foreign Legion hat, had the idea of starting a fishing team at Lasswell, and Mr. Bartlett, Lasswell's director of athletics, approved of the plan—it was going to be called the Lasswell Bass Masters.

And everyone had to turn in their iPads. Mrs. Moran, the science teacher who'd assigned the project on the layers of the Earth's atmosphere, came into my classroom and said, "What we're going to do is you need to get your iPad, gray case, black case, little wall pluggy-in thingy, and the long cord. So that's five things. You need to get them out right now. I'm going to get my kids, they're going to stand at the door, and you're going to get all your crap together. You're going to go with me."

"What if we lost our iPad?" said Bernard.

"Then you're going to get a six-hundred-and-fifty-dollar bill," said

Mrs. Moran. "LADIES AND GENTLEMEN. SHUT YOUR MOUTH. There's going to be three lines. One line for people that have everything that they need. One line for people that are missing things. And one line for people with broken iPads. Say you have a restricted iPad. Obviously if you have a restricted iPad, you've not been able to delete anything. Tell them that when you hand it over to them. So you're all going to wait here, with our wonderful substitute—"

"Mr. Baker!" said Tucker.

"Our wonderful substitute. And I'm going to bring my kids up here, and then we're all going to go together to the east gym."

They went off to the east gym, handed in their iPads, and returned, talking wistfully about lost apps and lost personal information. "I deleted everything," said Daisy. "I deleted my contacts, everything."

"No more iPad, no more iPad!" wailed Diana.

Soon Mrs. Moran came back in to say we had to attend freshman class elections. Two hundred ninth-graders and their teachers packed themselves into the cafeteria. There was no need for voting, though, because all the candidates were running unopposed. "Are you guys excited for your sophomore year?" said the current class president.

Cheering happened, followed by four echoing speeches from four girls—candidates for treasurer, secretary, vice president, and president— in which fund-raising successes and the word *awesome* figured prominently. The president-to-be closed by singing "We're All in This Together." Then she said, "What time is it? SOPHOMORE TIME!"

Yay! said the soon-to-be sophomores.

Back in class, April showed me the notes she'd made in the library for her Shakespeare paper. Her theme was love. "I just don't want to be behind anymore," said April, piling up overdue papers. "I'm trying to get ahead."

At the end of the day, Lionel held out his fist for me to bump it. "I'm sorry, man, I love you," he said.

"Knuckle it up," I said. I also bumped knuckles with Dixon and Stefan and Joel. "Take care, guys. Good times."

"Can I go to the band room?" asked Mira.

"Are you in tomorrow?" asked a silver-haired ed tech named Mrs. Ball.

"No, I'm not in tomorrow."

"See you later!" said Daisy. Bye! Bye!

The room was empty, but I didn't want to leave. I read some student poems that Mrs. Marsh had pinned to a corkboard. They all began with "I'm from." A dirt-biker wrote: *I'm from adrenaline rushes because of sports, snowmobiles and dirt bikes. / I'm from high land, mud bogs, and homegrown meat.* A girl wrote: *I'm from a town where we know each other's names. / Where we don't have to lock our doors at night.* Another girl, from a family who made maple syrup, said: *I'm from the trees that produce the sap / To the buckets that collect it all.*

I loved these poems, these children, these six brick schools that made up Regional School Unit 66—I loved them with a Plutonic love. I loved the element cubes, and the rhombuses, and the glue guns, and the Mother's Day bags, and the playgrounds, and the three-hole punchers, and the Tennsmith metal benders, and the hairy elbows, and the Pajama Days, and the Superhero Days, and the taxonomy-of-learning posters, and the antonym eggs, and the whining robots, and the stink bugs, and the Sharpies, and the SMILE folders, and the book buckets, and the lunch counts, and the whole broken, beautiful, wasteful, totally crazy educational system I'd been a part of. I hadn't been a good teacher, but I'd passed out a lot of worksheets, and I'd learned a universe of things I hadn't known. I packed away my computer, squirted a last squirt of hand sanitizer on my hands, and wrote a note for Mrs. Marsh, saying that the students were alert, funny, and good-natured, as always.

Boop. "Please excuse this interruption. Field hockey camp paperwork needs to be turned in to Mrs. Murphy ASAP. Thank you."

I took a drink at the drinking fountain. "Hi, Mr. Baker," called Tucker, waving.

I stood in the hall, watching the last kids leave. I saw April at her locker. "How did it go today?" I asked her.

"Good," she said. "I got a whole page done."

"Fantastic," I said. "Great job."

Bong, bong, bong, bong, bong, bong.

Outside, a wind was coming up, and the second-wave buses were idling, waiting to begin their rural wanderings. My Scrabble mug clanked against something in my briefcase. I noticed that I still had the substitute badge hanging around my neck and went back to the office to return it. "Awesome," said Paulette.

I got in the car and turned on the engine. I thought, There are no key terms. There are no themes, no thesis sentences. There are no main ideas. Life's curriculum is infinite. Most of the interesting things we know we can't explain. Most of what we need to know we were not taught. Stay classy, Lasswell. I drove home. Day Twenty-eight was over.

In fact, for me, the whole school year was over.

ABOUT THE AUTHOR

NICHOLSON BAKER is the author of ten novels and five works of nonfiction, including *The Anthologist*, *The Mezzanine*, and *Human Smoke*. He has won the National Book Critics Circle Award, the Hermann Hesse Prize, and a Katherine Anne Porter Award from the American Academy of Arts and Letters. He lives in Maine with his wife, Margaret Brentano; both their children went to Maine public schools.